International Perspectives on Social Policy, Administration, and Practice

More information about this series at http://www.springer.com/series/7

Shaun Grech • Karen Soldatic
Editors

Disability in the Global South

The Critical Handbook

Springer

Editors
Shaun Grech
Centre for Global Disability Research
The Critical Institute
Attard, Malta

Karen Soldatic
Institute for Culture and Society
Western Sydney University
NSW, Australia

International Perspectives on Social Policy, Administration, and Practice
ISBN 978-3-319-42486-6 ISBN 978-3-319-42488-0 (eBook)
DOI 10.1007/978-3-319-42488-0

Library of Congress Control Number: 2016952124

Printed on acid-free paper

This Springer imprint is published by Springer Nature
The registered company is Springer International Publishing AG
The registered company address is: Gewerbestrasse 11, 6330 Cham, Switzerland

Acknowledgements

We would like to thank our wonderful contributors for lending their knowledge and commitment and for patiently working with us throughout this lengthy project. We would also like to thank the series editors for giving us the opportunity to publish this edited collection.

Finally, and not least, we would like to extend our infinite gratitude to Kelly Somers, who has done a superb job with editing and supporting us throughout in keeping the whole project together.

Contents

Part I Placing Disability

1 **Disability and Development: Critical Connections, Gaps and Contradictions** 3
Shaun Grech

2 **Disability and Global Health** 21
Leslie Swartz and Jason Bantjes

3 **Disability Studies: Developments in Anthropology** 35
James Staples and Nilika Mehrotra

4 **Counting Disabled People: Historical Perspectives and the Challenges of Disability Statistics** 51
Arne H. Eide and Mitchell Loeb

5 **The Place of Disability** 69
Dan Goodley and Leslie Swartz

6 **From 'Sensing Disability' to Seselelame: Non-dualistic Activist Orientations in Twenty-First-Century Accra** 85
Kathryn Linn Geurts and Sefakor G.M.A. Komabu-Pomeyie

7 **Playing Disability, Performing Gender: Militarised Masculinity and Disability Theatre in the Sri Lankan War and Its Aftermath** 99
Neloufer de Mel

8 **Religion After the Medical Miracle: Recovering "Disability" as Religious Analytic of Social Suffering** 117
Sharon V. Betcher and Mary Nyangweso Wangila

Part II Connecting Disability

9 **Livelihoods and Disability: The Complexities of Work in the Global South** 133
Jill Hanass-Hancock and Sophie Mitra

10 **Begging and Disability: A Paradigmatic Way to Earn One's Living** 151
Carolina Ferrante and Eduardo Joly

11 **Don't Forget Us, We Are Here Too! Listening to Disabled Children and Their Families Living in Poverty** 167
Mary Wickenden and Jean Elphick

12 **Questioning Human Rights: The Case of Education for Children and Youth with Disabilities in Ethiopia** 187
Hisayo Katsui, Elina Lehtomaki, Abebe Yehualawork Malle, and Shuaib Chalklen

13 **Reflexive Re-storying of Inclusive Education: Evidence from India and South Africa** 199
Nidhi Singal and Nithi Muthukrishna

14 **Disability and Poverty: Complex Interactions and Critical Reframings** 217
Shaun Grech

15 **Disablism, Deprivation and Selfhood: Imagining the Subjective Nature of Oppression in Worlds of Poverty** 237
Brian Watermeyer and Sumaya Mall

Part III Intersectionalities

16 **Race, Ethnicity and Disability: Charting Complex and Intersectional Terrains** 255
Deborah Stienstra and Leon Nyerere

17 **Disabled People in Conflicts and Wars** 269
Maria Berghs and Nawaf Kabbara

18 **Disability and Forced Migration: Intersections and Critical Debates** 285
Maria Pisani, Shaun Grech, and Ayman Mostafa

19 **The Fluid Connections and Uncertain Spaces of Women with Disabilities: Making Links Across and Beyond the Global South** 303
Janet Price and Nidhi Goyal

20 **Violence Against Disabled Women in the Global South: Working Locally, Acting Globally** 323
Leanne Dowse, Carolyn Frohmader, and Aminath Didi

21 **'Locked in Space': Rurality and the Politics of Location** 337
Alexandra Gartrell and Elizabeth Hoban

22 **Disability and HIV: Critical Intersections** 351
Ruth Evans, Yaw Adjei-Amoako, and Agnes Atim

23 **Social Protection, Chronic Poverty and Disability: Applying an Intersectionality Perspective** 365
Marguerite Schneider, Zitha Mokomane, and Lauren Graham

Part IV Interventions

24 **The Hauntings of Slavery: Colonialism and the Disabled Body in the Caribbean** 379
Stefanie Kennedy and Melanie J. Newton

25 **From Colonialism to Postcolonialism and Contemporary Empire** 393
Siobhan Senier and Beatriz Miranda-Galarza

26 **Global Financialisation and Disability: Can Disability Budgeting be an Effective Response in the South?** 407
S. Janaka Biyanwila and Karen Soldatic

27 **Global Institutions and Their Engagement with Disability Mainstreaming in the South: Development and (Dis)Connections** 423
Tsitsi Chataika and Judith A. McKenzie

28 **A Local Critique of Global Mental Health** 437
China Mills and Bhargavi Davar

29 **Community-Based Rehabilitation and Disability-Inclusive Development: On a Winding Path to an Uncertain Destination** 453
Pim Kuipers and Louis Paluku Sabuni

30 **Disability-Inclusive Disaster Risk Reduction: Vulnerability and Resilience Discourses, Policies and Practices** 469
Kim Spurway and Thao Griffiths

31 **Critical Silences: Disability, Networked Technologies and the Global South** 483
Anupama Roy and Sarah Lewthwaite

Part V Activism and Research Across Cultures

32 **Whose Knowledge, Whose Voice? Power, Agency and Resistance in Disability Studies for the Global South** 503
JosAnn Cutajar and Casimir Adjoe

33 **Revising and Using the Social Model in the Global South: A Venezuelan Exploration** 517
Manuel Aramayo, Mark H. Burton, and Carolyn Kagan

34 **Disability Research in the Global South: Working from a Local Approach** 531
Marcia Rioux, Paula Campos Pinto, Jose Viera, and Rados Keravica

35 **Australian Indigenous People with Disability: Ethics and Standpoint Theory** 545
John Gilroy and Michelle Donelly

36 **Global South–North Partnerships: Intercultural Methodologies in Disability Research** 567
Karen R. Fisher, Xiaoyuan Shang, and Jiawen Xie

37 **Embodying Disability in the Global South: Exploring Emotional Geographies of Research and of Disabled People's Lives in Guyana** 583
Vera Chouinard, Cora Belle, Halima Khan, and Norma Adrian

Index 599

About the Editors

Shaun Grech, Ph.D. is Director of The Critical Institute (www.criticalinstitute.org) and Global Disability Watch (www.globaldisability.org). He is also Visiting Fellow at Manchester Metropolitan University and editor-in-chief of the international journal Disability & the Global South.

Karen Soldatic, Ph.D. is an Australian Research Council DECRA Fellow (2016–2019), Institute for Culture and Society, Western Sydney University. She is the head of research, Global Disability Watch (www.globaldisability.org), and Affiliate Fellow at The Critical Institute, Malta, and Centre for Disability Research, Policy and Practice, University of Colombo, Sri Lanka.

Introduction: Disability in the Global South

This book has been long in the making. Though the process of drawing in the right authors, working with all the different perspectives and approaches and putting it all together can be taxing, it has nevertheless been a profound and rewarding learning experience for us. We have reflected with each of the authors, discussed potential directions and approaches and often been directly challenged on our thinking. We were strongly convinced of the need for this interdisciplinary volume, and initially we each held strong views on what we were trying to do with the substantive content of each chapter, yet this handbook was shaped by the diverse, committed and critical authors working with us and their reflexive scholarship. We are excited to see this timely, sizeable collection finally published, featuring established and emerging academics and activists from global North and global South working collaboratively from and across a wide range of disciplines, covering a broad range of issues.

This critical handbook, the very first of its kind, emerged from the key concerns that came up as we talked about disability in the global South, the fledgling field called 'disability and development' and the spaces and voices in between and on the edges of these disciplinary regimes, whether in the form of a quiet conversation or more direct concerns about a bold policy convention, such as the United Nations Convention on the Rights of Persons with Disabilities (UNCRPD) or the World Report on Disability by the World Health Organization and World Bank. Many of the 'voices' we heard came from disciplinary peripheries: of disability studies, international development, sociology, anthropology, critical pedagogy and postcolonial theory, among others. Theorists and activists started hinting that not all is well and straightforward in uncritical stances, whether in talking about disability and poverty, inclusive education, defining and enumerating disability, childhood, health and community-based rehabilitation (CBR), the Sustainable Development Goals (SDGs) and their potential, development and the list goes on. Others challenged the dominance of Eurocentric disability tenets and readings of history, the ignoring of colonialism and geopolitics, the disembodied readings of disability in contexts of rural poverty, the challenges and limitations of rights in practice and the colonising of knowledge and its production (see Campbell 2009; Grech 2009, 2011, 2015; Erevelles 2011; Meekosha 2011; Soldatic 2013, 2015; Soldatic and Grech 2014;

Ghai 2015). From these broad and diverse perspectives, a handful of common threads and imperatives became apparent to us:

1. The process of knowledge production and power relations embedded therein and, in turn, the need for spaces that prioritise, privilege and learn from epistemologies and practices of the South
2. The need to question and engage critically with established and hegemonic notions, including rights, development and mainstreaming
3. The complexity and heterogeneity of disability across differing contexts and landscapes
4. The requirement to historicise and geopoliticise disability
5. The awareness that critical questioning necessitates critical practice and vice versa
6. The commitment that, whatever we do, we must challenge disablism, including in and through our own discourse and practices

As more grey literature is written, and as more of this tries to capture the lived experience of disability, the global South, poverty and families and communities, the more insistent our concerns became. In our own debates, we became acutely aware that there was a dearth of critical voices (particularly those from the global South) in the growing interdisciplinary area of disability in the global South. Disability studies, and its global North focus and tendencies, have not been too receptive to opening its geopolitical scope and remit. Similarly, scholarship focusing on colonialism, postcolonial identities and bodies often too quickly absorbs northern ideas of disability without exploring localised discourses, practices and processes. We started noticing a pattern within the burgeoning field of disability and development. Empirical work often excludes the voices of disabled people in the global South, especially those living in poverty, and mainstreaming discourses, largely dominated by global North professionals and their institutions, do little to acknowledge or include recent innovations from other fields, including disability studies, resulting in theoretical engagements that are weak and often monodisciplinary. In the bid to simplify and contain, some discourse has indeed become 'legitimate' and hegemonic, and is sometimes used to push aside and resist knowledge and perspectives that are constructed differently, that put forward uncomfortable questions and create epistemic unease. Reports continue to be written, some trying to compare and contrast disability statistics, to frame a coherent cross-cultural definition of what disability might mean. Others write manuals and publish toolkits on how to 'do' 'disability-inclusive development', or evaluate inclusive disability practices, but basic questions go unanswered, such as: Do we really know what disability is? Can we really define and contain disability across cultures, contexts, ideologies, (geo)politics and socio-economic terrains? Should we question and reflect on our practices? Whose voices and knowledge count? And this, on the contrary to what some positivists would claim, is not a project of theoretical abstraction; it is one of (self-)reflexive, responsible, responsive and respectful practice, through acknowledging local counterpoints of reflection and perhaps resistance. There has never been a more opportune time to be questioning and critical, with the advance of the SDGs and this newly defined 'interest' in disability in fields such as international development.

This collection is a result of some of these tensions and anxieties. This handbook is far from complete, but we believe it does some justice to igniting an earnest and much-needed debate that we hope will be taken up and built upon by others. We hope to see a dialogue between theorists, activists and practitioners that is open and safe, which is not bound and limited by paradigmatic, discursive, ideological, historical, locational, ontological and epistemological territorialism. This handbook is no more and no less than a call for a debate that dislodges fixities, that is inclusive and that never stops short of the ultimate goal—to challenge and disrupt oppression and to work in genuine partnership for social justice and transformative change.

The Book Structure and Parts Explained

This book is made up of five parts traversing conceptual, practice, intersectional and research terrains. They are linked by and through critical approaches to established discourses motivated by a quest to question, challenge and disrupt fixities whether in disciplines, approaches or paradigms.

Part I: Placing Disability

The first part maps out key conceptual, theoretical and disciplinary domains or spaces within and through which disability is often positioned and debated, but also framed and impacted. They influence how disability is often understood, researched, talked about and even intervened in. This part positions disability within disciplines and field areas, spaces that are material, discursive, epistemological and ontological and that try to frame spaces and bodies that are too often fluid and complex yet culturally, ideologically and contextually positioned and perhaps multidimensional. Disabled bodies and experiences, like the global South, can hardly be captured or generalised, calling instead for constant, engaged and critical analyses including around established discourses and practices in now hegemonic framings such as those positioned within international development or global health. This opening part provides the reader an overview of established theoretical and practical approaches and how these 'encounter' and/or face up to disability and localised understandings while simultaneously examining the dominance of the growing global agenda in relation to disability. In the introductory chapter, Grech maps out the intersection between disability and development, arguing that despite the establishment of the 'disability and development' sector (a 'new' field of thought and practice); hype around notions of disability-inclusive development (DID); and the recent mentioning of disability in the Sustainable Development Goals (SDGs), disability continues to linger on the fringes of development theory, policy and practice.

He notes how there is a worrying pattern of dominance by often unquestioning and uncritical global North voices, including around neoliberal globalised development, its collateral and whether it is necessarily 'good' for disabled people to be included within it. Grech goes on to argue that despite the connections between disability and development, studies in each area have yet to come together and critically engage with and learn from each other, and the voices of those from the global South and how these 'encounter' development are rarely heard. This perpetually leaves a vacuum and a terrain occupied by more dominant global North voices coopting and defining how disability is to be understood, 'intervened' in and how progress is to be measured and documented. Grech goes on to argue for a critical approach that poses uncomfortable questions, including on the merits (or otherwise) of development, an approach that necessitates interdisciplinary engagements, where the voices from the global South are no longer denied, but prioritised and built upon.

Swartz and Bantjes shift the critical focus towards another dominant field, that of global health, identifying core conceptual, ideological and political issues that are crucial to understanding disability in relation to global health, but which they argue remain under-theorised. The authors are clear from the outset that while disability is clearly connected with health, and while disabled people too often encounter critical access barriers, disability is frequently underestimated and also radically misunderstood in traditional global health accounts. This underestimation, Swartz and Bantjes argue, is itself a political act, one of misrecognition. They emphasise that a central problem in the field of global health is the silence around disability in health policies at local and global levels, with the implication that intervention moves little beyond mere awareness raising. Much of this work, they go on to argue, is descriptive, depending on existing data and where critical evaluations remain scarce.

Staples and Mehrotra complement these opening two chapters, positioning disability studies within anthropological readings, offering the reader critical insights into the possibilities of a deeply situated anthropological project enabling nuanced and grounded understandings of disability. The contributors are clear that connections between disability and anthropology have been shortcoming overall, highlighting how ethnographic studies engaging with disability have until recently been scarce, leaving a vacuum dominated by global North perspectives. While the situation may be changing, the authors argue there is a productive space, including the theoretical and methodological contributions anthropology has and continues to make, directly and indirectly to the study of disability. Staples and Mehrotra embark on a critical analysis of the spaces for connection including within and through key thematic and theoretical interests within the discipline such as power, representation, personhood, embodiment, culture and ontology, as well as citizenship and human rights.

Beyond the realm of disability framings and cultural understandings, one key area that has and continues to dominate discourse and efforts of those involved in disability in the global South has been the almost obsessive endeavour to enumerate and measure disability, too often driven by the motivation to compare and contrast. In their chapter, Eide and Loeb critically engage with the allusive character of statistics when attempting to count disability globally. In a terrain characterised by statistical gaps and dramatic differences (including between so-called 'low-income' and 'high-income' countries), counting disability is complex and at best unprecise. Differences in definition of disability, prejudice in some cultural contexts that may lead to underreporting, high mortality and an overall complexity of highly diverse societies make homogenising and standardisation a virtual impossibility. The authors highlight how more complex and also multidimensional understandings of disability, including the connections between the person and his/her environment, have opened up the terrain to more nuanced and complex dimensions of the disability experience and hence definition. Eide and Loeb contend that while different understandings and models of disability may and perhaps do complicate attempts at measuring and comparing, dynamic and co-existing models may open a space for finding some or other common ground within this complexity and to perhaps reframe what we understand as viable statistics and how we go about generating them.

These four initial chapters are followed by the work of Goodley and Swartz who explore the global–local nexus of disability knowledges to articulate the various complexities and troubles of conceptualising disability across a range of geopolitical spaces. The authors engage in critical disability studies to articulate a position and discourse that might start with disability, but, which they state, never actually ends with it, a position constantly vigilant of ontological, theoretical, political, cultural, social and material complexity and fluidity. This disability can hardly be captured, encapsulated or controlled when this complexity is further magnified as one thinks about the 'place' of disability, that is, where and when disability appears and how it (re)emerges geopolitically, temporally and epistemologically. The authors, through an engaged lens, embark on these varied terrains, to possibly map and locate disability, while remaining constantly vigilant that this process may, perhaps inevitably, involve a range of national and theoretical border crossings.

Geurts and Komabu-Pomeyie continue on the critical journey and questionings of issues around the mapping, definition and understandings of disability, this time opening the space to the subjective and the sensory terrain. They expose the limitations of western thought in relation to sensory understandings, practices and cultures, which, they argue, have very serious implications for disability studies. Reporting on fieldwork in Accra, Ghana, the authors highlight how bodily feeling is a vital source of information about environment, self-making and moral knowledge. They expose how disability activists in Accra exhibit the influence of 'seselelame' in their reflections on navigating and confronting ableist cultural practices and more broadly how disability too is 'sensed'. This chapter embarks on a journey navigating disability through the senses, opening up terrains for exploring disability subjectivity and embodiment beyond a northern canon. The authors usefully engage a space to argue that sensory experience is framed culturally and how a concept of disability sensibilities helps us dialogue across differences.

In her chapter, de Mel further grounds and positions disability within a geopolitical context, this time looking at the relationship between disability and masculinity in the context of the Sri Lankan war to ask what specific characteristics constitute war-related impairment and its registers of affect on military/militarised men. The chapter positions war, masculinity and the disabled male body within the specific Sri Lankan political, gendered and cultural context to critically interrogate what the connections between these three dimensions may mean for both disability and masculinity studies. De Mel goes on to focus on what she calls aesthetic activism on disability in Sri Lanka by analysing the applied and devised theatre of the Sunera Foundation, a civil society organisation that has worked with Sri Lankan disabled youth, including disabled soldiers, since 1998. The chapter reinforces the need to move beyond simplistic and rigid conceptualisations and framings, analysing the implications for expanding and operating through more nuanced frames to see the 'conditions' of disability.

This part rounds off with an exploration and positioning of disability within religious discourse, offering a religious analytic. Betcher and Wangila move beyond secular accounts in dominant strands of disability studies, arguing that religions have always used disability, to think with, about and through numerous issues, including corporeal anomaly. The authors, for example, articulate how the Christian West justified its 'humane imperialism' by reading disability as degeneracy in need of medical remediation. They go on to embark on a critical journey into how disability became for Christianity the external boundary of what counts as human kin and kind. Betcher and Wangila argue that the Christian missionary colonialism towards the South, was heavily inflected with the deployment of the metaphor of disability as an affect-inflected, geopolitical map. Consequently, this chapter reconsiders the metaphorical plethora of religious thought regarding disability.

Part II: Connecting Disability

The previous part signals to the reader and indeed supports a conceptual road map for the chapters that follow. The part 'Connecting Disability' acts as an effective and critical connector opening up for further interrogation the spaces between disability and a range of socio-economic, cultural, political and contextual terrains and how these (re)frame disability within context and how they challenge and even shift established discourses, whether about poverty, livelihoods, education or human rights. The chapters provide rich grounded examples from Africa, Central and South America and South Asia. In their chapter on livelihoods, Hanass-Hancock and Mitra push the epistemological and practical boundaries of a thematic within disability and development that, though often mentioned, has rarely been critically opened up for questioning. The authors map out key barriers confronted by disabled people that lead to compounded livelihoods and their impacts on impoverishment, but are quick to emphasise that in practice little information does exist. They are also quick to highlight that critical issues have rarely been interrogated, including the limited and constraining notion of livelihoods as paid employment, notions that rarely account for the complexity and heterogeneity of rural livelihoods. They also contest the idea that making disabled people participate in the labour market may not necessarily be a feasible solution for all disabled people, or even harmless, especially when other critical environmental conditions are encountered. The authors argue that improving livelihoods necessitates before anything an incisive understanding of what livelihoods are like on the ground, how they are built and how they in turn interact with and impact employment possibilities and chances of decent work.

Ferrante and Joly shift the envelope of what is framed as livelihoods and how a living may be earned, moving their focus towards the widespread practice of begging and the types of relationships it affords. Drawing on qualitative research in the city of Buenos Aires, the authors note how in a context where demands, including to employment, are consistently met by a resounding 'no', disabled people are forced to resort to begging. This operates within a hegemonic charity view of disability which is reflected in the begging for alms. The authors argue that within this context, the language of rights would seem insufficient in reversing what are structural foundations of these forms of vulnerability.

Katsui and colleagues take forward the critical debate on human rights and the unquestioning fate in rights and legislation, this time within the context of education for children and youth in Ethiopia. Focusing on the politics of education as a basic human right, they question in the process the challenges and opportunities implicit in realising the CRPD, in particular, in including disabled children and youth in the mainstream education system. Katsui and colleagues outline how despite ratifying the CRPD, there are numerous gaps and contradictions including the government's own interpretation of the CRPD and rights. The authors explain, for example, how in 2009, at the same time as the CRPD was ratified, the Ethiopian parliament issued a law forbidding civil society organisations (CSOs) from promoting human rights, especially the rights of women, children and disabled people. The implications are not only discursive but also in policy and practice, limiting advocacy for a human rights-based approach and even more widely limiting what legislation, policies and rights can achieve in practice.

Singal and Muthukrishna follow this critical thread through a comparative exploration of the mantra of inclusive education in India and South Africa and what this has come to yield or mean in practice in these contexts. The authors take a critical approach and push forward a dialogue that takes on current northern hegemonic assumptions in relation to the education of disabled children, while identifying epistemological and practical ways forward. They contend that the issues that must be questioned are many, including the fact that despite the incorporation of inclusive education in policies, it has varied and often ambiguous understandings in different contexts. This is not to mention the lack of debate on how to go about operationalising inclusive education in ways that respond to the realities and priorities of local settings. Consistently within this chapter is the call for debates to be reclaimed and owned by the global South, away from the northern lens that has dominated them.

Assumptions have come to dominate other dimensions of discourse, and a prominent one has been the frequent reference to the disability and poverty relationship, one framed as a mutually reinforcing cycle. In his chapter, Grech argues that the dynamics operating between this representation have in practice rarely been how their positionality, subjectivity and intersectionality are understood in light of shifting global forces. They address the feminist critique of disability as it incorporates new gender theory and a broadened geopolitics of globalisation. These theories, the authors argue, have opened avenues for a provisional politics of embodied interdependency and transformative connections which lead to hopes of what they call a geopolitically aware ethics of flourishing.

Dowse and colleagues extend the focus on gendered experiences of disability, looking at issues of violence on women in the global South. They adapt analyses of the global disabled women's movement explaining the differing repertoires required in building global feminist solidarities across the North–South divide. The authors note how the disproportionate lack of research on the nature, prevalence, impact and prevention of violence against disabled women and the deep silence that ensues is a clear indication of the crucial and urgent need for action on gendered-disability violence in the global South. They express how this violence is a pressing human rights concern, highlighting the nature and foci of international activities and campaigns to address such violence.

Violence, migration, conflict, gendered experiences, poverty and the various intersectionalities are also bound to locality. In their chapter, Gartrell and Hoban focus on rurality to expand disability intersectional engagements, adding a layer of depth that is not often recognised. The authors argue that there remains limited research examining the intersectionality between rurality and disability and the diversities and forms of disadvantage that emerge within and through this spatial relationship. They sustain their argument stating that macro-level structural forces together with household micro geographies and poverty can lock disabled people in feminised, domestic home spaces, typically at the bottom of local social hierarchies. The spatial boundedness of many disabled people's lives often results in their exclusion from globalised processes of development, with severe socio-economic, cultural and personal impacts.

Evans and colleagues examine the intersections between disability and HIV. While select grey documents have made reference to this relationship, the authors argue it has remained largely unexplored in disability studies, epidemiology, global health and associated fields, and disability issues have been in large also neglected in global and national HIV policy responses. Evans et al. insist that this is a serious gap with serious consequences. In this chapter, they critically explore these connections and the implications for disabled people with HIV in terms of their access to healthcare in the global South. They traverse various terrains including conceptualisations of disability, bodies and health identities and then examine issues of vulnerability for disabled people including to HIV, violence and stigma and the barriers to access to sexual health and HIV prevention and treatment programmes. Focusing on sub-Saharan Africa, they also examine recent policy and other initiatives, including by DPOs and networks to tackle discrimination and advance their claim for the right to health, providing an understanding of differing local and national contexts of vulnerability, activism and policy engagement on these issues.

To reveal the significance of the intersectional lens for disabled people, the closing chapter for this part by Schneider and colleagues engages with the connections between social protection, chronic poverty and disability. The author's central thesis is that being disabled, poor or in need of social protection is a critical identity in their own right. But when these come together, they not only intersect but create a series of outcomes for disabled individuals and their families, which are more than the sum of the individual components. The authors map out critical features of social protection as a strategy for managing risk and promoting development and follow this up with an analysis of the interaction of such a strategy with poverty and disability.

Part IV: Interventions

The fourth part moves on to draw out a number of interventions in the lives of disabled people that have in the process framed disability historically, socially and geopolitically. The chapters engage with the continuity of processes of colonisation, while simultaneously drawing out localised practices of resistance within the present. They thus traverse the significance of disability across time and space within and through the colonial, journeying into times of coloniality. Kennedy and Newton's chapter historicises disability, positioning it within the plantation slavery in the 17th- and 18th-century British Caribbean, one of the earliest zones of the Atlantic World to adopt a system of colonial exploitation based on African enslavement and sugar plantations. Drawing on Frantz Fanon's work, the authors highlight how the slave trade and plantation slavery are the historical underpinnings of systematised and violent African diasporic impairment. The authors force the reader to rethink trends among global North disability historians, which position mid-19th-century Europe and North America as the locations and era in which impairments took on new meanings with the onset of industrialisation. Kennedy and Newton argue that capitalism already existed in the early modern period causing negative social stereotyping of physical anomalies and impairments, changing the perception of impairment in the process. The authors insist that the colonial Caribbean confounds this chronology of disability history and undoes teleological distinctions between the early modern and modern. The authors advocate for histories of disability and colonialism that are attentive to different patterns of colonial exploitation and racialisation and the distinct legacies of disablement that they have produced.

The next chapter by Senier and Miranda-Galarza pushes the frontiers and timelines of colonialism focusing on contemporary forms of empire. Senier and Miranda-Galarza are firm in the statement that decolonisation did not end colonialism. While postcolonialism has come to describe what happened after European powers were overthrown, imperialism did not stop, but was instead perpetually recreated and reframed. As disability is positioned within this postcolonial or neocolonial condition, the authors contend that a thorough postcolonial history of disability experience, activism and culture in the global South is yet to be written. They argue that critical conversations between the two fields of postcolonialism and disability are still lacking despite the deep commitments in each to interdisciplinarity. The authors go on to map out some of postcolonial theory's keywords and concerns, while critically pondering postcolonial studies and disability studies and their (dis) engagements as many of the world's poorest and most disenfranchised populations continue to be beholden to the forces of neoliberalism and globalisation.

The part moves on to new forms of global governance that aim to bring disability into what Fiona Kumari Campbell has termed 'geopolitical knowledges' and the forms of resistance across the global South to contest and subvert global hegemons. Biyanwila and Soldatic explore the emergence of southern counter narratives to global financialisation and the promise of participatory budgeting processes as a strategic orientation of contestation. The authors provide an incisive critique locating the 2008 crisis within neoliberal strategies of financial deregulation launched in the mid-1990s, examining how the normalisation of financialisation mechanisms, processes and practices reproduces the marginalisation and exploitation of disabled people in the global South. They argue that new forms of colonialism are enacted through global finance capital located in the global North and how this increasingly influences the development landscape. They go on to explore the increasing role of identity budgeting, as a counteracting southern tool of social justice.

Chataika and McKenzie open up the critique of development, pointing a critical optic at global institutions and the extent to which they are engaging with and/or mainstreaming disability in their operations. The authors review disability inclusion processes within development prior to the adoption of the CRPD, and then reflect on the impact of this convention as well as the World Report on Disability, exploring, in the process, possibilities as to how these can be used to catalyse inclusive development efforts by global institutions. Chataika and McKenzie offer a grounded critique of how global governance programmes are implemented in the global South, opening spaces for consideration of a range of critical areas for consideration if inclusive development is to become a reality for disabled people in the global South.

Mills and Davar, in their chapter on global mental health, expose how global mental health agendas and discourse impact on disabled people's lives, pathologising and isolating psychiatrised peoples. They critically look at a host of human rights abuses that occur within psychiatric institutions and forced or coerced psychiatric treatment, both within institutions and within community settings, a form of torture and ill-treatment. This chapter, grounded in decolonising discourse, explores how epistemologies of the South and of the psychiatrised in the South mobilise the local to challenge and resist a single psychiatric approach to mental health and well-being that claims to be global—as currently embodied in advocacy for 'global mental health'. The authors recognise the need to directly problematise global mental health by questioning how a single model can claim to account for and 'treat' psychosocial distress experienced globally and specifically in contexts of persistent poverty and entrenched inequality.

Kuipers and Sabuni further the debate, illuminating a host of critical issues, raising questions and even contradictions about the now established discourse and practice called community-based rehabilitation (CBR). The authors historicise and then examine aspects of the evolving nature of CBR, which have over the years facilitated its emergence as a global service model. Kuipers and Sabuni hold that CBR and related approaches have had both positive and negative dimensions and, in turn, see constructive as well as possibly unproductive directions in the evolutionary paths ahead. The authors are clear in recognising that the CBR model can and should evolve further to more adequately respond to the needs of disabled people. Nevertheless, they argue that the road ahead is bumpy and requires paradigmatic and practical changes. They argue, for example, that the emphasis of CBR and disability-inclusive development (DID) remains dependent on 'upstream' agendas of management, policy and international declarations, reflecting primarily the interests and priorities of some NGOs and international bureaucrats rather than those of disabled people in the global South. They further note conceptual problems, including the fact that the evolving nature of CBR has made it quite ill-defined, resulting in a lack of identity and direction in some crucial dimensions.

Spurway and Griffiths engage with one of the more recent global narratives: disaster management. They open their chapter explaining how to date very little has been written on the topic of disability and disaster, with the issue almost completely ignored in literature, policy and practice. The chapter goes on to critically interrogate some of the key trends in the study and practice of disaster risk reduction and management through the lens of disability. They set out some of the conceptual parameters of current debates in disaster scholarship and then analyse existing data on disability and disasters and the current growth in awareness and recognition by the international community of the importance of disability-inclusive disaster risk reduction and humanitarian action. The chapter compares and contrasts some key commonalities and intersections between disaster and disability theory. They argue that integration and linkages between the sectors have strengthened in line with a growing consensus that disasters are the result of unsustainable development strategies and that the best way to prevent future humanitarian crises or natural disasters is to promote sustainable, equitable and inclusive development policies and practices.

The final chapter of this part by Roy and Lewthwaite traverses the biopolitics of the global, shifting attention towards digital networked technologies. Critically, Roy and Lewthwaite reveal the bifold process of enforcing technological fixes as a core development project within the global South for disabled people and the bio-security impacts of creating disability, for example, via the e-waste that is shipped to southern spaces and places from nation states and large transnational corporations. The authors examine the narratives that dominate mainstream understandings of technology and digital divides alongside more nuanced debates in areas relevant to disabled people. Recognising various evolutionary stages, the authors provide an in-depth exploration while highlighting silences in technology and disability discourse, ones that they claim continue to be occluded by the arrangement of social, geopolitical, economic and cultural forces that shape our technologies and day-to-day lives. Situating digital technologies in a geopolitical frame, the authors then offer an incisive critique of these critical silences in light of rampant contradictions and biopolitical effects offered by the mantra of capitalist development.

Part V: Activism and Research Across Cultures

This final part fleshes out critical concerns and directions for decolonising advocacy and research, offering readers an opportunity to explore new, critical and emerging research and practice alliances giving voice and advancing disabled people's rights and their struggles for recognition, redistribution and representation. This part brings together strategies and critical reflections on ways in which localised knowledges and practices can be recognised and built on. The central point of connection is the ethical commitment to move beyond the restraints of hegemonic global North epistemological, discursive, ontological and practical foundations to look towards and prioritise instead situated local knowledges. This part begins with Cutajar and Adjoe's account of local actors' transformation of global disability knowledge production through representative practices of knowledge disruption. They provide a sharp critique of the one-way transfer of knowledge between North and South, West and the rest, delineating analytical issues that need to be incorporated in disability studies for the global South. Using Ghana and Malta as fluid case studies, the authors argue that theories from the global North are not always transferable and do not always account for the fact that the causes and interventions in impairment also lie beyond the capacity of the nation state. At the same time, they argue for the need to explore the fact that the epistemologies and enunciative codes borrowed from the North may well help academics in the South reinterpret who they are. This chapter therefore explores the points of connection between location, positionality, dependency, neocolonialism, agency and resistance. The authors stress that national and global mobilisation can take place when disability scholars and activists recognise the multiplicity of disabled and impaired identities and orient themselves towards the politics of diversity within unity.

Aramayo and colleagues chart a similar critical and questioning terrain in respect to global North epistemologies, this time reflecting on the social model of disability and if/how it can be used and revised within the Venezuelan context and experience. The authors set off by stating that while they value an approach to understanding disability and 'what is to be done' to improve the situation, they also acknowledge the need to be vigilant of the ways in which ideological, theoretical and institutional reforms can be hard to understand and that enthusiasm for the positive elements can obscure other elements that are less helpful. Reflecting on the social model, Aramayo et al. chart various directions in which the social model has developed within context, at times in contradictory ways, but also possibly fluidly where local disability activists adapt, alter and change global disability knowledge frameworks through collective organisation. They conclude by saying that it makes more sense to see these social models as pragmatic theories of action that include some explicit and implicit propositions about the nature of disability in the national social context of the time.

Rioux and colleagues build upon their worldwide study of disability rights realisation engaging with disability research in the global South in ways that work from a local approach. Working through one piece of transformational research, the authors weave in the recognition of rights, justice and power stressing how these cannot be separated in the fundamental design and implementation of research and the transfer of knowledge. Knowledge, they argue, is not unidirectional but bidirectional, insisting there are no fixed rules for grounded research. Nevertheless they argue that one key connecting factor is the philosophy through which organisations view and operate, in particular, in regard to how they view their role in development and human rights work. They reveal the practices of embedded partnership-building while revealing necessary reflexive processes required to build international disability solidarity. In particular, they provide effective road maps for a transformative model of North–South research with an agenda based on disability rights, where disabled people are not mere pawns or beneficiaries of research, but instead proactive and activist stakeholders.

In their chapter on indigeneity and disability, Gilroy and Donnelly offer a very rare and critical piece on disability—Indigenous standpoint theories and research methodologies. Locally grounded and culturally embedded, Gilroy and Donnelly's chapter focuses on Australia to reflexively examine the role of research in establishing the white-settler enterprise and its continuity under the conditions of neoliberal capitalism. It explores the historical foundations of colonisation, colonialism and research on impairment and disability and then provides a critique of the current approaches used to address the ethics of research involving Indigenous disabled people. The authors argue that despite national ethical guidelines on research involving Indigenous people, these guidelines remain ineffective when it comes to addressing the ways in which Indigenous disabled people are framed and also disempowered in disability research methodology and epistemology. In response to this, Gilroy and Donnelly insist that the Indigenous standpoint theory (IST) may be a useful avenue and approach to critique how research presents, frames and defines Indigenous disabled people and to infuse local Indigenous communities' philosophies and cultures into the research process. It can also promote the decolonisation of research in the area of disability while empowering Indigenous disabled people.

The final two chapters focus on the techniques of building comprehensive research partnerships. Fisher et al. use a South–North research partnership between Chinese and Australian researchers to explore and discuss a range of emerging practical tensions and to explore how these may be managed in and through decisions made about research subject, design, methods, analysis and knowledge, among others. The authors argue that these questions and issues are constantly emerging because approaches to disability research are contested in any context also on account of epistemological and methodological differences in disciplinary approaches. The chapter illustrates various dilemmas and attempts at their resolution, rounding off with a critique of statements claiming universal application of global North disability research methods.

The final chapter in the handbook by Chouinard and colleagues engages with the emotional geographies of research with a special focus on Guyana. The contributors draw on feminist conceptions of reflexivity to explore the emotion-laden nature of the research process itself and the challenges of negotiating emotional reactions of researchers and participants in the interview process. In a constant reflexive and vigilant process, the authors illustrate research encounters, what they call altered research practices. They also adopt a feminist, embodied, emotional geographic conceptualisation of forces shaping disabled people's lives and activism in a global capitalist order to explore impairment, disability and responses to disability issues by activists in Guyana.

We hope the reader finds this handbook as nuanced, engaging and challenging as we do, and we hope it contributes to shifting fixities and opening up spaces for critical thought, research and practice. We reiterate our previous statement that this handbook is neither complete nor comprehensive, but we feel that a broad, complex and heterogeneous thematic such as disability in the global South can perhaps never be. Having said this, we hope this project is one step towards an ongoing reflexive, critical project and approach, where the challenge of disablism and oppression, whether discursive or material, never shifts out of focus and where the study of disability in the global South is not a mere academic project, but one of critical praxis and transformative decolonising change.

Shaun Grech
Centre for Global Disability Research
The Critical Institute
Attard, Malta

Karen Soldatic
Institute for Culture and Society
Western Sydney University
NSW, Australia

References

Campbell, F. K. (2009). *Contours of Ableism*. London: Palgrave McMillan.

Everelles, N. (2011). *Disability and difference in global contexts: Enabling a transformative body politic*. New York: Palgrave Macmillan.

Ghai, A. (2015). *Rethinking disability in India*. Delhi: Routledge.

Grech, S. (2009). Disability, poverty and development: Critical reflections on the majority world debate. *Disability & Society, 24*(6), 771–784.

Grech, S. (2011) Recolonising debates or perpetuated coloniality? Decentring the spaces of disability, development and community in the global South'. *International Journal of Inclusive Education, 15*(1), 87–100.

Grech, S. (2015). *Disability and poverty in the global South: Renegotiating development in Guatemala*. London: Palgrave.

Meekosha, H. (2011). Decolonising disability: Thinking and acting globally. *Disability & Society, 26*(6), 667–682.

Soldatic, K. (2013). The transnational sphere of justice: Disability praxis and the politics of impairment. *Disability & Society, 28*(6), 744–755. Retrieved from http://dx.doi.org/10.1080/09687599.2013.802218.

Soldatic, K. (2015). Colonial productions: Disability, indigeneity and the formation of the white masculine settler state of Australia. *Social Identities: Journal for the Study of Race, Nation and Culture, 21*(1), 53–68. Retrieved from http://dx.doi.org/10.1080/13504630.2014.995352.

Soldatic, K., & Grech, S. (2014). Transnationalising disability studies: Rights, justice and impairment. *Disability Studies Quarterly, 34*(2). Retrieved from http://dsq-sds.org/article/view/4249/3588.

Part I
Placing Disability

Chapter 1
Disability and Development: Critical Connections, Gaps and Contradictions

Shaun Grech

Introduction

The World Report on Disability (WHO and World Bank, 2011) estimates that around 15 per cent of the world's population are disabled people, that is, close to one billion people. It goes on to state that the majority of these, approximately 80 per cent, are located in the global South. Many of these people are said to live in rural areas in conditions of poverty and extreme poverty. It perhaps comes as no surprise that the bulk of disabled people may be located within the southern space, because poverty always has provided and continues to provide multiple conditions for the creation and maintenance of impairment. The numbers of disabled people continue to rise on account of hunger and malnutrition, inaccessible health care and rehabilitation, unsanitary living conditions, violence and conflict as well as 'development' in increasingly turbulent times. Disability has perhaps always been disproportionately present in these spaces if we are to historicise and position it within the violent colonial and the geopolitical asymmetries sustaining the current condition of coloniality (see Grech 2015).

Despite the likely imprecision of these rough estimates, they have come to serve specific purposes, as political and lobbying tools for those fighting for rights and access to services, but also to include disability in international development. This process came to be known as 'disability mainstreaming', culminating in more recent discourse suggesting the need for 'disability-inclusive development'. Much of this discourse emerged from the fringes of, and more often from outside, international development, reflecting disability's profound exclusion from the development sector and psyche. Indeed, the connections drawn between disability and development are very recent, and published and grey literature on the subject was scarce right until the end of the 1990s. Much of the belated attention in fact emerged from global

S. Grech (✉)
Centre for Global Disability Research, The Critical Institute, Attard, Malta
e-mail: S.Grech@criticalinstitute.org

S. Grech, K. Soldatic (eds.), *Disability in the Global South*,
International Perspectives on Social Policy, Administration, and Practice,
DOI 10.1007/978-3-319-42488-0_1

health and disability-specific international organisations, among others, many of which are located in the global North. These efforts turned into concerted lobbying to find a place for disability in the development agenda and practice. The inclusion of a disability component in the post-2015 Sustainable Development Goals (SDGs) is the culmination of this lobbying, and while disability is not one of the goals per se, many are hopeful that disability will be given the attention it deserves in development priorities and practice, including poverty reduction.

Yet, one is still to see what the discursive linkages between disability and development, including those in the United Nations Convention on the Rights of Persons with Disabilities (CRPD), will translate into in practice (if at all) for disabled people, especially rural people who are too often off the policy and practice radar. Indeed, the 'inclusion' of disability in development seems to highlight more of a forced absorption rather than a wilful, informed and committed embrace. It is a fact that the development sector has not been too quick to acknowledge disabled people as legitimate development 'subjects' in policy, research and practice (Grech 2015). One therefore may question what dramatic changes can be expected over the coming years.

Unfortunately, in the midst of much enthusiasm, critical issues and questions are frequently cast outside the realm of research, theoretical questioning and reflexive practice. These include, among others, questions around development itself and its willingness and capability to include disabled people in earnest and on their own terms; whether it is willing to change its (disabling) practices and whether including disabled people in development is necessarily 'good' or beneficial to them. The questions are many, but the silence remains deep, perhaps in the bid not to rock the boat, or because faith is indeed unwavering in the benefits of development as it stands.

This chapter maps out and questions the connections between disability and development in an effort to critically discuss *some* issues and gaps in the disability/development nexus and the disability-inclusive development discourse. These are far from comprehensive but are a partial and fragmented account that perhaps raises even more questions. Nevertheless, I hope that these can serve to generate much-needed debate and critical reflection in the field now called 'disability and development'.

From Disability Mainstreaming to Disability-Inclusive Development

Before addressing the main discursive linkages between disability and development, it is best to first briefly historicise the disability/development nexus. The lobbying to include disability in development, as I articulated earlier, is not only very recent, but it has also largely emerged from outside development, a project embraced and promoted by disability organisations as well as academics. This coincided with growth in the international disability movement, work towards the CRPD, more rights-based approaches being promoted within development and broader shifts in disability conceptualisations towards more socially constructed and rights-based framings, including the social model of disability (see Oliver 1990).

While the assumed numbers of disabled people in the global South, and the conditions they were said to be facing, were a substantial call for visibility and action, it is no secret that it was the conspicuous absence of disability within development that triggered a moderate 'movement'. The Millennium Development Goals (MDGs) had been set and disability was nowhere to be seen; development report after another ignored disability; and policies and measures addressing poverty reduction, health, HIV/AIDS, education, gender equality, humanitarian concerns, environmental and climatic issues, among others, were designed and set without disability within their scope and remit. In the meantime, practices such as community-based rehabilitation (CBR), strongly promoted by the World Health Organization, were growing exponentially to fill this void, alongside international organisations working in these so-called 'developing countries'.

Inspired by gender mainstreaming, many took this lobbying very seriously, calling for what they framed as 'disability mainstreaming'—promoting the idea that disability needed to be infused within all aspects and processes of development (see Albert 2006). Others (see CBM 2008) went further, suggesting the need for a twin-track approach that not only mainstreamed disability within existing development strategies and practice, but also targeted disabled people to ensure that all their needs were addressed.

Over the years, emerging debates capitalised on and promoted strongly the idea of 'inclusive development' or rather the idea that development should work in inclusive ways and not exclude anyone (see Gupta et al. 2014). This discourse was in fact borne out of the fact that so-called economic development continued to exclude and leave many behind, especially the poorest and most marginalised, those whom development was supposed to prioritise and serve. Some development agencies, organisations and even donors, such as the World Bank, USAID and the UK Department for International Development (2000), latched on, and references to disability in grey documents as well as internal disability policies were quickly shaped up (see Lord et al. 2010). Some even produced guidelines on how they intended to include mainstream disability in their development work, and others went as far as suggesting how to go about measuring disability-inclusive practices (see Wissenbach 2014). These efforts were further solidified and backed by prominent global measures such as the CRPD. Article 32 of the convention even provided for issues concerning development cooperation, suggesting the need to make development inclusive by providing a comprehensive framework for governments. The World Report on Disability published by the WHO and World Bank in 2011, the first report of its kind, contained a whole section devoted to disability and development, emphasising how 'disability is a development issue, because of its bidirectional link to poverty' and concluding that 'disability should be a part of all development strategies and action plans' (WHO and World Bank 2011: 265). It then went on to rearticulate the call for disability mainstreaming, defining it as the 'process by which governments and other stakeholders ensure that persons with disabilities participate equally with others in any activity and service intended for the general public', a process, the report goes on, that 'requires effective planning, adequate human resources, and sufficient financial investment' (WHO and World Bank

2011: 264–265). The World Report is not a legal document, and it is interesting to note that there is little guidance on what mainstreaming would entail in practice. However, alongside the CRPD, it has served as a tool for disability visibility in global policy while shifting discourse on the possibility of a disability/development intersection.

Discourse on the need for disability mainstreaming has remained consistent over the past years, fusing more intensely with the notion of inclusive development and shaping into disability-specific concepts and measures, including calls for 'disability-inclusive development' (DID) (see van Veen 2014). Motivated by the need to render disability more visible to the development sector, the hope was and continues to be one of a development that is completely planned, implemented and evaluated with disability in mind, a disability that is not only infused, but that also traverses all aspects of development. While few actually know what DID is or what it entails, it has over the past couple of years shaped into a catch-all phrase, perhaps a means, an end or both. Some donors have even started singing to this popular tune, a number even offering guidelines and manuals on how this could be achieved (see for example Australian Government 2015).

Despite the lingering questions and uncritical connections, 'disability and development' have not only been joined discursively, they have over the past 10 years come to stand in as a referent for 'global disability', marking a fluidly defined field of practice and, more recently, of study. 'Disability and development' consultants are increasing in number, universities are gearing for some or other course on disability and development, and manuals continue to be written on how to measure or include disability, capture the disability and poverty relationship, evaluate CBR or monitor inclusive practices.

While many issues remain unquestioned and uncontested, the arguments used by those lobbying and trying to create connections between disability and development have been reasonably consistent. Over the next sections I outline, albeit briefly, some of these major arguments.

Disability and Poverty

While the sheer numbers of disabled people assumed to populate the world and the global South have provided quite the impetus, the most prominent argument linking disability and development has been and continues to be the frequent reference to the relationship between disability and poverty, one too often framed as a binding and mutually reinforcing cycle (see Chap. 14 in this volume, Grech 2016). The idea is simple: poverty exacerbates and/or intensifies impairment, while the onset of disability intensifies or leads to poverty. More guesstimates and arguments emerged suggesting that disabled people encounter disproportionate barriers in employment and livelihoods, education, health and rehabilitation, infrastructure, social protection and other key areas (see Berman Bieler 2006; Mitra 2010; UNESCO 2012). These are problems that haunt the poverty landscape, in particular in rural areas, but which are experienced in more intense ways by disabled people as they meet a host of disability-specific barriers. The result is a deep, often chronic and intergenerational poverty marking disabled people and their families as those among the poorest of the poor. This simple equation (disability = poverty) worked well for those lobbying the international development sector, concerned (at least in theory) with poverty and its reduction. If disabled people are among the poorest of the poor, then it would be difficult if not impossible to reduce this poverty if this population were excluded.

While the frequent reference to this relationship has become a staple in disability and development discourse, much is based on hearsay. There is still lack of research, in particular critical qualitative research that looks at this relationship in informed, contextualised, sensitive and non-generalising ways, and, as I argue in Chap. 14 of this volume, theoretical interdisciplinary engagements remain weak. Anthropological and other research (see Ingstad and Whyte 2007) highlights many complexities, including ideological and religious or spiritual beliefs which frame disability and the disability experience in multifaceted, yet contextualised, ways, while others such as Grech (2015) have critiqued the notion of disability and poverty as a cycle. Unfortunately, much of this critique remains on the periphery of dominant discourse. This relationship is frequently mentioned in grey documents and 'fact' sheets are drawn up, just as disability and poverty are measured and compared using dubious census data, but the truth is that we know little about this relationship. Simplifications and generalisations dominate in the bid to contain it and, importantly, the voices of those who live this poverty and disability remain grossly invisible.

Exclusion from the MDGs and the Need to Include Disability in the SDGs

Alongside the frequent reference to disability and poverty, the exclusion of disability from the MDGs provided some impetus to further the disability/development connection. It alerted to profound neglect and abandonment of disability in the development agenda while providing a platform for lobbying to address disability within these MDGs, and to then make sure that disability was not excluded from successive goals post-2015. Many used the exclusion of disability from the MDGs to argue that disability was not only relevant to but also cross-cut every single goal, with the implication that if disability was not addressed, it would have compromised the achievement of each and every goal (see for example Groce 2009). These arguments, as well as the lobbying, strengthened in the run-up to the formulation and eventual agreement of the SDGs in 2015. The inclusion of a disability component in the 17 SDGs is hailed as a major achievement and success, with aspirations and hopes running high as I write. The UN itself boasted a participatory process in the formulation of these goals, and even presents attractive schematics of what disability-inclusive SDGs may look like (UN 2015).

But these are early days indeed, as it is for the CRPD, to see if and how things will change for disabled people, especially those in the poorest rural areas, where political promises mean little to those left to their own devices. It is not overly cautious to warrant that a marginally critical and questioning optic is required, especially if recent history is to serve as a lesson, and if disability activists and their allies are to be prepared when commitment falters, and strategies fail or are not contextually informed and adapted. The multiple failures of the MDGs, not least the increasing inequality, are a harsh reminder. Let's also not forget that while politically attractive, the SDGs are not legally binding by international law, leaving national and local governments to their own devices. On an even more basic level, while disability is mentioned in the SDGs, it is not included as a goal in its own right, as gender equality is. This impacts not only the visibility of disability as a core theme, but may well mean that inclusion of disability will be tokenistic, an exercise in box ticking, with disability subsumed under other core objectives.

The Rights-Based Approach to Development

While disability and poverty and reference to the MDGs were strong points for lobbyists, some (see Albert and Hurst 2005) resorted to the broader move towards a rights-based approach in development (RBA) as a point of entry for disability. Poverty in the case of the RBA is no longer an issue of charity but the denial of rights. This in turn supports the idea that what is required are fundamental changes to systems and structures, including legal ones. Attention therefore shifts from solely focusing on prevention and rehabilitation towards equal rights and participation in all spheres of life. This approach, it is not hard to see, bears strong similarities to that espoused by the disability movement.

While discourse and literature on the RBA to development per se rarely contemplated disability, it opened a marginal space for the consideration of disabled people as potential development subjects (at least at the level of rhetoric), when in theory the RBA emphasises a focus on those who are marginalised and excluded.

Once again, though, critique of the RBA in practice, and more broadly of rights, including the CRPD, and how these and other policies pan out in reality were and continue to be left out of any disability and development discussion. As I argue elsewhere (see Grech 2009, 2015), while rights and policies may look good on paper, they mean very little in practice for the poorest who struggle to eat, who have more immediate and practical needs, who may not even know what their rights are and who do not have the means to seek redress. All of this alongside lack of political commitment and resources, economic crises and neoliberal cost-cutting (discussed later) leaves a vacuum filled only by good intentions.

In Practice: Where is Disability?

The 'inclusion' of a disability component in the SDGs is a celebration of these lobbying efforts, and we will surely be hearing more about disability in development, including in donor funding requirements. Still, it is necessary to reflect on the past and present to learn about and be prepared for the future. The first issue to contend with is perhaps the most obvious: To what extent is disability included in development? To reiterate, the lobbying only emerged and continues because disability remains marginalised in development. So where are we now?

Development study textbooks are continually being published, but disability continues to hover outside much of this content bar the odd mention here and there. Development journals and courses remain lacking in disability content, perhaps reflecting the notion that disability is still not seen as a completely legitimate development thematic at a par with gender, childhood or ethnicity, for example. Development theorising is also not too quick to join disability with other key development issues: governance, participation, chronic poverty, social exclusion and so on. In fact, it is important to note that the few writings that do appear in development journals and books are largely written by those working outside development studies.

More broadly, disability is still to find a legitimate and stable place in humanitarian issues, governance, poverty, education, conflict, environmental degradation and climate change—staple development themes. As one world report is published after another, disabled people appear to be inexistent in crises such as wars, environmental disasters and forced migration. This is despite the fact that these same wars are a major cause of impairment, and disabled people are among those most disadvantaged when it comes to fleeing or reconstructing their lives (see Pisani and Grech 2015). The various intersectionalities are left disproportionately unexplored and untheorised, including the situations confronting disabled refugees, women, children and ethnic minorities, left in ontological shadows even when disability cross-cuts multiple and interacting key development areas.

Disability has also until recently lingered on the fringes of or outside development policy. Disability has not been a priority for donors, an exclusion cascading down to policymakers, practitioners and others. Policy exclusions have been manifest, for example, in the frequent elimination of disability from the Poverty Reduction Strategy Papers (PRSPs). Evidence from a range of countries and continents (see Griffiths et al. 2009) has highlighted how, despite years of lobbying for inclusion, disabled people were rarely mentioned in, and much less influenced by the PRSP process. Overall, this scenario is not surprising, considering that even gender (despite longer standing periods of lobbying) has not been adequately accommodated in the PRSP process. While the situation may well change in the coming years, it does not necessarily mean that donor conditions and, even more basically, their practices will. In a development guided by the god of neo-liberal globalisation (see Harvey 2014), the exclusive focus remains on economic growth in individualising capitalist markets rather than equity, rights, inclusion and social justice (discussed later).

Mainstream development programmes, including those aimed at poverty reduction, have done a spectacular job of excluding disabled people or failing to adapt projects to their needs and demands. In 2010, Riddell estimated that less than 5 per cent of all overseas development assistance was allocated to disability projects and programmes. Over the past years, evidence has highlighted how disabled people are regularly bypassed in a range of programmes, including micro-credit, income generation (e.g. public works) and disaster relief (see IFRC 2007; Cramm and Finkenflügel 2008; Grech 2015). Those with intellectual impairments, mental health problems and serious, multiple and chronic impairments are seldom even considered. This exclusion seems compounded and often reinforced by the assumption that disabled people may be indirectly included in mainstream poverty reduction, health or population-specific projects such as those addressing women and children, when in practice they are not. The reality is that disabled people too often continue to be reframed as a specialist issue, someone else's concern. In my own practice, I have all too often heard the phrase 'we don't do disability here' uttered by development and other organisations working on poverty reduction or gender issues. Commentators have suggested that organisations sometimes feel that they lack expertise in the area, or that disability is irrelevant, one of many competing priorities, or too costly to address (see Mwendwa et al. 2009; Grech 2015). Local and national governments in the global South, just like international organisations, often regard disability as an issue to be dealt with by civil society and charitable institutions aided by funds and donations, an approach some contend (see Ingstad 2001) was imported by colonial powers and their missionaries. Overall, these exclusions are critical when many programmes, with some flexibility, a change in attitude and inclusion of disabled people in planning and implementation, can in fact accommodate disabled people too, for example by lowering water pumps to make them usable by wheelchair users or ensuring that all latrines are accessible right from design stage.

Disability and Development: (Un)Critical Ways Forward

As the field now called 'disability and development' grows, many issues and questions remain, not least about the field itself and approach. Disability and development as an area still struggles to define an identity, including as an academic field, even as the mass of largely grey literature grows (see Source n.d.). In practice, empirical work on disability, in particular that steered and conducted by disabled people in the global South, remains scarce. Even more seriously, the voices and perspectives of disabled poor people, especially those in rural areas, are seldom heard and contemplated, too often drowned in the perspectives of so-called experts and professionals. This is what is framed as 'knowledge' and then exported from the global North to the rest of the world, a design known too well in development (see Comaroff and Comaroff 2012). In practice, even disabled people's organisations claiming to represent all disabled people are too often composed of the privileged urban elite, sometimes unknowing and usually detached from the realities of their poorest rural constituency (see Grech 2015). Poverty is rarely lived on the skin of those 'doing' policy talk, consultancy or academia.

Theorising on disability in the global South continues to be weak, subjected to a discourse of generalisations and simplifications in the bid to contain and even measure disability. In the process, there are few interdisciplinary engagements and debates between disciplines including anthropology, rural development, disability studies and, paradoxically enough, development studies.

At the disability/development intersection, the concerns are many, and questioning and theorising is not a matter of abstraction, but one of necessary reflection for informed, contextualised, responsible and responsive practice. These include how disability rights pan out in practice (and if they do have any impact on disabled people); geopolitical asymmetries and the production of impairment; colonialism and neocolonialism; and a critique of development and its implications for disabled people (see for example Grech 2011, 2015; Meekosha 2011; Soldatic and Grech 2014).

At this juncture, there is no better time than now to be asking questions. While it is impossible to address all these issues and questions in this short chapter, I will attempt to outline some.

Colonialism: The Uncomfortable Roots of 'Development'

It is clear that development itself needs questioning, not least as to how it stands in relation to, engages with, frames and 'acts' on poverty and disability. But to do this, one needs to historicise development and its colonial origins, because these are far from benign. Indeed, while the development industry formalised itself post-decolonisation in the 1950s, the actual birth of development came much earlier with the first wave of colonialism in the Americas accompanied by the colonial project of ideological, cultural, social and economic domination accommodating the impending rise of global capitalism. As McMichael (2008:26) emphasises, development 'became an extension of modern social engineering to the colonies as they were incorporated into the European orbit … *development was a power relationship*' (italics in original). While a detailed discussion of colonialism is beyond the scope of this chapter (see Grech 2015 for an in-depth analysis), one must contend with its dynamics and effects because its legacies and modus operandi provide the ideological and racial foundations for 'development' in post/neocolonial settings, identities and the geopolitical asymmetries that maintain them. Even more basically, they legitimise certain development actors (those legitimate to 'develop' and 'civilise' the Other) while delegitimising others (those unwilling/incapable of developing themselves). Engaging with the colonial is a pivotal concern not only for positioning and historicising disability, but above all because the only common experience in these fragmented, complex and heterogenous histories and contexts (the simplified and homogenised 'global South') is often that of having been colonised.

The violent colonial encounter was a source of not only impoverishment, but also impairment and death, disabling subaltern subjects. The focus on export commodities, the privatisation of property, the introduction of an economic value on food, and the exploitation of land beyond sustainable use meant environmental and land degradation, reduced food availability and shifted age-old sustainable cultivation patterns, often leading to starvation and consequently disease and impairment. The hazardous forced labour in mines and the violence of the colonial encounter were a cause not only of death, but also of injury and impairment for those who survived. The focus on production and exportation for the world market, an order founded on the extraction of labour through slavery or serfdom, also implied that those who were seen as unfit (among them, disabled people) or schismatic to the European presence and order had to be normalised (to function and produce) or else be subjugated and isolated. Colonial humanitarian models, for example, brought church organisations and western medical professionals in for the 'treatment' of disabled people, importing measures such as the institution, which often isolated disabled people (especially mental health institutions) from their families, communities and the public sphere, inflicted much suffering and destroyed traditional ways of caring for disabled people within communities. It is not difficult to see how these patterns are not only perpetuated, but also renovated in neo-liberal measures and assaults on so-called developed countries in contemporary times (discussed later), marking colonialism, the birth of *homo oeconomicus* and the logic of globalised capitalism as the unifying historical fibre and narrative.

To return to the question 'who does development?', colonialism framed development as a civilising mission and as a civilising force to be performed by civilised/developed actors in the name of global capitalism, a colonialism that introduced racial otherness as the ideological key to domination (see Quijano 2008). This legacy is far from over and continues to provide the psychological, ideological and material foundations of development, because it has always been the white, civilised, developed subject that 'develops' the Other—the one antithetical and resistant to development (see Fanon 1963). The native is repositioned as the one 'outside the normative subject of Western modernity' (Cutajar 2008:29), in need and even desiring this intervention. These discourses serve to reposition and maintain the superiority of the global North, its economies, epistemologies and practices, including the treatment of disability, perpetually opening a space for intervention, practices of thinking and acting—beneficial and even civilising, yet infinitely colonising. In the meantime, local and informal ways of doing 'development', of surviving despite all odds, are ignored, discarded or resisted. Escobar (1995: 54) notes how development too often 'relies on the perpetual recognition and disavowal of difference'.

The Sometimes Destructive Nature of 'Development': On Neocolonial Tendencies

Questioning development also involves contending with its hegemonic neo-liberal globalising logic and agenda, and its repercussions, especially on those it claims to work in favour of. From the 1950s model of development as economic growth through to theories of modernisation, the brief but peripheral appearance of 'dependency theory', the basic needs approach and more contemporary notions of development as neo-liberal globalisation, development is about the opening up of national economies to participate in the global market. The implications and consequences, though, are exclusionary at best, impoverishing and devastating at worst. The neo-liberal measures used to achieve this economic growth and then imposed on 'developing countries' through Structural Adjustment Programmes and Poverty Reduction Strategy Papers remain the same: reductions in public expenditure; removal of price distortions (e.g. subsidies); trade liberalisation and mass privatisation, including of health, education and water. While fragile global South economies are subjected to the whims of volatile global markets, powerful global North economies continue to protect themselves, their agriculture and their banks. There has not been and never will be a level playing field. The economy of extraction based on colonial slavery and serfdom is perpetuated and the modalities are renegotiated as appropriation of cheap and exploitative labour by foreign-owned multinationals (e.g. sweatshops). In this process, the dynamics of domination favouring the global North and its companies, and the control of the periphery, remain intact. This argument was in fact clearly articulated over four decades ago by Latin American dependency theorists (e.g. Frank 1967), who posited that underdevelopment was a result of an international system of political and economic structures favouring the rich countries (the core), through exploitation and extraction of surpluses of the poor countries (the periphery). This system, they argued, trapped the poorer countries of the periphery in a perpetual state of powerlessness and led to structural dependence on rich countries through international capitalism. What emerges most clearly from this is that the rules of the neo-liberal game are not the same for every country and depend on the perpetuation of inequalities and polarisation of income and wealth.

The outcomes continue to be consistent and catastrophic in these fragile economies, including enhanced poverty and inequality, conflict, environmental degradation and forced migration. Those who suffer most are the most vulnerable populations. Neo-liberal development itself contributes to impoverishment and disablement, implying that the disability/development analysis requires an understanding and reconstitution of poverty and development within the geopolitical domain, 'how poverty is produced, and the relationships between processes that produce wealth and poverty' (Nustad 2001: 488). For example, the privatisation of water, while enriching foreign and national companies, often makes it unaffordable to the poorest, contributing to the risk of impairment such as river blindness and other water-borne diseases. This is critical when almost half the global South countries suffer from diseases caused by lack of clean water. Development also often entails massive environmental destruction (e.g. deforestation and soil erosion through logging by multinationals or water contamination by mining companies) accompanied by dramatic ill health and impairment, conflict, displacement and social and economic impacts. And let's not forget the tragedies of conflict and illegal wars such as those in Iraq, for which the global North has more than a cursory responsibility for- conflict in the name of interventionist 'democracy', of civilising 'development'. But the notion of development as a source of impairment, as disabling itself, is rarely addressed by those lobbying for disability mainstreaming or disability-inclusive development, an impairment disembodied materially and geopolitically as with many social constructionist accounts. Soldatic and Grech (2014) argue how even the CRPD, in its exclusive focus on disability (abandoning impairment and the bodily experience), marginalises the experiences of 'groups engaging in repertoires of action within the *logos* of impairment' because 'transnational claims for disability justice … naturalize impairment and negate the production of impairment under global structural processes of violence' (n.p.).

Overall, the resulting impoverishment, inequality and human suffering have often pitched the neo-liberal and globalising projects of development as 'new incarnations of neocolonialism' in a world order where 'capitalism … not only allows for but requires the perpetuation of coloniality' (Moraña et al. 2008:12). Despite the prefix *post* in postcolonial, colonialism has not ended, but is instead perpetuated indefinitely. Quijano (2008:187) observes how race continues to provide the ideological (and economic) legitimisation for the lower wages earned by the 'inferior races' for the same work performed as white people, what he calls 'the global capitalist coloniality of power'. What emerges clearly is that just like the act of colonising was interpreted by the colonisers as a 'moral' obligation to civilise the racially inferior subjects they conquered, neo-liberalism too is not simply an economic theory and associated practices; it remains 'a hegemonic discourse of a civilising model' (Lander 2000: 11–12, my translation).

While disability and poverty are drawn together to support arguments for including disability in development, questions linger and are hardly addressed: How can development contribute to poverty reduction among disabled people if it continues to exclude, impoverish and even disable? Is this at all possible when inequality continues to rise, pushing further to the margins those disproportionately disadvantaged—those 'outside' development? And critically: Is development necessarily good for disabled people? Few lessons have in fact been learnt from gender mainstreaming, including the problems with development itself and the implications for women, which has a far longer history in development (see True 2010).[1]

Neo-liberalism and the 'Unproductive' Body

Positioning disability within the hegemonic neo-liberal agenda means questioning and reframing if and how disability exists, and is constructed and 'treated' within the neo-liberal development logic, psyche and intervention. This is far from a cursory concern. At the most basic level, the neo-liberal agenda and the associated cuts in public expenditure cannot possibly permit any genuine inclusion of disability in development, since disability-inclusive development requires resources, political

[1] The reasons for the failure of gender mainstreaming have been various including implementation problems, ineffectiveness, devaluation of the importance of local contexts and lack of sensitivity to political scenarios and change, among others.

will and commitment, and a solid policy environment. Where economic growth (premised on strong individualised bodies) may be prioritised above anything else, where resources are allocated to realise predetermined development goals in a short time span, or where development means quick results based on aggregated data, it is not hard to see how disabled bodies and minds may slip between the cracks. The SDG target 17.18 and its call for disaggregated data to account for disability is a positive way forward, but generating this data will not be a simple or precise endeavour, not least on account of different disability definitions, methods and, let's not forget, costs and political inconvenience. Neo-liberal globalised development calls for and reconfirms economic growth as the ultimate means and end, a development predicated on normalised, ableist and heteronormative ideologies and practices, a clear paradox in the rhetoric of inclusive development—development is not for every 'body'. Development necessitates docile able bodies and minds to function and produce; the rest are to be corrected (cheaply) to function and produce, or removed—burdensome bodies on individualistic economies. Disabled bodies who may be too 'slow' or 'unproductive' therefore fall outside development, almost inimical to development. The practices, including development priorities and the dispensing of funds, maintain these patterns. Despite the fact that not all donors are the same, many are in practice more concerned with quick, effective and visible results by circulating time-bound funds rapidly. As a result, attention will likely continue to be directed towards populations closer to the poverty line, those easier to 'pull' out of poverty. Disabled people and others living in chronic poverty who require extended time and resources, fundamental organisational changes (including ideological ones) and flexibility, and who may not produce immediately visible and quantifiable results over the short term, will most likely continue to be left out. They are instead (re)constructed as *the problem,* responsible for their own predicament, even resistant to development efforts. Disabled bodies in the global South are therefore repositioned as neocolonised subjects, or more accurate still, as *neocolonised bodies*, the bodies positioned at the anxious intersection of the economic, the cultural and political, the global and the local. In the process, the development field and those working within it continue to lack contact with disabled people and have limited knowledge of disability. Inclusion is slow, and strategies and programmes remain exclusive and unadapted.

The complexity and heterogeneity of disability, too, are rarely understood with the due importance and critical diligence they deserve in one-size-fits-all discourse and 'solutions'. What about those, for example, with intellectual impairments whose needs and situations will likely be misunderstood, who will be perceived to be unreceptive to (development) intervention, because they may well 'function' better within small-scale agriculture and family economies, or who may after all not be able to work?

The questions linger on. How can disability be included in or benefit from development if the ableist neo-liberal rules of the game do not change? Will disabled bodies ever be considered 'development subjects' capable of 'developing'? Is mainstreaming at all possible without commitment, resources, a coordinated strategy and a development sector educated in disability, including conceptually?

The Complexity and Heterogeneity of Disability

The inclusion of a disability component in the SDGs may well be a step forward, but containing disability in a word, a definition, a measure or an indicator is far from easy and not quite suitable given the complexity and heterogeneity of disability. A host of literature, including feminist writings within disability studies (see Garland-Thomson 2010; Shakespeare 2013; Grech, 2015), has emphasised how disabled people and their experiences are far from homogeneous, mediated by and varying alongside a host of gender, racial, locational, personal (including type of impairment), subjective, socio-economic, cultural, psycho-emotional and many other dimensions, themselves dynamic and changing. This includes religious and spiritual beliefs, too often cast aside in a development sector that desperately strives to be secular in increasingly unsecular times.

Disability is mentioned with ease, including in the SDGs, giving the impression of a coherent group of people, feeding into the illusion that we know who or what we are talking about, and above all, that 'solutions' can be fit for all and sundry, whatever and wherever they may be. This is very dangerous in a development sector too often bent on simplifying and generalising, including poverty and how it should be addressed, too often decontextualised and depoliticised, where communities and people become an undifferentiated mass. Context, cultures, ideologies and circumstances interact with, construct and frame disability and disability experiences differentially and are dynamic. These are in turn renegotiated and reframed by individuals, meeting a plethora of responses to disability but also to so-called development. What is perhaps constant is the need for time, flexibility and grounded, responsive and dynamic knowledge and practices willing to 'complexify' rather than contain disability, because the meaning of disability too is 'fluid, dynamic and shifting, constantly (re)negotiated' (Grech 2015). Disability across cultures, contexts, spaces and places can be hardly encapsulated in all embracing static models, goals or strategies.

Conclusion

This chapter has briefly engaged with the connections and critical gaps in the disability and development debate and practice. As mentioned at the start, there are far too many issues that need discussion and unpacking. That disability is mentioned in the SDGs is a positive discursive move, but how things pan out in practice depend on much critical reflection and, above all, contextualised and responsive practice. More importantly, the questioning and challenging of disablism must never slip out of focus, including that which is motivated and maintained by our own discourse and 'interventions', including 'development'. This is real transformational practice, this is real 'development'.

Time and will are indeed needed for those working in development to learn about disability, to question, reflect, adapt, deconstruct and discard what doesn't work for disabled people and what may even harm them and their families. Development must be on people's own terms, and disabled people must own and define the process, whatever shape 'development' takes. It is development that must respond and adapt, not disabled people. But before doing any of this, development has to engage with disability not as a mere adjunct to the list of development subjects, but one that cross-cuts, challenges and even dislodges development and its ideologies and practices, a disability that provides myriad theoretical, ontological and epistemological opportunities (learning and other) to understand, develop, question, challenge and even reframe development altogether. Development theory, research and practice need a major overhaul if theorists, researchers and practitioners are to stop working and 'developing' without disability in mind, and are to learn about and become conversant with disability discourses, theory and practice. If not, they will continue to feed back into a development sector side-lining disability as someone else's research and practice concern.

A reflexive, critical and political stance is long overdue among those working in disability and development, because simplification and containment of disability, poverty and geopolitics can no longer do. We need to not only reflect critically on the complexity of disability across space, place and time, but also learn about, contest and challenge the ideologies and mechanics of the development sector itself, even if this means rocking the boat or delaying the process of 'inclusive development'. Whether disabled people are included in development or not, the reality is that the poorest, including disabled people, continue to survive on their own accord, using their own means, and it is these means and strengths that we need to build upon and ensure that we do not trample upon or destroy discursively or materially. Openly listening and learning from disabled people, their families and communities, and prioritising their voices is the critical starting point, even when these voices may go against our own subjectivities, definitions and approaches to disability and development.

Bringing disability and development together does not mean uncritically absorbing disability into development. It also does not mean simply including development tenets in existing disability frameworks and discourse. Elsewhere (see Grech 2012), I highlight how we urgently need to decolonise the disability and global South/development debate through a critical transnational disability studies that is (self)reflexive, emphasises uncertainty and contingency, and encourages a great deal of critical questioning, learning and the challenging of epistemological, ontological and practical fixities. This project is transdisciplinary, transboundary, open to debate and, before anything else, willing to decolonise debates to make 'present and credible, suppressed, marginalised and disaccredited knowledges' (Santos 2007: 16) and practices.

References

Albert, B. (Ed.). (2006). *In or out of the mainstream? Lessons from research on disability and development cooperation*. Leeds: The Disability Press.

Albert, B., & Hurst, R. (2005). *Disability and a human rights approach to development*. London: Disability KaR.

Australian Government. (2015). *Development for all 2015–2020: Strategy for strengthening disability-inclusive development in Australia's aid program*. Canberra: Commonwealth of Australia.

Berman Bieler, R. (2006). *The MDGs, disability and inclusive development.* Presentation at the World Congress on Communications for Development, Rome, October.
CBM. (2008). *CBM and the twin-track approach to disability and development.* Germany: CBM.
Comaroff, J., & Comaroff, J. L. (2012). *Theory from the South.* London: Paradigm.
Cramm, J. M., & Finkenflügel, H. (2008). Exclusion of disabled people from microcredit in Africa and Asia: A literature study. *Asia Pacific Disability Rehabilitation Journal, 19*(2), 15–33.
Cutajar, J. (2008). Knowledge and post-colonial pedagogy. *Mediterranean Journal of Educational Studies, 13*(2), 27–47.
DFID. (2000). *Disability, poverty and development.* London: DFID.
Escobar, A. (1995). *Encountering development: The making and unmaking of the Third World.* Princeton: Princeton University Press.
Fanon, F. (1963). *The wretched of the Earth.* New York: Grove.
Frank, A. G. (1967). *Capitalism and underdevelopment in Latin America.* New York: Monthly Review Press.
Garland-Thomson, R. (2010). Integrating disability, transforming feminist theory. In L. J. Davis (Ed.), *The disability studies reader* (pp. 353–373). New York and London: Routledge.
Grech, S. (2009). Disability, poverty and development: Critical reflections on the majority world debate. *Disability & Society, 24*(6), 771–784.
Grech, S. (2011). Recolonising debates or perpetuated coloniality? Decentring the spaces of disability, development and community in the global South. *International Journal of Inclusive Education, 15*(1), 87–100.
Grech, S. (2012). Disability and the majority world: A neocolonial approach. In D. Goodley, B. Hughes, & L. Davis (Eds.), *Disability and Social Theory: New developments and directions* (pp. 52–69). London: Palgrave Macmillan.
Grech, S. (2014). The spaces of poverty: Renegotiating place and disability in the global South. In K. Soldatic, A. Roulstone, & H. Morgan (Eds.), *Disability, spaces, and places of policy exclusion* (pp. 48–63). Abingdon: Routledge.
Grech, S. (2015). *Disability and poverty in the global South: Renegotiating development in Guatemala.* London: Palgrave.
Grech, S. (2016). Disability and poverty: Complex interactions and critical reframings. In S. Grech & K. Soldatic (Eds.), *Disability in the global South: The critical handbook.* New York: Springer.
Griffiths, M., Mannan, H., & MacLachlan, M. (2009). Empowerment, advocacy and national development policy: A case study of disabled peoples' organizations in Bolivia. In M. MacLachlan & L. Swartz (Eds.), *Disability & international development: Towards inclusive global health* (pp. 105–117). New York: Springer.
Groce, N. (2009). Disability, poverty, human rights and the need for accurate data to promote action. *ALTER European Journal of Disability Research, 3*(3), 185–187.
Gupta, J., Baud, S., Bekkers, R., Bernstein, S., Boas, I., Cornelissen, V. et al. (2014). *Sustainable development goals and inclusive development.* POST2015/UNU-IAS Policy Brief #5. Tokyo: United Nations University Institute for the Advanced Study of Sustainability.
Harvey, D. (2014). *Seventeen contradictions and the end of capitalism.* London: Profile Books.
IFRC. (2007). *Micro-credit: ARwandan experience.* Kenya: IFRC.
Ingstad, B. (2001). Disability in the developing world. In G. L. Albrecht, K. D. Seelman, & M. Bury (Eds.), *Handbook of disability studies* (pp. 219–251). Thousand Oaks, CA: Sage.
Ingstad, B., & Whyte, S. R. (Eds.). (2007). *Disability in local and global words.* Berkeley, CA: University of California Press.
Lander, E. (2000). Ciencias sociales: Saberes coloniales y eurocéntricos [Social sciences: Colonial and eurocentric knowledges]. In E. Lander (Ed.), *La colonialidad del saber: Eurocentrismo y cienciassocials* (pp. 11–41). Buenos Aires: CLACSO–UNESCO.
Lord, J., Posarac, A., Nicoli, M., et al. (2010). *Disability and international cooperation and development: A review of policies and practices.* Washington, DC: The World Bank.
McMichael, P. (2008). *Development and social change.* Los Angeles: Pine Forge Press.

Meekosha, H. (2011). Decolonizing disability: Thinking and acting globally. *Disability & Society, 26*(6), 667–682.

Mitra, S. (2010). Disability cash transfers in the context of poverty and unemployment: The case of South Africa. *World Development, 38*(12), 1692–1709.

Moraña, M., Dussel, E., & Jáuregui, C. A. (2008). Colonialism and its replicants. In M. Moraña, M. E. Dussel, & C. A. Jáuregui (Eds.), *Coloniality at large: Latin America and the postcolonial debate* (pp. 1–20). Durham: Duke University Press.

Mwendwa, T. N., Murangira, A., & Lang, R. (2009). Mainstreaming the rights of persons with disabilities in national development frameworks. *Journal of International Development, 21*(5), 662–672.

Nustad, K. G. (2001). Development: The devil we know? *Third World Quarterly, 22*(4), 479–489.

Oliver, M. (1990). *The politics of disablement*. Basingstoke: Macmillan.

Pisani, M., & Grech, S. (2015). Disability and forced migration: Critical intersectionalities. *Disability and the Global South, 2*(1), 421–441.

Quijano, A. (2008). Coloniality of power, Eurocentrism, and social classification. In M. Moraña, M. E. Dussel, & C. A. Jáuregui (Eds.), *Coloniality at large: Latin America and the postcolonial debate* (pp. 181–224). Durham: Duke University Press.

Riddell, R. C. (2010). Poverty, disability and aid: International development cooperation. In T. Barron & J. Ncube (Eds.), *Poverty and disability* (pp. 27–109). London: Leonard Cheshire International.

Santos, B. D. (2007). Beyond Abyssal thinking: From global lines to ecologies of knowledges. *Eurozine*, 1–33. Retrieved April 18, 2015, from http://www.eurozine.com/pdf/2007-06-29-santos-en.pdf.

Shakespeare, T. (2013). *Disability rights and wrongs revisited*. London: Routledge.

Soldatic, K., & Grech, S. (2014). Transnationalising disability studies: Rights, justice and impairment. *Disability Studies Quarterly, 34*(2). Retrieved from http://dsq-sds.org/article/view/4249.

Source. (n. d.). Retrieved January 28, 2016, from http://www.asksource.info/.

True, J. (2010). *Mainstreaming gender in international institutions*. New York: Routledge.

UN. (2015). Disability-inclusive sustainable development goals: 2030 Agenda for sustainable development. United Nations Enable. Retrieved December 3, 2015, from http://www.un.org/disabilities/documents/sdgs/disability_inclusive_sdgs.pdf.

UNESCO. (2012). *Global initiative on out-of-school children*. Paris: UNICEF and UNESCO.

van Veen, S. C. (2014). *Development for all: Understanding disability inclusion in development organisations*. Netherlands: VU University.

WHO and World Bank. (2011). *World report on disability*. Geneva: World Health Organization. Retrieved from http://whqlibdoc.who.int/publications/2011/9789240685215_eng.pdf.

Wissenbach, L. (2014). *Pathways to inclusive development: How to make disability inclusive practice measurable?* Germany: GTZ.

Chapter 2
Disability and Global Health

Leslie Swartz and Jason Bantjes

The World Report on Disability published in 2011 by the World Health Organization and the World Bank, amassed a wide range of evidence that, across the globe, people with disabilities have poorer access to health care and poorer health outcomes than nondisabled people. The disparities are especially great in low-income contexts, within which most people in the world find themselves. The disparities relate to almost every aspect of health and health care. Here is a nonexhaustive list, adapted from the World Report, detailing some of these discrepancies:

- People with disabilities are more likely than others to be the targets of violence and hence of intentional injury.
- Rates of nonintentional injuries among people with disabilities are also greater than among others. For example, burns in infancy, which are almost nonexistent in wealthy countries but not uncommon in lower income countries (Frenkel 2002), may occur more commonly among disabled as opposed to nondisabled children.
- People with disabilities have a greater risk of premature death than nondisabled people. In wealthier countries, the life span for many disabled people has increased; this change appears not to be as strong in low- and middle-income countries.
- People with disabilities are more likely not to receive the health care that they seek (across the spectrum of curative, preventive and promotive services); these gaps appear to be greater in low- and middle-income countries.

L. Swartz (✉) • J. Bantjes
Department of Psychology, Stellenbosch University, 2023 R W Wilcocks Building, Corner Ryneveld and Victoria Streets, Stellenbosch, Western Cape 7602, South Africa
e-mail: Lswartz@sun.ac.za

S. Grech, K. Soldatic (eds.), *Disability in the Global South*,
International Perspectives on Social Policy, Administration, and Practice,
DOI 10.1007/978-3-319-42488-0_2

- People with disabilities may experience particular barriers to sexual and reproductive health services, partly because of myths about disabled people's asexuality or hypersexuality.
- In the global South people with disabilities may be at greater risk of HIV infection than others, with reduced access to care and support services (see Groce et al. 2013).

These are just a few examples of a pervasive problem. Even at the level of health policies, people with disabilities are commonly excluded or hardly mentioned, as recent analyses of such policies in some low- and middle-income countries have shown (MacLachlan et al. 2012).

It is well established that poor health globally is associated with less access to resources, and that where the rates of illness are highest, the care resources are fewest (Benatar 2013). Public health, furthermore, focuses on the health of populations as a whole and it could be argued that a focus on particular needs, such as those of people with disabilities, would be inequitable because of an implicit assumption among public health practitioners that it is more expensive and time consuming to treat such people. This argument has deep roots, but any reluctance to engage with particular challenges faced by people with disabilities in terms of health, in our view, links to a number of unacceptable prejudices. Chief among these is the belief that disability and impairment are far rarer than they actually are. The WHO's latest estimate is that there are over a billion people with disabilities globally, of whom between 110 million and 190 million experience substantial difficulties (WHO and World Bank 2011). Even if this estimate, which corresponds to about 15 per cent of the world's population having disabilities, can be questioned on a range of methodological grounds, what is clear is that disability is frequently underestimated and therefore radically misunderstood. This underestimation in itself is a political act, an act of misrecognition, even in the field of global health which is centrally concerned with issues of social justice. There is urgent need for good-quality global data comparing access to adequate health care and rehabilitation services for disabled as opposed to nondisabled people, but indications are that disability is associated with compromised health-care access (WHO and World Bank 2011).

A central problem in the field of global health is simply the silence around disability in health policies at local and global levels (MacLachlan et al. 2012; Mannan et al. 2012). As a result, some of the interventions regarding disability and health occur, as they should, at the level of rather basic awareness raising, but fail to move much beyond this. Much of the work in the field is descriptive, demonstrating the issues and the problems, and the World Report summarizes this information well. However, as the report is dependent on existing data, it does not go far beyond this descriptive level. There are rather few reports of evaluated interventions regarding disability and global health. The burgeoning field of global mental health has established a corpus of randomized controlled trials which attempt to assist people with psychosocial disabilities (Patel et al. 2013), but this field is still rather young and the conceptual framework of global mental health is hotly contested (Swartz 2012; see also the chapter by Mills and Davar (2016) in this volume, which takes a critical look at the rapidly developing global mental health field).

In this chapter we seek to identify core conceptual and ideological issues that are crucial for understanding disability in relation to global health but which are under-theorized. We will not review all the work that has been done in the field of global health, but will raise some conceptual and political issues which need to be considered by those interested in disability and health worldwide. We begin our argument by sketching some critical issues surrounding how we think about disability, health and power as they affect the global South. Following this, we focus on disability and health as social issues. This leads to a discussion of the ethics of distribution and exclusion. We then consider what it may mean to rethink global health from a disability perspective, and the implications of this thinking for processes of transformation in global health.

Power, Disability, and Global Health: Some Critical Issues

Just as there are established associations between poverty and poorer health outcomes, so there are associations between disability and poverty. There are higher rates of disability in poor populations, and disability itself can lead to impoverishment through a range of pathways, including decreased access to education and employment. In contexts where resources are scarce, it falls on family members to care for disabled relatives and as a result these family members may have reduced opportunity to work or to seek health care. The relationship between disability, poverty, and ill health is complex and multidirectional, and any attempts to change the situation will need to take account of this complexity. As Meekosha and Soldatic (2011) demonstrate, to separate health or disability from a range of other social issues related to global imbalances in wealth and power would be a disservice to our understanding of these interrelated issues. Indeed, questions of global justice and rights cannot be fully addressed without considering the bodies and embodied experiences of those on whom global forces of inequality operate, and operate with the most profound consequences (Grech 2009, 2011; Soldatic 2013; Soldatic and Grech 2014). In very many cases, impairments, like ill health, do not just 'happen'—they are the consequence of social and political arrangements. And the consequences of impairment and ill health are equally socially mediated.

The imposition of power from the global North may appear abstract, but is experienced viscerally by bodies (Meekosha 2011). Nixon (2011), in relation to environmental issues, speaks of 'slow violence' against the poor in the global South. This is a useful concept. Historically, overt and easily identifiable violence, including killing, was a well-known feature of colonial regimes; current relationships of power have consequences for bodies even if the pathways are commonly obscured (Grech 2012). Knowledge from the global North about the colonized body, especially the 'deviant' or non-normative colonized body, had and continue to have profound consequences for people's experiences of their lives, and indeed of their own bodies (Mashingaidze 2010). Nowhere is the entanglement between ideas about disability, health, and political deviance more clear than in the history of Robben Island, off

Cape Town, South Africa. This island once housed an asylum for people known as "lepers," "lunatics," "feeble minded," and "insane," but became far better known as the place where political prisoners opposed to the apartheid regime, including Nelson Mandela, were incarcerated (Deacon 1995; Swartz 2010). There are also links between dominant ideas about race and dangerous sexuality, and ideas about disability and dangerous sexuality. Some of the myths and fears held in the global North about hypersexuality of people with disabilities, and the potential that people with disabilities may have to spread sexually transmitted diseases, are very similar to anxieties about the bodies of black colonized people (Butchart 1998; Frawley 2012; Hook 2012; Shakespeare 2013a; Rohleder et al. 2014).

Disability and Health as Social Issues

At the heart of much of the success of disability movements since the 1960s has been the recognition that disability and ill health are not the same thing. Historically, the field of disability has been seen as falling under the remit of medicine and health care, with medical professionals viewed as experts on people with disabilities and their lives. The social model of disability questioned this medical expertise and, along with other liberation movements, has championed the idea of the insider as the true expert. Disability came to be seen as a political and rights issue as opposed to a medical issue. Thomas (2007, 2012) has shown clearly how both disability and health issues need to be looked at in social terms, as issues intertwined with realities of inequality and intolerance of diversity. She notes further that there are intersectionalities, both between disability and health status, and between these issues and others, which would include gender, race, social class, and sexual orientation, for example. It is not possible, furthermore, to provide practical skills for health professionals on issues regarding health care for people with disabilities without basing these skills in a social analysis. Many of the practical challenges in relation to health care for disability rest on patterns of misrecognition and on health professionals simply not thinking about people with disabilities as mainstream health-care users (Shakespeare and Kleine 2013).

It is important to take these issues further in the global health context. Struggles against the "medical model" within the disability arena have a parallel within the global health movement. The famous Alma-Ata Declaration of the World Health Organization of 1978 defines health as "a state of complete physical, mental and social wellbeing, and not merely the absence of disease or infirmity." Health is viewed as "a fundamental human right" and "the attainment of the highest possible level of health is a most important world-wide social goal whose realization requires the action of many other social and economic sectors in addition to the health sector" (WHO 1978: para. 2). The Alma-Ata Declaration states further:

> The existing gross inequality in the health status of the people particularly between developed and developing countries as well as within countries is politically, socially and economically unacceptable and is, therefore, of common concern to all countries. (WHO 1978: para. 3)

The recognition that health is a sociopolitical and human rights issue has, if anything, become clearer since 1978 (Goldberg 2013). The world has faced and continues to face sociopolitical and economic obstacles in the fight against communicable diseases, notably HIV/AIDS, tuberculosis, and malaria (Remais et al. 2013), and in dealing with an increasing number of people living with noncommunicable diseases including those of lifestyle, such as hypertension and diabetes (Ebrahim et al. 2013), and those associated with ageing, such as the dramatic rise in the number of people living with dementia worldwide, and especially in lower income countries (Prince et al. 2013). The recognition of the sociopolitical embeddedness of health and disease issues, therefore, is not something which is unknown in the global health field—it forms the bedrock of developments in health care and policy affecting most of the world's inhabitants. It is certainly true to say that there are huge commercial interests at play in how health care travels through the world, with health care increasingly viewed as a commodity which only the rich can afford (Pellegrino 1999; Maketa et al. 2013; Phadke 2013). This is of course a product of the global privatization and commodification of health care in a neoliberal, market-oriented context (Coburn 2000; Horton et al. 2014). Many contemporary global health efforts recognize the centrality of acting on the social determinants of health to achieve health care globally (Marmot et al. 2008).

The global health system, functioning within a global economic system dominated by neoliberal policies, has found profit through marketing technological and pharmacological products, developed with expertise in the global North, to people in the global South (see, for example, Petryna et al. 2006; Towghi 2014). The sociopolitical problem of inadequate health-care systems can in this way be presented as "solved" or at least mitigated by the apparently global technical pharmaceutical fix, an issue which is dealt with more fully by Mills and Davar (2016) in relation to global psychopharmacology.

These analyses from the anthropology of global health may seem to be worlds away from discussions in disability studies, but they are instructive and add a dimension which is crucial to understanding the intersections between disability and global health. We suggested earlier that critiques of the "medical model" in mainstream disability studies echo similar critiques from a global health perspective of a particular manifestation of medical discourse and practice—in short, if the medical model is bad for disability, it is equally bad for global health. The examination of commodified global health practices takes the argument further though. Just as a narrow technicist approach to health care can be used to obscure the socially embedded nature of health and health care, it may also obscure the socially embedded nature of disability. For example, the "Joint position paper on the provision of mobility devices in less resourced settings" prepared by WHO and USAID (2011), notes that assistive devices for mobility are not sufficiently available in low-income contexts. Furthermore, where these devices are available, there are no trained personnel to assist users and potential users of them. Devices may also be inappropriate to the terrain in some cases. Two potential consequences of this situation are, first of all, that wheelchairs and similar devices, even when available, may be underutilized (indeed the sight of unused or broken wheelchairs is common in health facilities in low-income contexts); and second, the devices themselves may cause health problems. For example, badly fitting wheelchairs and prostheses may lead to pressure sores which, if not properly treated, may lead to death (Chalklen et al. 2006).

Visagie, Scheffler, and Schneider add a further layer to this discussion. In their study of wheelchair provision by health-care personnel in a rural setting in South Africa, they found that "only persons with a better prognosis were referred for wheelchairs, whereas those with poorer prognoses or lower levels of functioning were not referred" (Visagie et al. 2013: 3). Though these practices, as the authors point out, were not sanctioned by formal rules or policies, they expose some of the value issues which may influence decisions made by health-care providers under conditions of constrained resources. There is an implicit assessment here regarding which lives are more valuable and more worth supporting.

It is easy in a context such as this to condemn the behavior of health-care personnel making such choices, and we do not wish to suggest that the choices are correct. In the section which follows, however, we explore the need for a perspective on ethics as it affects both global health and disability issues.

Ethics of Distribution and Exclusion

As we have mentioned, the global maldistribution of resources and opportunities affects both health status and disability, and there are indications that inequality may increase in the future (Benatar et al. 2003; Benatar 2013). In addition, catastrophes, disasters, and global climate change pose major threats both to public health and to the participation of people with disabilities in society at large (McMichael 2013). Though there is now a burgeoning literature on disability, disasters and climate change, and health issues (Mitchell and Karr 2014), it remains the case that the particular vulnerability of people with disabilities in the global South to the health effects of climate change and disasters is not always considered. In an excellent recent review, McMichael (2013) highlights how vulnerability is repeatedly mentioned in relation to poverty, and at times in relation to what may be termed psychosocial disability issues, but disability as a whole is not given full attention. It is probably not surprising that given the scale of environmental threats to the world, some anthropologists of global health have written:

> Although global health conceptually includes all peoples regardless of social, economic, and political contexts, its ethical and moral commitment is to the most vulnerable. However, and given the impending and hitherto unprecedented scale of global catastrophe that environmental destruction, mass species extinction, and anthropogenic climate change presage, global health might benefit from redefining the vulnerable to include all of us. (Janes and Corbett 2009: 169)

Though they note the issue of particular vulnerabilities, these authors are correct in stating that all people are vulnerable to the health effects of environmental catastrophe. The strong probability is that all the issues well known to affect health and health care for people with disabilities—including access to health care, physical and attitudinal barriers, and secondary health complications through lack of management or mismanagement of impairments—are likely to be increased under times of social strain, social instability, and resource constraints. Indeed, within the Nazi system's abuse of concepts of public health to justify genocide, part of the reason given for murdering people with disabilities was on the grounds that scarce resources in times of war should not be squandered on people deemed economically unproductive (Evans 2010).

Rethinking Global Health from a Disability Activism Perspective

Let us return now to the Alma-Ata Declaration, which defined health as "a state of complete physical, mental and social wellbeing, and not merely the absence of disease or infirmity" (WHO 1978: para. 2). If we examine this definition wearing a disability activism lens, we are forced to confront the implication of the phrase "not merely the absence of disease or infirmity." Here, the "absence of disease or infirmity" is positioned as a necessary, though not sufficient, condition for health. It is not altogether clear what the WHO means by "infirmity" and the term seems to be taken for granted as self-explanatory in much writing about global health. Indeed, in a recent thoughtful article on the need for changing paradigms in the global health context, Bhatia and Rifkin repeatedly mention what they term "control of disease and infirmities" (2013: 460). These authors, in keeping with developments in how health and health care are understood, are critical of the dominance of reference to biomedical approaches to "control" disease and infirmity, and they correctly point out that the determinants of health, and hence key solutions to health problems, are sociopolitical and economic. But, along with many other authors, they do not question the idea that "infirmity," like "disease," needs to be controlled. Dictionary and commonsense definitions of "infirmity" suggest an overlap with the term "impairment" as used in the disability context. And many of the struggles in the disability movement have been precisely against the idea that impairment should be controlled—or even be thought of as being controlled—in a similar way to how we think about controlling disease (Oliver 1998; Nussbaum 2007). Looked at this way, quite apart from any other problem with the Alma-Ata Declaration and how it has come to be used, it is possible to see an element of disablism built into the very definition of health. By definition, a person with an impairment ("infirmity") cannot be seen to be healthy. This bias in the definition of health can be argued to be unintentional or even unconscious, and there are many in the global health field who would probably be offended by the accusation of disablism. But new developments in disability studies and especially in the contemporary application of psychoanalytic insights to understanding disablism (Watermeyer 2013) would argue that it is precisely these unconscious, unexpressed biases—these silences—which hold power to continue to exclude and oppress people with disabilities. The unexpressed and unacknowledged is much more difficult to deal with than is the overt expression of hostility or exclusion.

It has become increasingly clear that the Alma-Ata definition of health, which forms the bedrock of much global health policy and practice, has its limitations, partly because of an implicit bias towards biomedical solutions, as Bhatia and Rifkin (2013) suggest. Furthermore, as Huber et al. (2011) propose, the very notion of "control" of disease or infirmity may be inappropriate in a contemporary context, and may in fact always have been inappropriate. They go on to note how the focus and goals of global health should not be about eliminating disease or infirmity, but about the opportunities and capacities people have to manage themselves and their health in their specific contexts. This goal of self-management is not without its critics, including those linking it to neoliberal ideologies, that is, "responsibilization" or the idea that the individual is responsible for his/her health despite the fact that drivers of health conditions are sociopolitical and economic (see, for example, Ellison 2014; Foley 2009). Nevertheless, the core idea here of appropriate adaptation to context will be familiar to anyone working in the field of disability. This does not mean that the context itself should not be interrogated and changed, but rather that the principle of contextuality, of living with impairment or with illness, represents an attack on conventional notions of biomedicine as a universal source of cure. This attack, coming as it now does from the field of global health, has clear resonance with the attacks on the "medical model" in disability studies. Consider a recent contribution by a medical sociologist discussing the goal of research in the global health field:

> Medical and public health interventions come with promises of relieving the burden of suffering, curing disease, enhancing wellbeing, preventing the onset of disability, and—the ultimate trump card—saving lives. The underlying notion is that much contemporary disease causes unnecessary pain and anguish, which can be effectively avoided or manipulated with public health interventions such as screening or vaccination campaigns and biomedical treatments. These promises are tied into regulatory, organizational, and behavioral scripts … Inevitably, however, such scripts underestimate the complexity of the social world and unintended consequences multiply. Hence, the reality of health workers and patients no longer matches the promises, requiring remediation work to realign interventions and expectations. (Timmermans 2013: 3)

This quote could be edited with the change of only a few words to reflect long-standing concerns in the disability field. Once again, the goal of preventing disability is presented with what may be regarded by readers familiar with disability studies as a degree of naïveté, given the complexity and ferocity of debates about preventing disability (Shakespeare 2013b). Clearly, there is a great deal of synergy between contemporary thinking in global health and disability studies, but it appears that the contribution of disability studies thinking to global health has not yet been optimized. The questions at the interface between global health and disability should, perhaps, not just be "How can disability issues be better integrated and taken seriously in global health programs?" but also "How can global health learn from disability research and activism?" It is with some suggestions regarding this latter question that we conclude this chapter.

Transforming Global Health Through Disability Thinking

In his work on issues of disability and the global South, Grech (2009, 2011) notes that the gaze of disciplines constructed in the colonizing world has been brought to bear as a form of expertise ostensibly to "solve" problems of the global South but also as a form of disciplinary control. Max-Neef (2005), furthermore, notes that the huge problems of the world, including those of poverty, environmental degradation, and issues of health, cannot be solved by disciplines working alone but require a broader, transdisciplinary perspective. In this regard, disability studies, which by its nature should be interdisciplinary (and questioning of the boundaries between disciplines), have much to offer global health.

MacLachlan et al. (2012) propose that for global health to be truly inclusive, the needs of people with disabilities must be taken into account. The mechanism by which this is proposed, though, is not primarily through new technologies or products, but rather through processes of care (MacLachlan 2009). There are many specific issues to consider, including the complexities of community-based rehabilitation (see Kuipers and Sabuni (2016) in this volume; Mannan and MacLachlan 2013), but underpinning all the practical steps and programs which need to be considered is an orientation towards creating and sustaining supportive networks for people through their lives. This emphasis is very different from seeing global health as being solely about the elimination of disease and/or impairment.

African thinking on disability has emphasized the importance of interrelatedness of people within the contexts in which they live (Mji et al. 2011; Owusu-Ansah and Mji 2013). Ideas about independence as a goal for people with disabilities are questioned in an African context in which mutuality and supportive networks are considered to be what make people human (Owusu-Ansah and Mji 2013). It is no coincidence that ideals of independence are associated with ways of thinking which tend to be dismissive of a range of indigenous practices, including practices related to how people live their lives in the context of disability and ill health. These indigenous practices, which are commonly community based and dependent on social networks, constitute an obvious challenge to views of global health as a set of discrete technological challenges which can be solved by the export of technologies and products developed in the global North (Smith 1999; Farmer 2003).

Conclusion

The idea that humanness is best understood in the ways in which all people depend on and are responsible for others has resonance with research into the ethics of care. In the field of disability, Kittay (2013) has shown how care for a person with a severe impairment is not only worth doing but also part of being human. Tronto (2010, 2013), along with Kittay, notes that foregrounding the work of care requires a new kind of politics—a politics which recognizes and even values vulnerability, and which makes care work visible. It is a truism that throughout the world, most health care, as well as most care for people with disabilities, occurs in private domestic spaces and not as part of large-scale formal interventions. The substantial literature that is now available on the lives of people with disabilities, including the burgeoning corpus of disability life writing (Couser 1997, 2004, 2012), attests powerfully to this fact. Disability studies not only emphasize the social and political determinants of both disablement and health problems, but also suggest a way of approaching global health challenges. This is by understanding interrelatedness, respecting and supporting empowering social practices, building solidarity, and creating a society which allows for and supports a range of bodies. If, in a disability study paradigm, the "medical model" was historically part of what has been termed "enforcing normalcy" (Davis 1995), then disability studies have much to offer global health. A key challenge is for people who work in the area of disability, especially in the global South, to help global health as a paradigm, or a set of paradigms, begin to question the "normalizing" assumptions of current health practices. True inclusion in global health is less about reaching common, taken-for-granted health goals than it is about supporting people through their lives, and in the varied contexts within which they live.

References

Benatar, S. (2013). The quest for justice in global health. *Hastings Center Report, 43*(6), 45–46.

Benatar, S. R., Daar, A. S., & Singer, P. A. (2003). Global health ethics: The rationale for mutual caring. *International Affairs, 79*(1), 107–138.

Bhatia, M., & Rifkin, S. B. (2013). Primary health care, now and forever? A case study of a paradigm change. *International Journal of Health Services, 43*(3), 459–471.

Butchart, A. (1998). *The anatomy of power: European constructions of the African body*. London: Zed Books.

Chalklen, S., Swartz, L., & Watermeyer, B. (2006). Establishing the secretariat for the African decade of persons with disabilities. In B. Watermeyer, L. Swartz, T. Lorenzo, M. Schneider, & M. Priestley (Eds.), *Disability and social change. A South African agenda* (pp. 93–98). Cape Town: HSRC Press.

Coburn, D. (2000). Income inequality, social cohesion and the health status of populations: The role of neo-liberalism. *Social Science & Medicine, 51*(1), 135–146.

Couser, G. T. (1997). *Recovering bodies: Illness, disability, and life writing*. Madison: University of Wisconsin Press.

Couser, G. T. (2004). *Vulnerable subjects: Ethics and life writing*. Ithaca: Cornell University Press.

Couser, G. T. (2012). *Memoir: An introduction*. New York: Oxford University Press.

Davis, L. J. (1995). *Enforcing normalcy: Disability, deafness, and the body*. New York: Verso.

Deacon, H. (1995). *The island: A history of Robben Island*. Cape Town: David Philip.

Ebrahim, S., Pearce, N., Smeeth, L., Casas, J. P., Jaffar, S., & Piot, P. (2013). Tackling non-communicable diseases in low-and middle-income countries: Is the evidence from high-income countries all we need? *PLoS Medicine, 10*(1), e1001377. doi:10.1371/journal.pmed.1001377.

Ellison, J. (2014). First-class health: Amenity wards, health insurance, and normalizing health care inequalities in Tanzania. *Medical Anthropology Quarterly, 28*(2), 162–181. doi:10.1111/maq.12086.

Evans, S. E. (2010). *Hitler's forgotten victims: The holocaust and the disabled*. Stroud: History Press.

Farmer, P. (2003). *Pathologies of power: Health, human rights and the new war on the poor.* Berkeley: University of California Press.
Foley, E. (2009). *Your pocket is what cures you: The politics of health in Senegal.* Brunswick, NJ: Rutgers University Press.
Frawley, P. (2012). Sex and disability. *Culture, Health & Sexuality, 14*(10), 1233–1234.
Frenkel, L. (2002). 'You get used to it': Working with trauma in a burns unit of a South African children's hospital. *Psychodynamic Practice, 8*(4), 483–503.
Goldberg, D. S. (2013). Global health care is not global health: Populations, inequities, and law as a social determinant of health. In G. Cohen (Ed.), *The globalization of health care* (pp. 403–420). New York: Oxford University Press.
Grech, S. (2009). Disability, poverty and development: Critical reflections on the majority world debate. *Disability & Society, 24*(6), 771–784.
Grech, S. (2011). Recolonising debates or perpetuated coloniality? Decentring the spaces of disability, development and community in the global South. *International Journal of Inclusive Education, 15*(1), 87–100.
Grech, S. (2012). Disability and the majority world: A neo-colonial approach. In D. Goodley, B. Hughes, & L. Davis (Eds.), *Disability and social theory: New developments and directions* (pp. 52–69). London: Palgrave Macmillan.
Groce, N. E., Rohleder, P., Eide, A. H., MacLachlan, M., Mall, S., & Swartz, L. (2013). HIV issues and people with disabilities: A review and agenda for research. *Social Science & Medicine, 77*, 31–40. doi:10.1016/j.socscimed.2012.10.024.
Hook, D. (2012). *The mind of apartheid: A critical psychology of the postcolonial.* London: Routledge.
Horton, S., Abadía, C., Mulligan, J., & Thompson, J. J. (2014). Critical anthropology of global health 'takes a stand' statement: A critical medical anthropological approach to the US's Affordable Care Act. *Medical Anthropology Quarterly, 28*(1), 1–22.
Huber, M., Knottnerus, J. A., Green, L., Horst, H. V. D., Jadad, A. R., Kromhout, D., et al. (2011). How should we define health? *British Medical Journal, 343*(6), d4163. doi:10.1136/bmj.d4163.
Janes, C. R., & Corbett, K. K. (2009). Anthropology and global health. *Annual Review of Anthropology, 38*, 167–183.
Kittay, E. F. (2013). *Love's labor.* New York: Routledge.
Kuipers, P., & Sabuni, L. P. (2016). Community-based rehabilitation and disability-inclusive development: On a winding path to an uncertain destination. In S. Grech & K. Soldatic (Eds.), *Disability in the global South: The critical handbook.* New York: Springer.
MacLachlan, M. (2009). Rethinking global health research: Towards integrative expertise. *Global Health, 5*(6). doi:10.1186/1744-8603-5-6.
MacLachlan, M., Amin, M., Mannan, H., El Tayeb, S., Bedri, N., Swartz, L., et al. (2012). Inclusion and human rights in African health policies: Using EquiFrame for comparative and benchmarking analysis of 51 policies from Malawi, Sudan, South Africa & Namibia. *PLoS ONE, 7*(5), e35864. doi:10.1371/journal.pone.0035864.
Maketa, V., Vuna, M., Baloji, S., Lubanza, S., Hendrickx, D., Inocêncio da Luz, R. A., et al. (2013). Perceptions of health, health care and community-oriented health interventions in poor urban communities of Kinshasa, Democratic Republic of Congo. *PLoS ONE, 8*(12), e84314. doi:10.1371/journal.pone.0084314.
Mannan, H., & MacLachlan, M. (2013). Disability and health: A research agenda. *Social Inclusion, 1*(1), 37–45.
Mannan, H., McVeigh, J., Amin, M., MacLachlan, M., Swartz, L., Munthali, A., et al. (2012). Core concepts of human rights and inclusion of vulnerable groups in the disability and rehabilitation policies of Malawi, Namibia, Sudan, and South Africa. *Journal of Disability Policy Studies, 23*, 67–81. doi:10.1177/1044207312439103.

Marmot, M., Friel, S., Bell, R., Houweling, T. A., & Taylor, S. (2008). Closing the gap in a generation: Health equity through action on the social determinants of health. *The Lancet, 372*(9650), 1661–1669.

Mashingaidze, T. M. (2010). Power, disease and prejudice: A historiographical overview of the syphilis contagion in colonial Sub-Saharan Africa, 1890s–1950s. *Sephis, 6*(3), 41–53.

Max-Neef, M. A. (2005). Foundations of transdisciplinarity. *Ecological Economics, 53*(1), 5–16.

McMichael, A. J. (2013). Globalization, climate change, and human health. *New England Journal of Medicine, 368*(14), 1335–1343.

Meekosha, H. (2011). Decolonising disability: Thinking and acting globally. *Disability & Society, 26*(6), 667–682.

Meekosha, H., & Soldatic, K. (2011). Human rights and the global South: The case of disability. *Third World Quarterly, 32*(8), 1383–1397.

Mills, C., & Davar, B. (2016). A local critique of global mental health. In S. Grech & K. Soldatic (Eds.), *Disability in the global South: The critical handbook*. New York: Springer.

Mitchell, D., & Karr, V. (Eds.). (2014). *Crises, conflict and disability: Ensuring equality*. London: Routledge.

Mji, G., Gcaza, S., Swartz, L., MacLachlan, M., & Hutton, B. (2011). An African way of networking around disability. *Disability & Society, 26*, 365–368.

Nixon, R. (2011). *Slow violence and the environmentalism of the poor*. Cambridge, MA: Harvard University Press.

Nussbaum, M. (2007). *Frontiers of justice: Disability, nationality, species membership*. Boston: Belknap.

Oliver, M. (1998). Theories of disability in health practice and research. *British Medical Journal, 317*, 1446–1449.

Owusu-Ansah, F. E., & Mji, G. (2013). African indigenous knowledge and research: Original research. *African Journal of Disability, 2*(1), 1–5.

Patel, V., Minas, H., Cohen, A., & Prince, M. (Eds.). (2013). *Global mental health: Principles and practice*. New York: Oxford University Press.

Pellegrino, E. D. (1999). The commodification of medical and health care: The moral consequences of a paradigm shift from a professional to a market ethic. *Journal of Medicine and Philosophy, 24*(3), 243–266.

Petryna, A., Lakoff, A., & Kleinman, A. (Eds.). (2006). *Global pharmaceuticals: Ethics, markets, practices*. Durham, NC: Duke University Press.

Phadke, A. (2013). Contradictions of the health-care system in India and a strategy for health-care for all. *Indian Journal of Public Health, 57*, 231–235. http://www.ijph.in/text.asp?2013/57/4/231/123256.

Prince, M., Bryce, R., Albanese, E., Wimo, A., Ribeiro, W., & Ferri, C. P. (2013). The global prevalence of dementia: A systematic review and metaanalysis. *Alzheimers & Dementia, 9*(1), 63–75.

Remais, J. V., Zeng, G., Li, G., Tian, L., & Engelgau, M. M. (2013). Convergence of non-communicable and infectious diseases in low-and middle-income countries. *International Journal of Epidemiology, 42*(1), 221–227.

Rohleder, P., Eide, A. H., & Swartz, L. (2014). Excluded from a health crisis? HIV/AIDS and people with disabilities. In D. Mitchell & V. Karr (Eds.), *Crises, conflict and disability: Ensuring equality* (pp. 58–64). London: Routledge.

Shakespeare, T. (2013a). *Disability rights and wrongs revisited*. London: Routledge.

Shakespeare, T. (2013b). Nasty, brutish, and short? On the predicament of disability and embodiment. In J. Bickenbach, F. Felder, & B. Schmitz (Eds.), *Disability and the good human life* (pp. 93–112). Cambridge: Cambridge University Press.

Shakespeare, T., & Kleine, I. (2013). Educating health professionals about disability: A review of interventions. *Health and Social Care Education, 2*(2), 20–37.

Smith, L. T. (1999). *Decolonizing methodologies: Research and indigenous peoples*. London: Zed Books.

Soldatic, K. (2013). The transnational sphere of justice: Disability praxis and the politics of impairment. *Disability & Society, 28*(6), 744–755.

Soldatic, K., & Grech, S. (2014). Transnationalising disability studies: Rights, justice and impairment. *Disability Studies Quarterly, 34*(2). Retrieved from http://dsq-sds.org/article/view/4249.

Swartz, S. (2010). The regulation of British colonial lunatic asylums and the origins of colonial psychiatry, 1860–1864. *History of Psychology, 13*, 160–177. doi:10.1037/a0019223.

Swartz, L. (2012). An unruly coming of age: The benefits of discomfort for global mental health. *Transcultural Psychiatry, 49*, 531–538. doi:10.1177/1363461512454810.

Thomas, C. (2007). *Sociologies of disability and illness. Contested ideas in disability studies and medical sociology*. Basingstoke: Palgrave Macmillan.

Thomas, C. (2012). Theorising disability and chronic illness: Where next for perspectives in medical sociology? *Social Theory & Health, 10*(3), 209–228.

Timmermans, S. (2013). Seven warrants for qualitative health sociology. *Social Science & Medicine, 77*, 1–8.

Towghi, F. (2014). Normalizing off-label experiments and the pharmaceuticalization of homebirths in Pakistan. *Ethnos, 79*(1), 108–137.

Tronto, J. C. (2010). Creating caring institutions: Politics, plurality, and purpose. *Ethics and Social Welfare, 4*(2), 158–171.

Tronto, J. C. (2013). *Caring democracy: Markets, equality, and justice*. New York: NYU Press.

Visagie, S., Scheffler, E., & Schneider, M. (2013). Policy implementation in wheelchair service delivery in a rural South African setting. *African Journal of Disability, 2*(1). doi:10.4102/ajod.v2i1.63.

Watermeyer, B. (2013). *Towards a contextual psychology of disablism*. London: Routledge.

WHO. (1978). *Declaration of Alma-Ata*. World Health Organization. Retrieved September 26, 2014, from http://www.who.int/publications/almaata_declaration_en.pdf.

WHO and the United States Agency for International Development. (2011). *Joint position paper on the provision of mobility devices in less resourced settings*. Geneva: World Health Organization.

WHO and World Bank. (2011). *World report on disability*. Geneva: World Health Organization.

Chapter 3
Disability Studies: Developments in Anthropology

James Staples and Nilika Mehrotra

Introduction

Despite the proliferation of disability studies (DS) in the USA and Britain over the last three decades, anthropology a discipline committed to understanding alterity, has contributed surprisingly little to the study of disability. There have been relatively few ethnographic studies that engage directly with disability; fewer still explicitly engage with the broader interdisciplinary arena of DS to document and analyse the experience of disability in the global South. Until recently, this has meant that DS has been dominated by the concerns of disabled people, policymakers and service providers in western, industrialised countries, rather than expanding to explore the different ways in which disability might be configured cross-culturally (e.g. see Miles 2002; Mehrotra 2011; Grech 2011, 2012). Ingstad and Whyte noted this gap in their pioneering edited collection *Disability and Culture* (1995) 20 years ago; Kasnitz and Shuttleworth made the same point a few years later (2001a, b); and, according to Rapp and Ginsburg (2012; Ginsburg and Rapp 2013), the lacuna still remains. Why that should be so is a matter of speculation. Rapp and Ginsburg, based on their own experiences in the USA, ultimately favour a Freudian explanation: that anthropologists, fearful of the loss that disability ultimately brings to us all, in one form or another, are in denial (2012: 174). Linton (1998) suggests that the lack of interest shown by anthropologists in disability corresponds with the fact that there are so few disabled anthropologists, and that those who do make it within the academy become marginalised. 'Indiana Jones in a wheelchair', to borrow Kasnitz and Shuttleworth's (2001a) image, is not a picture easily conjured up, other than as parody. By the same token, we would also

J. Staples (✉)
Brunel University London, Middlesex, UK
e-mail: James.Staples@brunel.ac.uk

N. Mehrotra
Jawaharlal Nehru University, Delhi, India

S. Grech, K. Soldatic (eds.), *Disability in the Global South*,
International Perspectives on Social Policy, Administration, and Practice,
DOI 10.1007/978-3-319-42488-0_3

suggest (based on anecdotal evidence from conversations with colleagues over the years) that some anthropologists might implicitly consider 'the disabled' as inherently less interesting—because they are assumed to be intrinsically unable to engage fully in social life—as creators and consumers of culture than more mainstream representatives of the populations being studied. Despite Mead's injunction back in the 1950s for us to study human beings in all their diversity, this is an understanding of disabled people that persists (Mead 1953).

None of this is to suggest, however, that anthropological engagement with disability has been stagnant over the last couple of decades. This chapter sets out to draw together the various fragments of anthropology's encounters with disability—which dates right back to the early twentieth century—and, in reviewing some of the discipline's more recent engagements with the topic, to explore the distinctive contribution that a fine-grained ethnographic approach can bring to our collective understanding. Given that there have been a number of essays that extensively review what we might categorise as the anthropological literature on disability (e.g. Kasnitz and Shuttleworth 2001a, b; Reid-Cunningham 2009; Ginsburg and Rapp 2013), we make no attempt here to provide a comprehensive bibliographical account, even though we flag the need for reviews that include more anthropologists trained and employed outside the USA and western Europe.

Rather, we set out to explore in a more general sense the theoretical and methodological contributions anthropology has made, directly and indirectly, that may be pertinent to the study of disability, particularly beyond the industrialised settings that provide the backdrop for many studies across the social sciences and humanities. In setting out a vision for how anthropology might make a more central contribution to theorising disability in non-western contexts, we also examine how the key thematic and theoretical interests we identify within the discipline—such as power, representation, personhood, embodiment, culture and ontology, as well as more recent foci on citizenship and human rights (Mehrotra 2011; Ginsburg and Rapp 2013)—might intersect with experiences and understandings of disability cross-culturally to throw new light on them.

Anthropological Interest in Disability

One of the first recorded studies in anthropology that focused specifically on disability was Ruth Benedict's essay 'Anthropology and the Abnormal' (1934). In tune with the broader Boasian thrust of her work, her argument is a culturally relativist one. She argues that what may appear abnormal or undesirable in one cultural configuration—in the case she describes, epilepsy—in another might be highly valued. For the Shasth tribe of California, for example, epileptic seizures were, according to Benedict, not symptoms of a 'dreaded disease', but a pathway to shamanic authority. 'Most peoples', as she puts it, 'have regarded even extreme psychic manifestations not only as normal and desirable but even as characteristic of highly valued and gifted individuals' (1934: 60). Jane and Lucien Hank were similarly ahead of the curve in recognising the cultural contingency of disability. 'The disfiguring scar in Dallas', as they characterise it rather neatly, 'becomes an honorific mark in Dahomey' (1948: 11). The language used by the Hanks might well reflect the ethnocentrism of the time in which they were writing, but their account of the anthropologist's task as being to 'describe the social status accorded the physically handicapped in various foreign cultures' (1948: 11) is prescient in recognising that a physiologically similar difference might be recognised and experienced in different ways cross-culturally. The questions posed by Whyte and Ingstad, nearly 50 years later—and which suggest why anthropology might be an important contributor to DS—were remarkably similar: 'How are the deficits of body and mind understood and dealt with in different societies? How is an individual's culturally defined identity as a person affected by disability? What processes of cultural change shape local perceptions of disability?' (1995: 3).

So, given anthropology's historical interest in disability (see Reid-Cunningham 2009 for a more detailed account), one that dates back almost to its inception as an academic discipline in the UK and the USA, why is anthropology so little recognised within DS, and why has anthropology's interest in the post-World War II years apparently been so sporadic? To these questions we turn in the next section.

Placing Anthropology in Disability Studies

When anthropologists have engaged with disability as a topic of study, they have, historically at least, given little recognition to the wider interdisciplinary arena of disability studies, as Kasnitz and Shuttleworth have noted (Kasnitz and Shuttleworth 2001a: 26–27). Although Ingstad and Whyte in their edited volume, for example, note in passing the work done by sociologists and psychologists (1995: 3), its contributors are criticised by Kasnitz and Shuttleworth for 'omitting references to work in disability studies by scholars without an anthropology degree' and for a lack of precision in problematising key terms. This accusation of disciplinary 'parochialism' (Kasnitz and Shuttleworth 2001a: 27) could well be applied to a number of ethnographic studies, Staples's own earlier work included (2003; 2007), that might nevertheless be considered rich in their analysis of the experiences of disabled people, even when they do not necessarily use the term disability or engage explicitly with DS. Indeed, we suspect that many ethnographers—again, Staples included, before 2003—may have been only obliquely aware of the terminological, theoretical and methodological wrangling among disability scholars in the UK and the USA that had been going on at least since the 1970s (e.g. Zola 1979, 1981; Oliver 1984, 1985). Our ethnographic encounters with disability had, in many instances, come about by serendipity, by encountering people who identified (or were identified by others) as disabled while in the field. The first port of call for theoretical or comparative material through which to analyse these encounters was, for the most part, the anthropological canon. Robert Murphy (1987), for example, in seeking out material to help him make sense of his own experience of paraplegia, turns to theorists such as Victor Turner (1967) and his work on liminality rather than, say, the work of Zola or Oliver on the social model.

This does not negate the value of such anthropological work to DS: indeed, in some cases, it may be made stronger by throwing a different kind of light on problems than that afforded by the particular foci of DS theory. So, while taking on board their arguments, we would take a more benign view than Kasnitz and Shuttleworth of earlier anthropological inattention to the paradigms that had already been forged by DS scholars and activists. As Whyte and Ingstad suggest in their subsequent collection (2007), in what might be seen as an indirect response to Kasnitz and Shuttleworth's critique:

> [A]nthropologists continue to produce penetrating ethnographies of great relevance to the study of disability, which are not explicitly identified as works of disability scholarship. These works can be sources of inspiration and challenge because they provide a variety of perspectives (Whyte and Ingstad 2007: 6).

Whyte and Ingstad then go on to cite Cohen's work (1998) on Alzheimer's disease in India and Petryna's (2002) on biological citizenship after Chernobyl as examples of ethnographic work relevant to DS, regardless of whether their authors classify themselves under its interdisciplinary umbrella. Joao Biehl's work with young Brazilian woman Catarina (2005), someone who would fit universal categorisations of disability but who did not herself use the term, or Julie Livingston's focus on 'debility' in Botswana (2005) might also be cited as sources useful to DS, precisely because they do not sit their analyses within its dominant frameworks.

Such caveats aside, anthropologists have increasingly acknowledged the potential usefulness of DS that Staples began to recognise in his own work (2005; 2011a). While no mainstream DS scholars were cited in Whyte and Ingstad's introduction to *Disability and Culture*, for example, the opening chapter of their 2007 collection, *Disability in Local and Global Worlds*, references several, particularly UK, sociologists (e.g. Barnes et al. 1999; Shakespeare and Watson 2001; Barnes et al. 2002; Corker and Shakespeare 2002), and situates itself much more firmly within the field of DS. The ways in which terms such as 'impairment' and 'disability' have already been intensively interrogated and problematised by DS scholars, for example, clearly demand that we no longer take these terms for granted.

While contemporary anthropological accounts of disabling experiences remain relatively thin on the ground, those produced in the last decade or so do engage more directly with DS. In his monograph on disability and the state in China, for instance, Kohrman (2005) draws upon the theoretical work of a number of disability scholars (Hughes and Paterson 1997; Frank 2000; Landsman 2001; Corker and Shakespeare 2002; Tremain 2002; Kasnitz 2003) who not only work in DS, but also build on earlier studies to go beyond the dualism of impairment/disability, a perspective that has dominated certain strands of DS. In so doing, Kohrman demonstrates how anthropology might fruitfully engage with DS without being straitjacketed by its theoretical orientations.

Positioning Disability Scholarship Within Anthropology

As implied in our introduction, the issue for anthropologists who study disability is not just how they situate themselves in relation to DS, but also where they are situated within their own discipline. We already noted the problem of marginalising disability, and disabled scholars, *within* anthropology. But one sub-area of anthropology that has offered a particularly fertile space for ethnographic work on disability to take root is medical anthropology (Inhorn and Wentzell 2012: 14–15). In the USA, this might be dated back to the formation of a disability research interest group within the Society for Medical Anthropology (SMA)—itself a section of the American Anthropological Association (AAA)—which was established by Louise Duval in the 1980s (Duval 1986; Goldin 1988), and a few years later developed by Devva Kasnitz, herself a disabled scholar (Kasnitz and Shuttleworth 2001a, b). Pioneering works on adult deafness (Becker 1983), limb reduction defects (Frank 2000) and dwarfism (Ablon 1984, 1988) were among the early anthropological contributions to DS for which the SMA group is credited as having served as a crucible (Inhorn and Wentzell 2012: 15).

While the intersections between medical anthropology and DS have clearly been productive, Rapp and Ginsburg—in an edited collection devoted to celebrating medical anthropology's half-century as a distinctive sub-discipline (Inhorn and Wentzell 2012)—also find it ironic that anthropological work, often strongly critical of the medicalisation of disability, should find a home within medical anthropology in particular (2012: 165–166). Medical anthropologists themselves, of course, also tend to take a critical approach towards medicalisation, but their central interests, however culturally relative in their framing, are in matters of illness and disease. These interests clearly intersect with those of DS scholars, but are not inimitable to them: the bodily states that, in certain contexts, underpin disability do not necessarily define individuals as ill or as suffering, but sometimes as different in ways that may be valued in their own right. The state of being deaf, for example, might be seen as constitutive of culture (Groce 1985), in the sense of 'culture' as valued patterns of behaviour shared by social groups, rather than a threat to it. Deafness might even, as Friedner's (2014, 2015) more recent work confirms, be constituted as an identity ripe for capitalist exploitation.

In some ways, then, disability might better be seen as an identity category more akin to those of ethnicity, race, gender or sexuality than to categories of ill health. Certainly, disability activists in the USA picked up on these connections in working from templates forged by their predecessors in the civil rights movement, and from which the related interdisciplinary areas of gender studies, race/ethnicity studies and queer studies similarly emerged (Clare 2001; Ferguson and Nusbaum 2012: 70). But here, too, in recognising the similarities we should avoid seeing disability as structurally identical to these categories. Rapp and Ginsburg write:

> Disability is a different form of difference: unlike the deeply embodied categories of race and gender, from which one can only enter or exit very rarely and with enormous and conscious effort … disability can happen in a heartbeat, turning one's vantage point around and implicating others (2012: 173).

Or, as Tom Shakespeare wrote in a similar vein: 'There is nothing intrinsically difficult about being black, excepting in particular social contexts. Yet, whatever the social context, there are impairments which cause suffering, pain and premature death' (1998: 670).

Rather than standing aloof from medical anthropology or, indeed, the other interdisciplinary configurations from which anthropologists working on disability have already gained valuable insights and made useful contributions, we agree with Rapp and Ginsburg's suggestion that, while continuing to embrace these connections, ethnographic research on disability should now move beyond narrow sub-disciplinary boundaries (2012: 166).

Moving South ...

Until this point, as will have become clear, our focus has been largely on anthropology's encounter with disability scholarship in the so-called West, and in the USA in particular. This is largely because DS developed first, and most powerfully, in these locations (Grech 2011; see also Aramayo et al. 2016, in this volume). As such, many studies have focused disproportionately on the disabling contexts constituted by industrialisation and on the rise of capitalism (see e.g. Oliver 1990: 25–39). Even when the ethnographic work or case histories on which studies were based took place in the global South, its theoretical framing was forged by the Euro-American academy for which it was, by and large, written. Most histories of DS, for example, are framed against the backdrop of American campaigns for civil rights and the independent living movement. Even scholars from the global South, as Ghai (2003) points out in respect of Indian disability activists, have often been in thrall to western-inspired structuralist models because of their own social positions within educated, liberal urban elites. Disability legislation in these contexts (such as the Persons With Disabilities Act 1995 in India) consequently reflects this discourse, while disability rights organisations are criticised for being overly dominated by the interests of middle-class men (Ghai 2003; Mehrotra 2011: 68), such as campaigning for concessions in air travel or special parking facilities, which remain irrelevant to the disabled poor.

Where studies of disability have emerged elsewhere beyond Europe and America, it is vital that we recognise and consider the different contexts against which they have developed, and ensure that local, on-the-ground realities are accounted for in constructing appropriate models (see e.g. Meekosha 2004; Grech 2011, 2012; Meekosha and Soldatic 2011; Soldatic and Grech 2014). In India, for example, the numbers of students studying disability, certainly at Delhi and Jawaharlal Nehru universities, has been on the increase (Karna 1999; Chakravarti 2008; Vaidya 2008) and other universities, notably Indira Gandhi National Open University and Ambedkar University in Delhi (Mehrotra 2011: 70, fn 7), have been keen to establish new programmes. Anthropologists are especially well placed to study the contexts within which scholarly foci on disability have been developed, but contributions from other disciplines, such as history, are also vital in carrying out this task. Mehrotra's work (2004a, b, 2006, 2011; see also Addlakha 2013), for example, explores how local women's movements, environmental movements and, more recently, Dalit and anti-caste movements have shaped studies of disability in India, as well as set out the frames of reference through which disability might be understood and experienced. We recognise that there are both conjunctions and disjunctions between these influences and those that have moulded disability discourse elsewhere, such as the movements for civil rights, anti-racism and feminism. In a globalising world, these backdrops are profoundly interrelated and dialogic, even as they speak across one another.

Without the resources and structures of organisations such as the AAA, for example, DS in postcolonial settings often have a more 'chequered history' (Mehrotra 2011: 65) and struggle to get heard. Values that might be taken as read in an American or a British setting, such as those espoused by the independent living movement, might be anathema to those for whom a notion of the individual self is secondary to what Roland described as the 'familial self' (1988). That many in the global South might conceptualise themselves as more continuous with those around them than with those from nations more steeped in individualism has been well rehearsed in anthropology (see e.g. Geertz 1983; Strathern 1988; Marriott 1989; Staples 2003, 2011a). Several studies in Jenkins's volume *Questions of Competence* (1998) offer examples and demonstrate why differing notions of what constitutes the self are relevant to how disability is perceived. Devlieger, for example, draws on his ethnographic work with both the Songye of Zaire and the Shona of Zimbabwe to argue that, in these African contexts, any disruption in a person's physical or mental capacities is interpreted as a consequence of 'wronged relationships', whether with people, nature, ancestors or God (1998; see also Devlieger 2007). Whyte picks up on a similar emphasis on relationships in her study of the Nyole people of rural Uganda, among whom 'competence is a property of social relations, not just of individuals' (1998: 154). Consequently, campaigns central to the disability rights movement in the global North, such as the promotion of independent living, struggle to find relevance when applied in settings, like those we have described, where the same value is not placed on personal autonomy. Such models need to be reinterpreted in culturally specific terms, with 'independence', in this example, being recast as applying not to individuals but to the family or wider social group (Lang 2001; Singit 2008; Mehrotra 2011: 71). As others have argued (e.g. Grech 2011, 2012; Meekosha and Soldatic 2011; Soldatic and Grech 2014), we also need to be open to new perspectives from which to explore disability, which emerge from people's everyday experiences in particular settings, rather than hoping simply to adjust models formulated for western settings.

We must also recognise that the very notion of disability, as it has emerged and developed as a category in DS, is problematic precisely because of its universalising tendencies. The reticence of some anthropologists to engage more fully with DS discourse might well be a consequence of that. More importantly, however, the imposition of universal analytical categories can, in some cases, serve to alienate disability activists (those from northern nations and the local activists who work through their NGOs) from disabled people in the global South whose causes they wish to support. Disability—or whatever terminologies used by people disadvantaged by how their bodies are accommodated in society—needs first to be understood in people's own terms and in relation to their particular experiences, away from 'the imagined universal moral sphere' constituted by the international disability community (Friedner and Osborne 2013: 43).

The Value of Anthropology

The question we now move to focus on, then, is what, specifically, DS might gain from further developing a relationship with anthropology.

First, and perhaps most obviously, we might cite the usefulness of anthropology's focus on alterity, and the comparisons between different ways of doing difference that this makes possible. At the same time, anthropologists' traditional focus on the global South—and, in particular, the access western anthropologists were afforded by colonialism—also offers particularly rich material from which cross-cultural comparisons might be made. The ethnographic canon offers nuanced contextual material about the social institutions of non-western societies, which is essential if our comparisons are to go beyond superficial similarities and differences, as well as specific case studies of how disability might be configured in different ways by different peoples.

That is not to say, of course, that all anthropological work is conducted in the global South. Much of the earlier work by anthropologists on disability—Benedict aside—had a specifically western focus: for example, Edgerton's ethnography of 'mental retardation' in the USA (1967); Ablon's work on America's 'little people' (1984); or Groce's monograph on deafness in Martha's Vineyard (1985), to name just three. Nor is it to suggest that anthropologists have a monopoly on the global South while sociologists write about industrialised settings, even though the most influential sociological work on disability (most likely because of the bias in favour of English-language publication) has indeed focused on the UK and the USA (Oliver 1990; Barnes et al. 1999).

The fact remains, however, that anthropology has led the field in offering case studies beyond the USA and western Europe. Ingstad and Whyte's 1995 volume, for instance, draws on ethnographic work from across Africa (Kenya, Uganda, Botswana and southern Somalia), central Borneo and Nicaragua, with only 2 of the 14 chapters focusing exclusively on western contexts (Monks and Frankenberg 1995; Murphy 1995), and a third exploring disability in the context of migration from Turkey to Sweden (Sachs 1995). Their 2007 volume further extends this scope, including chapters on Japan, China, Israel and India.

What the ethnographic documentation of disability in different places around the globe offers DS is, in short, firm evidence that disability is a relative phenomenon, that the social ramifications of having a particular kind of body are not a natural given, but are shaped by the wide configuration of circumstances in which one is situated. The experience of disability in, say, Vietnam might have as much to do with Buddhist notions of karma and local ideas concerning reciprocity, as Gammeltoft (2008) argues, as it does with people's capacities to operate within the industrialised working environments that, according to Oliver (1990), have determined how disability is experienced in the British context. In addition to defining *what* might be considered disability and how that difference might be interpreted and experienced, different cultural contexts also literally shape bodies in different ways: different kinds of diet, childbirth practices or types of work performed, for instance, all have a profound impact on the kinds of bodies people have.

The capacity for cross-cultural comparison is, of course, only one feature of anthropological inquiry and, as Kasnitz and Shuttleworth (2001a) set out very clearly, an increasingly contested one. Defining people by reference to discrete 'cultures' has rightly been criticised as over-determining human motivation and action, and, as a referent of difference, can sometimes be utilised as a euphemism to mask or neutralise inequalities. Claiming that blacks and whites were *culturally* different, for example, was an argument used to justify apartheid in South Africa (Kuper 1999). The more recent 'ontological turn' in anthropology might be understood by some as a rephrasing of 'culture', although others would argue that an ontological approach recognises multiple worlds rather than the multiple representations of a single world favoured by an approach that foregrounds cultural differences (Carrithers et al. 2010). It might also suggest possibilities for understanding radical alterity in its own terms.

Beyond this, however, anthropology is about more than just cultural (or even ontological) difference and comparison. In a paper presented to the AAA in Chicago in 2003, Shuttleworth and Kasnitz reviewed several theoretical orientations which, although not necessarily unique to anthropology, have nevertheless been central in interpreting ethnographic data. Goffman's (1963) work on stigma, for instance, has been particularly influential in theorising difference (see e.g. Staples 2011b, c), while Turner's (1967) notion of 'liminality'—which enables us to identify disabled people as 'betwixt and between' dominant understandings of normality—has also been informative. Robert Murphy, for example, utilises Turner's insights in making sense of his status as a disabled person (1987). Mary Douglas's anomaly theory (1965) allows for something similar: those categorised as disabled would be those who fall between the dominant cultural categories of a given society. While an anomalous social position might on the one hand be debilitating, in some circumstances it might also be seen as empowering, as it was for the people with epilepsy that Benedict described. Such framing allows for this potential in ways that the social model, which defines disability negatively in terms only of social constraints, does not. Work in anthropology that draws on the paradigm of embodiment (Scheper-Hughes and Lock 1987; Csordas 1990) also helps to bring the visceral, experiencing body back into the picture, as demonstrated by, for example, Geyla Frank's intimate portrayal of one woman's experience in her book *Venus on Wheels* (2000; see also Staples 2003), Emily Cohen's work on prosthetics in Colombia (2012) or Nicholas Rattray's portrayal of disability and urban space in highland Ecuador (2013).

More recently, as Ginsburg and Rapp (2013) set out, a turning of the anthropological lens onto human rights, citizenship and sociality (see e.g. Friedner 2014, 2015; and Pisani et al. 2016, in this volume), eugenics, social movements and state policy also serve to demonstrate the value of anthropology to the understanding of disability in contemporary contexts, wherever in the world it might be invoked.

Finally, but perhaps most importantly in terms of anthropology's usefulness, is the discipline's focus on long-term ethnographic fieldwork. The 'deep hanging out' of participant observation can lead to new perspectives on the lifeworlds of disabled people, with the focus on disability as a 'thing' decentred as a result. Staples's biography of an Indian man affected by leprosy (2014), for example—in common with Frank's telling of Diane DeVries's life story (2000)—demonstrates how thickly layered explanations, gathered over a longer period of time than other research methods, such as surveys or questionnaires, can help us to situate better the experiences of disabled people within a complex web of other identities, social relations and historical circumstances. While shorter case histories often capture stylised accounts of the experience of bodily differences, accounts that emerge out of long-term ethnographic fieldwork tend to be more nuanced and fully drawn (see Staples 2007, 2014: xvii), taking into account such factors as gender, age, class and caste and ethnicity (see Mehrotra 2006, 2013). They can also demonstrate that stigma, usually understood as wholly negative, can be transformed in certain circumstances to value, as shown in Friedner's work (2014; 2015; Friedner and Osborne 2013; see also Staples 2003). Rather than attempting to map anthropological methods onto other disciplines—which runs the danger of researchers deploying a kind of 'ethnography lite'—our recommendation here would be that multiple-disciplinary teams working on disability should, whenever possible, include an anthropologist alongside social workers, epidemiologists and other professionals.

Ethnographic Writing

Although the experience of ethnographic fieldwork is, self-evidently, different from the writing up of that experience as ethnographic text, there is clearly a link between the two, with anthropology—as perhaps the closest to the humanities of all the social sciences—demonstrating innovative ways of how to best communicate knowledge about disability. Indeed, anthropologists working in the field of disability might have something useful to offer to their own discipline, as well as to DS more generally, since it has been more forward than other sub-disciplines in experimenting with styles of writing. In part, we suspect that this is because trying to capture the experience of, for example, profound intellectual or bodily alterity is not always straightforward within the confines of accepted academic formats. As several examples demonstrate (Frank 2000; Nakamura 2013; Staples 2014), life histories, narrative approaches and auto-ethnography (Murphy 1987; Martin 2007) can situate disability in wider contexts in ways that make sense to those whose experiences are being described (Ginsburg and Rapp 2013: 4.3). Angrosino's (1998) set of short stories, which emerged out of his fieldwork in a community of people with intellectual impairments (or 'mental retardation', the American phrase he uses to describe it), goes a step further—using fiction in an attempt to capture both the subjectivities and the complexities of the lives he evokes. Again, unconventional writing styles are not likely to be embraced with equal verve by all the disciplines that contribute to DS—and nor should they be—but should rather be situated alongside other genres to offer more textured, multifaceted and reflexive perspectives on disability.

Conclusion

In reviewing the literature for this chapter we encountered a number of tentative answers to the question of why anthropology has apparently been reticent to engage with disability as an object of study, ranging from the suggestion that anthropologists are in denial of the pervasiveness of disability to the claim that romanticised images of anthropology are ill served by informants (or practitioners) in wheelchairs or brandishing white canes. On closer inspection, however, we observed that it is not disabled people *per se* who are left out of anthropological inquiry, sidelined though they might be. There are, if one seeks them out, studies that go back almost a century. Rather, it is the realm of disability *studies* that anthropologists have given a wide berth. This, we would argue, is because the tendency of DS to seek out universal analytical categories through which disability might be better understood jars with contemporary anthropology's focus on the local and the particular, and on theory grounded in specific data rather than on applying pre-existing theory to the situations we encounter. As a consequence, anthropological inquiries into the experiences of disabled people have, until recently, been rather scattered and fragmented, with explicit links seldom drawn between them, let alone with the wider corpus of work on disability.

Paradoxically, the fact that anthropological studies have not been tethered to the dominant theoretical models of DS has allowed for greater 'blue sky thinking'. They are useful to DS precisely because they have been produced as critical outsider accounts. More recently, as the newer work reviewed here demonstrates very well, anthropologists have slowly been finding ways of acknowledging and engaging constructively with DS theory, without being trapped in webs of theory spun largely for western, industrialised contexts, and the particular civil rights struggles they were formulated to assist.

Looking to the future, we would suggest that the inherent tensions between DS (a discipline that necessarily works towards universal categorisations of what 'disability' might mean) and anthropology (a discipline committed to working with local notions of bodily difference that might fit only partially, if at all, into DS's theoretical frames) are not simply going to dissolve. Such tensions, however, can be creative. As long as we remain committed to a mutual engagement, there is great potential for ethnographic insights to inform and give nuance to theory, while the theoretical insights of DS may open up, rather than shut down, routes towards understanding people's quotidian experiences of negatively construed bodily differences, across the full gamut of sociocultural, political and economic boundaries.

References

Ablon, J. (1984). *Little people in America: The social dimension of dwarfism*. New York: Praeger.

Ablon, J. (1988). *Living with difference: Families with dwarf children*. New York: Praeger.

Addlakha, R. (Ed) (2013). *Disability studies in India: Global discourses, local realities*. Delhi: Routledge.

Angrosino, M. V. (1998). *Opportunity house: Ethnographic stories of mental retardation*. Walnut Creek: Altamira Press.

Aramayo, M., Kagan, C., & Burton, M. (2016). Revising and using the social model in the global South: A Venezuelan exploration. In S. Grech & K. Soldatic (Eds.), *Disability in the global South: The critical handbook*. New York: Springer.

Barnes, C., Mercer, G., & Shakespeare, T. (1999). *Exploring disability: A sociological introduction*. Cambridge: Polity Press.
Barnes, C., Oliver, M., & Barton, L. (Eds.). (2002). *Disability studies today*. Cambridge: Polity Press.
Becker, G. (1983). *Growing old in silence*. Berkeley: University of California Press.
Benedict, R. (1934). Anthropology and the abnormal. *The Journal of General Psychiatry, 10*, 59–80.
Biehl, J. (2005). *Vita: Life in a zone of social abandonment*. Berkeley: University of California Press.
Carrithers, M., Candea, M., Sykes, K., Holbraad, M., & Venkatesan, S. (2010). Ontology is just another word for culture: Motion tabled at the 2008 meeting of the group for debates in anthropological theory, university of Manchester. *Critique of Anthropology, 30*, 152–200.
Chakravarti, U. (2008). Burden of caring: Families of the disabled in urban India. *Indian Journal of Gender Studies, 15*(2), 341–363.
Clare, E. (2001). Stolen bodies, reclaimed bodies: Disability and queerness. *Public Culture, 13*(3), 359–365.
Cohen, L. (1998). *No aging in India: Alzheimer's, the bad family, and other modern things*. Berkeley: University of California Press.
Cohen, E. (2012). From phantoms to prostheses. *Disability Studies Quarterly, 32*(3). Retrieved from http://dsq-sds.org/article/view/3269/3103.
Corker, M., & Shakespeare, T. (Eds.). (2002). *Disability/postmodernity: Embodying disability theory*. London: Continuum.
Csordas, T. J. (1990). Embodiment as a paradigm for anthropology. *Ethos, 18*, 5–47.
Devlieger, P. J. (1998). (In)competence in America in comparative perspective. In R. Jenkins (Ed.), *Questions of competence: Culture, classification and intellectual disability* (pp. 54–75). Cambridge: Cambridge University Press.
Devlieger, P. (2007). The production of disability culture among young African–American men. *Social Science & Medicine, 64*(9), 1948–1959.
Douglas, M. (1965). *Implicit meanings*. London: Routledge.
Duval, L. (Ed) (1986). *Disability & culture*. Self-published newsletter. Oyster Bay, NY.
Edgerton, R. B. (1967). *The cloak of competence*. Berkeley: University of California Press.
Ferguson, P. M., & Nusbaum, E. (2012). Disability Studies: What is it and what difference does it make? *Research and Practice for Persons with Severe Disabilities, 37*(2), 70–80.
Frank, G. (2000). *Venus on wheels: Two decades of dialogue on disability, biography, and being female in America*. Berkeley: University of California Press.
Friedner, M. L. (2014). Deaf Capital: An exploration of the relationship between stigma and value in deaf multilevel marketing participation in urban India. *Medical Anthropology Quarterly, 28*(4), 502–518.
Friedner, M. L. (2015). Deaf bodies and corporate bodies: New regimes of value in Bangalore's business process outsourcing sector. *Journal of the Royal Anthropological Institute*.
Friedner, M. L., & Osborne, J. (2013). Audit bodies: Embodied participation, disability universalism, and accessibility in India. *Antipode, 45*(1), 43–60.
Gammeltoft, T. M. (2008). Childhood disability and parental moral responsibility in northern Vietnam: Towards ethnographies of intercorporeality. *Journal of the Royal Anthropological Institute, 14*(4), 825–842.
Geertz, C. (1983). From the native's point of view: On the nature of anthropological understanding. In *Local knowledge: Further essays in interpretive anthropology* (pp. 55–70). New York: Basic Books.
Ghai, A. (2003). *(Dis)emodied form: Issues of disabled women*. New Delhi: Har-Anand Publications.
Ginsburg, F., & Rapp, R. (2013). Disability worlds. *Annual Review of Anthropology, 42*, 4.1–4.16. doi:10.1146/annurev-anthro-092412-155502.

Goffman, E. (1963). *Stigma: Notes on the management of a spoiled identity*. Harmondsworth: Penguin.
Goldin, C. (1988). *Disability research in anthropology: Ethnographic contributions and theoretical implications*. Paper Presented at the American Anthropological Association Annual Meeting, Phoenix.
Grech, S. (2011). Recolonising debates or perpetuated coloniality? Decentring the spaces of disability, development and community in the global South. *International Journal of Inclusive Education, 15*(1), 87–100.
Grech, S. (2012). Poverty, disability and education: Debating inclusivity in the majority world. In A. Azzopardi (Ed.), *Roots to inclusive education* (pp. 51–69). Germany: VDM.
Groce, N. (1985). *Everyone here spoke sign language: Hereditary deafness on Martha's vineyard*. Cambridge: Harvard University Press.
Hank, J., & Hank, L. M. (1948). The physically handicapped in certain non-occidental societies. *Journal of Social Issues, 4*(4), 11–20.
Hughes, B., & Paterson, K. (1997). The social model of disability and the disappearing body: Toward a sociology of impairment. *Disability & Society, 12*(3), 325–340.
Ingstad, B., & Whyte, S. R. (Eds.). (1995). *Disability and culture*. Berkeley: University of California Press.
Inhorn, M. C., & Wentzell, E. A. (2012). *Medical anthropology at the intersections: Histories, activisms, and futures*. Durham: Duke University Press.
Jenkins, R. (Ed) (1998). *Questions of competence: Culture, classification and intellectual disability*. Cambridge: Cambridge University Press.
Karna, G. N. (1999). *United nations and the rights of disabled persons: A study in Indian perspective*. New Delhi: APH Pub Corp.
Kasnitz, D. (2003). *A sociocultural model of impairment-disability*. Paper presented at the inaugural conference of the Disability Studies Association, Lancaster, UK, September 4–6.
Kasnitz, D., & Shuttleworth, R. P. (2001a). Engaging anthropology in disability studies. In L. J. Rogers & B. B. Swadener (Eds.), *Semiotics and dis/ability: Interrogating categories of difference* (pp. 19–41). Albany: State University of New York.
Kasnitz, D., & Shuttleworth, R. P. (2001b). Introduction: Anthropology in disability studies. *Disability Studies Quarterly, 21*(3), 2–17.
Kohrman, M. (2005). *Bodies of difference: Experiences of disability and institutional advocacy in the making of modern China*. Berkeley: University of California Press.
Kuper, A. (1999). *Culture: The anthropologists' account*. New Haven: Harvard University Press.
Landsman, G. (2001). *Models of disability: Agency, identity, and mothers of disabled children*. Paper presented at the annual meeting of the American Anthropological Association, Washington, DC.
Lang, R. (2001). *Understanding disability from a South Indian perspective*. Paper presented at the 14th annual conference of the Society of Disability Studies, Winnipeg, Canada.
Linton, S. (1998). *Claiming disability: Knowledge and identity*. New York: New York University Press.
Livingston, J. (2005). *Debility and the moral imagination in Botswana*. Bloomington: Indiana University Press.
Marriott, M. (1989). Constructing an Indian ethnosociology. *Contributions to Indian Sociology, 23*, 1–39.
Martin, E. (2007). *Bipolar expeditions: Mania and depression in American culture*. Princeton: Princeton University Press.
Mead, M. (1953). National character. In A. L. Krober (Ed.), *Anthropology today* (pp. 642–647). Chicago: Chicago University Press.
Meekosha, H. (2004). Drifting down the gulf stream: Navigating the culture of disability studies. *Disability & Society, 19*(7), 721–733.
Meekosha, H., & Soldatic, K. (Eds) (2011). Special issue: Disability and the global South. *Third World Quarterly, 32*(8).

Mehrotra, N. (2004a). Understanding cultural conceptions of disability in rural India. *Journal of Indian Anthropological Society, 39*, 33–45.

Mehrotra, N. (2004b). Women, disability and social support in rural Haryana. *Economic & Political Weekly, 39*(52), 5640–5644.

Mehrotra, N. (2006). Negotiating gender and disability in rural Haryana. *Sociological Bulletin, 55*(3), 406–426.

Mehrotra, N. (2011). Disability rights movements in India: Politics and practice. *Economic and Political Weekly, 46*(6), 65–72.

Mehrotra, N. (2013). *Disability, gender and state policy: Exploring margins*. Jaipur: Rawat Publications.

Miles, M. (2002). Disability on a different model: Glimpses of an Asian heritage. *Journal of Religion, Disability and Health, 6*(2–3), 89–108.

Monks, J., & Frankenberg, R. (1995). Being ill and being me: Self, body, and time in multiple sclerosis narratives. In B. Ingstad & S. R. Whyte (Eds.), *Disability & culture* (pp. 107–134). Berkeley: University of California Press.

Murphy, R. (1987). *The body silent*. New York: W.W. Norton.

Murphy, R. (1995). Encounters: The body silent in America. In B. Ingstad & S. R. Whyte (Eds.), *Disability & culture* (pp. 140–158). Berkeley: University of California Press.

Nakamura, K. (2013). *A disability of the soul: An ethnography of Schizophrenia and mental illness in contemporary Japan*. Ithaca: Cornell University Press.

Oliver, M. (1984). The politics of disability. *Critical Social Policy, 11*, 21–33.

Oliver, M. (1985). Discrimination, disability and social policy. In M. Brenton & C. Jones (Eds.), *The yearbook of social policy 1984–5* (pp. 74–97). London: Routledge and Kegan Paul.

Oliver, M. (1990). *The politics of disablement*. London: Macmillan.

Petryna, A. (2002). *Life exposed: Biological citizens after Chernobyl*. Princeton: Princeton University Press.

Pisani, M., Grech, S., & Mostafa, A. (2016). Disability and forced migration: Intersections and critical debates. In S. Grech & K. Soldatic (Eds.), *Disability in the global South: The critical handbook*. New York: Springer.

Rapp, R., & Ginsburg, F. (2012). Anthropology and the study of disability worlds. In M. C. Inhorn & E. A. Wentzell (Eds.), *Medical anthropology at the intersections: Histories, activisms, and futures* (pp. 183–205). Durham: Duke University Press.

Rattray, N. A. (2013). Contesting urban space and disability in Highland Ecuador. *City & Society, 25*(1), 25–46.

Reid-Cunningham, A. R. (2009). Anthropological theories of disability. *Journal of Human Behavior in the Social Environment, 19*, 99–111.

Roland, A. (1988). *In search of the self in India and Japan: Toward a cross-cultural psychology*. New Jersey: Princeton University Press.

Sachs, L. (1995). Disability and migration: A case story. In B. Ingstad & S. R. Whyte (Eds.), *Disability & culture* (pp. 210–225). Berkeley: University of California Press.

Scheper-Hughes, N., & Lock, M. M. (1987). The mindful body: A prolegomenon to future work in medical anthropology. *Medical Anthropology Quarterly, 1*(1), 6–41.

Shakespeare, T. (1998). Choices and rights: Eugenics, genetics and disability equality. *Disability & Society, 13*(5), 665–681.

Shakespeare, T., & Watson, N. (2001). Making the difference: Disability, politics, and recognition. In G. L. Albrecht, K. D. Seelman, & M. Bury (Eds.), *Handbook of disability studies* (pp. 546–564). Thousand Oaks: Sage.

Singit, N. (2008). Scent of freedom. *Combat Law: The Human Rights and Law Bimonthly, 7*(1), 50–53.

Soldatic, K., & Grech, S. (2014). Transnationalising disability studies: Rights, justice and impairment. *Disability Studies Quarterly, 34*(2). Retrieved from http://dsq-sds.org/article/view/4249/3588.

Staples, J. (2003). Disguise, revelation and copyright: Disassembling the south Indian leper. *Journal of the Royal Anthropological Institute, 9*, 295–315.

Staples, J. (2005). Leprosy in south India: The paradox of disablement as enablement. *Review of Disability Studies, 1*(4), 13–28.

Staples, J. (2007). *Peculiar people, amazing lives: Leprosy, social exclusion and community-making in south India*. Delhi: Orient Longman.

Staples, J. (2011a). At the intersection of disability and masculinity: Exploring gender and bodily difference in India. *Journal of the Royal Anthropological Institute, 17*(3), 545–562.

Staples, J. (2011b). Interrogating leprosy 'stigma': Why qualitative insights are vital. *Leprosy Review, 82*(2), 91–97.

Staples, J. (2011c). Nuancing 'leprosy stigma' through ethnographic biography in South India. *Leprosy Review, 82*(2), 109–123.

Staples, J. (2014). *Leprosy and a life in South India: Journeys with a Tamil Brahmin*. Lanham: Lexington Books.

Strathern, M. (1988). *The gender of the gift*. Berkeley: University of California Press.

Tremain, S. (2002). On the subject of impairment. In M. Corker & T. Shakespeare (Eds.), *Disability/postmodernity: Embodying disability theory* (pp. 32–47). New York: Continuum.

Turner, V. W. (1967). *The forest of symbols: Aspects of Ndembu Ritual*. Ithaca: Cornell University Press.

Vaidya, S. (2008). *A sociological study of families of autistic children in Delhi*. Ph.D. thesis, Jawaharlal Nehru University, New Delhi, India.

Whyte, S. R. (1998). Slow cookers and madmen: Competence of heart and head in rural Uganda. In R. Jenkins (Ed.), *Questions of competence: Culture, classification and intellectual disability* (pp. 153–175). Cambridge: Cambridge University Press.

Whyte, S. R., & Ingstad, B. (2007). Introduction: Disability connections. In B. Ingstad & S. R. Whyte (Eds.), *Disability in local and global worlds* (pp. 1–29). Berkeley: University of California Press.

Zola, I. (1979). Helping one another: A speculative history of the self help movement. *Archives of Physical Medicine and Rehabilitation, 60*, 452–456.

Zola, I. (1981). *Missing pieces: A chronicle of living with a disability*. Philadelphia: Temple University Press.

Chapter 4
Counting Disabled People: Historical Perspectives and the Challenges of Disability Statistics

Arne H. Eide and Mitchell Loeb

Introduction

Over more than three decades, the need for refining and improving disability definition and measurement, and using those tools to analyse the life experiences of individuals with disability, has been advanced through international initiatives and policy documents. With respect to the former, the work of the World Health Organization in the development of the International Classification of Functioning, Disability and Health (ICF) (WHO 2001) and the formation, in 2002, of the United Nations Washington Group on Disability Statistics have been paramount. In terms of policy, the focus of the international community has been directed to issues of disability in recent decades, highlighted with the World Program of Action Concerning Disabled Persons (UN 1982; 1993), The Standard Rules on the Equalization of Opportunities for Persons with Disabilities (UN 1994) and more recently in the UN Convention on the Rights of Persons with Disabilities (Article 31) (UN 2006) and the Report by the High-Level Panel on the Post-2015 Development Agenda (Chap. 4, page 23) (UN 2013a). Estimation of disability prevalence in a population, statistics on access to basic services and descriptions of the status of living conditions are regarded as important for policy development, for planning purposes, for resource allocation, for monitoring, impact assessments and comparisons across groups, for awareness building and as a foundation for advocacy work and improved dialogue between stakeholders, including disabled

A.H. Eide (✉)
Department of Health, SINTEF Technology and Society, PB 124 Blindern,
Oslo 0314, Norway
e-mail: ArneHenning.Eide@sintef.no

M. Loeb
National Center for Health Statistics/Washington Group on Disability Statistics,
Washington, DC, USA

S. Grech, K. Soldatic (eds.), *Disability in the Global South*,
International Perspectives on Social Policy, Administration, and Practice,
DOI 10.1007/978-3-319-42488-0_4

people's organisations (DPOs) and relevant national authorities (Madans et al. 2004). Reliable and valid disability statistics are seen as instrumental for monitoring the implementation of the UN Conventions, and to ensure the human rights of people with disability. This understanding has also been adopted by the international disability movement, as exemplified by the recent resolution of the International Disability Alliance supporting an inclusive post-2015 development agenda for persons with disability in Africa (point 6) (IDA 2014). This chapter draws some historical lines to illustrate the development of the discourse on disability and uses this as a background for a critical examination of current possibilities and challenges in disability statistics.

The state of disability statistics globally, and particularly in low-income countries, has been described by several authors (e.g. Eide and Loeb 2006b; Mont 2007b; Loeb et al. 2008). In many low-income countries, data are scare and of variable quality. Reported disability statistics are largely limited to measures of prevalence collected through the national census, and tend to be impairment-based, identifying only a small portion of individuals with disability, i.e. the visibly and severely disabled. Typically, reported prevalence rates in low-income countries are in the area of 2–4 per cent, while the corresponding figures for high-income countries may be 15 per cent or higher. While the definition of disability operationalised is a main reason for this gap in global disability statistics, other reasons include the understanding of disability, negative cultural attitudes and prejudice leading to underreporting, high mortality and complexity of societies (Loeb 2013).

Problems associated with infrastructure and a lack of training of survey enumerators may exacerbate difficulties associated with data collections in low-income countries. These data collections are further hampered by the general lack of awareness of issues associated with disability by survey administrators, data collectors and the general population. This lack of sensitivity also may impact survey results, leading to underreporting and yielding low prevalence rates.

Conceptually, a paradigm shift has occurred in our broader understandings of disability—from a previously medically oriented, individualistic, person-oriented (within the skin) ideology, to a more social-oriented model that focuses on the interaction between the individual (with a health condition) and their environment, resulting in reduced ability to participate in society. This current emphasis on the equalisation of opportunities and *human rights* is manifested in the UN Convention on the Rights of Persons with Disabilities (CRPD) (UN 2006). The Convention represents a major shift away from viewing people with disabilities as objects of charity, medical treatment and social protection towards a view as full and equal members of society, with all concomitant human rights (WHO 2011: 3).

Clearly, the theoretical model underlying any operationalisation and measurement intended to represent a concept as complex as disability, will strongly influence *what* we measure and *how*. The CRPD (Article 31) requires states to collect statistical data on disability, specifically to enable assessment of implementation of the Convention and "to identify and address the barriers faced by persons with disabilities in exercising their rights". In focusing on a human rights approach to measuring disability, the discourse on what, how and why, shifts from a purely epidemiological and/or economic perspective to a rights perspective. This further invites a more binding commitment to the role, involvement and ownership of individuals with disability and DPOs in research. Recent years have witnessed several examples of participatory approaches highlighting inclusion and ownership as a means to ensure relevance, application and empowerment.[1]

The existence of different models of disability may on one hand complicate the development of disability statistics, leading the field to evolve in different directions, using different terminology that would reduce cross-national comparability and thwart collaboration. On the other hand, the dynamic created by three co-existing main models (medical, social and interactional)[2] may also be seen to drive the interest for finding a common ground upon which to establish a new generation of disability statistics as required under the CRPD.

Conceptual Models

Two important conceptual models influenced disability research in Europe and the USA during the 25 years preceding the turn of the 21st century. The first was the development of the disablement or Nagi model by Saad Nagi (1965, 1991) for the US Social Security Administration, and the other was the International Classification of Impairments, Disability and Health (ICIDH), developed by Philip Wood for the World Health Organization (WHO 1980), which later evolved into the ICF (WHO 2001). Other models within the same time period, e.g. the extension of the Nagi model by Verbrugge and Jette (1994), the model developed by the National Centre

[1] Examples of participatory approaches in research include 1) SAFOD Research Program, funded by DFID and run by the Southern Africa Federation of the Disabled (http://www.safod.net/programs.html); 2) Living conditions among people with disability in southern Africa. Funded by the Norwegian disability movement and run by SAFOD in collaboration with SINTEF; 3) The Cross-Cutting Disability Research Program, run by the Leonard Cheshire Disability and Inclusive Development Centre, funded by DFID (http://www.ucl.ac.uk/lc-ccr/ccdrp).

[2] In many instances, the understanding of disability, i.e. the underlying model, is not necessarily formulated in an explicit manner when disability research and statistics is implemented and published. Further, implicit or explicit understandings of disability are often not very precise and perhaps even superficial, as for instance many researchers referring to ICF without really explaining how it influences the research. The following examples are intended to illustrate how the different models influence current research. Firstly, application of the medical model is found in continued collection of impairment data by national statistical offices, in particular in low-income countries (see e.g. https://unstats.un.org/unsd/demographic/sconcerns/disability/disab2.asp), and in much of the work with core sets derived from the ICF classification system (see e.g. http://www.icf-research-branch.org/download/viewcategory/5.html). Secondly, the social model has heavily influenced qualitative and in particular anthropological disability research (e.g. Ingstad and Whyte 1995), and also statistics through mapping of facilitators and barriers for participation (e.g. the Facilitators and Barriers Survey (Gray et al. 2008)). Thirdly, elements of an interactional model may be found in research on disability and poverty where the focus is on the exchange between an individual and his/her environment (see e.g. Eide and Ingstad 2011), and also may be found in comprehensive surveys incorporating all elements in the ICF model (e.g. Eide and Jele 2011).

Table 4.1 The ICIDH and Nagi models of disability (Jette 1994)

The Nagi scheme						
Active pathology	→	Impairment	→	Functional limitation	→	Disability
Interruption or interference with normal processes		Anatomical, physiological, mental or emotional abnormalities/loss		Limitation in performance at the level of the whole organism or person		Limitations in performance of socially defined roles and tasks within a sociocultural and physical environment
ICIDH						
Disease	→	Impairment	→	Disability	→	Handicap
The intrinsic pathology or disorder		Loss or abnormality of psychological, physiological or abnormalities or loss		Restriction or lack of ability to perform an activity in normal manner		Disadvantage due to impairment or disability that limits or prevents fulfilment of a normal role

for Medical Rehabilitation Research (NIH 1992), and the Quebec Classification by Fougeyrollas et al. (1999) can be viewed as modifications and extensions of these two schemes (Jette 1994). While there are many similarities between the Nagi model and ICIDH, they differ somewhat with regard to their handling of the relational aspects of disability/handicap (see Table 4.1). Altman (2001) also provides a comprehensive overview of these models.

While rudimentary statistics, or rather counting, of people with disabilities took place long before 1980, ICIDH and the Nagi model initiated a new basis for the collection of disability statistics. The demand for statistics on human functioning and disability greatly increased following the International Year of Disabled Persons (1981), the adoption of the UN World Programme of Action Concerning Disabled Persons (1982), and the release of the Standard Rules on the Equalization of Opportunities for Persons with Disabilities (UN 1994). Currently, two major tracks in developing global disability measures can be identified. We address these in the following sections.

The WHO Track

The World Health Organization has initiated several studies that feature different methodologies for measuring disability. The global burden of disease (GBD) study was initially conducted in 1990 and used the disability-adjusted life year (DALY) to measure burden of disease. This time-based measure combines years of life lost due to premature mortality and years of life lost due to time lived in states of less than full health, attempting to address some of the criticism over previous mortality-based measures for the effect of public health interventions (Mont 2007a). The assumptions underlying DALY were, however, still without regard for the context in which the health conditions occur[3] (Allotey et al. 2003). While DALY measures are derived by expert panels, the QUALY (Quality-Adjusted Life Year) emerged to account for subjective valuations of individuals living with different disorders. QUALY was also developed by WHO for the same purpose as DALY, i.e. to combine a measure on mortality and disabling conditions for particular health states. Both measures have contributed to advancing our understanding of disability, but also strongly link disability to health (Mont 2007a), which has attracted substantial criticism from authoritative scholars within disability studies (see e.g. Part 1 of Oliver and Barnes 2012). Measures based purely on medical conditions may run the danger of devaluing the lives of individuals with disability. In addition, the disregard of environmental influence as well as individual and contextual differences and determinants in experiencing disability is simply not compatible with the ICF and the influence of the social model on current understandings of disability.

WHO further conducted the World Health Survey (WHS) from 2002 to 2004, collecting demographic, wealth and health information for 70 countries to provide insight into the functioning of health systems. While in particular the GBD but also the WHS are illness related, the WHS instrument is highly influenced by the evolution of ICIDH and its successor, the ICF. Disability in the WHS is represented by a combined measure of impairments through functional limitations (seeing and concentrating) and activity limitations/participation restriction (moving around, self-care).

The revisions and debate around ICIDH culminated in a new classification that was adopted by WHO in 2001: The International Classification of Functioning, Disability and Health. The ICF represents a *biopsychosocial model* of disability/the disablement process and is an attempt at merging a medical, a social and an interactional model of disability (Fig. 4.1).

The novel aspects of ICF lie not only in the interrelationship between its components, linking the medical (health condition) with the impairment (physiological) and defining concepts of *activity limitations* and *restrictions in social participation*, but also in its inclusion of personal/individual and environmental components in

[3] DALYs combine time lived with a disability and time lost due to premature mortality. Years lost due to premature death is calculated on the basis of standard expectancy of life. Years lost due to disability is calculated on the basis of developed weights reflecting loss of functional capacity. The critique of DALYs concerns both their technical and conceptual basis. A major point is that DALYs are a narrow measure that oversimplifies human lives and does not take into account individuals' different ability to cope with their functional limitation, nor does it include efforts by family, friends and communities to reduce barriers, and contextual differences in support systems are excluded (Anand and Hanson 1997). From the perspective of disability studies and the social model of disability, it is the very idea of medicalising disability and making it a health issue, for instance through health-related classifications and measures. Disability is viewed as a social and not a medical phenomenon, and DALYs are problematic as they devalue the lives of individuals with chronic illnesses or functional limitations.

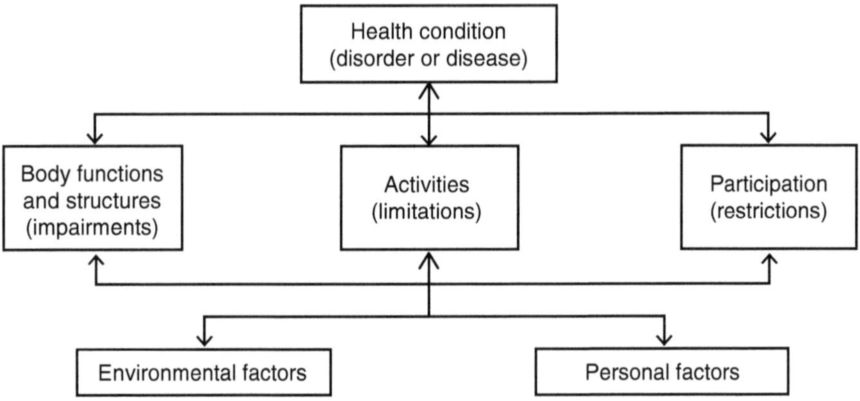

Fig. 4.1 The ICF model (WHO 2001)

defining disability. According to Jette: "The ICF framework holds great promise to provide a synthesis of earlier models of disablement and to provide … a universal language with which to discuss disability and related phenomena" (2006: 733). The development of the ICF has established a conceptual framework for more advanced studies and analyses of disability as a general human phenomenon.

WHO developed an earlier disability assessment scale, the World Health Organization Disability Assessment Schedule (WHODAS), into WHO DAS 2.0 (Üstün et al. 2010). This measurement integrates an individual's level of functioning in major life domains and directly corresponds with ICF's activity and participation dimensions. The aim of WHO DAS 2.0 was to develop a single generic instrument for assessing health status and disability across different cultures and settings. The instrument covers six different domains: cognition, mobility, self-care, getting along, life activities and participation. In 2014 WHO embarked upon the development of a Model Disability Survey (MDS), which is aimed at incorporating all dimensions of disability inherent in ICF: to gather information on the health status of an individual, limitations in the capacity to function, as well as the features of the environment that facilitate or create barriers to functioning, in order to make a determination of the lived experiences of people with disability. The MDS draws on existing data collections and experiences, including the studies that have been carried out in sub-Saharan Africa over the last decade (see e.g. Eide and Loeb 2011).

The UN Track

The World Programme of Action specifically requested the United Nations to develop systems for the regular collection and dissemination of information on disability. Collection of disability statistics by the United Nations Statistical Division (UNSD) started in the early 1980s with the establishment of a database (DISTAT)

Table 4.2 Disability questions in census: Namibia 2001 (UN 2013a, b, c)

Has [name] any type of permanent disability or limitation (yes/no)? (Up to three answers is possible)	– None
	– Blind
	– Deaf
	– Impaired speech
	– Impairment of hands
	– Impairment of legs
	– Mentally disabled
	– Others, specify
	– Don't know

that would house disability data from member countries, and the development of methodology and tools for data collection. While efforts to improve disability statistics reported to DISTAT have been carried out, the database is typically hampered by conceptual and methodological variation between countries, thus reducing global comparability (UN 2003). And, even though a broader range of data was requested, DISTAT remains largely a compilation of prevalence data.

The questions in Table 4.2 from Namibia are found in DISTAT and are presented here as an example of impairment-based measures, clearly influenced by a medical, individual model of disability. The data generated through such questions will typically identify severe and/or visible disability (impairments). The WHO has for several decades applied an estimate on disability prevalence of 10 per cent (WHO 1981, 2011). More recently, as reported in the World Report on Disability (WRD), Technical Note C (WHO 2011), WHO has adjusted the global estimate for disability to 15 per cent based on population ageing and the rapid spread of chronic diseases, as well as improvements in the methodologies used to measure disability in populations. There remains, however, limited empirical evidence for estimates in this range from low-income countries, and estimates provided by WHO appear to be influenced by disability statistics from the industrialised world and the methodology chosen to depict disability in the WRD.

In general, reported prevalence figures have tended to be low, around 2–5 per cent in low-income countries, while high-income countries have reported much higher figures, typically 12–15 per cent and higher (Mont 2007b; Loeb 2013). While these differences may be explained by several factors, it is assumed that variation in operationalisation of disability is a main cause, and behind this implicit or explicit differences in the applied understanding of disability.

While reported disparities in global estimates of disability persist, it is nevertheless the case that the understanding of disability has broadened with the emergence of the social model and the attempt to merge the medical and social models in ICF. It is thus logical that the current understanding should yield higher estimates than previous, narrower definitions.

Table 4.3 Washington City Group on Disability Statistics: short set of disability questions

Because of a health problem:	
1.	Do you have difficulty seeing, even if wearing glasses?
2.	Do you have difficulty hearing, even if using a hearing aid?
3.	Do you have difficulty walking or climbing steps?
4.	Do you have difficulty remembering or concentrating?
5.	Do you have difficulty (with self-care such as) washing all over or dressing?
6.	Using your usual (customary) language, do you have difficulty communicating (for example understanding or being understood by others)?

An International Seminar hosted by the United Nations Statistical Division (UNSD) in 2001 addressed the disparate means of disability data collection. Based on the recognition that statistical and methodological improvements were needed at an international level in order to facilitate cross-national comparison of disability data, the United Nations Statistical Commission (UNSC) authorised the formation of the Washington City Group on Disability Statistics (WG). The City Group format is used by the UNSC to address various recognised problems in survey measurement and methodology. City Groups comprise representatives from national statistical agencies globally. The Secretariat of the WG is located at the National Center for Health Statistics, the official health statistics agency of the United States. The objectives of WG were to guide the development of a small set or sets of general disability measures, suitable for use in censuses, sample-based national surveys or other statistical formats, and to recommend one or more extended sets of survey items to measure disability or principles for their design, to be used as components of population surveys or as supplements to specialty surveys. WG first developed a short set of questions intended for censuses. This set was finalised in 2006. The WG's approach in operationalising disability through the ICF was to focus first on limitations in basic activities that would or could result in social exclusion. Identifying the subpopulation at risk of social exclusion was the primary goal of the WG—and this approach has been recommended by the UN in its Principles and Recommendations for Population and Housing Censuses (2nd Revision) (United Nations Statistics Division 2008: 178–183, 292–294). Among the recommendations outlined in the document are several that pertain specifically to the measurement of disability and the approach of the WG. If such an approach is adopted internationally it would go a long way to decreasing the disparity in reported disability statistics and adding to the cross-national comparability of disability measures.

The decision to begin with the development of a short set of questions suitable for censuses derived from an understanding that many countries, in particular low- and middle-income countries, only have the means to collect disability data through a decennial census. For many of these countries, the cost of conducting a nationally representative population survey is prohibitive. WG did, however, later (in 2010) develop an extended set of questions intended for surveys that featured additional domains of functioning beyond those included in the short set and other aspects of

Table 4.4 Survey sample prevalence measures (n = 28,010), Zambia 2006 (Loeb et al. 2008)

Disability prevalence	*n*	%
P1: at least 1 domain is scored "some difficulty"	4053	14.5
P2: at least 2 domains are scored "some difficulty"	3090	11.0
P3: at least 1 domain is scored "a lot of difficulty"	2368	8.5
P4: at least one domain is scored "unable to do it"	673	2.4
PM (in multiple domains): more than 1 domain is scored "some difficulty"	1718	6.1

functioning, such as functioning with and without the use of assistive technologies. A module on child functioning and disability is currently being developed and tested in collaboration with UNICEF.

Each of the questions in Table 4.3 has four answer categories: (1) No, no difficulty, (2) Yes, some difficulty, (3) Yes, a lot of difficulty, and (4) Cannot do it at all. Combining the six questions yields a scale of activity limitations based on six domains of functioning with a range from 6 to 24. This summary variable can then be used either as a continuous variable—as a general measure of functioning in a population—or with a cut-off point or threshold that can be used to distinguish between those who are "disabled" and those who are not; or eventually, as a combination of the two with a cut-off point and a continuous measure (severity of activity limitations). Based on data from a study in Zambia applying the above six questions (Eide and Loeb 2006a), Loeb et al. (2008) were able to use the six questions to demonstrate how different cut-off points produced different prevalence rates.

The innovative aspect of the results presented in Table 4.4 is firstly a clear demonstration of how the operationalisation of disability influences prevalence estimates. Secondly, and more importantly, these results contribute to disentangle disability measurement from a fixation on a single measure of disability. Disability—or functioning—is seen as a continuum and relevant for all human beings when operationalised as limitations in doing daily life activities. By introducing several cut-off points, the WG short set measure offers different degrees of sensitivity towards activity limitations and may be applied according to the population group that is intended to be identified for analysis. Thus, if the purpose is to apply a wide definition of disability encompassing everyone who has at least some difficulty within at least one of the six functional domains, this will yield around 15 per cent. If the purpose is to identify those with severe and mostly visible impairments, the least sensitive cut-off point can be operationalised, yielding a prevalence rate of 2.4 per cent. By applying the six WG questions in a census or during the screening procedure in a survey, the data will contain the possibility for analysing and comparing different groups based on their level of activity limitations. Some of the difference between high- and low-income countries may be explained through the different screening procedures capturing different segments of the population of disabled people, as suggested by Mont (2007a).

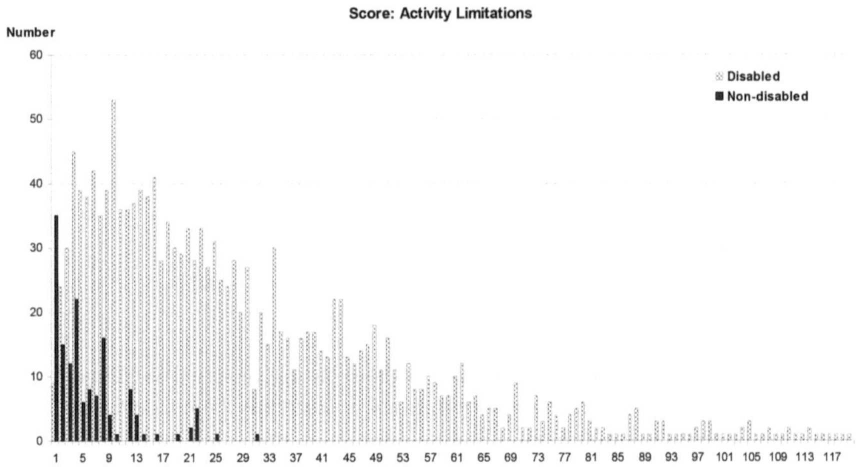

Fig. 4.2 Activity limitations among individuals who qualify/do not qualify as disabled

Treating disability/activity limitations as a continuous variable yields new possibilities in operationalising disability statistics.

Figure 4.2 shows another example from the Zambian data, where both those identified as having a disability according to the WG short set of questions and a small sub-sample of those identified as not having a disability were asked to respond to a series of questions on limitations in doing daily life activities (Activity and Participation Matrix, see Appendix 5 in Eide and Loeb 2006b: 185). The results, a composite score of activity limitations (Eide and Loeb 2006a), are represented in the Fig. 4.2. Of particular interest is the continuum from low levels of activity limitation to higher that is demonstrated, and the finding that some individuals who did not identify as disabled using the WG short set of questions are represented on the activity limitations continuum at the low end of the continuum with lower percentages than those who identify as disabled. With respect to the latter, this may be a manifestation of the fact that results from the short set of questions will represent the majority of, but not all, persons with limitation in the six basic actions, and represent the most commonly occurring limitations in basic actions.[4] A further implication of this finding is the support it provides to our understanding of disability, in terms of activity limitations, as a general human phenomenon, relevant and applicable to all. On this ground, activity limitations can be included in general population-based surveys, yielding a new angle to the study of functional limitations—and an interesting opening for mainstreaming disability statistics.

[4] Due to limitations of the census format, not all functional domains could be included, so that some of those identified as not having a disability may have other functional limitations that were not identified using the short set.

ICF: Challenges and Possibilities

Both the current WHO initiative to develop a Model Disability Survey and the work by the Washington City Group on Disability Statistics are firmly rooted in the ICF. This is also the case for most other recent attempts at developing disability-related measures. The ICF has attracted substantial interest from researchers across all disciplines (e.g. Borg et al. 2010; Bickenbach 2011; Madden et al. 2013). A review of ICF-related scientific articles between 2001 and 2009 (Cerniauskaite et al. 2011) listed a total of 672 papers, of which many were concerned with the measurement of disability within the framework. This documented interest in the research community can be regarded as a strong indication that the ICF will dominate the area of disability statistics. This is reflected in the fact that the ICF has been adopted and promoted in recent key documents, including the Community Based Rehabilitation (CBR) Guidelines (WHO 2010), The World Report on Disability (WHO 2011) and the UN Convention on the Rights of Persons with Disabilities (UN 2006). The ICF has as one of its main objectives to develop a common language, or terminology, on human functioning; and in so doing it is also attempting to gather the different research traditions under a single definitional umbrella of disability.

According to Jette (2006), there are however important challenges to be addressed with regard to the measurement of ICF concepts that need to be resolved in order for it to succeed as an international standard for research. Paramount is the internal coherence of the ICF model and the ability to distinguish clearly among dimensions and categories within the ICF framework. One example here is the distinction between *Activity limitations* and *Restrictions in social participation*. The question has been whether these constructs are distinct or largely overlapping. Jette et al. (2003) and Eide et al. (2007) were both able to identify distinct constructs, but factor analyses revealed sub-dimensions to the overall constructs of activity and participation (see Table 4.5). This implies potential for refining the model and thus making it more precise in both describing the disablement process and as a basis for measuring disability.

Bearing in mind that comparability between the two reported sets of sub-dimensions should be made with care due to methodological differences, these two examples nevertheless provide support in understanding the overall constructs of activity, participation and barriers as distinct, and also that identifying sub-dimensions may be a viable path for further development of the ICF model.

The second major challenge with the ICF is identified by Jette (2006) who is concerned with the need for developing sound assessment instruments that can be applied to the measurement of the various components in the ICF model. This is both to utilise the potential for knowledge generation inherent in the model, and for the purpose of further developing the constructs in the model and the model as such. According to the World Report on Disability:

> Using the ICF, as a universal framework for disability data collection related to policy goals of participation, inclusion, and health will help create better data design and also ensure that different sources of data relate well to each other. The ICF is neither a measurement tool nor a survey instrument—it is a classification that can provide a standard for health and disability statistics and help in the difficult task of harmonizing approaches across sources of disability data. (WHO 2011: 45)

Table 4.5 Sub-dimensions of activity and participation

Jette et al. (2003)	Eide et al. (2007)
Activity	Activity
– Basic mobility	– Social activities
– Daily activities	– Individual care
	– Education
	– Daily activities
Participation	Participation
– Social/role participation	– Social relationships
	– Individual care
	– Education
	– Daily activities
	Environmental barriers
	– Social and systems barriers
	– Mobility barriers

While the ICF does offer a set of questions for these three domains (activity, participation and environmental barriers/facilitators), the checklist is intended for use in clinical, rehabilitation or social work settings, and the empirical support is limited. An important distinction needs to be highlighted between using the ICF for clinical data collections versus for population statistics. Coding ICF components for purposes of classification in clinical settings is fundamentally different from the development of survey questions (based on the ICF framework) for inclusion in population censuses and surveys. This discussion is further elucidated in the ICF practical manual (WHO 2013, Chap. 5).

A range of different measures exists for activity (see for instance Long and Pavalko 2004; Harvey et al. 2008; Jagger et al. 2010), participation (e.g. Gray et al. 2006; Chang et al. 2013) and environmental barriers (Whiteneck et al. 2004; Maart et al. 2007; Gray et al. 2008). Many of the measures and others referred to by these sources are developed for specific contexts and impairment groups. Concerning the personal factor domain in ICF, this is explicitly not treated by WHO due to "the large social and cultural variance associated with them" (WHO 2001: 8). Personal factors fall outside the realm of health condition or health state, but comprise features that are both particular to the individual and relevant to their disability experience. These include age, gender, race, lifestyle, personal and health habits, social background, education and employment. While not itemised in the ICF, many personal characteristics are routinely collected in censuses and surveys, and they do impact disability and intervention outcomes. Personal factors clearly influence both activity and participation, and the lack of attention to personal factors has inspired substantial research into the subjective experiences of participation (e.g. Hammel et al. 2007; Witsø et al. 2011). This largely qualitative research contributes knowledge that may influence future measurement of activity and participation.

What Kind of Disability Statistics Do We Need?

The interest in disability statistics has been growing following the adoption of the ICF in 2001. Further growth in interest and activity in the field can be expected in connection with the UN Convention (CRPD), which requires ratifying countries to collect appropriate information, including statistical and research data, in order to formulate and implement policies (CRPD Article 31). Further renewed interest in disability measurement has followed the development of post-2015 sustainable development goals that would require disaggregation of information based on disability status.

Limiting disability statistics to counting and measuring level of functional limitation evidently provides a fragmented picture of disability. With a wider scope, disability statistics can provide a wealth of information on all aspects of living with a disability and generate knowledge that can contribute to a human rights approach to disability as required by the CRPD. In order to meet the needs of people with disability, to level the playing field, those at risk of restricted social participation need to be identified and their challenges met. There is little point, however, in "counting cases" without the ability to meet the needs of those who are counted, and there may even be a risk that measuring disability prevalence is used as evidence that action is planned or taken. Once valid and reliable data are collected, it then becomes incumbent upon governments to create the policies that would meet the needs of people with disability. The goal of counting people with disability is to still the voice of discrimination and ultimately achieve social equity.

Including people with disabilities in economic development activities is a key to achieving the UN Millennium Development Goals (UN 2013b) of ending poverty and hunger, providing universal education, and improving health outcomes. With the CRPD as backdrop, increased attention has been given recently to interventions aimed at the inclusion of disabled people in social and economic life. In order to achieve such aims, it is necessary not only to generate indicators and statistics that can reveal unjust discrimination in any form, but such indicators should also enable monitoring and assessment of the impact of policies and programmes on the lives of disabled people (Mont and Loeb 2008). Population data can be analysed to identify those areas where social participation is lagging behind—for example in education, in employment or in housing—and actions or policies can be enacted that would address these inequities and attempt to increase inclusion and social participation, which should be the ultimate goal for any intervention in this area.

A human rights approach to disability requires that disability statistics have the clear purpose of describing the situation for individuals with disability, in order to analyse facilitators and barriers for inclusive policies and measures, i.e. to ensure that individuals with disability get the same opportunities as everyone else in a society. A broad understanding of disability, as in the ICF, is required for disability statistics to play a central role in policy-making and implementation, monitoring and assessment of effectiveness. Policy without a basis of evidence and good science may be highly problematic in many ways, including in regards to inclusion and equity (Eide et al. 2012). Unfortunately, in most low- and many middle-income countries in the world, this is exactly what is happening today.

An example that can guide future disability statistics is the initiative taken by the Southern Africa Federation of the Disabled in collaboration with the Norwegian Federation of Organisations for Disabled People around the turn of the century. Based on the understanding of disability as promoted by ICF, a series of studies on living conditions among people with disabilities have been undertaken in eight different southern African countries (see for instance Eide et al. 2011). These studies are basically a broad mapping on the level of living, using a broad set of largely existing and tested measurement scales for functioning, mental and physical health, environmental barriers, individual characteristics, activity limitations, participation and access to basic services (see for instance Eide and Jele 2011). These studies thus contain indicators that can enable analyses of all dimensions in the ICF model, including various aspects of social participation. The comparative element in the study, i.e. between individuals with and without disabilities, different socio-economic groups, impairment types, rural or urban and gender, reveals differences that can guide policy, practice, resource allocation and so forth. By describing and analysing disparities between groups concerning access to basic services, inclusion and social participation, this is an example of how research can promote a human rights approach to disability.

Conclusions

Our understanding of disability and the way it is measured has evolved over the past few decades; and that paradigm shift has been captured and promoted through the development and implementation of the ICF. According to the Practical Manual for using the ICF (WHO 2013: 83): "the ICF can be used as a universal framework for disability data collection related to policy goals of participation or inclusion. Its use can improve how data are collected and increase the probability that different sources of data relate well to each other". The ICF is, however, neither a measurement tool nor a survey instrument but a classification. The structure and language of a classification like the ICF differ from that of a questionnaire, so it is not possible to use the classification directly as a data collection tool in surveys. Therefore the ICF is best suited as a reference text or framework rather than as a source of questions. While the ICF is key for current attempts at establishing global disability statistics, different understandings of disability exist in parallel and contribute to blurring the basis for defining, identifying and thus counting and measuring disability. The ICF presents a model for defining disability and operationalising components of functioning for survey research. But disability and the ICF model that is used to operationalise it are complex, and no simple, single set of questions can capture that complexity in a thorough manner.

The Practical Manual points out that given the inherent limitations of the survey format, it would not be feasible to create a questionnaire that covered the entirety of

the ICF in either scope or level of specificity: "The objective of a population-based survey should be to develop a coherent, relevant, valid and feasible set of questions that meets the purposes of that survey" (WHO 2013: 83). While this statement may reflect the relative complexity of capturing the entirety of the disability experience (including health conditions, bodily functions, activity limitations, participation restrictions as well as the personal and, not least, environmental factors that impact these) in a single questionnaire, it may be seen as self-limiting. In fact, the living condition studies referred to earlier attempt to capture all dimensions in the model (ICF) and are evidence of the feasibility of this work.

A sound and agreed basis for defining and measuring disability is important for many reasons, including the goal of establishing cross-national comparability of disability statistics that will provide individual countries with the ability to collect and analyse disability data in a manner that is consistent with the international community. This would also meet the requirements established in the CRPD. While the Millennium Development Goals made no mention of people with disabilities, this deficiency has been rectified as we move into the post-2015 development agenda with the anticipated design of Sustainable Development Goals.

The long-standing search for a definition and approach to measuring disability remains unfinished—it is work in progress. Such data are needed to assess whether people with disabilities are left behind or if they have proper opportunities and human rights. Mitra (2013), among others, recommends using and implementing globally the instruments developed by the WG as an international standard for assessing the equalisation of opportunities and monitoring the UN Convention and post-2015 sustainable development goals. It is also necessary, however, to bring together current experiences and initiatives that have paved the way—and continue to pave the way—for the development of disability statistics nationally and internationally. Disability statistics serve multiple purposes, and it is argued that the struggle to achieve a global standard on the measurement of disability may, in fact, act as a diversion from the inherent complexity that invites different measures for different purposes (Mont 2007a). Rather than offering the basis for a global standard measure on disability, ICF offers a conceptual model of disability that allows for the establishment of a common point of reference and a common language upon which to base our understanding of disability. It attempts to move beyond a medical definition that is based on individual pathology and towards a concept based on the consequences of disease for functional capacity and social participation. Once we move outside the body of the individual, beyond the physical impairment, to include environmental barriers and facilitators to participation, only then will we begin to fulfil the human rights aspects of collecting disability statistics.

The ICF offers the basis for a new generation of disability statistics that focus on the environment and not the person. Recognition of the complexity of disability, the penetration of a social and interactional understanding, and the human rights approach to disability inherent in the CRPD, inevitably impacts our means of defining and measuring. The overarching purpose should be the role of disability statistics in providing empirical evidence that would lead to policies of inclusion, reducing barriers for full inclusion and participation in society.

References

Allotey, P., Reidpath, D., Kouame, A., & Cummins, R. (2003). The DALY, context and the determinants of the severity of disease: An exploratory comparison of paraplegia in Australia and Cameroon. *Social Science and Medicine, 57*, 949–958.

Altman, B. M. (2001). Disability definitions, models, classification schemes and applications. In G. L. Albrecht, K. D. Seelman, & M. Bury (Eds.), *Handbook of disability studies* (pp. 97–122). New York: Sage Publications.

Anand, S., & Hanson, K. (1997). Disability-adjusted life years: A critical review. *Journal of Health Economics, 16*, 685–702.

Bickenbach, J. E. (2011). Monitoring the United Nations Convention on the Rights of Persons with Disabilities: Data and the international classification of functioning, disability and health. *BMC Public Health, 11*(Suppl 4), S8. Retrieved from http://www.biomedcentral.com/1471-2458/11/S4/S8.

Borg, J., Larsson, S., Östergren, P.-O., & Eide, A. H. (2010). The friction model—A dynamic model of functioning, disability and contextual factors and its conceptual and practical applicability. *Disability and Rehabilitation, 32*(21), 1790–1797.

Cerniauskaite, M., Quintas, R., Boldt, C., Raggi, A., Cieza, A., Bickenbach, J. E., et al. (2011). Systematic literature review on ICF from 2001 to 2009: Its use, implementation and operationalisation. *Disability and Rehabilitation, 33*(4), 281–309.

Chang, F.-H., Coster, W. J. C., & Helfrich, C. A. (2013). Community participation measures for people with disabilities: A systematic review of content from an International Classification of Functioning, Disability and Health perspective. *Archives of Physical Medicine and Rehabilitation, 94*(4), 771–781.

Eide, A. H., Amin, M., MacLachlan, M., Mannan, H., & Schneider, M. (2012). Human rights, social inclusion and health equity in international donors' policies. *Disability, CBR & Inclusive Development, 23*(4), 24–40. doi:10.5463/DCID.v23i4.144.

Eide, A. H., & Ingstad, B. (2011). *Disability and poverty: A global challenge*. Bristol: The Policy Press.

Eide, A.H., & Jele, B. (2011). Living conditions among people with disabilities in Swaziland: A national, representative study. SINTEF A 20047. Oslo: SINTEF Technology & Society.

Eide, A. H., Jelsma, J., Loeb, M. E., Maart, S., & Ka' Toni, M. (2007). Exploring ICF components in a survey among Xhosa speakers in Eastern & Western Cape, South Africa. *Disability and Rehabilitation, 30*(11), 819–829.

Eide, A. H., & Loeb, M. E. (2006a). Reflections on disability data and statistics in developing countries. In B. Albert (Ed.), *In or out of the mainstream? Lessons from research on disability and development cooperation* (pp. 89–104). Leeds: University of Leeds\Disability Press.

Eide, A. H., & Loeb, M. E. (2006a). *Living conditions among people with disabilities in Zambia: A national representative survey*. SINTEF Report No. A262. Oslo: SINTEF Health Research.

Eide, A. H., & Loeb, M. E. (2011). Living conditions among people with disabilities in southern Africa: A comparative analyses. In A. H. Eide & B. Ingstad (Eds.), *Disability and poverty*. London: The Policy Press.

Eide, A. H., Loeb, M. E., Nhiwatiwa, S., Munthali, A., Ngulube, T. J., & van Rooy, G. (2011). Living conditions among people with disabilities in southern Africa: A comparative analysis. In A. H. Eide & B. Ingstad (Eds.), *Disability and poverty* (pp. 55–71). London: The Policy Press.

Fougeyrollas, P., Cloutier, R., Bergeron, H., St Michell, G., Cote, J., Cote, M., et al. (1999). *The Quebec classification: Disability creation process*. Quebec: International Network on the Disability Creation Process.

Gray, D. B., Hollingsworth, H. H., Stark, S., & Morgan, K. A. (2006). Participation survey/mobility: Psychometric properties of a measure of participation for people with mobility impairments and limitations. *Archives of Physical Medicine and Rehabilitation, 87*, 189–197.

Gray, D. B., Hollingsworth, H. H., Stark, S., & Morgan, K. A. (2008). A subjective measure of environmental facilitators and barriers to participation for people with mobility limitations. *Disability and Rehabilitation, 30*(6), 434–457.

Hammel, J., Magasi, S., Heinemann, A., Whiteneck, G., Bogner, J., & Rodriguez, E. (2007). What does participation mean? *Disability and Rehabilitation, 30*(19), 1445–1460.

Harvey, A., Robin, J., Morris, M. E., Graham, H. K., & Baker, R. (2008). A systematic review of measures of activity limitation for children with cerebral palsy. *Developmental Medicine and Child Neurology, 50*(3), 190–198.

IDA. (2014). *Inclusive post 2015 development agenda for persons with disability in Africa.* Nairobi: International Disability Alliance. Nairobi Declaration.

Ingstad, B., & Whyte, S. R. (1995). *Disability and culture*. Berkeley: University of California Press.

Jagger, C., Gillies, C., Cambois, E., Oyen, H. V., Nusselder, W., & Robine, J.-M. (2010). The Global Activity Limitation Index measured function and disability similarly across European countries. *Journal of Clinical Epidemiology, 63*(8), 892–899.

Jette, A. M. (1994). Physical disablement concepts for physical therapy research and practice. *Physical Therapy, 74*, 380–386.

Jette, A. M. (2006). Towards a common language for function, disability and health. *Physical Therapy, 86*(5), 726–734.

Jette, A. M., Haley, S. M., & Kooyoomjian, J. T. (2003). Are the ICF activity and participation dimensions distinct? *Journal of Rehabilitation Medicine, 35*, 145–149.

Loeb, M. E. (2013). Disability statistics: An integral but missing (and misunderstood) component of development work. *Nord J Hum Rights, 31*(3), 306–324.

Loeb, M. E., Eide, A. H., & Mont, D. (2008). Approaching disability prevalence: The case of Zambia. *ALTER European Journal of Disability Research, 2*, 32–43.

Long, J. S., & Pavalko, E. (2004). Comparing alternative measures of functional limitation. *Medical Care, 42*, 19–27.

Maart, S., Eide, A. H., Jelsma, J., Loeb, M. E., & Ka Toni, M. (2007). Environmental barriers experienced by urban and rural disabled people in South Africa. *Disability and Society, 22*(4), 357–369.

Madans, J. H., Altman, B. M., Rasch, E. K., Mbogoni, M., Synneborn, M., & Banda, J. (2004). *Washington Group Position Paper: Proposed purpose of an internationally comparative general disability measure*. Retrieved September 25, 2014, from http://www.cdc.gov/nchs/data/washington_group/WG_purpose_paper.pdf.

Madden, R. H., Dune, T., Lukersmith, S., Hartley, S., Kuipers, P., Gargett, A., et al. (2013). The relevance of the International Classification of Functioning, Disability and Health (ICF) in monitoring and evaluating community-based rehabilitation (CBR). *Disability and Rehabilitation*. doi:10.3109/09638288.2013.821182.

Mitra, S. (2013). A data revolution for disability-inclusive development. *Lancet Global Health, 1*(4), e178–e179. Retrieved from http://dx.doi.org/10.1016/S2214-109X(13)70016-0.

Mont, D. (2007a). Measuring health and disability. *Lancet, 369*, 1658–63.

Mont, D. (2007b). *Measuring disability prevalence*. Social Protection Discussion Paper No. 0706. Washington, DC: The World Bank.

Mont, D., & Loeb, M. (2008). *Beyond DALYs: Developing indicators to assess the impact of public health interventions on the lives of people with disabilities*. SP Discussion Paper No. 0815. Washington DC: The World Bank.

Nagi, S. (1965). Some conceptual issues in disability and rehabilitation. In M. B. Sussman (Ed.), *Sociology and rehabilitation* (pp. 100–113). Washington, DC: American Sociological Association.

Nagi, S. (1991). Disability concepts revisited: Implications for prevention. In A. Pope & A. Tarolv (Eds.), *Disability in America: Toward a national agenda for prevention* (pp. 309–327). Washington, DC: National Academy Press.

NIH. (1992). *National advisory board on medical rehabilitation Research. Draft 5: Report and plan for medical rehabilitation research.* Bethesda: National Institute of Health.

Oliver, M., & Barnes, C. (2012). *The new politics of disablement.* Hants: Palgrave Macmillan.

UN. (1982). *The United Nations world programme of action concerning disabled persons.* New York: United Nations.

UN. (1993). *World programme of action concerning disabled persons.* New York: United Nations.

UN. (1994). *The standard rules on the equalization of opportunities for persons with disabilities.* New York: United Nations. Retrieved August 2, 2014, from http://www.un.org/disabilities/documents/gadocs/standardrules.pdf.

UN. (2003). *Expert Group Meeting to review the United Nations Demographic Yearbook System, 10–14 November 2003. ESA/STAT/AC.91/6.*. New York: United Nations Secretariat. Statistical Division.

UN. (2006). *Convention on the Rights of Persons with Disabilities and Optional Protocol.* New York: United Nations. Retrieved from www.un.org/disabilities/convention/facts.shtml.

UN DISTAT. (2013). *Human functioning and disability.* United Nations Statistics Division. Retrieved September 25, 2014, from http://unstats.un.org/unsd/demographic/sconcerns/disability/disab2.asp.

UN. (2013a). *A new global partnership: Eradicate poverty and transform economies through sustainable development.* Report by the High-Level Panel on the Post-2015 Development Agenda. New York: United Nations.

UN. (2013b). *UN Millennium Development Goals.* Retrieved September 26, 2014, from http://www.un.org/millenniumgoals/.

United Nations Statistics Division. (2008). *Principles and recommendations for population and housing censuses (2nd revision).* New York: United Nations. Retrieved August 2, 2014, from http://unstats.un.org/unsd/demographic/sources/census/docs/P&R_Rev2.pdf.

Üstün, T. B., Chatterji, S., Kostanjsek, N., Rehm, J., Kennedy, C., Epping-Jordan, E., et al. (2010). Developing the World Health Organization Disability Assessment Schedule 2.0. *Bulletin of the World Health Organization, 88*, 815–823. doi:10.2471/BLT.09.067231.

Verbrugge, I., & Jette, A. (1994). The disablement process. *Social Science and Medicine, 38*, 1–14.

Whiteneck, G. G., Harrison-Felix, C. L., Mellick, D. C., Brooks, C. A., Charlifue, S. B., & Gerhart, K. A. (2004). Quantifying environmental factors: A measure of physical, attitudinal, service, productivity, and policy barriers. *Archives of Physical Medicine and Rehabilitation, 85*, 1324–1335.

WHO. (1980). *International classification of impairments, disability and handicap.* Geneva: World Health Organization.

WHO. (1981). *Disability prevention and rehabilitation: Report of the WHO expert committee on disability prevention and rehabilitation. Technical Report Series 668.* Geneva: World Health Organization. Retrieved from http://whqlibdoc.who.int/trs/WHO_TRS_668.pdf.

WHO. (2001). *International classification of functioning, disability and health.* Geneva: World Health Organization.

WHO. (2010). *Community-based rehabilitation. CBR guidelines.* Geneva: World Health Organization.

WHO. (2011). *World disability report.* Geneva: World Health Organization.

WHO. (2013). *How to use the ICF. A practical manual for using the International Classification of Functioning, Disability and Health (ICF).* Geneva: World Health Organization.

Witsø, A. E., Eide, A. H., & Vik, K. (2011). Professional carers' perspective on participation for older adults living in place. *Disability and Rehabilitation, 33*(7), 557–568.

Chapter 5
The Place of Disability

Dan Goodley and Leslie Swartz

Introduction

To think of disability inevitably conjures up thoughts of age, class, gender, sexuality, ethnicity, race, indigeneity and nationality. Such intersectional considerations are at the heart of what has been termed critical disability studies (Goodley 2011; Shakespeare 2013), where disability links together other identities as a moment of reflection that Lenny Davis (2002, 2006) coins as dismodernism. While critical disability studies might start with disability, they never end with it: remaining ever vigilant of ontological and theoretical complexity, as well as complexity in terms of political, cultural, social and material issues (Goodley 2011). Such complexity is extended further when one thinks about *the place of disability*: where and when disability appears. Disability emerges geopolitically (in terms of location), temporally (by way of differing historical moments) and epistemologically (considering, for example, disability's varied disciplinary dwellings). We are interested in those varied terrains where we might map and locate disability but this journey, perhaps inevitably, involves much crossing of national and theoretical borders. In this chapter we will consider a number of ways in which we might place disability, including a global north perspective, a supranational discourse and a global South response.[1] In our geo-theoretical journey we will consider the troubles associated with

[1]We have deliberately chosen 'global north' and 'global South' to unsettle the dominance of the former position and augment perspectives emerging from latter contexts.

D. Goodley (✉)
University of Sheffield, Sheffield, UK
e-mail: d.goodley@shef.ac.uk

L. Swartz
Stellenbosch University, Stellenbosch, South Africa

S. Grech, K. Soldatic (eds.), *Disability in the Global South*,
International Perspectives on Social Policy, Administration, and Practice,
DOI 10.1007/978-3-319-42488-0_5

conceptualising disability. We conclude by thinking through the complexities borne out of this recognition of the local and global placing of disability.

A Global North Perspective on Disability

A well-told story about disability studies is of the field's emergence in a transdisciplinary space in North America and Western Europe as a dynamic community of practice that brought together theorists, practitioners, activists and artists who shared an antipathy towards the dominant conceptualisations of disability. Two cultural extremes come to mind when one thinks of dominant hegemonies around disability: disability as immorality; and disability as medical specimen (Snyder and Mitchell 2001: 380). Moral positions, especially from Judeo-Christian traditions, have viewed disability as a sin (a punishment from God forgiven through divine intervention). Medical perspectives have dominated the discursive landscape, framing disability as pathology (a physical, sensory or cognitive failing that tragically 'handicaps' those 'afflicted'). Following Snyder and Mitchell (2001: 379), moral positions have included disability as a reflection of God's dismay (Ancient Greece), as evidence of an intimacy with God (Medieval Europe) and a divine response to parental wrongdoing (Renaissance period). Religious views of disability have been denounced by numerous western disability studies scholars for their inherent tendencies for pathologisation (Goodley 2011). The medical model, meanwhile, has been conceptualised as a perspective originating in western modernity (Christensen 1996; Sachs 2008). Where the church benefits from the moral position then the para/medical professions benefit from the medical model. The eugenics movement of the early 20th century in Western Europe and North America, which accompanied the rise in the status of science and its related practices, colonialism and capitalism, located the burden of disability in the unproductive flawed, weak and lacking individual (Fernald 1912). Following Naidoo (2009), medicine has conceptualised disability as a distinct pathology (a pathogenic view) rather than part of a continuum of dis/ease (a salutogenic position) or in terms of capacities and strengths (a fortigenic approach). The medical model encourages the disabled entity to be framed in terms of assisted suicide, euthanasia and antenatal termination. The human worth of disabled people is rendered highly questionable through the growing use of reproductive technologies. And as medicine intervenes so disabled bodies are made increasingly undesirable.

For the first British professor of disability studies, Mike Oliver (1990), moral and medical approaches each promote an *individual model of disability*, reducing the problem of disability to the flawed tragedy of individual personhood treatable through the interventions of charities and healthcare professionals. Simi Linton (1998) and Mark Sherry (2006) suggest that this individual discourse creates a number of 'fault lines': disability is cast as an essentialist condition (with organic aetiologies); disabled people are treated as objects rather than authors of their own lives; 'person fixing' rather than 'context changing' interventions are preferred; the power of health and social care professionals is increased and the tyranny of normality is accentuated. Disabled people are infantilised, constructed as helpless and viewed as asexual (McRuer and Wilkerson 2003: 10). For Paul Abberley (1987: 18), presenting the disadvantage of disability as the consequence of a 'naturalised impairment' or 'biological flaw' lets exclusionary society off the hook.

Global north disability studies seeks to dislodge disability from its medicalised origins and from strains of thinking which associate disability with moral failure (Herndon 2002: 122). 'Disability' is not natural. Disability is socially constructed. In Britain, the Union of the Physically Impaired Against Segregation, devised the following definitions to acknowledge the role of society and the presence of bodily difference:

> Impairment—lacking part of or all of a limb, or having a defective limb organism or mechanism of the body.
>
> Disability—the disadvantage or restriction of activity caused by a contemporary social organisation which takes no account of people who have physical impairments *(and or learning difficulties)* and thus excludes them from mainstream social activities [italic text added by the authors]. (UPIAS 1976: 3–4)

These definitions acknowledge the body (impairment) but politicise the body's engagement with the social world (disability). Impairment as a form of embodied difference is defined 'often within a medical context and disability is the negative social reaction to those differences' (Sherry 2007: 10). Disabled people are just that: people *disabled by* contemporary society. This forms the heart of what came to be termed the social model of disability (Oliver 1990, 1996; Shakespeare 1993; Hughes and Paterson 1997). As Goodley (2011) observes, *disability* is recognised as a phenomenon of cultural, political and socio-economic conditions (Abberley 1987), *disablism* recognises the psychological, cultural and structural crimes against disabled people (Thomas 2007) and *disablement* captures the consequences of disablism (Oliver 1990). At the centre of these different concepts is the UPIAS split of body (impairment) from society (disability).

A strong trope within global north disability studies theory and history pertains to the analysis of the relationship between disability, labour and capitalism. Vic Finkelstein (1981) famously argues that while early capitalism (phase 1) offered some inclusion in the community through disabled people's involvement in small-scale cottage industries, the rapid growth of manufacturing and machinery supplanted their contribution to a growing labour force. Phase 2 saw manufacturing industries such as coal and steel expanding. Mass migration from rural to urban areas increased exponentially. Industrialisation deskilled and impoverished disabled people who had previously worked in agrarian communities (Slee 1996: 99). Many disabled people, deemed incapable of offering labour, quickly joined the unemployed in the cities. Industrialisation demanded fit workers. Factories exposed uncompetitive workers. Institutionalisation provided a means of controlling non-viable workers and, in contrast, developed new forms of labour for those working in the factories (Barnes et al. 1999: 14–20). Phase 3, late capitalism, offers more opportunities for consumer groups and disabled people's organisations to challenge their exclusion from mainstream life. That said, while contemporary post-Fordist techno-driven economies might include some disabled workers, others might be further ostracised by this move from manufacturing to knowledge production.

More recently, the World Report on Disability (WHO and World Bank 2011) has argued that choices between the medical and the social model are somewhat spurious. Depending on the International Classification of Functioning (ICF) approach (World Health Organization 2007), the World Health Organization and World Bank have presented disability as both a medical and a social issue, as other chapters in this volume discuss (see, for example, Eide and Loeb 2016). What tends to be obscured in these ‘global’ documents, however, is that global north disability studies and their products, as promoted by bodies such as the WHO and the World Bank, tend to be emblematic of the cultural contexts from which the theories emerged. These theories come from the global north. Questions must be raised about the specificities and particularities of global north analyses that, if left unchecked (and worse, exported to other parts of the globe), suffer from a lack of critical evaluation.

First, global north analyses often portray a distinctive contrast between self and other, the individual and their community, and body and society. To follow the critical psychologist Edward Sampson, the distinctions of body/mind and individual/society are deeply entrenched within the Eurocentric modernist psyche and mindset. For Ken Gergen,

> modernism is typically traced to that historical period in which culture moved from the so-called Dark Ages of medievalism (characterized by an unquestioning adherence to totalitarian royal or religious decree) to the Enlightenment (promising the bounded and sacred sanctuary of the mind, autonomous capacities and the beginnings of systematic human science). (Gergen 2001: 803–804)

The drawing of a boundary between nature and culture is distinctive to modernity (Tremain 2000). The individual we have come to cherish is a ‘post-Cartesian entrenchment of the notion that the self-possessive inviolability of the bounded body grounds the autonomous subject’ (Shildrick 2007: 225). For Sampson (1985: 1204) ‘to centre order within the persona is a peculiarly Western worldview’ that the individual will be the main architect of order and coherence. We associate a singular individual with control, connect many with chaos and are led to view the collective world as potentially threatening and disruptive. In a later paper, Sampson (1993) suggests that rich-income nations’ conception of human nature is primarily a white male of western ‘United Statesian’ character! Global north disability studies risks importing this peculiar modern man into its conception of the (impaired) individual. Ironically, the UPIAS (1976) definition actually maintains a rather medicalising conception of disability through its use of the language of individual lack. Moreover, global north rejections of religious disability discourse risk ignoring how faith communities replenish wider communities in ways that might be more inclusive than first thought (Valentine and Sporton 2009).

Second, global north scholars’ understandable emphasis on labour and capitalism (especially in the deeply class-divided contexts of nations such as Britain) emphasise capitalist economic forces associated with disablism. Disablement for many British disability activists is most evident in terms of labour participation, where disabled adults continue to be under-represented across the private and public sectors and actively discouraged from entering certain workplaces. That said, other forms of cultural production, community participation and involvement, and psychological and relational networks risk being obscured by centralising work and the economy.

Third, global north perspectives—especially those centred around the social model—have been criticised for ignoring the centrality of impairment to the lives of some disabled people (Shakespeare 2013), sidelining the importance of cultural and discursive factors in the framing of the meaning of disability (Tremain 2005) and failing to connect with the politics of other transformative perspectives, including critical race, queer and feminist approaches (Miles 2000; Sherry 2007; Thomas 2007).[2] While we do not have the space here to develop these critiques, what we are starting to witness in this brief expose of global north discourse are the dangers of generalising from the particular to the global. Critical disability studies seeks to address these limitations and the present absence of certain voices.

A Supranational Discourse of Disability

How we conceptualise disability will depend heavily on the kinds of place within which disability emerges. Let us think, then, pan-nationally (that is, across nation states). What attempts have been made to conceptualise disability across the world? The 2011 World Report on Disability is one example of an attempt to paint a comprehensive picture of the global position of disabled people. The World Report concludes that there are over one billion disabled people in the world, of whom nearly '200 million experience considerable difficulties in functioning'. This estimate suggests 15 per cent of the world's population live with an impairment. The theoretical framework on disability adopted by the authors of the report (theoretically representing nations from around the globe) is the ICF, a bio-psycho-social model which aims to

> represent a workable compromise between medical and social models. Disability is the umbrella term for impairments, activity limitations and participation restrictions, referring to the negative aspects of the interaction between an individual (with a health condition) and that individual's contextual factors (environmental and personal factors). (WHO and World Bank 2011: 3).

How then does disability emerge from this document? As Goodley has argued recently, the World Report works as an administrative text, targeting an international audience, saying many important things about the global positioning of disabled people:

> It is a text that will undoubtedly be used to bolster human rights programmes, inform anti-discriminatory legislation, and justify public funding of initiatives such as inclusive educa-

[2] For an overview of some of the key debates in disability studies see Goodley 2011.

> tion, accessible workplaces and anti-discriminatory cultural industries. This is an important report on an exigent matter. A lot of space is given to countries outside of Western Europe and North America. Emphasis is placed on environmental factors—such as participation restrictions—that can substantively reduce the life opportunities of people living with impairments. Key recommendations include the promotion of inclusive schools, stressing the importance of disability equality awareness and meaningfully drawing on the expertise of disabled people as consultants and co-workers. (Goodley 2014: 15–16)

Following Goodley (2014), disability is conceptualised in the World Report as a problematic phenomenon meriting an urgent response on the part of governments and their citizens. Simultaneously, by referencing the United Nations Convention on the Rights of Persons with Disabilities (CRPD), the World Report is a pragmatic document shared across the world by numerous policymakers and activists to contest the conditions of disablism. One recent observer celebrated the report's mass appeal:

> to inform governments of countries about the importance of disability, analyze scientific information, and provide recommendations for action at the national and international levels. The report successfully illustrates a great need for improved data, policies, and programs, while describing promising practices that can inform policy makers in addressing these needs. This report is highly recommended reading for anyone interested in a global view on disability and should be required reading for any students in disability and public health. (Krahn 2011: 141)

The World Report marks an opportunity for 'disabled people' in and across nation states 'to use its recommendations to bolster their collective struggle for a fairer and equitable society' (Oliver and Barnes 2012: 57). The report has inevitably received criticism and Goodley gives one example:

Oliver and Barnes (2012) give a typically Anglo-centric social model commentary, pivoting around three points of contention:

i. The World Report authors' owning of disability as a dynamic and complex relationship between an impaired person and the social world is something disability studies and organisations of disabled people have been saying for years.
ii. The report's emphasis on more systematic, objective and scientific methodologies for assessing disability risk invalidating disability research enacted in a politicised and more subjective manner.
iii. The report cannot be viewed as an objective document; 'we must clearly recognise that all social research is political and, perhaps more importantly, consider the political role of the WHO and the World Bank in sponsoring the Report. Both are structurally positioned to facilitate the ongoing development of global capitalism, which is based on the twin evils of domination and exploitation' (Oliver and Barnes 2012: 579) (Goodley 2014: 17).

Instead of rejecting the World Report one might, instead, productively read it as a cultural text. We might ask, where does the World Report place disability? As a supranational document—written with the aim to speak across geopolitical boundaries—the text toys with the possibilities of a universal response to disability. While the authors do acknowledge the culturally relative nature of disability's categorisation, the report, nevertheless, has to take disability out of a locality and place it in a register of a more global appeal. Yet, like all texts, the report 'has a constitutive character to it: disability is constructed and created through the workings of the text' (Goodley 2014: 17). So what does the report say and make of disability?

First, we should recognise that the World Report appears to draw on and develop an *interactionist model of disability*. This approach is associated with what some observers have termed the Nordic relational model of disability. Such a perspective approaches 'the study of disability with three main assumptions: (1) disability is a person–environment mis/match; (2) disability is situational or contextual; and (3) disability is relative' (Tøssebro 2004; Traustadóttir 2004). For Fiona Kumari Campbell (2009: 95), a relational model should be acknowledged 'for the ways in which it recognises the interactivity of impairment and disabling modes of socio-economic organisation' (Goodley 2011: 16). To more sceptical observers, an interactionist approach is in danger of smuggling in an unproblematic concept of impairment which leaves the body/mind split under-theorised and therefore uncontested (Goodley 2014).

Second, while the World Report seeks universal application, critical disability studies analyses that are emerging from the global South (and recognised in this book) urge us to incorporate historical, cultural, economic and political specificities of disability in different parts of the globe. Grech (2012: 59) makes the convincing argument that disability studies has not served the subject of majority world disability studies because 'it is dominated by white, Western, middle class academics engaging in debate imbued with ideological, theoretical, cultural and historical assumptions of Western urban post-industrialised societies'. 'Despite Western foundations', Grech continues:

> disability studies has reached hegemonic status in the disability and majority world debate as the exportation of its ideas (notably the social model of disability) from North to South continues unabated. This seems to be legitimised by numerous factors: the marginalisation/exclusion of disability in the development sector; the monopolisation of most things disability by the Western disability studies; and the assumption that disability theories and writings from the West are transferable across the globe with few or no modifications. (Grech 2012: 59)

As Goodley writes:

> the work of Anita Ghai (2006), Shaun Grech (2011, 2012), Karen Soldatic and Helen Meekosha (2012) (to name but a few) 'remind us, through reference to India, Guatemala and Australia, that different kinds of colonial histories, the suffering of indigenous groups and acute conditions of poverty will lead to different understandings of disablism'. A universalist approach risks whitewashing over the specifics of disability. Critical disability studies must seek to reinsert this cultural sensitivity. (Goodley 2014: 17)

In this regard, the collection edited by Ingstad and Whyte (2007) and the work of Devlieger (2005) have been key to developing cultural understandings of disability. As we show in the section which follows, however, even 'cultural' understandings present questions for the global South's response to these formulations.

A Global Southern Response

The Problem

Given the power of discourses developed in the global north and their export to the South, it becomes difficult to know what a response from the global South is, or should be. Part of the problem here is not only that disability is often seen in essentialised terms, as we have suggested earlier, but also that the difference between the north and the South, the global and the indigenous, is often cast as an essential and immutable difference. Colonists visiting the South had an interest in portraying local practices as essentially different from those in the north. This is a complex matter that we cannot give full attention to here, but the portrayal of the 'savage' as essentially different from the 'civilised' colonist from the north provided an ideological and apparently 'scientific' reason and justification for inferior treatment of the 'uncivilised' (Swartz 1998). If, for example, whole races of people are not fully human, or if they lack the intellectual capacity to make rational choices, then it follows that managing these groups with what would be seen as brutality for others, becomes necessary and even humane. Similarly, if primitive people have immutable belief systems, which are at odds with modern science, then it becomes a matter of cultural respect (rather than neglect) not to offer them what science has found to be the best forms of help. In apartheid South Africa, for example, it was commonly argued that the reason black people did not have equal access to mental health care was that they had cultural beliefs which made such care irrelevant and useless to them (Swartz 1998). A key flaw in this convenient line of essentialist reasoning is that in all cases it was those with power—the colonists and the masters of the apartheid system, for example—who decided for people what they did and did not believe and want. It was also possible at the stroke of a bureaucratic pen to exclude groups of people from care. At one time in South Africa, for example, by definition, only white people could be classified (using the term of the time) as 'mentally retarded' (Lea and Foster 1990).

In the context of this essentialising both of disability and of racial difference, as part of the broader project of what Dubow (1995) has termed 'scientific racism', it is hardly surprising that there are two contrasting images of disability and its manifestations in the global South, images which correspond uncomfortably closely to two images of the 'primitive' identified by Lucas and Barrett (1995). These authors describe 'primitivism' as a way western medicine describes the 'other' and, by implication and inversion, itself (see Said 1978). On the one hand, the 'primitive' is presented for western consumption as a 'Barbarian', as these authors put it—a dangerous force, out of control and a danger to order and civilisation. The obverse of the Barbarian is the 'Arcadian' view of natives happily living a prelapsarian existence, with civilisation presented as a danger to this natural state of being. What is interesting about this Barbarian/Arcadian split is that in the field of disability, it can occur in a number of permutations. Somewhat schematically, we can distinguish between views of disabled people themselves as either Barbaric or Arcadian on the one hand, and views of how societies in the South deal with disability and difference as either oppressive and cruel (Barbarian) or tolerant and inclusive (Arcadian). Well-placed and appropriate concern for the welfare of disabled people in the global South can rapidly lead to generalisations not necessarily based on evidence. For example, Bayat (2015) raises important concerns about the abuse and killing of disabled children in West Africa, but in the absence of research data claims that it is 'not unreasonable to speculate that both killing and abuse of this vulnerable population is more widespread than reported' (Bayat 2015: 2). This kind of statement is useful rhetorically for Bayat's argument but not necessary for it—any case of abuse or killing is sufficient for concern—and it contributes to an overall typification of barbaric practices.

The Question of Ubuntu

Disability studies scholars and activists living and working in the global South have a complicated balancing act to perform. First, it is important that they speak out about and fight exclusion, oppression and abuse. No amount of cultural relativism can condone the abuse or even killing of people with albinism in Africa, for example (Hong et al. 2006). Second, because of dependence on funding from the north, it is becoming increasingly necessary to speak the language of the social model and the CRPD (Heap et al. 2009; Meyers 2014; Jonas et al. 2015). Third, and crucially, there is an impetus to rescue images of disability and the treatment of disabled people in the global South from abjection. The complexity of this balancing act can be seen in the writing of Owusu-Ansah and Mji, who open an article on African indigenous knowledge systems with the following:

> The thrust of this paper is to heighten awareness, stimulate new thoughts and generate discussion on the wealth of indigenous knowledge. African researchers need to persist in developing and using alternative methods of studying our reality and refrain from sticking to the research pathways mapped out by Western methodologies, within which many have been trained. Whilst it neither seeks to negate nor denigrate known Western methods of investigation, it intends to challenge researchers and African scholars in particular into alternative methods of inquiry as far as the investigation and preservation of indigenous knowledge is concerned for the development and empowerment of African peoples and particularly persons with disabilities. (Owusu-Ansah and Mji 2013: 1)

Later, they portray 'Afrocentricity' as fundamentally concerned with cultural immersion and respect of the other:

> It is noteworthy that Afrocentricity is not just about Africa or the African culture. Instead, its fundamental aim is that all cultural centres must be respected and not impaired by colour or geography. Instead, to be 'centred' is to be located as an *agent*, not as 'the *other*' … the basis of which is equal and respectful mutual exchange and synthesis of information. To this end, Afrocentricity encourages cultural and social immersion as opposed to scientific distance in research as well as the use of tools and methods indigenous to the people being studied. This way, indigenous peoples are active participants in the articulation of the views, wishes, concerns and research questions that they deem important to their cultural

> context and experience. Social immersion would provide researcher knowledge about and familiarity with the history, language, philosophy, and myths of the people under study, and reduce misinterpretation, perpetuation of myths and researcher imposition. (Owusu-Ansah and Mji 2013:1)

In support of this African approach, the authors mention the importance of collectivism in Africa but also draw on social model theorists and the fundamental social model argument that the voices of disabled people themselves must be heard in order for emancipation to occur. What they do not do is explore the possible tensions between a collectivist model of social organisation and a social model approach. A fundamental question here is the extent to which models of collective experience and decision-making in African contexts are truly inclusive.

The concept of *ubuntu* is widely drawn on in contemporary Africanist thinking and has been suggested as a model for disability studies in the postcolonial context (Mji et al. 2011; Chataika and McKenzie 2013; Kathard and Pillay 2013). According to Kathard and Pillay (2013: 86), 'Ubuntu is an African consciousness characterized by inter-connectedness of people, their communalism, solidarity, generosity, compassion, and care'. Here, Kathard and Pillay summarise a commonly presented optimistic view of *ubuntu* as a philosophy of complete inclusion and care, a system of thought constructed as an opposing force to dominant and inhumane practices from the north. Feminist scholars in particular, however (see for example Mangena 2013), have noted that the extent to which *ubuntu* grants equal rights may be seriously constrained by ideas of gender and lineage. For example, in an *ubuntu* context, it may be true to say that decision-making is done collectively but there may be constraints on who constitutes the collective. Female gender may limit access to decision-making, as may young age. Van Zyl notes:

> In Ubuntu … individual existence is expressed through communal interdependencies, sharing, reciprocal obligations, and responsibilities. Therefore in Ubuntu freedom is circumscribed by belonging in a community, primarily referenced through kinship. (Van Zyl 2011: 337)

Van Zyl's point is important here. According to her reading, *ubuntu* does not create conditions for inclusion; it promotes inclusion for those already considered to be part of a circumscribed community. It is by no means clear, in this view, that disabled people would automatically be seen to be included. It is also not irrelevant here that kinship is a key concept. Kinship is determined partly by definitions of personhood (only people defined as such may be deemed kin) and by sexuality (it is through procreation that kinship ties are extended). It is by no means clear in the global South, as is the case elsewhere in the world, that disabled people enjoy the same rights as others do to being considered fully human and legitimately sexual.

In light of these concerns, it is probably true to say that though disability scholars from the South have raised the issue of *ubuntu* as an important one in engaging with questions of disability and inclusion, there is not as yet sufficient critical engagement with the concept and what it may mean for disabled people. There may indeed be a degree of unevenness in the application of *ubuntu* concepts to groups of people with different impairments and different genders.

Religion

A key way in which disability is understood globally is in terms of religion. Though many texts will depict ideas about disability in the north as having emerged from a religious to a scientific paradigm, religious formulations remain key to how disability is widely understood and experienced (see Miles 2002; Grech 2012). In the global South, furthermore, it is not uncommon that the only provision for disabled people of crucial resources, such as education and health care, will come from faith-based organisations. Disability activists in southern Africa who participated in a research skills course, all of them well versed in the social model, were all practising Christians (Swartz 2013) and found it inconceivable that it was possible to engage with disability issues without coming from a faith-based orientation. Local beliefs about disability as divine punishment or being associated with sorcery share much with such beliefs worldwide and need to be engaged with. In recent years, there has been a deepening interest in how issues of faith need to be considered in the context of promotion of disability rights in the global South (Claassens et al. 2013). As in the case of *ubuntu*, there are both possibilities and challenges here as the balance needs to be sought between recognising the deleterious effects of religion on disabled people on the one hand and, on the other, utilising religion as an important resource in this regard. The centrality of belief to the experience of disability is perhaps one of the most serious challenges to disability studies theorists influenced by materialist analyses, and much work needs to be done in exploring points of agreement and tension across different approaches.

Conclusion

Critical disability studies—when it works well and with an ethics of openness to inquiry—is always aware of the inequities of globalisation. In this chapter we have moved in and out of north and South spaces to consider the complex ways in which disability is placed and understood. As we have shown, there is an urgent need to consider disability within a global politics of place and power, but the ways in which this field should be taken forward are not yet fully clear. We have shown how 'disability' has become an object created and shaped—indeed, to a degree, produced—by global forces. We have suggested, however, that in the context of global power imbalances it is extremely difficult for those in the global South constructed by such forces to speak back to the power not only of global colonial and neo-liberal interests, but also to the power of theorists in the north who, whatever their emancipatory agendas, are located differently from those with less access. This chapter (and others in this book) represents an attempt to think together from positions in the global north and the global South. This is not enough.

Wherever disability is spoken of without contextual qualifiers, it is important that those generally excluded from discussions participate. Disability studies (after the medical model) depend centrally on a politics of participation; it is important that efforts are made and resources are made available to extend participation in the framing of debates. This requires much more active participation from the global South. Furthermore, it is important to recognise the dynamic ways in which global north discourses of disability penetrate and mingle with global South practices and, conversely, how these latter practices resist or hybridise disability discourses.

When we speak of global South disability studies we should not romanticise these contexts as if they were untouched by the processes of colonisation—nor unaffected by the disability activism of comrades in other parts of the world. Disability as it appears in the place of the global South demands us to think again, from different and often under-represented contexts, about disability as a moment of reflection on the kinds of humanities that we value and the types of politics that we require. Rather than setting up global north and global South disability discourses as always in opposition, we would want to acknowledge differences and the differential ways in which power operates within and across the contexts, but also we would want to identify a shared disability commons for the development of disability politics. Following Hardt and Negri (2000), while mindful of geopolitical differences, when we place disability we should also seek to identify those political moments when disabled people are agitating in similar ways across the globe that demonstrate their part of a shared politics of disability.

Acknowledgements Parts of this chapter are reproduced by permission of Sage Publications, © from elements of chapters 1, 4 and 5 of D. Goodley (2011), *Disability Studies: An interdisciplinary introduction*, London: Sage.

References

Abberley, P. (1987). The concept of oppression and the development of a social theory of disability. *Disability, Handicap & Society, 2*(1), 5–19.

Barnes, C., Mercer, G., & Shakespeare, T. (1999). *Exploring disability*. London: Polity Press.

Bayat, M. (2015). The stories of 'snake children': Killing and abuse of children with developmental disabilities in West Africa. *Journal of Intellectual Disability Research, 59*(1), 1–10.

Campbell, F. K. (2009). *Contours of ableism: Territories, objects, disability and desire*. London: Palgrave Macmillan.

Chataika, T., & McKenzie, J. (2013). Considerations of an African childhood disability studies. In T. Curran & K. Runswick-Cole (Eds.), *Disabled children's childhood studies: Critical approaches in a global context* (pp. 152–163). London: Palgrave.

Christensen, C. (1996). Disabled, handicapped or disordered: 'What's in a name?'. In C. Christensen & F. Rizvi (Eds.), *Disability and the dilemmas of education and justice* (pp. 63–78). Buckingham: Open University Press.

Claassens, J., Swartz, L., & Hansen, L. D. (Eds.). (2013). *Searching for dignity: Conversations on human dignity, theology and disability*. Stellenbosch: SUNMedia.

Davis, L. J. (2002). *Bending over backwards. Disability, dismodernism and other difficult positions*. New York: New York University Press.

Davis, L. J. (2006). The end of identity politics and the beginning of dismodernism. On disability as an unstable category. In L. Davis (Ed.), *The disability studies reader* (2nd ed., pp. 231–242). New York: Routledge.

Devlieger, P. J. (2005, October). Generating a cultural model of disability. In *19th congress of the European Federation of Associations of Teachers of the Deaf (FEAPDA), October* (pp. 14-16).

Dubow, S. (1995). *Scientific racism in modern South Africa*. Cambridge: Cambridge University Press.

Eide, A. H., & Loeb, M. (2016). Counting disabled people: Historical perspectives and the challenges of disability statistics. In S. Grech & K. Soldatic (Eds.), *Disability in the Global South: The critical handbook*. New York: Springer.

Fernald, W. E. (1912). The Burden of Feeble-mindedness. *Journal of Psychoasthenics, 17*, 87–111.

Finkelstein, V. (1981). Disability and the helper/helped relationship. An historical view. In A. Brechin, P. Liddiard, & J. Swain (Eds.), *Handicap in a social world* (pp. 12–22). London: Hodder and Stoughton.

Gergen, K. (2001). Psychological science in a Postmodern world. *American Psychologist, 56*(10), 803–813.

Ghai, A. (2006). *(Dis)embodied form: Issues of disabled women*. Delhi: Shakti Books.

Goodley, D. (2011). *Disability studies: An interdisciplinary introduction*. London: Sage.

Goodley, D. (2014). *Dis/ability studies: Theorising disablism and ableism*. London: Routledge.

Grech, S. (2011). Recolonising debates or perpetuated coloniality? Decentring the spaces of disability, development and community in the global South. *International Journal of Inclusive Education, 15*(1), 87–100.

Grech, S. (2012). Disability and the majority world: A neocolonial approach. D. Goodley, B. Hughes and L. Davis (Eds.), In *Disability and social theory: New Developments and Directions*, (pp. 52–69). London: Palgrave Macmillan

Hardt, M., & Negri, A. (2000). *Empire*. Cambridge, MA: Harvard University Press.

Heap, M., Lorenzo, T., & Thomas, J. (2009). 'We've moved away from disability as a health issue, it's a human rights issue': Reflecting on 10 years of the right to equality in South Africa. *Disability & Society, 24*(7), 857–868.

Herndon, A. (2002). Disparate but disabled: Fat embodiment and disability studies. *NWSA Journal, 14*(3), 120–137.

Hong, E. S., Zeeb, H., & Repacholi, M. H. (2006). Albinism in Africa as a public health issue. *BMC Public Health, 6*(1), 212.

Hughes, B., & Paterson, K. (1997). The social model of disability and the disappearing body: Towards a sociology of impairment. *Disability & Society, 12*(3), 325–340.

Ingstad, B., & Whyte, S. R. (Eds.). (2007). *Disability in local and global worlds*. Berkeley, CA: University of California Press.

Jonas, O., Aseka, W., Kanter, A., Philpott, S., Combrinck, H., Budoo, A., et al. (2015). *African disability rights yearbook 2014*. Pretoria: PULP Press.

Kathard, H., & Pillay, M. (2013). Promoting change through political consciousness: A South African speech-language pathology response to the World Report on Disability. *International Journal of Speech-Language Pathology, 15*(1), 84–89.

Krahn, G. L. (2011). WHO world report on disability: A review. *Disability Health Journal, 4*(3), 141–142.

Lea, S., & Foster, D. (Eds.). (1990). *Perspectives on mental handicap in South Africa*. Cape Town: Butterworths.

Linton, S. (1998). *Claiming disability: Knowledge and identity*. New York: New York University Press.

Lucas, R. H., & Barrett, R. J. (1995). Interpreting culture and psychopathology: Primitivist themes in cross-cultural debate. *Culture, Medicine and Psychiatry, 19*(3), 287–326.

Mangena, F. (2013). The search for an African feminist ethic: A Zimbabwean perspective. *Journal of International Women's Studies, 11*(2), 18–30.

McRuer, R., & Wilkerson, A. (2003). Cripping the (queer) nation. *A Journal of Lesbian and Gay Studies, 9*(1–2), 1–23.

Meyers, S. J. (2014). The social model of disability under the shadow of the revolution: Ex-combatants negotiating identity in Nicaragua. *Qualitative Sociology, 37*(4), 403–424.

Miles, M. (2000). Disability on a different model: Glimpses of an Asian heritage. *Disability & Society, 15*(4), 603–618.
Miles, M. (2002). Some influences of religions on attitudes towards disabilities and people with disabilities. *Journal of Religion, Disability & Health, 6*(2–3), 117–129.
Mji, G., Gcaza, S., Swartz, L., MacLachlan, M., & Hutton, B. (2011). An African way of networking around disability. *Disability & Society, 26*, 365–368.
Naidoo, P. (2009). *An analysis of the experiences of children with cerebral palsy in therapeutic horse-riding*. University of Kwazulu-Natal, South Africa: Unpublished Ph.D. Thesis.
Oliver, M. (1990). *The politics of disablement*. Basingstoke: Macmillan.
Oliver, M. (1996). Defining impairment and disability: issues at stake. In *Exploring the divide: Illness and disability* (pp. 39–54).
Oliver, M., & Barnes, C. (2012). Back to the future: The world report on disability. *Disability & Society, 27*(4), 575–579.
Owusu-Ansah, F. E., & Mji, G. (2013). African indigenous knowledge and research. *African Journal of Disability, 2*(1), 1–5.
Sachs, R. (2008). *Disability support services*. Montgomery college. Retrieved January 5, 2009, from http://www.mc.md.us/departments/dispsvc/diversity.htm
Said, E. (1978). *Orientalism*. New York: Vintage.
Sampson, E. E. (1985). The decentralisation of identity: Toward a revised concept of personal and social order. *American Psychologist, 40*(11), 1203–1211.
Sampson, E. E. (1993). Identity politics: Challenges to psychology's understanding. *American Psychologist, 48*(12), 1219–1230.
Shakespeare, T. (1993). Disabled people's self-organisation: A new social movement? *Disability, Handicap & Society, 8*(3), 249–264.
Shakespeare, T. (2013). *Disability rights and wrongs revisited*. London: Routledge.
Sherry, M. (2006). *If I only had a brain. Deconstructing brain injury*. London: Routledge.
Sherry, M. (2007). (Post) colonising disability. Special issue of Wagadu. *Journal of Transnational Women's and Gender Studies, 4*, 10–22.
Shildrick, M. (2007). Dangerous discourse. Anxiety, desire and disability. *Studies in Gender & Sexuality, 8*(3), 221–244.
Slee, R. (1996). Disability, class and poverty: School structures and policising identities. In C. Christensen & F. Rizvi (Eds.), *Disability and the dilemmas of education and justice* (pp. 96–188). Buckingham: Open University Press.
Snyder, S. L., & Mitchell, D. T. (2001). Re-engaging the body: Disability studies and the resistance to embodiment. *Public Culture, 13*(3), 367–389.
Soldatic, K., & Meekosha, H. (2012). Moving the boundaries of feminist social work education with disabled people in the neoliberal era. *Social Work Education, 31*(2), 246–252.
Swartz, L. (1998). *Culture and mental health: A southern African view*. Cape Town: Oxford University Press.
Swartz, L. (2013). Between faith and doubt: Training members of disabled people's organisations in southern Africa in basic research skills. In J. Claassens, L. Swartz, & L. D. Hansen (Eds.), *Searching for dignity: Conversations on human dignity, theology and disability* (pp. 81–90). Stellenbosch: SUNMedia.
Thomas, C. (2007). *Sociologies of disability, 'impairment', and chronic illness: Ideas in disability studies and medical sociology*. London: Palgrave.
Tøssebro, J. (2004). Understanding disability: Introduction to the special issues of SJDR. *Scandinavian Journal of Disability Research, Special Issue: Understanding Disability, 6*(1), 3–7.
Traustadóttir, R. (2004). Disability studies: A nordic perspective. Presented at the *British Disability Studies Association Conference*, Lancaster, UK, 26–28 July.
Tremain, S. (2000). Queering disability studies. *Sexualities and Disability, 18*(4), 291–299.
Tremain, S. (2005). *Foucault and the government of disability*. Ann Arbor: University of Michigan Press.

United Nations. (2006). *Convention on the rights of persons with disabilities*. New York: UN. Retrieved from http://www.un.org/disabilities/convention/conventionfull.shtml. Accessed 15 June 2015.

UPIAS. (1976). *Fundamental principles of disability*. London: Union of the Physically Impaired Against Segregation.

Valentine, G., & Sporton, D. (2009). How other people see you it's like nothing that's inside: The impact of processes of disidentification and disavowal on young people's subjectivities. *Sociology, 43*, 735–751.

Van Zyl, M. (2011). Are same-Sex marriages UnAfrican? same-sex relationships and belonging in post-apartheid South africa. *Journal of Social Issues, 67*(2), 335–357.

WHO and World Bank. (2011). *World report on disability*. Geneva: World Health Organization.

World Health Organization. (2007). *International classification of functioning, disability, and health: Children & youth version: ICF-CY*. World Health Organization.

Chapter 6
From 'Sensing Disability' to Seselelame: Non-dualistic Activist Orientations in Twenty-First-Century Accra

Kathryn Linn Geurts and Sefakor G.M.A. Komabu-Pomeyie

Introduction

As some of Ghana's most excluded members of society, people whose bodies are marked as "impaired" have historically been stereotyped by strangers and family alike as unable to work (Kassah 2008), incapable of caring for themselves and others, and a burden on the wider society. Indeed, for people with disabilities in Ghana, James Charlton's metaphor of "peripheral everywhere" is apropos: they live in a "geography of exclusion, degradation, and dependency" (2010: 195). For example, labeling discourse has been shown to create powerful and derogatory views of children in Ghanaian schools, with teachers deploying local language terms such as *Asotowo* or *Buluu* that translate as idiot, fool, and feeble minded (Agbenyega 2003). Social attitudes about disability in Ghana have recently been documented in a study carried out by Jaqueline Slikker when she worked for the U.K. company VSO (Voluntary Services Overseas). Slikker's report describes practices which include "the use of abusive language" in public and private, "underrating of abilities" in a myriad of settings, outright desertion of people with disabilities by their families, and complete exclusion from social, economic and political aspects of life (2009: ix). The study also demonstrates a widespread belief that people with disabilities should live in institutions "because the society does not offer enough care and support in the communities" (2009: ix). Slikker reports that "32 % of the respondents are of the opinion that people with a physical disability should live in a special institution, compared to 53 % for people with a visual or hearing impairment and 39 % for

K.L. Geurts (✉)
Hamline University College of Liberal Arts, St Paul, MN, USA
e-mail: kgeurts@hamline.edu

S.G.M.A. Komabu-Pomeyie
Department- Ghana Office, Enlightening and Empowering People with Disabilities in Africa (EEPD Africa) and World Learning Global Advisory Council, Nsawam, Ghana

S. Grech, K. Soldatic (eds.), *Disability in the Global South*,
International Perspectives on Social Policy, Administration, and Practice,
DOI 10.1007/978-3-319-42488-0_6

persons with an intellectual disability" (2009: ix). She also explains how many employers fear "losing customers when having an employee with a disability" and how nearly 30 per cent of her survey respondents believed that people with disabilities were inherently less productive than non-disabled workers (Slikker 2009: ix). These findings provide a glimpse into Ghanaian society and reveal a significant orientation toward people with disabilities as having "special needs" and as dealing with significant "impairment". These statistics, as well as other portions of Slikker's study, seem to suggest that a social model of disability has not yet taken hold throughout Ghana (see Ghai 2002: 52 for a similar concern regarding India). On the other hand, in this setting we find a relatively robust disability movement with organizations such as Ghana Association of the Blind and Ghana National Association of the Deaf dating back to the 1960s (Nepveux 2009: 42–45; Grischow 2011; Geurts 2012). This chapter begins to address how some activist-leaders in Accra have been countering the negative perceptions captured in Slikker's study, and point toward the significance of utilizing local ways of knowing in efforts to attend to disability in global South contexts.

In April and May of 2010 we jointly conducted a series of interviews with individuals involved in Ghana's disability rights movement, and we focused our inquiries on the "feelingful", affective, and sensory dimensions of their work. All of our interviewees were individuals with physical or sensory disabilities, and all were active members of various disabled people's organizations (DPOs) such as the Ghana Blind Union, and Ghana Federation of the Disabled. Sefakor Komabu-Pomeyie herself is Ghanaian born and raised and a leader in this movement; she has held a number of prominent positions in the Ghana Society of the Physically Disabled. Kathryn Linn Geurts is a U.S. citizen who has conducted research in Ghana intermittently since the early 1990s, initially on "the senses" (Geurts 2002) and more recently on disability in Accra (Geurts 2009, 2012). Our collaborative interviews were aimed at eliciting sensory-rich stories from activists about some of their practices and experiences, and then collectively reflecting on how attentiveness to the senses helps to open up spaces of understanding and empathy as well as produce insight on more effective strategies of activism.

Philosopher and disability studies scholar Mairian Corker suggested that *sensibility* "inscribes, materializes, and performs" a "critique of binary thought" and is therefore a necessary conceptual tool for valuing experiences and narratives of disability, and also for developing responsible and responsive ways of collectively thinking up inclusive societies (2001: 36). In this chapter we ask how might residents of Accra enhance the inclusivity of their social and built landscape at the beginning of the 21st century? How might a *disability sensibility* contribute to that effort? When we bring the senses into our analysis of disability activism, how does that expand our understanding of social practices that are inclusive and exclusive? How does pairing sensibility with disability not only critique binary thought but also undermine a totalizing notion of ability? Corker argued (2001: 35) that there is an "erasure of disabled people's 'sensibility' by the normative bias of ontological imperialism." By ontological imperialism we understand her to mean a rationalist, masculinist, and dualistic way of being-in-the-world, and she advocated undermining this imperialism in part by foregrounding sensibilities. Sensibility, in her usage, refers to a "set of individual and collective dispositions to emotions, attitudes, and feelings" that are relevant to ethics, aesthetics, and politics (Corker 2001: 35). Sensibility implies embodiment of these dispositions, and is a critical conceptual tool if we hope to understand ways in which "people sense the world differently" (Corker 2001: 35). What happens, however, when we challenge the applicability of global North findings to a specific circumstance in the global South? (Meekosha 2011) If people sense the world differently, it behooves us to begin our excavation of local disability sensibilities by first attempting to understand local sensoriums.

Geurts's (2005) research has demonstrated that Euro-American/global North civilization has historically and traditionally valued extero-receptive sensory modalities such as sight, hearing, touch, taste, and smell; on the other hand, intero-receptive senses such as balance, proprioception, and kinesthesia have held great value in certain global South civilizations, such as in Anlo-Ewe cultural contexts of Ghana. In fact, new work in sensory anthropology challenges not only the five senses model, but also the notion that the experience of sensing is individualized and distinct. Sensations need to be understood instead as social and intersubjective. As David Howes, one of the pioneers of sensory studies, put it:

> To a greater or lesser extent, every domain of sensory experience, from the sight of a work of art to the scent of perfume to the savor of dinner, is a field of cultural elaboration. Every domain of sensory experience is also an arena for structuring social roles and interactions. We learn social divisions, distinctions of gender, class and race, through our senses. (Howes 2003: xi)

How do the senses illuminate distinctions made in social practices throughout Accra when it comes to living with disability? How do citizens of Accra learn social divisions separating "disabled people" as somehow different, and how do the senses underscore these orientations? In this chapter we will work with a concept of "disability sensibility" as we develop our claim that global South disability studies must take seriously local understandings of embodiment and self-making.

Ethnographic Context and Disability Sensibilities in Accra

In a conversation about what it is like when you are being disrespected because of your disability, our blind colleague Janet explained:

> Yes, you feel it because even the intonation, or the action [is detectable]. Maybe the person is in front of you, you are calling the person, and the person may not mind you. But you feel a shadow, as if something is standing in front of you. To me, I feel like a big shadow is in front of me.

As a blind person, Janet was clearly not viewing a shadow, but rather taking in the person's negativity or disdain through an array of sensory modalities. Without viewing the interaction, she still understood that the person she beckoned was engaging in a dynamic of disrespect. "Sensation lies at the interface of mind, body, and world" (Corker 2001: 40) and Janet's experience invites us to consider some of the culturally constituted means by which she moves from sound and motion to imagery of shadow. Corker suggests that:

> Sensibility engenders ways of being in and knowing our world that are materialized in contradictory bodies in process, and performed in shifting aesthetic, ethical, and political values. In short, sensibility is the rubric of "and so on" … that constantly inscribes the excessive domain of … "unintelligibility," and that depends on the joining of "reality" and imagination. (Corker 2001: 41)

A "reality" of vocal intonation and bodily motion ("the person is in front of you") or a failure of expected bodily movements ("you are calling the person, and the person may not mind you") was joined or fused by Janet with imaginings of shadow. Janet's disability sensibility, which included that rubric of "and so on", enabled her to fill in an array of sensory information not available to her through vision.

Kathryn's early research in Ghana (Geurts 2002) explored embodied ways of knowing and sensory-emotional experiences of health and well-being among Anlo-Ewe speaking Ghanaians. It established that at least some Ghanaian sensibilities foreground bodily feeling as a vital source of information about environment, self-making, and moral knowing, and it excavated an important indigenous phenomenon encapsulated in the term *seselelame* (literally "perceive-perceive-at-flesh-inside", or "feeling in the body"). While *seselelame* is an Ewe term, it captures dimensions of habitus[1] or being-in-the-world that are arguably more pan-African than restrictively Ewe, and Geurts has suggested that *seselelame* be treated as a local iteration of a broad African foundational schema (Geurts and Adikah 2006: 58). As such, *seselelame* functions as a kind of "template, a common underlying form that links superficially diverse cultural models" while simultaneously contributing to a "sometimes ineffable sense of 'style' or 'ethos'" characteristic of a particular social group (Shore 1996: 117). *Seselelame* spawns a fusion rather than atomization of the senses, an integration rather than splitting of mind–body communication. In Janet's account of feeling a big shadow, we can grasp how some dimensions of *seselelame* were at play. A fusion of vocalized sound and bodily motion conveyed rejection and a sensibility of the oppressiveness of a large, dark shadow surrounding her.

In her article "Sensing Disability," Corker argued that binary, dualistic thought was part of the dominant ontology and particularly problematic for disability theory because it propagated "masculinist notions of presence, visibility, material 'reality,' and identity as 'given'" (2001: 36). Inversely, this assigns a negative valence to the invisible, the non-present, non-material realities, and the fluid, transient dimensions of identity. In this value system, stress falls on the visible, superficial aspects of being; identity is assumed to be fixed and given; and presence is required to count. Hidden disabilities, non-presence, fluctuating materiality of bodily states and symptoms, and changeable and intersecting identities are devalued and discounted. A "categorical status of (a visible and present) 'disability'" is set up (Corker 2001:

[1] We follow Pierre Bourdieu's conceptualization of habitus and favor his definition of it as "history turned into nature" or a "durably installed generative principle of regulated improvisation" (1977: 78).

35). By this, we take Corker to have meant that when disability studies strives for a "universalized discourse" it erases a great deal of disability experience: it privileges visible and clearly present impairments as well as surface-level experiences of disability while erasing sensible/experiential aspects of disability (non-visible, deeper elements) (see e.g. Shildrick and Price 1998; Thomas 1999; Schillmeier 2010). Corker claims:

> Indeed, it could be argued that existing critiques of normativism within disability studies are themselves based on disablist models of emancipation from normativism that presuppose and reinforce the domination of particular "disabled ontologies." This process initiates a descent into injustice, which should be of concern to feminists and disabled people alike. (Corker 2001: 35)

We share Corker's concerns about a universalized discourse and concur with other scholars who have demonstrated the northern dominance of theoretical, ideological, cultural, and historical assumptions regarding disability (Grech 2009: 771). This chapter contributes, therefore, to a growing literature aimed at infusing disability studies with southern voices and approaches that challenge normative ontologies coming from the North (e.g. Ghai 2002; Ingstad and Whyte 2007; Meekosha 2011; Meekosha and Soldatic 2011; Grech and Soldatic 2014).

One of the dismaying things Kathryn heard during fieldwork in Accra was from a social worker who said, "It is only now that we are learning to be among them." This was at a conference entitled "Disability Institute", held at the British Council, to which virtually no people with disabilities had been invited. Despite the fact that our names were not on the list of attendees, a group of about 15 disability activists mobilized and showed up en masse at the registration desk, gently insisting on the necessity of our presence. During a break, while chatting with some of the social workers, Kathryn pointed out the irony of holding a gathering focused on disability services when so few people with disabilities were invited to participate (another instance of Charlton's "peripheral everywhere" metaphor). It was here that the social worker made her admission, meaning that it was uncomfortable for ostensibly middle-class, respectable, professional Ghanaians to "be among" those who society marks as impaired. Sefakor suggests that, like the individual Janet beckoned, the social worker too creates a shadow. Though some people have higher levels of education and an awareness of natural causes of impairment, many individuals in Accra still think people with disabilities are at best cursed and useless, and at worst contagious (somewhat of a generalization but supported by Slikker 2009). In view of this, many people avoid associating themselves with individuals with disabilities because of an entrenched belief that disability can spread and affect their own family as well as themselves. Sefakor believes that Janet's use of shadow makes reference to the way many people in Accra rarely see anything good in people with disabilities. This outlines the ethnographic setting in which we intend to develop a concept of disability sensibilities and connect it to a local iteration of a foundational schema referred to as *seselelame*.

Sensory Accra from a Disability Vantage Point

A member of the Ghana Society of the Physically Disabled named Tico described the following experience of using transportation (a combination of public and private) in Accra.

> "Mostly if you sit in tro-tro [typically a minivan] you will see that thing. If you go sit in the tro-tro like this, somebody will come sit beside you, and that fellow don't want your body to touch him like this."
>
> We asked Tico: "How do they show that they don't want their body to touch yours?"
>
> "By shifting themselves beside you, shifting away. That thing, too, is not fine," Tico said. "We are human beings. If they cut my body, blood will flow; if they cut you, blood will flow. We are all one. No one is different, but they don't want to be close to us."
>
> We asked Tico what he does when this happens on the bus or tro-tro, and he said that oftentimes he just keeps quiet. But, "If I want to react … I will ask him, 'Why are you sitting beside me shifting like that? Am I not a human being like you?' Then maybe he will feel something—that I talk to him or her like that."
>
> "How do people react?" we enquired.
>
> "Maybe he can't say *anything*—because of what you have asked him," Tico replied.
>
> At this point our colleague Mutala interjected: "They will regret what they have done to you. You know, the anger you can show to them is, well, you have to get down, or change cars, change where you are. If that person is treating you that way [shifting away from you], at least you have to let them know by acting. Not acting in violence, but acting in a sensible way—for he or she to see that what they are doing is not the right way, and you are not having any skin disease, a diseased body, or something of that sort that can be transferred from your body to his body. At least he or she needs to understand that disability is not in the body, not something that if you touch or sit near somebody that you can get infected. You have to lecture the person in a sensible way. But, oh! They can disrespect you! They can squeeze their face—as if you are something that is not needed in the society. It's very bad. … They need to be lectured."

The withdrawal of touch is striking in Tico's and Mutala's accounts. Haptic perception is highly valued in many sectors of Ghanaian society (Geurts 2002), so denying such interaction directly communicates rejection in ways that might not be so obvious in other cultural contexts where personal space is guarded and individuals are not accustomed to regular and fairly intense bodily proximity. Life in Accra is filled with extensive skin contact with strangers: crowded markets in which people jockey to obtain sometimes scarce goods; intersection cross-walks where you are pulled along amid a river of people creating current with their collective movement; a throng of people rushing toward a bus when only a few seats are available. The local foundational schema *seselelame* (feeling in the body) would suggest that withdrawing skin contact in ways described by Tico and Mutala points toward disability sensibilities that reproduce notions of contagion and shame.

Self-consciousness and shame were apparent in an interview with our colleague Esther as she reflected on trying to navigate inaccessible terrain throughout Accra. In this brief excerpt, Esther's frustration at trying to reach the Ministry of Transport (which lacks a ramp) is readily apparent.

> I feel badly. I look at myself, and say why, why? Why is this thing happening to me? Because if you're not a disable,[2] then you can climb this thing. I have to beg somebody, for

[2] "Disables" or "a disable" is Ghanaian English phrasing. It is not necessarily pejorative as many people with disability use it affectionately to refer to a claimed identity.

> the person to help me, to carry me up the steps. It's not good. Disables have to suffer. Before you can get to this place, go to this office, there has to be accessibility all over the place [by which she means that entrances must be made accessible].

Sefakor jumped into the conversation, explaining how Esther

> feels so lonely, so isolatory; even if people are there, she realizes she is the single soul that has such a situation. So if, for instance, she should just be walking and she meets a step, or something, she feels, "Ah! What a situation!" An isolatory environment. Though people surround her, she feels lonely.

Sefakor pointed out how some Ghanaians believe that if a person has an impairment in one part of the body, it results in a more generalized inability to do things. For instance, if a person walks with crutches, some people assume he or she is also not able to hear, and may even jump to the conclusion that the individual has mental illness. This may be in part due to a cultural emphasis on fusing rather than fragmenting sensory modalities, on synesthetic rather than atomized interpretations of sensory experiences. We continued discussing mobility challenges and Esther offered the following story:

> I feel sooooo ashamed of myself when I meet that situation. [Once] … I was going to Adabraka market and it rained that day and the whole place was very muddy. … when I raised the wheelchair up—just to avoid the mud—it was as if they rang bell … Everybody's eyes were on me, and I became so confused—because the question is: who is watching the able-bodied who just passed? Nobody watches them! But the moment a thing of that sort happens, then they start to look at you in a very different way—like [they are thinking], 'Will she fall? Will she really go through the mud?' And there will be no helping hand. This is a typical experience. And I feel very ashamed of myself. When it happens like that I become annoyed within myself, and it pains me that I am in this situation. So … if someone wants to come closer at times, I'm annoyed within myself already, so I don't open up. I don't want to look at anyone; I will just bend my head down.

It is striking that Esther used an aural analogy to draw attention to the intensely social dimension of the situation: it was as if someone *rang a bell* when she began maneuvering about the barrier of the mud. In many Ghanaian contexts, bells are rung to summon community members to a town square or public place for a collective action or decision, and bells are used in nearly all traditional music and dance events. In Esther's narration she worked to raise up the wheelchair and then Clang! Clang! Clang!—it was as if someone was ringing a bell. Her sensibility told her that this was a circumstance in which collective action would be called for. But her narration further revealed that there would "be no helping hand". Instead of a collective action to remove the barrier, she experienced "everybody's eyes … on me" and a feeling of confusion. An absolute avoidance of touch and the "gawking, gaping, and staring"[3] of "everybody's eyes" exhibits sensory distancing and objectifying. This is a society in which aurality (in the form of both talking and listening) plus tactility (or an abundance of touch) tend to be more highly valued than the visual sense (Geurts 2002). Withholding sound and touch, and over-emphasizing sight, demon-

[3] "Gawking, Gaping, and Staring" is the title of a 2003 essay by Eli Clare.

strates how the people around Esther "othered" her and made her to feel that she did not belong.

To reinforce an "othering" of people with disabilities throughout Accra, let us turn to a story that Sefakor related to Kathryn in 2010.

> "People see me every day, especially when you want to be a little bit active, when you want to do something they are doing—then their eyes are on you. For instance, if I should walk today to the bank. You can imagine!"
>
> Kathryn cracked up laughing and interjected ironically, "Oh! How can a disabled go to the bank!"
>
> "Exactly!" Sefakor retorted. "So you know what I've been doing as of late? I drive straight—you know you cannot park in front of the Nsawam Bank, you cannot park there, because of the cars passing. But me, I go and park there because of the … whatever … I want more attention! Just as I told you: if I know you are watching me, I will perform. The bank is a glass, so when I park there I know they are watching me before I even get down from the car, so when I enter the bank, oh! Eyes on me! I know how I do it myself, so I will enter and just turn and I see all eyes on me.
>
> "They are fond of doing that," Sefakor continued. "Yeah, that's Ghanaian society. They don't expect you to do some things. They see you in a very weird manner—very awkward situation that they want you to be [in] at times … So, when I realize you are looking at me, then I bring more things to you to watch! And people will really stare at you and you will feel bad; if you're not courageous enough you will feel bad and miss your steps. Yes. Some people can watch you, even as you are looking at them, I mean face to face, it still continues—they don't avert their eyes, at all. At times I meet them, I confront them … if they want to make it like they're not looking, then I give it to the person, and I leave."

Here we need to interrogate this "very weird manner" in which Sefakor suggested society expects people with disabilities to do things; the "very awkward situation that they want you to be [in] at times." How does Charlton's "peripheral everywhere" dovetail with Sefakor's "awkward situation?" What local understandings of embodiment and self-making help us to deepen a notion of disability sensibility in this particular global South locale?

Denise Nepveux's in-depth study of Ghanaian women with disabilities (2009) can provide insight as she emphasizes how their "social personhood is undermined" through persistent marginalizing processes, such as "rolelessness" (after Ghai), "inferior education" and livelihood efforts in "unsustainable trades", as well as constant "expressions of pity or contempt" by fellow Ghanaians. While the life-story narratives Nepveux presents demonstrate moving accounts of women "knitting themselves back into the fabric of their families, neighborhoods, and religious communities" (2009: xi), we are deeply struck by the intense struggle this takes. Nepveux's identification of an undermining of personhood resulting from social exclusion and structural vulnerability (2009: 26) gets to the heart of what Sefakor pointed to in her anecdote. A disabled woman is not supposed to drive a car and frequent the bank; rather, cultural expectations are for her to embody dependency, vulnerability, charity seeking, and pity.

What, then, are we to make of Sefakor's sensibility? She reflected that "When I realize you are looking at me, then I bring more things to you to watch!" And she cautioned that "if you're not courageous enough you will feel bad and miss your steps". Sefakor's whole-bodied approach is striking: her inclusion of what it can *feel like* to engage in defying social expectations and her recognition of potential pitfalls (missing your steps) attests to the presence of *seselelame*. Earlier we discussed Corker's (2001: 35) claim that disabled peoples' sensibilities get erased by "the normative bias of ontological imperialism" and here we can see social pressure toward enforcing that rationalist, masculinist, and dualistic way of being-in-the-world through social norms that would stop Sefakor from daring to drive herself to the bank. Corker claimed, however, that *sensibility* "inscribes, materializes, and performs" a "critique of binary thought" (2001: 36), and would therefore be a critical tool in our efforts to create greater social inclusion. In the accounts provided by Sefakor, Tico, and Esther, bodily feeling was prominent in disability sensibilities drawn upon in their acts of defiance or their insistence on inclusion. We will now turn to addressing more pronounced links between bodily feeling and political action, making "movement" a critical hinge.

Movement: Bodily Feeling and Political Action

Even as a body seems still, it moves, and is continuously engaged in sensation. This pertains to individual and to collective bodies—all are alive, sensual, and in continuous movement. It can be argued, therefore, that bodily knowledge is modal in comparison to cognitive/cerebral knowledge which is categorical (Laplantine 2015). Categorical thinking erects discrete spheres into which sorted and differentiated phenomena are placed; modal thinking fluidly moves among all sensible phenomena, resisting stasis and fixed (categorical) notions. Why should this distinction matter? A young Ghanaian non-disabled woman's story may help to answer this question.

When Efua (a pseudonym) learned of Kathryn's research about disability, she recounted a conversation she had recently had with an acquaintance we will call Kobena. Efua explained that Kobena was blind and yet he loved to "watch" television. "At first I laughed when he told me this", she said. "I couldn't even imagine a blind person watching a film". But then Kobena named a television show they both liked and proceeded to recite a few lines of dialogue, hum a cadence or two of music, and recount environmental sounds and the images they conjured in his mind. Efua was astounded at how much of the television show Kobena processed and remembered, and she remarked that it was probably more than she had even taken in. This created a bridge for her into his world, and it opened Efua up to understanding Kobena as more like herself than she had previously realized. A category and label of "blind" was eroded, if ever so slightly, through this intersubjectivity: as Kobena led Efua on an audio-visual journey through his mind's eye, she moved closer to his experience, thereby diminishing (if ever so slightly) some of the societal marking of people with disabilities as useless and incapable. At the point of the discussion with Kathryn, Efua had begun going to the cinema with Kobena on a regular basis; they had moved from acquaintances to friends. From this anecdote we can begin to grasp how bodily/sensory knowledge is modal and cognitive/cerebral knowledge is categorical, and we can begin to appreciate why a local foundational schema of *seselelame* is critical to disability sensibilities and activism in this particular global South context.

"Disability: Anybody's Lot, Any Time!" is a slogan frequently used among members of Ghana's disability movement (and is occasionally inscribed on t-shirts and signs). One of our interviewees reflected that for her, the saying meant, "I own mine already. You'll get yours one day". This idea that vulnerability to disabling circumstances is an existential human condition (not restricted to a select few) is something that our colleague Ellen, who had polio as a child, emphasized several times during her interview. She recounted:

> One woman in my house is saying she doesn't have a child, so she is also disabled. … At the end of the day, she has a problem. Everybody has problems; you can't [always] see them, but everybody has a disability inside. Mine is physical, but others can be inside. If you see somebody, don't look at them like that because at the end of the day, everybody has something.

We suggest that Ellen is exhibiting a modal, fluid, non-categorical kind of thinking. She is resisting a dualistic, either–or notion of who is disabled. Modal thinking is attentive to "the sensible" and can open up spaces of understanding and empathy, allowing for movement and shifts in perspective, and changes in feeling. Sefakor asked Ellen, "As you have that realization that everybody has a disability—hidden, a hidden disability—how do you feel?" Ellen responded:

> Formerly I was feeling bad to even go to people. Now I have confidence in me that at the end of the day I'm better than somebody—even if they are strong. A woman in our house was saying [about, and to Ellen], "You are somebody! God bless you! Because me, I don't even have passport. I don't know where the airport is"—which Ellen does, since she has traveled abroad in her capacity as a dancer in a "mixed ability" dance company. Ellen says, "Now I feel somehow confident, not that proud, but I say "God bless me. I have something in me that I have to appreciate." Now I can go anywhere I like. Unless maybe the step is in the way. But I can go anywhere I like, so I feel very good in me.

Ellen had become involved in Ghana's disability rights movement more than 10 years before we sat down to talk. In many ways her journey illustrates connections between individual bodily movement and political action-oriented social movements. She explained that she ran away from home, and her narration of why she left included a poignant detail. Because she had polio as a child, she would remain in the house with her grandmother all day while other family members went out to work or school. The grandmother would stare right past her and shout, "I'm looking for a human being to send!" ("to send" meaning to go out on an errand). "Look at this!" Ellen complained: "She says 'nobody is there to send' when I'm right in front of her." This harkens back to Janet sensing someone right in front of her and remarking that "it feels like a big shadow" –similar in terms of proximity and a sense of negativity and disrespect (invisibility, mockery, disdain, and outright rejection).

Ellen was recalling these experiences from the late 1990s. And as we spoke in June of 2010, she exclaimed:

> If my mother can't take care of me, oh well! [Kathryn interjected: Who can? Yeah.] Yes, you get it? [Kathryn replied yes.] So, *you* have to! Disable, don't [you] say, "I can't do this! I can't." Sometimes our disables, some of the disables on the roadside … you've got [to be] dutiful! You make your make-up … [suggesting they dutifully work hard to look good so

they can succeed]. It's not easy, but you have to fight. Ministries! [I go to the] ministries! I walk, walk, walk, walk, walk. Ehhh, Parliament! Go and come, go and come, go and … go and come …and ministries … go and come …fill [out] form … bring your passport picture … go … every day like that. [Sefakor asked Ellen, 'What are you looking for?' and Ellen responded:] A job!

Here Ellen was talking about having to support herself: referencing being "a disable" (disabled person) having to work at roadside sales; describing what we might call "pounding the pavement" while searching for a job. The repetition and duplication in her utterances (walk, walk, walk; go and come, go and come) revealed both how passionate, feisty, and determined Ellen was in her pursuit of employment, and how the local foundational schema of *seselelame* was at play in the bodying forth of her speech.

In earlier work (see Geurts and Adikah 2006: 55–58), Kathryn demonstrated how words, feelings, and sounds are put together differently in black Atlantic contexts when compared to Euro-American settings, and here we are adding another layer to those distinctions by bringing in Laplantine's ideas about modal and categorical thinking. "Categorical thought … attributes properties to those things it isolates from the flux of existence and cleaves to the logic of the excluded middle", whereas modal thinking encourages us "to focus on duration, modulation, and rhythm instead of essence and identity" and it is "sensitive to the slightest gradations and movements and affects" (Howes 2015). As a local foundational schema, *seselelame* supports modal, sensible thinking more robustly than categorical thought, and attention needs to be paid to these distinctions if we are to better grasp disability sensibilities in global South contexts.

Ellen's transition away from her family engendered a change in capacity. From television she learned about a group calling itself the Ghana Society of the Physically Disabled and secretly attended a meeting in a nearby town, lying to her family about where she went. When she realized that they were holding meetings every month in Accra, she decided to move there—to get away from her family and "join the others who are in the same situation". She recounted how intensively she concealed from her family that she was living on her own in Accra, insisting that she was living with one of the society's "president ladies". This was because they refused to believe a disabled person could manage on her own. They perceived Ellen and all "disables" as dependent, needing others to do everything for them. This point enraged Ellen. She recounted how they would pester her with questions like, "Who is going to fetch water for you? Who will cook for you?" but she felt like "any hardship I have, I will face it alone, just like the ables! But they want to discourage you-o!" Ellen refused to be dissuaded from living on her own, and that transition was accompanied by a tremendous feeling of change in capacity. Her declaration "just like the ables" conveys her feeling of strength and resilience, and reveals her sense of having the right to be treated like "able-bodied" members of society.

Ellen began working with a mixed-ability dance company and was thereby able to travel to Europe a number of times to perform.[4] We suggest that her gradual

[4] See DIN A 13 tanzcompany & Dance Factory Accra, *Patterns Beyond Traces,* https://www.youtube.com/watch?v=014ownuoS6Y.

engagement with a "movement" for disability rights, from the late 1990s to her current involvement in dance, has deeply altered her feelings. In the span of just a few years, we observed how her voice had gotten stronger, even derisive (at times) of those putting up barriers to her freedom. Distinctions consistently made between rich/poor, outsider/insider, able-bodied/disabled, and the individual good compared to collective well-being fit more with categorical thinking and are minimized in the disability sensibilities we have observed in Ellen as well as Tico, Mutala, and Janet. Remembering our earlier quote from Howes, that "every domain of sensory experience … is a field of cultural elaboration" (2003: p. xi), sensibilities and sensitivities are about responsiveness, and Ellen's disability sensibility exhibits this point well. She joined the movement in part because it provided a sense of connectedness and a feeling of belonging, much like the narratives presented by Nepveux (2009) under the title "In the Same Soup." As we talked with Ellen about various rallies and demonstrations we had all participated in, she indicated that this made her feel very strong. In English she offered the phrase, "Together we stand, divided we fall." In Twi she described the way one bristle in a broom is easily broken, but if they are together, all the bristles make a strong broom which is very difficult to break. Ellen commented that, "If we are all coming together, we fight, fight, fight".

Conclusion

What have we learned about disability sensibilities through this discussion of a small set of interviews? How has attending to local ways of knowing informed our understanding of how disability activists might work more effectively in Accra? Sefakor had a recent encounter which helps illuminate some of our ideas regarding these questions. Several years ago she established an advocacy, educational, and networking organization called Enlightening and Empowering People with Disabilities in Africa, and in her capacity as the founder of this group she experienced the following interaction.

> A woman from the United Kingdom recently came looking for me to talk about a YouTube video we posted which profiled a boy named Kelvin.[5] Kelvin has been deprived of his right to an education because he is in a wheelchair and the school building is not accessible. After viewing the video, the woman from the U.K. [who we shall call Susan] wanted to take care of all his educational needs.
>
> She came with a Ghanaian lady named Nancy [a pseudonym] who was not initially aware of Susan's mission. When she got to know the reason Susan was looking for me, Nancy took her aside and expressed, "Oh Susan, so it is because of this small boy—that's why you brought me here? I thought it was an elderly person you wanted to help; someone who could do something within some few months. You cannot reap what you are sowing, ooo. Look, look at him! He cannot walk at all! What profit is there in this one?" (Her words included *Kpor efe aforwudey wudey woda*, which means "Look at his weak and useless legs!")

[5] *Making A Difference*, http://www.youtube.com/watch?v=-m1y6ywdggU&feature=youtu.be.

> I was so annoyed, but also had some mixed feelings. I was confused about whether to encourage Susan in her mission or to sack both of them to take their wealth away [a Ghanaian English colloquialism]. To me, I sensed some exploitation, but I cannot lay hands on exactly what the motive was behind this. Looking at Susan's facial expression I could see that she was surprised by Nancy's words, but she didn't know that I had eavesdropped and heard everything. All the same, the moment Kelvin's parents saw her, they were immersed in Susan's charity or "support." Despite the fact that she is supporting them, I still feel so bitter about the whole scene, and I can never erase these words from my memory.

Nancy's response is very similar to the comment overheard at the Disability Institute conference (mentioned earlier) who exclaimed, "It is only now that we are learning to be among them." Sensibilities are about responsiveness, and Nancy's response to Kelvin entails a fixation on "the look" of what she categorizes as "weak and useless legs". In this instance there is minimal attention to "the sensible" and it results in distancing and "othering" which reinforces how modal and categorical thinking result in dramatically different sensibilities. If we are to truly honor diverse ways of being and knowing, to resist imposing global North frameworks onto global South circumstances, attention to these sorts of distinctions is critical. More than a decade ago, in her article "Sensing Disability", Corker suggested that if we truly value experiences and narratives of disability that will help us develop responsible and responsive ways of collectively thinking up inclusive societies (2001: 36) then we must attend to sensibilities and the sensible. She argued for scrutinizing and breaking away from the normative bias of ontological imperialism. Here, in material gathered through observant participation and ethnographic interviewing, we have an instance of a small group of activists living out what Corker called for. We conclude by encouraging more collaborative work to produce fine-grained descriptions from global South contexts with the hope that this will enhance and enliven the field of disability studies.

References

Agbenyega, J. (2003). The power of labeling discourse in the construction of disability in Ghana. In P. Jeffrey (Ed.), *Australian Association for Research in Education Conference Proceedings*. Deakin: AARE. Retrieved from http://www.aare.edu.au/publications-database.php/3695/the-power-of-labeling-discourse-in-the-construction-of-disability-in-ghana.

Bourdieu, P. (1977). *Outline of a theory of practice*. Cambridge: Cambridge University Press.

Charlton, J. I. (2010). Peripheral everywhere. *Journal of Literary & Cultural Disability Studies, 4*(2), 195–200.

Clare, E. (2003). Gawking, gaping, staring. *GLQ: A Journal of Lesbian and Gay Studies, 9*(1–2), 257–261.

Corker, M. (2001). Sensing disability. *Hypatia, 16*(4), 34–52.

Geurts, K. L. (2002). *Culture and the senses: Bodily ways of knowing in an African community*. Berkeley: University of California Press.

Geurts, K. L. (2005). Consciousness as "feeling in the body": A West African theory of embodiment, emotion and the making of mind. In D. Howes (Ed.), *Empire of the senses: The sensual culture reader* (pp. 164–178). Oxford: Berg Publishers.

Geurts, K. L. (2009). When you cannot headload—Balance, mobility, and the dis/abling of sensibilities in Metropolitan Accra. In R. Schonhammer (Ed.), *Korper, Dinge and Bewegung: Der Gleichgewichtssinn in materieller Kultur und Asthetik*. Facultas Verlags.

Geurts, K. L. (2012). Disabled Citizens of Ghana: 'Creating a Political Community' to Marshall Change. *Conference paper presented at the 55th Annual meeting of the African Studies Association*. Philadelphia, PA.

Geurts, K. L. & Adikah, E. G. (2006). Enduring and endearing feelings and the transformation of material culture in West Africa. In E. Edwards, C. Gosden, & R. Phillips (Eds.), *Sensible objects: Colonialism, museums and material culture* (pp. 35–60). Oxford: Berg.

Ghai, A. (2002). Disabled women: An excluded agenda of Indian feminism. *Hypatia, 17*(3), 49–66.

Grech, S. (2009). Disability, poverty and development: Critical reflections on the majority world debate. *Disability & Society, 24*(6), 771–784.

Grech, S., & Soldatic, K. (2014). Introducing disability and the Global South (DGS): We are critical, we are open access!". *Disability and the Global South, 1*(1), 1–4.

Grischow, J. D. (2011). Kwame Nkrumah, disability, and rehabilitation in Ghana, 1957–1966. *Journal of African History, 52*(2), 179–199.

Howes, D. (2003). *Sensual relations: Engaging the senses in culture and social theory*. Ann Arbor: University of Michigan Press.

Howes, D. (2015). Introduction to Laplantine. In F. Laplantine, *The life of the senses: Introduction to a modal anthropology*. London: Bloomsbury Academic.

Ingstad, B., & Whyte, S. R. (Eds.). (2007). *Disability in local and global worlds*. Berkeley: University of California Press.

Kassah, A. K. (2008). Begging as work: A study of people with mobility difficulties in Accra, Ghana. *Disability & Society, 23*(2), 163–170.

Laplantine, F. (2015). *The life of the senses: Introduction to a modal anthropology*. London: Bloomsbury Academic. Trans by Jamie Furniss.

Meekosha, H. (2011). Decolonising disability: Thinking and acting globally. *Disability & Society, 26*(6), 667–682.

Meekosha, H., & Soldatic, K. (2011). Human rights and the Global South: The case of disability. *Third World Quarterly, 32*(8), 1383–1398.

Nepveux, D. M. (2009). *In the same soup: Disabled women's narratives of belonging and survival in Accra, Ghana*. Unpublished dissertation. University of Illinois, Chicago.

Schillmeier, M. (2010). *Rethinking disability: Bodies, senses, and things*. London: Routledge.

Shildrick, M., & Price, J. (Eds.). (1998). *Vital signs: Feminist reconfigurations of the bio/logical body*. Edinburgh: Edinburgh University Press.

Shore, B. (1996). *Culture in mind: Cognition, culture, and the problem of meaning*. New York: Oxford University Press.

Slikker, J. (2009). *Attitudes towards persons with disability in Ghana*. Accra: VSO Ghana.

Thomas, C. (1999). *Female forms: Experiencing and understanding disability*. Buckingham: Open University Press.

Chapter 7
Playing Disability, Performing Gender: Militarised Masculinity and Disability Theatre in the Sri Lankan War and Its Aftermath

Neloufer de Mel

Introduction

The Sri Lankan civil war (1983–2009) is an exemplary site from which to open up questions about the relationship of disability, disablement and masculinity in a south Asian context in the first place, and second, the role of aesthetic interventions within disability activism.[1] Wars carry a particular paradox in relation to disability. They are the foremost cause of disable*ment:* the deliberate, wilful maiming of abled and physically strong military men and women as well as civilian populations in the war zones who are targeted for injury by landmines, bombing and shootings. Yet, precisely due to the large numbers of those disabled in war and the consequential 'threat' of disability to the labour market, capital and national interests (McRuer 2006: 303; Serlin 2006), enhanced policy interventions, rehabilitative medicine, prosthesis technology and service provisions by the state as well as non-state actors also develop. The Sri Lankan war and its aftermath are no exception. Arguably, disability services by both the Sri Lankan Government and the LTTE privileged their own combatants during the war. Nevertheless, it is the case that several important policy initiatives on disability also took root during this period.[2]

War-related impairment brings masculinity into crisis in particular ways. Disability threatens 'normative' masculinity in general, its condition often represented as emasculation. The demands of a competitive labour force contingent on

[1] The war was fought between Sri Lankan government security forces and the Liberation Tigers of Tamil Eelam (LTTE) over the establishment of a separate Tamil state.

[2] These include the 1996 Protection of the Rights of Persons with Disabilities Act (No. 28) and the National Policy on Disability (Ministry of Social Welfare of the Democratic Republic of Sri Lanka 2003).

N. de Mel (✉)
Department of English, University of Colombo, Colombo, Sri Lanka
e-mail: nelouferdemel@gmail.com

S. Grech, K. Soldatic (eds.), *Disability in the Global South*,
International Perspectives on Social Policy, Administration, and Practice,
DOI 10.1007/978-3-319-42488-0_7

able-bodied men, cultural cults of hyper-masculine ableism, and social expectations of men as independent, strong, self-reliant, resilient, efficient, reproductive and protective of family and nation—each of which are pegged to the able body—conspire ideologically to norm the able-bodied man. The consequence of this hegemonic naturalization of able-bodied masculinity on male disabled subjectivity is often a profound sense of difference and dis-ease. Disablement in war provides yet another register of experience particularly for disabled military men. Because of prior membership in able-bodied military corps and their disability following military engagement, and because militarism and militarization as ideology and process routinely offer romances on the maimed soldier for patriotic power (de Mel 2007: 114; Bourke cited in Zarkov 2007: 163), disabled soldiers tend to emphasize their difference from other disabled men. Foregrounding military disablement, and the experiences and narrative registers of disabled soldiers draws attention, therefore, to the diversity of the conditions and discourses on male disability.

This chapter focuses on the relationship of disability and masculinity in the context of the Sri Lankan war to ask what specific characteristics constitute war-related impairment and its registers of affect on military/militarized men. It thereby positions the role of war, masculinity and the disabled male body within a specific Sri Lankan political, gendered and cultural milieu to extrapolate what such a triangulation may mean for an understanding of both disability and masculinity. Thereafter, it focuses on aesthetic activism on disability in Sri Lanka by analysing the applied and devised theatre of the Sunera Foundation, a civil society organization that has worked with Sri Lankan disabled youth, including disabled soldiers, since 1998. The analysis draws on ideas on artistic social responsibility as outlined by Paulo Freire and Augusto Boal; applied/devised theatre as a field of practice and knowledge; and the question of aesthetic standards by which disability performance is judged. In doing so, the chapter flags what each of these points may mean for retracting, expanding and nuancing the frames through which we see the conditions of disability in a particular south Asian setting.

Disablement in War

If occupations, occupational segregation and occupational status are already gendered (Wickramasinghe 2012: 21), military work—or wars as acts of violence—is heavily reliant on men and a masculinity tied to physical prowess, risk-taking, courage and 'technical rationality'. These attributes are, in turn, linked to cultural notions of honour and shame, particularly in ethno-nationalist wars (such as the Sri Lankan war) where older men are called upon to be patriarchs in control of family and community while young men become heroic fighters in defence of the nation (and older women are elevated as 'mothers' of the nation) (Johnson 2005: 107–113; Zarkov 2007). While the Sri Lankan war did produce a significant number of female LTTE combatants and suicide bombers, their military training closely followed the male military model—a fact that both the female combatants and the LTTE were keen to emphasize (de Mel 2001). Current or recent wars, therefore, continue to interpolate the young male subject as vital to their success and invite a manliness that is embodied in the tall, muscular, well-groomed young man who undergoes demanding physical and technical military training and becomes a member of the military corps (Mosse 1985: 114). When this military/militarized body becomes disabled in war, its masculinised sense of self comes into crisis.

Fieldwork with disabled soldiers of the Sri Lankan army (de Mel 2007: 132–145; Gunawardena 2010: 25–40) indicates that away from the battlefield, these men experience nostalgia for the abledness, social status, privileges and military prowess they have lost. Occupying a liminal space, no longer reporting regularly to work or wearing the army uniform, their narratives are characterized by lament. They miss their military corps and its fraternal bonding, bemoan the abrupt end of their career prospects within the army and are keen to get back to 'a piece of the action' (Gunawardena 2010: 27–35). Disabled soldiers worry about their marriage prospects or abandonment by their wives or girlfriends (de Mel 2007: 108). They dislike their dependence on others in accessing public transport, banks and toilets (de Mel 2007: 133). Those interviewed during the 2002–2004 Sri Lankan peace process felt the enemy (LTTE) had already taken the upper hand and that their sacrifices had been in vain (de Mel 2007: 111). As Červinková (2005: 61–65) notes of Czech soldiers who mourned the post-socialist Czech army as it transitioned into membership within NATO, theirs was a 'melancholic masculinity'.

In the Sri Lankan context, the melancholia is sutured to a local culture that binds masculinity to duty (particularly familial) and householdership. The successful householder is a masculine ideal that many men aspire to and against which male achievement is judged (Osella et al. 2004: 16). The inability to adequately fulfil the role of breadwinner constitutes a significant site of anxiety for men in general and disabled men in particular. This is also the case for disabled soldiers of the Sri Lankan army even though they enjoy a regular salary until retirement, post-retirement pensions and welfare provisions from the military, unlike disabled male civilians or disabled ex-LTTE combatants who no longer have the LTTE to protect their interests.

A study of masculinities in four districts of Sri Lanka (de Mel et al. 2013) shows what is at stake. Key findings on householdership and local expectations of men in urban and rural settings were elicited from a sample of 1658 men and 653 women.[3] Using the Gender Equitable Men (GEM) Scale to measure gender attitudes, the study found wide acceptance, for instance, of the view that 'To be a man means providing for your family and extended family', affirmed by 70 per cent of male and 73 per cent of female respondents (de Mel et al. 2013: 23). Concomitantly, 60 per cent of male respondents noted frequent stress or depression due to lack of adequate income, 51 per cent declared frequent stress or depression because of having to provide for their families, and 46 per cent of males stated their occupations were not commensurate with their educational status or experience (de Mel et al. 2013: 60). This data indicates the extent to which the masculinization of householdership costs

[3] The study sought data on gender attitudes, male risk-taking behaviours and male perpetration as well as experiences of violence. The districts were Colombo and Hambantota (urban) and Batticoloa and Nuwara Eliya (rural). Respondents were aged 18–49 years.

men and the fact that not all men benefit equally from hegemonic ideas of masculinity (de Neve 2004: 64). For disabled men who are 'handicapped' in relation to able-bodied male peers, successful householdership and its social capital as core attributes and achievements of masculinity (de Neve 2004: 93) become fraught sites of internal tension and public negotiation.

Yet, while masculinity displays certain 'crisis tendencies', overall, the argument that it is in trouble is overrated and requires deeper historical and demographic nuance to understand how different models of masculinity emerge, shift and are produced over time (de Neve 2004: 62; Edwards 2006: 14). The local study (de Mel et al. 2013) bears this out. It found that there was popular support for gender inequitable decision-making within households that favoured men and patriarchy. Seventy-eight per cent of the male respondents stated, 'I think a women should obey her husband', while 40 per cent noted, 'I think the man should have the final say in all family matters', and 58 per cent declared, 'I think a woman cannot refuse to have sex with her husband' (de Mel et al. 2013: 25). About a quarter of male respondents answered that there are times when a woman deserves to be beaten, and 64 per cent noted that the wife's primary responsibility is towards the home and child care (de Mel et al. 2013: 23). The findings also revealed that ideas of masculinity associated with toughness, honour and violence circulated widely. More than half (57 per cent) believed that 'To be a man you have to be tough', while 58 per cent stated 'It is manly to defend your family honour even by violent means' (de Mel et al. 2013: 23). Such patriarchal, hyper-masculinist standpoints (including the appropriateness of physical violence to uphold honour) had the consensus of the female respondents, often at a higher level than the men (de Mel et al. 2013: 26). Emboldened during ethno-nationalist wars, these positions enabled each ethnic group to vigorously reinforce its 'own' values in reiteratively performing ethnicity. These performativities, in turn, permit the men of each group to wield power over 'their' women and 'other' men, including by forceful means.[4]

This ideological field permits men, including disabled soldiers, to leverage patriarchal masculinity, and disability's compensatory claims, towards their dominance within the household. Therefore, while masculinity comes under stress in some respects, disabled soldiers are nevertheless able to maintain their management of and access to power at least within the household. As Vijayan (2004: 364, 373) notes, a complementarity exists between different forms of masculinity (in this case between abled and disabled masculinities) so that even as masculinities gradually change or abruptly alter (as when military men are maimed on the battlefield), patriarchal conditions that enable hegemony and dominance to be masculine are already accommodated into that change.

Disabled soldiers also leverage their war hero status to reiteratively (re)assert their masculinity, an outcome of which is their differentiation from male disabled civilians.

[4]The return of caste-based arranged marriages in Jaffna after the war (Thiranagama 2014), assaults by Muslim vigilante males on Muslim women for using the internet (Thambiah 2011) and Sinhala, Tamil and Muslim opinion on masculinity as recorded in the masculinities study (de Mel et al. 2013) provide evidence.

Battlefields authorize male behaviours that would not find sanction elsewhere. They hold both a display of militarized, hyper-masculine aggression and 'effeminate' emotion when soldiers hold, comfort and openly weep over comrades wounded or killed in battle (Easthope cited in Eberwein 2001: 149). However, partly due to the singularity of the battlefield in this regard, and partly due to the need for disabled soldiers to recoup their heroism, their post-battlefield narratives are often only about military toughness—realigned now to mean the mental strength with which they cope with their disability. Gunawardena (2010: 29) noted of the disabled soldiers at the Rana Viru Sevana rehabilitation centre at Ragama, 'In the group "toughness" was the basis for the construction of relational masculine hierarchies with disabled civilian men being the most subordinate'. Machismo and martial pride in having fulfilled their civic duty in joining the army in the first place and, secondly, their costly sacrifice on the battlefield confer on amputee and visually impaired soldiers in particular a prestige unavailable to disabled male civilians (Gunawardena 2010: 33).

This was a social capital endorsed during the war by the *Rana Viru* (War Hero) discourse that deployed war-related disability and its pain to ideological/patriotic use. Many popular Sinhala songs hailed disabled soldiers for their sacrifice. 'Soldier' by 6th Lane, '*Sanda sisile*' sung by Lucky Deva, and '*Enne avith langa redenna*', which became known as the 'Bravehearts song', hit the airwaves and were made popular through repeated broadcasts on local radio and TV channels. Renowned singers (Amaradeva, Dushyanth Weeraman, Ranidu) donated the proceeds of their concerts and CD sales to the Seva Vanitha Unit of the Sri Lankan army for its work with disabled soldiers and their families. In this manner a public donation drive based on *our* civic duty to care for disabled soldiers was realised, and with it the conferment of their special status.

Martial virtue, however, is double-edged. It provided, and continues to offer, disabled soldiers of the Sri Lankan army a coping mechanism because it permits self-esteem. Within states and societies at war, such honour produces a privileged, militarised ethno-nationalist disabled masculinity that disabled male civilians cannot claim. However, it also encourages a sense of entitlement that sutures disabled soldiers into 'wounded attachments' (Brown 1995; de Mel 2007: 112–15). This folds into resentment, particularly when public attention on them fades in the aftermath of war. Making military disability visible thereby becomes an ambiguous site, both necessary and risky for the expectations it promotes.

Making Disability Visible

The visibility that disability gained during Sri Lanka's civil war was largely due to the significant numbers of soldiers maimed in battle. While accurate data remains elusive, one estimate places the figure at 14,224 soldiers on the government side (Dias 2010), while another points to 15,000–20,000 (Dayaratne 2007). In the north of the country where the harshest battles were fought, it is estimated that 10 per cent of the population (both civilians and LTTE combatants) became disabled due to the war (Perera 2014).

These numbers warranted strong institutional support for disabled combatants on both sides of the conflict. In 2000, the Rana Viru Seva Authority was established by the Sri Lankan government to enable its disabled soldiers access to specially designed housing schemes known as Rana Viru Gammanas, health and rehabilitation services including counselling and prostheses fitting, vocational re-skilling and monetary compensation. This work also had the objective of uplifting the morale of the Sri Lankan army during the war by portraying the Sinhala nation as one that cared for its disabled warriors. Among the non-state agencies that supported disabled veterans was the Association of Disabled Ex-Service Personnel (ADEP). Established in 1994, its work included policy advocacy on their pension rights and livelihoods.[5] Using its non-governmental status, ADEP also made visible the condition of disablement as common to both Sri Lankan and LTTE militaries at two peace rallies it organized.[6] It thereby marked a negotiated peace as an alternative to wilful disablement in war.

On the LTTE side, rehabilitation wards were set up for its disabled combatants in Kilinochchi in the Vanni, a region then under LTTE control. Its disabled female combatants in particular were trained to work at its media unit, Nitharsanam, also based in the Vanni. However, LTTE policy of not returning its disabled combatants to their homes in Jaffna in the north or Batticoloa in the east, from where cadres were recruited, because it did not want to burden family members with their care, played into their invisible-isation (de Mel 2007: 147). This policy, as I have argued elsewhere (de Mel 2007: 112, 147), not only folded into the conventional biopolitics of segregating of people with disabilities, but was also a strategy of war because their seclusion meant keeping LTTE *casualties* of war away from public view.

The re-skilling of disabled combatants to work in outfits such as Nitharsanam pointed, nevertheless, to a planned programme of disability rehabilitation that the LTTE followed during the war. This programme included the provision, each month, of a hamper of dry rations to families of disabled combatants in addition to the payment of Rs9000 (US$70) to families of all combatants during the war (pers. comm. with NGO programme officer, Batticoloa, January 2015). Post-war, LTTE disabled ex-combatants have been victims of a fragmented, under-resourced programme of reintegration dominated by state security interests. The multiplicity of state agencies involved in their disarmament, demobilisation and reintegration (DDR) that act independently of each other has caused overlaps and confusion, while at the provincial level the DDR programme is overseen by under-funded councils (Krishnan 2012: 7). In post-war rehabilitation camps, skills retraining programmes and livelihood grants have lacked transparency. A disabled former LTTE Sea Tiger from the Batticoloa district told me that at his rehabilitation camp in Vavuinya, at which he spent a year, he was given a short course in masonry but not awarded the Rs5000 grant that some of the other rehabilitees were given. He was not aware of the criteria by which the grantees were chosen, nor how pledges of funding from international donors, such as

[5] For example, it campaigned for the issuance of three-wheeler driving licences for disabled veterans so they could engage in sustainable livelihoods (de Mel 2007: 115, 147).

[6] These rallies were held on Galle Face Green in the capital, Colombo, and in Kilinochchi, which was the de facto capital of the LTTE during the war.

International Organization for Migration and the International Committee of the Red Cross, had either run out or been mishandled (Sathkunanathan 2013; Perera 2014). The lack of information as well as faith in the rehabilitation programme (he reported that the masonry course was quite superficial) folded into a strong feeling of injustice (interview with disabled LTTE ex-Sea Tiger, January 2015).

Perera (2014) notes that eleven per cent of rehabilitated LTTE ex-combatants (both abled and disabled) are listed as unemployed. This is two and a half times the national unemployment rate. A significant factor preventing their employment is the military surveillance of all LTTE ex-combatants, subjecting them to constant scrutiny upon their return home (Krishnan 2012: 7; Sathkunanathan 2013). The unavailability of guarantors, who fear for their own security, also hampers the access of ex-combatants to bank loans, small start-ups and self-employment (interview with Divisional Secretary, Trincomalee, August 2013).[7] Moreover, ex-combatants are often stigmatized in their own communities for being members of the LTTE. DDR agencies have failed, therefore, to adequately prepare local communities on rehabilitee reintegration, and stigma coupled with surveillance conspire to disavow these ex-combatants the benefit of what should have been the state's nurturing of a 'social contract' with the community receiving them (Krishnan 2012: 7). For these reasons both abled and disabled LTTE ex-combatants remain as yet largely outside the labour force and the community. For disabled female ex-combatants, the result of such exclusion has been their marginalisation from even the modest, albeit important, civil society initiatives on disability currently underway.[8]

Sunera Foundation and Its Butterflies Theatre

In this context of paucity, the aesthetic work of the Sunera Foundation (SF) targeting people with disabilities, including disabled soldiers, is important to mark. While a nascent but already significant body of scholarship on disability in Sri Lanka focuses on policy, law and service provision for people with disabilities (Mendis 1997, 2014; Gunawardena 2010; Krishnan 2012; Samararatne 2012; Campbell 2013, 2014; Samararatne and Soldatic 2014), disabled performance art has received little attention. I build, therefore, on my earlier work (de Mel 2007) on SF's Butterflies Theatre, which included disabled soldiers in its cast and used their disablement for a critique of the war, to assess SF's applied theatre practice with disabled youth, including disabled soldiers, in the post-war context. I do so not only because aesthetic work has been at the forefront of the disability movement

[7] The government provides ex-combatants Rs25,000 as livelihood loans through the Bank of Ceylon but as of July 2014, only 1773 who qualify for such support have accessed the money (Perera 2014).

[8] Krishnan (2012: 7) provides the example of The Association of Women with Disabilities (AKASA), an organization based in the North Central Province that does important work with women with disabilities, often in coalition with other women's groups, but so far has excluded working with disabled female ex-combatants. (On the activities of AKASA, see also Samararatne and Soldatic 2014).

worldwide and is important to mark in the Sri Lankan context, but also because theatre holds particular conceptual tools and characteristics that make it an appropriate medium for interrogating and recognising disability as both exclusion and everyday performance (Sandahl and Ausslander 2005: 9).

In this section I focus on the body in performance and, in particular, the disabled body on stage, and what they mean for a politics of transformation that is promised in much of the applied/devised theatre work with people with disabilities. The performing body is not without gender and how masculinities are deployed in the SF theatre constitutes an important analytical vector. In discussing SF's theatre workshops and performances I highlight three axes: (1) its processes, (2) the issue of impact and (3) the criteria by which we judge disability performance. Each of these axes point to specific concerns around both disability and applied/devised theatre and how they play out in a Sri Lankan context.

'Performance', notes Kruppers (2003: 88), 'is the medium of the body … [and] relies on the complexities of presence for its aesthetic drive.' In turn, disabilities are most obvious when they are seen as variations, or even disfigurements, to the body (Davis 2006). This makes visible-ising the disabled body on stage a primary manoeuvre in interrogating its otherness. Yet, disability is irreducible to bodily disfigurement (Hall 2011: 1) or the physical body itself. A variety of impairments are not obviously evident on the body. More importantly, because of how we see bodies and how we apply particular social and cultural meanings to the body—whether it be abled or disabled—the body extends, both as a concept and a presence, beyond its own physicality (Katz 1999). We don't 'just' look at a body: we look and recognise it according to tacit rules that have a history. This history of looking is what makes up the field of visuality (Bleeker 2008: 1–2) and because the performing disabled body on stage acts as a signifier within visuality, it holds a powerful semiotic charge of sameness and otherness that provokes critical thinking on disability. Yet, for this to happen a certain reification of the body does take place within this theatre wherein disability is fused with, or marked on, the body on stage. The analytical purchase of this fusion/marking would be, then, to call into question such reifications when they merely repeat and fall short of rupture, and concomitantly, at what point and under what conditions rupture occurs. It is within this line of questioning that I examine the SF theatre—as artifice and a representational site—thereby opening up for critique its transformational promise.

If disability and what it embodies are both of the body and not merely questions of the body, it also always flags questions of the social. This includes stigma, at times grounded in religious belief (a common explanation within Buddhism is of disability as past bad karma (Liyanage 2014)) and at other times in gendered superstition that serves to keep disabled women, in particular, uninvited and outside of puberty and marriage rituals (Samararatne and Soldatic 2014: 10). A gendered biopolitics in the management of the disabled body is thereby evident and because this body is a placeholder of difference it is sometimes locked away, medicalised and even pathologised.[9] It is for these reasons that the SF's vision and mission state-

[9] Samararatne and Soldatic (2014: vi) found that even when women with disabilities in rural households, for instance, are not considered 'abnormal' and are encouraged by their families to cope and contribute to household economies, this integrative approach is challenged by the exclusions they

ments uphold principles of equality and non-discrimination of people with disabilities, envisions a society that fully recognizes and accepts the contribution disabled people make, and insists on their fullest integration.

Embodying its vision as a change agent, SF's signature metaphor is the butterfly: an iconic symbol of metamorphosis. Its early theatre was known as the Butterflies Theatre and its latest series of *Samanalayaya* workshops with disabled youth denote both a butterfly (*Samanalaya* in Sinhala) and a transformative *place* (*yaya*). Jehan Aloysius, who choreographed and directed *An Inspired Swan Lake* (2010) and *The Nutcracker* (2011) for SF, noted that his choice of the ballets was based on their narrative charge of transformation: from swan to human, from inanimate toy to dancing gingerbread men and mice (Aloysius, interview with the author, January 2015). With *An Inspired Swan Lake* Aloysius noted, 'I wanted the disabled cast including the disabled soldiers to feel sensuous and sexy. That was a new experience for them because disability is seen as asexual. That was the kind of change I sought'. Theatre performance is at its most transformative when it empowers an actor to inhabit a created character, thereby permitting one body to 'disappear' into another (Burns 2013: 6). It draws the spectator into an illusion, albeit one that is held within an ambiguous tension between similarity and difference, the actor and character, an originary presence and representation (Bleeker 2008: 9–11). It thereby transports us into the world on stage. Based on artfulness as well as artifice, the reconfiguration that occurs in theatre is a unique property of *performance*, whether on stage or in daily life.

Writing on applied theatre (often used interchangeably with devised theatre), Thompson (2003: 30) notes that one of its challenges is to create a relevant theatre in a space (such as a prison or hospital) where the most forbidden action is escape. This calls attention to how this theatre must offer its participants a pathway to reimagine both their individual and social locations. In doing so it locates itself within a rich genealogy of thought and practice on aesthetic work as social responsibility. From Aristotle, *c.*350 BCE, to Augusto Boal and Paulo Freire in the 1970s and up to today, art/theatre has been regarded as a change agent with the potential to conscientise the 'masses' on colonialism, revolutionary liberation and human rights (Freire 1972). Sommer (2014) has highlighted ongoing art literacy programmes, such as Pre-Texts in South America, and public art/pantomime/mime/poster and theatre projects that take on local issues in cities such as Bogota to emphasise the vital reformist role art can and must play in the world. Art has had a long history of being deployed for public good, and the use of forum, applied/devised, storytelling and playback theatre for community development, or the pedagogical deployment of literature in nation building, has marked art's validity itself as dependent on its

face in the public sphere. Krishnan (2012: 12) observes a similar pattern in his study of disabled female LTTE ex-combatants in Batticoloa. While Batticoloa's strong matrilocal structures provide a supportive network for these ex-combatants within family environments, their integration in the wider community falls short of expectations even in a context that has generally failed to deliver on combatant reintegration whether male or female (Krishnan 2012: 7). Disability exists, therefore, as an unstable sign, scripted by and through variables of gender, class and ethnicity. While there is an acceptance of the disabled body (even if conditional) within homes, it remains outside of politics and the public sphere.

transformative power. Within such a framework, art is not for contemplation or pleasure alone but also for civic action (Kushner cited in Nicholson 2005: 8; Sommer 2014: 53–61).

In Sri Lanka, applied theatre workshops have been held in rehabilitation and refugee camps targeting war survivors as well as those affected by the 2004 Asian tsunami, youth groups, disabled youth and soldiers, ex-LTTE child soldiers and combatants, and plantation workers. Thompson (2003: 15–16) defines applied theatre as primarily a participatory activity with people who would not usually perform theatre. It is, therefore, a theatre of inclusivity. Its politics celebrates freedom where fear and exclusion are dominant, even as it interrogates the escapism of a celebratory freedom when that liberty is founded on oppression. It is, therefore, also a theatre of critique. Where successful, it has pragmatically balanced the need to be relevant in difficult, taboo environments with the idealism it wishes to infuse on the possibility of transformation. It aims at offering a safe, intimate space and a process suited not only to movement and script development but also to collective storytelling appropriate for communities with experiences of exclusion, violence and vulnerability. For these reasons, 'Applied theatre programs can be a vital part of the way [vulnerable] people engage with their communities, reflect on issues and debate change' (my addition, Thompson 2003: 16). Given that it is process oriented rather than performance oriented, even if for many practitioners there is a consonance between the two (Nicholson 2005: 4), applied theatre is a popular choice for those who wish to use theatre in specific communities, institutions and groups for social change and therapeutic gain that is gradual and long term. In a context of stigma, conflict and scarcity, an applied theatre group, particularly if it has spent a long time together, has the potential to become a cohesive community bound by vulnerability and art.

For Boal, it was important that both his Forum Theatre participants and agentive spectators (spect-actors) got rid of the 'cop in their heads' (Sommer 2014: 58; also see Boal 1979), shedding habits and habitual thought. As the SF production of *An Inspired Swan Lake* proved, this included changing attitudes to gender and sexuality. Based on an already known ballet and musical score, *An Inspired Swan Lake* was not wholly a piece of devised theatre although Aloysius refers to it as such (cited in Ismail 2009). It was devised to the extent that even though participants worked to a known narrative, the acting and choreographic methods were devised, drawing on specific experiential frameworks. Counteracting the reluctance of the disabled soldiers to embrace a feminised dance form such as ballet (one soldier's anger at having to wear tights provides an example), Aloysius asked the soldiers to think of themselves, for instance, as a *Hansa Balakaya* or 'Swan Force'. This kept to their sense of militarised masculinity and drew on their familiarity with the concept of a military corps or battalion that dances/advances as a team forming a ballet d'corps (Aloysius, interview, January 2015).

Ballet offsets its own feminisation through dualistic gender relations. It is gender equal in its demand for great physical prowess and technique from both male and female dancers. Yet, mainstream ballet's narratives are characterised by strong male characters who, in stereotypical roles, lead, protect and fight over females with less agency (Jordan and Thomas 2010: 153). Aloysius kept to this gendered heteronormativity during rehearsals: for instance, devising a theatre exercise which required the male swan cast to chase the female swans as 'they would chase girls in the village' (Aloysius, interview, 2015). Failure to find a suitable female dancer as the lead swan led Aloysius, however, to cast the disabled soldier Thusitha Wimalasuriya in the role. This was a fortuitous move that enabled a compelling gender reversal. Wimalasuriya had to adopt a feminine, sensuous physicality (including wearing false eye lashes) when he played the swan, yet be within masculine heterosexuality as Nicholas when wooing Gabriella. This (hetero)sexuality was overtly visualised for us during the pas de deux of Nicholas and Gabriella when the disabled soldier's leg stump became his phallus. On the other hand, the homoerotic charge with which soldier and villain danced a pas de deux in the later production of *The Nutcracker* evinced the possibility of 'a macho soldier giving himself up totally to the homoerotic' (Aloysius, interview 2015).

The physicality of the dance form and its sexual and romantic expressions were novel experiences for many of the people with disabilities who took part in the productions (Aloysius, interview 2015). To overcome their inhibitions as well as create, the cast worked with the metaphor of 'body narratives' aimed not only at exploring the 'beauty of the human body' but also becoming 'absolutely comfortable in their bodies' (Aloysius cited in Ismail 2009). Disability as an embodied form was reified but towards rupture, and this is where the radicalness of *An Inspired Swan Lake* lay. It facilitated a safe space for the cast—whether abled or disabled—to connect with their bodies, involving their sensuality where this would have been otherwise taboo. As Edwards (2006: 123–4) notes, what is opened up in studying the body is not a series of dualisms but a variety of encounters that lead to overcoming such binaries. Polarities between ability and disability, male and female, soldier and civilian, sexuality and asexuality are thereby opened up for critique and located within power, inscriptions and norms that set up such dualisms in the first place, determining which bodies and behaviours pass muster and which do not. Aloysius's approach of asking the impaired cast to demonstrate their unique abilities in movements that abled members of the cast could not perform was aimed at unpacking such judgements (interview, 2015).

For the disabled soldiers, ballet also meant moving into a non-indigenous dance form, and Wimalasuriya's embrace of both classical ballet and contemporary dance is particularly significant in a context where militarized, ethnicised masculinity would otherwise reject such 'western' and 'effeminate' forms of aesthetic expression, and where Sri Lankan army soldiers have expressed dissatisfaction at performing *non-military* tasks in the country's post-war construction, hospitality and agri-business ventures. Following his training with Aloysius, Wimalasuriya has travelled abroad to perform as a dancer and to work with choreographers, such as Gerda König in Germany. His commitment to explore new frontiers, cross gender and caste lines in becoming a semi-professional dancer, and take up an art form that has been conventionally associated with the 'perfectly formed', graceful and agile body within mainstream choreographies that exclude people with disabilities, is evidence of his desire to reinvent himself. It also speaks of how an alternative dance culture embraces disability today and provides opportunities for new forms of self-expression.

In Sri Lanka, the aspiration to disabled dance and performance remains at an incipient stage and reflects both attitudinal neglect of the arts as a resource in the development of life skills and the unavailability of sufficient dance/art/theatre/music programmes for training people with disabilities. There is also a shortage of trainers and trained performers with the level of technical proficiency and choreographic vision required to emphatically serve the interests of artists who celebrate diversity (Smith 2005: 83). Against this background, distinctions between art as therapeutic practice that encourages the 'impaired' individual to integrate into society as opposed to an activism that emphasises disability rights and social inclusion on the basis of difference, or between inclusive casting aimed at the broadest outreach versus an auditioned casting aimed at high aesthetic standards, coexist in tension. In this context questions of criteria and of how we judge disability performance become sites of contention.

Judging Disability Performance

SF works with both inclusive and auditioned casting. Its current programme with disabled youth aims at a broad outreach and consists of 36 workshops per year, culminating in the *Samanalayaya* drama festival. The workshops, led by 30 trainers, are held once a week for three hours in 13 districts in community halls.[10] Potential participants are identified by a field manager through lists of people with disabilities in the area compiled by the District Secretariats. The field manager writes or visits the relevant families with information on the workshops. Following this initial contact, a model workshop is held for both parents and potential participants, after which enrolment takes place dependent on parental approval. The workshops are free of charge and participants are between 13 and 20 years of age with an equal gender balance. Although largely urban centred, the enrolment of approximately 1200 disabled youth in the *Samanalayaya* workshops as of 2014 indicates SF's fairly widespread outreach (Sunethra Bandaranaike, interview with the author, November 2014).

The inclusivity of the *Samanalayaya* workshops predicates that youth with a wide range of impairments take part and is in consonance with the use of drama for therapeutic practice (in this case largely though yoga, mime and movement therapy). The performances thereby stay within the category of disability theatre, that does not preclude the showcasing of exceptionally talented actor/dancers or choreography. Auditioned casting on the other hand aims at an integrated theatre in which abled and disabled performers are made equal with the ultimate goal of discarding the disability label altogether. In doing so it locates itself within activism on disability rights, access and diversity (Aloysius, interview 2015; Gerda König, interview with the author, January 2015). The promise of transformation is common to both approaches.

---

[10] Workshops are held in Badulla, Amaparai, Matara, Mawanella, Panadura, Dehiwela, Kurunegala, Galle and Kandy in the south of the country; in Hatton, and Maskeliya in the plantations; and Jaffna and Batticoloa in the north and east.

The politics of this promise is, therefore, important to analyse. Applied theatre practitioners have increasingly begun to worry about whether the claim of transformation is valid, too grand, and in whose interests it is made (Thompson 2003, 2009; Nicholson 2005). Those who raise these questions understand that meaningful change requires an arduous process. This is particularly the case when working with impairments that range from cognitive to severe physical disability. In an hour-long interview with me, Bandaranaike never once used the words 'empowerment' or 'change agent'—terms that are commonly used as outcomes of applied/devised theatre. She merely emphasized the joy the disabled participants experience on the stage:

> Marginal people feel they have no ability to do anything: that they are less than us and they feel it. And they feel strange. The collectivity in theatre helps them to start using their limbs, voices, make movements, and interact with others in a friendly non-judgemental space. That makes them feel very different from what they normally feel ... At the performances they love putting on make-up, getting into costumes. They feel great. What I have noticed of stage performances—we get stage fright, but they have no such fear. Without exception they adore it because this is the very opposite of what goes on in their lives. They love the applause. They love to take a bow on stage. It is a major event in their lives. (Bandaranaike, interview 2014)

This euphoria on stage supports Richard Schechner's view (cited in Nicholson 2005: 12) that applied theatre *transports* rather than transforms, although it does not preclude the latter. Bandaranaike's emphasis was on the importance of the transitory moment—of exuberance, visibility, applause and affirmation on stage—rather than a claim about disabled participants being agents of change. They may become such in the long term as they grow more independent and self-confident through the workshops which, importantly for Bandaranaike, also offer a 'non-judgemental space'. But her emphasis endorses Schechner's view that 'transportation', which is temporary and contingent, is a more realistic assessment of the impact of this theatre than transformation that seeks an ultimately stable and measurable set of coordinates.

Transportation also captures the temporary transformation of performers on stage. As Jones (2007: 239) notes, given that the body is the main tool with which participant-actors express themselves on stage, a series of changes can occur as they enter the stage. Within the role play that theatre demands they experience their own bodies differently, thereby altering their relationship with it. They become aware of the increased potential and range of movement their bodies are capable of, thereby becoming more cognizant of what they can achieve. These realizations facilitate, in turn, an altered perception on the part of others who look upon the disabled body. Yet, as Jones also states, within drama therapy (or the stage) the participant is in a heightened, *exceptional* state, within dramatic rules that are usually different from those outside of the therapeutic site or theatre stage. Therefore, even though a reiterative series of transportive moments has the potential to effect change in the long run, the workshops and theatre stage can, nevertheless, remain exceptional.

The exceptionality also marks the boundary between a devised/applied theatre process that is essentially private and the public outside. James Thompson (2009), writing of his experience of conducting applied theatre workshops at the Bindunuwewa camp in Bandarawela just three months before the massacre of its ex-LTTE child soldier detainees in 2000, notes that while the workshops became an intimate, private process with the camp's participants, no attempt was made to bridge the suspicion by which the village outside held the participants inside. What Thompson recalls, in hindsight, is that the essentially private workshop/rehearsal process of this theatre takes place in a highly contested public political field it often ignores. Unlike the suspicion by which the Tamil child soldiers at the Bindunuwewa camp were viewed by the surrounding Sinhala villagers, not many would discount the importance of a safe, empowering space for people with disabilities. Yet, disability has been explained on occasion as karmic sin and not particularly empathized with; nor is it a homogeneous category. As a result, apart from the conflictual private–public dynamic Thompson writes of, there can be competing interest from *within* a respective participant group itself.

A disabled soldier who took part in SF's early Butterflies Theatre stated, for instance, that at the initial workshops he resented being grouped with children with Down's syndrome (de Mel 2007: 129–130). Another flashpoint occurred at the rehearsals for *Flowers Will Always Bloom* (1999) when tension between the disabled soldiers and a war survivor whose brother had been killed by the Sri Lankan army spilled over to overt hostility. The *Rana Viru* discourse that privileges the disabled soldiers positioned them uneasily within an integrated theatre process that required collaboration with co-actors on an equal footing informed by mutual consent. Such mutuality is, as Sandahl and Ausslander (2005: 2) note, a key issue of insiderness and outsiderness that also marks disability performance in the everyday. At the Butterflies rehearsals this was a binary imported from the ethnic war. There is a 'messiness' in this theatre, therefore, which requires flexibility, self-reflection and constant labour. While its outcomes can be anticipated, they cannot be fixed or determined beforehand. This is why theatre scholars such as Schechner argue for the concept of transportation rather than transformation as a more realistic expectation.

The *Samanalayaya* performances with an all-disabled cast draw attention to themselves as sites of difference. Bandaranaike noted, 'At a performance we are conscious that we are watching disabled people. The context is of disability. Disability is written on their bodies, and the performances are to showcase the abilities of the disabled.' This begs an important question: in experiencing this theatre, how does one prevent 'a theatre of empathy folding into a theatre of charity'? (Aloysius, interview, 2015; see also Kruppers 2003: 74–77). Jones (2007: 291) writes that assessment of therapeutic success itself is notoriously difficult and contentious within the arts. Debates have centred around how 'there can be no absolute criteria within artistic judgment', that available criteria is 'highly value laden and specific', and that 'what occurs within an art form is too complex to be fully encompassed by a series of criteria' (Jones 2007: 291). Debates on standards and criteria are common to any marginal group that performs or writes for a dominant public, as postcolonial, black or women writers who have struggled at one time or another over how they are represented and legitimised well know (Huggan 2001; Nafisi 2014: 313). Disability and disabled performance as *difference* are often held up as exotic and expected to perform the same rites towards its own commodification (particularly so when seeking donor funding for disability projects). The challenge for an inclusive audience is, then, whether it should watch a disability performance through the lens of special needs or be alert to when the performance itself wants to move away from this tag. Aloysius stated:

> The move is towards a totally inclusive theatre where the division between ability and disability is no more. When you have a deaf dancer who moves to a spot on time, you have succeeded. The trainer should not train them as if they are disabled. They work hard to get onto the same page. Theatre is theatre. Not disability theatre. In order so that otherness and injustice are not erased, activism has to take place. Both are necessary and the process is more important than the production. But I want to create a consummate set of actors.[11]

The shift in contemporary performance to the 'post-dramatic', which moves away from the teleological well-made play, is eclectic in style and not reliant on language or the verbal sign, points to both the power of the theatre to position us in different ways and how contemporary theatre audiences have begun to change (Barnett 2008; Freedman cited in Bleeker 2008: 9). As the theatre audience changes so do its aesthetic goalposts. Admittedly the Colombo audience has had greater exposure to these forms of theatre of late through the work of companies like Floating Space, Center Stage, Stages and Mind Adventures than the provincial audiences to whom the *Samanalayaya* plays are first performed, even though the folk theatre familiar to the latter is replete with stylised abstraction. However, for both urban and provincial theatre audiences, unmooring disability performance in Sri Lanka from the labels of 'amateurish' or 'exotic' would require a decentring of the usual ways in which both performance and disability are produced and viewed. It is only then that disability performance can fulfil its potential as radical critique.

Conclusion

By foregrounding how the Sri Lankan civil war and militarized masculinity mediate disablement, disability and aesthetic work on disabilities in Sri Lanka, this chapter situates disability as a gendered and historically located field of experience. By marking the psychosocial states of disabled soldiers as well as post-war challenges to their reintegration (including ex-LTTE combatants), it draws attention to the diverse conditions, discourses, practices and performativities of disability and masculinity in a particular south Asian context.

The chapter also looked at the Sunera Foundation's disability performances taking into account its reformist vision and mission, workshop processes, methodologies of casting, and transformational promise. Analysing the performing body on stage, the chapter also drew attention to the properties of theatre that lend themselves to reconfiguration and the distinction between art/drama as therapeutic practice versus an art that emphasises integration on the basis of good performance values. Arguing that casting is a site where this distinction plays out, the chapter also posed questions on how we should judge disability performance.

By positioning the role of war, masculinity and the disabled male military body within a specific Sri Lankan political, gendered and cultural milieu to extrapolate

---

[11] Aloysius noted that Thusitha Wimalasuriya, the disabled soldier who took the lead role in *An Inspired Swan Lake*, had told him that 'he had never been tested like this before' (interview 2015).

what such a triangulation may mean for our understanding of both disability and masculinity, and by bringing in other analytical vectors of theatre, performance and performativity to the conversation, the chapter wove together seemingly disparate yet deeply connected insights into how and practices on disability, aesthetics and masculinities in Sri Lanka today.

Acknowledgement My thanks to Karen Soldatic for many thoughtful comments and critical insights on an earlier version of this essay, and to the participants of the Cultural Studies Colloquium of the University of California at Santa Cruz for their responses to this chapter.

References

Aloysius, Jehan. (2015). Interview with author, Colombo.

Bandaranaike, Sunethra. (2014). Interview with author, Colombo..

Barnett, D. (2008). When is a play not a drama? Two examples of postdramatic theatre texts. *National Theatre Quarterly, 24*(1), 14–23.

Bleeker, M. (2008). *Visuality in the theatre: The locus of looking*. London: Palgrave Macmillan.

Boal, A. (1979). *Theatre of the oppressed*. London: Pluto Press.

Brown, W. (1995). *States of injury: Power and freedom in late modernity*. Princeton: Princeton University Press.

Burns, L. M. S. P. (2013). *Puro Arte: Filipinos on the stage of empire*. New York: New York University Press.

Campbell, F. K. (2013). A review of disability law and legal mobilization in Sri Lanka. *Colombo: Law & Society Trust Review, 23*, 308.

Campbell, F. K. (2014). The terrain of disability law in Sri Lanka: Obstacles and possibilities for change. In S. Rao & M. Kalyanpur (Eds.), *South Asia and disability studies: Redefining boundaries and extending horizons*. New York: Peter Lang.

Červinkovǻ, H. (2005). The maladies of manhood in the Buzerplatz: Czech military officers in transition. In B. van Hoven & K. Hörschelmann (Eds.), *Spaces of masculinities: Critical geographies* (pp. 58–67). London: Routledge.

Davis, L. J. (Ed.). (2006). *The disabilities studies reader*. London: Routledge.

Dayaratne, A. (2007). *Sri Lanka: Disabled veterans battle high cost of prosthetics, unemployment*. Retrieved from www.irinnews.org.

de Mel, N. (2001). *Women and the nation's narrative: Gender and nationalism in twentieth century Sri Lanka*. New Delhi: Kali for Women and Rowman & Littlefield.

de Mel, N. (2007). *Militarizing Sri Lanka: Popular culture, memory and narrative in the armed conflict*. London: Sage.

de Mel, N., Peiris, P., & Gomez, S. (2013). *Broadening gender: Why masculinities matter*. Colombo: CARE International Sri Lanka.

de Neve, G. (2004). The workplace and the neighborhood: Locating masculinities in the south Indian textile industry. In R. Chopra, C. Osella, & F. Osella (Eds.), *South Asian masculinities: Context of change. Sites of continuity*. Delhi: Women Unlimited.

Dias, S. (2010). *Abhimansala to give life long care to War Heroes: Brave Hearts fund project of the Army*. Daily Mirror. Retrieved from http://www.dailymirror.lk/print/index.php/news/news/6336.html.

Eberwein, R. (2001). As a mother cuddles a child: Sexuality and masculinity in World War 11 Combat Films. In P. Lehman (Ed.), *Masculinity: Bodies, movies, culture* (pp. 149–166). New York: Routledge.

Edwards, T. (2006). *Cultures of masculinity*. London: Routledge.

Freire, P. (1972). *Cultural action for freedom*. Harmondsworth: Penguin.

Gunawardena, N. (2010). *Subverted Heroes: Narrative experiences of disabled veterans in post-war Sri Lanka*, M.A. Thesis. University of Leeds.

Hall, K. Q. (Ed.). (2011). *Feminist disability studies*. Bloomington: Indiana University Press.

Huggan, G. (2001). *The postcolonial exotic: Marketing the margins*. London: Routledge.

Ismail, A. (2009). Body narratives: Exploring the abled and Disabled. *The Sunday Times*, 25 October, Colombo: Wijeya Newspapers.

Johnson, M. (2005). Ethnic violence and crises of masculinity: Lebanon in comparative perspective. In B. van Hoven & K. Hörschelmann (Eds.), *Spaces of masculinities: Critical geographies* (pp. 105–114). London: Routledge.

Jones, P. (2007). *Drama as therapy: Theory*. Practice and Research, London & New York: Routledge.

Jordan, S., & Thomas, H. (2010). Dance and gender: Formalism and semiotics reconsidered. In A. Carter & J. O'Shea (Eds.), *The Routledge dance studies reader* (pp. 149–159). London: Routledge.

Katz, J. (1999). Dismembership: Jasper Johns and the body politic. In A. Jones & A. Stephenson (Eds.), *Performing the body: Performing the text* (pp. 170–185). London: Routledge.

Krishnan, S. I. (2012). *The transition to civilian life of teenage girls and young women ex-combatants: A case study of Batticoloa*. Colombo: International Center for Ethnic Studies.

Kruppers, P. (2003). *Disability and contemporary performance: Bodies on edge*. London: Routledge.

Liyanage, C. (2014). *Socio-cultural construction of disability and its challenges towards an inclusive society*. Paper presented at the Symposium on Exploring Disability: Towards an Inclusive Society, Center for Disability Research, Education and Practice, University of Colombo.

McRuer, R. (2006). Compulsory Able-Bodiedness and Queer Disabled/Experience. In D. Lennard (Ed.), *The disabilities studies reader* (pp. 301–308). London: Routledge.

Mendis, P. (1997). Act for the Protection of the Rights of Persons with Disabilities in Sri Lanka. *Asia and Pacific Journal on Disability 1:1*. Asia and Pacific Regional Committee of Rehabilitation International (RI) and the Regional NGO Network (RNN).

Mendis, P. (2014). *Keynote at symposium on Exploring Disability: Towards an Inclusive Society*. Faculty of Arts, University of Colombo

Ministry of Social Welfare of the Democratic Republic of Sri Lanka. (2003). *National Policy on Disability for Sri Lanka*. Retrieved from http://www.unicef.org/srilanka/disability_policy_(1).pdf.

Mosse, G. (1985). *Nationalism and sexuality: Middle-class morality and sexual norms in modern Europe*. Madison: University of Wisconsin Press.

Nafisi, A. (2014). *The republic of the imagination: A case for fiction*. London: Heinemann.

Nicholson, H. (2005). *The gift of theatre: Applied drama*. Basingstoke: Palgrave Macmillan.

Osella, C., Osella, F., & Chopra, R. (2004). Introduction: Towards a more nuanced approach to masculinity, towards a richer understanding of South Asian men. In R. Chopra, C. Osella, & F. Osella (Eds.), *South Asian masculinities: Context of change, sites of continuity* (pp. 2–33). Delhi: Women Unlimited.

Perera, A. (2014). *From tigers to Barbers: Tales of Sri Lanka's ex-combatants*. Inter Press Service

Samararatne, D. (2012). *Critical Reflections on Recognising and Enforcing Disability Rights within the Sri Lankan Legal Framework*. Paper presented at the University of Colombo Annual Research Symposium. Retrieved from http://archive.cmb.ac.lk/research/bitstream/70130/3375/1/AnnualResearchSymposium2012UniversityofColombo.176-178.pdf.

Samararatne, D., & Soldatic, K. (2014). *Rural disabled women's social inclusion in post-armed conflict in Sri Lanka Report*. University of New South Wales, Australia and Social Scientists Association Sri Lanka.

Sandahl, C., & Ausslander, P. (2005). Disability studies in commotion with performance studies. In C. Sandahl & P. Ausslander (Eds.), *Bodies in commotion: Disability and performance* (pp. 2–12). Ann Arbor: University of Michigan Press.

Sathkunanathan, A. (2013). *Sri Lanka Remembers to Forget*. Opendemoracy. Retrieved May28,2013,fromhttp://www.opendemocracy.net/opensecurity/ambika-satkuznanathan/sri-lanka-remembers-to-forget.

Serlin, D. (2006). The other arms race. In L. J. Davis (Ed.), *The disabilities studies reader* (pp. 49–66). London: Routledge.

Smith, O. (2005). Shifting Apollo's frame: Challenging the body aesthetic in theatre dance. In C. Sandahl & P. Ausslander (Eds.), *Bodies in commotion: Disability and performance* (pp. 73–85). Ann Arbor: University of Michigan Press.

Sommer, D. (2014). *The work of art in the world: Civic agency and public humanities*. Durham: Duke University Press.

Thambiah, M. (2011). Male Suspects Remanded, Female Suspects Granted Bail. *Sunday Times*, Colombo.

Thiranagama, S. (2014). Female militancy: Some reflections from Sri Lanka. In L. Fernandes (Ed.), *Routledge handbook on gender in South Asia* (pp. 115–128). Abingdon: Routledge.

Thompson, J. (2003). *Applied theatre: Bewilderment and beyond*. Bern: Peter Lang.

Thompson, J. (2009). *Performance affects: Applied theatre and the end of affect*. London: Palgrave Macmillan.

Vijayan, P. K. (2004). Developing powers: Modernization and the masculine hegemony of Hindu nationalism. In R. Chopra, C. Osella, & F. Osella (Eds.), *South Asian masculinities: Context of change, sites of continuity* (pp. 364–390). Delhi: Women Unlimited.

Wickramasinghe, M. (2012). *Towards gender equity/equality*. Colombo: International Labor Organization.

Zarkov, D. (2007). *The body of war: Media, ethnicity, and gender in the break-up of Yugoslavia*. Durham: Duke University Press.

Chapter 8
Religion After the Medical Miracle: Recovering "Disability" as Religious Analytic of Social Suffering

Sharon V. Betcher and Mary Nyangweso Wangila

Religions have used disability, like gender, to think with. After briefly essaying the ways religious systems think with and about corporeal anomaly, this chapter considers how the Christian West justified its "humane imperialism" by reading disability as degeneracy in need of medical remediation. Digging into the particulars of how disability became for Christianity the external boundary of what counts as human kin and kind, it considers two key historical epochs: (1) the early missional discernment of monstrosities at the ends of the earth which lent itself to the eschatological urgency of remediatory impulse (400–800 c.e.); and (2) modern realism which developed a picture of Jesus-as-Healer simultaneous to the western colonial and scientific age of discovery (Kwok 1998). That epistemological rendering of Jesus authorized the transgress of boundaries in the name of healing. This exemplary history follows one particularly strong and residual valence of Christian missional colonialism towards the South, a valence heavily inflected with the deployment of the metaphor of disability as an affect-inflected, geopolitical map. Health may be a still under-analyzed vector of imperialism, one that has been easily cloaked by religious affect. Consequently, this chapter, reconsidering the metaphorical plethora of religious thought regarding disability, insinuates "the anti-colonial politics of disabled persons" (Meekosha 2008) within the Christian gospels so as to interrupt that humanist reading and its trajectory of trespass.

S.V. Betcher (✉)
Independent Scholar, Washington, DC, USA
e-mail: sharon.betcher@gmail.com

M.N. Wangila
East Carolina University, Greenville, NC, USA

S. Grech, K. Soldatic (eds.), *Disability in the Global South*,
International Perspectives on Social Policy, Administration, and Practice,
DOI 10.1007/978-3-319-42488-0_8

Thinking with Disability

Most religions suggest that perceptions of disability constitute in themselves a spiritual delusion (Rao 2004: 118). Nonetheless, religions have developed rules of social conduct that short-circuit the basic spiritual truth that all beings are of ultimate spirit. While the major axial religions overtly acknowledge the human experience of suffering and insinuate that suffering can be companioned, even shared, disabled bodies are often caught in personal and systemically entrenched aversion to suffering. Disgust, fear and other prejudices can become consequently lodged in religious constructs such that Ultimate Reality—heaven or nirvana, for example—may be viewed as a realm without pain, a metaphysical construct that holds material bodies under judgment. Contrarily (and these strains can appear within the same religion), thinking Ultimate Reality as co-extensive with the material world, such that one lives radical finitude with spiritual nonjudgment, openness, and compassion, suggests the realm of everyday culture as the locus of spirit. Insisting that Daoism constitutes a religious cosmology more amenable to the experience of disability, Darla Schumm explains how:

> Western religions tend to place their trust in an invisible stability that somehow transcends the fleeting experience of time, whereas Daoism…celebrates the…mysterious creativity within the very fabric of time and space itself…. Daoism rejects a conflict dualism rooted in absolute distinctions between good and evil, heaven and hell, health and illness, ability and disability. Nothing is purely matter or spirit. All things are flowing in the midst of everything else. (Schumm and Stoltzfus 2011: 105–106)

That disability appears in the eyes of its beholders, even against the backdrop of contemporary evolutionary science and philosophical awareness of interdependent co-arising, suggests that one of the following conditions may be true: religious origin narratives do not appreciatively include material fluidity; religions can be more or less motivated by a sense of "natural order" and then cling to notions of kin and kind out of a sense of misplaced security; or metaphysical visions of God or Brahman refuse the reality of pain, thus rendering people with disabilities as not only materially but also spiritually deficient. When a religion supremely values a static, unchanging vision of the transcendental realm, a vision of an original state of health, of Eden, and/or of the body, that religious community may in turn handle biological mutability as auspicious or "tragic."

Affectively, religious aesthetics can be directed toward transcendental ideals, aspects that allow the subject to be free from embodied limitations and entanglements—like today's much touted "state of health." The religious performance of that transcendental aspiration, even as it has been assumed by cosmopolitan zones of secular liberalism, constitutes something of a "decency theology" (Althaus-Reid 2000: 9)—comparable to "ablenationalism," where economic and civil expectations have come to shape understandings of what is normal and proper for bodies (Snyder and Mitchell 2010: 113). Those religiously assumed expectations of what is, for example, "upright," a postural schema yoked with notions of morality, may be performatively out of reach for people living with corporeal anomaly or impairment. Consequently, people with disabilities and their families often take leave of religious communities (Kabue 2012: 16). Problematically, secular zones may be no freer of theology than are intentional religious communities.

Yet, if religious analytics seem, like cultures at large, to receive disability as negative, this constitutes but one spectral range of religious interpretation of disability. Reminding us that what constitutes western notions of health are not universal, postcolonial disabilities scholar Mark Sherry (2007) notes that among Flathead Indians depression might be not an illness, but a maturational horizon from which we have seen and chosen to carry the suffering of all beings—a position not unlike that for which a *bodhisatva* is praised. The Christian bible itself suggests diverse ways in which disablement has been a tool for generating spiritual value: Jacob's limp, a result of wrestling with a night visitant (Genesis), resonates with the historic sense that disability has sometimes been seen as a portentious visitation from the divine. If Paul's virtuosity was "made perfect in weakness" (2 Corinthians 12.9), then disability may serve as a teaching harness for the spiritual qualities of leadership as surely as illness marked the initiatory threshold of the Korean shaman. "In ancient literature," notes biblical scholar Simon Horne, "paradox is associated with inability in a particular way: within inability is striking capability .... As if to underline the axiom's truth, the authority held in greatest respect in ancient society for his insight into human and divine affairs was a blind person, the epic poet Homer" (1998: 89–90). The same might be said of stuttering Moses, who in Jewish history, led the Children of Israel out of Egyptian captivity (Exodus 4:10–12). The metaphor of disablement has in scripture also been deployed as a spiritual diagnostic: "You Pharisees are blinder than the blind" (John 9), Jesus purportedly asserted, borrowing the experience to suggest that sight was never a guarantee of insight. The sixteenth-century Christian theologian Martin Luther suspected that disability might be a test of Christians' strength to love through aversion and anxiety. Comparably, disability is perceived in Yoruba communities—where Obatala the deity, tasked with the responsibility of creating humans, got himself drunk in the process, thus yielding disability—as a social challenge rather than a symptom of sin. These examples begin to insinuate the diverse refractions of "thinking with disability," troubling the singular western notion of disability as deficiency.

Corporeal alterity appears before the beholder only insomuch as religio-cultural strictures desire sameness. Where that has happened, crips have been sequestered by Levitical laws, institutionalized in poorhouses or sanitariums, or hidden away by civic codes like "the ugly laws." The crip—again, exposed only to the extent that a system cannot tolerate alterity—then becomes a sign of the constructedness of human, even religious, sensibilities—a sign that nature not only radically differs within itself, but of the need for rethinking religio-cultural orders. Disability challenges religions to reconsider the ways in which, given evolutionary science, "there are no grounds for conceiving of it as an aberration" (Stiker 1999: 12). Without an extraterrestrial, metaphysical location—without a purported God's eye view—from which to judge, "each entity in the mesh [of nature] looks strange" (Morton 2010: 15). Reality is a "generator of differences, among which is disability" (Stiker 1999: 13). Religions can think with and value that generator of difference; but equally they can succumb to anxiety in the face of difference.

Colonial Mission Brings the Medical Miracle

Disability, theorist Helen Meekosha (2008) advises us, is a term developed in the western context. And indeed critical disability studies have tracked "the invention of the disabled body" to 19th-century western developments amid industrialization—namely, as the inverse of the sense of the norm, the normal and normalcy developed through statistics and set loose through public practices around nationality, race, public health, and criminality (Davis 1997: 9–10). We, however, push this history back, locating the affective precursors for this development within the western Christian history of salvation, which influences the affective arcs—the paternalism, shame and humiliation—within which people living with disabilities are still caught. Coming out of this salvation history, the stigmata of disability has become in western consciousness short-hand for remediation urgently needed (think, for example, of the "need" to remediate wheelchair-riding Jake Sully around which the plot of the 2009 movie *Avatar* silently pivots). Consequently, the adrenal rush of habituated urgency enculturated through salvific mission in relation to disability can easily occasion socio-political and somatic trespass. Always already, the presence of disability stigmata presumes the power of miraculous remediation, whether at the hands of religion or biotechnoscience. Here we consequently consider specific ways in which the Christian West justified its "humane imperialism" by resorting to reading disability singularly as degeneracy in need of miraculous remediation, given a religious metaphysics that rejects pain and evolutionary mutations as inherent to material existence. And degeneracy, we do well to remember, informed notions of race and gender as well as disability in the western eye (Betcher 2007: 49).

After the fall of the Roman empire, Christianity read morphological anomalies as indicative of a world gone ontologically awry and, comparably, of the inverse calibration of transcendental power of Spirit to reset Edenic wholeness without pain (Betcher 2007). The late 4th-century writings of Augustine not only links blindness, deafness or being born with "as little wit as the cattle" with humanity's "condemned origin," but theologically shades these experiences with guilt, that is, "God forbid we say this is done without its being deserved" (1957: 118, 115). Consequently, this theological landscape will be telescoped into an analytic of "brokenness" attuned not so much to "obedience to transcendental command," but—as critical disabilities scholar Lennard Davis has surmised—"to an intrinsic design of thing" (Schoolman 1991: xviii). Western Christianity, ruminating on the world's presumed fall from original grace and its ontological outcroppings (namely, defect), effectively set in motion, beginning no later than the 4th century, the development of a comprehensive, cultural optic deployed as map to rescale the monstrous bodies on its geographic margins and in its cultural midst (Schuld 2003: 151).

Western Christianity's impulse to assess the boundaries of humanity already implicit with Augustine would be ratcheted up by Christianity's missionary drive during the 7th to 10th centuries. If Augustine in one breadth bemoaned the ruined origins occasioning monstrous births, contrary to "the persistent norm of nature" (*City of God* XVI.8, 1984: 662), he simultaneously mused, leaning into the Greco-Roman teratological traditions, upon the monstrosities—cyclopses, pygmies, sciopods, and hermaphrodites—set as figures along territorial borders. Augustine, relying on Pliny's *Natural History* to supplement regional tales, believed the monstrous races limning borders to be continuous with the monstrous births known among any populace. But Augustine comparably believed that heaven held the miracle of remediation to normalcy for such bodies. Consequently, such spectacles reawakened human wonder and respect for "the vigorous power" of God (*On the Gospel of John* 8.2.1, 2007: 57).

We catch in Augustine the catalyst for conceiving the norm of nature, the consequent treatment of disability as guilt-ridden defect and expectation of remediation. Simultaneously, we note the instantiation of a geographical sense of mission driven by the same optic. Frightful curios were presumed to populate the uncivilized territories; the terratological encyclopedia consequently served as map of the ends of the earth, "disability" shading the moral and geographic territory through which Christianity must traverse to accomplish salvation. Christian evangelization takes shape as an act of pastoral concern, but a concern vested with the self-interested, internal urgency to extend the gospel to the ends of the earth so as to occasion the end of time and, hence, the return of God and the conditions of Eden. If for Augustine the monstrous were clearly "bodies of evidence" in and for divine power, they now become an eschatological keystone: evangelical mission proceeded as repair to the ends of the earth, which simultaneously necessitated remediation of the ravaged edges of humanity. The eschatological urgency of impulse to remediation aggravates against the morphological anomalies seen to be peopling the horizon of the Christian imaginary.

One now readily anticipates anthropologist Jean Comaroff's conclusions from her exploration of the relationships of medicine and imperialism in South Africa during the eighteenth and nineteenth centuries: "The early soldiers of Christendom were also the cutting edge of colonialism, and when they tried to domesticate the realities of the 'dark' interior [of Africa], they drew heavily on the iconography and practice of healing" (1993: 306). Modern colonialism—evolving hand-in-hand with the co-incident "birth of the clinic" as the lay form of clerical ministry (Foucault 1994) *and* with the scriptural "discovery" of the historical Jesus (Kwok 1998), now "remembered" as healer set against the "miserable, disabled wash of humanity" (Von Harnack 1908: 109)—advanced by laying out the template of disability as a geosocial map of the world. The zones of degeneracy identified through this optic mobilized the evangelical impulse of earlier eras of Christian mission, as missioners imitated the one they now saw as Jesus-the-Healer, the miracle worker. Already infused with the eschatological impulse to save, to teach, to rehabilitate, Christian mission-cum-modernization sailed towards "the poor, diseased heart of Africa" (British missionary Rev. W.C. Willoughby, cited in Comaroff 1993: 305), as it simultaneously worked feverishly at home to civilize the degenerate classes: racial others, the working class, people with disabilities. As "a climate of technical optimism and rational idealism" swelled in Europe and as Europe now looked through its telescopic optic, the stage was set for colonialism under the auspices of the new science of health (Comaroff and Comaroff 1991: 186). As Jean Comaroff succinctly concludes, "Metaphors of healing have justified 'humane imperialism'" (1993: 313). The optic of degeneracy—that is, seeing others as needy and suffering—occasioned colonial trespass.

Disability, along with its cognates of deficiency and degeneracy, has been one of the most significant memes in the colonial campaign to reinvent life-worlds in the global South. In this, disablement names as well an affective template for "colonizing consciousness" (Comaroff and Comaroff 1991: xi). "The essence of colonization," as Jean and John Comaroff explain, "inheres less in political overrule than in seizing and transforming 'others' by the very act of conceptualizing, inscribing, and interacting with them on terms not of their choosing; in making them into pliant objects and silenced subjects of our scripts and scenarios, in assuming the capacity to 'represent' them" (1991: 15). If "the silent power of the sign, the unspoken authority of habit, may be as effective as the most violent coercion in shaping, directing, even dominating social thought and action" (Comaroff and Comaroff 1991: 22), nothing works so well as the optic of disability set within the theatre of miracle, whether religious or scientific. "Colonial relations," Jean Comaroff concludes, "found an alibi in the ailing human body" (1993: 307). The template of deficiency remains an aspect of evangelical Christian, if also medical and scientific, mission moving from North to South today.

Because people living with disability tend to retreat from religion, having experienced their churches, synagogues, and sangas as places of exclusion (not just physically, but psychically and philosophically), it is important to note that religiously scaled affective maps of disability have migrated into and informed the supposedly secular, cosmopolitan realm where, as Gil Andijar puts it, "Christianity forgot and forgave itself" (2006: 63). Deconstruction of the religiously informed, political affects which crips regularly encounter—for example, the anticipation of deficiency, benevolent paternalism, fear of contagion—will therefore require attention not only within formal religious structures, but in the cosmopolitan secular zone. "The hardest science," historian of science Donna Haraway noted, demarcating the trajectory of western Christianity, "is always about the most pure spirit" (1991: 153). Even the medical miracle remains hinged to certain religious anthropologies, metaphysical assumptions and epistemological optics.

While the medical and religious senses of miracle as "miraculous remediation of disability" seem to vie for credible belief, their competition virtually forecloses any other particularly religious appreciation of disability. At the intersection of western culture and its ideology of health, "the 'savages' of colonialism are ushered, by earnest Protestant evangelists, into the revelation of their own misery, are promised salvation through self-discovery and civilization, and are drawn into a conversation with the culture of modern capitalism" (Comaroff and Comaroff 1991: xii). But hence they "find themselves enmeshed, willingly or not, in its order of signs and values, interests and passions, wants and needs" (Comaroff and Comaroff 1991: xii). These theatrics of religion and science, sunk in modern realism and deadlocked for power in the West, having for centuries played themselves out in the lives of people of the South, may occlude other epistemological ways of looking at and living health. But, as John and Jean Comaroff presciently remind us, "[E]ven as they are encompassed by the European capitalist system—consumed, ironically, as they consume its goods and texts—these 'natives' of other worlds often seek to seize its symbols, to question their authority and integrity, and to reconstruct them in their own image," in such a way as to "escape [the dominant order] without leaving it" (Comaroff and Comaroff 1991: xii, sic). Reconsidering the metaphorical plethora of religious thought regarding disability may then, we hope, insinuate "the anti-colonial politics of disabled persons" (Meekosha 2008) within the Christian gospels so as to suggestively interrupt this western reading and its self-authorization for colonial trespass.

Inside My Wound There Is a People

The all-consuming dialectic of pathology and health belies the raw exposure of lives laid bare by the socio-economic process of neocolonialism-cum-globalization. Most impairment across the world today is owed to such phenomena as residual landmines, industrialization moved to ecologically uncontrolled zones, exposure to pesticides among migrant laborers, the nuclearization of the South Sea Islands, militarization among gangs, tribes, and nations as well as within culture wars, where "gender trouble" has resulted in acid attacks. Against this socio-economic, ecological and political landscape, the analytic of "disability" seems but to open out the intensities of the pathologized body to global capital. "Disability," insomuch as it has named individuated, somatic or neurological deficit, becomes financially lucrative to the mobile, capitalist class as it harvests the geopolitical heaps of "wasted lives" (Bauman 2004) for intensive capitalist investment. As Jasbir Puar observes in terms of western interpretations of disability, "the knitting together of finance capitalism and the medical-industrial complex means that debility pays, and pays well" (2012: 149). People with disabilities in the global South will then be caught between this and the refusal of many governments to make social and educational inclusion a priority.

Philosopher Giorgio Agamben might use the term "bare life" to speak of these geopolitical fields of human lives devoid of value except as brought into economics as objects of finance capital (cited in Bauman 2004: 32, 40). Populations exposed through generations of impoverishment, chemical slow violence, militarization, and labor conditions, all of which aggravate impairment, become "valuable" to the global socio-economic system, a system of financial and corporate elites and the governments that open access gates for them, only as individuated and objectified "disability" awaiting medical remediation. Caught up in the theatrics of science and religion, "disability"—divested of socio-political considerations—seems an inadequate name for this scene of lives invalidated and fiscally disposed. People living with disabilities, which includes geosocial population swathes of the South, recognize that "miraculous remediation of disablement" simply returns one to the heap of people already made redundant, those set outside labor and political processes.

Because disability has marked an individuated body in need of miraculous remediation to normalcy, and because "disability" ties individuated consciousness to "living in prognosis" (an obsession which avoids socio-political analysis), Meekosha (2008) and Puar (2012) both worry about speaking of these scenes of exposure in terms of "disability," which in turn but marks a geographical region for imperial "benevolence." While surveying the living conditions of indigenous people in remote Australia, the conditions of workers in the export processing zones, and the disease consequences of wars, which themselves appear to be aggravated by northern resource extraction, Meekosha concludes that "concepts of disability and impairment seem hopelessly inadequate" to the experience of 66 per cent of the world's disabled people (2008). More adequate, she contends, would be the concept of "social suffering," since the analytic of "disability" deteriorates but to "the concept of personal tragedy" (Meekosha 2008). Given the West's ideology of health as the capaciousness of a normative body to which debility is but an extraordinary exception, "disability" evades socio-political and economic analysis. Puar likewise asserts—while thinking with Lauren Berlant's insight into "populations marked out for wearing out"—that "disability must be rethought in terms of precarious populations" (2012: 152, 154). So could the analytic of "disability" be socio-politically embedded in such a way as to capaciously enable what neo-marxist philosophers Michael Hardt and Antonio Negri call "this monstrous power of the flesh of the multitude to form a new society," to "change its own species" (2004: 193, 196)? If the South is today harbinger of the North (Comaroff and Comaroff 2012) and "the new world of monsters is where humanity has to grasp its future" (Hardt and Negri 2004: 196), could "disability" come to mean anything other than deficit of an individual *in extremis*? In this vein we look back at the religious plethora of meaning-making related to disability.

The refrain celebrating that "the blind see, the lame walk, the deaf hear" was set as banner headline and narrative emplotment for Jesus' ministry in the Christian gospels (Matthew 11.5; Luke 7.22). Christian literature has consequently been read to lift up Jesus-as-Healer working miraculous remediation of bodies disabled, a scene of incomparable importance not only to Christianity's "strong theology" (as already epitomized in Augustine), but to the aspirations of western biotechnoscience. Theological archaeology, digging into the textual strata and thus recalling that the liturgy was borrowed from days lived amid empire at the time of Isaiah (Isaiah 35.5), might rather lift up scenes of socio-political and economic dislocation. More particularly, the stigmata of blindness, deafness and lameness appear archaeologically consistent with the practices of slave holding:so as to prevent their flight, slaves were in ancient times blinded, hobbled or had their eardrums punched out. Under imperial duress, when oppressed people resorted to communication by means of "hidden transcripts" (Scott 1990: 27), as might be anticipated in terms of the Christian gospels, references to disablement—whether the madness of spirit possession (e.g., the possession by "Legions" likely referred to the occupation by the Roman army) or the marks of blindness, deafness and lameness—might well have served as protest against people's political enslavement, whether specifically economic or that occasioned when preoccupied by definitions not of their own choosing. The stigmata help them analytically remember the socio-economic and political conditions that brought about such suffering—namely, their exiles as slaves in Egypt and later in Babylon. Remediation comparably carries not so much the hope of "health" per se but of economic justice and political freedom. If so, the biblical metaphors of disablement and their "healing" may better be remembered as resistance to social and economic suffering. Chicana poet Cherie Moraga catches this sensibility when she writes, echoing Jesus' post-resurrection invitation to the disciples (John 20.27), "Put your hand inside my wound. Inside the valley of my wound there is a people" (cited in Davidson 2011 [2008]: 196). Unlike western notions of disability, these stigmata clearly carry awareness of political ground conditions and pose an analytic interruption within history.

Further, the Christian gospels can be read to pivot around one himself remembered as a disfigured slave-servant, who himself knew the ways humans could humiliate flesh and who queered that humiliation-cum-humility. This is not the Jesus that serves as northern liberalism's mirror of narcissism, but the tradition which interpolated Jesus as crip, a tradition stretching from Isaiah 53 in the Hebrew bible through the Christian gospel traditions to our contemporary, the historian of science Donna Haraway. Sounding a postcolonial call, Haraway urges us to "set aside the Enlightenment figures of coherent and masterful subjectivity, the bearers of rights, holders of property in the self," encouraging us to think beyond humanism by thinking with "brokenness"—specifically, by recalling Jesus as an historical grotesque. Interpolated through Isaiah's figuration of the suffering servant-slave, Jesus emerges as related to colonialism's "in\appropriate\d others" (Haraway 1992: 87).

Remembering Jesus as disfigured slave-servant has been pivotal for Dalit theology, the Indian theology of the "broken ones." The Dalits, also known as "The Untouchables," constitute 15–18 per cent of India's population and are the sociological result "of the caste system mentioned in the Rig Veda" (Rao 2004: 63, 81). For Arvind P. Nirmal, the founder of Dalit theology, God in Jesus—and Nirmal too interpolates Jesus through Isaiah 53's sketch of the disfigured slave—identifies God's self with the Dalits (cited in Rao 2004: 233). As Dalit theologian Moses P. P. Penumaka has likewise surmised, this affiliation of God with humiliated flesh then inverts metaphysics such that—contrary to the aristocratic notions of the ninth-century Hindu philosopher Shankara, if also Christianity's "strong theology"—God has been poured into and can only be encountered in the most radical embrace of finitude and flesh. In such a way, "the mundane sufferings of humble people are dignified by receiving a place in God's reality" (Penumaka 2006: 252).

Argentinian theologian Marcella Althaus-Reid echoed the insights of the Dalit theologians, lifting up the parallel between those people who live without a structured world—the socially, politically, sexually dis-identified and dispossessed—and Jesus, the bastard child of Mary, socially humiliated because she was impregnated during the Roman military occupation. Jesus, she asserted, must then be but a contaminated Messiah: "Jesus brings … contamination and contagion into Divine revelation" (Althaus-Reid 2005: 396). We embrace God at our own risk—at the risk of contamination, that is, which will yield an alternative law of tact or touch, an alternative body politics: the divine economy proves itself an alternative to the path of industry, of cultural comeliness.

"At the very moment when the name Israel is accorded to the Hebrew people, the subject of disability arises" (Stiker 1999: 28), Henri-Jacques Stiker observed in his religious history of disability. Stiker was thinking of Jacob wrestling with the nocturnal divine visitor, leaving him limping (see Genesis 32:23–33). Holmes Rolston III, however, recognizes the consistency between this scene and Israel as itself a "crip nation," as a people who have been formed by the economics, and human-on-human violence, of enslavement (Rolston 1994: 220). In the gospel stories, Jesus himself was initially remembered as uncomely and disfigured, like the suffering slave-servant (Isaiah 53), and thus reminiscent of stuttering Moses and limping Jacob. So one wonders if the gospel narratives were occasions of anticolonial Oedipal mimesis (Oedipus himself being a cripped and exposed infant), circulated so as to trouble the conscience of those in the Greco-Roman city. That paradigmatic scene of encounter with alterity and the importance of navigating it without fear, disgust or aversion has been recalled ever and again within religious practices beginning with reminders about "entertaining God or Christ unaware," in the stranger on the road as well as among the imprisoned, the hungry, the thirsty (see Matthew 25). At the least, these might help us remember to read Jesus as a figure within a series of tableaux, beginning with the night wrestler, left "crip" hero, Jacob (Sherwood 2006: 178), and the "limping nation" bearing his name (Rolston 1994: 220). That then allows for the further possibility that the cripped iconography at the heart of Christianity might interpolate us into different socio-political allegiances than but lending ourselves to the West's conceit of health.

In such ways Christians might insinuate crip disruptive readings of the ways in which the biblical text, in the scope of modern realism, assumed the marginalization of disability as ever assuredly deficit. Given "The power of the bible in the global South" (Jenkins 2006), this biblical archaeology becomes an important means of refusing the imperial vector, especially where it leans into strong theology: invoking disability need not raze or undercut resistance to social suffering, but could return us to care for the commons of social flesh. Only the medicalized arc of western interpretation (the body interpreted through what Davis called "the hallucination of wholeness"), along with its generation of the autonomous individual, prevents Christianity's sacred texts from being read in a way that these celebrate not miraculous cure of individual disablement by Jesus-as-Healer, but disruption of the economics enslaving bodies—thus situating disability as symptomatic of inherently socio-political and economic suffering.

What Notion of the Good Life Might Yet Come to Bear

Assuming the South to be a harbinger of conditions moving North (Comaroff and Comaroff 2012), crips—in ways comparable to the central characters we play in "dystopian" or postapocalyptic literature—prove pivotal to "living after the end of the world" (Morton 2010). The so-called dystopian literature—and the ironic "scare quotes" befit this form of literature, which wonders if there may be more fulfilling ways of living than we have experienced in the turbocapitalist strata—pivot crip characters front and center. As this "dystopian" literary implosion shows up the West's post-industrial, socially urbane and consumer chic "conceit of health," respect for suffering might well return to the religious agenda. Respect for suffering flies in the face of a modernity which presumed its biotechnoscientifically assured eradication. Bodies that have learned to tack through wakes thereof, including the riptides of social humiliation, may be welcomed companions.

It's intriguing to consider what might yet be thought, if the Christian scriptures were allowed to function as "dystopian" in relation to empire, initially Rome, now the global capitalist marketplace. What notions of the good life come to bear when the "ablenationalist" (Snyder and Mitchell 2010: 113) God no longer judges and sorts bodies? When the religious or medical miracle is no longer deployed to rehabilitate bodies back into the worker-armies of the upright and the consumer "cult/ure of public appearance" (Betcher 2007: 28–30)? A dystopian lens might at the least help us remember that wholeness has not necessarily been the mark of the spiritually authoritative. Such questions, disseminated as analytic prompts among communities "that identify with the social and economic realities the Bible portrays" (Jenkins 2006), may help us constitute a location from which we are able "to form alternative networks of existence and resistance to normative relations of consumption, competition, and class conflict" (Mitchell and Snyder 2010: 179).

To be sure, disability, experientially speaking, tends initially to be experienced as an aesthetic surplus that overwhelms the onlooker's rational thought processes. Morphological disabilities often elicit a visceral response—of culturally habituated disgust, thus skirting reason, self-control, and empathy. We cannot emotionally escape shared bio-affective social flesh — thus, we cringe at the guillotine amputation of another. Religious practitioners can be as stricken with avoidance as culture at large. But religions have developed affect practices to mitigate habituated aversions and thus be able to welcome and love the strange/r. Fears can be navigated with equanimity. Affective practices like seeing Buddha or Christ, even as disfigured grotesque (Isaiah 53), in the other are intended to expand our neuropolitical neighborhood, to open out an enlarged aesthetics. Religions—drawing on such ancient practices as carrying the pain of another (Buddhist *tonglen*), corpse meditation to traverse enculturated disgust, and alternative accounts of beauty—might help stretch the ethical breadth of living with alterity without inducing panic attacks.

Conclusion

In this chapter, we have shown that viewing disability as degeneracy in need of medical remediation short-circuits the basic religious truth that all beings are, in essence, spirit and therefore kin. To render people with disabilities as materially and spiritually deficient is to ignore diverse, enriching ways that disability has been lived and can be interpreted. Further, we have named several religious practices that meet the criteria of theory from the South for thinking disability as social suffering: (1) the Oedipal theatre of disabled alterity as central to the spiritual practice of welcoming and respecting divine presence; (2) insinuating disruptive readings of western medical-humanitarian colonialism by releasing clinical language to take in the imperial conditions of slavery in the political background of sacred texts.

Amid the diverse religious ways of considering disability, the optic of modern realism and Christian mission, moving hand-in-hand North to South, assumed disability as degeneracy and thereby justified its missional and medical imperialism. Postcolonial and dystopian literatures evidence another crip modality than that presumed by the

West, a view which we proposed using as an alternative optic for reading the Christian gospels, given "The power of the bible in the global South" (Jenkins 2006). In this view, the stigmata of disability, as lived by people of the global South, helps one to critique the economic and political conditions that occasion enslaving or wasting human life—as, for example, by making it carry an undue burden of precariousness. Sharon Snyder and David Mitchell appropriately remind us that "[b]ands of disabled people have produced viable alternatives to the consumptive models of capital and the expulsion of bodily imperfection in order to envision a meaningful contrast of life-styles, values, and investments adapted to life as discontinuity and contingency" (2010: 192). Reading the Christian gospels as dystopian in this way might release that future which is so hopefully monstrous (Derrida 1995: 386–387).

References

Althaus-Reid, M. (2000). *Indecent theology: Theological perversions in sex, gender and politics*. Abingdon: Routledge.

Althaus-Reid, M. (2005). *El Tocado* (*Le Toucher*): Sexual irregularities in the translation of God (The Word) in Jesus. In Y. Sherwood & K. Hart (Eds.), *Derrida and religion* (pp. 393–405). New York: Routledge.

Andijar, G. (2006). Secularism. *Critical Inquiry, 33*(Autumn), 52–77.

Augustine. (1957). Against Julian (trans. Schumacher, M.A.). In H. Dressler (Ed.), *The fathers of the church: A new translation* (vol. 35). Washington, DC: Catholic University Press.

Augustine. (1984). *The city of god* (trans. Bettenson, H.). London: Penguin.

Augustine. (2007). [c. 1888] On the gospel of John. In P. Schaff (Ed.), *Nicene and post-nicene fathers: First Series, Volume VII: St. Augustine: Gospel of John, First Epistle of John, Soliloquies*. New York: Cosimo Classics.

Bauman, Z. (2004). *Wasted lives: Modernity and its outcasts*. Cambridge: Polity Press.

Betcher, S. V. (2007). *Spirit and the politics of disablement*. Minneapolis: Fortress.

Comaroff, J. (1993). The diseased heart of Africa: Medicine, colonialism and the Black Body. In S. Lindenbaum & M. Lock (Eds.), *Knowledge, power and practice: The anthropology of medicine and everyday life* (pp. 305–329). Berkeley: University of California Press.

Comaroff, J., & Comaroff, J. (1991). *Of revelation and revolution: Christianity, colonialism, and consciousness in South Africa*. Chicago: University of Chicago.

Comaroff, J., & Comaroff, J. (2012). *Theory from the South: Or, how Euro-America is evolving toward Africa*. Boulder: Paradigm Publishers.

Davidson, M. (2011). *Concerto for the Lefthand: Disability and the defamiliar body*. Ann Arbor: University of Michigan. Original work published 2008.

Davis, L. (1997). Constructing normalcy. In L. J. Davis (Ed.), *The disability studies reader*. New York: Routledge.

Derrida, J. (1995). *Points…: Interviews 1974-1994*. Stanford: Stanford University Press. Trans Peggy Kamuf.

Foucault, M. (1994). *The birth of the clinic: An archaeology of medical perception*. New York: Vintage.

Haraway, D. (1991). *Simians, cyborgs, and women: The reinvention of nature*. New York: Routledge.

Haraway, D. (1992). Ecce Homo, Ain't (Ar'n't) I a woman, and inappropriate/d others: The Human in a post-humanist landscape. In J. Butler & J. W. Scott (Eds.), *Feminists theorize the political*. London: Routledge.

Hardt, M., & Negri, A. (2004). *Multitude: War and democracy in the age of empire*. New York: The Penguin Press.

Horne, S. (1998). 'Those Who Are Blind See': Some new testament uses of impairment, inability and paradox. In N. Eiesland & D. E. Saliers (Eds.), *Human disability and the service of god: Reassessing religious practice*. Nashville: Abingdon Press.

Jenkins, P. (2006). The power of the Bible in the global South. In *The Christian* Century (July 11, 2006). Retrieved December 12, 2013, from http://www.religion-online.org/showarticle.asp?title=3416

Kabue, S. (2012). Persons with disability in Church and society: A historical and sociological perspective. In S. Kabue & E. Mombo (Eds.), *Disability, society and theology: Voices from Africa* (pp. 3–23). Limuru, Kenya: Zapf Chancery.

Kwok, P.-L. (1998). Jesus/the native: Biblical studies from a postcolonial perspective. In F. F. Segovia & M. A. Tolbert (Eds.), *Teaching the Bible: The discourses and politics of biblical pedagogy*. Maryknoll: Orbis.

Meekosha, H. (2008). *Contextualizing disability: Developing southern/global theory*. Keynote paper given to Fourth Biennial Disability Studies Conference, Lancaster University, UK. September 2–4, 2008. Retrieved December 12, 2013, from http://wwda.org.au/meekosha2008.pdf.

Mitchell, D. T., & Snyder, S. L. (2010). Disability as multitude: Re-working non-productive labor power. *JLCDS, 4*, 2.

Morton, T. (2010). *The ecological thought*. Cambridge: Harvard University Press.

Penumaka, M. P. P. (2006). Luther and Shankara: Two ways of salvation in the Indian context. *Dialog, 45*(3), 252–262.

Puar, J. (2012). Coda: The cost of getting better: Suicide, sensation, switchpoints. *GLQ, 18*(1), 149–158.

Rao, A. (2004). *Soteriologies of India and their role in the perception of disability: A comparative transdisciplinary overview with reference to Hinduism and Christianity in India*. Piscataway: Transaction Publishers/Rutgers University.

Rolston, H., III. (1994). Does nature need to be redeemed? *Zygon, 29*, 205–229.

Schoolman, M. (1991). Introduction to William Connolly. In *The Augustinian Imperative: A reflection on the politics of morality*. Newbury Park: Sage.

Schuld, J. J. (2003). *Foucault and Augustine: Reconsidering power and love*. Notre Dame: University of Notre Dame Press.

Schumm, D., & Stoltzfus, M. (2011). Beyond models: Some tentative daoist contributions to disability studies. In Schumm & Stoltzfus, (Eds.), *Disability and religious diversity: Cross-cultural and interreligious perspectives*. New York: Palgrave MacMillan.

Scott, J. (1990). *Domination and the arts of resistance: Hidden transcripts*. New Haven: Yale University Press.

Sherry, M. (2007). (Post)colonizing disability. *Wagadu, 4*, 10–22.

Sherwood, Y. (2006). Passion-Binding-Passion. In V. Burrus & C. Keller (Ed.), *Toward a theology of Eros: Transfiguring passion at the limits of discipline*. New York: Fordham University Press.

Snyder, S. L., & Mitchell, D. T. (2010). Introduction: Ablenationalism and the geo-politics of disability. *JLCDS, 4*(2), 113–125.

Stiker, H.-J. (1999). *A history of disability* (Trans. W. Sayers. Foreward D. T. Mitchell). Ann Arbor: University of Michigan Press.

Von Harnack, A. (1908). *The mission and expansion of Christianity in the First Three Centuries*, vol. 1, (Trans. J. Moffatt). New York: G P Putnam's Sons.

Part II
Connecting Disability

Chapter 9
Livelihoods and Disability: The Complexities of Work in the Global South

Jill Hanass-Hancock and Sophie Mitra

Introduction

Four-fifths of the world population lives in the global South (United Nations 2011), where disability prevalence is higher and livelihood challenges are greater than in developed countries or the global North (WHO and World Bank 2011; Mitra and Sambamoorthi 2014). Yet, the majority of research on disability and livelihoods (including studies on employment and economic wellbeing) has been conducted in the global North (OECD 2003). In the North, it is well established that people with disabilities have worse outcomes on a set of economic indicators than people without disabilities including lower employment rates, wages and earnings. This raises the question of whether similar outcomes are found in the global South. Most people with disabilities living in the global South experience compounded livelihood challenges related to general economic disadvantage as well as disability. Social support grants are mostly absent (see Schneider et al. 2016, in this volume), raising the question of how people with disabilities can maintain livelihoods and be integrated in income-generating activities such as employment.

Little systematic information is available on the employment situation of people with disabilities in the global South, where employment refers to paid work for another individual or organization or through self-employment. The World Bank estimates that the employment rate of people with disabilities in the global South is 58.6 per cent for males and 20.1 per cent for females, compared with 71.2 per cent and 31.5 per cent for nondisabled males and females respectively in the global North (WHO and World Bank 2011). Mizunoya and Mitra (2013) in their analysis

J. Hanass-Hancock
South African Medical Reseach Council, Durban, South Africa

S. Mitra (✉)
Fordham University, Bronx, NY, USA
e-mail: mitra@fordham.edu

S. Grech, K. Soldatic (eds.), *Disability in the Global South*,
International Perspectives on Social Policy, Administration, and Practice,
DOI 10.1007/978-3-319-42488-0_9

of 15 countries in the global South estimate that in 13 of these countries, the employment rate of people with disabilities is lower than that of nondisabled people. In nine of the 15 countries, there is a statistically significant gap showing lower employment rates for people with disabilities. Overall, the evidence suggests that there is a disability gap in employment rates in the global South and that policies promoting access to employment may be particularly important for the economic well-being of people with disabilities and their families. The attempt to make people with disabilities participate in the labour market is not necessarily a feasible solution to address livelihood challenges for all people with disabilities (Soldatic 2013), however, and this becomes a serious issue when disability as well as environmental conditions vary extensively in the global South. In order to improve their livelihoods, it is necessary to understand how people with disabilities in the global South build their livelihoods and how livelihood affects employment and the type of decent work that they can access.

Livelihood is a complex concept incorporating different aspects of people's lives. In the context of disability literature, however, livelihood is often reduced to discussion around employment and income and does not consider the influence of other factors. The United Nations ESCAP 2012 report—Disability, Livelihood and Poverty in Asia and the Pacific—criticizes Narayan et al.'s (2000) definition of livelihood because it includes only 'the well-being derived from the adequacy and security of income and food'. UNESCAP (2012) argues that livelihood goes beyond these basic necessities and includes the dignity of people's lives. The UNESCAP report also mentions the sustainable livelihood framework and points out that it borrows ideas from the capability approach, which focuses rather on people's assets and capabilities. Even though the report criticizes the absence of a livelihood framework, it does not describe one itself and consequently does not reveal data on a number of crucial livelihood aspects.

The term 'livelihood' can be understood in different ways. This chapter uses the sustainable livelihood framework to guide a review of literature related to disability and livelihoods and the intersection with employment in the global South. Using this framework, livelihood describes the means of making a living or surviving and the ability to maintain or build long-term well-being (Chambers and Conway 1991; Bebbington 1999; UNESCAP 2012). This sustainable livelihood framework recognizes that multiple components (or capitals) contribute to overall livelihood and thus provides a lens through which to analyse the challenges and opportunities of people with disabilities in the global South more holistically. In reviewing the available literature, we attempt to reveal gaps in our thinking around disability and livelihood as well as to critically discuss how livelihood challenges may be related to employment issues.

Although there are variations in terminology, five principal resource types, or 'capitals', provide the basis for most sustainable livelihood frameworks (see Fig. 9.1) and may be described as follows: financial (economic), human (such as knowledge, health, work experience), social (emanating from relations of trust, reciprocity and exchange, and built through interactions between and within individuals and groups), physical (such as infrastructure, services) and natural (emanating from the natural environment) (Chambers and Conway 1991; Leach et al. 1997; Scoones 1998; Bebbington 1999; Farrington et al. 1999; Misselhorn 2009). These capitals are viewed

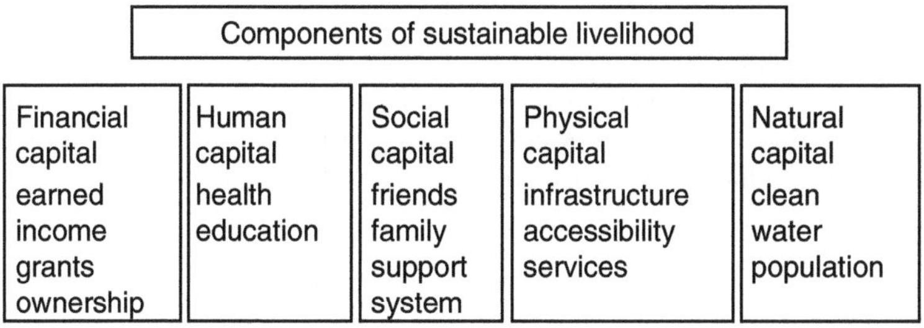

Fig. 9.1 Example of capitals in the sustainable livelihood framework (developed by Misselhorn at HEARD in Groce et al. 2013)

as providing the raw material from which people, and this includes people with disabilities, can fashion their livelihoods, but they can also encompass elements that constrain livelihood choices. The varying ability to access capitals explains many of the enormous economic and social inequities between individuals, households and communities, including people with disabilities. To illustrate, employment contributes to earned income and is considered within financial capital; however, other capitals may contribute to the person's ability to find employment, such as human capital via education. In the case of people with disabilities, these capitals may disproportionately and significantly influence employment and income opportunities.

This chapter critically reflects on the use of livelihood concepts in the context of disability and reviews the limited empirical evidence on employment for people with disabilities in the global South using the sustainable livelihood framework. Using a livelihood framework allows a systematic approach towards challenges and entry points for economic interventions to assure household well-being. This analysis is timely since it can inform policies related to the economic advancement of people with disabilities as governments, civil society organizations and international organizations implement the obligations arising from the Convention on the Rights of Persons with Disabilities (UN Convention on the Rights of Persons with Disabilities 2006).

Disability and Livelihood in the Global South

How impairment or disability may impact on employment is an empirical question (Mizunoya and Mitra 2013) and realities in the global South may differ from the global North. In an agrarian economy, as is often the case in the global South, many jobs are in the primary sector (agriculture, forestry, mining) and may involve heavy manual labour, which people with physical disabilities may not be able to do. People with hearing impairments or with mild intellectual or learning disabilities, on the other hand, may not experience barriers to physical labour. The effect of disability on employment will also depend on the workplace, its accessibility, available accommodations and transport, and whether there is discrimination that might prevent access to employment and/or might lead to lower wages (Baldwin and Johnson 2005; Mitra and Sambamoorthi 2008). The policy context is also relevant; for instance, vocational rehabilitation, disability insurance or social assistance programmes could facilitate, limit or not affect access to employment for people with disabilities depending on how they are designed and implemented.

Financial Capital

People may have access to various sources of financial capital, such as inherited wealth, labouring income, social grants and loans, depending on their circumstances. Lack of financial resources is often a direct result of exclusion or disadvantage in the labour market (UNESCAP 2012), but can also inversely be a barrier to employment through a variety of mechanisms (for example, the inability to afford the transport or communication channels that might facilitate job opportunities, or prohibitive business start-up costs required for self-employment). Financial resources via grants, pensions or other kinds of support can compensate the necessity to participate in the workforce.

Within the empirical disability literature, financial resources gained from employment have been substantially investigated (UNESCAP 2012; Soldatic 2013). This empirical literature reveals how those who are working are more likely to be self-employed (Loeb 2004; Mitra and Sambamoorthi 2008; Loeb et al. 2013). The UNESCAP (2012) report on Asia revealed for instance that people with disabilities are able and willing to work, but have fewer work opportunities than their peers. The same report revealed that women with disabilities are the least likely to be employed (UNESCAP 2012). On a similar note, Ingstad and Grut's (2007) work in Kenya shows that people with disabilities are not employed even if they have achieved adequate educational levels. Lack of employment or integration in the formal workforce has often been attributed in the literature to several factors, among them a lack of access to education and health, negative attitudes and stigma, a lack of motivation and a lack of disability accommodation in the workplace and supporting services, such as transport. However, little research assesses empirically which specific barriers people with disabilities experience when trying to access employment in the South.

In some countries in the global South, social support grants have been introduced to provide financial support to people with disabilities. For instance in South Africa people with disabilities who earn under a certain threshold are eligible for a disability grant; yet, in many families this grant is used to look after the whole family, leaving little for the disabled person (National Treasury and South African Revenue Service 2013). Literature on disability grants in the context of HIV shows that the grant has a positive impact on people's livelihoods, though the literature also questions if disability grants in the context of a generally impoverished population are 'a necessity or a reward' for not looking after one's health (see Nattrass 2005; Macgregor 2006; Phaswana-Mafuya et al. 2009). This has been argued in South Africa where HIV is endemic and disability grants are available, but it has been heard only anecdotally that people living with HIV who receive grants from the government may deliberately default on their antiretroviral treatment to worsen their health and thus qualify for the grant (Kagee 2014). As Kagee's recent review reveals, empirical evidence is rather lacking and more research needs to be done to clarify these speculations.

Human Capital

People's human capital is built in relation to their access to knowledge/education, health care and work experience. Lack of access to health and education may be a cause of disability but is also related to exclusion from the labour market. In particular, health and education have been linked to employability and income.

Health

Health issues reduce human capital when they lead to impairment. The literature argues that a lack of access to health care in the global South is the main barrier to health (Groce et al. 2011; WHO and World Bank 2011). The lack of access to timely, adequate health care and decreased health-seeking behaviour is highlighted as causing impairment-inducing illnesses, such as river blindness and malaria (Czechowicz et al. 2010; Rohleder and Swartz 2012; Frohmader and Ortoleva 2013; DHAT 2014; Van der Heijden 2014). Poverty is often discussed as a driving factor of poor health (see Swartz and Bantjes 2016, in this volume). Drawing on a nationally representative survey sample, Gilbert et al. (2008) find that blindness in Pakistan is more than three times higher in poor clusters than in affluent clusters, and that poor access to eye-care services is a significant causal factor. Similarly, Kuper et al. (2003) report how in Kenya, the Philippines and Bangladesh people with cataracts over the age of 50 are more likely to be in the lowest quartile of per capita expenditure, have lower asset ownership, and have lower self-rated wealth in all three countries. This type of literature does usually focus on a medicalized response to preventing impairment but does not provide evidence on how disability poses further challenges to accessing health care and how medical care or rehabilitation programmes may impact on the ability to earn a living.

A small but growing literature (Groce et al. 2011; WHO and World Bank 2011) argues that a lack of disability accommodation reduces access to health care, increasing health disparities for people with disabilities which, in turn, affect their prospects of employment or restrict the type of work and number of hours they are able to work (Ingstad and Grut 2007; Groce et al. 2011). In the context of HIV, lack of access to reproductive health services and information exposes people with disabilities to additional health risks, such as HIV and AIDS (Hanass-Hancock 2009; Chirawu et al. 2014). This is particularly disastrous for disabled women. Research in Zambia has shown how the double or triple burden of HIV, disability and gender increases health and social challenges and affects livelihoods with the loss of not only social support but also informal and formal modes of employment and income (Yoshida et al. 2014).

Education and Training

Central to human capital are levels of education and training. Poverty and disability influence education level and, in turn, future livelihood, with lack of education perpetuating the cycle of poverty among people with disabilities (see Wickenden and Elphick 2016, in this volume). Poor children are more likely to become sick, be uneducated and not have future prospects of employability, thus becoming dependent in adulthood (Victoria et al. 2003). Roughly one-third of the 77 million children out of school globally are estimated to be disabled children (UNESCO 2010). For instance, evidence from South Africa suggests that learners with disabilities are disproportionately represented in the groups of children who are out of school or lagging behind their peers in school (Filmer 2008; Fleisch et al. 2012). The same studies suggest that if children with disabilities have access to education (schooling) it reduces the likelihood that they will live in poverty as adults (Filmer 2008).

Access to education involves the physical access to an educational facility and the quality and relevance of education. Dhungana's and Kiani's qualitative studies with women with disabilities reveal that lack of access to employment is related to unsuitable vocational training (Dhungana 2006; Kiani 2009). In Dhungana's (2006) study, 12 of the 30 participants had received some form of vocational training; however, this was often not relevant to the local job opportunities. This indicates that education for people with disabilities cannot be a one-size-fits-all approach. Like anybody else, people with disabilities need to have access to education that is relevant to the available labour market and suitable to their impairment. In particular, vocational training may need to be conducted in the workplace rather than in isolated institutions. The accommodation of disability in the workplace itself in turn may need to be looked at and feasible solutions found.

Social Capital

People's access to social capital entails their ability to access support from their community as well as individual social networks (for example, there may not necessarily be many employers in poor communities). Stigma and exclusion from society, which people with disabilities may experience, can be a driving factor in lack of access to social capital. In turn, lack of access to social capital, in the form of employers or mentors, for example, is a disadvantage in finding employment.

Disability stigma has been described in a number of publications (Izumi 2007; Groce et al. 2011; WHO and World Bank 2011). Stigma reduces social participation, access to social networks and opportunities, including those for employment.

The literature argues that stigma and discrimination is another reason for high unemployment among people with disabilities (Groce et al. 2011). The workplace can be inaccessible, while employers and their staff may also neglect to reach out to disabled groups (such as by advertising jobs in places accessible to the blind) or have negative attitudes towards disability. Ingstad and Grut's study in Kenya reveals how stigma and discrimination may be linked to low employment rates, as even those people with disabilities who had achieved higher levels of education found themselves unemployed.

Disability stigma can intersect with other forms of discrimination. For instance, Kaori in a Zimbabwean study reveals that the double stigma of HIV and disability pushes the families of disabled children into a vicious cycle of stigma, poverty, food insecurity, abuse and neglect, and even premature death (Izumi 2007). Similarly, the Sepo study (ICDR and HEARD 2011; Yoshida et al. 2014) in Zambia revealed issues of double or even triple stigma related to disability, HIV and gender. The study highlighted the increased vulnerability and discrimination of women with disability who also live with HIV (ICDR and HEARD 2011). These women were more likely to be abandoned by their partner or less likely to have a partner, thus decreasing their social capital. Stigma and loss of support from partners has been reported in other studies. For instance, Dhungana (2006) describes how women who acquired impairment during adulthood frequently lost the financial support of their spouses and their families.

Poverty is linked to access to family support, community support, and education and knowledge, all of which form part of psychosocial security within a livelihood framework. Empirical literature often still uses a medical model of impairment and simplistically assumes causality from disability to poverty. For instance, Li et al.'s (2012) study in China using the National Sample Survey on Disability revealed a direct association between poverty (specifically income, which is part of financial capital) and the psychosocial support available for people with 'psychiatric disabilities'. Although Li et al. assume that psychiatric disability predicts poverty and social support, it is not possible to conclude from the presented data in which directions the associations work. It is also possible that poverty and lack of social support predicts psychiatric disability. More thorough research needs to be conducted to understand associations between complex phenomena such as poverty and disability and how this is influenced by livelihood components, including psychosocial support.

In addition, disability may also affect the employment prospects of the family members without disabilities who provide care. In this context, Hanass-Hancock and Casale (2014) discuss the potential interrelationships between caregiving, disability and poverty in Africa. Their exploratory model illustrates how co-existing experiences of disability and caregiving may lead to a vicious cycle of deteriorating well-being and loss of income opportunities as caregivers may be overburdened with care activities affecting their own health and time to earn an income (Buckup 2009). There is a lack of empirical evidence on the interplay of social support/caregiving and disability from the global South.

Physical Capital

People's physical capital is related to the infrastructure they can access, and how this infrastructure responds to their needs. Poor infrastructure (lack of safe transport, poor sanitation and housing) can be a cause of impairment and also be a barrier for people with disabilities in accessing transport or buildings (missing ramps etc.). Lack of access to physical capital consequently disadvantages people with disabilities in accessing services as well as employment. On the one hand, even if people with disabilities have access to health care and education, they may still face challenges to employment if work and trade places are not accessible or do not accommodate disability needs (e.g. no disabled toilet), transport is unsuitable (e.g. no door for a wheelchair), communication needs are not accommodated (e.g. sign language), and people's attitudes discriminate against them (Snyman 2009; UNESCAP 2012).

On the other hand, access to infrastructure and housing coupled with exposure to a number of environmental risks such as pollution may potentially lead to health issues and impairments, and ultimately to disability. There is an extensive body of evidence available on this link. In the 1980s, poor working conditions and the absence of effective injury prevention programmes in the global South were billed as leading to a very high sickness and accident rate: 'In such circumstances, the salary and social benefits of the worker are low, because productivity is well below its capacity. This vicious cycle also results in the worker's malnutrition and low working capacity, resulting in turn in greater vulnerability to disease and job-related accidents' (Shahnavaz 1987). This has the potential to lead to disability and loss of work opportunities.

Similarly, farmers who perform more manually oriented agricultural work, such as lifting or moving very heavy equipment or agricultural products and often using hand tools, are at risk of developing musculoskeletal disorders (Walker-Bone and Palmer 2002). Mechanizing agricultural practices is a practical way of reducing the incidence of impairments (Walker-Bone and Palmer 2002). This approach focuses only on the prevention of impairment, however, and avoids a discussion on how to address disability once it has occurred and how farmers may continue to work once they have become disabled. This is a recurring theme in empirical literature, which discusses prevention of impairment but not inclusion and accommodation of people with disabilities.

Natural Capital

People's natural capital is related to their environmental resources, including clean water, land and other natural resources, such as oil. Insufficient access to clean water, sanitation and safe housing has been associated with disability. Again poor environments, such as polluted rivers, water, air or food supply, or a lack of natural resources can be a cause of impairment or even death, while people with disabilities may have little or no access to natural capital (e.g. land). Further, Wisner et al. (2003) reveal that people with disabilities are prone to experience greater losses of their natural capital (land, housing and water sources) and to suffer more in situations where 'natural hazards' occur. A physical or intellectual constraint on being able to identify, avoid or escape harmful incidents or to protect property (such as during a fire outbreak at home, hurricane or earthquake) poses a threat to the survivial and livelihood of the person with disabilities. Such harm or loss may plunge them into more hardship and poverty.

The literature argues that where people live, work and develop their livelihoods can pose risks or opportunities to them (Wisner et al. 2003). For example, trachoma has been related to a lack of clean water and sanitation (Kuper et al. 2003). One could argue that the inability to change or avoid risky environmental conditions affects human capital and through this the ability to work; however, although there is empirical literature on disease and impairment, it is again missing in regards to disability inclusion and employment. Wisner et al. (2003) also argue that social processes and stigma can facilitate unequal access to opportunities and exposure to hazards, and relegates certain groups into areas with no choice of living conditions (people with disabilities, immigrants, people of certain ages and socio-economic class). Wisner et al. (2003) write that 'vulnerable groups (such as disabled people) find it hardest to reconstruct their livelihoods following disaster, and this in turn makes them more vulnerable to the effects of subsequent hazard events' (also see Spurway and Griffiths 2016, in this volume).

The links between livelihoods and disability are complex and we have attempted to summarize a large body of literature from a wide range of disciplines. While by no means all encompassing, the above discussion emphasizes that the links between livelihood capitals and employment, on the one hand, and disability on the other, are multifaceted and bi-directional. Disability directly affects all five capitals, most obviously human capital and through this the opportunity to work. The 'work–disability nexus' is most directly linked to financial capital, yet it has both direct and indirect links to other capitals through, for instance, the work, home and social environments, and access to health care and education, all of which may be influenced by income.

While this literature review is not exhaustive, it gives enough evidence that people with disabilities tend to be more often deprived in terms of livelihood capitals, and thus tend to be more likely to face multiple livelihood challenges. The review also highlights how empirical evidence is still often medical in nature. There is extensive literature available on the determinants of impairment related to livelihood failures (e.g. malnutrition, working conditions). There is also some evidence on the consequences of disability on livelihood capitals, often focused on a single capital (e.g. financial capital) in each study. Yet, the livelihood challenges determining or resulting from disability are multifaceted and inter-related. For instance, if the environment is not accessible, physical capital is affected, which may negatively impact on social capital, which may in turn influence employment opportunities and financial capital, which then reinforce a lack of social capital. Finally, our review also shows that there is little empirical literature on how to develop the livelihoods of people with disabilities in the global South, let alone on describing and assessing their livelihood situation.

Disability-Inclusive Livelihood Assessments in the Global South

People with disabilities tend to face multiple livelihood challenges in the global South. Efforts to improve their employment and livelihoods at a country, district or community level need to start with an assessment of the livelihood opportunities and outcomes of people with disabilities and the constraints they face in their human, social, physical, financial and natural capital. For instance, it could be argued that inaccessible physical environments prevent access to the workplace, while also claiming that lack of or inadequate education leads to low employability. Conversely, one could also challenge the notion that people with disabilities have to be part of the workforce and point to the unfairness of this expectation where health conditions may prevent a person from performing certain tasks.

In addition, different types of disability, different levels of severity, a person's sex, and location in urban or rural areas all may present constraints to a person's employment. Apart from understanding the local context, it is therefore essential to identify first the different groups of interest, and second the main livelihood failures and opportunities for each group.

While the inclusion of disability indicators in mainstream surveys and surveillance can provide some indication of numbers of people with disabilities, small-scale participatory research involving multiple stakeholders may go a long way in developing a deeper understanding of their livelihood situation and of the constraints to employment, an exercise that can inform disability policy and interventions (IRP, n.d.; United Nation Development Programme [UNDP] 2012; Nokrek et al. 2013). Stakeholders in participatory research on disability and livelihood would include, of course, people with disabilities who can contribute their expertise from lived experience. They could also include employers, service providers (e.g. social workers), and policymakers and advocates. Although new to the intersection of disability and development studies, participatory research in poverty assessments has become widespread (Chambers and Conway 1991; Chambers 2007) and could be tapped into for disability and livelihood assessments. There is a variety of participatory methods that can be used flexibly, depending on local resources (Chambers 2007). The activist origins of participatory work make it highly applicable to groups such as people with disabilities who are marginalized for a range of reasons.

Interventions in the Global South

A wide range of interventions could impact the livelihoods and social protection of people with disabilities. They include targeted public and private policies and legislation, as well as programmes and projects, for example in employment (United Nation Development Programme [UNDP] 2012). Some of these have been reviewed in detail in recent publications (United Nation Development Programme [UNDP]

2012; UNESCAP 2012; Mitra and Sambamoorthi 2014), including the World Report on Disability (WHO and World Bank 2011), which reviewed interventions related to employment, education, the environment and health-care services. Many of the interventions in the North have limited applicability to the global South, however, given their high costs or the very different nature of labour markets and living environments. At the risk of generalizing the context in the global South, given that resources are very limited and that opportunities are often found in the informal sector, it appears attention is needed on programmes that are community based and in the informal sector, whether such programmes are mainstream or targeted to people with disabilities.

Social protection interventions, such as cash transfer, food for work, training and microfinance programmes, may provide an alternative road to gainful work. The microfinance movement in the global South is based on the assumption that lack of access to credit is the main constraint facing the poor in improving their livelihoods, and programmes aim to reduce this constraint by providing small loans to small businesses. As a stand-alone programme, whether mainstream or targeted, microfinance has so far been shown to have mixed results in a small but expanding body of evidence (Dyer 2003). It may be necessary to understand microfinance as just one entry point to livelihood changes and that it will be more effective if combined with other livelihood entry points (e.g. improving social capital via increasing networks for the proposed business). This will be particularly relevant to people with disabilities who face multiple livelihood challenges.

At the same time, there is limited but positive evidence that comprehensive entrepreneurship programmes can assist businesses. Such programmes provide a combination of financial literacy, micro-credit and/or insurance schemes, market analysis, business development training, counselling and marketing assistance (Cunningham et al. 2010). When targeted, they include support services that meet the needs of people with disabilities, such as medical support or rehabilitation (Munoz et al. 2010).

Microfinance and entrepreneurship programmes are largely mainstream programmes provided by non-government organizations (NGOs). It remains to be seen to what extent people with disabilities access such programmes. To the best of our knowledge, very few NGOs running mainstream livelihood-related programmes do consider disability in their monitoring and programming. One exception is Trickle Up (2013), an NGO operating in Asia, central America and west Africa which operates microenterprise programmes and targets individuals (with disabilities, among others) who are not typically reached by other microfinance organizations. It should become standard for organizations, whether providing microfinance services, cash transfers or other mainstream livelihood-related programmes, to collect disability data as part of their monitoring and evaluation systems.

There are also livelihood-related interventions that are targeted at people with disabilities, such as sheltered employment, supported employment, disability management, job-seeker assistance, and employment quotas. Common in the global South is community-based rehabilitation (CBR). Since its inception in 1970, CBR has broadened in scope and is now multidimensional with health, education and social empowerment as well as livelihood components (see Kuipers and Sabuni

2016, in this volume). CBR interventions are very broad and may address a variety of livelihood constraints, including providing supports or adaptations in the workplace, teaching skills (ILO 2008), providing employment services (e.g. job search advice, guidance to developing relationships with employers), reducing employer discrimination, and promoting positive attitudes with respect to disabled people's employment, thus encouraging a labour force of people with disabilities.

Although CBR programmes can be found in many countries in the global South, evidence of their impact in general and on livelihood outcomes in particular is scarce and inconclusive. Some recent evidence is encouraging. A quantitative study by Biggeri et al. (2013) finds a positive effect on the well-being of people with disabilities, and particularly on their social capital, with increased participation within the family and society at large. Additionally, an emancipatory and participatory study by Deepak and colleagues (2014) had a similar result with CBR promoting collective action among people with disabilities and facilitating access to existing supports. Such evaluations remain scarce, however, and most of the study designs are inadequate for rigorous impact evaluation. A review of CBR evaluations by Sharma (2007) covered 21 studies published in peer-reviewed journals, with different methodologies. Only two studies used a randomized control trial design, six studies used a quasi-experimental design, and only one study measured the costs of the programme. Of course, CBR interventions are complex to evaluate in that they include multiple components of livelihoods. Such evaluations are resource intensive, which perhaps explains the dearth of evidence in this area. Further research is needed to evaluate the impact of CBR programmes on livelihoods and of other targeted interventions, such as the supply of assistive devices or vocational training.

Conclusion

To conclude, we describe what we perceive to be imperatives for policy and programmes, research and data in order to contribute to the improvement of livelihoods for people with disabilities.

Policy and Programme Imperatives

This chapter has identified a number of areas where action is needed to improve the livelihoods of people with disabilities. In particular, little is known on the extent to which they access livelihood-related policies and programmes (e.g. microfinance, disaster management, health) and how social protection programmes address disability. Although it is difficult to measure disability, a lot of progress has been made. It should become standard for organizations with mainstream livelihood-related programmes to collect disability data as part of their monitoring and evaluation systems.

In addition, little has been written about how mainstream programmes can be adapted to accommodate disability and counteract inequality. Some of these adjustments seem common sense and require a universal design of services. These can be at low cost in some cases, instead requiring awareness among management and staff for the adjustment to be made (e.g. movable ramps for buildings, training to change attitudes). Other adaptations, particularly those around reasonable accommodation, may need further thought and innovative ideas to suit resource-poor settings (and where assistive devices and assistant staff are expensive, for example). Policy needs to address the tension between disability accommodation and resource constraints in these settings and needs to include innovations in workplace legislation.

Research Imperatives

There is a need to conceptualize a comprehensive 'disability-orientated' livelihoods framework investigating all five capitals and not just isolated elements of the livelihoods concept (e.g. income, health, education). A livelihoods framework would allow disability research to analyse potential points of intervention holistically, and through this provide the pathway for innovative interventions that might enhance livelihoods among those experiencing, or vulnerable to, disability in the global South.

There is also a need to develop, pilot and evaluate targeted livelihood interventions for people with disabilities as well as inclusive practices in mainstream programmes. Community-based and informal programmes warrant more attention given the generally limited resources and areas of opportunity in the global South. Additionally, programmes that address multiple livelihood components such as CBR are promising, whereas those that address a single constraint (e.g. technical training) may not be sufficient. Very little evidence is available on CBR and, more generally, on livelihood programmes, whether mainstream or targeted, that are aimed at improving outcomes in the global South. Evidence-building is much needed to determine the impact of specific interventions and their relative effectiveness and cost.

A Call for Data

Little of the action or research imperatives noted earlier can take place without more data.

Disability indicators need to become standard in household surveys in the global South, as well as in the monitoring systems of NGOs and governments, to inform the development of disability-inclusive policies and programmes (see Eide and Loeb 2016, in this volume). More data collection and analysis, whether qualitative or quantitative, is also needed for strengthening disability-inclusive policies, programmes and research more generally, but particularly those focusing on the strengthening of livelihoods. The use of the Washington Group on Disability Statistics recommended questions on disability in surveys and monitoring systems would provide some of the necessary data in the global South. Given the scarcity of resources for research and evaluations in the global South in general, and on livelihoods and disability in particular, international development agencies have an important role in laying the seed for disability inclusion through funding and promoting the collection of data on disability in the global South.

References

Baldwin, M., & Johnson, W. G. (2005). *A critical review of studies of discrimination against workers with disabilities*. Cheltenham: Edward-Elgar.

Bebbington, A. (1999). Capitals and capabilities: A framework for analyzing peasant viability, rural livelihoods and poverty. *World Development, 27*(12), 2021–2044.

Biggeri, M., Deepak, S., Mauro, V., Trani, J., Kumar, J., & Ramasamy, P. (2013). Do community-based rehabilitation programmes promote the participation of persons with disabilities? A case control study from Mandya district, in India. *Disability and Rehabilitation,* 1–10. doi:10.3109/09638288.2013.823244.

Buckup, S. (2009). *The price of exclusion: The economic consequences of excluding people with disabilities from the world of work.* Geneva: International Labour Office (ILO).

Chambers, R. (2007). Participation and poverty. *Development, 50*(2), 20–25.

Chambers, R., & Conway, G. R. (1991). *Sustainable rural livelihoods: Practical concepts for the 21st century IDS discussion paper 296.* Brighton: IDS.

Chirawu, P., Hanass-Hancock, J., Aderemi, T., de Reus, L., & Henken, A. (2014). Protect or enable? Teacher's beliefs and practices regarding provision of sexuality education to learners with disability in KwaZulu-Natal, South Africa. *Sexuality and Disability, 32*(1).

Cunningham, W., Sanchez-Puerta, M., & Wuermli, A. (2010). Active labor market programs for youth: Teaching entrepreneurship: Impact of business training on microfinance clients and institutions. *Review of Economics and Statistics, 93*(2), 510–527.

Czechowicz, J., Messner, A., Alarcon-Matutti, E., Alarcon, J., Quinones-Calderon, G., Montano, S., et al. (2010). Hearing impairment and poverty: The epidemiology of ear disease in Peruvian schoolchildren. *Otolaryngology-Head and Neck Surgery, 142*(2), 272–277.

Deepak, S., Kumar, J., Ramasamy, P., & Griffo, G. (2014). An emancipatory research on CBR and the barriers faced by persons with disabilities. *Disability and Rehabilitation, 36*(18), 1502–1507. doi:10.3109/09638288.2013.800914.

DHAT. (2014). DHAT think tank report: Disability, HIV/AIDS and sexual and reproductive health and rights. In DHAT & SAT (Eds.), Harare.

Dhungana, B. (2006). The lives of disabled women in Nepal: Vulnerability without support. *Disability & Society, 21*(2), 133–146.

Dyer, S. (Ed.). (2003). Credit is a need and a right: Inclusive policy and practice in micro finance: Mobility international.

Eide, A. H., & Loeb, M. (2016). Counting disabled people: Historical perspectives and the challenges of disability statistics. In S. Grech & K. Soldatic (Eds.), *Disability in the global South: The critical handbook.* New York: Springer.

Farrington, J., Carney, D., Ashley, C., & Turton, C. (1999). *Sustainable livelihoods in practice: Early applications of concepts in rural areas natural resource perspectives* (vol. 42).

Filmer, D. (2008). Disability, poverty, and schooling in developing countries: Results from 14 household surveys. *The World Bank Economic Review, 22*(1), 141–163.

Fleisch, B., Shindler, J., & Parry, H. (2012). Who is out of school? Evidence from the Statistics South Africa Community Survey. *International Journal of Educational Development, 21*, 529–536.

Frohmader, C., & Ortoleva, S. (2013). *He sexual and reproductive rights of women and girls with disabilities*. Paper presented at the International Conference on Population and Development: Beyond, Geneva.

Gilbert, C. E., Shah, S. P., Jadoon, M. Z., Bourne, R., Dineen, B., & Khan, M. A. et al. (2008). Poverty and blindness in Pakistan: Results from the Pakistan national blindness and visual impairment survey. *British Medical Journal, 336*(7634), 29–32.

Groce, N. E., Amy Farkas, M. K., Schultink, W., & Bieler, R. B. (2013). Inclusive nutrition for children and adults with disabilities. *The Lancet, 1*, 180–181.

Groce, N. E., Kembhavi, G., Wirz, S., Lang, R., Trani, J.-F., & Kett, M. (2011). *Poverty and disability—A critical review of the literature in low and middle-income countries: UCL*. London: Leonard Cheshire Disability and Inclusive Development Centre.

Hanass-Hancock, J. (2009). Disability and HIV/AIDS—A systematic review of literature in Africa. *Journal of the International AIDS Society, 12*(34). doi:10.1186/1758-2652-12-34

Hanass-Hancock, J., & Casale, M. (2014). An exploratory model to illustrate the interrelationship between HIV, disability and care giving in southern Africa. *Journal of the Association of Nurses in AIDS Care, 25*(4), 351–363.

ICDR, DHAT, & HEARD. (2011). *Sepo Study Report*. Toronto: ICDR.

ILO. (2008). *Skills training through community based rehabilitation (CBR): A good practice guide*. Geneva: ILO.

Ingstad, B., & Grut, L. (2007). *Seeme, and do not forget me. People with disabilities in Kenya SINTEF Health Research*. Norway: SITEF.

IRP. (n. d.). Intervention strategy for sustainable livelihood recovery and selected case studies. In IRP (Ed.), *Unknown: International recovery platform (IRP)*.

Izumi, K. (2007). *"Forgotten Gifts"—Children with disabilities in Zimbabwe*.

Kagee. (2014). Do disability grants influence adherence to antiretroviral therapy? *African Journal of Disability, 3*(1), 6. doi:10.4102/ajod.v4103i4101.4100

Kiani, S. (2009). Women with disabilities in the north west province of Cameroon: Resilient and deserving of greater attention. *Disability & Society, 24*(4), 517–531.

Kuipers, P., & Sabuni, L. P. (2016). Community-based rehabilitation and disability-inclusive development: On a winding path to an uncertain destination. In S. Grech & K. Soldatic (Eds.), *Disability in the global South: The critical handbook*. New York: Springer.

Kuper, H., Solomon, A. W., Buchan, J., Zondervan, M., Foster, A., & Mabey, D. (2003). A critical review of the SAFE strategy for the prevention of blinding trachoma. *The Lancet Infectious Diseases, 3*(6), 372–381. doi:10.1016/S1473-3099(03)00659-5

Leach, M., Mearns, R., & Scoones, I. (1997). *Challenges to community based sustainable development: Dynamics, entitlements, institutions IDS Bulletin*. London: Institute of Development Studies.

Li, N., Pang, L., Du, W., Chen, G., & Zheng, X. (2012). Association between poverty and psychiatric disability among Chinese population aged 15-64 years. *Psychiatry Research, 200*(2–3), 917–920. doi:10.1016/j.psychres.2012.05.026.

Loeb, M. (2004). *Living conditions among people with activity limitations in Malawi*. Malawi: A National Representative Study.

Loeb, M., Eide, A. H., Jelsma, J., Mzolisi Ka, T., & Maart, S. (2013). Poverty and disability in Eastern and Western Cape Provinces, South Africa. *Disability & Society, 23*(4), 311–321.

Macgregor, H. (2006). 'The Grant is What I Eat': The politics of social security and disability in the post-apartheid South African State. *Journal of Biosocial Science, 38*(1), 43–55.

Misselhorn, A. A. (2009). *Is a focus on social capital useful in considering food security interventions? Insights from KwaZulu Nata*. Development Southern Africa.

Mitra, S., & Sambamoorthi, U. (2008). Disability and the rural labor market in India: Evidence for males in Tamil Nadu. *World Development, 36*(5), 934–952.

Mitra, S., & Sambamoorthi, U. (2014). Disability prevalence among adults: Estimates for 54 countries and progress toward a global estimate. *Disability & Rehabilitation*.

Mizunoya, S., & Mitra, S. (2013). Is there a disability gap in employment rates in developing countries? World development. *Elsevier, 42*(C), 28–43.

Munoz, W., Last, U., & Kimsean, T. (2010). *Good practices from the project: Towards sustainable income generating activities for mine victim and other persons with disabilities in Cambodia Employment challenges and success.*

Narayan, D., Patel, K., Schafft, A., Rademacher, & Kocj-Schulte, S. (2000). *Couves of the poor Volume 2 Can anyone hear us?* (vol. 2). New York: Oxford University Press for the World Bank.

National Treasury & South African Revenue Service. (2013). *2013 tax statistics*. Pretoria: National Treasury and SARS.

Nattrass, N. (2005). AIDS, unemployment and disability in South Africa: The case for welfare reform. *Southern African Journal for AIDS Medicine, 20*, 30–32.

Nokrek, P., Alam, M. A., & Muzzafar, A. (2013). *Livelihood challenges for extremely poor disabled people in the southwest coastal region of Bangladesh.* Shiree Working Paper No. 12. Dhaka, Bangladesh: Shiree.

OECD. (2003). *Towards more and better jobs: OECD Employment Outlook.*

Phaswana-Mafuya, N., Peltzer, K., & Petros, S. G. (2009). Disability grant for people living with HIV/AIDS in the Eastern Cape of South Africa. *Social Work in Health Care, 48*(5), 533–550.

Rohleder, P., & Swartz, L. (2012). Disability, sexuality and sexual health. In P. Aggleton, P. Boyce, H. L. Moore, & P. Richard (Eds.), *Understanding global sexualities: New frontiers* (pp. 138–152). London: Routledge.

Schneider, M., Graham, L., & Mokomane, Z. (2016). Social protection, chronic poverty and disability: Applying an intersectionality perspective. In S. Grech & K. Soldatic (Eds.), *Disability in the global South: The critical handbook.* New York: Springer.

Scoones, I. (1998). *Sustainable rural livelihoods: A framework for analysis.* IDS Working Paper 72. Brighten: Institute for Development Studies United Kingdom.

Shahnavaz, H. (1987). Workplace injuries in the developing countries. *Ergonomics, 30*(2), 397–404. doi:10.1080/00140138708969725.

Sharma, M. (2007). Evaluation in community based rehabilitation programmes: A strengths, weaknesses, opportunities and threats analysis. *Asia Pacific Disability Rehabilitation Journal, 18*(1), 46–62.

Snyman, A. E. (2009). *Factors with regard to the Attainment of Workplace Equality as perceived by People with Disabilities (Master).* University of South Africa, Johannesburg.

Soldatic, K. (2013). Appointment time: Disability and neoliberal workfare temporalities. *Critical Sociology, 39*(3), 405–419.

Spurway, K., & Griffiths, T. (2016). Disability-inclusive disaster risk reduction: Vulnerability and resilience discourses, policies and practices. In S. Grech & K. Soldatic (Eds.), *Disability in the global South: The critical handbook.* New York: Springer.

Swartz, L., & Bantjes, J. (2016). Disability and global health. In S. Grech & K. Soldatic (Eds.), *Disability in the global South: The critical handbook.* New York: Springer.

Trickle Up. (2013). *Disability, poverty and livelihoods: Guidance from Trickle Up.* Retrieved May 12, 2015, from http://www.trickleup.org/media/publications/loader.cfm?csModule=security/getfile&pageid=5056.

UN Convention on the Rights of Persons with Disabilities (2006).

UNESCAP. (2012). *Disability, livelihood and poverty in Asia and the Pacific.* An executive summary of research findings. Thailand: United Nations Economic and Social Commission for Asia and the Pacific (UNESCAP).

UNESCO. (2010). *EFA Global Monitoring Report 2010. Reaching the marginalized.* Oxford: Oxford University Press.

United Nation Development Programme [UNDP]. (2012). *Livelihood opportunities for persons with disabilities*. India: UNDP.

United Nations. (2011). Rural population, development and the environment. Department of Economic and Social Affairs. Retrieved May 1, 2012, from http://www.un.org/esa/population/publications/2011RuralPopDevEnv_Chart/ruralpopdevenv2011wallchart.html

Van der Heijden, I. (2014). *What works to prevent violence against women with disabilities.* Pretoria: What Works to Prevent Violence, Medical Research Council of South Africa.

Victoria, C., Wagstaff, A., Schellenberg, J., Gwatkin, D., Claeson, M., & Habicht, J. (2003). Applying an equity lens to child health and mortality: More of the same is not enough. *The Lancet, 362*, 233–241.

Walker-Bone, K., & Palmer, K. (2002). Musculoskeletal disorders in farmers and farm workers. *Occupational Medicine, 52*(8), 441–450.

WHO and World Bank. (2011). *World report on disability*. Geneva: World Health Organization.

Wickenden, M., & Elphick, J. (2016). Don't forget us, we are here too! Listening to disabled children and their families living in poverty. In S. Grech & K. Soldatic (Eds.), *Disability in the global South: The critical handbook*. New York: Springer.

Wisner, B., Blaikie, P., Cannon, T., & Davis, I. (2003). *At risk: Natural hazards, people's vulnerabilities and disasters* (2nd ed.). Abingdon: Routledge.

Yoshida, K., Hanass-Hancock, J., Nixon, S., & Bond, V. (2014). Using Intersectionality to Explore Experiences of Disability and HIV among Women and Men in Zambia. *Disability and Rehabilitation*.

Chapter 10
Begging and Disability: A Paradigmatic Way to Earn One's Living

Carolina Ferrante and Eduardo Joly

In the 21st century, to speak sociologically about begging as a survival strategy among those with disabilities sounds incongruent. Associating begging with disability seems more like the kind of segregation suffered by those with disabilities during the Middle Ages (Stiker 2000), evidencing the stigmatizing nature of what is currently understood as a deficiency from a biomedical perspective in western culture (Goffman 2001).

Today in Argentina, as throughout Latin America as a whole, there seems to be consensus that the symbolic struggles carried forth by the disability rights movement over the past four decades have succeeded in establishing disability as a matter of human rights, thereby dismantling previously dominant perspectives, such as assistance-dependent, charitable, and/or medical approaches (Rosales 2013).

In the sphere of local studies on disability one encounters optimism with regards to the living conditions of this minority, associated with the ratification of international treaties, such as the Inter-American Convention for the Elimination of All Forms of Discrimination against Persons with Disabilities (incorporated by Argentina in 2000 by virtue of Law 25.280) and the United Nations Convention on the Rights of Persons with Disabilities (ratified by Argentina via Law 26.378; hereupon CRPD). According to the UN, the CRPD would represent a "paradigm shift in attitudes and approaches towards persons with disabilities" (UN 2006). Such a "paradigm shift" is associated with the assumption of a perspective on disability that is rooted in what Mike Oliver (1998) calls the social model of disability. This model,

C. Ferrante (✉)
CONICYT-FONDECYT, Universidad Católica del Norte, Antofagasta, Chile
e-mail: caferrante@gmail.com

E. Joly
Fundación Rumbos, Buenos Aires, Argentina
e-mail: ejoly@rumbos.org.ar

S. Grech, K. Soldatic (eds.), *Disability in the Global South*,
International Perspectives on Social Policy, Administration, and Practice,
DOI 10.1007/978-3-319-42488-0_10

as conceived by a group of Anglo-Saxon people with disabilities in the 1970s, understands disability as a socio-political problem (Barnes 1998). Analytically, it distinguishes two dimensions: deficiency or impairment—understood as biophysical conditions of a personal nature—and disability—understood as the social disadvantage generated by a society that does not take into account people with impairments and thereby oppresses them (Barnes 1998). From this perspective, disability is no longer understood as a religious or medical concern, as was prevalent up till then, but rather as a creation intrinsic to capitalist societies (Palacios 2008). Designed with reference to the capable body, these societies erect physical and social barriers that restrict the participation of people with disabilities (Oliver 1998). Thereby, according to the social model of disability, in order to guarantee respect for this minority one must design policies that are capable of transforming the social structures that hinder participation.

Conceiving of disability as a socially construed problem, the CRPD promotes measures that would tear down those structures and achieve the inclusion of this minority. The change in perspective leads many authors to conclude that the conception of disability as a body in need of medical and/or social assistance is bygone (Eroles 2005; Acuña and Bulit Goñi 2010); nowadays, with the CRPD the most fashionable terms are respect, inclusion, and entitlement to rights.

Yet, even though in recent years one can observe significant formal advances in the struggle for recognition of people with disabilities, one can hardly assert that such a viewpoint has taken root in the social arena and in personal subjectivities. When focusing on the living conditions of these people, one cannot claim that inclusion has materialized in their everyday realities. The basic statistical data on the socioeconomic situation of this minority (i.e., highest educational level attained and occupation) was collected before the CRPD was sanctioned into law and has not been updated since (this data belongs to the National Disability Survey, carried out by the National Institute of Statistics and Census between 2002 and 2003). And the local shadow report on the country's application of the CRPD, drafted by organizations of people with disabilities, denounces non-compliance on most of its measures and with regard to laws currently in force (REDI et al. 2012).

Along these lines, and based on qualitative research in the city of Buenos Aires, we note that people with disabilities live their everyday lives in a world where "no" reigns supreme (Scribano 2009); that is, where one cannot get a job, nor an education, nor get around town, nor participate socially (Venturiello 2010; Ferrante 2012).

In this scenario, inclusion is but science fiction. And one need not have a disability or conduct research to take note of this reality. Any car driver in the capital city of Argentina, any subway or train passenger on her way to work, will come across people with disabilities claiming their fate to be a personal medical tragedy (Oliver 1998) that excludes them from society and drives them to plead for financial assistance, alongside other poor people begging for handouts. In the micro-scenario of giving and receiving alms by virtue of having a disability, we will find that the perception of disability as a personal medical problem is quite alive. Those who beg for alms because they have a disability, as well as those who give, tacitly accept that disability is an unfortunate matter affecting the body, which justifies lending social assistance. In this respect, we are quite far from the discourse that highlights awareness of people with disabilities and respect for their dignity. In the practice of begging "because one has a disability" we encounter a form of mercantilization of social contempt,[1] where stigma becomes justifiable as it proves that one is an authentically poor person (Bauman 2008).

Far from adhering to a notion that claims there is an essence to disability, we believe that the widespread resort to charity towards people with disabilities—emblematically revealed in begging for alms—as well as the cynicism present in the double discourse on their situation, speak of social relations associated with modes of domination promoted by capitalism. These social relations erect new forms of vulnerability, observable in the intersection between the global South and disability, bringing to the fore what is referred to as the new social question. In this context, the language of rights would seem insufficient to reverse the structural foundations of these new forms of vulnerability (Rosanvallón 2007). To advance this working hypothesis, which refutes the diagnosis of a paradigm shift, we will address the following questions: What is the rationale whereby lower class people with disabilities in a peripheral capitalist setting think of begging as "business"? What "explains" the generous disposition of those who "give" alms to others because they "have" a disability? What does the spectacle of a disabled body, as an invalid unfortunate recipient, tell us about the social relations promoted within today's capitalism in a country belonging to the global South and about the challenges facing the CRPD to materialize inclusion?

To address these questions we will rely on a critical reconsideration of the theoretical contributions of the Anglo-Saxon social model of disability,[2] on the sociology of the body and the emotions, and on empirical data gathered in qualitative research conducted in Buenos Aires.[3] This research entailed nine in-depth interviews with people with motor disabilities who beg, aged between 33 and 62 years old, and 10 in-depth interviews with adults who give alms.[4] Fieldwork was conducted between April and July 2013 at traffic lights, at subway and train stations, and at avenues in different spots of the city where people with disabilities beg.[5]

---

[1] The notion of social contempt, also known as social disrespect, is developed by Honneth (1993) when referring to privation, denial or disentitlement of rights.

[2] Disability Studies constitutes an unorthodox group of critical studies about disability that emerged in the 1970s in the Anglo-Saxon world, oriented to think about this problematic as cultural rhetoric (Skliar 2002).

[3] This research is entitled 'Begging practices and modes of domination among adults with acquired motor disabilities in today's City of Buenos Aires' and was conducted by Carolina Ferrante, financed by the Consejo Nacional de Investigaciones Científicas y Técnicas via a post-doctoral fellowship (2012–2014) at the Instituto de Ciencias de la Rehabilitación y el Movimiento, Universidad Nacional de San Martín.

[4] In order to preserve the confidentiality of respondents, we have used pseudonyms for their names. All gave their informed consent to participate in this study. Responses were translated into English by the authors.

[5] When we talk about begging we exclusively refer to begging for alms or handouts, and we do not include the homeless.

Begging: A "Chosen" Means of Life or "Amor Fati"?

On a cold winter morning in 2013, Javier, a 37-year-old man with a motor disability, who completed secondary school education, begs in one of the richest neighborhoods of Buenos Aires, seated on the ground with his crutches next to him and a sign that reads "I am disabled." He talks about how this practice became his means of survival:

> I do this on my own free will … The good thing about the street is that it always taught me to manage on my own, independently, the street taught me to get by. … Another good thing about the street is making money real easy, and that on a good day of work, like I say, you can make as much as 300 pesos. That's why I saw the 'business of pulling on someone's sleeve'[6] in a news bulletin and said to myself yes, it's like that, this is like a business, because a person comes and gives you a handout, even though there are people who use crutches but don't really need them, and because of them we all wind up losing.

Along similar lines, 48-year-old Andrés, who has polio sequels, and with elementary school education, asks for money from his wheelchair at a traffic light in the upper middle-class neighborhood of Palermo. He points out:

> Here I solely depend on myself; at a regular job I would have a boss, someone who would boss me around; here I'm independent, the work depends on me, I depend on myself alone, the work depends on my will, my charisma and my effort. Many disabled have jobs where they are taken in just to say 'I've got a disabled employee' and they kind of have them hidden in a corner. I don't like that because I'm a normal and regular guy.

For those who beg and have a disability, begging is clearly a form of self-employment, or a business venture in which they appeal to the "help" of people or to their sense of "solidarity." As narrated by respondents, this insistent begging for alms or handouts implies a certain degree of protection of one's honor, where one monetarily exploits the stigmatized body as a spectacle, extracting for oneself the surplus value of guilt generated in the other, without providing anything in return. That is why, according to respondents, begging for alms allows them to access "easy money." According to Marcelo Silberkasten (2006), the right to beg is the only right that has remained unaltered over time for people with disabilities and he names this legacy as the ideology of charity.

Far from constituting a chosen destiny, however, the exercise of begging among people with disabilities both entraps and subjects them within a relation of domination masked by the form of the body's deficit. Such an entrapping practice speaks of a lack of symmetry established by the state's definition of disability, as we shall see further on. When Pierre Bourdieu (1991) addresses how symbolic power or, more precisely, how a mode of symbolic violence is embodied, he speaks of *amor fati*, that is of love of destiny, of resigned acceptance of the conditionings associated with the assumption of arbitrary cultural and historical mores. To understand such conditionings one must analyze the links between capitalism, body politics, disability, and the production of "lumpenized subjectivities" (Bourgois 2010).

---

[6] "To pull on someone's sleeve," in Spanish *tirar de la manga*, is a popular expression in Argentina that means: "to request a loan of money insistently or take advantage of circumstances" (Academia Argentina de Letras 2008: 427). In that sense, the "business of pulling on someone's sleeve" refers to asking for alms or handouts associated with disability.

Capitalism, Body Politics, Disability, and Lumpenized Subjectivities

According to data in the World Report on Disability (WHO and World Bank 2011), about 15 per cent of the world's population has some kind of disability, and within that population 80 per cent is poor and unemployed. To understand these figures one must read them within the framework of the system of social relations in which they express themselves, that is, to interpret them within the context of contemporary capitalism.

In post-Fordist capitalist societies—characterized by job insecurity, competitiveness and inequality (Castel 2004—the pauperization of living conditions generates disability (Nabergoi and Bottinelli 2007). Hunger, violence, wars, addictions, and poor living and working conditions differentially disable the most deprived individual bodies.

In turn, and as demonstrated by the Anglo-Saxon social model of disability, bearing a visible disability that connotes distance from the capable body—and is thus presumed to be unproductive and incapable (Oliver 1998)—leads to the social exclusion of people with disabilities (Barnes 2008). Far from constituting a personal medical problem, a disability implies a relation of domination derived from a distancing of the disabled body from the parameters that define the "legitimate body" (Bourdieu 1991). Thus, the disabled body tenses those values that promote the social division of labor in the current stage of capitalism: the body's flexibility, presumed independence, performance in accordance with criteria of economic profitability, normality as biomedically defined, and beauty as joviality as established by the mass media (Scheper-Huges and Lock 1986).

Poverty and disability in the global South allow us to make visible some aspects privy to the Anglo-Saxon social model that demand rethinking and which have in recent decades been critically addressed within this model (Shakespeare and Watson 1995; Hughes and Paterson 2008; Morris 2008; Shakespeare 2013).

First of all, it becomes evident that the foundational difference between deficiency and disability posited in the Anglo-Saxon social model masks the ties between poverty and disability in the global South. Disability and deficiency mask an ideology that reifies an apparent normality which classifies useful and useless bodies, and deserving and non-deserving poor, and which legitimizes relations of domination (Rosato et al. 2009).

Second, we can no longer think, as was the case in the early days of the social model, that the disability experience is one of homogeneous oppression. Social class, gender, nationality, and context singularize the actual experience of disability. In this respect, Erving Goffman (2001) pointed out that stigma, more than an attribute, alludes to a language of relations, where the observer and the observed matter. In the case of begging, it is quite evident how this social interaction is possible in the context of other conditions allowed for in the forms that capitalist domination assumes in the global South.

Third, the theory of domination present in the Anglo-Saxon social model seems to impose a rather mechanical and omnipotent perspective, forgetting that it is only possible insofar as it counts on the complicity of the social agents involved

(Bourdieu 1991). This leads us to pay attention not only to the adjustments that reproduce domination (highlighting those social conditions that favor the development of specific subjectivities), but also to the resistances, inflections, and lack of a "perfect" domination.

In order to explore these elements and exploit the full potential of the materialist approach of the Anglo-Saxon social model, we introduce the theoretical discussion on the disabled body as indispensable in analyzing the links between capitalism and poverty in the global South (Shakespeare 2013). Here, Adrián Scribano's (2009, 2010) contributions to the sociology of the body and of the emotions allows us to consider that both the material consequences and the stigmatizing nature of disability are the result of the politics of bodies inherent in today's capitalism, insofar as they unveil the "strategies that a society accepts in order to respond to the social availability of individuals as part of the social structuring of power" (Scribano 2009: 1). These accompany the politics of emotions, which are influenced by the mechanisms that regulate sensations and by the mechanisms of social tolerance (Scribano 2010). The former allow organizing, categorizing, and classifying emotions, thereby configuring social sensibilities. The latter allow for systematic avoidance of social conflict.

The relations between capitalism and disability are masked by the ideology of normality (Rosato et al. 2009). This ideology, which relies on a hegemonic medical perspective of disability, naturalizes disability as a personal medical problem, derived from the body's distancing from what is understood to be the "normal" body, thereby masking the situation of oppression—inseparable from the capitalist mode of production—that legitimizes what is biomedically understood as a body defect or flaw, which in turn appears as the rhetoric used for social segregation. Thus, a desired normality stands in opposition to a rejected abnormality (Foucault 2000). An exciting, useful, beautiful, and healthy body that can be exhibited to the world stands in opposition to an isolated, boring, useless, ugly, and sick body.

Regarding these principles of appreciation, the state, as the guarantor of the asymmetrical relations associated with capitalism, plays a fundamental role insofar as it officially validates a concept of disability as personal deficit. By implementing authentic politics of disablement (Oliver 1998), such as officially certifying a disability, the state provides a biological basis to legitimize disability as a state of exception from working. Such a state or condition enables the person to receive social assistance (Rosato et al. 2009) without providing any kind of compensation in return.

Therefore, by assuming disability to be a medical tragedy (Oliver 2008), state policies produce schemes of perception (Bourdieu 1991) that generate domination and social contempt of people with disabilities (Rosato et al. 2009). By assuming that bearing a "disabled body" is an undesirable destiny, the figure of disability is created, whereby the "disabled" is "compensated" in his unchosen disadvantage, which precludes him from working.

Earlier we claimed that one of the inherent features of current capitalism is its segregating nature and inequality, whereby those bodies that cannot adapt to the needs described as constituent of the legitimate body, join the lists of "supernumerary individuals," that is, surplus population individuals (Castel 2004; Joly and Venturiello

2012). Within this group, people with disabilities are considered authentically poor: they are excluded not because they are "vagabonds" and don't want to work, but because they cannot work.

Paradoxically, within such a broad social category such as "the poor," disability becomes a subcategory that accounts for the deserving poor (Rosato et al. 2009)—those that inspire a kind of moral obligation (Bauman 2008). Thus, the official construction of disability carries with it a set of "symbolic gains" that imply the embodiment of symbolic violence (Bourdieu 1991). This incorporation implies recognition of the disabled as the carrier of a biological deficit, as well as ignorance of the arbitrary nature of the "disabled body" when its historical and social nature is acknowledged and therefore legitimized. By means of a set of compensatory policies, the domination of people with disabilities is produced and reproduced. In this web, the complex relations between capitalism, social class and state policies generate "lumpenized subjectivities" (Bourgois 2010). Within this politics of bodies and emotions, the ideology of normality becomes a mechanism that regulates sensations (Scribano 2009), which taxonomizes the disabled body as "sensibility at fault" (Cervio and D'hers 2012). This ideology permeates and manifests as what is commonsense in institutions, in the mass media and even among people with disability. As a formed identity, this sensibility is self-perceived as "disabled," as someone who needs to "be given" things or "helped" by virtue of a bodily disadvantage that does not allow him or her to participate in regular exchanges, and is thus exempt from having to give anything in return or in compensation (Silberkasten 2006).

The analysis so far allows one to infer that disability is a socially construed problematic that is exacerbated by the growing processes of globalization associated with capitalism today, especially in peripheral contexts. This mode of production generates a dynamic in which poverty disables and disability impoverishes even further (Joly 2008). As a result, lower-class people with disabilities must resort to social charity to survive (Barnes 2008). This charity manifests itself under four non-exclusive streams (Joly 2008): the transfer of family income, social security, assistance provided by religious and charitable institutions, and the development of begging.

"Opting" for this last strategy within a marginal economy (Bourgois 2010; Epele 2010) becomes a "job," which in formalizing begging for alms—exploiting the sense of pity in others and highlighting the social perception of the disabled body—mercantilizes and transforms social contempt into a means to earn a living (Honneth 1993). Whereas this image harks back to the Middle Ages and the institutionalization of begging among people with disabilities, it actually puts what is known as the "new social question" in center stage (Rosanvallón 2007). Just as the dysfunctions of 19th-century industrial society led to the social question and to the recognition of social rights, the regressive phenomena associated with contemporary capitalism, which reminds us of bygone crises, actually reveal "the failure of the concept of social rights as capable of offering a satisfactory framework within which to think the situation of [today's] excluded" (Pérez Sosto 2005: 19).

More precisely, the notion of a marginal economy refers to a set of processes that

> make use of and extract the material and human resources from vulnerable populations, which become profitable and extractable due to the inequality and vulnerability generated

> by the expropriation of the minimal conditions of traditional wellbeing that, in turn, was carried out in order to deliver wellbeing and the common good. (Epele 2010: 51)

Thus, disability becomes a label that "biologizes" a situation of social inequality and generates new modes of domination.

All Roads Lead to "The Street"

As discussed, the recurrence of begging results from a previous situation of inequality and vulnerability that is not visible when disability functions as justification for social exclusion and as deserving of commiserative responses from others.

State policies regarding disability in Argentina, and derived from the 1981 law *System of Comprehensive Protection of the Disabled* (22.431), limit themselves to: (1) carry out medical rehabilitation of the deficit, and (2) deliver a series of secondary benefits (free travel passes, pensions, exemption from paying import duties for cars) which, though legally acknowledged, are exceptionally exercised (Acuña and Bulit Goñi 2010). The spirit of this law is rooted in a conception of disability as a personal deficit to be rehabilitated, and in which the individual must seek to become normal in order to 'integrate himself' in society. This law hardly emphasizes the removal of disabling barriers; the available social benefits are to compensate the individual for his disadvantaged situation (as seen previously). Regarding work, this law timidly demands a job quota whereby 4 per cent of government jobs must be filled by disabled people, but according to non-government organizations that advocate for the rights of people with disabilities, compliance hardly reaches 1 per cent. Notably, this law was passed during the most recent military dictatorship and replaced law 20.923, passed by the Peronist government in October 1974 (Bregain 2012). Law 20.923, drafted by the National Socioeconomic Union of the Crippled, set a job quota whereby the government and private firms had to make up no less than 4 per cent of their labor force with 'disabled' people (Bregain 2012). This law also stipulated the creation of a National Commission of the Disabled, under the Ministry of Labor, composed of, among others, representatives of organizations of people with disabilities with the mandate to penalize those institutions that failed to comply with the job quota, a feature that is absent from law 22.431, which does not specify how this article is supposed to be implemented (Bregain 2012). Law 20.923 was never actually enforced and was among the first laws to be repealed by the dictatorship, which argued that to force a job quota for the disabled would infringe on the market's freedom (Bregain 2012). Repealing this 'disruptive' law was in tune with the neoliberal ideology of the military dictatorship.

In fact, law 22.431, which still rules over the fate of people with disabilities in Argentina, is rooted in a miserable conception of disability, wherein the person with a disability is a member of the 'deserving poor'. The incorporation of the CRPD has not led to substantial changes to this lack of recognition of people with disabilities. As a result of these politics of disablement in Argentina, and despite there being no up-to-date government data, organizations of people with disabilities estimate that 80 per cent of people with disabilities in the country are unemployed (Castillo Orué et al. 2013).

Bearing in mind that a non-contributive disability pension amounts to 1200 pesos (which amounts to 37.5 per cent of the minimum wage established in 2013), and in the context of a prevailing informal job market and labor flexibilization, it is not surprising that people with disabilities who hardly have an education are excluded from the job market and must resort to begging as a strategy to survive. By way of example, we have José, a young man aged 33, with amputations on all four extremities, who has completed secondary schooling and is from San Luis, a province in the Cuyo region, located in the central west of Argentina. He moved to the city of Buenos Aires 9 years earlier intent on rising socially but wound up begging on the streets:

> The fact is that not only those who govern but also businessmen label you as disabled simply because you are in a wheelchair, are deaf, blind or have minor mobility problems; they discard you, they turn you into a disabled person … They label you as totally disabled.

For José, as for other lower class people with disabilities without a university education, obtaining formal work in a highly competitive context, as characterizes late capitalism, is a complex feat. José narrates those difficulties:

> When I arrived from San Luis I started looking for a job and discovered I couldn't, not because I was in a wheelchair, not because the offices were up a staircase, but merely because they didn't want me. So I asked myself, what should I do? Should I go back to my hometown, lock myself in and sit and watch life roll by? Or should I resort to what they can't close down? … the streets … and here I am … without a life, working from eight in the morning to eight at night, to make just enough to eat and pay for my daughter's diapers. … The solution they denied me, I sought for myself, and found it on my own, and people deliver …

The persistence of miserable state policies, via governmental certification of disabilities, turns the disabled body into a body that is useless in the labor process. Fernando, a young man aged 30, completed elementary schooling. He acquired a triple amputation when he was nine years old after falling off the rooftop of a moving train while under the influence of drugs[7]:

> According to my disability certificate I'm 100 per cent disabled, which means that for the certificate I should be lying in bed, incapable of using the remote control to switch channels … do you get it? And that's precisely why it's tough to find a job, because nobody can employ me … How are they going to employ someone who is 100 per cent disabled, meaning he can't manage on his own? … It's up to me to accept and stick with this 100 per cent or find other means.

Along the same lines, 48-year-old Jorge, who has polio sequels and has been begging at traffic lights since the age of 16, points out that he hit the streets "out of need, not having a trade, and wanting to make a living on my own."

[7]This description reveals the social and economic vulnerability that predisposes certain bodies to suffer injuries. In this case, the conditions of public transportation put passengers at risk. Likewise, this accident is associated with "problematic consumption of drugs," a concept that seeks to skirt moralizing interpretations of this consumption and refers to drug use that can be problematic for an individual when it affects him adversely, whether occasionally or chronically, in one or more areas: 1) physical or mental health; 2) primary social relations (family, partner, friends); 3) secondary social relations (work, study); or 4) relations with the law, following the definition provided by El Abrojo (2007).

Thus, the "street" and "people's help" become a "job" that, by exploiting a sense of pity in others, mercantilizes the experience of social contempt (Honneth 1993) and becomes a means of subsistence. The act of generosity without any kind of possible reimbursement or compensation, as occurs in charity, creates a situation of lasting dependence that is a variant of the inequality perpetuated by the state itself. The extension of this practice not only infringes on the right to gainful employment in the formal job market, but also subjects people with disabilities within a relation of domination in which they are reduced to mere bodies deserving of medical and/or social assistance, masking the underlying inequality that configures disability as a situation of social exclusion. This is why questioning policies that establish disability as a personal medical tragedy has been the focus of the struggles pursued by the disability rights movement (Oliver 1998). Although traditionally charitable organizations have assisted people with disabilities, people have expressed their opposition to being reduced to mere objects of pity, as this image "harms their dignity and social prestige" (Drake 1998: 171). Specifically, the CRPD seeks to remove the question of disability from the field of assistance-dependent services (be they medical or social). Very little progress has been achieved in the fields of employment and education, however, to encourage such a change, beyond mere discourses.

The effectiveness of begging among people with disabilities leads us to ask about the generous disposition of those who give money to a person based on their disability. As Juan Pablo Matta (2007) points out, the effectiveness of begging depends on the possibility of generating a pathetic reaction among others. We have already mentioned that in the practice of begging because "one is disabled" the exploitation of a disability as a personal medical tragedy is the narrative of the social interaction. However, the ideology of normality (Rosato et al. 2009) is so strong in our society that in many cases pity emerges as a spontaneous emotion without the need for discourse or a special *mise-en-scene* on behalf of the person with a disability. José begs on an avenue in one of the richest neighborhoods in Buenos Aires, simply seated in his wheelchair and with a cloth bag hanging from his neck. He has no need for words; when people see his body lacking all four extremities, they spontaneously put money in his bag. José notes that he does nothing special to gain people's help:

> I'm harming no one here; I'm not forcing anyone to give me a handout. I'm here as their conscience. If they feel uncomfortable, let them give to me; and if not, it's fine, maybe tomorrow, or the day after, or when they can, when they see they have a few extra coins they'll give them to me.

Likewise, Andrés, who comes and goes at the traffic light of an avenue in one of the most upscale neighborhoods of the city, boasts he has never asked for a handout:

> I never asked for a coin, never knocked on a window, never said 'can you give me?'; when people just see me on the street struggling to survive, they acknowledge me and help me out.

In this respect, a 51-year-old man, educated to university level, after giving a bill to a person with a disability who was begging on the subway, says to the researcher that he "feels sorry" seeing him and that he gave him a handout because "I've known this man for a long time, I always give to him, I know for a fact that he can't walk, that's why I always give to him." Likewise, a young woman aged 24, who completed high school, says "I always give because I feel pity, because I know they don't have another chance. It's not like the kids who live on the streets, who maybe spend the money on something else."

Ramón, with incomplete elementary schooling and multiple amputations, who has been begging for nine years, says that people give money to him because:

> It's like they feel sorry for the disabled on the street. There are others who wonder and ask me about my problem. So I show them the scars from my various operations … I pull up my pants and show them, look, look, this is not a sham. And so they give to me. People are good and help you out.

In the interaction of giving and receiving, the body's deficit, the stigma, translates into a certificate that legitimizes that he who begs deserves the charitable help of the other, the giver. But why does the disabled body trigger pity? Or, in other words, what politics of the emotions goes hand in hand with a politics of bodies to trigger guilt and charity via a personal deficit, accepting as an assigned social destiny "being a deserving poor person" and masking the situation of inequality that underlies the act of begging?

What Does Begging Tell Us About Our Society?

According to David Le Bretón (2002), the pity the disabled body triggers is associated with ambivalence in the relations that are established with people with disabilities. On the one hand, they are formally recognized as individuals entitled to rights who deserve to lead a life like any other citizen. But on the other hand, when they struggle to get by day after day, they are marginalized and denied any possibility to be active (that is, productive) members of society, treated as inferior and condemned to social contempt.

This contradictory and cynical attitude says a lot about our society. Early on we noted that one of the striking characteristics of our world is the enormous inequality rooted in the capitalist mode of production. In this context, the politics of bodies establishes mechanisms that regulate sensations and mechanisms of social tolerance (Scribano 2009). In this regard, the dividing line between supernumerary bodies and useful ones is fragile and vulnerable. Faced with this, the citizens of peripheral countries must develop a set of moral properties, determined by what Scribano (2010) calls "the new neocolonial capitalist religion." This religion is formed by the following trinity: mimetic consumption, solidarity and resignation. Specifically,

> Social mandates are the 'new tables' of the Law. 'Consume and you will be happy' … 'Be good at least once a day' … 'Resign yourself! Because it's all you can do' …. Rooted in and at the service of this Moesian[8] trinity, wherein consumption that defines us as somebody,

[8] Moesian alludes to the Mobius tape. These three elements, which according to Scribano characterize today's capitalism (or better still, neocolonial religion), circle and reproduce themselves as in an endless tape, without a beginning or an end.

> solidarity that only benefits those who give, and resignation that leads one to accept one's limited capacity to act, there are social consequences with strong collective impact that are ritualized and intertwined. (Scribano 2010: 148)

We can venture that pity and guilt triggered in the interaction of giving alms to someone by virtue of "having" a disability is an act hued by resignation, whereby society accepts to condemn to social death those whose bodies fail to adapt to the demands of flexibility. In this regard, the generous deliverance of money, as a charitable practice, fails to revert the situation of domination, but instead further reaffirms it, generating mental relief in the giver by calming the guilt he or she feels (Silberkasten 2006). As pointed out by Eugenia Boito (2005: 6), a response of solidarity acts as a social fantasy that masks the "phantom of oppression, precluding possible explanations and actions when confronted with need."

Recapping Jorge's words, the disabled body is "like the conscience" of those citizens that "belong." To think of disability as a biological and personal problem and to relieve ourselves from the social pain generated by this social injustice by means spare change, constitutes a mechanism of social tolerance that allows us to live on a daily basis alongside such a degree of inequality and to calm our own fears of social death and the guilt triggered by this other, who is none other than our very vulnerable selves in an unfair and unequal world (Scribano 2010).

The widespread nature of these types of practice that seek society's charitable response when faced with people with disabilities reinforces the situation of inequality that generates the exclusion of this minority. As Juan Pablo Matta points out,

> Inequality is the point of departure and at the same time the point of arrival in the exchange surrounding pity. That is why, from a sociological perspective, inequality occupies a central place in the political, economic and ideological dimensions of this problematic. It appears as the basis and consequence of the practices that this exchange unleashes. (Matta 2007: 168)

Along similar lines, Slavoj Žižek (2011), in underlining the central role acquired by charity within current capitalism, cites a famous fragment from Oscar Wilde:

> [People] find themselves surrounded by hideous poverty, by hideous ugliness, by hideous starvation. It is inevitable that they should be strongly moved by all this. … Accordingly, with admirable, though misdirected intentions, they very seriously and very sentimentally set themselves to the task of remedying the evils that they see. But their remedies do not cure the disease: they merely prolong it. Indeed, their remedies are part of the disease. … But this is not a solution: it is an aggravation of the difficulty. The proper aim is to try and reconstruct society on such a basis that poverty will be impossible. And the altruistic virtues have really prevented the carrying out of this aim.

By Way of Conclusion

Based on the everyday experience of begging as exercised by people with disabilities, we have attempted, on the one hand, to show how those who beg feel it is a personal choice, interpreted as a kind of "business" venture. On the other hand, we have revealed how this practice and narrative make invisible a relation of domination via the form of a "personal deficit." We have contextualized this micro-practice in the broader sphere of charitable responses towards people with disabilities, associating these with the social structure that generates them. In this interaction of giving and receiving alms or handouts "because someone has a disability," via the biological discourse of a deficit, disability and social inequality are naturalized, along with a resigned and guilty acceptance of the unequal availability of individual bodies.

In Argentina we are far from dismantling the prevalent approach to disability rooted in helping/assisting the disabled. This approach expresses itself first of all in state policies oriented towards disability and materializes in both explicit and implicit ways whereby many people with disabilities (especially the poor) find their conditions of existence denied. These forms of social negation are both material and symbolic; they include the disablement of individual bodies, the exclusion from a social life (that is, social death coupled with stigma, and crystallized in lack of access to jobs, to an education and to social participation), and the principles of appreciation of what a disability is, emblematically portrayed in the institutionalization of social contempt via politics of disablement (Oliver 1998) that reduces people with disabilities to mere bodies deserving medical and/or social assistance. As we have seen, the act of generosity without possible compensation, as in the case with charity, creates a situation of lasting dependence that constitutes a variant of inequality perpetuated by the state itself. Associating this politics of disablement within the broader framework of the politics of bodies and emotions in the context of today's capitalism, we suggest that the micro-scenario of giving and receiving alms by virtue of having a disability constitutes a variant of social charity that in this mode of domination emerges in the process of excluding people with disabilities.

The persistence of these practices is the reason why we reject the diagnosis that the social model of disability is in force in Argentina. We believe that as researchers we must be critical in this aspect, given that to adhere to such affirmations would imply masking and being accomplices to a reality of social domination that assumes the name of disability. To stop and analyze these phenomena, associating them to the politics of bodies currently in place, can give us critical elements to rethink the modes of domination that capitalism assumes in peripheral contexts such as the global South.

This does not imply disregarding the Anglo-Saxon social model as an analytical tool for our social context, but rather suggests a threefold exercise. First, avoid a simplistic application that winds up postulating recognition as rhetoric rather than as practice. Second, in light of the specific situations promoted in peripheral contexts, use the sociological imagination and critical theory to come up with the necessary conceptual adjustments to think from this—peripheral—side of the world. This exercise can not only enlighten the study of disability but also its metonymic expression of the emergence of the new social question and new modes of vulnerability. Finally, in this direction and in this context certain questions come up that may not be as evident in developed contexts: Can the CRPD reverse the structural dynamics that lead to the exclusion of people with disability and that become visible in the practice of begging in territories of the global South? Here we cannot ignore that in the framework of individualizing social needs brought about by neoliberalism in most Latin American countries, the CRPD posits that the state must guarantee their satisfaction. But are these measures useful if they are used only to generate a discourse of good intentions and, in so doing, to make invisible the proliferation of modes of inequality? In this respect, Colin Barnes (2010), a representative of the Anglo-Saxon tradition, argues that the legal path promoted by the CRPD would seem insufficient to generate the social structural changes required to reverse the inequality suffered by people with disability.

It is therefore essential that sociology and the social sciences as a whole face the situations thus posited and actively intervene to make visible these ambivalences, while researching them in depth. As Esteban Kippen (2013: 131) notes, "one must perceive the mechanisms of exclusion as a prerequisite to start thinking about strategies of inclusion. In fact, without excluding processes, the whole discourse of integration makes no sense."

References

Abrojo, E. (2007). *El Equilibrista: guía educativa para el trabajo con adolescentes en prevención del uso problemático de drogas [The tightrope: Educational guide for working with adolescents in prevention of problematic drug use]*. Montevideo: El Abrojo.

Academia Argentina de Letras. (2008). *Diccionario del habla de los argentinos*. Buenos Aires: Emecé.

Acuña, C. H., & Bulit Goñi, L. G. (Eds.). (2010). *Políticas sobre la discapacidad en la Argentina. El desafío de hacer realidad los derechos*. Buenos Aires: Siglo Veintiuno.

Barnes, C. (1998), "Las teorías de la discapacidad y los orígenes de la opresión de las personas discapacitadas en la sociedad occidental". In Barton, Len (Ed.), *Discapacidad y sociedad* (pp. 59–76). Madrid: Ediciones Morata.

Barnes, C. (2008). La diferencia producida en una década. Reflexiones sobre la investigación "emancipadora" en discapacidad. In Barton, L. (Ed.), *Superar las barreras de la discapacidad* (pp. 381–397). Madrid: Ediciones Morata.

Barnes, C. (2010). Discapacidad, política y pobreza en el contexto del Mundo Mayoritario [Disability, politics and poverty in a majority world context]. *Política y Sociedad, 47*(1), 11–25.

Bauman, Z. (2008). *Trabajo, consumismo y nuevos pobres*. Barcelona: Gedisa.

Boito, M. E. (2005). *Una aproximación crítica a la fantasía solidaria como expresión de la materialidad de la ideología*. Paper presented at the IX Jornadas Nacionales de Investigadores en Comunicación. Las (trans)formaciones de las subjetividades en la cultura contemporánea. Reflexiones e intervenciones desde la comunicación. Villa María, Córdoba, Argentina.

Bourdieu, P. (1991). *El sentido práctico*. Madrid: Taurus.

Bourgois, P. (2010). *En busca de respeto. Vendiendo crack en el Harlem*. Buenos Aires: FCE.

Bregain, G. (2012). Historiar los derechos a la rehabilitación integral de las personas con discapacidad en Argentina (1946–1974). In L. Pantano (Ed.), *Discapacidad e investigación: aportes desde la práctica* (pp. 111–166). Buenos Aires: EDUCA.

Castel, R. (2004). *Las trampas de la exclusión. Trabajo y utilidad social*. Buenos Aires: Editorial Topía.

Castillo Orué, N. E., Guinard, L. M., & Mazzei, L. (2013). *La invisibilidad del desempleo en las personas con discapacidad en la Argentina*. Paper delivered at the X Jornadas de sociología de la UBA. 20 años de pensar y repensar la sociología. Nuevos desafíos académicos, científicos y políticos para el siglo XXI. Buenos Aires: Carrera de Sociología de la Facultad de Ciencias Sociales, Universidad de Buenos Aires.

Cervio, A., & D'hers, V. (2012). Cuerpos y sensibilidades en falta. Una aproximación a la noción de necesidad en contextos de segregación socio-espacial. In A. Cervio (Ed.), *Las Tramas del Sentir. Ensayos desde una sociología de los cuerpos y las emociones*. Buenos Aires: ESE Editora.

Drake, R. F. (1998). Una crítica del papel de las organizaciones benéficas tradicionales. In L. Barton (Ed.), *Discapacidad y sociedad*. Madrid: Ediciones Morata.
Epele, M. (2010). *Sujetar por la herida. Una etnografía sobre drogas, pobreza y salud*. Buenos Aires: Paidós.
Eroles, C. (2005). La discapacidad como eje de un movimiento de afirmación de derechos. In C. Eroles & C. Ferreres (Eds.), *La discapacidad: una cuestión de derechos humanos* (pp. 15–39). Buenos Aires: Nueva visión.
Ferrante, C. (2012). *¿Cambio de paradigma? De mirada social a sujetos en falta. La vigencia del asistencialismo a partir del análisis del origen y disolución de un club de básquet de la Ciudad de Buenos Aires*. Paper delivered at the "7 Jornadas Nacionales Discapacidad y Derechos Humanos. Universidad y Sociedad ¿qué estamos haciendo frente a las problemáticas de la discapacidad?", Universidad Nacional de Río Cuarto, October 31, November 1 and 2, Río Cuarto, Argentina.
Foucault, M. (2000). *Los anormales*. Buenos Aires: Fondo de Cultura Económica.
Goffman, E. (2001). *Estigma. La identidad deteriorada*. Buenos Aires: Amorrortu.
Honneth, A. (1993). *La lucha por el reconocimiento. Por una gramática moral de los conflictos sociales*. Barcelona: Grijalbo Mondadori.
Hughes, B., & Paterson, K. (2008). El modelo social de discapacidad y la desaparición del cuerpo. Hacia una sociología del impedimento. En Barton, Len (comp.) *Superar las barreras de la discapacidad* (pp. 107–123). Madrid: Ediciones Morata.
Joly, E. (2008). *Discapacidad y empleo. Por el derecho a ser explotados*. In Le Monde Diplomatique.
Joly, E. D., & Venturiello, M. P. (2012). Persons with disabilities: Entitled to beg, not to work. The Argentine Case. *Critical Sociology, 39*(3), 325–347.
Kippen, E. (2013). En torno a una conceptualización –(im)posible- de la discapacidad. In *Angelino, Alfonsina and Almeida, María Eugenia (Eds) Debates y perspectivas en torno a la Discapacidad en América Latina* (pp. 128–132). Paraná: Universidad Nacional de Entre Ríos, Facultad de Trabajo Social.
Le Breton, D. (2002). *La sociología del cuerpo*. Buenos Aires: Nueva Visión.
Matta, J. P. (2007). *El lado oscuro de la limosna. Análisis sociocultural de la dualidad limosna/lástima como variación del intercambio. Tesis de Licenciatura en Ciencias Antropológicas orientación Antropología Social*. UNICEN—FACSO—Olavarría.
Morris, J. (2008). Lo personal y lo político. Una perspectiva feminista sobre la investigación de la discapacidad física. In L. Barton (Ed.), *Superar las barreras de la discapacidad* (pp. 315–326). Madrid: Ediciones Morata.
Nabergoi, M., & Bottinelli, M. M. (2007). Discapacidad, pobreza y sus abordajes: Revisión de la estrategia de rehabilitación basada en la comunidad (RBC). In Facultad de Psicología—UBA, Secretaría de investigaciones. *Anuario de investigaciones, 14*, 159–165.
Oliver, M. (1998). ¿Una sociología de la discapacidad o una sociología discapacitada? In Barton, L. (comp.) *Discapacidad y sociedad*. Madrid: Morata, Fundación Paideai.
Oliver, M. (2008). Políticas sociales y discapacidad. Algunas consideraciones teóricas. In Barton, L. (Ed.), *Superar las barreras de la discapacidad* (pp. 19–34). Madrid: Morata.
Palacios, A. (2008). *El modelo social de la discapacidad: orígenes, caracterización y plasmación en la Convención Internacional sobre los Derechos de las Personas con Discapacidad*. Madrid: Fermi.
Pérez Sosto, G. (2005). Las manifestaciones actuales de la cuestión social. En Pérez Sosto, Guillermo (coord.) *Las manifestaciones actuales de la cuestión social* (pp. 9–16). Buenos Aires: Instituto Di Tella.
REDI, CELS, FAICA, FENDIM, ADC. (2012). Comité sobre los derechos de las personas con discapacidad. 8° período de sesiones/Evaluación sobre argentina. Informe alternativo. Situación de la discapacidad en Argentina—2008/2012. Retrieved from http://www.mindbank.info/item/1384
Rosales, P. (2013). Una mirada desde lo legal acerca de la discriminación por discapacidad, los estereotipos y la necesidad de toma de conciencia. Su tratamiento en la Convención sobre los

Derechos de las Personas con Discapacidad, ONU (ley 26.378). In Discapacidad, Justicia y Estado. *Discriminación, estereotipos y toma de conciencia* (pp. 3–66). Buenos Aires: Infojus.

Rosanvallón, P. (2007). *La nueva cuestión social: repensar el Estado providencia*. Buenos Aires: Manantial.

Rosato, A. et al (2009). El papel de la ideología de la normalidad en la producción de discapacidad. *Ciencia, Docencia y Tecnología, 39*, 87–105.

Scheper-Huges, N., & Lock, M. (1986). The Mindful Body: A Prolegomenon to Future Work in Medical Anthropology. *Medical Anthropology Quarterly, 1*. Trans. Gonzalez Martin, M. Material for the Seminario de Antropología Médica de la Facultad de Filosofía y Letras de la Universidad de Buenos Aires, p. 19.

Scribano, A. (2009). Una periodización intempestiva de las políticas de los cuerpos y las emociones en la Argentina reciente. *Boletín Onteaiken, 7*. Retrieved from onteaiken.com.ar/ver/boletin7/1-1.pdf

Scribano, A. (2010). ¿Por qué una mirada sociológica de los cuerpos y las emociones? A Modo de Epílogo. Iin Adrián Scribano and Carlos Figari (Eds.) *Cuerpo(s), Subjetividad(es) y Conflicto(s) Hacia una sociología de los cuerpos y las emociones desde Latinoamérica* (pp. 141–151). Buenos Aires: CLACSO-CICCUS.

Shakespeare, T. (2013). The social model of disability. In L. Davis (Ed.), *The disability studies reader* (pp. 214–221), New York: Routledge.

Shakespeare, T., & Watson, N. (1995). The body line controversy: A new direction for Disability Studies? In *Hull Disability Studies Seminar*.

Silberkasten, M. (2006). *La construcción imaginaria de la discapacidad*. Buenos Aires: Topía Editorial.

Skliar, C. (2002). Acerca de la anormalidad y lo anormal. Notas para un enjuiciamiento (voraz) a la normalidad. In ¿Y si el *Otro no estuviera ahí? Notas para una pedagogía (improbable) de la diferencia* (pp. 115–144). Buenos Aires: Escuela Marina Vitte CTERA- Miño y Dávila Editores.

Stiker, H. J. (2000). *A history of disability*. Ann Arbor: The University of Michigan Press.

UN. (2006). *Convention on the rights of persons with disabilities*. Retrieved December 12, 2014, from http://www.un.org/disabilities/default.asp?navid=15&pid=150

Venturiello, M. P. (2010). Los espacios físicos de la discapacidad: las experiencias de los cuerpos, las actividades y las redes sociales. In B. A. Bustos García & M. L. Martínez Sánchez (Eds.), *Cuerpo y discapacidad: perspectivas latinoamericanas* (pp. 89–130). México: Facultad de Filosofía y Letras, Universidad Autónoma de Nuevo León y Asociación Latinoamericana de Sociología.

WHO and World Bank. (2011). *World report on disability (Informe mundial sobre la discapacidad)*. Geneva: WHO.

Žižek, S. (2011). Video of the conference at The Royal Society for the encouragement of Arts, Manufactures and Commerce (thersa.org). First as tragedy, then as farce—RSA Animate, Primero Tragedia, Luego Farsa. Subtitles by the Programa de Estudios sobre Acción Colectiva y Conflicto Social. CEA-UE-Conicet. Córdoba.

Chapter 11
Don't Forget Us, We Are Here Too! Listening to Disabled Children and Their Families Living in Poverty

Mary Wickenden and Jean Elphick

Introduction

Discourses in the disability movement and disability research are predominantly focussed on adults. This volume, ironically, is further evidence of this bias. In this chapter we set out to illustrate why the lives of disabled children and young people and their families, especially those living in low-income settings globally, warrant more attention. We argue that their perspectives can and should be more actively sought. We draw on theory from childhood studies and disability studies, both of which maintain a bias towards consideration of those in the global North. We also draw on participatory research and project work, first with disabled children themselves in South Asia and Uganda, and second with parents in South Africa, to show that there is much to be learned by listening to both groups, encouraging their direct participation in research as well as in programme planning, implementation and evaluation.

Many of the issues commonly discussed in relation to the exclusion and oppression of disabled adults have their roots in childhood experiences (for those who have had impairments from early in life). Oppression often starts, is normalised and sometimes becomes internalised during childhood. Parents and caregivers are usually important mediators for their disabled children and can play a crucial role in either perpetuating or challenging such oppression. In this chapter we address the perspectives of disabled children themselves and those who look after and support them, whether their parents or other caregivers. Although much more could be said

M. Wickenden (✉)
University College London, London, UK
e-mail: m.wickenden@ucl.ac.uk

J. Elphick
Afrika Tikkun, Durban, South Africa

S. Grech, K. Soldatic (eds.), *Disability in the Global South*,
International Perspectives on Social Policy, Administration, and Practice,
DOI 10.1007/978-3-319-42488-0_11

separately about both groups, there is some logic in discussing them together as they are interconnected. Richard (2014) argues similarly (in the Indian context) that the well-being of disabled children and of their families is intertwined and reciprocally affected by each other, and that therefore they should be considered as a unit.

Disabled Children and Their Parents and Caregivers

Current estimates suggest that globally there are roughly 93 million children aged under 14 who have moderate or severe disabilities (World Health Organization and World Bank 2011; Lansdown 2012). This is both a staggering figure and most probably an underestimate. Better identification of and data about childhood impairment is needed in order to plan services and there are a number of initiatives that focus on this. It is recognised that the number of disabled children globally is probably rising (UNICEF 2008; Groce et al. 2011). Two contradictory factors are affecting prevalence: improved healthcare across the lifespan, better nutrition, education and environmental safety are preventing some types of impairment; however, the global focus on reducing infant mortality has resulted in the survival of more premature and vulnerable babies, some of whom have increased levels of impairment (Fujiura and Yamaki 2000; Maulik and Darmstadt 2007; Mont 2014).

What is certain is that the majority of the world's disabled children live in the so-called *majority world* (UNICEF 2013) alongside most of their nondisabled peers. Although we would not argue for using prevalence figures alone to advocate for improvements in people's lives, indisputably disabled children are a large, under-recognised, poorly served and marginalised group (Croft 2013). There is increasing evidence, although still inadequate and inaccurate, of their relative disadvantage in comparison with other children as exemplified by data from a range of sectors. As Mont succinctly reports, 'the evidence is clear that childhood disability diminishes a person's life chances' (2014: 20). For example, it is clear that they experience lower rates of school attendance: 'It is estimated that children with disabilities represent more than one-third of the 67 million children who are out of school worldwide' (Human Rights Watch 2010: 10). They also experience disproportionate corporal punishment; worse access to general healthcare as well as to impairment-related rehabilitation; and much higher levels of abuse and neglect (Human Rights Watch 2010; World Health Organization and UNICEF 2012). In addition, evidence is mounting that disabled children are disproportionately affected in settings where there is conflict or disaster (Trani et al. 2013).

Less clearly documented, but regularly reported anecdotally, is the frequent exclusion of disabled children from social participation both within their families and in their wider communities (Tisdall 2013). There are, however, some encouraging signs of more inclusive attitudes and of increased recognition of the need to acknowledge disabled children as agentive citizens alongside their peers (Feldman et al. 2013), though this varies greatly across regions and with cultural and socio-economic context.

During the last 30 years or so, the emergence and legitimisation of the concept of children's rights and the academic arena of childhood studies have both driven and responded to the idea that children and young people can be social actors, even though their competencies may be different from adults (UN 1989). Children are now seen as important contributors to society while they are growing up, rather than as people waiting passively to become adults who will then be productive and have voices (James et al. 1998). Increasingly nondisabled children are being included in consultations, either as part of research or in policy or practice contexts Christensen and James (2000). Although this trend started mainly in the global North, it is now increasing in the global South within the international development arena as it is recognised that children's views can and should inform interventions and service developments (Boyden and Ennew 1997; White and Choudhury 2007; Hart 2008; Stoecklin 2013).

In parallel to the near-universal recognition of children's and women's rights, disabled people via a global disability movement have successfully argued for disability rights, at least as adults. The changing perceptions and expectations about children's agency have generally not been extended to disabled children though, who remain largely excluded from participatory research and consultation (Morris 2003). Studies focussing on them tend to ask proxies, mostly adults around them, instead of asking disabled children themselves about their lives (Mahon et al. 1996). Additionally, large mainstream research projects about diverse aspects of nondisabled children's lives fail to include their disabled peers, even as a subgroup whose data might be disaggregated (Feldman et al. 2013). Disabled children and their parents have largely remained unrepresented and unconsidered in the broader international development agenda as well as arguably within the disability rights movement (Human Rights Watch 2010).

Parents, usually the mothers, of disabled children, particularly those with very stigmatised impairments (severe cognitive, communication or behavioural difficulties or multiple impairments), are often their primary carers. This is especially true where their children are excluded from early childhood development and educational provision. As part of extended parenting roles, they also take on duties as protectors, advocates, lobbyists and human rights defenders and quite often they are single mothers. Commonly, disabled children remain more dependent on their families as they grow up than their nondisabled peers because of lack of appropriate support, diminished opportunities and low expectations of them as potential autonomous citizens, parents, breadwinners or householders (Lorenzo 2012; Mont 2014). Consequently their parents' parenting roles often extend into their children's adulthood. Parents and caregivers are also those most likely to continue to negotiate access to essential services for their disabled children. This will include physically getting their children to facilities, speaking for them and assertively confronting stigma and exclusion. For some children and young people, expressing their own views will always be difficult and so, particularly for those with communication difficulties, parents and caregivers are usually, naturally and necessarily their proxies and closest allies.[1] The voices of disabled children's caregivers therefore need to be heard and amplified. Much as they may hope that their children will one day speak up and advocate for themselves, these adults inevitably play a vital role in fighting for the acceptance and valuing of their disabled children, as well as safety, appropriate services and access to human rights for them, when they are under 18 and beyond (Lansdown et al. 2013).

The Nature of Difference: Being a Different Kind of Child

In many societies disabled people of all ages are excluded and neglected by their communities through structurally violent processes (Farmer 1996). Powerful hegemonic, normative ideas about bodies and minds predominate in many cultures and subcultures (Paterson and Hughes 1999). Child development check-ups and surveillance are almost universal, and clearly serve a purpose in identifying children who are malnourished, sick or failing to meet developmental milestones. During this process impairment may be identified by the authorities (usually either health or education), whether or not it has already been noticed by the child's caregivers. Thus disabled children, once officially identified, are labelled and judged to be different from their peers. As a result of this recognition, they may then go on to experience a parallel, deeply stigmatising social rejection, which may be lifelong. They become a different kind of person in the eyes of society. In many contexts globally, one positive outcome of being 'classified' as disabled might be the opportunity to access some form of social grant or financial assistance. Yet, social protection schemes for disabled people are non-existent in many low- and middle-income countries. The recognition of an impairment does however bring, with more certainty, a whole range of negative, discriminatory and disadvantaging consequences for children and their families. This includes increased risks of abuse, neglect or bullying; poverty, violence, family or parental stress; and abandonment and diminished access to basic services such as mainstream healthcare and education (Goodley and Runswick-Cole 2011; Chataika and McKenzie 2013; Grech 2013).

Disabled children, and by association their families, often live in a state of reduced personhood and lack of agency, exemplified for instance by their regular exclusion from school. As Farmer suggests, in his case describing the structural violence experienced by the poor, they 'are not only more likely to suffer, they are also more likely to have their suffering silenced' (1996: 280). In many societies acquiring the label 'different' has implications for a person's identity and worth, and

[1] We recognise that relationships between parents and children are complex, and the roles and experiences of parents of disabled children are particularly so. In addition, there is evidence that much of the very common abuse (of all types) of disabled children takes place within the home. There is little data to suggest that mothers are implicated in this, thus they are usually their children's key protectors and advocates (African Child Policy Forum 2010; Save the Children and Handicap International 2011).

leads to judgements about the quality and value of their life (Albrecht and Devleiger 1999). As Mackenzie and Leach Scully (2007) argue, people without impairments often cannot, because of their own embodied experience, really put themselves in the position of the disabled person. Erroneous judgements about disabled people's lives are commonly made by wider society.

For all the recent international development focus on the elimination of poverty and on 'leaving no one behind' (UNA-UK 2013), it is clear that disabled people are often 'othered' so much that they become invisible in policies and strategies designed to improve the lives of the majority (Meekosha and Soldatic 2011; Wolbring et al. 2013). This exclusion and silencing are particularly true of disabled children (Singh and Ghai 2009).

The Perspectives of Disabled Children and Young People

Although children are increasingly being asked for their opinions on matters affecting them, disabled children's perspectives are missing, particularly in the global South and in contexts of poverty. When research about children and young people is being conceptualised, disabled children are often simply a 'non-category'. They are often actively excluded because it is anticipated that they will 'complicate' the data or make data collection methodologically difficult. Alternatively they may simply be forgotten or overlooked. A Ugandan mother of four children, one of whom was disabled, said: 'when people ask me how many children I have, I usually say three and then sometimes I mention "the other one"'.

Disabled children are forgotten when consultation with other children is being planned, for example about services, and it is assumed that as a subgroup they would either not have opinions or would be unable to express them. This is despite the great heterogeneity of their individual characteristics and social situations. Children vary in relation to type of impairment and support needs, living environments, life experiences and competencies. Thus there is a need for positive inclusive practices, including flexible research methodologies which make it possible to include them and to hear their distinct voices (Jans 2004).

When projects do include disabled children they most often focus just on those with physical impairments and occasionally those who are deaf or blind, but hardly ever on those with learning disabilities, complex or multiple impairments, or communication or behaviour difficulties. This selection bias serves, albeit unwittingly, to compound a 'hierarchy of exclusion' which continues to reinforce views of the most stigmatised as 'nonpersons'. The habitually negative responses of others to disabled children and an emphasis on their differences sows the seeds for their potential internalised oppression and continuation of their liminal status as adults (Mont 2014). To the small extent that there is currently some increased interest in disabled children, this is often couched in neo-liberal terms, emphasising the macroeconomic arguments for improving their health and education, so that they may become economically productive. We argue fundamentally that it is important disabled children and young people are brought into the mainstream because they are citizens like everyone else (Lansdown 2012).

Participatory Research with Disabled Children

The first author (Wickenden) has carried out research which deliberately seeks the views of disabled children through running disabled children's meetings in rural and urban sites in northern India, Sri Lanka and Uganda. These meetings are part of research projects aiming to explore disabled children's views of various aspects of their lives and the resources available to them in their communities. Meetings have been run in collaboration with local partner organisations, including universities and non-government organisations working in the disability sector, for example running school or community-based rehabilitation programmes. The underlying philosophy is always that of actively including disabled children with any type or severity of impairment if they and their parents agree. A range of different information and consent procedures as well as data collection activities have been trialled, aiming to provide adaptations to suit children's specific needs, to allow them all equal opportunities to participate. Their styles and levels of contribution of course vary. For example, sign language, symbols and pictures, adapted content and style of spoken language, and tactile materials as well as physical adaptations are used to enable the participation of children with deafness, learning and or communication difficulties, blindness and a variety of physical impairments, respectively.

Details of some methods and tools used are described and critiqued elsewhere (Wickenden and Kembhavi-Tam 2014). Selected key themes from the data are presented here with illustrative quotes. As can be seen, in some cases the children's communication or cognitive difficulties present challenges in interpreting their meanings. However, illustrating the possibility of consulting disabled children, whatever their skills, and presenting some of their responses is useful in challenging the common perception that they have nothing to say. Abbreviations of pseudonyms (mainly chosen by the children) are used to differentiate participants.

Social Relationships

The most important people in their lives named by disabled children are nearly always, clearly and unsurprisingly immediate family members: parents and siblings, closely followed by grandparents, uncles, aunts and cousins. These are people who they know love them, but who also provide for and look after them in practical ways (e.g. food, washing, taking them out, buying clothes and treats).

> Mummy cooks food, she makes tea and she even buys clothes for me. (Lak, 14-year-old girl, urban India)

There is an appreciation that their parents are the ones who do the most for them and there is a strong sense of being advocated for and protected by them:

> Who else will do so much effort the amount my father does? (Sh, 14-year-old girl, rural India)

Mention of specific impairment or disability-related help was rather rare, although perhaps implied:

> Because till today wherever I have to be taken for my foot, baba [grandfather] takes me. Baba has taken care of me most. (Po, 15-year-old girl, rural India)

Teachers also regularly featured positively for those children who attended school, as people who help them learn and look after them. A few children mentioned teachers' harsh attitudes, but it is unclear whether this was specific to them as disabled children or a more generic experience for all children.

Friends (classmates, neighbours) were also mentioned as people to 'chat to', 'play with' and 'have fun with', although disabled children commonly expressed a wish for more friends. A restricted range of friendships compared with nondisabled children and a desire for more friends and more social life has been noted by other authors (Cavet 1998). Having pets is also mentioned regularly as an important aspect of their lives.

Problematic Relationships

Given the prevalence of bullying and abuse of disabled children noted in the literature (UNICEF 2013), it is not surprising that this often comes up in group conversations, for example in this group of 8–11-year-olds in urban Sri Lanka:

Interviewer:	Is there anyone who calls you names?
A (girl, 11):	Yeah J, I can stand up to him, I will chase him and give him a whack

And in a group of the same age range in urban India:

Int:	K says that he does not like his friends that much because they beat him up. Does anybody else get beaten up in school?
Ki (boy, 9, with no speech):	(gestures) Me.
Int:	Ki do friends beat you up?
Ki:	(smiles and gestures) Yes.

Disabled children's solutions to these situations are usually couched in the language of acceptance of difference and of seeing everyone as equal.

> I don't like hitting. I like to love others. (Lak, 14-year-old girl, urban India, who had been teased)

Aspirations for Education and Work

Nearly all the children enjoyed going to school or wanted to go. In all the settings most children (approximately 90 per cent) had initially been refused admission to government schools despite government policies supporting inclusion. They attended alternatives such as NGO-run special schools or private schools with an inclusive ethos. In groups run for older children (12–18) there was commonly talk about getting work and wanting to be economically helpful to their families. In the context of poverty, disabled youth clearly saw themselves as potential active contributors rather than as the passive consumers and burdens they are so often portrayed as. They expressed a range of career aspirations and made no direct mention of potentially restricted access to work because of their disability. In reality their opportunities and choices in relation to employment are likely to be very limited. Those who had left school said they wanted more than anything else to work and contribute actively to their families economically, but it seemed that this was difficult to achieve.

> I like to study to become an educated person. (Po, 15-year-old girl who had left school at 12, rural India)
> If I can get some job. (Ja, 17-year-old boy who had left school at 14, rural India)
> I want to talk about dreams … I wish to be a vet. (A, 11-year-old girl, urban Sri Lanka)
> I wish I could be a dog trainer. (J, 11-year-old boy, urban Sri Lanka)
> Dreams … I wish to be running like a tiger and quicker (D, 9-year-old boy, urban Sri Lanka)

Impairment-Focussed Responses and Solutions

Discussion of impairment-focussed problems and solutions arose spontaneously in all the groups, although not in a pathologising or stigmatising way. There was a great deal of acceptance and practical discussion about ways of managing life with an impairment and most of this was in the form of socially inclusive solutions rather than about curative approaches to the impairment itself.

It was not obvious that any particular judgements were made by the children in relation to the status of different types of impairment within the groups, although this has been observed among disabled adults in other contexts, where a hierarchy of discrimination is known to exist among and between different impairment groups (Deal 2007). The children's attitudes and responses to dilemmas related to exclusion were overwhelmingly pragmatic and implicitly rights-based. Below are two excerpts from discussions in different groups about the same vignette. In the story (presented in picture form by the interviewer), Ranjith is a boy with a physical impairment who is being excluded from village cricket games.

8–11-Year-Olds in Rural Sri Lanka

Int.:	Now how can we take Ranjith to play cricket? He is finding it difficult to walk. If he goes alone he might fall. But he would like to go. What to do?
N (girl, 8):	Sad.
Int.:	Yes it's sad, but what shall we do to take him to the playground?
N:	Can't. [i.e. can't get there himself]
Int.:	Yes, can't, but … how to take?
N:	Take him in a wheelchair.
Int.:	Yes … [but] if there is no wheelchair how can we take the friend?
N:	Carry him on the back.
Pr (boy, 8):	Take him from the house and sneak him to the match!

12–18-Year-Olds in Rural Sri Lanka

Pr (girl, 14):	Ranjith should call his friends over and ask for help.
H (boy, 12):	Put two false legs on him so he can walk better.
L (girl, 14):	Take him to hospital … we can also get some donations/aid and get a false leg for Ranjith.

The last two quotes are rare examples of children suggesting impairment-focussed solutions (in contrast to or in addition to attitude change), and perhaps this is unsurprising in contexts with scarce availability of specialist rehabilitation services, aids and appliances. The children may have been unaware of the possibility of some impairment-related types of help (such as hearing and communication aids, prostheses, adapted home environments) which their disabled peers in high-income countries would regard as standard and their right to have. Often their ideas were limited to the idea that the person should go to the hospital.

Specialist rehabilitation services, such as provision of therapies and assistive devices, are in extremely short supply in many low-income settings globally (World Health Organization 2010). Even when they are available, they are often concentrated in urban settings and thus would require time and money from families to access them. Poor and rural families have little awareness of these possibilities and few resources to access them. For example, deaf children without hearing aids in the Ugandan group did not mention or demand these. This may be either because they did not know of their existence or because they knew their families could not afford them. In the same group a girl with amputated lower limbs did not mention prostheses, again probably because she had never seen these and perhaps did not see herself as 'deficient' in any way without them. This echoes numerous examples in the literature of people with impairments not perceiving the aspect of themselves that is seen as 'different' as disabling (Watson 2002).

Expressing Preferences and Opinions

Disabled children's initial responses to questions about their preferences and wishes (things to make a good life) were quite prosaic and arguably like those of nondisabled children in those communities. In some cases it seemed that they were unused to the idea of being asked about their opinions or preferences and in contexts of poverty, choice is in any case not usually a possibility. Their responses were mostly not related to impairment or disability at all and several times led to, in both India and Sri Lanka, long conversations about food that they did or did not like. This was clearly an important topic in settings where although there was little overt malnutrition, there wasn't an abundance of variety in the daily diet. When asked about things that might make life better, the Ugandan children talked first about wanting better school uniforms, sportswear and school bags. They also expressed a variety of opinions about other topics once some suggestions were presented in a neutral 'non-leading' way. Many of their views and opinions seemed unrelated to impairment or disability or only obliquely linked, and often appeared more overtly to be about poverty or exclusion. As described in the literature cited earlier, poverty and exclusion are both the cause and consequence of disability, but the children themselves did not make this link explicitly. The following quotes are selected examples.

Having Friends and Playing with Others

8–11-Year-Olds in Urban India

Int.:	Who likes playing with others and who likes playing alone?
Ksh (boy, 9):	When other children do not let me play, I feel bad.
Int.:	Kul, when other children play and you don't, then how do you feel about that?
Kul (boy, 8, with no speech):	(Points to sad face symbol.)

8–11-Year-Olds in Rural India

Int:	What about playing alone or with others?
Mother of a boy with severe learning disabilities who is often excluded:	He likes to be with other children.
Int.:	Now tell me who likes to be alone?
S (boy, 8, who had been attending school but was then often left at home as no one was available to carry him to school):	Nobody! I hate it.

12–18-Year-Olds in Urban India

Kin (boy, 12):	I don't like staying at home.
Shi (boy, 12, with no speech):	(Points to picture, like talking with friends).

Disabled children's social exclusion from school or community activities has been extensively described in the literature, although mainly through small-scale studies and anecdotes rather than in large-scale population-level data collection (World Health Organization 2010; UNICEF 2013). It was clear that the children in our studies in India, Sri Lanka and Uganda disliked being excluded from education, socialising and community activities that other children were involved in, saw school as a social place and wanted to be 'part of the gang' rather than being left at home.

Favourite Things and Activities

12–18-Year-Olds in Urban India

Int.:	What do you like to do?
Lak (girl, 14):	Like weddings.
Int.:	Lak, why do you like to go to weddings?
Lak:	Everybody dances there.
Int.:	And?
Lak:	We eat there.
Int.:	Ka, why do you like to go marriages?
Ka (boy, 12, with no speech):	(gestures/sign) Eating.
Int.:	Anything else?
Ka:	(gestures/sign) Dancing.

What Is Learned from Talking to Disabled Children Directly?

The findings from these exploratory projects echo those from the small but growing body of participatory research with disabled children, mainly undertaken in the global North (Boyden and Ennew 1997; Wickenden and Kembhavi-Tam 2014). This shows that disabled children see themselves overwhelmingly as more like their peers than different, in fact as ordinary young people (Davis et al. 2003; Kembhavi and Wirz 2009; Wickenden 2011). An important aspect of all children's evolving identity is to feel that they belong and are accepted as people (James 1999), and in most ways disabled children are no different in this aspiration from their nondisabled siblings and friends. However, they face constant challenges in being recognised in this way and in countering the habitual privileging of their 'difference' rather than their similarities with their nondisabled peers.

Disabled children are typically pragmatic about their need for assistance and impairment-related aids and adaptations, if they are aware of them; however, they do not want impairment or disability issues to dominate views of them and to overwhelm their identities as people. In fact they mention their impairments and disability rather rarely, unless these topics are introduced by someone else. They usually have similar interests and priorities to their peers and want to be included in mainstream activities, but with appropriate support and adaptation where they need it, so that they can join in meaningfully.

Meeting their impairment-related and access needs is an important part of enabling their inclusion, but in the disabled children's conversations it does not dominate over other types of wishes and aspirations for their lives and futures. However, they do express great dislike of tokenistic approaches, where the rhetoric suggests they are welcome but underlying attitudes are negative and serve only to exacerbate their exclusion. Even though they mostly do not know explicitly about the two United Nations human rights conventions under whose purview they fall—the Convention on the Rights of the Child (UN 1989) and the Convention on the Rights of Persons with Disabilities (UN 2006)—disabled children and young people articulated in practical ways their rights as citizens and their needs as people.

Perspectives of Parents and Caregivers of Disabled Children in Orange Farm, South Africa

In this section we discuss an example of some work with parents and carers of disabled children, where we can see that their perspectives mirror and support those of disabled children.

The second author (Elphick) has been facilitating a community-based rehabilitation programme in Orange Farm, a peri-urban community south of Johannesburg in South Africa. Here, mothers, grandparents and other relatives play the vital role of advocates as well as primary caregivers. They also encounter discriminatory attitudes and have to negotiate exclusionary systems during the course of raising their children (De Sas et al. 2014). We argue that it is important to recognise and encourage the agency, decision-making capabilities and motivation of caregivers, as well as that of their disabled children. Their years of experience in raising a disabled child in the context of poverty, discrimination and social marginalisation means they are able to provide relevant, first-hand insight into the lives and needs of their children. They are able to play a vital part in identifying and illuminating the problems they face in exclusionary societies. In addition, as the following case study will illustrate, they can also become important allies to researchers and development practitioners. Caregivers are able themselves to participate in planning and implementing intervention programmes for children as well as steering social change.

In South Africa, traditional and often harmful beliefs about disability stubbornly persist. Mothers are widely believed to have done something wrong and therefore 'deserve' the impairment affecting their child (Lansdown 2002; Hanass-Hancock

2012). In a country now famous for its equality-promoting constitution, with a full 20 years since the inauguration of the South African Bill of Rights, disabled people continue to experience high levels of discrimination, exclusion and social marginalisation (Bhabha 2009). In the sprawling informal settlement where this story originates, there are believed to be over 800 children with various impairments.

Life in Orange Farm is characterised by ubiquitous poverty, unemployment, domestic violence, HIV and tuberculosis affecting almost every household. Disabled children here are subject to frequent, almost routine, human rights violations. Reflecting the often-quoted statistics about disabled children's exclusion from school (Ford-Shubrook 2007), just a handful of the 800 disabled children currently access their non-progressive right to a basic education. The vast majority are cared for by unemployed single mothers who have been abandoned by the child's father and his extended family. Although there is a social grant available for all children, with more generous 'care dependency grants' available for children with diagnosed disabilities, less than half the caregivers entitled to these grants have managed successfully to navigate the laborious system required to access them (Saloojee et al. 2007). Further, disabled children are at extremely high risk of sexual abuse, an endemic problem disproportionately affecting the disabled population (Sicking et al. 2013). As one caregiver put it, 'everything comes down to discrimination' with respect to accessing state-provided health, education, social welfare and criminal justice services. These were the findings of a 2010 baseline study conducted by established NGO Afrika Tikkun. Finding an equitable and sustainable way of tackling these deep-rooted problems presented a bewildering challenge to the organisation.

To assist in choosing an intervention strategy that would cover the scope and scale of the situation, the baseline study asked parents of disabled children about their main concerns. This enabled the priorities for the intervention to be articulated by parents themselves, achieved by conducting focus group discussions, interviews and home visits. Despite the complex situation that families were encountering and the lack of education and literacy among the caregivers who participated, their desired priorities for assistance were unexpectedly forward-thinking and progressive. The parents wanted psychological support for themselves and they wanted to teach their communities about accepting and including their disabled children. They prioritised these over and above medical interventions, assistive devices, hand-outs like food parcels and other services. The caregiver of a 13-year-old child with multiple disabilities emphatically summarised:

> My main concern is for them to be treated with respect as they are human beings like everyone! And they have rights like everyone in South Africa who is having rights. They also have those rights. So I would like the community around us to treat us and our kids as normal families.

These sentiments were taken seriously and informed the strategic development of the programme that exists today. A community-based rehabilitation (CBR) empowerment programme was launched in the community in late 2011. A focus on empowerment is one of the key aspects suggested in the reconceptualisation of CBR developed by WHO (2010) as a cross-sectoral approach to improving the lives of disabled people, particularly in low- and middle-income countries. CBR is now seen fundamentally as a strategy for the promotion of human rights for disabled people. The empowerment component encourages the mobilisation of disabled people and their families to come together and form self-help groups capable of effectively communicating about the problems they face; participating politically; and aligning themselves with other similar movements promoting human rights (World Health Organization 2010).

This highly participatory intervention has been active for the past two years and, with modest programme inputs, has achieved some notable outcomes. Caregivers meet weekly on a Friday morning. They come wearing purple t-shirts emblazoned with the logo they designed for their self-help group, which they named Sidinga Uthando (meaning 'all we need is love'). The group has decided its mission is to change attitudes about disability. Armed with new-found human rights literacy they have decided to concentrate on promoting three key rights that are frequently not afforded to their children: equality, education and safety from violence. Each week they make an agenda that typically includes upcoming events they are involved in organising, feedback from members attending meetings in various other fora, lectures from guest speakers and peer-education sessions.

There is an implicit function of the group in addition to the agenda. The members value their weekly meetings where they are able to share their problems, and give or receive advice. One mother said:

> When I first came here, I cried tears and everyone came and hugged me. They started talking to me. It is easy for me now, I'm not angry anymore. I treat my child with more calm and understanding. But when you are at home, thinking it is me against the world—it's sad. There are people like you who face the very same problems, it's better now, because we come and talk and laugh.

The most notable of the numerous milestones achieved by the group is their successful lobby for the right to education for disabled children. The members of the Sidinga Uthando self-help group set their hearts on having a local, accessible school for their children to attend. Currently, the few children who have been accepted into schools travel daily to schools in neighbouring districts, at a prohibitive expense to their families. They do not attend the same schools as their nondisabled siblings, which are within walking distance from home, despite established inclusive education policies and the extension of the right to a basic education to all South African children (Engelbrecht 2006). Unfortunately the legacy of discriminatory policies from the Apartheid era persists and education for disabled children remains dependent on where they live and what their parents can afford (Soudien and Baxen 2006). Caregivers described how they had spent years applying to multiple 'special schools' to no avail.

In 2012, Sidinga Uthando members started to compile a database of children needing school placements, alongside collecting the requisite documentation for school admission. The caregivers not only added their own children's names to the database but also assisted in referring new families into the empowerment programme. Today 200 families are registered. Each child has been referred to the district office of the education department. In addition to formally making the department aware of the children, the compilation of documents showing each caregiver's journey to find a school was highlighted, as many of them had endured years of referral back and forth without resolution.

The group wrote letters of complaint and parliamentary submissions. They continued to populate their detailed database and to refer new members. Before long the education department began to acknowledge the scale of the problem in Orange Farm. The local district office called a meeting to discuss a way forward. The outcome was the establishment of a multi-stakeholder task team, headed up by an educational psychologist from the district. Representatives from different government departments, as well as NGO and parent representatives from Sidinga Uthando, started meeting monthly with the primary aim of having a new school built in the township to cater for the demonstrated needs of disabled children. The task team collaborated in compiling a submission requesting the urgent provision of inclusive education for disabled children in the area according to their educational support needs.

The submission made its way up through the bureaucratic structures to the provincial head of education. In mid-2013 a community meeting was called in Orange Farm. Representatives from the district office of the education department arrived to a room packed with family members of disabled children. After the initial pleasantries, a stamped and signed version of the submission was held up before the crowd. They were told that the submission had been successful and a school for 600 children would be budgeted for in the coming fiscal cycle. The school will be built within 3 years and temporary measures to cater for out-of-school children in the interim were promised. At the 2013 Christmas party of Sidinga Uthando, one mother commented: 'I am so happy concerning education because we challenged the Department of Education'.

The budget for building the school infrastructure alone will be 500 times the annual operating budget of the entire Afrika Tikkun empowerment programme. The strength of the empowerment programme model lies in the fact that not only is it built on a foundation motivated by its beneficiaries, but it is implemented by those same beneficiaries. The success of the empowerment programme and the Sidinga Uthando self-help group illustrates that even the most oppressed and marginalised people can work effectively to fight for the rights of disabled children despite living in contexts where human rights violations, social exclusion and poverty characterise life.

Conclusion

The examples and quotes given above illustrate clearly that both disabled children and their parents or caregivers see themselves as 'normal', without problematising this concept. The children overwhelmingly want to be seen by others as ordinary people, for who they are, not for what their difficulties are or for what they can or cannot do (Thomas 2004). They and their parents or caregivers are hurt and angered by overt structural or more subtle social-relational forms of disablism which often exclude them from mainstream activities in their communities. Only by actively seeking out disabled children's and their parents' perspectives through participatory research and other consultations, and taking these findings into account in policy and programming alongside the views of their nondisabled peers, can policymakers and service providers really claim to be acting inclusively.

Disabled children's agency and competence as people and in voicing their perspectives need to be recognised in a variety of cultural contexts globally, not just in the global North. Some authors suggest there needs to be a recognition of 'disabled children's childhoods' as an arena for discussion (Curran and Runswick-Cole 2013). However, our research suggests that disabled children and their parents and carers would prefer to be included within mainstream childhoods arenas than to be singled out for separate consideration.

In relation to the status and potential amplifying of children's voices through consulting with them, we are not advocating a fundamentalist position that would necessarily give these or any children's views precedence over those of adults around them. Rather we argue that their perspectives should be heard *alongside* significant adults such as family members, caregivers and teachers who look after and support them. Asking them directly will build a complete picture of their lives and concerns, and facilitate improvement of their well-being in ways that they approve of.

We have set out to show there is mounting evidence that disabled children and their families are often excluded and are cast in disempowered positions, especially in low-income settings. Our examples of participatory work directly with disabled children in South Asia and Uganda, and with caregivers in South Africa, demonstrate that both groups have important things to say and do, however. Listening to the perspectives and priorities of disabled children and their caregivers in poor contexts globally can reveal and highlight valuable and perhaps surprising information about them and their lives. This can aid understandings about them, challenge stereotypes and assist in catalysing new initiatives, with the power to bring about material, structural and social changes in otherwise exclusionary and oppressive societies. Hearing disabled children's and their parents' voices directly helps to humanise them and reinforce their rights to be treated as agentive citizens. We are advocating for the inclusion of disabled children's and their parents' perspectives in mainstream research, policy and action agendas. Direct involvement of both groups is essential in arguing for equality and inclusion of disabled people in the global South. Our case studies from Asia and Africa provide real examples of the potential for fruitful and revealing outcomes through deliberately seeking out the seldom heard voices of the real experts—the disabled children and their families.

References

African Child Policy Forum. (2010). *Breaking the Silence: Violence Against Children with Disabilities in Africa.* Addis Ababa: The African Child Policy Forum. Retrieved from https://app.box.com/s/6sx37rls7t0m5c90yps3/1/116120024/1019081819/1

Albrecht, G., & Devleiger, P. (1999). The disability paradox: High quality of life against all odds. *Social Science & Medicine, 48*, 977–988.

Bhabha, F. (2009). Disability equality rights in South Africa: Concepts, interpretation and the transformation imperative. *South African Journal of Human Rights, 25*(2), 217–223.

Boyden, J., & Ennew, J. (1997). *Children in focus—A manual for participatory research with children*. Stockholm: Radda Barnen.

Cavet, J. (1998). Leisure and friendship. In C. Robinson & K. Stalker (Eds.), *Growing up with disability* (pp. 97–110). London: Jessica Kingsley.

Chataika, T., & McKenzie, J. (2013). Considerations for an African childhood disability studies. In T. Curran & K. Runswick-Cole (Eds.), *Disabled children's childhood studies: Critical approaches in a global context* (pp. 152–163). Basingstoke: Palgrave-Macmillan.

Christensen, P., & James, A. (Eds.). (2000). *Research with children: Perspectives and practices*. London: Routledge Falmer.

Croft, A. (2013). Promoting access to education for disabled children in low-income countries: Do we need to know how many disabled children there are? *International Journal of Educational Development, 33*, 233–243.

Curran, T., & Runswick-Cole, K. (Eds.). (2013). *Disabled children's childhood studies: Critical approaches in a global context*. Basingstoke: Palgrave-Macmillan.

Davis, J., Watson, N., & Cunningham-Burley, S. (2003). Learning the lives of disabled children: Developing a reflexive approach. In P. Christensen & A. James (Eds.), *Research with children: Perspectives and practices* (pp. 201–224). London: Routledge Falmer.

De Sas, K. Z. O., Elphick, J., & Elphick, R. (2014). Standing by themselves: Caregivers' strategies to ensure the right to education for children with disabilities in Orange Farm, South Africa. *Childhood, 21*(3), 354–368.

Deal, M. (2007). Aversive disablism: Subtle prejudice toward disabled people. *Disability & Society, 22*(1), 93–107.

Engelbrecht, P. (2006). The implementation of inclusive education in South Africa after Ten years of democracy. *European Journal of Psychology of Education, 21*(3), 253–264.

Farmer, P. (1996). On suffering and structural violence: A view from below. *Daedalus, 125*(1), 261–283.

Feldman, M. A., Battin, S. M., Shaw, O. A., & Luckasson, R. (2013). Inclusion of children with disabilities in mainstream child development research. *Disability & Society, 28*(7), 997–1011.

Ford-Shubrook, A. (2007). *Disability inequality within Orange Farm: Barriers to education for children with disabilities within a township community in Johannesburg, South Africa*. London: University of London.

Fujiura, G. T., & Yamaki, K. (2000). Trends in demography of childhood poverty and disability. *Exceptional Children, 66*(2), 112–130.

Goodley, D., & Runswick-Cole, K. (2011). The violence of disablism. *Sociology of Health & Illness, 33*(4), 602–617.

Grech, S. (2013). Disability, childhood and poverty: Critical perspectives on Guatemala. In T. Curran & K. Runswick-Cole (Eds.), *Disabled children's childhood studies: Critical approaches in a global context* (pp. 89–104). Basingstoke: Palgrave-Macmillan.

Groce, N., Kett, M., Lang, R., & Trani, J. (2011). Disability and poverty: The need for a more nuanced understanding of implications for development policy and practice. *Third World Quarterly, 32*(8), 1493–1513.

Hanass-Hancock, J. (2012). The intersection of disability and HIV in eastern and southern Africa In *Global HIV/AIDS politics, policy and activism: Persistent challenges and emerging issues.* vol 2 *Pager.*

Hart, J. (2008). Children's participation and international development: Attending to the political. *The International Journal of Children's Rights, 16*, 407–418.

Human Rights Watch. (2010). *Barriers to full realization of humans rights for women and children with disabilities*. New York: Human Rights Watch.

James, A. (1999). 'Learning to be friends': Participant observation amongst English schoolchildren (the Midlands, England). In C. W. Watson (Ed.), *Being there: Fieldwork in anthropology* (pp. 98–120). London: Pluto Press.

James, A., Jenks, C., & Prout, A. (1998). *Theorizing childhood*. Cambridge: Polity Press.

Jans, M. (2004). Children as citizens. Towards a contemporary notion of participation. *Childhood, 11*(1), 27–44.

Kembhavi, G., & Wirz, S. (2009). Engaging adolescents with disabilities in research. *ALTER. European Journal of Disability Research., 3*, 286–296.

Lansdown, G. (2002). *Disabled Children in South Africa: Progress in implementing the Convention on the Rights of the Child*. Cape Town: Committee on the Rights for Disabled Children.

Lansdown, G. (2012). *Using the human right framework to promote the rights of children with disabilities: Working paper. An analysis of the synergies between CRC, CRPD, CEDAW.* New York: UNICEF.

Lansdown, G., Groce, N., Deluca, M., Cole, E., Berman-Bieler, R., Mitra, G., Farkas, A., Sabbe, L., & Burlyaeva-Norman, A. (2013). *Children and young disabled people: Fact sheet.* New York: UNICEF.

Lorenzo, T. (2012). *Advocating for equality in accessing livelihood assets for disabled youth* in South African Human Rights Commission *South African Human Rights Commission Equality Report—Commentaries on equality: Race, gender, disability and LGBTI Issues* (pp. 42–45). Johannesburg: SAHRC.

Mackenzie, C., & Leach Scully, J. (2007). Moral imagination, disability and embodiment. *Journal of Applied Philosophy, 24*(4), 335–351.

Mahon, A., Glendinning, C., Clarke, K., & Craig, G. (1996). Researching children: Methods and ethics. *Children & Society, 10*, 145–154.

Maulik, P., & Darmstadt, G. (2007). Childhood disability in low and middle income countries: Overview of screening, prevention, services, legislation, and epidemiology. *Pediatrics, 120*, 1–55.

Meekosha, H., & Soldatic, K. (2011). Human rights and the Global South: The case of disability. *Third World Quarterly, 32*(8), 1383–1398.

Mont, D. (2014). *Childhood disability and poverty*. LCD Working Paper 25. Leonard Cheshire Disability. Retrieved from http://www.ucl.ac.uk/silva/lc-ccr/centrepublications/workingpapers/WP25

Morris, J. (2003). Including all children: finding out about the experiences of children with communication and/or cognitive impairments. *Children & Society, 17*(5), 337–348.

Paterson, K., & Hughes, B. (1999). Disability studies and phenomenology: The carnal politics of everyday life. *Disability & Society, 14*(5), 597–610.

Richard, B. (2014). Families well-being and inclusion: Rethinking priorities for children with cognitive disabilities in Ladakh. *Childhood, 21*(3), 308–323.

Saloojee, G., Phohole, M., Saloojee, H., & Ijsselmuiden, C. (2007). Unmet health, welfare and educational needs of disabled children in an impoverished South African peri-urban township. *Child: Care, Health and Development, 33*(3), 230–235.

Save the Children & Handicap International. (2011). *Out from the shadows. Sexual violence against children with disabilities*. London: Save the Children UK. Retrieved from http://www.savethechildren.org.uk/sites/default/files/docs/out_of_the_shadows_5.pdf.

Sicking, L., Hanass Hancock, J., & van Brakel, W. (2013). *The challenges of reporting, investigating, and prosecuting of sexual violence among disabled people in south Africa*. Amsterdam: HEARD UKZN.

Singh, V., & Ghai, A. (2009). Notions of self: Lived realities of children with disabilities. *Disability & Society, 24*(2), 129–145.

Soudien, C., & Baxen, J. (2006). Disability and schooling in South Africa. In B. Watermeyer, L. Swartz, & T. Lorenzo (Eds.), *Disability and social change: A South African agenda* (pp. 149–163). Pretoria: HSRC Press.

Stoecklin, D. (2013). Theories of action in the field of child participation: In search of explicit frameworks. *Childhood, 20*, 443.

Thomas, C. (2004). Developing the social relational in the social model of disability; a theoretical agenda. In C. Barnes & G. Mercer (Eds.), *Implementing the social model of disability; theory and research*. Leeds: The Disability Press.

Tisdall, E. (2013). The transformation of participation? Exploring the potential of 'Transformative Participant' for theory and practice around children and young People's participation. *Global Studies of Childhood, 3*(2), 183–193.

Trani. J., Kett, M., Bakhshi, P., & Bailey, N. (2013). Disability, vulnerability and citizenship: To what extent is education a protective mechanism for children with disabilities in countries affected by conflict? Chapter 10 In Singal, N. (Ed.), *Disability, poverty and education.* Oxford: Routledge

UN. (1989). *Convention on the Rights of the Child.* Retrieved from www.ohchr.org/english/law/pdf/crc.pdf.

UN. (2006). *Convention on the Rights of Persons with Disabilities.* Retrieved from http://www.un.org/disabilities/default.asp.

UNA-UK. (2013). *Global development goals: Leaving no one behind.* London: UNA-UK.

UNICEF. (2008). *Monitoring child disability in developing countries: Results from the multiple indicator cluster surveys.* New York: UN.

UNICEF. (2013). *State of the world's children: Children with disabilities.* New York: UNICEF.

Watson, N. (2002). Well I know this is going to sound very strange to You but I don't see myself as a disabled person: Identity and disability. *Disability & Society, 17*(5), 509–527.

White, S., & Choudhury, S. (2007). The politics of child participation in international development: The dilemma of agency. *The European Journal of Development Research, 19*(4), 529–550.

Wickenden, M. (2011). 'Talk to me as a teenager': Experiences of friendship for disabled teenagers who have little or no speech. *Childhoods Today, 5*(1), 1–35.

Wickenden, M., & Kembhavi-Tam, G. (2014). Ask us too! Doing participatory research with disabled children in the global south. *Childhood, 21*(3), 400–417.

Wolbring, G., Mackay, R., Rybchinski, T., & Noga, J. (2013). Disabled people and the post-2015 development goal agenda through a disability studies lens. *Sustainability, 5*, 4152–4182.

World Health Organization. (2010). *Community-based rehabilitation guidelines.* Geneva: WHO. Retrieved from http://www.who.int/disabilities/cbr/guidelines/en/.

World Health Organization and UNICEF. (2012). *Early childhood development and disability: A discussion paper.* Geneva: WHO. Retrieved from http://apps.who.int/iris/bitstream/10665/75355/1/9789241504065_eng.pdf.

World Health Organization and World Bank. (2011). *World report on disability.* Geneva: WHO and World Bank. Retrieved from http://www.who.int/disabilities/world_report/2011/en/.

Chapter 12
Questioning Human Rights: The Case of Education for Children and Youth with Disabilities in Ethiopia

Hisayo Katsui, Elina Lehtomaki, Abebe Yehualawork Malle, and Shuaib Chalklen

Introduction

The UN Convention on the Rights of Persons with Disabilities (CRPD) marks a historical groundbreaking moment, providing the first ever disability rights instrument. The convention has not only marked a step forward in rendering visible the lives of people with disabilities but also in acknowledging that human rights violations persist and that rights have to be respected, protected and fulfilled. The CRPD has further promoted a human rights-based approach to disability (HRBAD). The significance of this approach is that it is based on the principles of non-discrimination and equality and involves all human beings in the mainstream discourse, including those with disabilities. Secondly, the approach requires rights-based processes and goals instead of those based on charity, which have thus far dominated the disability discourse. Thirdly, the approach stipulates that it is the state's obligation to secure the human rights of the people concerned. Fourthly, this approach demands inclusive and accessible international cooperation. These four focal points are significant for people with disabilities in the global South in achieving the ultimate goal of equality (Katsui and Kumpuvuori 2008). Evidence concerning the operationalisation of the HRBAD is invaluable for assessing global and country-level commitments to the realisation of the CRPD.

H. Katsui (✉)
University of Helsinki and Abilis Foundation, Helsinki, Finland
e-mail: hisayo.katsui@helsinki.fi

E. Lehtomaki • A.Y. Malle
University of Jyväskylä, Jyväskylä, Finland

S. Chalklen
Independent Researcher, South Africa, South Africa

S. Grech, K. Soldatic (eds.), *Disability in the Global South*,
International Perspectives on Social Policy, Administration, and Practice,
DOI 10.1007/978-3-319-42488-0_12

This chapter focuses on the politics of education as a basic human right. We analyse the challenges and opportunities implicit in realising the CRPD and operationalising the HRBAD with a case study on the inclusion of children and youth with disabilities in the regular education system of Ethiopia. The country is a significant example as the headquarters of the African Union and the United Nations Economic Commission for Africa are located there, and many African and international high-level meetings convene in the capital, Addis Ababa. Therefore, the Ethiopian Government's interpretation and realisation of the CRPD has policy-level connections and implications beyond the country's borders in Africa, when more than half the countries in sub-Saharan Africa have ratified the CRPD. Moreover, exploring the case of Ethiopia in relation to the realisation of the CRPD is important because of the somewhat contradictory situation concerning the human rights-based approach.

The Government of Ethiopia ratified the CRPD on 1 June 2010, thereby making the convention part of the law of the nation; based on Article 9(4) of the 1994 Constitution of the Federal Democratic Republic of Ethiopia, 'all international agreements ratified by Ethiopia are an integral part of the law of the land'. In 2009, however, during the ratification process, the Ethiopian parliament issued a law forbidding civil society organisations (CSOs) from promoting human rights, especially the rights of women, children and people with disabilities, thus limiting advocacy for a human rights-based approach to development (Yeshanew 2012). This prohibition of advocacy for human rights is unique in sub-Saharan Africa and, therefore, Ethiopia represents a special case, particularly in relation to the ratification and realisation of the CRPD. Yet CSOs[1] receiving foreign aid and working with children and people with disabilities are allowed to provide services. In this specific context, education for children and people with disabilities is considered a service.

Understanding the CRPD as a starting point for progressive realisation of basic human rights, we investigate how the right to education of people with disabilities and the denial of this right have influenced their (1) access to primary education, and (2) participation and advancement in education. The aim is to describe the particular situation in Ethiopia, and analyse the gaps and challenges. Finally, African collaboration in realising the right to education of people with disabilities is discussed.

Using education as a case, the realisation of the HRBAD and the CRPD is analysed through education policy and programme documents and reports. The existing situation is highlighted with the lived experiences of people with disabilities and comments by organisations of people with disabilities (DPOs), education professionals and government officials who were interviewed between August and October 2013 in Ethiopia (Katsui et al. 2014). Altogether 50 people were interviewed. The majority of the interviews were conducted with or by an Ethiopian research assistant with a disability. Pseudonyms have been used for participants whose comments are included in this chapter.

---

[1] Civil society organisations (CSOs) refers to non-governmental, not-for-profit, voluntary organisations formed by a group of people. Both organisations for people with disabilities and organisations of people with disabilities (DPOs) are CSOs. In this chapter, we use DPOs when the organisation is managed and controlled by and for people with disabilities.

Access to Education for Children with Disabilities

In the global South, most children and youth with disabilities are excluded from education though exact data are not available for all countries (United Nations 2011). Ethiopia is among those sub-Saharan African countries in which over one million children are likely to be out of school (UNESCO 2014).

The government has made investments in education and has exerted efforts to reach the Millennium Development Goal of achieving universal primary education for all by 2015. Ethiopia's public spending on education is one of the highest among countries in the global South. In 2010–2011, Ethiopia spent 4.6 per cent of its gross domestic product on education, and increased this to 5.2 per cent in 2011–2012 (World Bank 2013: 10). As a result, the net enrolment rate (NER) in primary education (grades 1–4) increased from 69.9 per cent in 2004–2005 to 98.2 per cent in 2012–2013 for boys, and from 65.1 per cent to 92.8 per cent for girls (Ministry of Education of Ethiopia [MoE] 2013a). This achievement of increased enrolment has been overshadowed by poor quality education and high dropout rates (Ministry of Education of Ethiopia [MoE] 2013b), which are of particular relevance to children with disabilities in the global South (Bines and Lei 2011; Jennings 2011).

The NER of children with disabilities was reported at 3.2 per cent in 2011–2012 (Ministry of Education of Ethiopia [MoE] 2012). More children with disabilities are enrolled in urban primary schools (4.6 per cent) than in rural ones (2.3 per cent) (Education Management Information System 2012, cited in Ministry of Education of Ethiopia [MoE] 2013b). On average, there are more boys than girls with disabilities in all grades, reflecting the tendency for parents to keep girls with disabilities at home (Jennings 2011). Similar to other low-income countries, being a girl with a disability in combination with other factors significantly increases the risk of exclusion (Hunt 2008: 28). This is reflected by many representatives of Ethiopian DPOs who maintain that education statistics on children and people with disabilities in Ethiopia are not trustworthy because many of them, especially girls and women, are not officially registered but 'hidden at home'. Education professionals suspect that the NER of children with disabilities would be even lower than the official statistics:

> There are many street children in Addis. But they are not registered. They are not included in the current government statistics. The same goes for children with disabilities. They are also not included in the statistics. That is the reason that the enrolment rate of children in Addis is almost 100 per cent, but this is not true. (A senior education professional)

In Ethiopia, regional states and districts are not yet capable of systematically collecting data on the number of children with disabilities who are out of school and those who are 'hidden at home' (Wapling 2010: 15, 38). The existing statistical information relies on reports from schools and observations by teachers concerning students with easily identifiable disabilities (Ministry of Education of Ethiopia [MoE] 2013a). The rough categories used for disaggregating data are 'blind, physically disabled, deaf, intellectually disabled, and other' (Ministry of Education of Ethiopia [MoE] 2013a: 36). The statistics, though limited, may help make children with disabilities become more visible in the development of the education system while more efforts are urgently needed to include all children with disabilities in education. At the same time, there is a danger that only children belonging to these few categories are expected to be registered and go to school; thus the statistics may work against the HRBAD and inclusion in education.

The 2007 national census defined disability categories on the basis of activity limitations in line with the CRPD and WHO definitions. However, the data collection produced a disability prevalence rate of 1 per cent, which is lower than in the previous 1994 census and significantly lower than the global average prevalence rate of 15 per cent (World Health Organization (WHO) and The World Bank 2011). Applying the rate of 15 per cent in a population of about 90 million would result in almost 13 million people with disabilities in Ethiopia instead of the less than one million figure identified in the 2007 census. A baseline study commissioned by the African Decade of Persons with Disabilities (Ministry of Labour and Social Affairs [MOLSA] [MOLSA] 2010: 18, citing World Health Organization (WHO) and The World Bank 2011) concluded that 'The number reported by both censuses is far less than other estimates. Understandably, part of the reason for the underestimation is the presence of strong cultural barriers to declare oneself or one's own child as disabled'.

In Ethiopia, disability is still regarded as a problem and a private issue instead of a social reality, let alone a human rights issue. As a result, many parents of children with disabilities are ashamed and reluctant to let their children appear in society, inhibiting them from fulfilling their potential, obtaining access to education and leading independent lives (Teferra 2005). An example of how families can be informed and convinced about the right to education and the possibility of school access is provided by Aida, who was brought to a school in a rural area farther away from her home village after a CSO approached her family and told them about the educational possibilities for children with visual impairments.

> The person who visited my family had a visual disability and told my parents that education would be important for me. My family was not ready to send me to school and was reluctant to let me go so far away from home. I was only seven years old. But this person came to visit us a few times, and my family finally decided to send me to a special school for students with visual disabilities. Until I left home for school, I was at home and not allowed to leave the house because of my disability. (Aida, a girl with a visual disability, 11th grade)

In Ethiopia, as in many other countries in the global South, identifying and finding all children with disabilities (often hidden at home) and having appropriate diagnosis and assistance requires more effort and efficient collaboration between community leaders and workers, families and healthcare professionals, and the social and education sectors (Njelesani et al. 2011; Croft 2013). Even where health care and diagnostics are available, disability prevalence rates vary due to differences in definitions and the purposes of using information (Eide et al. 2011). This lack of information, a situation whereby children with disabilities are not counted even in the demographic statistics and where birth certificates are not issued, making it impossible to cross-check the number of children in a school area, contributes to a high NER, as in the case of Ethiopia.

Students with Disabilities: Greater Risk of Dropping Out

The quality of education in sub-Saharan Africa is a concern. The all-round poor quality of the education system increases the risk of students dropping out and contributes to weak learning outcomes in general, more so of children with disabilities who have accessed primary education. One of the most important factors for improving quality is teacher development. Sub-Saharan African countries need about 225,000 more teachers annually to be able to provide primary education for all children (UNESCO 2014). In Ethiopia, the number of qualified teachers needed for primary education is far beyond the capacity of teacher education institutions; alternative programmes and in-service training to update skills are therefore urgently needed (Abebe and Woldehanna 2013). In regions where children with disabilities are enrolled in regular schools, teachers report on their need for capacity development, materials and support to enable the learning of these children (Jennings 2011).

Ministry of Education statistics show that nationally, the average pupil–teacher ratio at the primary level (grades 1–8) was 49.4 pupils per teacher in 2012–2013, although regional differences are observed. For instance, in the Somali region, the ratio was as high as 102.5 (Ministry of Education of Ethiopia [MoE] 2013a: 30). This has an adverse effect on the teaching and learning process and hence on the quality of education. Poor quality education reduces families' motivation to send their children to school (Jennings 2011; UNESCO 2014). The situation is exacerbated by the fact that teachers have reportedly been required to give passing grades to almost all students to enable them to advance to the next level with a view to reducing dropout rates and increasing the enrolment rates in schools at all levels.

> When I started to teach at the university, I gave 'failing' marks to several students. The head of the department came to me and instructed me not to give 'failing' marks to any student even when their exam marks are very poor. I can show you this. This is the exam result for this semester. You can see that there are no 'failing' grades on this list. I am not allowed to fail students. This seems to be the national policy now. … That's why even university graduates are not qualified employees today. (A university lecturer in education)

In sub-Saharan Africa, due to very limited access to schools, little is known about how children with disabilities advance and succeed in education (Hunt 2008; Lehtomäki et al. 2014). Many observable barriers in physical environments, such as distance between home and school and inaccessible school facilities, are challenging, particularly for children with mobility difficulties and visual disabilities. Water and sanitation are serious problems. According to the latest government report on education in Ethiopia, 40.7 per cent of primary schools have water facilities while 8 per cent do not have latrines at all (Ministry of Education of Ethiopia [MoE] 2013a: 37). This water and sanitation problem is of particular importance for girls and children with disabilities (Jones and Reed 2005).

Two girls who completed the eight years of primary school with good grades and proudly continued their studies talked about the challenges in advancing their education. At the time of the interviews, they were attending the 11th grade in a regular secondary school in the same rural area where they attended primary school. Each of the girls received a small amount of monthly allowance provided by a CSO, which receives funding from abroad. The girls claimed that the allowance was too small to live on because the monthly rent of the room they shared was the same amount. As the girls transitioned from the special primary school to the secondary school, they faced many challenges, including lack of accessible educational means, attitude of teachers and peer pupils and poverty.

> No special attention is paid to students like us in our school. For example, teachers do not know how to teach us. Teachers only write on the blackboard and do not read what is written there. So we are often not learning what others learn in the same classroom. (Sofia, a girl with a visual disability, 11th grade)
>
> I am still afraid of students with no disabilities. I have no confidence in speaking with them because I was in the special school. It's difficult to become friends with them. (Aida, a girl with a visual disability, 11th grade)

Poverty deeply affects the realities of people with disabilities (Eide and Ingstad 2011), including participation in education. In a quantitative study in four African countries, findings highlight how the mean size of households with family members with disabilities was bigger because those households required extra hands for support. The study concluded that households with members with disabilities tended to be worse off compared with households without because they had more mouths to feed (Eide et al. 2011). Therefore, even when children with disabilities manage to access education, the poverty of their families challenges their advancement and survival. The two girls above said that many former classmates had not continued their studies.

> Many classmates at the primary school are now on the streets begging for money because they were too poor and also not good enough to continue their study. They do not have a place at home (to go back to) because they lived here. (Sofia, a girl with a visual disability, 11th grade)

In circumstances where children with disabilities are not in school due to disabling environments both inside and outside district-run schools, CSOs and church groups provide alternative services for them (Jennings 2011: 2; Ministry of Education of Ethiopia [MoE] 2013b: 17). They run many of the special schools while rehabilitation is left mostly to CSOs. The 2009 'CSO law' introduced restrictions on the relevant work of CSOs. It classifies CSOs based on the law under which they are formed, the nationality of their members and their source of funds; the restriction in the law is reserved for work on human and democratic rights, gender equality, the rights of children and people with disabilities, and conflict resolution, while judicial support is given only to Ethiopian CSOs. The latter are those formed under Ethiopian law with full membership and control by Ethiopians, and which do not use more than 10 per cent of funds from foreign sources (Proclamation no. 621/2009, Articles 2 and 14). Other CSOs, both Ethiopian and international 'charities', are allowed to work only in service delivery and development issues, and there is no reference to rights in their interventions. The law limits CSOs, their sources of funding and areas of operation and, consequently, implementation of the human rights-based approach in development cooperation with Ethiopia. To illustrate the impact of the law, the CSO supporting Sofia and Aida plans to discontinue funding for the special school and graduates in the near future.

During the interviews with the two girls, their observations suggested the educational environment was challenging for youth with disabilities at schools. The girls were not literate in braille though they had completed their primary education in a special school for students with visual disabilities. This is often the case in Ethiopia due to a lack of braille materials as well as a lack of teachers trained in Braille (as mentioned by a staff member of an organisation of blind people). Furthermore, in the regular secondary school where the language of instruction is English, these young students most probably had difficulties due to their weak English proficiency. They were not able to respond to simple questions in English, such as 'How are you?' and 'Is it true?' The interviews were held in their mother tongue through an interpreter who also had a disability. In addition to general poverty, these facts indicate that they are disadvantaged in many ways, which explains the high dropout rates of children and youth with disabilities from schools. Hence good quality education as a right is hardly recognised in reality.

The girls were asked 'If you did not attend school, what do you think you would be doing now?' They both answered 'I would have been at home'—as is the case for 97 per cent of children and youth with disabilities in Ethiopia. The young students were uncertain about their future but hoped to become professionals—one wanted to be a teacher and the other a baker—as any girl of their age would dream within this context.

To investigate how the human rights-based approach can be utilised in education, we need to ask how we can turn teachers and education authorities into important duty-bearers responsible for those who are left behind without reasonable accommodation in schools. An equally important question is how different sectors and actors at all levels in society can collaborate to realise these rights, as ratified by the government, in an effort to end exclusion and reduce poverty.

Do Disability Rights Matter?

The reports and experiences of people with disabilities powerfully depict the severe stigma attached to disability in Ethiopia as families do not problematise the non-education of their children. Many parents do not yet know that their children with disabilities have an equal right to education (Jennings 2011). Mainstream policy and practice have often unintentionally, or even intentionally, excluded children with disabilities and reinforced their exclusion. The selected interviews indicate that without institutionalised mechanisms, disability rights will not be automatically mainstreamed at any or all levels, whether local, national, regional or global. This is because the priority is low among other priorities for duty-bearers. For instance, increasing the NER of children in general is the priority of the government while the quality of education is secondary, let alone the right to education of children with disabilities.

The possibilities to claim rights and the capacity of both duty-bearers and rights-holders are limited. Rights-holders, children and youth with disabilities and their families, hardly have the means to claim their rights due to multi-layered poverty and power relations (Grech 2009). On the other hand, duty-bearers, such as teachers, school leaders, education authorities and families, do not problematise that children with disabilities do not go to school. In the Ethiopian context where the vast majority of children with disabilities, about 97 per cent according to the official statistics, are not in schools, this situation is the social norm. Inequality is not politicised because it is seen as a natural matter of fact for many duty-bearers and rights-holders, which consequently reinforces the status quo of exclusion. Educational exclusion tends to contribute to further exclusion in society and increases poverty among families who have children with disabilities. This national context complicates the operationalisation of the HRBAD.

The interviews with the two girls mentioned earlier revealed that without the possibility of education facilitated by CSO staff, they would have most probably remained at home. Many other DPO representatives also described this scenario.

In Ethiopia, this high level of exclusion can be explained by the result-based management centred on cost-effective thinking that has prevailed among stakeholders and which has undermined the principles of a HRBAD. More precisely, there is a disincentive to address the needs of children and people with disabilities because, for instance, enrolling 10,000 non-disabled children in schools is considered 'more effective' than enrolling 9000 children with and without disabilities. In this context, operationalisation of a HRBAD itself becomes challenging without principles, such as non-discrimination and equality. That is, the very power structures that a HRBAD tries to challenge hamper its operationalisation, especially in terms of reducing inequality. In other words, the approach itself needs to be elaborated on in its relevance and validity in each specific context, and even questioned. When people are more advantaged, objectively quantifiable impacts of intervention are greater than for those whose capacity is made to be much more limited (Katsui 2012). For instance, children without a disability tend to benefit from national educational efforts as shown in the increasing NER statistics, while many children with disabilities too frequently remain uneducated. Furthermore, powerful actors make strategic decisions based on competing priorities and leave behind less powerful actors, without listening to their voices, which means that disability rights are not prioritised in practice. How can people with disabilities be heard and included in education in Ethiopia? Could there be a solution through African collaboration?

Politics for the Human Rights-Based Approach to Disability in Africa

As Oinas and Jungar (2008: 255) emphasise: 'There are no neutral agendas, there is no pre-discursive embodiment and there are no politics-free zones where stakeholders can unite in terms of absolute good'. Frediani (2010: 185) states that the HRBAD undermines local agencies' own identification of values and priorities, and maintains a situation where 'approaches to development can explicitly incorporate this reflexivity of their [the agencies'] role in the process of moving from rhetoric to transformation, without being coerced, manipulated, and co-opted into preconceived goals'. Values based on local context and individuals are often not only undermined but even overruled by universal norms. In other words, although human rights has been a 'discursive process, not a static set of prescriptive values' that were 'formed in the process of struggle and debates' (Meekosha and Soldatic 2011:

1387), the human rights-based approach tends to depoliticise itself. A critical reflection is needed to examine how the approach is applied in the reality where it is used. When many modalities are identified in development and disability discourse, such as empowerment, mainstreaming and community-based rehabilitation (European Commission 2010: 48; Norwegian Agency for Development Cooperation (NORAD) 2012), to name a few, the human rights-based approach needs to be continuously questioned in terms of its validity in a specific context and, moreover, negotiated by the duty-bearers and rights-holders.

This chapter focuses on disability rights and their realisation, particularly the right to education of children and people with disabilities in Ethiopia where the HRBAD is constrained on account of the political climate. The case of Ethiopia reveals that both local and international disability-specific efforts face challenges and multi-layered resistance, resulting in a reinforced and extremely unequal status quo. Most of the international and bilateral cooperation agencies and funding charities either have little or no knowledge, or are not interested in the issue of disability on account of a lack of awareness and trust in the potential and capacity of people with disabilities. Their representatives are unaware of their governments' commitments to the CRPD and MDGs, including 'Education for All'. Professionals do not appear to question contradictory information, such as the near 100 per cent NER reported, as 97 per cent of children with disabilities are not in school. Though the CRPD defines inclusive education as the approach to ensure the access and participation of children with disabilities, in many low-income countries, inclusive education has been interpreted with reference to other marginalised groups, such as girls, ethnic and linguistic minorities and rural children. Children with disabilities are usually the last to be included (Bines and Lei 2011).

Inequality may be reinforced or even increased unless duty-bearers in the global South and North increase their capacity, dialogue and change their paradigm from 'intervention effectiveness' to 'development effectiveness', thereby encompassing inequality reduction as a central objective. For instance, existing statistics are not rigorous in elaborating on those who are excluded from educational opportunities and in analysing the root causes of such exclusion (UNESCO 2014). The very power structures that the HRBAD should deconstruct are taken for granted in too many development interventions. Priorities favour the more powerful, such as the more empowered, richer, stronger, healthier and so forth, thereby reflecting existing power structures. This is evident in current trends of educational development as more investments are being made in the education of children and young people of rich families in urban areas; this simultaneously results in the neglect of disadvantaged children and youth, including those with disabilities (UNESCO 2014).

At the grassroots level in the global South, many children and people with disabilities remain at home, hidden or overprotected. They do not have enough capacity to claim their rights due to disempowering power structures and disenabling environments. Educational exclusion worsens their situation. Therefore, representative organisations of people with disabilities have to play a major role in filling the gaps of both rights-holders and duty-bearers at different levels until sufficient capacity is built. Eide and Ingstad (2011) emphasise the capacity building of DPOs and people with disabilities, and knowledge production for advocacy.

When successful, the HRBAD and its critical analysis bring about transformation in theory and practice. People with disabilities at the grassroots level, including rights-holders, need knowledge, capacities and channels to claim their rights from duty-bearers. Initiatives aimed at including the voices of students and girls with regard to their education and participation have proven powerful in transformations when these groups have been included in local, national and international development dialogues (e.g. Kiragu et al. 2011).

Disability rights do matter for children and people with disabilities who comprise 15 per cent of the total global population. This chapter advocates making duty-bearers accountable for their duties at all levels and pressuring for collaboration between them, particularly through the African Union. Without voice and powerful representation, African disability stakeholders have missed important opportunities for advocacy. For instance, the United Nations High-level Meeting on Disability and Development in September 2013 was a historic opportunity to promote inclusive sustainable development and reduction of inequality for the post-2015 agenda. This meeting could have been an opportunity to question the inclusiveness of future sustainable development goals and donor accountability, particularly with reference to Article 32 of the CPRD which explicates that development cooperation has to be inclusive and accessible and must highlight the gaps and failures in global development (United Nations 2011). Disability rights in Africa have not been a priority in the global context, when realities in so-called 'rich countries' require a lot of structural changes in terms of disability rights. Hence, when not represented, the reality for people with disabilities will never become a priority among many competing priorities.

In the disability community in Africa, we find a number of cross-disability as well as single disability pan-African and sub-regional federations of DPOs. At present, however, none of the existing regional or sub-regional DPO federations is recognised by the African Union as the authoritative, representative voice of people with disabilities in Africa. The very diversity has been one of the biggest challenges for African DPOs to become agents of change at the continental level, thereby hampering their participation at regional, national and local levels. Consequently, the voices of African people with disabilities have hardly been heard.

The African Union has been undergoing a number of developments in the field of disability at three levels: legal, programmatic and institutional. The new African Union Disability Architecture (AUDA) will seek to promote equality as enshrined in the International Disability Architecture, which consists of the CRPD and other international human rights and development instruments. The AUDA would benefit greatly from representatives and ownership of African people with disabilities if there were such an organ as an African Disability Forum (ADF).

A consultative meeting on the creation of the ADF took place in November 2012 at the UN Conference Centre in Addis Ababa. An interim working group meeting among members with diverse regional, disability, gender and age profiles was organised in December 2013 in Addis Ababa. The launch event of the forum was planned in 2014. The ADF will seek to strengthen and unify the representative voices of DPOs and people with disabilities in Africa. The African continent is immense with regional and in-country diversity, and therefore one organisation cannot be expected to fully reflect and represent such diversity. Rather, the ADF would include and build upon existing structures, capacities and successes, including the more marginalised groups among people with disabilities. Ownership and representation need to remain in the hands of African people with disabilities in order to strengthen their capacity as well as that of duty-bearers. As diverse and structural challenges at all levels intertwine, so too must the solutions, not only in the education sector but beyond.

References

Abebe, W., & Woldehanna, T. (2013). *Teacher training and development in Ethiopia: Improving education quality by developing teacher skills, attitudes and work conditions*. Oxford: Young Lives, Oxford Department of International Development, University of Oxford. Retrieved February 4, 2014, from http://www.younglives.org.uk/files/working-papers/yl-wp103-abebe-woldehanna.

Bines, H., & Lei, P. (2011). Disability and education: The longest road to inclusion. *International Journal of Educational Development, 31*, 419–424.

Croft, A. (2013). Promoting access to education for disabled children in low-income countries: Do we need to know how many disabled children there are? *International Journal of Educational Development, 33*, 233–243.

Eide, A. H., & Ingstad, B. (Eds.). (2011). *Disability and poverty: A global challenge*. Bristol: The Policy Press.

Eide, A. H., Loeb, M. E., Nhiwatiwa, S., Munthali, A., Ngulube, T. J., & van Rooy, G. (2011). Living conditions among people with disabilities in developing countries. In A. H. Eide & B. Ingstad (Eds.), *Disability and poverty: A global challenge* (pp. 55–70). Bristol: The Policy Press.

European Commission. (2010). *Study of disability in EC development cooperation*. Retrieved October 15, 2013, from http://ec.europa.eu/europeaid/what/social-protection/documents/223185_disability_study_en.pdf

Federal Negarit Gazeta. (2009). *Proclamation no. 621/2009. Proclamation to provide for the registration and regulation of charities and societies*. Addis Ababa: Federal Democratic Republic of Ethiopia. Retrieved August 11, 2014, from http://www.molsa.gov.et/Amharic/Resources/Documents/Charities%20and%20Societies%20Proclamation.pdf

Frediani, A. A. (2010). Sen's capability approach as a framework to the practices of development. *Development in Practice, 20*(2), 173–187.

Grech, S. (2009). Disability, poverty and development: Critical reflections on the majority world debate. *Disability & Society, 24*(6), 771–784.

Hunt, F. (2008). *Dropping out from school: A cross-country review of literature*. CREATE Pathways to Access No. 16. Brighton: Consortium for Research on Educational Access, Transitions and Equity, University of Sussex. Retrieved February 4, 2014, from http://www.create-rpc.org/pdf_documents/PTA16.pdf

Jennings, M. (2011). *Social assessment for the education sector, Ethiopia*. London: Department for International Development, Social Development Direct. Retrieved November 20, 2013, from http://www.sddirect.org.uk/uploads/pdfs/social-assessment-education-ethiopia.pdf

Jones, H., & Reed, B. (2005). *Water and sanitation for disabled people and other vulnerable groups: Designing services to improve accessibility*. Leicestershire: Water, Engineering and Development Centre, Loughborough University. Retrieved August 1, 2014, from https://wedc-knowledge.lboro.ac.uk/details.html?id=16357

Katsui, H. (2012). *Disabilities, human rights and international cooperation: Human rights-based approach and lived experiences of Ugandan women with disabilities*. Publication Series No. 8. Helsinki: The Center for Human Rights of Persons with Disabilities.

Katsui, H., & Kumpuvuori, J. (2008). Human rights-based approach to disability in development in Uganda: A way to fill the gap between political and social spaces? *Scandinavian Journal of Disability Research, 10*(4), 227–236.

Katsui, H., Ranta, E. M., Yeshanew, S. A., Musila, G. M., Mustaniemi-Laakso, M., & Sarelin, A. (2014). *Reducing inequalities: A human rights-based approach in Finland's development cooperation with special focus on gender and disability. A case study on Kenya and Ethiopia.* Turku: Institute for Human Rights.

Kiragu, S., Swartz, C., Chikovore, J., Lukalo, F., & Oduro, G. Y. (2011). Agency, access, silence and ethics: How young people's voices from Africa can contribute to social and educational change in adult-dominated societies. In C. Day (Ed.), *International handbook of teacher and school development* (pp. 254–263). London: Routledge.

Lehtomäki, E., Tuomi, M. T., & Matonya, M. (2014). Educational research from Tanzania 1998–2008 concerning persons with disabilities: What can we learn? *International Journal of Educational Research, 64*, 32–39.

Meekosha, H., & Soldatic, K. (2011). Human rights and the global south: The case of disability. *Third World Quarterly, 32*(8), 1383–1397.

Ministry of Education of Ethiopia [MoE]. (2012). *Education statistics annual abstract: 2004 EC.* [2011/12 GC.]. Addis Ababa: Ministry of Education. Retrieved December 13, 2013, from http://www.moe.gov.et/English/Resources/Documents/eab04.pdf

Ministry of Education of Ethiopia [MoE]. (2013a). *Education statistics annual abstract: November 2005 EC.* [2012/13 GC.]. Addis Ababa: Ministry of Education. Retrieved January 5, 2014, from http://www.moe.gov.et/English/Resources/Documents/eab05.pdf

Ministry of Education of Ethiopia [MoE]. (2013b). *Social assessment of the General Education Quality Improvement Program Phase 2.*

Ministry of Labour and Social Affairs [MOLSA]. (2010). *Baseline study on the status of persons with disabilities and the influence of the African decade pronouncement in Ethiopia.* Addis Ababa: Federal Democratic Republic of Ethiopia. Retrieved August 11, 2014, from http://www.molsa.gov.et/English/SWD/Documents/Baseline%20Study%20Final%20report_ADDP.pdf.

Njelesani, J., Couto, S., & Cameron, D. (2011). Disability and rehabilitation in Tanzania: A review of the literature. *Disability and Rehabilitation, 33*(23–24), 2196–2207.

Norwegian Agency for Development Cooperation (NORAD). (2012). *Mainstreaming disability in the new development paradigm: Evaluation of Norwegian support to promote the rights of persons with disabilities.* Retrieved January 16, 2013, from http://www.norad.no/en/tools-and-publications/publications/evaluations/publication?key=389256

Oinas, E., & Jungar, K. (2008). A luta continua!—South African HIV activism, embodiment and state politics. *Development Dialogue, 50.* Retrieved December 9, 2009, from http://www.nai.uu.se/research/researchers/elina_oinas/publications/Development_dialogue_50_art12-2.pdf

Teferra, T. (2005). *Disability in Ethiopia: Issues, insights and implications.* Addis Ababa: Addis Ababa University.

UNESCO. (2014). Teaching and learning: Achieving quality for all. *Education for all global monitoring report 2013/14.* Retrieved January 30, 2014, from http://www.unesco.org/new/en/education/themes/leading-the-international-agenda/efareport/reports/2013

United Nations. (2011). *Disability and millennium development goals: A review of the MDGs process and strategy for inclusion of disability issues in millennium development goal efforts.* New York: United Nations. Retrieved February 4, 2014, from http://www.un.org/disabilities/documents/review_of_disability_and_the_mdgs.pdf.

Wapling, L. (2010). *Exploratory mission to assess the opportunities for inclusive education in Ethiopia.* London: Handicap International.

World Bank. (2013, September). *International Development Association Project Appraisal Document for a General Education Quality Improvement Program II.*

World Health Organization (WHO) and The World Bank. (2011). *World report on disability.* Geneva: WHO. Retrieved December 15, 2013, from www.who.int/disabilities/world_report/.

Yeshanew, S. A. (2012). CSO law in Ethiopia: Considering its constraints and consequences. *Journal of Civil Society, 8*(4), 369–384.

Chapter 13
Reflexive Re-storying of Inclusive Education: Evidence from India and South Africa

Nidhi Singal and Nithi Muthukrishna

Introduction

Over the past few decades, inclusive education has become an integral part of the global discourse on education. This was most notable in the 1990s, with the adoption of the Salamanca Statement and Framework for Action on Special Needs Education (UNESCO 1994). This statement was very influential in shaping the vision of inclusive education as 'the hallmark of service provision for children with disabilities' internationally (Rao and Kalyanpur 2015: 11). It was unequivocal in calling on the international community to endorse the approach of inclusive schooling: 'We call upon all governments and urge them to [...] adopt as a matter of law or policy the principle of inclusive education, enrolling all children in regular schools, unless there are compelling reasons for doing otherwise' (UNESCO 1994: ix). Over the years, inclusive education has been accorded great legitimacy across the world, setting in motion decades of deliberation and passionate debates reflecting on its theoretical underpinnings, practicality and perceived effectiveness (see for example Strogilos 2011; Lim and Thaver 2014). The Salamanca Statement itself was very powerful in equating inclusive schooling with visions of an inclusive society and with economic issues. For example, it noted:

N. Singal (✉)
University of Cambridge, Cambridge, UK
e-mail: sn21@cam.ac.uk

N. Muthukrishna
University of KwaZulu-Natal, Durban, South Africa

S. Grech, K. Soldatic (eds.), *Disability in the Global South*,
International Perspectives on Social Policy, Administration, and Practice,
DOI 10.1007/978-3-319-42488-0_13

> Regular schools with this inclusive orientation are the most effective means of combating discriminatory attitudes, creating welcoming communities, building an inclusive society and achieving education for all; moreover, they provide an effective education to the majority of children and improve efficiency and ultimately the cost effectiveness of the entire education system. (UNESCO 1994: xii).

While the concept of inclusive education has had global spread, and has been incorporated in various national and international policies, it has varied and often ambiguous understandings in different contexts (see Rose 2010; Artiles et al. 2011; Donohue and Bornman 2014). Slee (2001) has argued that despite the impressive growth in interest and enthusiasm around inclusive education throughout the world, how it is defined and implemented, and for whose benefit, remains at best incompletely understood. Since the calls for inclusion in the early 1990s there has been a lot written and discussed around inclusion, especially in countries such as Australia, the UK and the USA. A simple Internet search of texts around inclusive education in the UK, for instance, will inundate anyone with the high volume of journal articles, monographs, professional books and magazines about inclusive schooling and inclusive practices.

Research on inclusive education in southern contexts (here we are particularly focusing on Africa and south Asia) tends to be dominated by studies addressing government and teachers' understandings of 'inclusive education' and/or attitudes towards individuals with disabilities (for example, Parasuram 2006; Agbenyega 2007; Bornman and Donohue 2013). These concerns on access and attitudes, as Singal and Jeffery (2011) note, are primarily first-generation issues and are devoid of deeper engagement with issues such as the quality and impact of schooling on students with disabilities. Additionally, a significant amount of existing work tends to adopt northern countries as a reference point for developing inclusive practices (Singal 2006; Schuelka and Johnstone 2012). It is common to come across training and development packages and toolkits which are developed in the North and translated into various local languages for southern consumption. For example, the Index for Inclusion (Booth and Ainscow 2002), translated and exported to over 40 countries, and the UNESCO-funded Teacher Education Resource Pack (UNESCO 1993), the result of a project titled 'Special Needs in the Classroom' carried out in around 50 countries, were underpinned by certain assumptions about school improvement and pedagogy which were not culture or value free. There has been little parity in the exchange of ideas between countries of the South and the North (Armstrong et al. 2011); rather, the flow of information has been unidirectional, from the North to the South. Thus, existing debates around inclusive education in the South, we would argue, have ignored important contextual and cultural specificity, and have largely failed to engage with the strengths and tensions within existing educational and broader socio-cultural systems.

The discourse around inclusive education in southern contexts is constructed around three central premises. First, inclusive education is strongly linked with the vision of an inclusive society (UNESCO 1994) and is regarded as a mechanism for achieving social justice. Second, inclusion is viewed as being financially desirable, as Lynch notes:

> If segregated special education is to be provided for all children with special educational needs, the cost will be enormous and prohibitive for all developing countries. If integrated in-class provision with a support teacher system is envisaged for the vast majority of children with special educational needs, then the additional costs can be marginal, if not negligible. (Lynch 1994: 29)

Finally, inclusive education has been linked to the development of educational systems for the benefit of all children (e.g. see Sebba and Ainscow 1996). Ainscow (1995) argued that when teachers develop a wider range of different pedagogical responses to pupils who experience difficulties in their learning, it enables the reformation of ordinary education, to make it more comprehensive. However, what remains conspicuously absent in all these debates is how to operationalise inclusive education in practice in such a way that it responds to the realities and priorities of local settings (e.g. Donohue and Bornman 2014).

Interestingly, even though inclusive education has occupied a vast amount of research space in countries such as the UK, Florian and Linklater (2010) remind us that many classroom teachers remain uncertain about how to *do* inclusion in practice. Others such as Miles and Ahuja acknowledge that 'Northern countries clearly do not have all the answers' (2007: 135), noting that in England considerable efforts have been made to promote inclusive education, though school attendance and dropout rates are a matter of significant concern as is the variation in special education provision across local authorities. More recently, commentators such as Farrell (2010) have begun to question the relevance and the practicality of inclusion for all children with disabilities. In some ways the most powerful critique for reconsidering this all-encompassing focus on inclusive education has come from Lady Mary Warnock, who was chair of the commission which introduced the terminology of special educational needs (SEN) and other related policies in England. Warnock, writing with reference to children with special needs, noted:

> It is their right to learn that we must defend, not their right to learn in the same environment as everyone else … whatever may be the merits of deploying the rhetoric of human rights in the demand for inclusion for the disabled in society as a whole, it cannot be argued a priori that values within a school must be identical to values in the society of adults. (Warnock 2005: 36)

It is important to explicitly state here that in putting forward these arguments, we are not making a case for not supporting the education of children with disabilities; rather, by raising these issues we are highlighting the complexities inherent in the realisation of inclusive education in everyday practice. While such critical voices are beginning to emerge in northern contexts, inclusive education in countries of the South remains an ideal which nations are being pushed to achieve through the 'exhortations of first world aid agencies, and international donors' (Armstrong et al. 2011: 33). The irony of the situation is that while 'disability' is being reclaimed in southern contexts, as evident in the work of Grech (2011) and Meekosha and Soldatic (2011), the field of education, particularly in relation to debates around the education of children with disabilities, has remained largely dominated by a northern lens (Schuelka and Johnstone 2012; Singal and Muthukrishna 2014).

More recently scholars have begun to argue that while inclusive education is propagated as the solution to educational problems faced in southern contexts, it is primarily based on 'a set of globally-generated, validated and disseminated assumptions about the educational needs of students' (Le Fanu 2011: 5), which do not necessarily hold true in these settings. Others have been more forthcoming in acknowledging that 'the growth of 'inclusive education' in the developing world … in part reflects the export of first-world thinking to countries which reinforces dependency' (Armstrong et al. 2009: 12). This results in a scenario where models of inclusive education are (seemingly) seamlessly transported from one context to the other, the underlying assumption being that such models will work without any expectation of country-based stakeholders to adapt these or, more importantly, feel a sense of ownership.

It must also be acknowledged that such transference focuses attention on what is not happening in these settings, rather than engaging in a more nuanced exploration of educational priorities and realities in local contexts (as illustrated by Kalyanpur 2014 in the case of Cambodia). By reproducing deficit discourses, the real opportunities which are accorded within local contexts to support learning of children with disabilities remain unacknowledged. This is not to disregard the real challenges that are present in many southern contexts, where educators work with limited budgets and so on, but the fact that there is no endeavour to engage with enablers in the existing system frames these countries as deficit oriented.

It has naively been assumed that inclusive education policies framed at a global level can be reproduced neatly in local contexts, and when this does not happen the failure is seen as resulting from lack of political will or teacher indifference, rather than the appropriateness of the policies being questioned. By drawing on the work of Ball et al. (2011a, b) we argue that an in-depth understanding of the context of how and why people (teachers, parents and young people themselves) make decisions is centrally important. Even though this body of research (Ball et al. 2011a, b) was conducted in UK secondary schools, what is most powerful in their framework is a delineation of 'context', while exemplifying its multidimensionality. They argue that context consists of situated contexts (such as locale, school histories, intakes and settings); professional contexts (e.g. values, teacher commitments and experiences); material contexts (e.g. staffing, budget, buildings, technology and infrastructure) and external contexts (e.g. pressures and expectations from broader policy context, legal requirements and responsibilities). Examination of these dimensions enables a deeper understanding of how different variables inform, frame and indeed limit various stakeholders' responses to policy. Further, Ball et al. (2011a, b) stress the localised nature of policy enactment and that teachers are active agents in the mediation of policy, though in their enactments of policy they may not emerge as coherent subjects and may work in contradictory and ambiguous ways. In our study we were interested in the notion of teachers as policy actors in the context of globally influenced inclusive education policy imperatives in India and South Africa, and in exploring ways in which teachers find spaces to *perform* their agency as they select, interpret and modify policy in line with contextual demands and circumstances. Our view is that the role of context in shaping teacher enactments of inclusive education policy is critical to the study of inclusive education policy implementation.

In this chapter we wish to take forward a dialogue which is not only critical of current northern hegemonic assumptions in relation to the education of children with disabilities but also identifies ways of moving forward. The aim is to draw on research evidence from the field to challenge and expand the existing discourse around inclusive education, while being mindful of building a new grand universal theory. In order to achieve the stated aims we will examine how 'inclusive education' policies are practised in schools in two national settings: India and South Africa. While the contexts are markedly different, they share particular similarities in relation to the presence of a policy discourse which has been significantly influenced by international declarations, such as the Convention on the Rights of Persons with Disabilities (United Nations 2006). Additionally, in both these countries, the 1990s saw the widespread introduction of toolkits and other guidance legitimised by international bodies such as UNESCO (1993, 2004). Finally, given the common history of colonialism, schooling systems in both these countries are influenced by the period of the British Raj and, even more crucially, the modern intelligentsia continue to look towards the North for solutions to many of their country problems (Breidlid 2013). We begin by examining briefly the policy contexts in India and South Africa before moving on to discuss the two research projects from which we draw the data to support our arguments.

Educational Policies for Children with Disabilities in India and South Africa

Similar to other southern countries, education in India and South Africa is an important part of the government agenda, with particular attention given to addressing concerns about educational inequity among various groups and the general quality of schooling. In South Africa, Education White Paper 6 makes a commitment to the provision of quality and equitable education for all learners irrespective of diversity and the protection of the right to education (Department of Education 2001). In India, the Sarva Shiksha Abhiyan, literally meaning the 'Campaign for Universal Education', is considered one of the most significant education initiatives globally. It is within these national contexts that our research projects were situated. In both country contexts, the rights of children with disabilities are clearly affirmed in legislation and policy in that they cannot be excluded from schooling on the basis of disability. Further, there is a commitment that all social institutions should challenge inequity and fundamental inequalities. India and South Africa have both ratified the Convention on the Rights of Persons with Disabilities (CRPD). Article 24 of the Convention states that, 'States Parties shall ensure that [...] persons with disabilities can access an inclusive, quality and free primary education and secondary education on an equal basis with others in the communities in which they live'. It is interesting here to note how the notion of 'inclusive' has been elaborated upon differently at the policy level in the two countries.

India

In recent years India has made significant progress in improving access to primary education; however, significant challenges remain in relation to quality and continued exclusion of some groups (De et al. 2011). Official data highlights that mainstream enrolment of children with special needs (CWSN, in India this term is synonymously used with children with disabilities (Singal 2014)) has increased sharply from 566,921 in 2002–2003 to 2.35 million in 2012–2013. Not surprisingly, these statistics are contested (see Singal 2014 for a detailed discussion). Additionally, analysis of recent school data, which is collected through the District Information System for Education (DISE), highlights large interstate variations in enrolment of CWSN at the elementary level. Even in states such as Kerala where the overall enrolment of children is high, the group which is most likely to be disproportionately marginalised from schooling is children with disabilities, even when controlling for variables such as gender and socio-economic factors. Moreover, the data reveals that children with certain types of disability, such as autism and cerebral palsy, face far greater disadvantage than others (Singal 2014). While the focus has remained on enrolment, a recent NCERT survey of Class V examined the learning outcomes of children, including those with disabilities, across 27 states and 4 union territories. In the sample, 6 per cent of the students belonged to the physically challenged group (NCERT 2012: xxvii) and in various tasks they did 'substantially worse than the rest of the population' (NCERT 2012: 113), scoring on average 12 scale points lower than their (non-disabled) peers in reading comprehension, even after controlling for background characteristics.

The education of children with disabilities was addressed in the earliest national policies, such as the 1986 National Policy of Education (Ministry of Human Resource Development 1992), and was a focus of the District Primary Education Programme (DPEP) in the 1990s. This programme was central in introducing the concept of inclusive education at the national level. While DPEP had a very specific mandate on mainstreaming all children with disabilities, a more nuanced approach has been adopted in the ongoing national programme, Sarv Skiksha Abhiyan (SSA). SSA is focused on improving access and the quality of teaching and learning for all children, including CWSN, who are addressed under the framework of 'inclusive education'. SSA notes that it adopts a 'zero rejection policy' so that no child is left out of the education system (SSA 2007). Over the last few years there has been a move away from a dual system—mainstream and special—to a more expansive understanding, wherein a multi-option model of educating CWSN is now being implemented. An important aim of this model has been to reach out to more CWSN and also to provide them with appropriate need-based skills, be it vocational, functional literacy or simply activities of daily living, in the most appropriate learning environment.

An additional impetus to the education of children with disabilities has been the passing of the Right to Education Act 2009, which mandates the right to free and compulsory education for *all* children in the 6–14 age group. This commitment to education is supported through the efforts of the Ministry of Social Justice and Empowerment, which framed the National Policy for People with Disabilities: 'Education is the most effective vehicle of social and economic empowerment. … free and compulsory education has to be provided to all children with disabilities up to the minimum age of 18 years' (Government of India 2006: 7).

While it could be argued that India has one of the strongest policy frameworks for supporting the education of children with disabilities, low rates of enrolment and poor learning outcomes remain of central concern.

South Africa

In South Africa, the apartheid system had made access to quality education limited to the minority white population with the result that since democratic elections in 1994, education for all has been a critical imperative of government. Access to basic education for *all* is guaranteed in the Constitution of the Republic of South Africa of 1996 and is supported by the South African Schools Act of 1996, which instituted the right of access to quality education without discrimination for all children aged 5–16 years.

In recent years the poor quality of education outcomes has become a growing concern (Carnoy et al. 2012), in addition to the emergence of bimodality of educational achievement (Spaul, unpublished thesis, 2012), where access to quality schooling and higher levels of education leading to better employability is determined by the socio-economic status of the family. Similarly, exclusion of children and youth with disabilities remains a concern as there are approximately 467,000 children of school-going age who are not attending school (Moeketsi 2012), and this is a gross underestimation. Studies suggest that schools, including special schools, sometimes deny educational access to children with disabilities and other learning difficulties in ways that subvert policy and legislation in South Africa (Muthukrishna 2013; Muthukrishna and Ebrahim 2014).

Education White Paper 6, *Special Needs Education: Building an Inclusive Education and Training System* (EDWP6) (Department of Education 2001), is the key policy document on inclusive education in South Africa. It moves beyond focusing only on disability and proposes the concept of 'barriers to learning' of various kinds, namely, systemic barriers (e.g. overcrowded classrooms, inaccessible school buildings); societal barriers (e.g. poverty, lack of safety and security in schools, the impact of HIV/AIDS); pedagogical barriers (e.g. unqualified or under-qualified teachers, inappropriate teaching and assessment methodologies); and intrinsic barriers (e.g. neurological, sensory, physical and intellectual disabilities). In order to address these, the EDWP6 proposed varying levels of support to learners, including:

- The Special School as Resource Centre(SSRC), designated to provide high-level support to those who experience severe barriers to learning, as well as support to neighbouring schools and communities; the Full Service School, which provides a moderate level of support and, similar to SSRC, serves as a resource and referral centre. FSSs have slightly greater resourcing and staffing than mainstream schools.

- The Institution Level Support Team, a school-based support to identify and address the support needs of teachers and work with the local community.
- The District Based Support Team, a further support structure with its core responsibility being to plan, budget and programme for additional support needs of the district, and teacher development initiatives.

Since 2001 the focus has been on the implementation of the EDWP6 at the national and provincial levels through these initiatives such as whole school development and teacher professional development (Department of Education 2010; Republic of South Africa, Department of Education 2010a, b).

Overview of the Two Research Projects

India

The research in India was undertaken in a small rural community in the state of Karnataka. It is one of the few states to have a Draft State Policy on Inclusive Education (Sarva Siksha Abhiyan [SSA] [SSA] 2006), which supports the need to improve the education of children with disabilities. This policy highlights a strong commitment to issues of equity, emphasising not only access, but also issues of quality and progression. Singal's (2014) analysis of DISE suggests that the percentage of CWSN identified in the total elementary school population in the state increased from 1.13 per cent in 2010–2011 to 1.53 per cent in 2012–2013, with more or less equal participation for boys and girls (1.7 % and 1.3 %). Children with loco-motor disabilities constituted the highest group among the overall school-going population of CWSN (21.2 %).

The findings presented in this chapter are drawn from a small village school which was part of a larger project. The school offered classes up to Grade 8 and had 250 students and seven teachers. The school building was a permanent all-weather structure with eight rooms, including the principal's office, which also served as a common room for the teachers. Since there were not enough rooms or teachers, multi-grade teaching was common.

Data was collected using semi-structured interviews with the head teacher, focus group discussions with teachers and semi-structured interviews with support staff visiting the school. The aim of these focus groups was to gain a better understanding of how teachers perceived their role, the nature of planning they undertook to address the needs of children in their classroom, their perceptions about children with disabilities, and also their reflections on their professional readiness to meet the diverse needs of learners. Eighteen hours of school and lesson-based observations were also conducted.

South Africa

The research in South Africa also took place in a rural area, in the province of KwaZulu-Natal. Adopting a case-study approach, different institutions which are the focus of the inclusive education strategy in South Africa, namely the Special School as Resource Centre (SSRC) and the Full Service School (FSS), along with a mainstream school, were included in the project (for more details see Muthukrishna and Morojele 2014). The FSS and the mainstream school taught children with disabilities, including those with mild to moderate intellectual disabilities and those with hearing impairments. Each school had an Institution Level Support Team (ILST). The participants in the project were school principals and key members of school management, selected teachers and therapists at three institutions, and learning support educators, who were members of the District Based Support Team (DBST). The KwaZulu-Natal Department of Education, as part of its inclusive education strategy, built a Centre for Care and Support at the FSS. The role of the centre was in line with the national model of Care and Support for Teaching and Learning (Republic of South Africa, Department of Education 2010a). Primary data was gathered through individual semi-structured interviews, focus group interviews, informal observations of the school environment and culture, classroom observations, and participatory research tools such as photo-voice and ranking activities. Secondary data included available demographic information, school policies, minutes of school meetings and various other policy texts, such as the school mission statement, students' books, lesson plans and photographs of events.

Both the projects, in India and South Africa, generated vast amounts of data, which were handled by the respective national research teams using a combination of analytical approaches. Here we discuss two key themes—reflexivity and grounded responses to exclusion and inclusion, and global enactments in local spheres: positioning teachers as partners—to enable a more nuanced exploration of the debates in these countries.

Key Comparative Findings

Reflexivity and Grounded Responses to Exclusion and Inclusion

Reflective practice and reflexivity have long been regarded as of critical importance in enhancing teachers' awareness of their own thoughts, behaviours and actions, and for creating opportunities for professional growth (for example Cunliffe 2004; Stingu 2012). Osterman and Kottkamp (1993) and Thomas and Packer (2013) have argued that professional knowledge and development is grounded in experience, practice and in reflexive action. Evidence of this was seen in the South African study where teachers described constant tensions between having agency to respond to immediate needs and concerns, and the policy demands being made on them. Thus, policy implementation is made an unpredictable process as teachers are both policy actors *and* subjects. This can result in contradictions, tensions and resistance becoming evident in the course of the implementation process (Ball et al. 2011a, b).

For example, at the FSS in South Africa, ILST members made the decision to begin two 'remedial classes' for learners who were not performing at grade level in literacy and numeracy. Teachers stressed that the aim was to reintegrate these children into regular classes as soon as possible. An ILST member explained:

> Right now we have introduced remedial classes … we are trying … and it is working. Once the learners do well, they go back to the mainstream class. It is working. The Teaching Assistants go to these classes and also to other classes. Because there are some learners who do not want to go back, they want to stay in the remedial class.

This initiative may be viewed by policymakers as in conflict with the vision of inclusive education proposed in EDWP6 and aligned to a medical/deficit approach. However, what one can gauge is that teachers respond reflexively to what they view as their contextual priorities and the support needs of their learners. As Ball et al. (2011b) elucidate, teachers need to deal with the nuances of their context, and in such a scenario policy implementation can become complex and can often be regarded as contradictory to the intended policy reform.

Emerging from this study was also evidence of how teachers engaged in collective thinking and action, and drew on their own biographies, values and situated knowledge to make decisions and choices in response to contextual realities. Data highlighted how teachers in the three schools came to understand EDWP6 through the lens of their contextually informed values and priorities. Teachers in these schools clearly believed that teaching and learning in the classroom could not be divorced from the psycho-social realities of their schools and local communities. The philosophy of *ubuntu* and Christian and Hindu values were voiced by participants. These philosophical and religious beliefs were central and rather powerfully linked to the notion of rights and inclusion. It is argued that a person with *ubuntu* has allegiance to and affirms one's fellow human beings, and has a sense of community, compassion and shared concern for the rights of others (Tutu 1999; see also Chataika and McKenzie 2016, in this volume). This interdependency, where the focus is not only on asserting one's rights but also sharing concern for others, was significant. This is best illustrated in the example where a teacher in the primary school had initiated a garden project that served the school community as well as the children who attended the school. The rationale for setting up this garden was a shared belief that poverty was the most pervasive barrier to learning in the community. As a teacher explained:

> Because we said if we can start this school garden project and just sustain it, then maybe just give those learners who are coming from these impoverished backgrounds, to give them food parcels. Because … sometimes we can see that in the classrooms they would feel, you know dizzy and they sleep … Sometimes they come to school without anything in the stomachs … so when they enter the classrooms, they cannot concentrate for long periods.

While mainstream teachers were responding to the reality of poverty, teachers at the SSRC noted that their efforts focused on ensuring that their learners could lead an independent life in the future. For them, forging partnerships to create opportunities for work experience was an important focus, particularly given that adults with disabilities were more likely to be excluded from employment.

Both these examples illustrate how materialities and contingencies were being played out in teachers' efforts. At the mainstream primary school, the critical issue was that of poverty alleviation and at the SSRC, it was life skills and future employment, thus revealing the localised nature of policy actions. Also highlighted here is teacher agency where teachers were working towards responding to the child and not just delivering the prescribed curriculum. Working within prevalent socio-cultural norms they were able to draw on networks of support in the wider community. Nkambule et al. (2011) stress the critical importance of a culture in social institutions, such as schools, that is value driven and where responses to child and family well-being are systemic and contextual in nature.

While the study found genuine and creative attempts at policy implementation where teachers drew on available and often limited resources, there were ample tensions. At the FSS, for example, lack of resources, inadequate staffing and large class size were raised as some key barriers to inclusive education policy implementation. The FSS and the SSRC were not fully equipped in terms of material and human resources. For example, the principal at the SSRC had to draw on external funding sources to address the shortage of Braillers. Inadequate funding made it difficult for the ILST at the FSS to hold workshops for teachers from surrounding schools who wanted to understand the various implementation strategies that had emerged since EDWP6 (for example, Department of Education 2010; Republic of South Africa, Department of Education 2010a, b).

Global Enactments in Local Spheres: Positioning Teachers as Partners

In the Indian school, it was clearly evident that teachers recognised an amplified focus on disability issues in government policies. In many ways teachers were central in enacting policy imperatives: for example, they conducted surveys of out-of-school children in the neighbouring communities and actively encouraged parents to enrol their children, including those with disabilities. Interviews with teachers highlighted that they were willing to accommodate children with disabilities in their classroom and, compared to earlier studies, teachers were found to be more open and willing (Shah et al. 2014 also highlight some of these changing trends).

Interestingly, while on one hand teachers argued that all students have different types of ability and can be good or bad at different things, they felt that children with disabilities were, in most cases, particularly poor at grasping concepts and were not necessarily able to learn easily. These teachers did not necessarily see children with disabilities in an entirely negative light, rather they acknowledged that some children were simply more difficult to teach than others, particularly given the realities of existing mainstream classrooms. As noted by one teacher:

'They can come easily to the school, and there isn't any problem. There is no problem from teacher side, or student side, they are just below average students. They don't give any problems to other students; they mingle with all students happily'. Thus, while some teachers perceived children with disabilities as less academically able, it did not result in them being denied access; rather teachers reframed their own roles. Teachers argued that their central role was in supporting social inclusion for this group of students, while the students' academic learning would be best supported by experts (such as inclusive education resource teachers, as mandated under SSA). Here it is important to note that in framing these arguments, teachers were very articulate in relation to the day-to-day demands being made on them, such as having a large syllabus to cover; concerns that a vast majority of students were first-generation learners with little support for learning available at home; and the continued shortage of basic teaching and learning materials.

Paramount among their narratives was the real failure of government to engage with the teachers when rolling out the inclusion agenda. Teachers did not see themselves as partners in these changes. They discussed the policy in terms of it being imposed on them, noting that it was something 'they had been told to do'. Teachers re-enacted official mandate by arguing that the main purpose of opening up mainstream classrooms for children with disabilities was 'letting children be together', wherein they learned to socialise with peers and became familiar with the norms of social functioning, while relegating efforts towards supporting their learning and curriculum access to the background. Teachers either adopted an approach of non-engagement in the child's learning or sought simple accommodations, such as giving students reduced parts of the curriculum and longer time on tasks, including examinations.

It is significant that teachers did not simply reject inclusion. In focus group discussions they were nuanced in debating the purpose of special and mainstream settings (Singal 2014). Teachers were conflicted in their views about the value of children with disabilities attending mainstream settings and they articulated a range of dilemmas around purpose, participation and outcomes. There were interesting points of departure in teacher narratives and this was best exemplified in the following exchange when teachers in the focus group were asked what they thought was the role of schools in the lives of children with disabilities. Here some lively debates took place:

> [Here or nearby] there is no special school for disabled. They come to mainstream and they feel that I am also student of this school like others. If we send them to special school, he might have a feeling that I have some problem. But they come to mainstream school, they won't get that feeling. Government also have the feeling and that is why they gave money to provide ramps, special toilets for them. Governments gave Rs 50,000 for the special toilet to be built in school. Like this so many benefits are being given by the government, it's better they to come to school here. (Teacher, male, 10 years of experience, School 1)
>
> We have to improve them. It is the responsibility of the teacher. At any cost without any inferiority complex we have to teach them. They have to mingle with other children. I picked these things from the training. (Teacher, male, 15 years of experience, School 1)

In another exchange, a teacher's struggle between her beliefs regarding the perceived negatives of special provision, while articulating her own perceived inability to meet the learning needs of children with disabilities, was clearly evident. She noted, 'If we send them to special school they suffer from inferiority complex because they would get to know that they have been treated differently because of the problem'. In response to this, another teacher noted, 'If there is no special school, its fine but we definitely need a special teacher in our school'. While teachers were conflicted about the role of special schools, they did reflect on the benefits and positive implications of having children with disabilities in their mainstream classroom. As another teacher elaborated:

> The [child with disability] doesn't feel that they are different. He will mingle with all children. They play with other children and feel that they also have to win words of appreciation from the teachers. Because they come to school, they are able to have these feelings. They have enthusiasm to study. If they're only in a group of disabled children then it's not fair, he should mingle with others as well. They happily play with other students. (Teacher, female, 17 years of experience, School 2)

The aim of highlighting these dilemmas is to problematise discussions which provide homogenised constructions of teachers' perceptions of and attitudes towards children with disabilities as predominantly negative (Sharma and Desai 2002; Sharma et al. 2008). Evident in the narratives of teachers in this study were competing ideologies of special education with embedded beliefs of deficiency and need versus a social rights framing of teacher policy enactment. In undertaking such an analysis where one highlights teachers' conflicts and dilemmas, and positions them as 'knowers' of their classrooms, we gain a better insight into the oppressive nature of essentialised and medicalised discourses around disability, and at the same time recognise that teachers make spaces to assert their own agency.

The inclusive education discourse in southern contexts has viewed mainstream teachers primarily through a deficit lens, that is, with an assumption that they are unwilling or unable to teach children with disabilities. Therefore, there is a need to open up the space for dialogue with teachers, which positions them as partners in the educational development agenda, not as a problem. What is currently missing is a respect for teachers' concerns, an acknowledgement of their real struggles and effective partnership models in supporting the inclusive education reform agenda. Furthermore, as attempted in this study, future research on inclusive education policy implementation needs to examine the processes that shape the way teachers think, talk and act in the face of policy imperatives; how and why they ascribe particular meanings; and what competing ideologies are embedded in these meanings. Such a focus is likely to illuminate how local enactments of global agendas can be precarious, and often disempowering, for those who are meant to enact them at the local level within given contextual demands and constraints. These enactments are further overlaid with varied values, interpretations, interests and commitments of the policy actors, namely teachers, as discussed in this research.

Concluding Reflections

We began this chapter by foregrounding the need for developing a more nuanced understanding of inclusive education in southern contexts. An understanding which is appreciative of the realities of the South, rather than one anchored in a largely deficit view of educational systems, teachers and other stakeholders. We have argued for a shift away from the pursuit of a global doctrine towards 'inclusive education' reflected in international declarations and donor-funded interventions, to the incorporation of local meanings. A monolithic understanding of inclusive education needs to be contested because of the diversity and complexity of local contexts in which international and national policies are enacted. Interventions aimed at creating inclusive schools and communities must begin with an in-depth analysis of engaging with local policy actors and their biographies—How do they understand policy imperatives? What do they view to be their situated needs and priorities? What do they consider to be enabling and constraining influences? And what are the key social support networks that can be drawn upon? In the same vein, Kozleski et al. argue how 'universalizing policies such as EFA [Education for All] de-privilege local knowledge and practice in favour of global agendas that may not benefit the ecologies of local communities' (Kozleski et al. 2009: 27).

Our findings from the field lend support to the need to undertake a more situated analysis which acknowledges both strengths and struggles. Our findings show how teachers assert their agency and enact policy in different ways, with many unintended consequences. There needs to be a deeper acknowledgement of the sometimes very limited real choices that teachers are working with in many southern contexts but also a greater appreciation of situated values and priorities that determine stakeholder action. For example, the practices adopted by South African teachers were underpinned by reflexivity—thinking from within experiences (Bolton 2010)—and responded to familial notions of schooling and social influences that negatively impact access to quality education. Inclusion is an ongoing process involving reflexivity and negotiation. It is a process which is embedded in and shaped by unique existing material conditions, social relations, and interpersonal actions undertaken in response to situated needs and priorities.

A concern is that in current times the focus is on developing a decontextualised grand narrative around inclusive education, without an acknowledgement of local complexities. For example, mainstream teachers in India did not provide neat accounts of rejection of the child with disabilities, rather they posed real dilemmas, similar to those being voiced in many other contexts, even those which are plush with resources and funding. The paradoxes and tensions teachers face in everyday practice should be placed under scrutiny and engaged with in a positive way for advancement of learning. Involving teachers in examining their own practices and reflecting on localised tensions should be a critical component of teacher development programmes. Such reflexivity in teacher professional development enables an 'openness to different perspectives and paradigms; activation of the "sociological imagination", and … emancipatory activity which can lead to positive social change'

(Duarte and Fitzgerald 2006: 21). Nurturing and fostering teacher agency, according to Priestley, Robinson and Biesta, is 'strongly connected to the contextual conditions within which it is achieved and not as merely a capacity or possession of the individual. Agency is achieved in particular situations and through particular actor-environment transactions' (Priestley et al. 2011: 4).

The uniqueness of the contextual dimensions in the two countries indicate that implementation of inclusive education is indeed a very complex process, and success mainly depends on the extent to which the agency and capabilities of the local stakeholders are harnessed, supported and optimised. Further, sustainable implementation of inclusive education is a culmination of multiple players acting in collaboration within schools and their communities. We have focused on teachers to provide analytical depth, rather than to make invisible the range of other stakeholders (most significantly people with disabilities) who need to be part of these critical conversations to enable localised understandings of inclusive education policy implementation, as stressed by scholars and practitioners working in disability studies (Connor et al. 2008). Such an emphasis on shared knowledge and participatory engagement is crucial to developing an understanding of inclusion, which is socially situated and culturally responsive.

The arguments made in this chapter also highlight the absence of rigorous evidence which could be drawn upon to assess the impact of current inclusive education policies (Bakhshi et al. 2013). Similarly, in a review of various implementation programmes on inclusive education in developing countries it was noted that there is 'insufficient empirical evidence on the effects of projects under the aegis of international organisations. It is alarming that governments and other organisations proceed in developing or implementing inclusive education without actual knowledge on possible outcomes' (Srivastava et al. 2015: 190). During times of evidence-based policy developments this lacuna of rigorous research, drawing on both quantitative and qualitative research traditions, is most felt in the field of disability and education in southern contexts. As we move forward, developing a more coherent research agenda must be based on a deeper understanding and appreciation of contextual realities, and must also recognise and privilege the voices of people with disabilities—those in classrooms and also those who occupy spaces outside these structures. As Ferguson and Nusbaum stress, 'the voice of individuals with disabilities is a necessity in the production of research and scholarly work and is central to the epistemology of disability' (2012: 78).

References

Agbenyega, J. (2007). Examining teachers' concerns and attitudes to inclusive education in Ghana. *International Journal of Whole Schooling, 3*(1), 41–56.

Ainscow, M. (1995). *Education for all: Making it happen. Keynote address presented at the International Special Education Congress*. England, April: Birmingham.

Armstrong, A. C., Armstrong, D., & Spandagou, I. (2009). *Inclusive education: International policy and practice*. London, UK: Sage.

Armstrong, D., Armstrong, A. C., & Spandagou, I. (2011). Inclusion: By choice or by chance? *International Journal of Inclusive Education, 15*(1), 29–39.

Artiles, A. J., Kozleski, E. B., & Waitoller, F. R. (2011). *Inclusive education: Examining equity on five continents*. Cambridge: Harvard Education Press.

Bakhshi, P., Kett, M., & Oliver, K. (2013). *What are the impacts of approaches to increase the accessibility to education for people with a disability across developed and developing countries and what is known about the cost-effectiveness of different approaches?* London: EPPI-Centre, Social Science Research Unit, Institute of Education, University of London.

Ball, S. J., Maguire, M., Braun, A., & Hoskins, K. (2011a). Policy subjects and policy actors in schools: Some necessary but insufficient analyses. *Discourse: Studies in the Cultural Politics of Education, 33*(4), 611–624.

Ball, S. J., Maguire, M., Braun, A., & Hoskins, K. (2011b). Policy actors: Doing policy work in schools. *Discourse: Studies in the Cultural Politics of Education, 33*(4), 625–639.

Bolton, G. (2010). *Reflective practice: Writing and professional development*. London: Sage Publications.

Booth, T., & Ainscow, M. (2002). *Index for inclusion. Developing learning and participation in schools*. London: CSIE.

Bornman, J., & Donohue, D. K. (2013). South African teachers' attitudes toward learners with barriers to learning: Attention-deficit and hyperactivity disorder and little or no functional speech. *International Journal of Disability, Development and Education, 60*(2), 85–104.

Breidlid, A. (2013). *Education, indigenous knowledges, and development in the global south: Contesting knowledges for a sustainable future*. New York: Routledge.

Carnoy, M., Chisholm, L., & Chilisa, B. (2012). *The low achievement trap: Comparing schooling in Botswana and South Africa*. Cape Town: HSRC Press.

Chataika, T., & McKenzie, J. (2016). Global institutions and their engagement with disability mainstreaming in the south: Development and (dis)connections. In S. Grech & K. Soldatic (Eds.), *Disability in the Global South: The critical handbook*. New York: Springer.

Connor, D. J., Gabel, S. L., Gallagher, D. J., & Morton, M. (2008). Editorial: Disability studies and inclusive education—Implications for theory, research, and practice. *International Journal of Inclusive Education, 12*(5–6), 441–457.

Cunliffe, A. L. (2004). On becoming a critically reflexive practitioner. *Journal of Management Education August, 28*(4), 407–426.

De, A., Khera, R., Samson, M., & Kumar, A. K. S. (2011). *PROBE revisited*. OUP Catalogue: A report on elementary education in India.

Department of Education. (2001). *Education white paper 6—Special needs education: Building an inclusive education and training system*. Pretoria: Republic of South Africa.

Department of Education. (2010). *National support pack*. Durban: MIET Africa.

Donohue, D., & Bornman, J. (2014). The challenges of realising inclusive education in South Africa. *South African Journal of Education, 34*(2), 1–14.

Duarte, F., & Fitzgerald, A. (2006). Guiding principles for a reflexive approach to teaching organisation studies. *Journal of University Teaching and Learning Practice, 3*(1), 15–23. http://jutlp.uow.edu.au/2006_v03_i01/pdf/duarte_007.pdf. Accessed 5 March 2013.

Farrell, M. (2010). *Debating special education*. Oxon: Routledge.

Ferguson, P. M., & Nusbaum, E. (2012). Disability studies: What is it and what difference does it make? *Research & Practice for Persons with Severe Disabilities, 37*(2), 70–80.

Florian, L., & Linklater, H. (2010). Preparing teachers for inclusive education: Using inclusive pedagogy to enhance teaching and learning for all. *Cambridge Journal of Education, 40*(4), 369–386.

Government of India. (2006). *National Policy for Persons with Disabilities*. Retrieved from http://socialjustice.nic.in/nppde.php. Accessed 10 Sept 2013.

Grech, S. (2011). Recolonising debates or perpetuated coloniality? Decentring the spaces of disability, development and community in the global South. *International Journal of Inclusive Education, 15*(1), 87–100.

Kalyanpur, M. (2014). Distortions and dichotomies in inclusive education for children with disabilities in Cambodia in the context of globalisation and international development. *International Journal of Disability, Development and Education, 61*(1), 80–94.

Kozleski, E. B., Artiles, A. J., Fletcher, T., & Engelbrecht, P. (2009). Understanding the dialectics of the local and the global in education for all: A comparative case study. *International Critical Childhood Policy Studies Journal, 2*(1), 15–29.

Le Fanu, G. (2011). *Paper presented at the 11th UKFIET conference*. Oxford: UK. Reconceptualising inclusive education in international development.

Lim, L., & Thaver, T. (2014). Inclusive education in the Asia Pacific region. *International Journal of Inclusive Education, 18*(10), 975–978.

Lynch, J. (1994). *Provision for children with special educational needs in the Asia region*. World Bank Technical paper No. 261. Asia Technical Series. Hampshire: Microinfo.

Meekosha, H., & Soldatic, K. (2011). Human rights and the global South: The case of disability. *Third World Quarterly, 32*(8), 1383–1397.

Miles, S., & Ahuja, A. (2007). Learning from difference: Sharing international experiences of developments in inclusive education. In *Sage handbook of special education* (pp. 131–145). London: Sage.

Ministry of Human Resource Development. (1992). *NPE 1986: Programme of Action 1992*. Government of India: New Delhi.

Moeketsi, S. (2012). *Many disabled kids not in school*. Retrieved from http://www.iol.co.za/news/south-africa/many-disabled-kids-not-in-school-1.1428147#.VB2nIxZWhu1. Accessed 14 July 2014.

Muthukrishna, N. (2013). The geographies of the schooling experiences of children labelled ADHD. *The Anthropologist, 15*(2), 145–156.

Muthukrishna, N., & Ebrahim, H. (2014). Motherhood and the disabled child in contexts of early education and care. *Childhood: A Global Journal of Child Research, 21*(3), 339–349.

Muthukrishna, A., & Morojele, P. (2014). South Africa case study. In MiET Africa (ed.), *South Africa case study. A North-South Partner-Driven Co-operation Project: Teaching for inclusion and democracy.* Durban: MiET Africa.

NCERT. (2012). *National Achievement Survey, Class V*. New Delhi: National Council of Educational Research and Training.

Nkambule, T., Balfour, R., Pillay, D., & Moletsane, R. (2011). Rurality and rural education: Discourses underpinning rurality and rural education research in South African postgraduate education research 1994-2004. *South African Journal of Higher Education, 25*(2), 341–357.

Osterman, K. F., & Kottkamp, R. B. (1993). *Reflective practice for educators: Improving schooling through professional development*. Newbury Park, CA: Corwin Press.

Parasuram, K. (2006). Variables that affect teachers' attitudes towards disability and inclusive education in Mumbai, India. *Disability & Society, 21*(3), 231–242.

Priestley, P., Robinson, S., & Biesta, G. (2011). *Mapping teacher agency: An ecological approach to understanding teachers' work.* Retrieved from http://www.stir.ac.uk/media/schools/education/documents/teacheragency/Mapping%20teacher%20agency_final.pdf . Accessed 16 Nov 2014.

Rao, S., & Kalyanpur, M. (2015). *South Asia and disability studies. Redefining boundaries and extending horizons*. New York: Peter Lang.

Republic of South Africa. (1996a). *Constitution of the Republic of South Africa, Act 108 of 1996.* Pretoria: Government Printer.

Republic of South Africa. (1996b). *South African Schools Act 84 of 1996.* Pretoria: Government Printers.

Republic of South Africa, Department of Education. (2010a). *Guidelines for Inclusive/Full Service Schools*. Pretoria: Republic of South Africa.

Republic of South Africa, Department of Education. (2010b). *Guidelines for inclusive teaching and learning*. Pretoria: Republic of South Africa.

Rose, R. (2010). *Confronting obstacles to inclusion: International responses to developing inclusive education*. London: Routledge.

Sarva Siksha Abhiyan [SSA]. (2006). *The draft state policy on inclusive education in Karnataka.* Bangalore: MHRD.

Schuelka, M. J. & Johnstone, C. J. (2012). Global trends in meeting the educational rights of children with disabilities: From international institutions to local responses. *Reconsidering Development, 2*(2). Retrieved from http://reconsideringdevelopment.org/issues/iii/global-trends-in-meeting-the-educational-rights-of-children-with-disabilities/. Accessed 10 Sept 2013.

Sebba, J., & Ainscow, M. (1996). International developments in inclusive schooling: Mapping the issues. *Cambridge Journal of Education, 26*(1), 5–18.

Shah, R., Das, A., Desai, I., & Tiwari, A. (2014). Teachers' concerns about inclusive education in Ahmedabad, India. *Journal of Research in Special Educational Needs*, n/a–n/a. doi:10.1111/1471-3802.12054.

Sharma, U., & Desai, I. (2002). Measuring concerns about integrated education in India. *Asia and Pacific Journal on Disability, 5*(1), 2–14.

Sharma, U., Forlin, C., & Loreman, T. (2008). Impact of training on pre-service teachers' attitudes and concerns about inclusive education and sentiments about persons with disabilities. *Disability & Society, 23*(7), 773–785.

Singal, N. (2014). *Role of inclusive education in enhancing children's personal, social and educational well-being.* Final report submitted to CBM.

Singal, N., & Jeffery, R. (2011). Inclusive education in India: The struggle for quality in consonance with equity. In A. J. Artiles, E. B. Kozleski, & F. R. Waitoller (Eds.), *Inclusive education: Examining equity on five continents.* Boston: Harvard Education Press.

Singal, N., & Muthukrishna, N. (2014). Special issue: Education, childhood and disability in countries of the South: Re-positioning the debates. *Childhood, 21*(3), 293–307.

Slee, R. (2001). Social justice and the changing directions in educational research: The case of inclusive education. *International Journal of Inclusive Education, 5*(2–3), 167–177.

Spaul, N. (2012). *Equity & efficiency in South African primary schools: A preliminary analysis of SACMEQ III South Africa.* Unpublished Masters of Commerce thesis, Faculty of Economic and Management Sciences, University of Stellenbosch, Stellenbosch.

Srivastava, M., Boear, A., & Pijl, S. J. (2015). Inclusive education in developing countries: A closer look at its implementation in the last 10 years. *Educational Review, 67*(2), 179–195.

SSA. (2007). *Inclusive education in SSA.* New Delhi: MHRD.

Stingu, M. M. (2012). Reflexive practice in teacher education: Facts and trends. *Procedia: Social and Behavioral Sciences, 33*, 617–621.

Strogilos, V. (2011). The cultural understanding of inclusion and its development within a centralised system. *International Journal of Inclusive Education, 16*(12), 1241–1258.

Thomas, S. B., & Packer, D. (2013). A reflective teaching road map for pre-service and novice early childhood educators. *International Journal of Early Childhood Special Education, 5*(1), 1–14.

Tutu, D. (1999). *No future without forgiveness.* New York: Random House.

UNESCO. (1993). *Teacher education resource pack: Special needs in the classroom.* Paris: UNESCO.

UNESCO. (1994). *Salamanca statement and framework for action on special needs education.* Paris: UNESCO.

UNESCO. (2004). *Changing teaching practices using curriculum differentiation to respond to students' diversity.* Paris: UNESCO.

United Nations. (2006). *Convention on the rights of persons with disabilities and optional protocol (adopted on December 13, 2006).* New York: UN.

Warnock, M. (2005). *Special educational needs: A new look.* No. 11 in a series of policy discussions. Published by the Philosophy of Education Society of Great Britain.

Chapter 14
Disability and Poverty: Complex Interactions and Critical Reframings

Shaun Grech

Introduction

The relationship between disability and poverty has been acknowledged with reasonable conviction in recent years. Various commentators have expressed how disability and poverty are bound together, one feeding into the other, a relationship typically presented as a mutually reinforcing cycle (World Health Organization and World Bank 2011). Within this discourse, sometimes supported by schematic representations, it is said that poverty exacerbates and/or intensifies impairment or vulnerability to it, while the barriers encountered by disabled people result in a greater chance of falling into or experiencing more intense poverty. As a result, disabled people are said to be among the poorest of the poor. The argument that impoverishment is what typifies many of these disabled lives, supports the efforts of those who insist that disability is not only relevant to, but cuts across international development policy, research and practice. This has come to be known as disability mainstreaming (see Chap. 1 in this volume, Grech 2016). The emphasis on the disability/poverty relationship has remained a strong linchpin in negotiations with the United Nations to get some or other disability component into the coveted Sustainable Development Goals (SDGs), and now forms a key discursive component in the new rhetoric on 'disability-inclusive development'.

But while this relationship is too frequently mentioned with uncritical confidence, there remains a dearth of empirical work, especially qualitative research, and in particular that focused on rural areas. Research looking at the dynamics operating

S. Grech (✉)
Centre for Global Disability Research, The Critical Institute, Attard, Malta
e-mail: S.Grech@criticalinstitute.org

S. Grech, K. Soldatic (eds.), *Disability in the Global South*,
International Perspectives on Social Policy, Administration, and Practice,
DOI 10.1007/978-3-319-42488-0_14

between this representation, ideally in longitudinal, intergenerational ways, and which critically listens to and learns from the experiences of disabled people, families and communities remains scarce (Grech 2015). The voices and narratives of disabled people, especially those living in extreme poverty, are notably absent, too often spoken for by so-called professionals and experts or by privileged urban disabled people's organisations (DPOs), including those in the global South. Overall, quantitative methods and positivist approaches dominate because numbers, generated or collated, pull money for research bids, driven by the illusion of cross-cultural reliability, replicability and rigour.

It is not only research that is lacking, but also adequate theoretical interdisciplinary engagement with this relationship, ideally employing epistemologies from the South (see Santos 2014) with a view to learning and expanding theoretical knowledge in grounded and responsive ways. While some critical literature has emerged on disability and development in recent years (see, for example, Miles 2007; Grech 2009, 2011), critical theoretical debate on the poverty/disability relationship is scant.[1] Perhaps the questioning and critique of this taken-for-granted and oft-simplified relationship, challenges or dislocates the sense of false security and authority of lobbyists, academics and others. Or it may contest the attempts by those trying to standardise a schematic of this relationship or the efforts by some positivists attempting to enumerate and compare dimensions of this relationship across the global South with (most likely) unrealistic expectations. Others still, among them international organisations and consultants exporting 'knowledge', may lose some ground (and money) if their discourse and 'solutions' to the poverty of disabled people are pushed under a critical optic.

In the meantime, as research, critical questioning and theoretical work are pushed further into the background, what we are left with is largely anecdotal evidence, a few tentative numbers and a handful of schematic representations of this so-called cycle in grey documents, written by perhaps well-intentioned, but still assuming, overconfident/authoritative/simplifying academics and organisations. This chapter seeks to critically debate this relationship, contesting some of the standard discourse, with a view to generating (I hope) new debate, research and theoretical developments in understandings around this relationship.

The Disability and Poverty Cycle: Historical Developments, Uncontested Terrains

References to the disability and poverty relationship in the global South are relatively recent, dating back only to the late 1990s, at the same time that possible connections between disability and international development started to be considered (see Chap. 1 in this volume, Grech 2016). This discourse, it must be clear,

[1] One of the very few offerings critically debating and reframing this relation is that by Grech (2015).

emerged from the margins of, and even more often from outside the development epistemological and practical space—from global health, for example. This, however, does not mean that writing on the two 'conditions' of disability and poverty separately and/or together did not exist before this time. Indeed, disability studies, a global North field focused specifically on disability in the global North, was expanding exponentially to highlight issues of disablism and exclusion, including poverty of disabled people, largely in response to more social constructionist understandings of oppression (see Oliver 1990). Outside the disability studies space, some academics and organisations published a handful of publications highlighting some aspects of the disability experience in so-called majority world countries (see, for example, Coleridge 1993; Ingstad and Whyte 1995; Charlton 1998). In the meantime, powerhouses such as the World Health Organization (WHO) sought (sometimes obsessively) to define and streamline disability in the bid to measure it, later promoting some or other miracle pill for all disability in the global South. Notions such as community-based rehabilitation, for example, became particularly prominent and hegemonic (see, for example, Helander 1992; Kuipers and Sabuni 2016 (Chap. 29 in this volume). Before disability was identified as an issue in its own right within the arena of development—an issue only recently formalised with the Sustainable Development Goals—and before disability and poverty were connected in a cyclical relationship, disability had on occasion been unwittingly assumed by some even inside the broader 'poverty' discourse. Disabled people were occasionally mentioned among groups labelled as socially excluded (Sen 1999), marginalised (Elwan 1999), the most vulnerable and chronically poor (Lwanga-Ntale 2003), and those assumed to be caught in a cycle of intergenerational poverty (Yeo 2005). This marginal attention to the poverty of disability was not so much explored or understood through adequate disability or non-disability focused research and practice, as much as inferred. Important anthropological offerings, such as those by Ingstad and Whyte (1995, 2007), though not specifically focused on this relationship, provided an invaluable window into close, cultural, grounded readings of disability and also the experience of poverty in its various manifestations.

The earliest high-profile incarnation of disability and poverty as a relationship in a publication, both causal and consequential, came with a report by Elwan (1999), closely followed by one by the British Department for International Development (DFID 2000). These publications, though not supported by empirical work, contributed to the elaboration of the idea that this relationship was not simply one of connection, but a mutually reinforcing 'cycle'. Disability, it was said, feeds into poverty, and poverty in turn feeds into disability in what seems to be an endless cycle (see Fig. 14.1 for an example). The idea here is that poverty is a major cause of, or makes people more vulnerable to impairment through access barriers to health, livelihoods, education, services, clean water, accidents, poor sanitation, unsanitary and unhealthy living and working conditions, inadequate infrastructure, and unsafe transport, among myriad other causes. These early documents speculated that up to 50 per cent of impairments in the global South were a result of poverty and hence preventable. Notwithstanding the virtual absence of research to

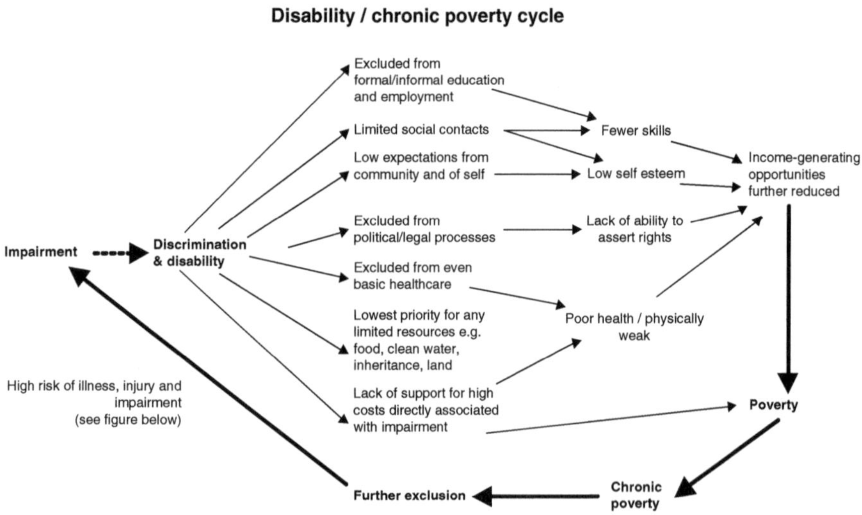

Fig. 14.1 Disability and poverty as a cycle (Yeo and ADD 2001)

back these assertions, confusion between the terms 'disability' and 'impairment', and the ignoring of the notion of disablism (see Thomas 2007), as Fig. 14.1 highlights, this was framed as a relationship characterised and constructed by and through barriers—those confronting the poor and those facing disabled people. As these multiple barriers meet and bind, disabled people, this discourse suggests, are those on the losing end, confronting multiple and combining exclusions: socially, politically, economically and culturally. For those living in conditions of chronic poverty who are already disabled, fragmented or absent work opportunities, inadequate health care and rehabilitation, among other things, mean a perpetuated cycle that opens spaces for secondary impairments and disease. Poverty is intense, chronic and likely enduring, even over generations. Yeo and Moore (2003) developed the concept further, calling it a 'vicious circle' to articulate how this is a relationship, or rather a trap, that is difficult to slip out of, a cycle which is difficult to break. A host of guesstimates have emerged in recent years suggesting how around one in five of the poorest people are disabled people (World Health Organization and World Bank 2011). Less than 2 per cent of disabled people in the global South are said to have access to health care and rehabilitation, and only around 2 per cent have access to adequate education, with girls disproportionately disadvantaged (World Health Organization and World Bank 2011). Other statements emerged, as amply documented in this handbook, to suggest that violence, discrimination, isolation, racism and disablement may be realities faced by many disabled people in the global South, some (for example, women, ethnic minorities and lower castes) more than others.

As Fig. 14.1 illustrates, it is not difficult to see that the focus on barriers (exclusion, limited opportunities, fragmented access, etc.), away from the individualising and problematising of disabled bodies and minds, is inspired by the social model of disability (see Oliver 1990). Turning the spotlight away from bodily and individual limitations dominant in medical models, the shift here is towards socially constructed and generated hindrances impinging on access and the well-being of disabled people. In turn, the implication is that the focus of analysis and 'intervention' must be the socially enacted barriers (as opposed to 'correcting' the disabled person), and critically these analyses and practices must be multidimensional and multitiered.

This argument served well those lobbying to include disabled people in all spheres of development (poverty reduction, health, education, rights, etc.), a process that came to be known as mainstreaming (see Chap. 1 in this volume, Grech 2016). For a number of stakeholders and organisations, assumptions about the existence of the disability/poverty relationship came to form a solid basis for measures they developed and promoted, and hence a justification for their own existence, for example community-based rehabilitation (see CBM n.d.; Kuipers and Sabuni 2016; and Chap. 29 in this volume)).

Over the years, literature has been mounting to restate the existence of this relationship (see Eide and Ingstad 2011; Groce et al. 2011; Palmer 2012). For some it has become an academic project, for others it has provided a lobbying tool, and for others still, including organisations, it has legitimised their presence and work in the global South and hence the need for funding. Some have also shaped a career out of disability and poverty consultancy in the field now called 'disability and development'. Donors and others, including the World Bank, latched on to the mainstreaming and later disability-inclusive development discourse, producing some or other document or policy rearticulating this relationship as one of the linchpins for considering disability in their work. The DFID-ESRC issuing of a fund for research entitled 'Disability, inequality and poverty' in 2013 was not only the first and largest of its kind (up to £2 million), but it also marked a critical shift in discourse in a sector (development) that, despite the changes in rhetoric, continues to struggle with the idea that disability is a genuine development issue (see Grech 2011, 2016; Chap. 1 in this volume). Indeed, the exclusion of disability from the Millennium Development Goals (MDGs) was clear evidence of this, an exclusion that paradoxically came to serve as a major lobbying tool to make sure it was included in the revamped goals post-2015. This assumed disability/poverty bind had to be the 'entry point' in the same way that the gender/poverty connection had to be made and emphasised over and over by those who had earlier pushed for gender-inclusive development.

However, and despite the continued mentioning of this relationship, especially in grey literature, one statement that still echoes is that there remains a dearth of empirical research on this relationship (Groce et al. 2011; Grech 2015). Qualitative research, despite an increase in recent years, remains particularly lacking, especially that focused on rural areas. Overall, and too often, the existence of this disproportionate and has contributed to an approach to the study of this relationship that is virtually atheoretical and almost invariably uncritical and unreflexive. In the schematics that are drawn up, the collating of numbers, and the interpretation of findings, the analysis is hardly subjected to in-depth theoretical probing. The cyclical relationship and its focus on the disabled individual does not seem to allow space for more macro, global and historical issues to be considered. This leaves the disability and poverty relationship outside the realm of theoretical study and development by those working in other fields such as history, postcolonial theory, critical sociology, politics and even development. For example, historicity, issues of power and the colonial encounter are flagrantly excluded, even when much of the current poverty context (social, economic, cultural and political) is not only referent to, but constituted in and through to the colonial woven into contemporary coloniality.

It is through an in-depth, informed, historicised analysis that land distribution (and landlessness), race and racism, agricultural aspects, geographical dispersion, and even 'development' can be adequately understood (Grech 2011). History constructs contexts, but also the barriers and modes of resistance encountered within these, for example by indigenous communities and disabled people, and which in turn must be an object of study in a disability/poverty relationship that, too, has historical roots and needs to therefore be studied in historical terms. Disability and how it is understood and 'treated' in local and national spaces is also constructed historically because disability, just like poverty, is a historical 'condition'. For example, colonisers imported missionaries alongside medical and charity models, too often encroaching on or destroying local forms of community care and informal 'rehabilitation' developed over centuries—practices that till today continue to be ignored or simply dismissed as traditional or folkloric (Grech 2012). As disability and poverty are analysed within and in relation to dominant narratives such as 'development' or 'community-based rehabilitation', issues such as the exportation/imposition of western knowledge and practice (including development) and the delegitimisation of southern voices emerge. They highlight concerns of academic neoimperialism and geopolitical power asymmetries accrued over history, including who gets to study and intervene in disability and poverty, and whose conceptualising and practice matters. This includes colonising disability and poverty research, issues well documented among those proposing attention to indigenous methodologies and research (Tuhiwai Smith 2002; see also Gilroy and Donelly 2016 (Chap. 35 in this volume). Deeper questions, including about the roots of development in colonialism, whether development itself can be a source of impairment and disabling, and whether the cycle of disability/poverty can be broken through a neo-liberal development sector, too often remain unaddressed (see Grech 2016 (Chap. 1 in this volume)).

Overall, in this process of atheoretical, uncritical generalisation around the disability/poverty nexus, a host of issues are perpetually silenced, intentionally or otherwise. In the following sections, I discuss a number of these concerns, which have seldom been addressed.

As Fig. 14.1 illustrates, it is not difficult to see that the focus on barriers (exclusion, limited opportunities, fragmented access, etc.), away from the individualising and problematising of disabled bodies and minds, is inspired by the social model of disability (see Oliver 1990). Turning the spotlight away from bodily and individual limitations dominant in medical models, the shift here is towards socially constructed and generated hindrances impinging on access and the well-being of disabled people. In turn, the implication is that the focus of analysis and 'intervention' must be the socially enacted barriers (as opposed to 'correcting' the disabled person), and critically these analyses and practices must be multidimensional and multitiered.

This argument served well those lobbying to include disabled people in all spheres of development (poverty reduction, health, education, rights, etc.), a process that came to be known as mainstreaming (see Chap. 1 in this volume, Grech 2016). For a number of stakeholders and organisations, assumptions about the existence of the disability/poverty relationship came to form a solid basis for measures they developed and promoted, and hence a justification for their own existence, for example community-based rehabilitation (see CBM n.d.; Kuipers and Sabuni 2016; and Chap. 29 in this volume)).

Over the years, literature has been mounting to restate the existence of this relationship (see Eide and Ingstad 2011; Groce et al. 2011; Palmer 2012). For some it has become an academic project, for others it has provided a lobbying tool, and for others still, including organisations, it has legitimised their presence and work in the global South and hence the need for funding. Some have also shaped a career out of disability and poverty consultancy in the field now called 'disability and development'. Donors and others, including the World Bank, latched on to the mainstreaming and later disability-inclusive development discourse, producing some or other document or policy rearticulating this relationship as one of the linchpins for considering disability in their work. The DFID-ESRC issuing of a fund for research entitled 'Disability, inequality and poverty' in 2013 was not only the first and largest of its kind (up to £2 million), but it also marked a critical shift in discourse in a sector (development) that, despite the changes in rhetoric, continues to struggle with the idea that disability is a genuine development issue (see Grech 2011, 2016; Chap. 1 in this volume). Indeed, the exclusion of disability from the Millennium Development Goals (MDGs) was clear evidence of this, an exclusion that paradoxically came to serve as a major lobbying tool to make sure it was included in the revamped goals post-2015. This assumed disability/poverty bind had to be the 'entry point' in the same way that the gender/poverty connection had to be made and emphasised over and over by those who had earlier pushed for gender-inclusive development.

However, and despite the continued mentioning of this relationship, especially in grey literature, one statement that still echoes is that there remains a dearth of empirical research on this relationship (Groce et al. 2011; Grech 2015). Qualitative research, despite an increase in recent years, remains particularly lacking, especially that focused on rural areas. Overall, and too often, the existence of this disproportionate and has contributed to an approach to the study of this relationship that is virtually atheoretical and almost invariably uncritical and unreflexive. In the schematics that are drawn up, the collating of numbers, and the interpretation of findings, the analysis is hardly subjected to in-depth theoretical probing. The cyclical relationship and its focus on the disabled individual does not seem to allow space for more macro, global and historical issues to be considered. This leaves the disability and poverty relationship outside the realm of theoretical study and development by those working in other fields such as history, postcolonial theory, critical sociology, politics and even development. For example, historicity, issues of power and the colonial encounter are flagrantly excluded, even when much of the current poverty context (social, economic, cultural and political) is not only referent to, but constituted in and through to the colonial woven into contemporary coloniality.

It is through an in-depth, informed, historicised analysis that land distribution (and landlessness), race and racism, agricultural aspects, geographical dispersion, and even 'development' can be adequately understood (Grech 2011). History constructs contexts, but also the barriers and modes of resistance encountered within these, for example by indigenous communities and disabled people, and which in turn must be an object of study in a disability/poverty relationship that, too, has historical roots and needs to therefore be studied in historical terms. Disability and how it is understood and 'treated' in local and national spaces is also constructed historically because disability, just like poverty, is a historical 'condition'. For example, colonisers imported missionaries alongside medical and charity models, too often encroaching on or destroying local forms of community care and informal 'rehabilitation' developed over centuries—practices that till today continue to be ignored or simply dismissed as traditional or folkloric (Grech 2012). As disability and poverty are analysed within and in relation to dominant narratives such as 'development' or 'community-based rehabilitation', issues such as the exportation/imposition of western knowledge and practice (including development) and the delegitimisation of southern voices emerge. They highlight concerns of academic neoimperialism and geopolitical power asymmetries accrued over history, including who gets to study and intervene in disability and poverty, and whose conceptualising and practice matters. This includes colonising disability and poverty research, issues well documented among those proposing attention to indigenous methodologies and research (Tuhiwai Smith 2002; see also Gilroy and Donelly 2016 (Chap. 35 in this volume). Deeper questions, including about the roots of development in colonialism, whether development itself can be a source of impairment and disabling, and whether the cycle of disability/poverty can be broken through a neo-liberal development sector, too often remain unaddressed (see Grech 2016 (Chap. 1 in this volume)).

Overall, in this process of atheoretical, uncritical generalisation around the disability/poverty nexus, a host of issues are perpetually silenced, intentionally or otherwise. In the following sections, I discuss a number of these concerns, which have seldom been addressed.

Measuring and Comparing: Problems with Method and Approach

Recent attention to the economic mapping of the relationship between disability and poverty (Trani and Loeb 2012; Mitra et al. 2013) acknowledges intransigent difficulties not only in quantitatively measuring the relationship, but also in generalising the outcomes across countries and even within countries. Representational generalisation made from one context to another is open to multiple criticisms, including that of universality. But there are other concerns, including methodological ones.

Firstly, the questions on which such studies are based are usually answered by one individual. In many cases, children under the ages of 14 or 18 are not included. This not only excludes the voices of children, but serves to maintain the emphasis on a market-led measurement of disability and poverty where only a person who has direct access to the employment market will be counted. Importantly, much of the labour performed by the rural poor, for example, is in the informal sector, including work in kind, which means that it is difficult to frame this labour in traditional conceptualisations of work, especially if it is unremunerated. In relationship to this, families and communities continue to be excluded in research, not considered important in a relationship viewed as pertinent only to and experienced by the disabled individual.

Secondly, even if the questions asked about disability in household surveys were the same in every study, and definitions of disability were streamlined, it is not possible to account for different methods, the different interpretations and meanings of 'disability' and other terms used, such as 'livelihoods', 'health', 'mobility', 'independence' and even 'poverty' on the ground and between people. These are localised notions that vary and that need to be constantly understood and (re)negotiated. Any representation of levels of disablement and hence poverty caused by impairment will be subjectively framed within the constructs of an individual's experience within and through their own culture, history and context at every level, from the micro (family) to the macro (societal). This complexity cannot be reliably captured through multivariance measures. It also cannot be remotely captured without adequate, contextualised understandings of what Grech (2014) calls the 'spaces of poverty' within which disability as well as poverty are variably lived, framed, (re) constructed and survived, every single time.

Thirdly, regardless of the similarity in methodology and data analysis in any two countries, the number of dissimilarities in the quality of the original data is such that any generalisable comparison is rendered unreliable. Much of what people understand (if at all) and how they reply is determined by the methods used, who the researcher is, if he/she belongs and/or is known in the community, trust, personal (dis)like (both ways), his/her skills and traits (as a researcher, interviewer and a sensitive human being), and knowledge of the local context, among others. Power relationships are not only present, they are too important to be dismissed in unreflexive ways because they frame the research process and outcomes. Even if one asks the same questions off a piece of paper (many times drafted hundreds of miles away), it does not mean that he/she is being understood in the same way and is generating quality reliable data that can be compared. Researchers also sometimes have the tendency to stick to the beaten track, meaning that many perspectives are blatantly excluded, especially those that may differ, even by virtue of their language and/or location, for example indigenous people in rural areas. Speaking about language, much is also lost in translation. Even the type of impairment determines who gets to participate in a study and if his/her perspectives are considered valid and legitimate. People with intellectual impairments continue to be flagrantly excluded, too often spoken for by others. The type of impairment also impacts how people respond and how a question is understood (if at all) and answered. Other issues that are important here include feelings of pressure to participate in a study, for example through a powerful gatekeeper. People may also not be familiar with the notion of research, and an unknown person with a questionnaire can be very intimidating in isolated rural areas (see Grech and Goodley 2012 for more on critical issues in disability research).

Overall, it is not clear what is to be gained by quantitative comparisons between countries, an exercise that runs the risk of universalising the experiences of individuals and families, experiences that are clearly unique and diverse in both detail and depth—this is ultimately what gives data 'quality'. They may also lead to much disappointment when researchers come in and go back out with a piece of a paper without engagement with participants as human beings, without a relationship, and without research leaving something behind.

Defining Disability and Poverty

Moving away from the methods themselves, another critical concern is the problem in defining poverty as well as disability. The quest to define poverty in international contexts has long troubled researchers, especially those trying to move beyond simplistic monetary notions (see, for example, Lister 2004). The definition of disability, too, has preoccupied stakeholders such as the WHO (see Chap. 4 in this volume, Eide and Loeb 2016) who have overzealously attempted to not only define, but also to standardise the meaning of disability through some or other model of framework—always with the purpose of comparative measurement—however open they may claim to be (see, for example, the International Classification of Functioning, Disability and Health). The erroneous idea is that if people can be defined and categorised, they and aspects of their own lives (access to employment, poverty, etc.) can consequently be counted, and these numbers can then be compared. But this task has and continues to elude researchers, who deep down may indeed know that it is impossible to define and to measure.

First of all, and however 'participatory' processes may claim to be, it is ultimately professionals who make up definitions. Disabled people, especially the poorest rural people, are rarely given the space and authority to define themselves.

Some people may not want to even define themselves; 'disability' as a notion may not exist within their particular cultural, ontological, spiritual and/or cosmological space, or may be framed in other localised terms (that need qualitative probing). People may even want to frame themselves outside the space of disability but, as happens most often, there is no box to tick in a standardised questionnaire and the data is confined to irrelevance.

The truth is that there isn't and never will be a single definition of disability. While more flexible models such as the social model of disability have contributed invaluable political tools highlighting the complexity and social dimensions of disability, they too have sometimes tried to capture disability with authority, being sometimes punitive towards perspectives that raised critical/difficult questions, for example those around the body, pain and impairment. It is undeniable that the social model of disability emerged out of very specific global North contexts, to explain and act within these very specific spaces. On closer inspection, theoretical elements of the social model of disability may fall short of being transformational in certain global South contexts, not least because this model may be hardly known, and because it may face deep problems when faced by poverty contexts in the global South. Grech (2009, 2015), for example, expresses concerns over the dichotomisation of 'impairment' and 'disability', when pain, impairment and impairment effects (Thomas 1999) are real and daily concerns for those living in the most extreme rural poverty. They also condition every aspect of how poverty is defined, lived, how it is resisted and what disabled people prioritise and demand. In contexts of fragmented or absent health care, pain may be deep and consistent. Where livelihoods are dependent on hard physical labour, pain may be both a cause of greater (at least economic) impoverishment as well as a consequence of the enhanced inability to medicate. Pain and, indeed, its relief may take precedence above all other immediate needs and demands, and disability itself may well be defined in impairment or corporeal terms (as 'ill health' or 'disease', for example) (see Grech 2015). In such spaces, any devaluation of the experience of pain and ill-health limits understanding of pain as a critical dimension of disability/poverty connections. It may also consequently diminish and weaken the dramatic need for quality and consistent health care, especially among those in dispersed rural areas with few or no formal safety nets. If issues such as pain or repeated unmedicated seizures from epilepsy or unavailable assistive devices are not overcome, a person's capabilities are ultimately and immediately curtailed. Indeed, for the social model to have any currency in context, it requires enough medical and financial resources, political will and commitment—resources and will the neglected poor in the global South are well accustomed to not being entitled to. Looking at the relationship between disability and poverty as a cycle based on the social model of disability assumes a given level of available services and resources akin to those found in the global North. This is not only ridiculous, it also runs the risk of homogenising and simplifying a diverse global population made up of individuals with differing financial and practical priorities situated in different cultural, economic and geopolitical contexts. Overall, the materialist social model diminishes the attention paid to the embodied experiences of disability in the exploration of the relationship, resulting in a disembodied disability/poverty nexus. It is also important to explore the experience of disability and the impacts of poverty on a range of disabled bodies, because different bodies experience disability as well as poverty differently. For example, someone with a learning disability or intellectual impairment can still perform a number of agricultural tasks dependent on physical strength, while someone with spinal cord injury may not. These factors condition how poverty shifts and is experienced.

Just as poverty is considered multidimensional and highly complex in terms of definition and measurement (see Alkire and Foster 2011), so is disability complex, multifaceted and dynamic over context, time and space. It inherently defies simple definition and is subject to cultural, social, spiritual/religious, political, geographical and, importantly, personal and subjective interpretations, continuously in flux (Grech 2009). There are dimensions of the disability and human experience, including pain and wellbeing, that are not only hard to define across persons, cultures and places, they are well-nigh impossible to measure. Elsewhere (see Grech 2015) I go on to argue that disability can only be remotely understood over space and time and through longitudinal research working with families and communities, because circumstances, family situations, attitudes, policy and macro factors and processes, and indeed the experience of poverty change over time, and this forces us to consistently ask anew, what is disability for people within very specific micro contexts across time? How is poverty understood and continuously reframed as the experience of disability itself shifts? Should we be speaking instead about a dynamic disability/poverty relationship or a spectrum of relationships? Disability sits more comfortably on a continuum of interaction between bodies and minds and the economy, politics, culture, environment and society, imbued within a deep and complex subjective dimension, and is therefore both mutable and in motion. It is consequently difficult, if not impossible, to reliably capture and measure the relationship between two such multidimensional and continually evolving 'conditions' of life.

It is not only 'disability' and 'poverty' individually that can create difficulties in definition and statistical measurement, but also comparisons between disabled and non-disabled people, not least because one needs to know what it means to be 'non-disabled' and the dimensions associated with it within very specific and diverse spaces, hence drawing attention to learning about personhood within the space of the norm or the normative. Findings from Trani and Loeb (2012), for example, show no significant difference between the 'assets' held by disabled people compared to people who are not disabled. This hovers like an impending storm cloud over the status quo of established linkages between disability and poverty, in particular the notion that disabled people are more harshly impacted by poverty, and the authors are compelled to look again at their own definition of 'assets' and how they have been understood and analysed in the studies in question. One would expect such a subjective notion as 'assets' to create mass conceptual confusion not only among researchers, but also participants. Relationships, community networks and other valued dimensions may well be considered 'assets', especially in reducing the so-called vulnerability to poverty, ill health and even disability (as a social condition), even if they may not strictly have monetary value. Overall, it reinforces the dangers of assuming a universal understanding of terminology—disability, poverty, assets, livelihoods, and the list goes on—that can be misleading, not least across academic disciplines. The problem of semantics in capturing and measuring multidimensional concepts such as these remains a critical concern.

Not All are Disabled, Disproportionately Poor or 'Differentially' Poor

The cyclical representation of this relationship stresses that poor people are at higher risk of, or more vulnerable to, impairment, and disabled people are poorer. While this may be reasonably true and understandable, it still runs the risk of setting in motion a generalised, generalising and simplified discourse, especially among those seeking to take empirical shortcuts. It not only assumes a linear and inevitable progression from poverty to disability and vice versa, but it also makes gross assumptions about people's vulnerability as the intermediary connector between these. In the process it diminishes people's agency and ability to buffer against impending or more intense poverty or impairment, and their resilience. Vulnerability is indeed a human condition and is not exclusive to the poor or disabled: it is part and parcel of being human. Furthermore, substantial literature has emerged from disability studies (Runswick-Cole and Goodley 2013), studies on poverty (Akter and Mallick 2013) and other areas to emphasise resilience and resistance among the poor, disabled people and their families. They do not simply 'slip into' poverty and/or impairment without fighting back. But this resistance and resilience slips out in cyclical framings of the disability/poverty relationship, removing altogether the chance to recognise and build upon existing strengths. Overall, disabled people may also not feel differentially poor, or themselves want to be prioritised (including in poverty reduction) vis-à-vis others, such as their own families.

It is no surprise that not all poor people are disproportionately disabled, and not all disabled people are more vulnerable to or necessarily entrapped in poverty, at least more than others. The assumption of this cyclical relationship also insinuates that disabled people experience a different type of poverty than others, with attending differential needs—and this consequently requires a different type of 'intervention' (Grech 2015). This not only dismisses the experience of poverty as a shared experience and narrative, but also isolates even further disabled people from ordinary poverty analyses and practice, pitching them as subjects outside this research and experiential space, and perhaps the development sector altogether. It also does not consider if or how poverty in itself may be disabling and whether the poorest, too, may indeed consider themselves 'disabled' irrespective of the presence of impairment.

Ignoring these issues becomes rather dangerous when, for many, the immutable assumption of this path (disability to poverty and vice versa) means a lack of necessity to research and probe further, including points where the cycle is interrupted on a daily basis by the poor themselves. Subjective notions of vulnerability (including what people understand by this within their very specific contexts and whether people do indeed feel 'vulnerable' or more vulnerable than others), ability to resist and what disabled people and their families understand by 'poorer' or 'more disabled' than others are open spaces for critical research.

A Cycle: But Do Poverty and Disability Ever Meet?

Elsewhere in my critique of the notion of a disability/poverty cycle (see Grech 2015), I argue that a problem with the cyclical representation (as in Fig. 14.1) is that while disability and poverty constantly feed into each other, they never seem to actually meet. This cycle paradoxically separates both, epistemologically and practically, relegating each to its own space of inquiry and practice—an ironic position when most are speaking about disability-inclusive development. Importantly, it limits the space to engage with points of encounter, to look at disability as a condition of poverty and vice versa.

It is undeniable that the cyclical relationship creates a good case to at least acknowledge disability in poverty reduction efforts. It also opens a space for looking at the possibility or, rather, risk of impairment in poverty contexts, perhaps normalising the existence and presence of disability among the poor, at least epistemologically. But it also succeeds in perpetually dichotomising the two—disability and poverty—as two extremes of the cycle. For many it continues to imply the inability to look at similarities between disability and poverty, or rather understanding poverty through disability and vice versa, including in the theories employed. Those engaging with this relationship have been in the main those outside disciplines such as disability and development studies. For example, there is little engagement with development literature and issues therein: power inequalities imbued in the processes of participation (Cooke and Kothari 2000); inequality and geopolitical asymmetries; poverty dynamics; and chronic poverty, among other thematics. This weakens the analysis when looking, for example, at the impacts of disability on the poverty of children, poverty traps and multiple dimensions of impoverishment operating in complex and multidirectional ways. Using development frameworks can also bring the situation of disabled people in chronic poverty to the fore. At the same time, it provides the space to ask what may be particular about disability that requires in-depth interdisciplinary analyses.

Notions from disability studies and critical disability studies, and other theory of disability, have also not been employed in the disability/poverty analysis, leaving critical dimensions such as the experience of pain, embodiment, discursive constructions of disability and gendered experiences (such as those explored in feminist disability studies) untouched. Works from the peripheries of critical disability studies (see, for example, Soldatic and Grech 2014) critically questioning issues such as rights in poverty contexts are also excluded, even though they offer a brief window of questioning as tó why rights and the simple fate in measures such as the UN Convention on the Rights of Persons with Disabilities (UNCRPD) may offer little to buffer against deep, entrenched barriers in the most extreme chronic poverty (see Grech 2009, 2015).

Finally, 'poverty' is also momentarily pulled out of the cycle to reappear again with greater intensity among disabled people, but in practice what ties both 'conditions', so to speak, is ultimately the perpetual presence of poverty. This never goes away and understanding it in its full complexity in nuanced, contextualised ways must be and remain the key focus.

Families: Poverty and Disability Are a Family Affair

The cyclical relationship and the barriers that seem to be encountered as a result of disability would also appear to be confined to the disabled individual. On the contrary, emerging ethnographic evidence (see Ingstad 1997; Grech 2015) suggests that disability is lived by families, suggesting that we should be speaking about and researching 'disabled families' or 'disabled households' as opposed to focusing exclusively on the disabled individual. Indeed, families often have to work harder to accommodate loss of labour and provide for the health, food and other needs of the disabled person, with the consequence that they themselves have to reduce their own consumption. And these impacts feed back into how disability and poverty are lived and experienced by both individual and family, especially when family members suffer from ill-health and/or impairment as a consequence.

The analytical and practical implications of this point are very important. This disability/poverty relationship must be explored from the perspective of the family or household and must include family and even community experiences and impacts. This can only be accommodated through adequate and engaged household analyses. Furthermore, many of these impacts can hardly be captured precisely or enumerated. These include, for example, psycho-emotional aspects (see Reeve 2002), religious dimensions, and issues of stigma within communities that can only be considered through narrative. Finally, it highlights yet again the need to view this relationship as a fluid, complex, multidimensional, heterogeneous and also bi-directional relationship that is permeable to the experiences of others.

Is the Cycle Ever Interrupted?

The final piece of critique emerges yet again in relation to the notion of a disability/poverty cycle: is the circle ever interrupted? And, if yes, are these interruptions recognised? While I am sceptical of simplistic discourse about the poor 'pulling themselves out of poverty', one issue that arises here is that the cycle as is traditionally represented, does not seem to ever be interrupted, not momentarily, not even internally by the poor themselves. The concern here is not whether people stop becoming disabled or stop experiencing more intense poverty, but whether they do find ways of resisting on a daily basis together with their families and communities, and whether the 'vicious cycle' leaves any space for engaging theoretically, in research and in practice with the daily forms of resistance and resilience. Ultimately, and in the absence of formal safety nets, more often than not, the poor survive on their own against all odds in the harshest conditions, and they enable the survival of their disabled members. This leads us to some other questions: can this focus on a poverty/disability trap render invisible the agency of these disabled and poor families? Can it limit the analysis in learning from these local and even personalised interventions in their own lives, which can contribute to understanding the relationship while offering the means to build on these in practice? And finally, how does it contribute to often exoticising/demonising discourse when it comes to the so-called treatment of disabled people in the homogenised global South?

Conclusions

This chapter has briefly explored some emerging, though seldom explored critical issues in research and discourse on the disability/poverty relationship. It seeks to promote the idea, not that qualitative, critical, theoretical efforts are more valuable than quantitative ones in seeking to understand this relationship, but that numbers cannot do without narrative and the prioritising of voice, and that adequate in-depth analysis cannot do without critical and theoretical thought and reflection, however much it slows down the process or complicates matters. Our task is not to contain this relationship. It is to understand it, however long or however complex it makes the task. An adequate analysis has to move beyond hearsay and simplistic statements and requires an openness and alertness to the heterogeneity generated even by the simple idea of this relationship, not to mention the various and multidirectional dynamics operating within it.

The argument here is simple. We cannot contain this relationship (and most likely never can) without first opening it up to critical exploration through different disciplines. We need all the theory we can manage, and we need an analysis that is not only interdisciplinary but also transdisciplinary and critical. Studying this relationship with a critical theoretical eye does not have to be a project of abstraction, as (ironically) some academics and organisations in the field would have it. Instead, learning and in-depth study should be the task that any serious and open academic and organisation should be embarked on. Engaged practitioners, however much one may deny it, need critical reflection and theory, too. Working together is a priority in a process that must be inclusive, especially of voices and critical perspectives from the global South, especially those that challenge, critique and contradict even the notion of a cycle. Findings are of minimal use unless underpinned by cultural, historical, political and geopolitical knowledge and responsiveness.

Fundamentally, attention to context is key, defying any claim to universalism while calling for a better understanding of the continuum of difference within the disability and poverty relationship alongside diligence and depth in understanding difference and the complexity that arises. Previously assumed causal and consequential relationships are shown in this light to be fragile, while a more nuanced understanding of the relationship, one imbued with a range of causes and consequences for individuals and communities, is strengthened. This is a relationship that is fluid, dynamic and heterogeneous over space and time, and that can hardly be captured in neat and static models. But to do this we cannot do without narrative, without a space prioritising subjectivity and subjective understandings, whatever the chaos it creates and however it dislocates the quest for standardisation and generalisability. It can also hardly be captured in exclusive and exclusionary ways, especially when the voices of families and communities are not adequately considered. Instead, this relationship is perhaps best framed, as Grech (2015) suggests, as a *dynamic association* that demands understanding of not only different framings and understandings on the ground, but also of intergenerational impacts, without ever losing sight of poverty, the spaces of poverty and what it means to live within these spaces as the critical starting point—a poverty that ultimately embraces and includes all within its fold, disabled or not.

Finally, exploring the relationship between poverty and disability must not be confined to an academic project, but one of praxis, motivated by the need to question, challenge and shift disablism, including that resulting from poverty and its structural, historical and discursive causes. The final goal should be one where reciprocal responsibility and social justice are the key objectives and targets.

References

Akter, S., & Mallick, D. (2013). The poverty–vulnerability–resilience nexus: Evidence from Bangladesh. *Ecological Economics, 96*, 114–124.

Alkire, S., & Foster, J. (2011). *Understandings and misunderstandings of multidimensional poverty measurement*. Oxford: Oxford Poverty & Human Development Initiative.

CBM. (n.d.). *The twin-track approach*. Retrieved from http://www.cbm.org/The-Twin-Track-approach-250816.php. Accessed 6 Nov 2015.

Charlton, J. I. (1998). *Nothing about us without us: Disability oppression and empowerment*. Berkeley, CA: University of California Press.

Chen, S., & Ravallion, M. (2007). *Absolute poverty measures for the developing world, 1981–2004*. Washington, DC: World Bank.

Coleridge, P. (1993). *Disability, liberation and development*. Oxford: Oxfam.

Cooke, B., & Kothari, U. (Eds.). (2000). *Participation: The new tyranny?* London: Zed Books.

Department for International Development (DFID). (2000). *Disability, poverty and development*. London: DFID.

Eide, A. H., & Ingstad, B. (Eds.). (2011). *Disability and poverty: A global challenge*. Bristol: Policy Press.

Eide, A. H., & Loeb, M. (2016). Counting disabled people: Historical perspectives and the challenges of disability statistics. In S. Grech & K. Soldatic (Eds.), *Disability in the Global South: The critical handbook*. New York: Springer.

Elwan, A. (1999). *Poverty and disability: A survey of the literature*. Washington, DC: World Bank.

Filmer, D. (2008). Disability, poverty, and schooling in developing countries: Results from 14 household surveys. *World Bank Economic Review, 22*(1), 141–163.

Gilroy, J., & Donelly, M. (2016). Australian indigenous people with disability: Ethics and standpoint theory. In S. Grech & K. Soldatic (Eds.), *Disability in the Global South: The critical handbook*. New York: Springer.

Grech, S. (2009). Disability, poverty and development: Critical reflections on the majority world debate. *Disability & Society, 24*(6), 771–784.

Grech, S. (2011). Recolonising debates or perpetuated coloniality? Decentring the spaces of disability, development and community in the global South. *International Journal of Inclusive Education, 15*(1), 87–100.

Grech, S. (2012). Disability and the majority world: A neocolonial approach. In D. Goodley, B. Hughes, & L. Davis (Eds.), *Disability and social theory: New Developments and Directions* (pp. 52–69). London: Palgrave Macmillan.

Grech, S. (2014). Disability, poverty and education: Perceived barriers and (dis)connections in rural Guatemala. *Disability and the Global South, 1*(1), 128–152.

Grech, S. (2015). *Disability and poverty in the global South. Renegotiating development in Guatemala*. London: Palgrave Macmillan.

Grech, S. (2016). Disability and development: Critical connections, gaps and contradictions. In S. Grech & K. Soldatic (Eds.), *Disability in the global South: The critical handbook*. New York: Springer.

Grech, S., & Goodley, D. (2012). Doing disability research in the majority world: An alternative framework and the quest for decolonising methods. *Journal of Human Development, Disability, and Social Change, 19*(2), 43–55.

Groce, N., Kembhavi, G., Wirz, S., Lang, R., Trani, J. F., & Kett, M. (2011). *Poverty and disability: A critical review of the literature in low and middle-income countries*. London: University College London.

Helander, E. (1992). *Prejudice and dignity*. New York, NY: Karpf.

Ingstad, B. (1997). *Community-based rehabilitation in Botswana*. Lewiston, NY: Mellen.

Ingstad, B., & Whyte, S. R. (1995). Introduction. In B. Ingstad & S. Whyte (Eds.), *Disability and culture* (pp. 137–139). Berkeley, CA: University of California Press.

Ingstad, B., & Whyte, S. R. (Eds.). (2007). *Disability in local and global worlds*. Berkeley, CA: University of California Press.

Kuipers, P., & Sabuni, L. P. (2016). Community-based rehabilitation and disability-inclusive development: On a winding path to an uncertain destination. In S. Grech & K. Soldatic (Eds.), *Disability in the global South: The critical handbook*. New York: Springer.

Lister, R. (2004). *Poverty*. Cambridge: Polity Press.

Loeb, M., Eide, A. H., Jelsma, J., Ka Toni, M., & Maart, S. (2008). Poverty and disability in Eastern and Western Cape Provinces, South Africa. *Disability & Society, 23*(4), 311–321.

Lwanga-Ntale, C. (2003). *Chronic poverty and disability in Uganda*. Ithaca, NY: Cornell University ILR School.

Miles, M. (2007). *International strategies for disability-related work in developing countries: Historical, modern and critical reflections*. Farsta, Sweden: Independent Living Institute. Retrieved from http://www.independentliving.org/docs7/miles200701.html. Accessed 24 Nov 2013.

Mitra, S., Posarac, A., & Vick, B. (2011). *Disability and poverty in developing countries: A snapshot from the world health survey*. Washington, DC: World Bank.

Mitra, S., Posarac, A., & Vick, B. (2013). Disability and poverty in developing countries: A multidimensional study. *World Development, 41*, 1–18.

Mohanty, C. T. (2003). *Feminism without borders: Decolonizing theory, practicing solidarity*. Durham, NC: Duke University Press.

Mont, D. (2007). *Measuring disability prevalence*. Washington, DC: World Bank.

Mont, D., & Nguyen, C. (2013). *Spatial variation in the disability-poverty correlation: Evidence from Vietnam*. London: University College London.

Oliver, M. (1990). *The politics of disablement*. Basingstoke: Macmillan.

Palmer, M. (2012). Disability and poverty: A conceptual review. *Journal of Disability Policy Studies, 21*(4), 210–218.
Reeve, D. (2002). Negotiating psycho-emotional dimensions of disability and their influence on identity constructions. *Disability & Society, 17*(5), 493–508.
Runswick-Cole, K., & Goodley, D. (2013). Resilience: A disability studies and community psychology approach. *Social and Personality Psychology Compass, 7*(2), 67–78.
Santos, B. (2014). *Epistemologies of the South: Justice against epistemicide*. London: Routledge.
Sen, A. (1999). *Development as freedom*. Oxford: Oxford University Press.
Soldatic, K., & Grech, S. (2014). Transnationalising disability studies: Rights, justice and impairment. *Disability Studies Quarterly, 34*(2). Retrieved from http://dsq-sds.org/article/view/4249. Accessed 7 Dec 2015.
Thomas, C. (1999). *Female forms: Experiencing and understanding disability*. Buckingham: Open University Press.
Thomas, C. (2007). *Sociologies of disability and illness contested ideas in disability studies and medical sociology*. Basingstoke: Palgrave Macmillan.
Trani, J. F., & Loeb, M. (2012). Poverty and disability: A vicious circle? Evidence from Afghanistan and Zambia. *Journal of International Development, 24*(1), 19–52.
Tuhiwai Smith, L. (2002). *Decolonizing methodologies: Research and indigenous people*. London: Zed Books.
World Health Organization and World Bank. (2011). *World report on disability*. Geneva: WHO.
Yeo, R. (2005). *Disability, poverty and the new development agenda*. London: Disability Knowledge and Research Programme, DFID.
Yeo, R., & ADD. (2001). *Chronic poverty and disability*. Somerset: Action on Disability and Development. Retrieved from http://www.addc.org.au/documents/resources/add-chronic-poverty-and-disability_990.pdf. Accessed 7 Dec 2015.
Yeo, R., & Moore, K. (2003). Including disabled people in poverty reduction work: Nothing about us, without us. *World Development, 31*(3), 571–590.

Chapter 15
Disablism, Deprivation and Selfhood: Imagining the Subjective Nature of Oppression in Worlds of Poverty

Brian Watermeyer and Sumaya Mall

Introduction

The World Report on Disability (WHO and World Bank 2011) is a significant contribution to developing our knowledge of the life circumstances of disabled people in the developing world. Yet, there remains a paucity of data regarding structural barriers, discrimination, and life experiences of disabled people living in poverty. Exploring these realities means traversing a mosaic of cultural and economic differences, in order to learn not only about material realities, but also the meanings these hold in specific contexts. This chapter represents an initial attempt at exploring the psychological layer of disability experience in contexts of poverty. As should be clear, it is reasonable to say that we have little material to work with, and our models of analysis have uncertain cross-cultural validity. Therefore this chapter is more a stimulus for discussion than a theoretical proposition.

There are several conceptual, ethical and epistemological questions to consider when addressing ethnographic material, which emerge throughout the chapter. A starting point is the relationship between disability and poverty, which some have characterized as a 'vicious cycle' (Mitra 2006). This is the matrix in which many disabled people become trapped and where subjective experience coalesces. Precisely how disability and poverty influence one another in specific contexts is a key question. Next are difficulties with cross-cultural research more generally, relating to

B. Watermeyer (✉)
University of Cape Town, Cape Town, South Africa
e-mail: brian.watermeyer@uct.ac.za

S. Mall
University of the Witwatersrand, Johannesburg, South Africa
e-mail: sumaya.mall@gmail.com

S. Grech, K. Soldatic (eds.), *Disability in the Global South*,
International Perspectives on Social Policy, Administration, and Practice,
DOI 10.1007/978-3-319-42488-0_15

ethnocentrism and stereotyping. The disability movement's role as a politicized struggle for liberation can lend itself to promoting a specific orthodoxy, which may confound understanding. Further, exploring the psychological nature of disability inequality and impairment is, in itself, a highly controversial matter.

For many disability studies scholars, psychology is defined by its history of medical pathologization (Goodley and Lawthom 2005). Recently though, interest in psychological perspectives on disability inequality has been growing, as the role of emotion in its perpetuation becomes recognized (Watermeyer 2012a, 2013). Some argue that political movements flounder through not attending to the emotional experience of their constituency. While work on the critical psychology of disablism is in its infancy, these questions pertain powerfully to the developing world.

The main body of the chapter comprises snapshots of ethnographic data, with ideas about the psychological impressions of lived experience. With an entire world of cultural contexts to make sense of, it was necessary to focus on a particular data set, localized at least in terms of continents. We draw almost exclusively on African data, in particular on Ingstad and Eide's (2011) important edited volume. This subject matter is presented as a means to think experimentally with psychological ideas and invite further research. The chapter rests on conceptual and empirical material discussed elsewhere in this book (Grech and Soldatic 2016), beginning with the demographic, economic and structural details of the majority world's disabled population. Grech (2016) provides a critical review of what we know. The mutually reinforcing, often malignant relationship between disability and poverty is examined in detail in Buell, Grech and Brogna's chapter (2016). The purpose of this chapter is to populate these contextual frames with subjective life, through imagining the possible psychological impressions left by lifeworlds which are often brutal. Some critics believe that as much as half the impairment in the developing world could be prevented by such measures as improved sanitation and drinking water, alleviation of malnutrition and reforms in labour policy (Barnes and Mercer 2005). Good governance, an equitable economy and basic measures of community safety would reduce impairment prevalence substantially. But to the peoples of the many regions we will visit later in the chapter, such services and resources are simply not part of life.

Psychological Aspects of Disability and Poverty: Careful Perspectives

Impressions of the treatment of disabled people in under-researched areas of the global South are liable to ethnocentric distortions. For example, generalizing myths of abuse and neglect in low-income nations have been criticized (Ingstad 2001). Our psychological analysis must be sure to begin from reliable accounts of social responses to the disabled individual, remaining candid about the very real paucity of data (Grech 2009). In terms of psychological theory, questions of cross-cultural applicability, as well as emancipatory potential, are central. The 'bottom-up' epistemology of liberation psychology, concerned as it is with local, contextual and subversive knowledge, is a useful point of departure (Martin-Baro 1994).

One implication is that researchers resist surface impressions, instead collecting thick descriptions of the structural constraints and subjective nature of lifeworlds (Fraser and Nicholson 1990). For example, Grut et al. (2011) point out how, with families in dire poverty, the extra labour demands of a disabled child can push parents beyond the threshold to despair. What may appear as neglect or abuse may then, on closer examination, be better understood as simple desperation—helplessness in the face of impossible odds. From a middle-class vantage point it is almost impossible to imagine the pain of not having the resources to care for one's children, to see them in pain and going hungry. At play here is the structural violence of a state which fails to provide basic health care, nutrition and much else. To Grut et al., the key method of changing the lives of disabled children in such circumstances is to 'help the family regain a viable way of life' (2011: 163).

There can be little doubt that supporting rather than pathologizing families in such circumstances is the only useful course of action. Yet, from a psychological perspective, understanding social positioning means exploring the impression left on identity by family-based socialization (Watermeyer 2013). Accounts from the global South have also highlighted abuses based in so-called traditional beliefs about the meaning and cause of congenital disability, but there is bias in how these are viewed as representative of nations, or the developing world as a whole (Ingstad 2001). Here, too, the effect of such beliefs on the growing identity of disabled children deserves close attention. In families the cultural symbolism of disability becomes operationalized in formative relationships, laying the groundwork for social positioning (Watermeyer 2012a). For example, Helander's (1995) account of the Hubeer of southern Somalia's belief that caring for a disabled child is a merciful, religious duty must carry imprints for families and selves. Similarly, consider the predicament of a disabled child who is aware that her presence severely aggravates her family's already precarious socio-economic position. Even in middle-class circumstances, some congenitally disabled people describe early experiences of feeling like a source of trouble, rather than joy, to their family (Asch 2006). Contributing to family hardship may deepen feelings of guilt, seemingly so ubiquitous in relationships around disability (Watermeyer 2013). A lack of social service support intensifies dependence on family for assistance, potentially harming both relationships and selves (Watermeyer and Swartz 2008). In a world where the social roots of disability inequality remain poorly understood, it is very difficult to feel entitled to essential help and care. The misery emanating from a combination of poverty and impairment may thus be directed inward as self-blame, reducing the number of disabled voices demanding change.

In the balance of this chapter, we examine aspects of monograph material on disability and poverty, extrapolating possible psychological significance of these.

Specific Exclusion in a Field of Deprivation

Set against a dearth of data, a series of studies on the living conditions of disabled people in four southern African countries by Eide et al. (2011) represents an important step. Collaboration between SINTEF Health Research, the Norwegian Federation of Organizations of Disabled People, the Southern African Federation of the Disabled (SAFOD), and national ministries, facilitated data collection in Zimbabwe (Eide et al. 2003), Namibia (Eide et al. 2003), Malawi (Loeb and Eide 2004) and Zambia (Eide and Loeb 2006). The investigation provides a broad account of disabled life in low-income countries, allowing comparison across groups and contexts. Findings showed differences in living conditions experienced by (1) disabled and non-disabled people, and (2) households with and without a disabled member (Eide et al. 2011). Gaps between requirements and delivery of all services were higher for disabled than non-disabled people, with vocational training, social support services, assistive device provision and counselling showing the most extreme shortfalls (Watermeyer 2002; Eide et al. 2011). Often such deprivations occur amid limited awareness of human rights or the means to exercise these, as well as a shortage of national resources for delivery (Grech 2009).

Material deprivation is never psychologically sterile, always bringing meaning-making to render it intelligible (Watermeyer and Swartz 2008). Deprivation easily becomes connected to impairment, as the most evident marker of separation between those who have and those who do not, and impairment connects to self. Even where deprivation is the rule, differences across the impairment marker are often substantial. When one sees other children climbing onto an inaccessible school bus which transports them to an inaccessible school, it is hard to avoid giving in to the implication that one does not belong with other children and that school is 'not for you'. Where 'rights' are a foreign incongruity, this resignation is even harder to resist. People battered by structural violence quite sensibly expect more of the same — expectations which are largely realized. Too little attention has been paid to how such expectations may settle in the self as confirmation of low worth (Watermeyer 2012a). The high salience of the impairment marker may cause disabled people to join others in a projection which sees all difficulty as emanating from the impaired structure or system of the body (Watermeyer 2013). As noted by Davids (1996) with regard to race, this means that the 'problem' of disability inequality settles as something intrinsic to the individual, colouring the self. In a world which consistently singles one out for deprivation, psychological survival may come at the cost of accepting this as what one deserves. Here, hope can be emotionally costly, as it may pave the way for further losses.

Unemployment is rife in southern Africa, and higher among disabled people (Eide et al. 2011). Further, disability households are less likely to have any form of income than non-disability households (Eide et al. 2011). Thus, disability disadvantages everyone in the home (Braathen and Loeb 2011). Muderedzi and Ingstad (2011) provide this example from Zimbabwe. Rural women had the task of fetching water for their household, which had to be carried over long distances. There were reports of a two-hour walk to taps or wells, taken twice daily. This trek was worsened for some by having to carry their disabled child in addition to the water, resulting in less water for the household. Seeing the labour of others would, for many, raise feelings of helplessness and guilt, potentially distorting already taxed relationships (Watermeyer and Swartz 2008).

Feeling that one causes hardship to loved ones can foster an enduring persona based on guilt-ridden accommodation. When gratitude is so salient, healthy self-expression is constricted. Individuals who develop in this way may literally not know their needs, let alone be able to express these in a healthily assertive manner (Winnicott 1960). The result may be lives of silent suffering, and an unarticulated belief that one's belonging is contingent on compliance and inauthenticity (Watermeyer and Swartz 2008). In material circumstances of misery, the desolation of such a life may be immense.

Going to School: A Litany of Barriers

Across the four countries in the southern African investigation, disabled children were two to three times more likely than others to not go to school (Eide et al. 2011). Rural disabled children were at a yet greater disadvantage, with between 25 and 40 per cent never having attended school. Literacy correlated closely, with half of all disabled people being illiterate (Eide et al. 2011). Notably, disabled children who were admitted to school achieved at similar levels to non-disabled peers. Given other, ongoing barriers, this suggests exceptional effort by such children (French 1993; Watermeyer 2009). Exclusion factors were multiple, beginning with physical accessibility. This pertained not only to built structures, but also to transportation (Grut et al. 2011). Data from Kenya found disabled children unable to walk the often long distances to schools. In rarer instances, where school buses were provided, these were not accessible, and families with disabled children were less likely to afford fares (Grut et al. 2011). Learning materials, apparatus and teaching skills for sensorily impaired children were often not available. Beyond these more obvious barriers, many children were taken out of school because of inaccessible toilets (Eide et al. 2011). The toilets were typically an enclosed hole in the ground, often surrounded by faeces and a foul stench. Physically impaired children would have to crawl through the mess to make their way to a toilet which, in addition, was unsafe to use (Grut et al. 2011). Also from Kenyan data, many parents removed disabled children from school because of peers' and teachers' prejudice and unwillingness to assist. Similarly, Howell (2006) found that attitudinal barriers in South African schools reduced the possibility of higher education enrolment among disabled young people.

When only others go to school or engage in vocations, it is quite rational to feel discarded. With exclusion comes a message of profound difference and the worthlessness of one's potential contribution, and hence oneself. We all know the pain of being left out. Trusting our belonging is a universal human struggle; arguably, all carry an unconscious anxiety that one's place in the family or community is somehow conditional and could be withdrawn (Corker 1994; Watermeyer 2013).

The ongoing messages of un-belonging implicit in exclusion may re-evoke and aggravate such anxiety. As other children's talents are validated and developed, disabled children may feel hopelessly left behind, consigned to the junk-heap of those seen as having nothing to offer to the community, the world. While not impossible, it is hard to grow a healthy and entitled sense of self in the face of denigration (Watermeyer 2013). For children steeped in these meanings, faith in one's capacity to grow is desperately hard to come by.

Even where disabled children are admitted, life in barrier-ridden schools presents immense physical and emotional demands. For example, where large-print learning materials for a partially sighted child are unavailable, practical and emotional responsibility for 'overcoming' this obstacle tends to fall on the individual and his or her family. French (1993) notes how sight-impaired people may easily fall into excessive effort, such as working very long hours, in a manner which may border on self-harm. Sight-impaired university students in South Africa reported print access concerns as a twofold challenge. First was the laborious, unreliable and time-consuming business of having material translated into an accessible form (Braille, audio); second, and often more exhausting, was the emotional work of remaining hopeful and energetic in the face of massively unfair access (Watermeyer 2000). Disabled school children may face an expectation of silent 'integration', rather than the provision of the means for real inclusion, fostering anxiety and self-blame.

The point has been made that human rights discourse, if it is to be useful, requires national resources (Grech 2009). Yet it costs nothing to recognize a disabled child's right to be in school. The simple recognition of the right to inclusion among teachers and others is a first step, but a difficult one. Until hidden emotional resistance to disability inclusion is thoroughly discussed, it remains a barrier to the basic act of *thinking about* the experience and needs of the disabled child (Rustin 1991; Watermeyer 2013). Human rights discourse speaks to intention, not just material allocation. Awareness of social justice directs communities towards seeking home-grown, if imperfect, solutions, even when abandoned by the state. Careful political conscientization has intrinsic value, but has to be based on an authentic conversation about the emotional evocations of impairment. As in race, responses to the impaired body are heavily shaped by strong unconscious feelings, including fear, shame, hatred and identification (Watermeyer 2013). Until teachers and others are supported in understanding their own resistances, imagining the predicament of the disabled school child will remain too threatening.

The Community and the State: Neglectful Parents

All children and vulnerable adults, including disabled people, require specific forms of care; this group is a subset of the human family, where care is a universal necessity for survival. In early life this may be provided by parents, and later fulfilled by a network of supportive relationships. In disabled lives this care may fail, perhaps due to rejection, but more often because family members may already be battling poverty or other adversity. Families need resources and support to provide care (Watermeyer and McKenzie 2014). This 'care for the carers' falls to the community and then to the state. When our parents cannot cope, we hope that these entities will catch us. One view of parenting (in the broadest sense) sees humans as needing experiences of containment—that is, being 'thought about'. Simply put, this implies having one's experience seen, accepted and responded to (Frosh 1991; Rustin 1991). Failure of 'parents' to see or manage one's needs may settle psychologically as confirmation that one is, at some intrinsic level, unmanageable to others. A world of constant barriers to participation recapitulates this message in the lives of disabled people (Watermeyer 2012b). These ideas are not difficult to defend where modernity dominates, as the principle of autonomy is a lynchpin. There is much to learn about how developing contexts may differ.

To South Africans the notion of *ubuntu* is very familiar, embodying ethics of communal interest, generosity, social cohesion and equality, as personified in the life of Nelson Mandela (1918–2013). But this picture is far removed from much African data on life with disability. Consider, for example, evidence from South African Xhosa culture. Here, mothers may be accused of bad behaviour, which 'explains' infantile impairment; many fathers will subsequently abandon wife and child (Hansen and Sait 2011). The knowledge of having brought punishment and abandonment to one's mother *because of one's very nature* is very hard to bear. In particular, it is important to note how experiences of deprivation interact with malignant stereotypes about disability. In the face of hardship it is more difficult to internally resist the hateful imputations of a prejudiced community.

Abandonment by the 'parental net' is brought to life in the following example from Malawi (Braathen and Loeb 2011). People with albinism have little or no pigment in their skin, and may also carry a sight impairment. Accounts from across Africa detail extreme prejudice, shunning and even genocide (Ladizinski et al. 2012). One effect of the condition is susceptibility to sunburn. All informants in the Malawian study constantly suffered sunburn, and were too poor to buy sunscreen or protective clothing (Ladizinski et al. 2012). Children walking long distances to school are scorched by the harsh African sun, causing chronic pain and skin damage. The need is for a simple resource, based on the act of being 'remembered' by 'parents'; to be 'forgotten' is to be burnt again and again. And to be burnt is to be forgotten. What we see is a failure of 'parenting' to protect from the elements in a very basic way. Parents are not supported ('parented') and must watch their children suffer, also un-parented. With victimization commonplace, we may wonder whether the sun's punishment is felt as a consequence of hated characteristics (Sinason 1992; Clegg 2006). One parent told of how her son had been refused school entrance because he had too many blisters and sores from the sun.

A critical psychoanalytic view of disability discrimination (Watermeyer 2013) sees the disabled figure as a container for projections. Disabled people are psychologically scapegoated to carry parts of the human condition that we find difficult to own, such as shame, abjection and dependence; in the words of Tom Shakespeare (1994), disabled people are 'dustbins for disavowal'. Situations of deprivation or abuse can present disabled people as vulnerable or damaged, contributing to the adhesiveness of projections. In this sense there may be an unconscious 'psychic payoff' (Marks 1999) for the majority in the continued suffering of the disabled figure, through reaffirmation that it is this Other—not us—that is the 'real' holder of shame and vulnerability. The story of albinism and sunburn in Malawi may, in this sense, be powerfully symbolic of a more pervasive unconscious dynamic regarding othering in disability.

Disabled and Displaced

Conflicts in many parts of the developing world lead to displacement of vast numbers of people, including a higher proportion of disabled individuals due to war-related injuries. Life for all in refugee or IDP (internally displaced person) camps is spartan and unpredictable; for disabled people these hardships are multiplied.

The conflict in northern Uganda was the backdrop to a study by Muyinda and Whyte (2011), focusing on the experiences of displaced disabled people. Between 1996 and 2004 an estimated 1.2 million people in the region were displaced, and living in IDP camps or other temporary accommodation (Muyinda and Whyte 2011). Displacement often means losing livelihoods as well as homes. Land, livestock and possessions are left behind, deepening poverty and food insecurity. Where food, water and shelter are in short supply, and competition is fierce, disabled people are at great risk. Simply moving about in a sprawling, unfamiliar camp may be near impossible for a physically or sight impaired person. The rudimentary sanitation facilities will be unusable to many, rendering further indignity amid the misery of hunger and dislocation. Susceptibility to cold and infection, along with limited health services, are threats to life itself. Muyinda and Whyte (2011) found few assistive devices in the camps, leaving physically impaired people immobilized. Despite incalculable hardships of life for disabled IDPs, Ugandan politicians and programme managers showed little awareness, seeing disability as a long-term rehabilitation issue rather than immediately life-threatening (Muyinda and Whyte 2011).

It is likely that most refugees and IDPs experience feelings of abandonment, perceptions which are not inaccurate. The misery and hardship of people torn from their homes, separated from loved ones, and left in inhuman circumstances are part of an experience of being forgotten by the parental state. Of note for disabled people is how, when all are struggling for survival, the extra needs of impairment may be further marginalized. It is harder to make demands of people who themselves are barely managing to stay alive.

Evidence shows that some disabled people experience belonging in disablist society as tenuous or conditional (Watermeyer and Görgens 2013). A partly unconscious suspicion that one's place in the community is not secure may be brought painfully into view by being 'left behind' in the struggle for survival. To be alone in one's exceptional vulnerability, when all live in danger, is an especially acute abandonment. Disabled people may find themselves in situations where essential assistance comes at a great, even life-threatening, cost to the carer. The impulse to disguise one's needs, engendering further suffering, may be difficult to resist. The need for physical assistance, along with commonly held anxieties about impairment, means that disabled people often feel called to be silent regarding personal struggle (Watermeyer and Swartz 2008). In adversity, such entitlement would be even further reduced, leaving disabled people more alone in the physical and emotional suffering shared by all.

The shortage of assistive devices such as wheelchairs, tricycles, calipers, crutches and white canes may have life-threatening implications in times of war. The physical and psychological vulnerability of disabled displaced persons without such resources is almost unthinkable, potentially exposing people who have been hurt by lifelong imputations of damage to overwhelming feelings of shame (Watermeyer 2012b).

Physical Disability and Mobility in the Developing World: An Incarceration Without Walls

Mutua (2001) describes having lived in Kenya and the USA, and compares physical access for wheelchair users. In low-income contexts such as Kenya, some mobility-impaired people exist in a 'uniquely paradoxical state of being—present, yet completely invisible' (Mutua 2001: 105). No accessible transportation can literally mean imprisonment in the home, destroying any chance of participation. In our home city of Cape Town a local activist estimates that we might have around 50,000 people with mobility impairments; we ask ourselves, 'where are they?' A sprinkling of wheelchair users can be found on streets or in other public places. Most are in their homes, of which many will be shack dwellings in informal settlements sprawled on the city's outskirts, with no formal assistance or accessible sanitation (Watermeyer and Görgens 2013). Recently we have seen the very small beginnings of a bus service which is wheelchair accessible, but its roll-out will take much of the coming decade. Without transportation one cannot go somewhere to look for a job, let alone keep one. Buses, trains and taxis in Cape Town have never been wheelchair accessible. On rare occasions when a wheelchair user is permitted to enter a minibus taxi, this involves the indignity of being lifted by strangers and then being required to pay two fares—one for the person, and one for the wheelchair.

On top of the palpable reality of poverty, an environment impregnable to physically impaired people carries malignant messaging. Collision with barriers that completely block agency can feel like an obliteration of self. At the very least, environments prepared only for others signal unwelcome; 'as the world goes about its business, inanimate structures whisper "why are you here?"' (Watermeyer 2013: 161). Lack of access means limited self-determination, strangling spontaneity (Murphy 1995). Muyinda and Whyte (2011) observe how immobility increases poverty, while poverty undermines access to the means of mobility, including money and assistive devices. For anyone, this vicious circle would represent a powerful assault on hope and the human spirit.

Assistive Devices: Access and Implications

According to a WHO estimate in 2001, as little as 1 per cent of disabled people in the developing world receive any form of institutional or community-based rehabilitation (Barnes and Mercer 2005). Among northern Ugandan mobility-impaired people, Muyinda and Whyte (2011) found that less than half of an urban sample, and less than a third of an IDP camp sample, had mobility devices, with complex implications besides those already described. The lack of devices reduced the possibility of overcoming social barriers to physical assistance (Muyinda and Whyte 2011). Someone in a wheelchair was likely to be pushed by a stranger, or helped with pumping water at a borehole. Non-ambulatory people crawling on the ground or sight-impaired people without white canes tended to be passed by (Muyinda and Whyte 2011). A beggar who moved on all fours described people behaving as if they did not see him, while pushing a wheelchair user up a hill, or helping him or her with heavy items. At play are feelings of shame and vulnerability, evoked in the observer by exposure to a visibly disabled person. The awkwardness of such feelings is managed through projection into the disabled person, who is experienced as a personification of vulnerability (Watermeyer 2006, 2013). Apparently, the interaction is manageable for the observer when the 'un-control' represented by the disabled person can be symbolically mastered by the act of assistance, as in pushing a wheelchair. But where assistive devices are absent, the pricking of vulnerability is too acute, evoking a more primitive response. The consequence is avoidance and denial of the disabled individual, as well as the shared human frailty of which he or she is a harbinger. It is a violent rejection, communicating that one's needs and struggles have no place here. Carried to its logical conclusion, the implication calls the very humanness of the disabled person into question.

Debates about the 'oppressive' prizing of independence in 'western' disability studies are familiar (French 1993; Hughes 2001). The notion of the independent subject is viewed as culturally specific, a product of the discourses of neo-liberal autonomy and humanistic psychology (Treacher 1989). In practice though, this view sets up an unreal binary with the developing world, seeing 'traditional' societies as embracing interdependence and eschewing the modernist discomfort with need (Watermeyer 2013). Muyinda and Whyte's (2011) account evidences disquiet, raised by perceived helplessness which brings intimate physical care into view. A wheelchair may act as a foil, insulating one from close contact with assumed vulnerability. In developed world critiques of independence (e.g. French 1993; Watermeyer and Swartz 2008), one argument is that impairment-related needs are marked as unacceptable, while 'non-disabled needs' are normalized. Rather than an idealized, *ubuntu*-oriented view of African positions on dependency, it is likely that a complex system of acceptable and unacceptable dependencies pertains; this requires exploration.

Sanitation and Selfhood

The vicious cycle of disability and poverty can impinge on the sense of self in a variety of ways. It may reduce the possibility of finding a spouse (Sentumbwe 1995; Rossiter 2001), leave one unable to support one's children, restrict one from attending social gatherings, and much else (Muyinda and Whyte 2011). Across rural Africa, a burning issue for physically impaired people is dignified and private access to latrines (Muyinda and Whyte 2011). Water-borne sanitation is an unlikely luxury in many parts of the continent, presenting hardships and health risks to all, but intolerable difficulties to disabled people. Unusable latrines can mean daily humiliation for physically impaired people, who are forced to rely on family, friends or strangers for intimate bodily assistance.

Muyinda and Whyte (2011) assessed sanitation circumstances in Ugandan IDP camps. Latrines were too few and very basic, comprising mud and wattle huts covering a rudimentary hole in the dirt. Most were surrounded by flies and a foul smell, and moisture oozing up from below ground, indicating holes which were too shallow or over-used. Latrines were often surrounded by excrement, inside as well as outside of the huts, as some people did not use them appropriately (Muyinda and Whyte 2011). Physically impaired people would have to either be carried or crawl through the faeces of others. If this was managed, many would not have the strength to squat over the latrine opening, especially as most latrines lacked the recommended cement slabs for safety and stabilization. Assistance would therefore extend to the person being held over the latrine. It is painful to contemplate the misery which these circumstances might create. Occupying a disablist world means living in the face of a hail of projections—that is, shameful, unwanted parts of self which are disowned and attributed to the disabled individual (Marks 1999). To survive, the self must attempt to rebuff all it can of this emotional waste, reiterating at some unspoken level that 'this is not mine, this is not me' (Watermeyer 2009). But material inequality makes this task much harder. When, for example, one is forced to come into contact with the excrement of others, imputations of shame and inferiority are harder to resist. Instead, the reality of inhuman conditions serves as a malignant confirmation of the denigration which is at the heart of everyday ill-treatment. Indignity and humiliation is easily turned inward as self-deprecation, through the individualizing logic which emerges from a lack of material access.

Disability, Reproductive Health and Dignity

A number of studies have found inadequate reproductive health services in southern African countries. But besides the broad lack of services, reproductive health care for disabled women has its own difficulties. Health workers often assume that disabled women are not sexually active, and do not require education and resources for birth control or protection from infections (Mgwili and Watermeyer 2006; Mall 2012). Disabled women may consequently be excluded from ante-natal classes or post-natal clinics (Grut et al. 2011). Where beliefs which see disability as punishment exist, a disabled woman who, despite her ascribed 'guilt', chooses to have a baby may suffer hateful treatment. This is painfully evident in responses to disabled women in South African reproductive health clinics. The assumption that disabled women either are not privy to, or do not desire or deserve fulfilling sexual contact was repeatedly found (Grut et al. 2011). Responses began with surprise and confusion at the presence of disabled women at the clinics. A disabled woman seeking contraception was assumed to be afraid of being raped, but later questioned about her sexual life in a fetishized, faintly hostile manner (Grut et al. 2011). On seeing a pregnant disabled woman one staff member remarked in passing that 'men have such low morals'. The implication seems twofold. First is the assumption that if a disabled woman is pregnant she must have been raped. Second, and more disturbing, is the view that a man who would choose a sexual relationship with a disabled woman must be of 'low morals' (Grut et al. 2011).

Sexuality is a fundamental part of humanness, no matter whether or how it is expressed (Shakespeare et al. 1996). Seeing disabled people as asexual communicates a disqualification from full human belonging, constructing 'disabled experience' as separate—and a menace—to that which 'we' have in common (Žižek 1990; Davis 2002). In the words of Robert Murphy, disabled people are culturally positioned as 'neither fish nor fowl … they are human beings, but their bodies are warped or malfunctioning, leaving their full humanity in doubt' (1995: 131). Sinason (1992) sees ascriptions of asexuality as evidence of unconscious fear that disabled people, and the shared human frailty which they represent, will multiply and overwhelm 'civilization', as well as the self. The condemning of disability experience to a shadowy place outside of 'real humanness' is evident. Such symbolic violence makes it harder for members of oppressed groups to exercise compassion for the self, constraining psychological integration (Watermeyer 2009). Disabled women cast out from sex and reproduction have to overcome powerful signals that their needs are illegitimate, in order to treat their struggles and losses with loving acceptance (Watermeyer 2009). Everything in the studies cited seems to militate against this self-love.

Disability or Death

In many parts of the developing world hardships are such that safety risks are a necessary part of everyday life. In South Africa illegal miners find their way into disused and unstable mineshafts — death or disablement is commonplace. Across the continent, women in poverty perform sex work with little protection from an epidemic of gender-based violence, and inadequate sexual health care. The outcome may be HIV infection, injury or death. Post-conflict regions harbour landmines and other explosive devices, lying in wait to maim or kill. Here, gathering the materials of survival means chancing one's life.

Taksddal (2011) investigated the lives of agrarian Cambodians occupying mine-ridden territory. For these people, avoiding mined areas means surrendering to starvation. In rural villages this researcher came upon large numbers of people disabled by mines. After losing one or more limbs, many individuals had gone into debt to pay medical expenses, before returning to mined areas to continue small-scale agriculture or wood collecting. One farmer commented, ‘I can sit at home and starve to death, or I can plough my fields in danger’ (Taksddal 2011: 192). Another remarked, ‘the only safe thing to do is to sit and die’ (Taksddal 2011: 195). The horror of such an existence, in which oneself and one’s children are at constant risk of a violent death, is difficult to comprehend. Although the psychiatric paradigm of trauma and recovery has many problems when applied to developing contexts (Summerfield 1999; Kaminer and Eagle 2010), the reality of having to re-enter daily the environment in which one’s body was torn by an explosion is brutal. Husum and Edvardsen (2011) observe that, from the insular safety of middle-class modern life, the horror of women, children and men being torn to pieces in their homes by bombing is beyond imagination. What is it like to have lost a child or children, and to have no choice but to remain in circumstances where at any time another might be taken? Or to see one’s child struggling with a trauma-related physical impairment, while his or her siblings remain in danger? Poverty and disability demand political advocacy, as it is through the action and inaction of governments that suffering continues. Everything in this chapter is a call to political action.

Conclusion

Developing knowledge about the psychological ways that disability oppression works is a broad project, which has only just begun. We believe it essential that psychological conceptualization is carefully tracked back to social causes, preventing individualization. At most, this chapter has provided some food for thought on what internal meanings there might be in lives combining disability and poverty. But even with this limited data, it is reasonable to say that in most parts of the world disabled people are positioned unequally in material, relational and existential terms. This last domain, resonant as it is with European history, denotes that if people are treated differently, this will often lead to feeling different, about the world, the society, the self. To us, this statement is sufficiently broad to disqualify it as a stereotype. Instead, it makes thought-space available for imagining, and asking, how experiences feel.

The notion of internalized oppression, in the context of black consciousness writing, is not foreign to Africans; it is of Africa. Analogous questions regarding disability and subjectivity should not be too hard to ask. Peter Coleridge’s interviews with disability activists in the developing world led him to conclude that, ‘For many disabled people, rejection is catastrophic: it provokes despair and retreat, which in turn widens the gap and produces further rejection and stereotyping’ (Coleridge 1993: 37). He goes on to compare the psychological impressions left by disablist treatment to those of physically abused children, women who live in fear of violence, and communities subjected to intergenerational institutional discrimination (Coleridge 1993). To us these statements ring true; both physical and symbolic violence are harmful. Careful relativism is essential in cross-cultural research, but is to be distinguished from a mistaken smoothing over of subjective harm. Whether one is poor, female, homosexual, HIV positive or disabled, being forgotten is being forgotten. Understanding and investing in the subjective states of oppressed peoples has the potential to lead us beyond the divisions of traditional identity politics, to caring societies based on recognition of shared humanity. We do not know what we can become without knowing who we are. For the global disability movement, progression to a more nuanced politics means having the courage to embrace this truth.

References

Asch, A. (2006). Appearance-altering surgery, children's sense of self, and parental love. In E. Parens (Ed.), *Surgically shaping children: Technology, ethics, and the pursuit of normality* (pp. 227–249). Baltimore: Johns Hopkins University Press.

Barnes, C., & Mercer, G. (Eds.). (2005). *The social model of disability: Europe and the majority world*. Leeds: Disability Press.

Braathen, S., & Loeb, M. (2011). 'No disabled can go here'…: How education affects disability and poverty in Malawi. In B. Ingstad & A. Eide (Eds.), *Disability and poverty: A global challenge* (pp. 71–92). Bristol: The Policy Press.

Buell, S., Grech, S., & Brogna, P. (2016). Disability and poverty: Complex interactions. In S. Grech & K. Soldatic (Eds.), *Disability in the global South: The critical handbook*. New York: Springer.

Clegg, J. (2006). Understanding intellectually disabled clients in clinical psychology. In D. Goodley & R. Lawthom (Eds.), *Disability and psychology: Critical introductions and reflections* (pp. 123–140). Basingstoke: Palgrave Macmillan.

Coleridge, P. (1993). *Disability, liberation, and development*. Oxford: Oxfam.

Corker, M. (1994). *Counselling: The deaf challenge*. London: Jessica Kingsley.

Davids, M. F. (1996). Frantz Fanon: The struggle for inner freedom. *Free Associations, 6*(38), 205–234.

Davis, L. (2002). *Bending over backwards: Disability, dismodernism, and other difficult positions*. New York: New York University Press.

Eide, A., & Loeb, M. (Eds.). (2006). *Living conditions among people with activity limitations in Zambia*. Oslo: SINTEF Health Research.

Eide, A., Loeb, M., Nhiwatiwa, S., Munthali, A., Ngulube, T., & van Rooy, G. (2011). Living conditions among people with disabilities in developing countries. In B. Ingstad & A. Eide (Eds.), *Disability and poverty: A global challenge* (pp. 55–70). Bristol: The Policy Press.

Eide, A., Nhiwatiwa, S., Muderedzi, J., & Loeb, M. (2003a). *Living conditions among people with disabilities in Zimbabwe: A representative, regional study*. Oslo: SINTEF Unimed, Norway.

Eide, A., van Rooy, G., & Loeb, M. (2003b). *Living conditions among people with disabilities in Namibia: A national, representative study*. Oslo: SINTEF Unimed, Norway.

Fraser, N., & Nicholson, L. J. (1990). Social criticism without philosophy: An encounter between feminism and postmodernism. In L. J. Nicholson (Ed.), *Feminism/postmodernism* (pp. 19–38). New York: Routledge.

French, S. (1993). What's so great about independence? In J. Swain, V. Finkelstein, S. French, & M. Oliver (Eds.), *Disabling barriers—Enabling environments* (pp. 44–48). London: Sage.

Frosh, S. (1991). *Identity crisis: Modernity, psychoanalysis and the self*. London: Macmillan.

Goodley, D., & Lawthom, R. (2005). Epistemological journeys in participatory action research: Alliances between community psychology and disability studies. *Disability & Society, 20*(2), 135–151.

Grech, S. (2009). Disability, poverty and development: Critical reflections on the majority world debate. *Disability & Society, 24*(6), 771–784.
Grech, S. (2016). Disability and development: Critical connections, gaps and contradictions. In S. Grech & K. Soldatic (Eds.), *Disability in the global South: The critical handbook*. New York: Springer.
Grech, S., & Soldatic, K. (Eds.). (2016). *Disability in the global South: The critical handbook*. New York: Springer.
Grut, L., Olenja, J., & Ingstad, B. (2011). Disability and barriers in Kenya. In B. Ingstad & A. Eide (Eds.), *Disability and poverty: A global challenge* (pp. 153–170). Bristol: The Policy Press.
Hansen, C., & Sait, W. (2011). 'We too are disabled': Disability grants and poverty politics in rural South Africa. In B. Ingstad & A. Eide (Eds.), *Disability and poverty: A global challenge* (pp. 93–118). Bristol: The Policy Press.
Helander, B. (1995). Disability as incurable illness: Health, process, and personhood. In B. Ingstad & S. Whyte (Eds.), *Disability and culture*. Los Angeles: University of California Press.
Howell, C. (2006). Disabled students and higher education in South Africa. In B. Watermeyer, L. Swartz, M. Schneider, T. Lorenzo, & M. Priestly (Eds.), *Disability and social change: A South African agenda* (pp. 164–178). Pretoria: HSRC Press.
Hughes, B. (2001). Disability and the constitution of dependency. In L. Barton (Ed.), *Disability, politics, and the struggle for change* (pp. 24–33). London: David Fulton Publishers.
Husum, H., & Edvardsen, O. (2011). Poverty as trauma: Methodological problems when reality gets ugly. In B. Ingstad & A. Eide (Eds.), *Disability and poverty: A global challenge* (pp. 207–224). Bristol: The Policy Press.
Ingstad, B. (2001). Disability in the developing world. In G. L. Albrecht, K. D. Seelman, & M. Bury (Eds.), *Handbook of disability studies*. London: Sage.
Ingstad, B., & Eide, A. (Eds.). (2011). *Disability and poverty: A global challenge*. Bristol: The Policy Press.
Kaminer, D., & Eagle, G. (2010). *Traumatic stress in South Africa*. Johannesburg: Wits University Press.
Ladizinski, B., Cruz-Inigo, A., & Sethi, A. (2012). The genocide of individuals with albinism in Africa. *Archives of Dermatology, 148*(10), 1151.
Loeb, M., & Eide, A. (Eds.). (2004). *Living conditions among people with activity limitations in Malawi: A national representative study*. Oslo: SINTEF Health Research, Norway.
Mall, S. (2012). HIV prevention issues for Deaf and hard of hearing adolescents: Views of parents, teachers, adolescents and organizations serving the Deaf community (Unpublished doctoral dissertation). Stellenbosch University, Stellenbosch.
Marks, D. (1999). *Disability: Controversial debates and psychosocial perspectives*. London: Routledge.
Martin-Baro, I. (1994). *Writings for a liberation psychology*. Cambridge: Harvard University Press.
Mgwili, N., & Watermeyer, B. (2006). Physically disabled women and reproductive health care: Some psychoanalytic reflections on experiences of discrimination. In B. Watermeyer, L. Swartz, M. Schneider, T. Lorenzo, & M. Priestley (Eds.), *Disability and social change: A South African agenda*. Cape Town: HSRC Press.
Mitra, S. (2006). The capability approach and disability. *Journal of Disability Policy Studies, 16*(4), 236–247.
Muderedzi, J., & Ingstad, B. (2011). Disability and social suffering in Zimbabwe. In B. Ingstad & A. Eide (Eds.), *Disability and poverty: A global challenge* (pp. 171–188). Bristol: The Policy Press.
Murphy, R. (1995). Encounters: the body silent in America. In B. Ingstad & S. Whyte (Eds.), *Disability and culture* (pp. 140–158). Los Angeles: University of California Press.
Mutua, N. K. (2001). The semiotics of accessibility and the cultural construction of disability. In L. J. Rogers & B. B. Swadener (Eds.), *Semiotics and dis/ability* (pp. 103–116). Albany: State University of New York Press.
Muyinda, H., & Whyte, S. (2011). Displacement, mobility and poverty in northern Uganda. In B. Ingstad & A. Eide (Eds.), *Disability and poverty: A global challenge* (pp. 119–137). Bristol: The Policy Press.

Rossiter, J. C. (2001). Shareholder commentary. In L. Rogers & B. Swadener (Eds.), *Semiotics and dis/ability* (pp. 97–99). Albany: State University of New York Press.
Rustin, M. (1991). *The good society and the inner world: Psychoanalysis, politics and culture*. London: Verso.
Sentumbwe, N. (1995). Sighted lovers and blind husbands: Experiences of blind women in Uganda. In B. Ingstad & S. Whyte (Eds.), *Disability and culture* (pp. 159–173). Los Angeles: University of California Press.
Shakespeare, T. (1994). Cultural representation of disabled people: Dustbins for disavowal? *Disability & Society, 9*, 283–299.
Shakespeare, T., Gillespie-Sells, K., & Davies, D. (1996). *The sexual politics of disability: Untold desires*. London: Cassell.
Sinason, V. (1992). *Mental handicap and the human condition: New approaches from the Tavistock*. London: Free Association Books.
Summerfield, D. (1999). A critique of seven assumptions behind psychological trauma programmes in war-affected areas. *Social Science & Medicine, 48*, 1449–1462.
Taksddal, M. (2011). 'My story started from food shortage and hunger': Living with landmines in Cambodia. In B. Ingstad & A. Eide (Eds.), *Disability and poverty: A global challenge* (pp. 189–206). Bristol: The Policy Press.
Treacher, A. (1989). Be your own person: Dependence/independence, 1950–1985. In B. Richards (Ed.), *Crises of the self: Further essays on psychoanalysis and politics* (pp. 131–146). London: Free Association Books.
Watermeyer, B. (2000). Psychoanalysis and Disability: An exploration of the utility of psychoanalytic methods and analyses in the interrogation of social responses to impairment (Unpublished masters dissertation). University of Cape Town, Cape Town.
Watermeyer, B. (2002). Disability and psychotherapy: An ideologically charged relationship in community mental health service provision. In L. Swartz, K. Gibson, & T. Gelman (Eds.), *Reflective practice* (pp. 85–98). Pretoria: HSRC Press.
Watermeyer, B. (2006). Disability and psychoanalysis. In B. Watermeyer, L. Swartz, M. Schneider, T. Lorenzo, & M. Priestley (Eds.), *Disability and social change: A South African agenda* (pp. 31–43). Pretoria: HSRC Press.
Watermeyer, B. (2009). Claiming loss in disability. *Disability & Society, 24*(1), 91–102.
Watermeyer, B. (2012a). Is it possible to create a politically engaged, contextual psychology of disability? *Disability & Society, 27*(2), 161–174.
Watermeyer, B. (2012b). Disability and counter transference in group psychotherapy: Connecting social oppression with the clinical frame. *International Journal of Group Psychotherapy, 62*(3), 393–417.
Watermeyer, B. (2013). *Towards a contextual psychology of disablism*. London: Routledge.
Watermeyer, B., & Görgens, T. (2013). Disability and internalised oppression. In E. J. R. David (Ed.), *The psychology of marginalized groups*. New York: Springer.
Watermeyer, B., & McKenzie, J. (2014). Mothers of disabled children: In mourning or on the march? *Journal of Social Work Practice*. doi:10.1080/02650533.2014.889103.
Watermeyer, B., & Swartz, L. (2008). Conceptualising the psycho-emotional aspects of disability and impairment: The distortion of personal and psychic boundaries. *Disability & Society, 23*(6), 599–610.
WHO and World Bank. (2011). *World report on disability*. Geneva: World Health Organization. Retrieved from http://whqlibdoc.who.int/publications/2011/9789240685215_eng.pdf. Accessed 3 Dec 2011.
Winnicott, D. W. (1960). *The Maturational Process and the Facilitating Environment: Studies in the Theory of Emotional Development*. New York: International UP.
Žižek, S. (1990). Eastern Europe's republics of Gilead. *New Left Review, 183*, 50–62.

Part III
Intersectionalities

Chapter 16
Race, Ethnicity and Disability: Charting Complex and Intersectional Terrains

Deborah Stienstra and Leon Nyerere

Disabled people around the world are often defined in terms of their impairments or conditions, with little thought to intersections with race and ethnicity or other socially constructed identities and experiences. Using intersectionality, this chapter asks: Whose bodies matter? Who do states protect? How do disabled people contribute? and Of what benefit are human rights in an intersectional approach? We also ask in what ways do racialised relations of power intersect with disability to construct and reinforce global and local inequalities? Through this we expose critical assumptions about and complexities in exploring race, ethnicity and disabilities in the global South and between the global South and North.

Intersectionality is a dynamic tool to analyse and transform power relations and a unique interdisciplinary space for engaging with various disciplines and in social movement activity. We explore how intersectionality helps us to understand the structural locations and multiple experiences that are created, reproduced and sustained in racialised and disability inequalities around the globe. In particular we ask a series of theoretical questions that arise from this intersectional analysis, including the following: Whose bodies matter? Who do states protect? How is disability used to constitute and sustain racialised inequalities? How do discourses and practices of race render disability invisible? Drawing upon the transformative aspects of intersectionality, we ask to what extent can human rights conventions, like the United Nations Convention on the Rights of Persons with Disabilities, be used to identify and respond to these intersections and begin to transform these global inequalities?

D. Stienstra (✉)
University of Manitoba, Winnipeg, MB, Canada
e-mail: deborah.stienstra@umanitoba.ca

L. Nyerere
Independent Scholar, Calgary, Alberta, Canada

S. Grech, K. Soldatic (eds.), *Disability in the Global South*,
International Perspectives on Social Policy, Administration, and Practice,
DOI 10.1007/978-3-319-42488-0_16

Why Intersectionality?

Intersectionality has been widely discussed and used in academic and non-academic work for application and analysis, as a theoretical and methodological paradigm, and as a lens for political interventions (Morris 2007; Cho et al. 2013). Intersectionality offers a dynamic and flexible approach to discuss sameness and difference in experiences and treatment, and has been widely used in critical race theory, feminist theory (Crenshaw 1995; McCall 2005; Cho et al. 2013) and among those who look at the intersections of race and disability (Erevelles 2011; Stienstra 2012; Annamma et al. 2013; Liasidou 2014). It has been used by activists in transformative politics and practice (Native Women's Association of Canada (NWAC) 2010; Chun et al. 2013) and requires a level of reflexivity by those using it.[1]

While intersectionality can be seen as additive—one set of inequalities added to another creating more intensified experiences of oppression—many scholars argue for intracategorical or intercategorical frameworks. McCall (2005) suggests that intracategorical intersectionality allows for exploration of the range of diversities and difference *within a group* and embodied in a particular social location. Erevelles argues that the intercategorical approach to intersectionality is most useful in looking at the intersections of race and disability globally because it 'continues to insert complexity into analyses of multiple differences by examining the structural context where social categories are (re)constituted, without having to resort to an additive approach that will always be incomplete' (Erevelles 2011: 101). The importance of intersectionality for this chapter is its ability to interrogate both multiple locations and identity experiences as well as explore the structural contexts within which those experiences are constituted and maintained. To analyse and engage using intersectionality requires thinking and doing at many levels, including asking who is included and excluded; who has access to resources and why; and what are the different manifestations of global inequalities such as racism, ableism and sexism in different times and places.

But intersectionality offers more than a tool to analyse current and past inequalities. As Chun and colleagues (2013) suggest, it can also be a strategy for transformative change in power relations from the collective action of those who have been marginalised. This requires activists to move beyond recognition of their exclusion as a result of their identities to a politics formed using those identities. We also ask to what extent an intersectional approach to race and disability can be or become transformative for people with disabilities?

[1]As co-authors we each reflect different locations in the diverse power relations in the world. Stienstra is a professor in disability studies, racialised white, settler and, perhaps unexpectedly, first-generation immigrant. She has written previously on race and ethnicity as it intersects with disability, and uses intersectionality extensively. Nyerere came to Canada as a refugee from Sudan, is racialised black, completed his master's degree in disability studies and is currently a disability service provider. His thesis was on the situation of people with disabilities in Sudan. He is actively involved with the South Sudanese diaspora in Canada.

Why Does Race Matter?

Too often, research around disability ignores race and critical race theory does not engage with disability. As the late Chris Bell (2010) reminded us, disability studies is often 'White' disability studies, with implicit assumptions that people with disabilities are primarily white and that any differences based in race and ethnicity do not change experiences of disability. Compounding this invisibility of race are the historical associations between race and disability, 'justifying the brutality of slavery, colonialism, neocolonialism and the continued exploitation of people of color in contemporary times' (Erevelles 2011: 102), making many people of colour unwilling to associate with disability. In the global North, there is increasing attention to the ways in which race is used to 'normalise'—'labeling a student "at-risk" for simply being a person of colour, thereby reinforcing…norms of whiteness, and signaling to many that the student is not capable in body and mind' (Annamma et al. 2013: 11).

Complexities of race and disability are intensified when we consider the global South and the on-going practices of colonisation and globalisation that reinforce racialised disparities. As Erevelles (2011) suggests, by focusing on the global South, or what she refers to as the Third World, we are necessarily addressing race. She argues this must be done in ways that are not simplistic but reflect the Third World in the global North as well as in the global South. 'I deploy the term "Third World" in a much more expansive way to expose how the social, political and economic conditions of global capitalism produce spaces of extreme exploitation and oppression in both the imperialist states and their former colonies' (Erevelles 2011: 122). We follow Erevelles' lead in addressing race in this way. We also recognise and draw from emerging attempts to bring together critical disability studies and critical race theory, recognising their points of contact and challenges to each other (Annamma et al. 2013; Liasidou 2014).

Whose Bodies Matter?

As we write this chapter, conflict has re-emerged in South Sudan. Popular media paint the conflict as ethnic or tribal in nature (Van Dijken 2014). Some recognise the war as an extension of the conflict within Sudan prior to South Sudan's independence in 2012 and its place as a weak or fragile state (Eckhard and Gaus 2014; Prunier 2014). Others argue that global oil interests play a significant role in the conflict (Medani 2014; Raghavan 2014). Rarely do bodies and people come into the analysis except to account for those who are in leadership positions or are victims and refugees of the conflict.

Our retelling of the South Sudan conflict gives an opportunity to ask key questions related to the intersections of race and disability. First, an intersectional analysis reminds us that bodies and people do matter. Conflicts are not abstract—they involve women and men, boys and girls, those who are soldiers and civilians and those who live with the repercussions of an oil-based economy and the choices governments make in (re)building states. Once we recognise that bodies do matter, we must ask whose bodies matter and in what ways do experiences of race and disability intersect to create or perpetuate inequalities?

The people and bodies in South Sudan and around the world have diverse experiences. They are gendered and have gendered experiences. Women and girls experience different forms of violence than men (Dowse et al. 2016, in this volume). They are racialised and part of diverse ethnic and religious communities. South Sudan has multiple ethnic divisions, most notably the Dinka and Nuer. But this conflict also reflects the tensions with Sudan. Before being divided into two nations in 2012 (Sudan and South Sudan), within the country there were inequalities based on the intersections of disability, race and ethnicity and religion. The demographic makeup of Sudan included people of Arab descent and different Black African groups. The northern part of the country was and is still made up of ethnic Africans (Black) and Sudanese Arabs. The Sudanese Arabs have been in control of the country since it gained its independence in 1956 (Deng 2006). Both groups are predominantly Muslim. The southern part of the country, which is now the republic of South Sudan, was and is made up of mainly Black Africans who were predominantly Christian. There are also those who practise indigenous spiritual traditions. Before the disintegration of the country, Sudanese Arabs were on the top of the social pyramid while Black Africans were at the bottom (Sharkey 2008). People of Black African origin were not only discriminated against because of their race but also for practicing religions other than Islam.

The bodies in South Sudan reflect human variations, including impairments and conditions, many caused by war. The International Red Cross estimates that 50,000 people are physically impaired in South Sudan, many as a result of landmines and the effects of conflict (IRIN 2013). This does not account for those labelled intellectually disabled or with mental health concerns, including post-traumatic stress disorder. As many have argued, women, men, girls and boys with disabilities are among the most marginalised in the world (World Health Organization and World Bank 2011; UNICEF 2013). In South Sudan, experiences of disability are also shaped by the conflict and how the impairment was acquired. 'Those who were wounded in the war, they discriminate against the "natural" disabilities [of those] who have acquired disabilities through diseases … They discriminate against us, the naturally disabled, saying we did not do anything to liberate South Sudan' (IRIN 2013). In this way, war is used to justify inequalities among people with disabilities.

In South Sudan, ethnicity and religion intensify experiences of exclusion as a disabled person. One activist in South Sudan suggests that there are 'bad' attitudes to disability within South Sudan's dominant ethnic group, the Dinka people.

> First, when a child with a disability is in the family, that family calls that child a curse from God, maybe as something that has been done wrong by the parents … the child is kept indoors so that he or she is not seen, and stays there until dying or suffering there without the notice of the government or the entire community. (IRIN 2013)

Race and ethnicity work together with disability to make certain bodies invisible to their communities as well as to their governments.

'Whose bodies matter?' is a question to ask in the context of all conflict and in the international arms trade. We recognise that war remains a major cause of disability worldwide (Meekosha 2011; Berghs and Kabbara 2016, in this volume). International actors increasingly acknowledge the role of landmines and other explosive devices in disabling people during and after conflict. We have not yet asked about how race and disability intersect in those effects. Few have asked questions about how racialised inequalities between the global South and North shape the presence of conflicts across the world. Who is funding arms trades and how does this shape or sustain existing racialised and disability inequalities? How do racialised inequalities shape global responses to conflict? What are the racialised discourses that shape patterns of global health responses to conflict and crises? Who benefits and who does not from global campaigns to end landmines? To what extent do these reflect structural racialised inequalities and assumptions about disability?

In the example of South Sudan, race and ethnicity work together with ableist assumptions to keep disability invisible. Why is this? In discussions of the ethnic tensions, why is disability erased? To what extent does this happen when we look at the combatants, or refugees and others who have been displaced (Pisani et al. 2016, in this volume)? The invisibility and silence around disability is not unusual. Around the globe, people with disabilities are often invisible. This invisibility may be a result of the conflation of human experiences to those of people without disabilities; it may be due to the segregation of people with disabilities in separate spaces of asylums, institutions or special classrooms (Erevelles 2011). Do race and ethnicity create unique experiences of disability? Does disability create unique experiences of racial and ethnic tensions? Do the intersections of race and ethnicity intensify the invisibility of disability?

Asking 'whose bodies matter?' in terms of the intersections of race and ethnicity with disability is also important for understanding the longstanding colonial and imperialist relationships between the global North and global South (Grech 2011). Erevelles (2011) argues that these colonial relationships are not limited to countries of the global South but include racialised communities of black, Asian, Latino and indigenous peoples in North America, Europe and Australia, and may be evident in internal colonisation. From this perspective we recognise that disabled bodies from the global South are understood as disposable—used for labour until they are injured or unable to work and then set aside (Grech 2011, 2012). The global North has benefited tremendously from the global South by exploiting cheap raw materials and labour during colonial times (Kennedy and Newton 2016, in this volume) and continues to through neocolonial practices (Senier and Miranda-Galarza 2016, in this volume). The colonial legacy has left many countries, especially in Africa, the Middle East and parts of Asia, in conflict and economic deficit. Conflict, neocolonialism and global economic markets rely on the labour and bodies of people in the global South and build upon racialised and gendered assumptions about whose bodies are fit for this work and are unnecessary once they are disabled or injured from the work.

This racialised disregard for bodies is evident in the effects on people in the global South who work in manufacturing cheap goods for the global North, lacking workplace health and safety protections that are found in most workplaces in the global North. Meekosha (2011) outlines the longstanding health and safety concerns, recognising that the disability studies literature has done little to address these issues. The disabling nature of factories in the global South gained prominence in 2013 with the fires in Bangladeshi factories that provided clothing for many stores in the global North. Yet as companies such as Loblaws and Kmart outlined their responses, few discussed their corporate social responsibility in the context of understanding their complicity in the creation of disability and the assumption of bodies as disposable.

This analysis of the links between race, ethnicity and disability in terms of whose bodies matter reminds us to ask about the ways in which resource extraction in northern regions of Canada or other parts of the global North rely on the intersections of race and disability. Communities in the global North, and especially indigenous communities, have also experienced colonisation. For Aboriginal people with disabilities especially in northern Canada, we see these experiences of internal colonisation reinforce their invisibility and justify their displacement from their home communities to 'service centres'—hub cities or towns that host major services, often the only locations where people with disabilities can receive treatment, care and education for complicated needs (Stienstra 2015). In times of crisis, caused by labour supply being redirected to resource extraction, for example, people with disabilities are seen as 'disposable' as disability services are subsequently not available, forcing their displacement to Canada's south and outside their cultural communities (Stienstra 2015). These same communities and their services are put under significant stress as they deal with fly-in, fly-out workers, increasing violence, skyrocketing housing prices and an inadequate infrastructure to deal with these social concerns and the demands of an increasing population. These policies and practices in the global North are reflective of some countries' development policies in the global South. Canada, for example, has recently refocused its development assistance on supporting countries that can provide resources for the global economy, including through mining. We can ask who pays the costs associated with these developments: whose cultures, lands and ways of life are most affected as a result of these policies? In what ways do dominant assumptions about race and ethnicity together with disability practices reinforce the inequalities within 'internal colonies' of Canada and other white settler societies as well as in the global South?

Who Do States Protect?

Race, ethnicity and disability also intersect to shape experiences of who is allowed to be a citizen as well as which citizens can access what they need. Beginning at these intersections we see at least three different sets of questions arise: How do disability and race or ethnicity intersect to exclude certain bodies from state protection or citizenship? How do race or ethnicity and disability intersect to reduce or remove the access to services that citizens in the global South may have? How are the intersections of race and ethnicity with disability used to frame and sustain possible contributions of people with disabilities to reconstruction and state-building?

Excluding the 'Other'

In the global North assumptions and practices related to race, ethnicity and disability are used to exclude certain bodies from citizenship—especially disabled bodies from the global South. The immigration policies of northern countries, including Australia, Canada, the UK and the USA, are based on assumptions that disabled people cannot contribute to economies in combination with racialised assumptions about those from the global South to justify the exclusion of disabled people from the global South as immigrants. Dossa argues that it is the intersection of race and disability which constructs disabled people as unfit for waged work and racialised people with disabilities 'as the Other of the Other' (2009: 34). In this way, Canadian and other northern immigration policies bar the entry of applicants with disabilities, arguing that they will put excessive burden on the health system, thus equating disability with illness, and that people with disabilities are primarily burdens rather than contributing members of a society, and thus cannot become immigrants who will be productive and contribute (Soldatic and Fiske 2009; El-Lahib and Wehbi 2012).

The anti-disability immigration policies in both Canada and Australia disadvantage disabled people from the global South more than those from the global North and remind us to ask how these differences are related to racialised inequalities. Soldatic and Fiske argue that beliefs about white superiority remain at the core of Australian society:

> Whilst the White Australia Policy and associated slogans such as 'Australia for the white man' have been formally discarded, the underlying framework of Australian identity continues to maintain the centrality of whiteness as the norm against which otherness is measured. (Soldatic and Fiske 2009: 292)

This is evident in the example of thirteen Australians with disabilities who were unlawfully detained. Of those, 11 were remarked upon because their ethnicity was 'different' (Soldatic and Fiske 2009). Twelve of the thirteen were immigrants from the global South who had obtained Australian citizenship but it was their 'otherness' that raised suspicion and led to their detention. In other words, these individuals were spotted because they did not fit into the white Australian normative framework.

The intersections of exclusion based on race and disability found in immigration policies of countries in the global North can be traced to the colonial era. During colonial times in New Zealand, ships' captains were instructed to ascertain that passengers boarding their ships were not 'deemed to be a lunatic or [persons] who would become a burden requiring charitable aid' (Meekosha 2011: 674). In Australia, 'the 1901 Immigration Restriction Act was aimed to control the entry of unwanted people, including those defined in terms of "race", criminal status and certain forms of disability' (Meekosha 2011: 674).

The immigration policies adopted by the global North barring disabled people from entering their countries marginalise this group on three different levels. First, they are from the global South, which make them undesirable as a result of the colonial legacies and related racism that perpetuates their exclusion. Second, they are poor as a result of being both from the global South and a person with disabilities, which makes it difficult for them to afford immigration processes and pay for any health or social services once they enter the global North. Third, being disabled closes the door for them because of the perception that their types of body cannot contribute as required of new immigrants.

Access to Services

Even when people with disabilities are citizens, the intersections of race, ethnicity and disability can change their access to services and opportunities to participate in the labour force. Citizens with racialised bodies and disabilities have less opportunity to participate in the labour market and face difficulties accessing services. For example, in Latin America and the Caribbean, indigenous people, Afro-descendants, and people with disabilities have less capacity to generate income because of their lower levels of human capital, lower remuneration in the labour market, and lower access to high-quality jobs (Gandelman et al. 2011). Disabled people participate less in the labour market compared to the rest of the population in part because of transportation obstacles and costs, and barriers to productivity in the workplace.

The intersections of race, ethnicity, religion and disability in Sudan and South Sudan illustrate similar barriers. Sharkey (2008) argues that the Sudanese government's economic and political policies benefit one racial group more than the other and that these differences have been reinforced since colonial times. 'Arab' dominated regimes in the northern Sudan have treated non-Arabs and Arabs as though they have different entitlements. Those who are considered Arabs are treated as citizens while those who are perceived as non-Arabs are treated as subjects. Sharkey (2008) argues that when British and Egyptian forces began to colonise Sudan in 1898, there was no such thing as a self-identified 'Sudanese Arab' among Muslim elites in Sudan. At that time, to be Arab was to be Muslim and to be free. The term 'Arab' connoted high status while a deeply entrenched slave trade was associated with the term 'Sudanese'. In the view of high-status Muslims who regarded themselves as Arabs, being Sudanese meant being black, and being black, in turn, meant having low social status. The British colonial authorities preserved and respected these local status hierarchies and reinforced them through education policies, by favouring high-status 'Arab' males for the academic educations that would lead to administrative jobs, in the process co-opting these men and thwarting their resistance to the regime. Meanwhile, they guided those of slave descent, whom the British in the early years of the twentieth century variously called 'Sudanese' or 'detribalised blacks', into army careers and manual jobs (Sharkey 2008: 29).

These racialised disparities continue in Sudan and create uniquely unequal situations for people with disabilities. Nyerere's (2011) small qualitative study on barriers to inclusion of people with disabilities in Sudan suggests that race, ethnicity, religion and disability intersect to create and reinforce unequal access to services. Three-quarters of the research participants identified themselves as Black, Christian and disabled, and said they faced discrimination on race, religion and disability grounds, which contributed to the barriers they experienced accessing health services and aid provided by the government, including access to assistive devices. One participant suggested that disabled people who identified themselves as Christian were singled out by health professionals based on their Christian names. Once service providers knew the person was a Christian, their attitudes towards that person would change. But if a person identified themselves as Black, disabled and Muslim, service providers would give them more positive treatment. A second participant said that it was difficult to live in northern Sudan as a disabled Christian. She said it was tempting for disabled Christians to convert to Islam just to get out of the hardship they were facing; in fact, some disabled Christians from the south had changed their faith because they were too poor to afford food. A third participant added that Muslims would encourage disabled Christians to convert to Islam so they could get help.

Nyerere's research suggests that the intersections of race, religion and disability result in unique barriers and experiences but also reflect inequalities. The comments of participants illustrate that being disabled, Black Christian Sudanese makes them outsiders and invisible in Sudanese society. As Black Africans, they are seen as lesser citizens who sit at the bottom of the social pyramid. That status is intensified because they have impairments, which can make them invisible as well as powerless. Finally, their minority religion, Christianity, means that they have less access to services in a society led by Muslims. If they were Black and Muslim, the participants suggested, they would have been treated better. They also indicated that disabled Arab Muslims who came from the dominant political and economic group were offered better services and treatment. The resulting economic and political inequalities in turn create disparities between disabled people based on race and religion. This research reminds us to ask the extent to which race, ethnicity, religion and disability interact to create invisibility and inequalities among people in the global South.

Other related questions arising from this work are the extent to which governments perpetuate these intersectional inequalities or use the racialised inequalities to perpetuate certain policies and practices. There is no literature that indicates the Government of Sudan actively discriminated against disabled Christians or people of Black African descent, but it remains an important area for further research. Loeb (2009) suggests that fragile states and post-conflict states not only raise new challenges for people with disabilities, but can also intensify negative attitudes towards disabled people. Scarce resources may mean that people with disabilities are served last or not at all. For instance, Loeb says, as the economic situation deteriorated in Zimbabwe, people became less and less tolerant toward those deemed to be a burden on their families, with the result being widespread abuse and neglect of children with disabilities. When people of south Sudanese origin left Sudan following South Sudan's independence, many families left their disabled loved ones behind because of economic hardship (Nyerere 2011). Using the intersectional lenses of race, ethnicity and disability, we can ask the extent to which race, ethnicity and religion intensify or change experiences of disability and access to services in fragile states.

This modest literature suggests key questions to consider. To what extent are racialised inequalities used to justify unequal treatment of people with disabilities? Are the racialised priorities of a government, including for example Arabisation and Islamisation by the Sudanese government or the colonisation of indigenous people in Canada and other states, used to justify inequalities of treatment among people with disabilities? Is disability conflated with a racialised minority? How do the racialised tensions affect the willingness of people to identify themselves as disabled and seek or receive the supports they need? Do racialised practices intensify the invisibility of people with disabilities? How do the intersections of race and disability shape economic access for people with disabilities in the global South? To what extent do global and regional efforts post-conflict recognise and address the racialised experiences of children and adults with disabilities? To what extent do these practices reinforce racialised differences among people with disabilities by failing to address the needs of disabled people? To what extent do international donors and agencies recognise racialised inequalities among people with disabilities and provide culturally specific services?

Disabled People as Contributors to Their Country's Development

Race and ethnicity intertwine with disability in constructing disabled people from the global South as unable to contribute to their countries' development. This is most evident in fragile and conflict-affected countries where reconstruction efforts fail to include people with disabilities. Children, and especially girls, with disabilities are most likely to be out of school in conflict and fragile-affected states (Trani et al. 2011). In addition, development assistance initiatives rarely address the needs of children and adults with disabilities in conflict-affected countries. To what extent do discourses and practices related to race and ethnicity as well as historical inequalities resulting from colonisation reinforce the invisibility of disabled people in global development? How do development initiatives of the global North build upon these racialised and disability inequalities?

Not only do programs not address the needs of people with disabilities, many reconstruction efforts fail to use inclusive design principles in building schools, hospitals and other public buildings. For example, after Hurricane Mitch in Honduras, not one foreign donor country required that accessibility standards be met and as a result the rebuilt schools failed to include wheelchair access (Stienstra et al. 2002). Why is it that many governments in the global North require universal access as part of the building codes within their own countries but fail to incorporate this when they work in the global South? Finally, many rebuilding efforts post-conflict fail to bring women and men with disabilities as participants to the table.

Even in countries committed to mechanisms such as the United Nations Security Council Resolution 1325 on Women, Peace and Security, women with disabilities remain unrecognised as community leaders who can contribute to peace processes (Stienstra 2013). In what ways are assumptions about people with disabilities as victims perpetuated through post-conflict reconstruction and reconciliation processes (Berghs and Dos Santos-Zingale 2011)? How is race used to reinforce or challenge these portrayals?

Human Rights

One of the hopes for many disabled people around the world is the ratification and implementation of the United Nations Convention on the Rights of Persons with Disabilities (CRPD). Many disabled peoples' organisations around the world are using the Convention to press for their rights and inclusion in their own societies. Some South Sudanese people with disabilities see the Convention as an opportunity to insert their needs and interests into and to challenge existing systems. For example, even though Sudan had ratified the CRPD, some argue the government was not implementing certain articles that were of benefit to people with disabilities (Nyerere 2011). In Juba, people with disabilities used the Convention to voice their discontent with how they were being treated (Stephen 2009). They complained they were restricted from accessing the physical environment, transportation, information and communication, technological systems and facilities openly provided to the public. They also demanded their inclusion in key administrative systems starting from the lowest government level to the highest authority.

Yet human rights instruments, including the CRPD, are contested because they are framed primarily around northern ways of understanding human rights and may be 'diversionary' in the struggles of daily living (Meekosha and Soldatic 2011). In addition, they do little to address intersectional experiences including those based in Aboriginality, race and ethnicity, as well as the way in which disability is created through colonial and imperial relationships. Some attention is beginning to be paid to using the Convention together with the Declaration on the Rights of Indigenous Peoples to promote the rights of indigenous people with disabilities (Demas and Shackel 2012). This work is complex given the intersections of indigeneity and disability. Demas and Shackel (2012) argue that some indigenous world views and practices may already be inclusive of people with disabilities, and that the experience of indigenous people with disabilities is complicated by both colonial and ableist legacies and practices. In addition to addressing these inequalities at the community level, they suggest that the CRPD together with the Declaration offers an opportunity to monitor and advance the rights of indigenous people with disabilities.

As we argued earlier, intersectionality has a transformational element to it—it is not only about identifying inequalities but also about bringing change in those relationships. As Chun et al. (2013) argue, intersectional work enables progressive politics in which people can derive their identities from their politics rather than their politics from their identities, and thus give new meanings and action to their embodied social identities. Meekosha and Soldatic (2011) encourage us to think more about how this could be done in the context of disability rights and the CRPD. They suggest that 'impairment is not, in fact, always "natural", but the outcome of deeply politicised processes of social dynamics in bodies, that then become medicalised and then normalised through a raft of moral discursive and real practices' (Meekosha and Soldatic 2011: 1393). This may include colonial practices in indigenous communities, such as introducing alcohol as a means of social control. In the case of South Sudan, historical and continuing conflicts result in widespread disabling practices which emerge in the context of global oil, the relationship with Sudan, and a variety of racial and religious differences.

It is not sufficient to look at disability within the existing definitions of the CRPD, especially in countries of the global South; we need to recognise how the ongoing processes of colonisation, racialised inequalities and other structural inequalities work together with disability and impairment. This requires solidarity across and between those in the global North and South. These networks can enable us to act together to recognise and redress the global violence at work in conflict, exclusionary immigration policies, global factories that rely on disposable bodies, and development assistance programs that reinforce the isolation and invisibility of people with disabilities.

Conclusion

Understanding the intersections of race, ethnicity and disability matters. Recognising the different experiences at these intersections as well as the systemic or structural ways in which historical and current racial inequalities work to keep disability invisible, or the ways that disability disparities intensify racialised inequalities, helps to make greater sense of what happens in the global South or the global South in the global North. Intersections of race, ethnicity and disability also help us to move together, recognising our diversities, in our work to end these inequalities and create networks of solidarity and support.

References

Annamma, S. A., Connor, D., & Ferri, B. (2013). Dis/ability critical race studies (DisCrit): Theorizing at the intersections of race and dis/ability. *Race, Ethnicity and Education, 16*(1), 1–31. doi:10.1080/13613324.2012.730511.

Bell, C. (2010). Is disability studies actually white disability studies? In L. J. Davis (Ed.), *The disability studies reader* (3rd ed., pp. 374–382). New York: Routledge.

Berghs, M., & Dos Santos-Zingale, M. (2011). A comparative analysis: Everyday experiences of disability in Sierra Leone. *Africa Today, 58*(2), 19–40. doi:10.1353/at.2011.0044.

Berghs, M., & Kabbara, N. (2016). Disabled people in conflicts and wars. In S. Grech & K. Soldatic (Eds.), *Disability in the global South: The critical handbook*. New York: Springer.

Cho, S., Crenshaw, K. W., & McCall, L. (2013). Toward a field of intersectionality studies: Theory, applications, and praxis. *Signs: Journal of Women in Culture and Society, 38*(4), 785–810.

Chun, J. J., Lipsitz, G., & Shin, Y. (2013). Intersectionality as a social movement strategy: Asian immigrant women advocates. *Signs: Journal of Women in Culture and Society, 38*(4), 917–940.

Crenshaw, K. (1995). Mapping the margins: Intersectionality, identity politics and violence against women of colour. In K. Crenshaw, N. Gotanda, G. Peller, & K. Thomas (Eds.), *Critical race theory: The key writings that informed the movement* (pp. 357–383). New York: New Press.

Demas, D., & Shackel, D. (2012). *Giinawind bigo ji wiijii'iweyang (nothing about us without us) Understanding our rights: First Nations people with disabilities engage in human rights education*. Toronto: Disability Rights Promotion International.

Deng, F. M. (2006). Sudan: A nation in turbulent search of itself. *The Annals of the American Academy of Political and Social Science, 603*(1), 155–162. doi:10.1177/0002716205283021.

Dossa, P. (2009). *Racialized bodies, disabling worlds: Storied lives of immigrant Muslim women*. Toronto: University of Toronto Press.

Dowse, L., Frohmader, C., & Didi, A. (2016). Violence against disabled women in the global South: working locally, acting globally. In S. Grech & K. Soldatic (Eds.), *Disability in the global South: The critical handbook*. New York: Springer.

Eckhard, S. & Gaus, A. (2014, February 5). No surprises in South Sudan, or in the Central African Republic [blog post]. *Le monde diplomatique*. Retrieved February 21, 2014, from http://mondediplo.com/blogs/no-surprises-in-south-sudan-or-in-the-central

El-Lahib, Y., & Wehbi, S. (2012). Immigration and disability: Ableism in the policies of the Canadian state. *International Social Work, 55*(1), 95–108. doi:10.1177/0020872811407941.

Erevelles, N. (2011). *Disability and difference in global contexts: Enabling a transformative body politic*. New York: Palgrave Macmillan.

Gandelman, N., Ñopo, H., & Ripani, L. (2011). Traditional excluding forces: A review of the quantitative literature on the economic situation of indigenous peoples, Afro-descendants, and people living with disability. *Latin American Politics and Society, 53*(4), 147–179. doi:10.1111/j.1548-2456.2011.00136.x.

Grech, S. (2011). Recolonising debates or perpetuated coloniality? Decentring the spaces of disability, development and community in the global South. *International Journal of Inclusive Education, 15*(1), 87–100. doi:10.1080/13603116.2010.496198.

Grech, S. (2012). Disability, communities of poverty and the global South: Debating through social capital. In A. Azzopardi & S. Grech (Eds.), *Inclusive communities: A critical reader* (pp. 69–84). Rotterdam: Sense Publishers.

IRIN. (2013, February 18). Scant help for South Sudan's disabled. *IRIN humanitarian news and analysis*. Retrieved December 11, 2013, fromhttp://www.irinnews.org/report/97496/scant-help-for-south-sudan-s-disabled

Kennedy, S., & Newton, M. (2016). The hauntings of slavery: Colonialism and the disabled body in the Caribbean. In S. Grech & K. Soldatic (Eds.), *Disability in the global South: The critical handbook*. New York: Springer.

Liasidou, A. (2014). The cross-fertilization of critical race theory and disability studies: Points of convergence/divergence and some education policy implications. *Disability & Society, 29*(5), 724–737. doi:10.1080/09687599.2013.844104.

Loeb, M. (2009). The effect of failed states on the well-being and lives of people with disabilities. In M. MacLachlan & L. Swartz (Eds.), *Disability and international development: Towards inclusive global health* (pp. 13–30). New York: Springer.

McCall, L. (2005). The complexity of intersectionality. *Signs: Journal of Women in Culture and Society, 30*(3), 1771–1800. doi:10.1086/426800.

Medani, K. M. (2014, January 14). South Sudan is divided by the spoils of oil, not ethnicity. *The Guardian*. Retrieved February 21, 2014, from http://www.theguardian.com/commentisfree/2014/jan/14/south-sudan-divided-oil-ethnicity-violence

Meekosha, H. (2011). Decolonising disability: Thinking and acting globally. *Disability & Society, 26*(6), 667–682. doi:10.1080/09687599.2011.602860a.

Meekosha, H., & Soldatic, K. (2011). Human rights and the global South: The case of disability. *Third World Quarterly, 32*(8), 1383–1397. doi:10.1080/01436597.2011.614800.

Morris, M. (2007). *Using intersectional feminist frameworks in research: A resource for embracing the complexities of women's lives*. Ottawa: CRIAW.

Native Women's Association of Canada (NWAC). (2010). *What their stories tell us: Research findings from the Sisters in Spirit initiative*. Ottawa: Native Women's Association of Canada.

Nyerere, L. (2011). *Understanding disability in Sudan*. Unpublished Master's Thesis. University of Manitoba, Winnipeg.

Pisani, M., Grech, S., & Mostafa, A. (2016). Disability and forced migration: Intersections and critical debates. In S. Grech & K. Soldatic (Eds.), *Disability in the global South: The critical handbook*. New York: Springer.

Prunier, G. (2014, February 3). South Sudan: It all began so well. *Le monde diplomatique*. Retrieved February 21, 2014, from http://mondediplo.com/2014/02/03southsudan

Raghavan, S. (2014, February 21). South Sudan crisis: How the oil that's fuelled deadly conflict might help stop it. *The Star*. Retrieved February 21, 2014, from http://www.thestar.com/news/world/2014/01/21/south_sudan_crisis_how_oil_is_fuelling_the_countrys_deadly_conflict.html

Senier, S., & Miranda-Galarza, B. (2016). From colonialism to postcolonialism and contemporary empire. In S. Grech & K. Soldatic (Eds.), *Disability in the global South: The critical handbook*. New York: Springer.

Sharkey, H. (2008). Arab identity and ideology in Sudan: The politics of language, ethnicity, and race. *African Affairs, 107*(426), 21–43. doi:10.1093/afraf/adm068.

Soldatic, K., & Fiske, L. (2009). Bodies 'locked up': Intersections of disability and race in Australian immigration. *Disability and Society, 24*(3), 289–301. doi:10.1080/09687590902789453.

Stephen, J. J. (2009, December 21). The disabled demand affirmative action: People with disabilities in Central Equatoria State have requested to be granted affirmative action by the government. *Gurtong*. Retrieved December 18, 2013, from http://www.gurtong.net/ECM/Editorial/tabid/124/ctl/ArticleView/mid/519/articleId/2917/The-Disabled-Demand-Affirmative-Action.aspx

Stienstra, D. (2012). Race/ethnicity and disability studies: Towards an explicitly intersectional approach. In N. Watson, A. Roulstone, & C. Thomas (Eds.), *Routledge handbook of disability studies* (pp. 376–389). New York: Routledge.

Stienstra, D. (2013, May 21). Making disability visible: Inclusive reconstruction in fragile and conflict-affected states [blog post]. *Centre for International Policy Studies Blog*. Retrieved December 17, 2013, from http://cips.uottawa.ca/making-disability-visible-inclusive-reconstruction-in-fragile-and-conflict-affected-states/

Stienstra, D. (2015). Northern crises: Women's relationships and resistances to resource extractions. *International Feminist Journal of Politics, 17*(4), 630–651 doi: 10.1080/14616742.2015.1060695.

Stienstra, D., Fricke, Y., D'Aubin, A., & Team, R. (2002). *Baseline assessment: Disability and inclusion in World Bank activities*. Winnipeg: Canadian Centre on Disability Studies.

Trani, J., Kett, M., Bakhshi, P., & Bailey, N. (2011). Disability, vulnerability and citizenship: To what extent is education a protective mechanism for children with disabilities in countries affected by conflict? *International Journal of Inclusive Education, 15*(10), 1187–1203. doi:10.1080/13603116.2011.555078.

UNICEF. (2013). *State of the world's children 2013: Children with disabilities*. New York: United Nations Children Fund.

Van Dijken, K. (2014, February 3). South Sudan ravaged by ethnic violence. *Al Jazeera*. Retrieved February 21, 2014, from http://www.aljazeera.com/indepth/features/2014/02/south-sudan-ravaged-ethnic-violence-2014236519937368.html

World Health Organization & World Bank. (2011). *World report on disability*. Geneva: World Health Organizatiocxn.

Chapter 17
Disabled People in Conflicts and Wars

Maria Berghs and Nawaf Kabbara

> *He was telling me about what it was like for disabled people living in the town when it fell to the rebels. As he told me about the fear and 'constraints' they lived under, I remembered the awful story of the looting of the workshop and being told of his own involvement in violence. I asked him if he had ever been involved in violence during the civil war or before. He evaded the question and told me a story about a woman with polio who was so beautiful that one of the rebel commanders recruited her and then later apparently made her his wife. He said, 'We used to see her walking through the town with a huge knife hung around her neck.' He pointed half way down his body and illustrated the shape of what looked like a machete.*[1]
>
> *Presently, the peace movements are not on the forefront these days. But I think disabled people should be like the ambassadors of peace and human rights in the world. (Hersey 2001, para. 36)*

Introduction

This chapter begins with two quotes illustrating the heterogeneity and complexity of disabled people's experiences during conflicts. They describe marginalised histories, such as those of female fighters or peace activists. Historically, disabled people have been and continue to be created as well as situated in war economies. They are

[1] Fieldwork notes, Sierra Leone, 2011.

M. Berghs (✉)
University of York, York, UK
e-mail: mariaberghs@gmail.com

N. Kabbara
Balamand University, Koura, Lebanon

S. Grech, K. Soldatic (eds.), *Disability in the Global South*,
International Perspectives on Social Policy, Administration, and Practice,
DOI 10.1007/978-3-319-42488-0_17

vulnerable and suffer. Yet, they also participate in conflicts as fighters, spies, factory workers, cooks, cleaners, nurses, doctors and communication specialists, as well as protesters and activists (e.g. Nielsen 2012).

There is a dearth of literature on the subject linked to a history of North–South disparities in the creation and embodiment of impairment. This is despite the fact we know disabled people are mainly located in the global South (WHO 2011). Conflicts are also a cause of impairment and leave disabled people susceptible to early death, violence and multiple impairments. Collier et al. (2003) point out that civil wars predominantly affect low-income countries but are also indicative that neoliberal development policies have failed. Meekosha (2011), too, argues that global capitalism is now implicated in neoliberalism in the arms trade, nuclear weaponry and appropriation of land and resources in the global South, fuelling the inequality at the root of conflicts. Furthermore, Leaning and Guha-Sapir (2013) note that while their incidence has decreased globally, armed conflicts have become more protracted, with over 300 million people now living in conditions of 'violent insecurity'.

Data on disability in conflicts and war is skewed towards a rarefied medical humanitarianism (Berghs 2014). The emphasis is on forms of biomedical or epidemiological measurement, assessing 'burden' of disability and cost-effectiveness (as in Disability Adjusted Life Years—DALYs), instead of focusing on social protection, resilience or prevention of violence within societies. There is scant evidence of statistics, prevention and monitoring of disability in conflict and post-conflict situations (Kett and van Ommeren 2009; World Health Organisation [WHO] 2011; Handicap International [HI] 2012). Though there are efforts at ensuring accountability and transparency in aid, for example through The Sphere Project, within such oversight and guidelines there has been a lack of action in evaluating and assessing the implementation of the United Nations Convention on the Rights of Persons with Disabilities (CRPD) in conflict situations.

While Article 11 of the CRPD is focused on the protection of disabled people during humanitarian emergencies,[2] the situation is different in practice. Lord (2014: 156) elucidates how the myriad barriers that disabled people face in 'accessing education, employment, health, rehabilitation and an adequate standard of living' are exacerbated during times of conflict, and yet there has been 'no operational interrogation and guidance' given about CRPD implementation in such situations. All too often this has concentrated on UN refugee camps without taking into account the changing nature of conflicts and how humanitarianism implicates disablism. For example, it is still unclear how much money is actually spent on disabled people in relief efforts, what mainstreaming and accommodation mean during a conflict, and if organisations gain consent and give compensation for images they use to get humanitarian funding. Data connected to the CRPD is also specialised and has not been adapted to contexts of internal displacement or post-conflict realities.

[2] The CRPD contains 50 articles. Article 11 makes specific reference to international humanitarian and human rights law to ensure the protection of persons with disabilities during situations of risk, such as armed conflicts or humanitarian emergencies.

Additionally, terrorism and the 'war on terror' engage in a militarised and mediatised typology of 'us' versus 'them' while validating the able-bodied male soldier, fighter, rebel or martyr, a validation which often continues post-conflict. There is an invisibility correlated to the long-term effects of conflict on civilians, who are affected the most, particularly disabled women, the elderly, youth and children (Ahlen 1997; Ghobarah et al. 2004; Human Rights Watch [HRW] 2010). We know almost nothing about civilian casualties and impairments during and post-conflict, such as those caused by the Iraq wars, while data on military impairment is stringently collected (Hyndman 2007). Moreover, conflicts and humanitarian emergencies in the global South are traditionally seen in terms of threat to health and hence human security (Ong et al. 2009).

In this chapter, this current understanding of disability in conflicts and wars is repositioned. We begin by illustrating the narrow public health focus in medical humanitarianism despite the changing nature of conflicts. We argue that such an approach misses existing populations of disabled people, which has consequences for reintegration and social protection. Secondly, we examine how indirect impairments result from sites of vulnerability in conflict and post-conflict situations. Thirdly, we illustrate the long-term consequences of conflict and highlight where action is needed. We locate impairment and disabled status, noting issues of intersectionality on ethnicity, gender, social status and impairment/s. Finally, we illustrate the potential of inclusion as an important resource for peace but illustrate its limits with a case study.

The Changing Nature of Conflicts: Rethinking Medical Humanitarianism

The nature of conflict is changing from intra to inter-state and is more geographically dispersed and prolonged, as evidenced in the eastern Democratic Republic of Congo (Leaning and Guha-Sapir 2013). Conflicts are also becoming complex emergencies, in the way that several humanitarian crises may combine, including, for example, mass population displacements, food insecurity, epidemics and political, religious or ethnic instability, such as in Syria. Pederson (2002) notes how conflicts now disproportionately affect certain groups or specific populations in the global South, such as indigenous communities, as well as religious and ethnic minorities. Additionally, certain locations are targeted, such as sites of mineral resources; agricultural and water supplies; telecommunications, transport and civilian infrastructures; religious sites; and fe/male bodies as symbolic sites of honour, family and community (re)production (Pederson 2002).

The changed nature of conflicts should mean a rethinking of how impairment occurs, how and why disabled people are affected and what should be incorporated into services long term. Despite this, both policy and practice reveal a short-term and often disjointed focus on specialised medical and emergency relief services. Additionally, the potential and ethics of medical humanitarianism to contribute to sustainable training, knowledge, protection and empowerment of communities during conflicts and displacement has received minimal attention or has been co-opted by the military (Banatvala and Zwi 2000). A purely medical focus also means the political and socio-cultural framing of issues of inequality is lost (e.g. gender-based violence) (Ticktin 2011) and explains why 'disability' disappears.

Due to the link to medical humanitarianism, global public health analyses of conflict usually focus on direct and indirect causes of impairment (Ghobarah et al. 2004). Direct impairments are linked to the immediate physical consequences of violent conflict, such as becoming wounded during an air raid, being hit by a bullet, stepping on a land mine or being raped as a weapon of war. The indirect consequences are linked to experiences of displacement, psychological ill health (from witnessing violence, for example) and/or lack of basic needs (shelter, sanitation, water, food, healthcare, etc.). People can be affected by direct and indirect forms of impairment in that they may gain injuries and then be forced to flee, being impaired further due to displacement or inadequate food provision in refugee camps.

During a conflict, the medical, rehabilitative and other immediate needs of the population affected by direct impairments takes necessary precedence. Yet, the instantiation of this hierarchy post-conflict depends on the outcome of the conflict, which affects how people who fought and gained impairments are perceived (whether as heroes, saviours, martyrs or villains) and if services are provided. For example, both Bruun (1995) and Meyers (2013) note the changing notions of citizenship, gender and sacrifice that underlie the continued valorisation of impaired ex-combatants in Nicaragua. Socio-cultural, religious, economic and political context is important, however, as French (1994) illustrates in Cambodia where Buddhist notions of karma and compassion are interwoven. The identities of former soldiers who become wounded by land mines become ambivalent due to a karmic 'devaluation' of their bodies and lives (French 1994: 77). Similarly, both Gundawara (2010) and Lamichhane (2014) found disjunctions between internal perception of heroism and sacrifice of impaired veterans, and external community treatment and services available.

As post-conflict security is often a concern, male ex-combatants generally gain initial priority over civilians, or even women and children in their own ranks, in terms of disarmament, demobilisation and reintegration, social security, compensation, equipment, or training programmes. Most of these programmes tend to be short term, however. The rebuilding of inclusive and conjoined health and social care services as part of the overall infrastructural services of the state is rarely planned for in humanitarianism. We proceed to examine the consequences of a focus on direct impairment for the pre-existing populations of disabled people.

The Forgotten Disabled

The existing, pre-conflict populations of disabled people are often forgotten during a conflict and in relief efforts. The focus is mostly on medical and rehabilitative provision for conflict-related direct physical impairment (Berghs 2012; Burton et al.

2013). The destruction of infrastructure and services that disabled people depend on, such as specialised or inclusive schools, institutions, day centres, disabled people's organisations (DPOs), medical services and rehabilitation clinics, is rarely reported on (Grove et al. 2010; World Health Organisation [WHO] 2011; Miles 2013).

Additionally, resources such as medical aid and rehabilitation services are diverted to veterans or civilians who gain direct impairments. Miles (1990) explains how, in Afghanistan, this meant disabled people were forced to rely on informal care and community-based rehabilitation (CBR). He goes on to note how this disproportionately affected families and women in particular, with resources in communities often becoming stretched. Working in Palestine, Burton et al. (2013) note that the focus on physical impairment affects statistics and welfare provisions, resulting in marginalisation of disabled people, especially women. Nagata (2008) found that disabled women in Jordan and Lebanon experienced double discrimination, especially those with 'non-physical' impairments, such as congenital or intellectual. Yet, she elucidates how negative attitudes are 'multidimensional' and 'consisting of the interlocking facets of cognitive, cultural, behavioural and economic factors' (Nagata 2008: 17).

Understanding these multidimensional attitudes is fundamental to explaining why disablement and marginalisation within a disabled population occurs. For instance, we know that disabled children are particularly neglected post-conflict (Ahlen 1997). Aid to 'disabled war veterans' is also prioritised over aid and provisions, such as education or prosthetics, for disabled children (Miles 2013). Often, direct injuries such as those from wars or mines are valorised, while children with other types of acquired (e.g. AIDS) or congenital (e.g. epilepsy) impairments can have stigmatised identities in hierarchies of 'recognition' (Tomlinson and Abdi 2003). This 'recognition' is shaped by social, cultural and economic factors (Tomlinson and Abdi 2003), which can be influenced and changed.

The above-mentioned research illustrates that if no assessment is made of service provision needs for an existing and often diverse disabled population, this can contribute to neglect and/or stigmatised identities. Furthermore, an initial focus on victims with physical impairments to the detriment of all other types of impairment can lead to competition and corruption in order to access limited resources. This can result in the creation of hierarchies between victims accessing aid as well as between disabled people (Berghs 2012). Global disability policy, definitions and funding trends also impact on identities and hierarchies, for example, in the post-conflict interventions implemented by non-government organisations (NGOs), such as those linked to medical aid, mental health or human rights (Berghs and Dos Santos-Zingale 2011). The impact of humanitarian interventions and funding trends on the creation of disabled identities and DPOs, societal attitudes and psycho-social resilience among disabled people has not yet been adequately investigated.

Representation in NGOs and DPOs has been limited mostly to educated men with physical impairments, whereas those with no education, women and parents groups are often marginalised (Nagata 2008; Berghs 2012). In this way, hierarchies of impairment and people (men) who can 'speak' to certain western definitions of disability are further instantiated. It is also becoming increasingly important to be able to verbalise needs in English, write project proposals, fight for disability 'rights', and understand global disability policy (Wehbi 2011a). The focus of international disability policy priorities during a conflict also affects how sites of vulnerability are created as well as indirect forms of impairment.

Indirect Impairments: Contested Sites of Vulnerability

Disability during conflict is usually understood in terms of 'vulnerability' without questioning why and how. Looking at North–South inequalities in greater depth, De Jong (2010: 74) argues that the propensity for conflict is linked to:

1. Inequality
2. Rapidly changing demographic characteristics
3. Lack of democratic processes
4. Political instability
5. Ethnic composition of ruling group different from the population at large or ethnic groups straddling interstate boundaries
6. Deterioration of public services
7. Severe economic decline
8. Cycles of violent revenge.

How the CRPD and a global policy focus on poverty ties into the potential reduction of conflict has not been explored. Instead there has been a superficial emphasis on consequences of armed violence, identification of weapons such as mines, and 'risk' of 'disability' to development, where disability is viewed as inhibiting development processes (Handicap International [HI] 2012). The 'risk' linked to disability exists in conflict and post-conflict settings. Disabled people suffer death, exploitation, torture, gender-based violence, social isolation and impairment due to the conditions in which they live during a conflict. Those who are mentioned most are linked to the movement of civilians within a nation as internally displaced people (IDPs) and/or movement of people outside a nation's borders as refugees (UNHCR 2013).

The United Nations High Commissioner for Refugees (UNHCR) views disabled people as 'invisible' or 'vulnerable', noting they are at risk from physical, emotional and sexual abuse because of conditions in camp settings, but the agency does not implement any disability model or approach that empowers people (Mirza 2011; Miles 2013; UNHCR 2013). A focus on these barriers also means that other sites of vulnerability to impairment linked to community, domestic spaces and reproduction are ignored (Das and Addlakha 2001; Berghs 2011).

Dos Santos-Zingale and McColl (2006) illustrate how disabled people are not invisible or necessarily abandoned by families or communities as they become displaced, but that social support and resources are needed. Intersectionality is also important as gender, age, religion, ethnicity and association between fighting forces and type of impairment interact, making certain people more vulnerable during and/or after conflict. For example, Grove et al. (2010) and Rohwerder (2013) argue that particular population groups, such as those with intellectual disabilities, are often not considered or included in disability planning or guidelines—when fleeing, in refugee camps and post-conflict. Grove et al. (2010) elucidate how impairments such as intellectual disabilities or autism also make a person more susceptible to injury or even death, due to lack of knowledge about violence and technology, and 'grooming' into violence, as well as use by military forces.

Environment is also an intersectional consideration because the contexts in which people are located often makes them more vulnerable to impairment. In Syria, millions of people have become displaced but 79 per cent of refugees are located in urban spaces, not camps (Sami et al. 2014). This means that we need to rethink the concept of where disability mainstreaming occurs (i.e. camps) and what the disability demographic entails in a middle-income country with a predominantly young population. In such a context, attention needs to be placed on ensuring mobility, strengthening existing disability services and DPOs, paying attention to youth needs and ensuring social protection grants in (inter)national disability mainstreaming. Yet, most guidelines still focus on mainstreaming disability in traditional refugee camps. Mirza (2011) notes that these guidelines are routinely flouted and basic services, equipment, security and camp layouts remain inaccessible. She details the inadequacy of services in understanding demographic changes in terms of increases of chronic illness, mental health, and advanced medical treatment needed by disabled people, as well as the linkages between such care, pharmaceuticals and social integration (Mirza 2011).

In keeping with the importance of intersectionality, specific guidelines and inclusive services also need to be developed for children and young people, especially girls with any type of impairment, since they are more vulnerable to exploitation and marginalisation in camps (Ahlen 1997; Hynes 2004). Programmes also lack consideration of the need to localise both global and local resources, for example, in terms of ensuring medical provision alongside indigenous ways of healing (Berghs 2011). Similarly, employment and education of disabled people and mobilisation of DPOs and activists as a means of (re)integration post-conflict have been neglected. Wehbi (2011a) speaks about a lack of coordination, collaboration and mistrust leading to the exclusion of civil society and DPOs in Lebanon. This is a missed opportunity because it leads to a lack of inclusive rebuilding and misunderstanding of what causes short- and long-term impairment and disablement.

Long-Term Effects of Conflict

The long-term consequences of protracted conflict on disabled people and the creation of impairment need more research. This calls for a longitudinal or life-course approach (Priestley 2007) to see how identities, single and multiple impairment(s), health and social care needs differ as the age of populations and their environments change. A life-course approach can also explore how the concept of disability is changing intergenerationally, whether passed on biologically (e.g. HIV/AIDS) and socially (e.g. stigma), or through ascription of a new kinship identity (e.g. amputee) (Berghs 2012). Yet, research, funding and planning to understand the long-term effects of conflict on disability is rarely available (Wehbi 2011a).

Inhorn and Kobeissi (2006) usefully note how there are six long-term effects of conflict on civilians: physical, mental, reproductive/demographic, social structural, infrastructural, and environmental. We briefly discuss each of these in turn in an effort to illustrate what is missing from current debates in relation to disability.

Physical

We know very little about civilian deaths and creation of impairment despite the fact that poorly resourced health systems contribute to death, illness and impairment (Banatvala and Zwi 2000; WHO 2011). With the focus on public health, the effects of malnutrition, communicable and non-communicable diseases, unsanitary conditions and lack of access to water are given substantial attention post-conflict. For example, Miles and Medi (1994) found that while conflict in Mozambique had resulted in impairment among children, most actually gained indirect impairments due to a mix of effects created by the long-term consequences of the conflict, such as malnutrition. Insurance provision, necessary implementation of user fees for services and a lack of (paid) professionals, medication, assistive devices, prosthetics and rehabilitation programmes affect impairment, too. Growing privatisation under neo-liberalism is also a threat to access to health and social care services (Berghs 2013). Likewise, the impact of landmines, chemicals and circulation of (small) arms can last for generations and will need long-term planning of services. Long-term effects of conflict and links to impairment need to be identified so that services can be planned and implemented adequately.

Mental

In post-conflict situations, there are increases in mental health needs such as for counselling, social care and specialised psychiatric services. Inhorn and Kobeissi (2006) cite lack of infrastructural development and trained professionals, as well as not prioritising mental health as detrimental to well-being. The evidence base for many interventions affecting disabled people does not exist, especially in the field of gender-based violence and mental health (Blanchet et al. 2013). Likewise, while there is a lot of data on western veterans, there is very little information on culturally sensitive, indigenous or communal interventions for disabled people. Institutionalisation, stigma, western diagnoses (following the *Diagnostic and Statistical Manual of Mental Disorders* 5) and links to pharmaceutical companies also influence how mental health care is accessed and why. Thus, coping strategies involving cheap and freely available pharmaceuticals, alcohol and/or drugs develop in society (Inhorn and Kobeissi 2006). More research is needed to explore the long-term mental health impact of conflict.

Reproductive/Demographic

Lives are disrupted during a conflict, as families, gender relations and patterns of reproduction undergo profound changes. Marriage is a means of societal integration for disabled people but when most men are fighting or community ties are disrupted, there may be earlier, delayed or no marriages taking place. Periods of conflict also have reproductive consequences for disabled women and men with lack of access to reproductive services, antenatal, postnatal and emergency care. There may also be an increase in perceived need for certain services or technologies to prevent impairment, such as antenatal screening in Vietnam (Gammeltoft 2013). Correlations exist between lack of access to reproductive services (e.g. screening and contraception) and war-time sexual violence, increases in Sexually transmitted infections (STIs), infertility, infant deaths and children born with impairments. Disabled people often face discrimination in services and institutions ensuring neglect, segregation, sterilisation or institutionalisation. For example, Human Rights Watch (2010) documented high rates of physical and sexual abuse of disabled women post-conflict, but a lack of access to reproductive services, health education and STI testing continues. Lack of access to reproductive services pre- and post-conflict is important to understand demographically.

Social Structural

The social structure of society changes during a conflict and the informal CBR systems that families and communities are supplied with may collapse. Programmes implemented by NGOs that superficially mainstream disability may also increase poverty and marginalisation of disabled people (see Wehbi 2011a). There could be rising violence on account of (small) arms and the circulation of drugs, often with links to criminal networks and gangs, which leads to rises in specific types of impairment (e.g. spinal cord injuries caused by bullet wounds) (Buchanan 2011; Handicap International [HI] 2012). Conflict and post-conflict societal upheaval may last for decades with the threat of bombs, drones and violence profoundly affecting communities. Hill and Hansen (2011) describe how in Northern Ireland, a state of terror with bombs going off meant that those with mobility problems were forced to stay at home, leading to greater social isolation. Social isolation has also been identified as a risk factor when it comes to exploitation of disabled people (Grove et al. 2010). The consequences of societal breakdown, lack of evaluation of disability programming during a conflict and post-conflict, and the programmes that empower disabled people to survive must be urgently addressed.

Infrastructural

Conflict destroys most of the limited infrastructure that exists for disabled people. Vocational workshops, institutions such as day centres, and schools need to be rebuilt. Post-conflict rebuilding can offer an opportunity for inclusive design and mainstreaming of disability in all infrastructural development. For instance, while education is disrupted, new opportunities present themselves to rebuild educational and vocational systems through inclusive practices (Miles 2013). Such interventions will have little impact, however, if issues in the current educational system, notably that teachers lack training and know-how and are often unpaid, are neglected. Likewise, ensuring suitable skills training, micro-credit programmes, and employment in the formal and informal economy are particular concerns post-conflict, but there will be gross difficulties in improving disabled people's situation if societal attitudes remain negative, barriers persist in transportation systems, or there is no economy to contribute to. Therefore, we need to understand more about what enables the entire social and physical infrastructure to become inclusive and robust post-conflict.

Environmental

The exploitation of resources and environmental impact of conflicts will be felt for generations. Yet, the impact of new forms of impairment on indigenous communities and women is rarely investigated (Ngo et al. 2012). Likewise, disability rights and intergenerational rights in terms of creation of differing forms of impairment are rarely advocated (Soldatic 2013). North–South hierarchies in bodies and body parts are thus still correlated with inequalities, especially in countries with histories of violence or conflict that are undergoing political transitions (see Scheper-Hughes 1996). This is exemplified in biopolitical claims for genetic reproductive harm, such as the use of Agent Orange in Vietnam, nuclear testing in the southern hemisphere and the use of depleted uranium in Iraq, which are rarely upheld. Reflections on newer forms of biosociality, or social identities based on biological, genetic or medical conditions (such as HIV/AIDs), chemical and environmental harm, and the links between conflict, violence and activism remain unexplored.

Inclusion for Peace

The above sections illustrate the importance of including disabled people, DPOs and activists in any conflict and post-conflict planning, especially as a resource for peace. Disabled people and their families are involved in protest and activism in veterans' organisations, camp committees, grassroots civil society organisations, DPOs, NGOs, human rights organisations, transitional justice initiatives, and national politics (Wehbi 2011a, b). Men, women and children who become wounded during conflicts or are affected by various forms of violence are involved in fights for justice, reparations and other forms of restitution (Buchanan 2011; Hill and Hansen 2011; Berghs 2012). They often have an important role symbolically within a country and they have used this status to advocate for peace, protest, riot or revolution (Nagata 2008; Berghs 2012; Kabbara and Abou Khalil 2014).

In spite of a digital divide and the dangers of activism in countries undergoing transitions, people are using new technological tools such as smartphone cameras, YouTube and crowd-sourced funding to gain a voice, film and advocate their own needs on their own terms (French and Swain 2014). If the CRPD is adhered to and mainstreaming is implemented, humanitarian aid should allow DPOs and activists to gain resources to ensure advocacy and much-needed inclusion. The post-conflict reality is not there yet, however, as illustrated by the following case study.

Case Study: The Disability Movement in Lebanon

Before the civil war in Lebanon in 1975, disability as an issue was omitted from the political agenda. The charity paradigm was the dominant approach. The violence in the country between 1975 and 1990 left thousands of people with impairments and led to the development of societal awareness. The first response came from the military and militia organisations within each sectarian community. These groups, supported by religious and other societal institutions, felt the need to build medical and rehabilitation institutions and programmes to deal with injured militia men as well as civilians within their own communities. Their intervention was both institutional and community based. In the 1980s, the second response began when disabled people, supported by international NGOs, organised their own programmes and actions.

The most important innovation of the disability community during that period was the decision to put aside demands for rights and play an active role in ending the violence. Accordingly, DPOs and prominent activists began to join anti-war and anti-violence campaigns. Many activities were implemented including a blood donation campaign in 1985 and a sit-in on the crossroads between the two fighting camps in 1986. The most significant action was the 1987 peace march organised by the disability movement in collaboration with the non-violence movement. This march traversed the country from north to south in protest against the continuation of violence and militia control.

Post-conflict, the disability movement adapted to a new role and devised a strategy based on two pillars. The first was to consolidate disability rights by lobbying for a new law on disability. The second was to keep the disability movement as an 'avant garde' social force working to strengthen social peace and reconciliation and to push for reforms. The law became a reality in 2000. Nonetheless, after 14 years, it is far from being implemented. Kabbara (2014) found that health care was still not properly provided, most schools and public transport were inaccessible, employment opportunities were rare, and government funds were mostly supporting care institutions at the expense of adopting integrative programmes and projects. The government and international community had not included disabled people in developing emergency plans to deal with displacement.

From 1992 to 2006, Lebanon witnessed a series of wars and violence as a result of confrontations between the Lebanese resistance and Israel, which was occupying parts of South Lebanon. The Lebanese disability movement was actively facing the challenges resulting from the displacement of people due to war in 1993, 1996 and 2006. This displacement meant the move of thousands of people to the capital and out of southern areas, especially in 2006.

Investigating this, Kabbara and Abou Khalil (2014) made five findings. Firstly, disabled people were neglected during wars, emergencies and catastrophes. They dealt with displacement either by themselves or with the support of relatives; there was no indication of aid or support provided by government institutions. Secondly, civil society was mobilised but this was delimited to basic relief, aid during displacement and medical care. Thirdly, there was a lack of inclusion by the government, forcing DPOs to find a role for themselves. Fourthly, the ministry was ineffectual and the relief council offered only general aid without paying attention to the special needs of disabled people. It is worth mentioning, however, that the council, upon the request of the Prime Minister, distributed financial aid to those who were injured during the war. Finally, in spite of its anti-war and civil rights activities, the disability movement in Lebanon is virtually alone in viewing disability as a human rights issue, struggling to ensure participation in elections and advocate for political inclusion.

The challenges facing the disability community in 2014 include the Syrian crisis and internal sectarian violence, which is once again becoming a serious issue. Many of the same mistakes are being made in the provision of aid to refugees, and the disability community again finds itself at the vanguard of peace, non-violence and inclusion for the rights of all people.

Conclusion

In this chapter, we showed how a medical humanitarianism that focuses on direct and indirect physical impairment depoliticises the issue of how and why 'disability' occurs and does not contribute to the sustainable rebuilding of health and social care services. We argued that a medical humanitarianism thus neglects existing populations of disabled people, which has further consequences for reintegration and social protection. Additionally, despite the focus on the impaired veteran, we showed how many indirect impairments and sites of vulnerability arose due to lack of understanding of the changing nature of conflicts, humanitarian emergencies and nature of displacement for disabled people and civilians.

There is a need for more inclusive planning and serious commitment to disability and gender mainstreaming in relief efforts. We have shown how complex the needs are for future research in keeping with the changed nature of conflicts, their diverse long-term impacts and the importance of intersectionality. Research also has a tendency to indicate who is being silenced and overlooked, such as the aged, youths and children.

The evidence presented in this chapter illustrates how disabled people in the global South are a crucial resource for peace and greater equity but are currently being marginalised. The possible legislative clout that the CRPD could have in a humanitarian setting and its overall implementation in conflict and post-conflict settings continues to be ignored. There is a need for actual implementation, evaluation and clarity on the utilisation of the CRPD to influence humanitarianism. This can only happen if disabled people, activists and DPOs are viewed as key resources and included in humanitarian work by NGOs, international organisations, governments, ministries and councils.

Acknowledgements We would like to thank the reviewers for their detailed editing and helpful comments.

References

Ahlen, E. (1997). *Inventory of documentation about children with disability in armed conflict and displacement*. Stockholm: Radda Barnen.

Banatvala, N., & Zwi, A. B. (2000). Public health and humanitarian interventions: Developing the evidence base. *BMJ, 321*, 101–105.

Berghs, M. (2011). Embodiment and emotion in Sierra Leone. *Third World Quarterly, 32*(8), 1399–1417.

Berghs, M. (2012). *War and embodied memory: Becoming disabled in Sierra Leone*. Aldershot: Ashgate.

Berghs, M. (2013). The global economy of care. In J. Swain, S. French, C. Barnes, & C. Thomas (Eds.), *Disabling barriers-enabling environments*. London: Sage.

Berghs, M. (2014). The new humanitarianism: Neoliberalism, poverty and the creation of disability. In C. Schuland-Vials & M. Gill (Eds.), *Disability, human rights and the limits of humanitarianism* (pp. 27–44). Aldershot: Ashgate.

Berghs, M., & Dos Santos-Zingale, M. (2011). A comparative analysis: Everyday understandings of disability in Sierra Leone. *Africa Today, 58*(2), 19–40.

Blanchet, K., Sistenich, V., Ramesh, A., Frison, S., Warren, E., Hossain, M. et al. (2013). *An evidence review of research on health interventions in humanitarian crises*. Harvard School of Public Health and the Overseas Development Institute: Department for International Development (DfID) and Wellcome Trust.

Bruun, F. J. (1995). Hero, beggar, or sports star: Negotiating the identity of the disabled person in Nicaragua. In B. Ingstad & S. R. Whyte (Eds.), *Disability and culture* (pp. 53–80). Los Angeles: University of California Press.

Buchanan, C. (2011). The health and human rights of survivors of gun violence: Charting a research and policy agenda. *Health and Human Rights, 13*(2), 50–63.

Burton, G., Sayrafi, I., & Abu Srour, S. (2013). Inclusion or transformation? An early assessment of an empowerment project for disabled people in occupied Palestine. *Disability & Society, 28*(6), 812–825.

Collier, P., Elliott, V. L., Hoeffler, A., Raynal-Querol, M., & Sanbanis, N. (2003). *Breaking the conflict trap: Civil war and development policy*. Washington: World Bank/Oxford University Press.

Das, V., & Addlakha, R. (2001). Disability and domestic citizenship: Voice, gender and the making of the subject. *Public Culture, 13*(3), 511–531.

De Jong, J. T. V. M. (2010). A public health framework to translate risk factors related to political violence and war into multi-level preventive interventions. *Social Science & Medicine, 70*(1), 71–79.

Dos-Santos-Zingale, M., & McColl, A. (2006). Disability and participation in post-conflict situations: The case of Sierra Leone. *Disability & Society, 21*(3), 243–257.

French, L. (1994). The political economy of injury and compassion: Amputees on the Thai-Cambodia border. In T. Csordas (Ed.), *Embodiment and experience: The existential ground of culture and self* (pp. 69–99). Cambridge: Cambridge University Press.

French, S., & Swain, J. (2014). Disability and social inclusion in the information society. In J. Swain, S. French, C. Barnes, & C. Thomas (Eds.), *Disabling barriers, enabling environments* (pp. 279–286). London: Sage.

Gammeltoft, T. (2013). Potentiality and human temporality: Haunting futures in Vietnamese pregnancy care. *Current Anthropology, 54*(S7), S159–S171.

Ghobarah, H., Huth, P., & Russett, B. (2004). The post-war public health effects of conflict. *Social Science & Medicine, 59*, 869–884.

Grove, S., Grove, N., & Myerscough, T. (2010). Intellectual disability and war: Issues for consideration. *Journal on Developmental Disabilities, 16*(1), 85–93.

Gundawara, N. (2010). *Subverted heroes: Narrative experiences of disabled veterans in post-war Sri-Lanka*. Submitted for the Degree of Master of Arts in Disability and Gender, The School of Sociology and Social Policy, The University of Leeds.

Handicap International [HI]. (2012). *Armed violence and disability: The untold story*. Brussels: Handicap International.

Hersey, L. (2001). *Interview with Dr. Nawaf Kabbara. Disability World, 8*. Retrieved from http://www.disabilityworld.org/07-08_01/il/kabbara.shtml. Accessed 24 Apr 2014.

Hill, M., & Hansen, N. (2011). Disability and conflict. Untold stories from the north of Ireland. In T. Matyók, J. Senehi, & S. Byrne (Eds.), *Critical issues in peace and conflict studies: Theory, practice, and pedagogy* (pp. 97–114). Plymouth: Lexington Books.

Human Rights Watch [HRW]. (2010). *As if we weren't human*. New York: HRW.

Hyndman, J. (2007). Feminist geopolitics revisited: Body counts in Iraq. *The Professional Geographer, 59*(10), 35–46.

Hynes, P. H. (2004). On the battlefield of women's bodies: An overview of the harm of war to women. *Women's Studies International Forum, 27*, 431–445.

Inhorn, M. C., & Kobeissi, L. (2006). The public health costs of war in Iraq: Lessons from post-war Lebanon. *Journal of Social Affairs, 23*, 13–47.

Kabbara, N. (2014). *Status of young persons and women with disability in Lebanon*. Paris: UNESCO.

Kabbara, N., & Abou Khalil, J. (2014). The July-August 2006 war in Lebanon: The impact on persons with disabilities. In D. Mitchell & V. Karr (Eds.), *Crises, conflict and disability: Ensuring equality* (pp. 218–223). London: Routledge.

Kett, M., & van Ommeren, M. (2009). Disability, conflict and emergencies. *The Lancet, 374*(9704), 1801–1803.

Lamichhane, K. (2014). Social inclusion of people with disabilities: A case from Nepal's decade-long civil war. *Scandinavian Journal of Disability Research*. doi:10.1080/15017419.2013.861866.

Leaning, J., & Guha-Sapir, D. (2013). Natural disasters, armed conflict, and public health. *New England Journal of Medicine, 369*, 1836–1842.

Lord, J. E. (2014). Persons with disabilities in international humanitarian law—Paternalism, protectionism or rights? In C. Schuland-Vials & M. Gill (Eds.), *Disability, human rights and the limits of humanitarianism* (pp. 155–178). Aldershot: Ashgate.
Meekosha, H. (2011). Decolonising disability: Thinking and acting globally. *Disability & Society, 26*(6), 667–682.
Meyers, S. (2013). Wounded warriors or one of the crowd?: Civil war, citizenship, and disability in Nicaragua. *Peace Studies Journal, 6*(4), 22–36.
Miles, M. (1990). Disability and Afghan reconstruction: Some policy issues. *Disability & Society, 5*(3), 257–267.
Miles, S. (2013). Education in times of conflict and the invisibility of disability: A focus on Iraq. *Disability & Society, 28*(6), 798–811.
Miles, M., & Medi, E. (1994). Disabled children in post-war Mozambique: Developing community based support. *Disasters, 18*(3), 284–291.
Mirza, M. (2011). *Unmet needs and diminished opportunities: Disability, displacement and humanitarian healthcare*. Geneva: UNHCR.
Nagata, K. K. (2008). Disability and development: Is the rights based model of disability valid in the Arab region? An evidence-based field survey in Lebanon and Jordan. *Asia Pacific Rehabilitation Journal, 19*, 60–78.
Ngo, A. D., Brolan, C., Fitzgerald, L., Pham, V., & Phan, H. (2012). Voices from Vietnam: Experiences of children and youth with disabilities, and their families, from an Agent Orange affected rural region. *Disability & Society, 28*(7), 955–969.
Nielsen, K. E. (2012). *A disability history of the United States*. Boston: Beacon.
Ong, A., Kindhauser, M., Smith, I., & Chan, M. (2009). Global health agenda for the twenty-first century. In R. Detels, R. Beaglehole, M. A. Lansang, & M. Gulliford (Eds.), *Oxford textbook of public health* (pp. 1713–1729). Oxford: Oxford University Press.
Pederson, D. (2002). Political violence, ethnic conflict, and contemporary wars: Broad implications for health and social well-being. *Social Science & Medicine, 55*, 175–190.
Priestley, M. (2007). *Disability and the life course: Global perspectives*. Cambridge: Cambridge University Press.
Rohwerder, B. (2013). Intellectual disabilities, violent conflict and humanitarian assistance: Advocacy of the forgotten. *Disability & Society, 28*(6), 770–783.
Sami, S., Williams, H. A., Krause, S., Onyango, M. A., Burton, A., & Tomczyk, B. (2014). Responding to the Syrian Crisis: The needs of women and girls. *The Lancet, 383*, 1179–1181.
Scheper-Hughes, N. (1996). Small wars and invisible genocides. *Social Science & Medicine, 43*(5), 889–900.
Soldatic, K. (2013). The transnational sphere of justice: Disability praxis and the politics of impairment. *Disability & Society, 28*(6), 744–755.
The Sphere Project. (2013). *Humanitarian charter and minimum standards in humanitarian response*. Rugby: Practical Action Publishing. Retrieved from http://www.sphereproject.org/.
Ticktin, M. (2011). The gendered human of humanitarianism: Medicalising and politicising sexual violence. *Gender & History, 23*(2), 250–265.
Tomlinson, S., & Abdi, O. A. (2003). Disability in Somaliland. *Disability & Society, 18*(7), 911–920.
UNHCR. (2013). *Displacement: The new 21st century challenge*. Geneva: UNHCR.
Wehbi, S. (2011a). Crossing boundaries: Foreign funding and disability rights activism in a context of war. *Disability & Society, 26*(5), 507–520.
Wehbi, S. (2011b). Lebanese disability rights activists: War-time experiences. *Women's Studies International Forum, 33*(5), 455–463.
World Health Organisation [WHO]. (2011). *World report on disability*. Geneva: WHO.

Chapter 18
Disability and Forced Migration: Intersections and Critical Debates

Maria Pisani, Shaun Grech, and Ayman Mostafa

Introduction

Every day people are pushed to flee their homes as a result of persecution, conflict and generalised violence or human rights violations. These are collective and yet unique trajectories marked by fear, violence, death and untold tragedies. Millions of human beings have been displaced by the ongoing crisis in Syria, which has been described as the 'greatest humanitarian crisis' of contemporary times (Guterres 2015). It is a reality that is spatially specific; the vast majority of the world's displaced people are also hosted in the global South, in the poorest countries in the world. Beyond the human experience, in a globalised and ever-connected world, nation states are changing, engaged in a constant dialectical process of (re)negotiating, where histories are rediscovered and reframed, and where futures are fluidly (re)constructed. Despite sometimes desperate efforts to strengthen national borders, one can safely say that this forced human movement is not going to diminish any time soon. It is set to grow and forge new paths as wars continue to be waged, conflicts escalate, infrastructure breaks down, economies weaken and livelihoods and personal security are threatened.

Despite the growing numbers, these populations are too often unheard as they move or settle, their rights and voices subjugated. Critically, they are too frequently homogenised with little or no alertness to context, culture, religion or gender, but

M. Pisani (✉)
Department of Youth and Community Studies, University of Malta, Msida, Malta
e-mail: maria.pisani@um.edu.mt

S. Grech
Centre for Global Disability Research, The Critical Institute, Attard, Malta
e-mail: s.grech@criticalinstitute.org

A. Mostafa
Independent researcher, Msida, Malta

S. Grech, K. Soldatic (eds.), *Disability in the Global South*,
International Perspectives on Social Policy, Administration, and Practice,
DOI 10.1007/978-3-319-42488-0_18

especially dis/ability. Disabled people represent a significant number of refugees and forced migrants, not only on account of the fact that many flee wars—a source of impairment—but simply because of the sheer numbers of disabled people in every single country. Rough estimates, such as those offered by the World Health Organization, suggest that 15 per cent of the world's population are disabled (WHO and World Bank 2011). One can therefore speculate that around 7.5 million of the 51 million displaced people in the world may well be disabled people. Given the nature of forced migration, however, where people are fleeing war, conflict, 'development' and natural disaster, the number is more than likely significantly higher than the numbers reported. For example, a recent study stated that 22 per cent of surveyed Syrian refugees had an impairment, just under a third (6 per cent) of whom claimed to have a severe impairment (HelpAge International and Handicap International 2014). Televised images of disabled people from Syria reaching Europe are starting to make the news. In practice, displaced persons may have lived with their disability all their lives; impairments may be a direct result of environmental and structural factors, including poverty, and unhealthy and unsafe living and working conditions, as well as conflict or natural disasters. Many others become disabled in the migratory journey, experiencing a change of dis/ability status and identity alongside multiple (re)negotiations as they transit across space and time. Disabled people therefore migrate, too.

Despite the scale of forced human movement, the reality is that disability and forced migration are rarely put together, in policy, research and practice. They are two parts of a different equation for those theorising and those working in practice, whether in humanitarian contexts, development, international relations, politics and even disability studies. The ramifications are that those working in migration remain unaware of and lack understanding in disability, and those working in disability remain uninformed about migration. Research on disability and forced migration remains embryonic; theory is scarce, perhaps reflecting an ableist view of migrating bodies in migration studies and a persistent global North/Eurocentric disability studies inalert to migrant disabled people (see Grech 2011). Indeed, the little research that does exist (see, for example, WRC 2008; Berghs 2012) has emerged from peripheral spaces.

This chapter[1] attempts to bring disability and forced migration closer together under a critical lens to explore points of contact, intersections and gaps as we work towards a migration studies that is critical, interdisciplinary, alert to and informed by disability—what we call 'critical migration studies'. Our attempts to theorise and understand disability and forced migration are framed within the broader processes of neo-liberal globalisation. In this chapter we highlight how containment policies and the securitisation of borders enacted by the donor countries of the global North have contributed to protracted refugee contexts in the global South, the illegalisation and racialisation of the forced migrant reaching the North, loss of life, and the violation of human rights of disabled people. We make the case that the hegemony of the nation state within disability studies fails to provide an adequate

[1] An earlier version of this chapter (Pisani and Grech 2015) was published in the journal *Disability and the Global South.*

framework for understanding the lived realities of the disabled non-citizen. We do not claim to provide a comprehensive account of disability and forced migration; rather, this chapter marks a humble attempt to stimulate further debate on an issue that urgently deserves theoretical engagement, a critical interrogation of humanitarian intervention and practice, and legal and policy change in order to ensure rights and social justice for disabled forced migrants.

Framing Forced Migration

Any attempts at understanding what this deceptive term might mean have often been based on distinctions between forced and voluntary migration. The former is often associated with refugees, war and persecution, while voluntary migration is linked with economic migration. Such a dichotomy is problematic. The fine line between fleeing one's home in search of safety and the means of subsistence, we contend, is inherently blurred and complex because human security must necessarily incorporate socio-economic threats and not be limited to violence and persecution. Indeed, in this regard, to be disabled and living in extreme poverty in parts of the global South, with little or no access to health care and rehabilitation, fragmented or non-existent formal safety nets, and constrained family support, constitutes a very serious threat to security and survival (see, for example, Grech 2015). If there is one population existing at the junctures of a poverty that is violent, one that kills, it is disabled people, and survival in scarcity, pain and ill-health triggers flight—it always has, it always will. Forced migration therefore needs to be (re)negotiated and reframed because it occurs along a spectrum; because each individual is complex and multifaceted; and because each person is, in turn, motivated and constrained by a complex mix of structural forces that shift over time and space (Betts 2009: 2).

For the purpose of this chapter, forced migration is understood as the movement of individuals resulting from an existential threat (that may have social, economic, political, cultural, ideological and religious dimensions) and which includes, among others, persons displaced as a result of war, persecution, conflict, poverty, famine, natural disasters, ill-health, disability and environmental disasters. As such, this definition includes, but is not limited to, those persons labelled as refugees[2] and internally displaced persons (IDPs)[3] (see also Betts 2009; IASFM 2014). A note of caution is warranted, however, because such labels and categories are far from unproblematic, as discussed later.

---

[2]Article 1a of the 1951 Geneva Convention defines refugees as people who, 'owing to a well-founded fear of persecution, on the grounds of race, religion, nationality or membership of a social group, find themselves outside their country of origin, and are unable or unwilling to avail themselves of the protection of that country'.

[3]The United Nations defines IDPs as 'persons or groups of persons who have been forced or obliged to flee or to leave their homes or places of habitual residence, in particular as a result of or in order to avoid the effects of armed conflict, situations of generalized violence, violations of human rights or natural or human-made disasters, and who have not crossed an internationally recognized State border' (OCHA 2004).

Neo-liberal Globalisation: Dividing and Displacing

Framing and understanding forced migration is not possible without understanding what drives it. Far from occurring in a vacuum, forced migration is historical, contextual, political and politicised. An understanding of the experiences of displaced disabled people in the global South must be positioned within neo-liberal globalisation and global processes of change. With the onus on economic growth and only meagre attention to human dimensions and impacts, such as inequality and impoverishment, the neo-liberal framework has proven to be detrimental to poor people's rights and livelihoods in the global South, in particular to disabled people (Grech 2011). While exact numbers are unavailable, an estimated 20 per cent of the world's poorest, especially those residing in rural areas, are said to be disabled people (WHO and World Bank 2011). The relationship between disability and poverty has been reasonably acknowledged as a mutually reinforcing cycle in popular 'disability and development' discourse (see Chap. 16 in this volume, Grech 2016a). Yet, this relationship has been seldom theorised, and geopolitical and historical factors and asymmetries that trigger poverty in the first place have hardly been engaged with by those looking at disability in the global South (Grech 2011). These factors include neo-liberal globalisation, too often framed as the object and trajectory of 'development'—a neo-liberal globalisation rooted in capitalism, colonialism and the Atlantic trade (see Grech 2016b, Chap. 1 in this volume).

The geopolitical and historical relationships between the global North and South, and the mechanisms of unequal development and social inequalities (between and within countries), continue to generate the structural conditions propelling people to flee their homes. Poverty, inequity and destruction of communities make for fragile and unstable states, many of which are associated with corrupt regimes, human rights abuses and the repression and persecution of minority groups. Paradoxically, though by no coincidence, such states often also host a disproportionate number of displaced people.

Among those who are displaced are disabled people: those who, in the hetero-normative, ableist, productive and individualist neo-liberal framework guiding 'development' and national policies and the amassment of wealth, are persistently (re)constructed as unproductive, fragile, lacking—a burden. Their resistance is constrained (though they are not weak!) and their capability to escape may be slowed down by the weight of their bodies and/or the absence of support by their families or others, themselves pushed towards flight, as their world and what they know collapses (see Mostafa 2015). For those who manage to escape, the road to safety is a long one, a narrative rarely told, wherein 'protection' continues to be undifferentiated, ill informed by other bodies, ontologies, geographies, contexts and cultures. Research (see, for example, WRC 2008; Mirza 2011) has demonstrated how the protection challenges faced by the general population of displaced persons are intensified for disabled people, and yet they are the least visible and the most excluded and vulnerable.

Illegal Bodies

Crucial to our understanding of forced migration is the knowledge that disabled people who flee their homes are often compelled to seek protection and safety beyond their nation state. As such, forced migration is intrinsic to global politics,[4] neo-liberalism, sovereignty and the disparate interests of the citizen and non-citizen (Pisani 2012).

Indeed, as demonstrated in this chapter, the decision to leave one's home does not translate into the right to be granted permission to enter another country. The increasing securitisation of borders and stricter border controls must be seen within the broader context of North–South relations. The intensification of migration, interacting with global transformations, has led to an increasing number of refugees and migrants reaching the global North. This has been met with an emphasis on containment, wherein every effort has been made to limit South–North migrant flows (Koffman et al. 2000; Pisani and Grech 2015). This new phenomenon has coincided with the fracturing of the refugee label (Zetter 2007). Usage of terms such as 'illegal immigrants', 'clandestine' and 'irregular migrants' has become a common strategy adopted by states to restrict access to protection. Often shrouded in racialised speech, such discourse resonates with a colonial past that remains so very present, feeding into contemporary social and political practices that serve to reproduce domination and inequality and maintain the status quo. Importantly, they (re) enact boundaries and divisions.

Label, Categorise, Exclude

Categories, terminology and labels matter because they frame, as well as uphold, power relations, and these have real effects on the individuals they seek to define. Homogenisation plays a key part in this, not only in simplifying—thus distorting—this process, but also in removing, criminalising and perhaps pathologising all that does not fit. In a similar fashion, traditional social model theorists (see, for example, Oliver 1994) have long argued how disablism results from a society insensitive to, ill informed about, and enacting barriers (including attitudinal ones) towards disabled people. In this case, society is constructed and organised around a dominant non-disabled frame that not only does not cater for disabled people, but also excludes and (re)positions them perpetually outside the norm—disabled people are those it is legitimate to exclude. The medical profession, medical labels and infinite interventions/violations on disabled bodies and minds have served, and continue to serve, this purpose.

[4] As Betts (2009: 2) indicates, even in the case of IDPs, where their own state is unwilling or unable to assure protection, there is a broader international responsibility to guarantee such individuals access to their rights and receive protection.

Comparisons with 'illegal bodies' help us to reflect on where disabled bodies fit within normative discourses on legality. Indeed, driven by states' migration policies and legal and operational concerns, such normative distinctions pay little attention to a given individual's particular needs. They dictate, among other things: who is considered as 'assistable'; who can/should be assisted by the international community and how; who will qualify for legal protection and who won't; where funds should be directed to and how they should be spent; and who will be granted access to rights. A prime example is the situation in Libya post 'revolution' in 2011, a situation that highlighted the shortcomings of the international protection regime as well as the rigid categorisation dictating who is deserving of protection and assistance and who is not. Médecins Sans Frontières reported on its frustrations in dealing with so-called mixed flows fleeing the conflict in Libya. Different 'categories' of migrants, including migrant workers, IDPs, asylum seekers and refugees, were all displaced as a result of the conflict in Libya and forced to cross the border to Tunisia. Needless to say, each 'category' and, indeed, each individual faced the horrors that accompanies such a context—as such, the rigid categorisation was impossible to relate to on the ground. Yet, the differentiation marked the difference between life and death, wherein individuals were ineligible for assistance, compelling some humanitarian actors to question the ethical and legal grounds for such rigid (and legally defined) categorisation, calling instead for a response based on human need (see Bach Baouab et al. 2012).

Such categorisation means that many are left to fall between the cracks, their demands becoming illegitimate, ergo, no one's responsibility. This includes disabled people. The exclusions that displaced disabled people face are, in fact, many and well beyond those documented in empirical research (see, for example, Shivji 2010), including physical or communication barriers, stigma and, notoriously, lack of services, including specialised and adapted health care and rehabilitation, services that are contextually and culturally informed, sensitive and responsive.

The debate, then, we would argue, has to move forward and beyond labelling and legal categorisation to incorporate broader issues of discourse, construction of subjects, the right to rights and borders.

National Security Takes Precedence Over Human Security

Dictated by affluent countries of the global North, the emphasis on securitisation, containment and the externalisation of borders has been extended to countries in the global South, undermining forced migrants' ability to access human rights. The majority of displaced people are being hosted by countries in the global South, in the Middle East, Asia and Africa. These so-defined least developed countries host 86 per cent of the world's refugees (UNHCR 2015). This appears to challenge the discourse of burden propagated by certain global North countries and regions, including the European Union, that they are shouldering a disproportionate weight of those who flee. There is, as always, little or no reference to history and the obligations that come with it. Indeed, as Chimni (2009: 11) has convincingly argued, while asylum seekers have always existed in the global South, restrictive access to international rights has been longstanding and deliberate, grounded in what he calls the 'myth of difference between second and third world refugees'.

Tightening border controls and restricting access to protection have not reduced flows; rather, the need to find security has led forced migrants to search for alternative routes, and this has triggered the proliferation of often unscrupulous smuggling and trafficking networks and evermore precarious routes. The escalation of deaths in the Mediterranean is testimony to this. The onus on national security has therefore come at the cost of human security. The need to turn to smuggling networks has also impacted the financial costs of seeking safety, as Zetter (2007: 187) has argued: 'refugee status becomes a commodity to be bought, which only the more wealthy can afford, rather than a right'. A 'right', then, is increasingly beyond the reach of the poorest of the poor—the poverty/disability nexus being so strong ensures the pervasive presence of disabled people among those not entitled to rights, and for whom they are unachievable. In spite of this, the tragic state of affairs in Syria has seen an increasing number of disabled refugees reaching Europe.

For those who try to make the journey, the human costs are staggering. Beyond untold human rights violations, thousands continue to perish in the sea, in the desert and in trucks (see, for example, the situation in the Sahara desert, the Mediterranean sea, the waters surrounding Australia, and on the Mexico–USA border, among others). Of course, such routes are not open for all. For example, research conducted with Syrian refugees demonstrated a higher prevalence of impairment in Jordan (25.9 per cent) than in Lebanon (20 per cent), the difference in part being explained by the Jordanian border being easier to access, suggesting disabled people had a better chance of making the crossing (HelpAge International and Handicap International 2014). In a similar fashion, recent evidence is emerging to highlight the impairments caused on the Mexican border as irregular migrants (largely from Central America) attempt to cross into the United States on the infamous train *la bestia*.

In our work as academics, activists and practitioners, we have listened to many asylum seekers and humanitarian actors recount stories of the journey across the Mediterranean.[5] Mostafa (2015) provides a firsthand account of how disabled people of all ages were often among the first to die: because of dehydration, lack of medication, constrained ability to swim, confusion and chaos at times of crisis and lack of knowledge and the unpreparedness of humanitarian intervention around disability issues. The reasons are complex and varied, but the outcome is too often absolute and irrevocable. The challenges that displaced people face during forced migration are intensified for disabled people, who may also experience difficulties in physically moving, hearing, seeing, communicating or understanding (UNHCR 2011). This reality, though, cannot—and must not—be divorced from the securitisation of borders, issues of sovereignty and citizenship, and the North/South divide (see Soldatic and Grech 2014). The Greece–Turkey border would be a case in point,

[5] In 2014 more than 3000 individuals drowned in this body of water. The number of deaths in the early months of 2015 suggest that even more will lose their lives this year.

wherein barbed-wire fencing, landmines, thermal night-vision cameras and border patrols are among the means used to prevent what is constructed as a national security threat. The razor-wire fence set up on the Serbian–Hungarian border is another more recent example. The upshot of such 'securitisation' measures has led to many migrants losing limbs in their efforts to cross the border and reach Europe (Council of Europe 2010). And so it is, the emphasis on national security pushes human security to the margins.

Social Relationships and Networks

Introducing a meso level of analysis helps us to understand the forced migration process in terms of social relationships extending from the country of origin to the country/ies of transit, the host society and within ethnic communities and families, among others (Anthias 2012).

Established support structures break down in a time of crisis, which is paradoxically also the time when social relationships become even more vital in accessing resources, be it when crossing borders and negotiating travel, surviving in camp settings or other places of 'transit', or considering options for return or resettlement. Research has demonstrated, however, that when caught up in the crisis, and when forced migration contexts become increasingly protracted, many disabled people do not receive support along the way (see HelpAge International and Handicap International 2014). The support systems that do exist are often overstretched, unprepared for disability, or break down in the midst of a crisis, including disabled people's organisations.

Migration out of the most deprived areas is further made difficult since poor people often lack the economic capital necessary to travel, the cultural capital required to access information, and the social capital and networks required to negotiate a new space (Castles 2003). Where poverty intersects with disability, the situation becomes more complex; the costs of disability (for the individual and the family) can be broad, including less time and possibility for productive labour, and fewer possibilities to 'bridge' their capital and invest in social relationships beyond the immediate family and/or community (see Grech 2015). This is a serious concern as, in the absence of formal safety nets and serial violations of rights and abuses, for better or for worse, what enables people to survive are immediate relationships. For poor disabled people, then, the decision and possibility to flee is also influenced by the existence of and participation in social networks, meaning that those with fewer social networks may be more likely to turn to smugglers who are dishonest. This exposes them to further risk of violence, robbery, rape and trafficking and more precarious routes. This is a critical concern for disabled women and girls, who are more vulnerable to sexual abuse, violence and trafficking, especially in situations of conflict (see also Buscher 2014). Such a reality cautions once again against homogeneous and essentialist categories, to look instead at the complexity and multiple positions of disabled forced migrants, how disability intersects with gender, age, socio-economic status and legal status, and how social relations of power never shift out of focus (see also UNHCR and Integra 2015).

We're All About Rights ... Just Not Yours

The imposition of human rights and liberal democratic norms by the global North in the global South can be juxtaposed with policy measures and discursive practices that contribute to the securitisation of the richer countries of the North which seek to contain the 'immigrant threat'. With some 145 nation states party to the 1951 Geneva Convention and the 1967 Protocol, it is by far the most broadly ratified refugee treaty. And yet, the wealthiest and most powerful of these states have disregarded their international obligations with brazen disdain. Take, for example, the European Court of Human Rights judgement (Council of Europe 2010) on Italy's violation of *non-refoulement* or the Australian authorities' refusal to comment on accusations that they paid smugglers to return asylum seekers to the coast of Indonesia (Aljazeera 2015).

In the global South, national borders demarcated and imposed during colonial times are today reinforced by donor capital. Contradictions abound. The year 2015 witnessed ongoing disputes between the EU nations on mandatory 'burden' sharing. While agreement was made to relocate less than half the asylum seekers, the overriding solution was to mobilise funds to neighbouring states (including Turkey, Serbia and the former Yugoslav Republic of Macedonia) for 'refugee-related actions' (European Commission 2015).

Couched in political discourse that emphasises national security concerns and which constructs the forced migrant as 'illegal' (see Pisani (forthcoming)), forced migrants are denied the possibility—and right—to access the asylum system and protection in the global North, and remain in a state of limbo in overcrowded, protracted refugee contexts. Disabled migrants are particularly disadvantaged (see Soldatic and Fiske 2009).

Humanitarian Spaces Are Political Non-disabled Spaces

The proximity to a crisis should not determine the level of responsibility individual states assume for displaced people, but so it is.[6] The implications here are complex and diverse. For the purposes of this chapter, analysis is limited to the issue of disability and possibilities for resettlement, and the consequences for disabled people in humanitarian spaces.

The securitisation of borders in the global North has contributed to the reproduction of protracted refugee contexts in the South. This, combined with a breakdown in cooperation between countries of origin and donor countries, dwindling funds (as money is directed to 'emergency' contexts), host-country resistance to integration, and limited possibilities for resettlement, has led to an ever-growing number of forced migrants remaining in a state of limbo, either in camps, rural settlements or

[6] For a review on how protracted refugee situations impact regional security, see Milner 2014.

cities. There are an estimated 51 million displaced people in the world today, the vast majority in protracted settings, with little hope for change or an end to their predicament any time soon—hopeless futures (Aleinikoff 2015).

Focusing on the issue of camps, Hyndman (2011) reminds us that such spaces are not politically neutral. Political humanitarianism plays out as the pawn in the continuity of the colonial order; aid comes at great costs, serving the interests of the global North (see also Chimni 2009). Aid is granted to refugee-producing countries on conditionality of containment and stemming migrant flows to the donor countries, and funds are managed by international organisations often established to safeguard the interests of the northern countries, maintaining the civilising mission. The insidious abuse of power by northern countries remains steadfast; the imposition of policies and practices are rarely in the best interests of the poorest or most vulnerable. Instead, they are directed by political and economic gains, and the reproduction of 'humanitarian' spaces where liberal democratic 'norms', including human rights, are non-existent: a depoliticised space wherein, by virtue of their political—and ontological—exclusion, lives are suspended, reduced to 'bare life' and outside the reach of law (see Agamben 1998).

Writing on refugee camps within the African context, Crisp (2002) describes a harrowing scenario wherein basic human rights are completely inaccessible and basic needs unattended to. Where protracted refugee contexts intersect with disability, the situation can be nothing short of toxic. The conditions experienced by disabled people living in camps have been sometimes documented (see, for example, Handicap International 2008; *Forced Migration Review* 2010 special issue). The absence of disaggregated data on the number of disabled people, a lack of consistency in the identification of disabled people, definitional problems, unclear or absent policies on inclusion, shortages in funding and lack of evaluation tools and processes not only contribute to the marginalisation of disability as a subject of study and practice in migration and humanitarian affairs, but they also coincide with, and contribute to, significant challenges and barriers for disabled people on the ground.

In short, despite Article 11[7] of the Convention on the Rights of Persons with Disabilities (CRPD), which extends rights to situations of risk and humanitarian emergencies, the needs and rights of disabled people are consistently and systematically excluded, their very existence ignored ontologically and practically. Their security is assigned to the biopolitics of administration—the disabled body is rendered docile, this time through indifference and inaptness in 'dealing with' and responding to it. While disability theorists have spoken at length about this docility being caused by medical practices in the global North (see, for example, Oliver 1994), in the global South, and in these conditions of flight, docility is paradoxically caused by the absence of such practices, being the bare minimum to keep them alive (Grech 2009).

[7] Article 11 of the CRPD on situations of risk and humanitarian emergencies states: 'States Parties shall take, in accordance with their obligations under international law, including international humanitarian law and international human rights law, all necessary measures to ensure the protection and safety of persons with disabilities in situations of risk, including situations of armed conflict, humanitarian emergencies and the occurrence of natural disasters.'

Such realities extend to forced migration contexts in Europe. Research conducted in Malta (UNHCR and Integra 2015) documented how disabled people were more likely to remain stuck in refugee camps and 'open centres'. An often precarious legal status, lack of access to employment, restricted information and access to education, inter-ethnic discrimination and broader experiences of racism, coupled with the conspicuous absence of mainstream disability services, all contributed to the isolation (physical and ontological) of disabled forced migrants. Often, disabled people are among those more likely to remain in protracted refugee contexts since the challenges related to return may also be accentuated. The outcome of such a scenario is that camps become, as Kett and Trani (2010: 15) describe, 'de facto "welfare camps"'.

Do Rights Cross Borders?

The CRPD marks the first and only international agreement to put down the rights of persons with disabilities in international law. Article 11 of the CRPD has the potential to be an important tool in ensuring the protection of all disabled people in all aspects of humanitarian response. In ratifying the convention, nation states are committing themselves to international obligations. In the global North these obligations are often systematically ignored: militarised border controls, detention centres and resettlement opportunities are just some examples. Certainly, despite extraordinary efforts to keep forced migrants at bay, national borders are porous, and some people do manage to reach the richer countries of the North. Needless to say, those who do make it tend to be the most resourceful and not necessarily those in most critical need. That said, disabled people often do manage to cross these borders, which is testimony to the extraordinary determination and agency of human life.

Detention centres have become an important component of deterrence[8] and securitisation. While the duration of detention varies from country to country, it is not uncommon for forced migrants to be administratively detained for many years. Indeed, the detention centre is, as Agamben (1998: 174) has argued, the definitive paradigm of the 'state of exception', wherein 'the normal order is de facto suspended'. The values normally associated with a 'liberal democracy'—justice, rights, equality and so on—are discarded; seemingly a state can imprison thousands of people where no crime has been committed. Such is the lot of the 'illegal body': the cost of state security is borne by the politically insecure, and this will include disabled people. The obligation on states to provide 'reasonable accommodation' is enshrined within the CRPD. Juxtapose this, for example, with the detention conditions on Manus Island, which hosts one of Australia's offshore processing centres:

[8] Research has demonstrated how, in reality, detention does not act as a deterrent. Asylum seekers and migrants are generally not informed of such policies, do not communicate the information to others considering the journey, and may also perceive detention as unavoidable (International Detention Coalition 2015).

> One of the asylum seekers detained on Manus Island is a person with dwarfism. Despite his obvious difficulty in going about daily life at the detention centre, and in spite of his repeated requests for simple accommodations that would make his life easier—such as a stool to allow him to use the toilet without assistance—the centre had taken no steps that would afford him a measure of dignity and autonomy, in violation of Australia's and Papua New Guinea's obligations under the UN Convention on the Rights of Persons with Disabilities. (Amnesty International 2013: 8)

The report goes on to state that one individual was denied the use of crutches as these were deemed a security threat (Amnesty International 2013: 44). Similar scenarios are commonplace elsewhere. The effects are a travesty of human rights wherein the sovereign state would appear to be the source and cause of human insecurity. Alas, it would appear that, in the case of 'illegal' bodies at least, donor countries are not accountable to the same liberal democratic 'norms' as they enforce on countries of origin.

Beyond the impact of the immediate environment, Crock et al. (2011) have documented some of the many challenges disabled people experience during the refugee determination process, and how disability can impact a person's eligibility for protection. Such barriers include, but are not limited to: difficulties in understanding the asylum process; difficulties in communicating; behavioural difficulties; and problems in presenting a coherent and consistent testimony. The authors conclude that the Geneva Convention presents some 'intractable' problems for some disabled asylum seekers, which begs the following question: in the absence of refugee protection, how will their rights be protected? Similar critiques have emerged from those working on disability issues in the global South (see Grech 2009; Soldatic and Grech 2014), contesting if and how rights travel across borders, how these are upheld (if at all), and how they benefit disabled people in the midst of extreme poverty. When few even know what their rights are (and much less of transnational tools such as the CRPD), where there are few or no organisations lobbying, or when lobbying may be dangerous, and when disabled people and their families have few or no means to seek redress, it is no exaggeration that many slip outside protection. It is hardly surprising, then, that the rights of the poor and those who are disenfranchised, including disabled people, are rarely upheld, even in contexts where policies, laws, organisations and institutions are not lacking.

The Unproductive Foreign Body: A National Security Threat

Migration entrenches the citizen/non-citizen dichotomy, establishing—in law—the normative distinction between the citizen who 'belongs' and the non-citizen who doesn't. While this distinction is clear, the status of migrant is established along a hierarchy of rights. Increasingly restrictive immigration policies impede access to the labour market and, together with racialising discourse, ensure a pecking order that is massaged by temporal and spatial factors and ranked by *inter alia* legal status, nationality, 'race' and ethnicity, gender and disability. Upon ratification of the CRPD a number of states (among them the USA, Canada and the UK) included a reservation excluding immigration policy from the enshrined obligations, arguing that such obligations are only due to nationals and that, in essence, the non-citizen disabled person would amount to an economic and social burden on the state, ergo a threat to the state. UNHCR, the Office of the High Commission for Human Rights and the UN treaty-monitoring bodies have found such reservations to be too broad, contrary to the principles of the CRPD, discriminatory, and a violation of states' international obligations (see, for example, UNHCR 2009; Crock et al. 2011; Yeo 2015). The impacts of such reservations are lived out by disabled people and their families, wherein some families are also forced to leave a disabled family member behind.

'Rights', then, are de facto assigned to the citizen imbued with humanity, while the disabled, non-productive non-citizen is stripped of these. All too often, all this occurs within a political discourse that seeks to nullify and, in particular, 'illegalise' the southern body; the uncivilised body is a demonised one, further sustaining and justifying the need to divide and separate (see Fanon 1963). Terms such as 'illegal' and 'clandestine' thrown around in political and public discourse are hegemonic discursive practices that define and represent the 'illegal' body, fuelling fear, 'securitisation' and heightened nationalism among citizens, and reinforcing hard-line policies—and the negation of rights.

All this is part and parcel of a post-Cold War shift in discourse on the part of western governments, a return to a colonial era, where inequality is somehow justified as natural. This is where refugees are increasingly being labelled as 'economic' or 'illegal' migrants—an unwanted burden—while contemporaneously and paradoxically, the illegalisation process ensures a steady supply of a cheap, exploitable workforce that meets the demands of the labour market (Pisani 2011). The relation of domination is reproduced as different forms of discrimination intersect: the broken, southern, racialised, illegalised body is rendered docile. And so, the state asserts its sovereign muscle, enforcing a survival of the fittest scenario that selects the desirables from the masses of the 'wretched of the earth' (Fanon 1963). Such a reality sits comfortably with the neo-liberal ideologies at work. In short, it is not about rights, it is about productivity, and the onus is placed upon the security of the state, rather than the human being. This is a familiar scenario among disabled citizens, including in countries such as the UK, who in the midst of austerity measures continue to be pitched as 'scroungers', those framed as unproductive bodies illegitimately trying to claim resources of more 'legitimate' others. They are hence an economic burden, but also those the government can offload responsibility to for anything constructed as mishap. The result is that the government is no longer the responsible party for socio-economic and other inequalities, but people themselves are, hence providing an effective deflection of population anger towards this new Othered.

Reflecting further, it is clear that not all 'productive' is the same 'productive', especially when this productivity is inextricably linked with constructions of race and whiteness within an imaginary global North normative and narrative, both of which have powerful historical antecedents. Within this scenario, some are perceived as even more 'unproductive' and 'burdensome' than others. The disabled body and mind, in particular, is an unwelcome and unwanted threat to the wellbeing of the nation state, a nation state that is built on fostering functional, independent, self-vigilant and surveilling individuals, a nation state increasingly obsessed with offloading the care of citizens, and where serving the interests of businesses and banks remains the priority. Within this narrative is another narrative, one that requires the demonising of these subjects to promulgate a rejection incited by the state, but upheld by the popular—pitching people against each other in a battlefield of misplaced alliances, where nationhood and citizenship become critical variables in differentiating between those who are 'deserving' and those who are not.

The Hegemony of the Nation-State Mindset

In much emerging discourse, including that within global North disability studies, one can witness a number of assumptions, including a notion of rights premised on citizenship, hence weakening the claims of those who do not fit or slip outside this space. Categories such as 'refugee' and 'IDP' are constructed in relation to the nation state, ergo, one cannot exist without the other. It follows, then, that a nuanced and informed understanding of the experiences of disabled forced migrants must move beyond what Pisani (2012) calls the 'citizenship assumption': a statist hegemony that is ubiquitous even within disability studies. Barnes and Mercer (2009: 515), for example, have argued that disability theory, specifically the social model of disability, and practice is grounded in the notion that society has failed to 'remove the wide-ranging social, economic and environmental barriers that underpin the social exclusion of disabled people and the denial of their basic citizenship rights'. Like others, they appear to take citizenship as a given or to assume it—the right to citizenship rights is not questioned. Elsewhere, Barnes and Mercer (2006) place emphasis on the importance of a democratic, bottom-up process in order to pursue citizenship rights, but there are limitations to advocating for a democratic process for the excluded non-citizen who lacks political leverage (see Pisani 2013).

As we have demonstrated in this chapter, social justice cannot be pursued and framed within sovereign structures and liberal democratic norms that not only disregard the role of neo-liberal globalisation in causing and shaping the experience of forced migration, but also assume the right to citizenship rights, thus excluding the non-citizen, ergo the illegalised disabled body. At the forced migration, disability and nation state nexus, the 'right to rights' cannot be assumed. Forced migration studies, and indeed empirical work on disability and forced migration, demonstrates how the dynamics of social relations go beyond national borders; as such, so must the theories and methods used to study them (see also Castles 2003). This would imply and support the call for what Grech (2015) calls a 'Critical Transnational Disability Studies', one that must move beyond the nation state as a framework of analysis, with the implication that theories and the assumptions upon which they are built also need to be questioned and perhaps (re)negotiated.

Conclusion

This chapter has briefly but critically engaged with disability and forced migration within dominant and hegemonic frames, discourses and structures that not only produce forced migration, but also reproduce social inequalities between the global North and South—a reality that needs to be historically contextualised. Failure to critically engage with the history of colonialism risks ignoring the deep fractures that have never ceased to exist and serves to perpetuate inequality. Within this narrative, disabled people are often among the poorest, yet too frequently ignored within humanitarian practice and migration studies. Poor people are more vulnerable to impairments and encounter greater barriers, including to health and education, which are intensified throughout the forced migration process: from fleeing one's home, to the breakdown in support structures and community relations, to protracted displacement contexts where the rights and needs of disabled people are often pushed to the periphery. This is where their voices are largely unheard and their rights ignored as they try to cross borders marked by danger, impairment, death and insecurity. Enhanced border controls and the emphasis on containment has ensured the illegalisation and racialisation of the forced migrant, contributing to the protraction of refugee contexts, the need to take ever more dangerous routes to reach some form of protection, and harsher detention policies, all perpetuating the logic of the colonial era.

Beyond the protection of a state, the disabled non-citizen occupies a toxic space wherein the right to rights cannot be assumed. This chapter concludes by calling on disability studies to not only transnationalise its focus, but also to move beyond the statist hegemony: excluded from democratic structures and possessing no political clout at the ballot box, the illegalised disabled body cannot make the claim to 'equal citizenship'. More broadly, engaging with disability and forced migration entails critical dialogue across sectors and services, and across theory and disciplines. Fields such as disability studies need to urgently engage with migration, to not only inform other areas, but also to challenge its own eurocentrism and to broaden its epistemological horizons. The same applies to migration studies, looking at transit, at change, at different bodies that move and cross borders.

References

Agamben, G. (1998). *Homo sacer*. Stanford: Stanford University Press.

Aleinikoff, T. (2015, February 25). *From dependence to self-reliance: Changing the paradigm in protracted refugee situations*. Retrieved March 11, 2015, from UNHCR Global Views: http://blog.unhcr.org/globalviews/changing-the-paradigm-in-protracted-refugee-situations/.

Aljazeera. (2015, October 29). Amnesty: Australian officials paid people smugglers. *Aljazeera*. Retrieved December 8, 2015, from http://www.aljazeera.com/news/2015/10/amnesty-australian-officials-paid-people-smugglers-151028230421588.htm.

Amnesty International. (2013). *This is breaking people: Human rights violations at Australia's asylum seeker processing centre on Manus Island, Papua New Guinea*. London: Amnesty International. Retrieved September 14, 2014, from http://www.amnesty.org/en/library/info/ASA12/002/2013/en.

Anthias, F. (2012). Transnational mobilities, migration research and intersectionality: Towards a translocational frame. *Nordic Journal of Migration Research, 2*(2), 102–110.
Bach Baouab, T., del Valle, H., Derderian, K., & Ponthieu, A. (2012). Looking beyond legal status to human need. *Forced Migration Review, 39*, 19–20.
Barnes, C., & Mercer, G. (2006). *Independent futures: Creating user-led disability services in a disabling society*. Bristol: The Policy Press.
Barnes, C., & Mercer, G. (2009). Disability culture: Assimilation or inclusion? In G. L. Albrecht, K. Seelman, & M. Bury (Eds.), *Handbook of disability studies* (pp. 515–534). New York: Sage.
Berghs, M. (2012). *War and embodied memory: Becoming disabled in Sierra Leone*. London: Ashgate.
Betts, A. (2009). *Forced migration and global politics*. Chichester: Wiley-Blackwell.
Buscher, D. (2014, February). *Preventing gender-based violence: Getting it right*. Retrieved September 13, 2014, from Humanitarian Practice Network: http://www.odihpn.org/humanitarian-exchange-magazine/issue-60/preventing-gender-based-violence-getting-it-right.
Castles, S. (2003). Towards a sociology of forced migration and social transformation. *Sociology, 37*, 13–34.
Chimni, S. B. (2009). The birth of a 'Discipline': From refugee studies to forced migration studies. *Journal of Refugee Studies, 22*(1), 11–29.
Council of Europe. (2010, February 4). *Commissioner for human rights: Criminalisation of migration in Europe: Human rights implications*. Retrieved October 18, 2014, from Council of Europe: https://wcd.coe.int/ViewDoc.jsp?id=1579605#P99_13092.
Crisp, J. (2002). *No solutions in sight: The problem of protracted*. San Diego: The Center for Comparative Immigration Studies.
Crock, M., McCallum, R., & Ernst, C. (2011). Where disability and displacement intersect: Asylum seekers with disabilities. *Discussion paper prepared for the Vulnerable Persons Working Group; International Association of Refugee Law Judges World Conference*. Bled, Slovenia.
European Commission. (2015, September 23). *Managing the refugee crisis: Immediate operational, budgetary and legal measures under the European Agenda on Migration*. European Commission. Retrieved October 24, 2015, from http://europa.eu/rapid/press-release_IP-15-5700_en.htm.
Fanon, F. (1963). *The wretched of the earth*. New York: Gove Press.
Forced Migration Review. (2010). Disability and displacement special issue. *Forced Migration Review,* 35. Retrieved from http://www.fmreview.org/disability/access.
Grech, S. (2009). Disability, poverty and development: Critical reflections on the majority world debate. *Disability and Society, 24*(6), 771–784.
Grech, S. (2011). Recolonising debates or perpetuated coloniality? Decentring the spaces of disability, development and community in the global South. *International Journal of Inclusive Education, 15*(1), 87–100.
Grech, S. (2015). *Disability and poverty in the global South: Renegotiating development in Guatemala*. London: Palgrave.
Grech, S. (2016a). Disability and poverty: Complex interactions and critical reframings. In S. Grech & K. Soldatic (Eds.), *Disability in the global South: The critical handbook* (pp. xx–xx). New York: Springer.
Grech, S. (2016b). Disability and development: Critical connections, gaps and contradictions. In S. Grech & K. Soldatic (Eds.), *Disability in the global South: The critical handbook* (pp. xx–xx). New York: Springer.
Guterres, A. (2015, February 26). *Open briefing on the humanitarian situation in Syria*. Retrieved March 9, 2015, from UNHCR: http://www.unhcr.org/54ef66796.html.
Handicap International. (2008). *Toolkit on protection of persons with disabilities*. Handicap International.
HelpAge International and Handicap International. (2014). *Hidden victims of the Syrian crisis: Disabled, injured and older refugees*. London: HelpAge International and Handicap International. Retrieved October 18, 2014 http://www.helpage.org/newsroom/latest-news/hidden-victims-new-research-on-older-disabled-and-injured-syrian-refugees/.
Hyndman, J. (2011). A refugee camp conundrum: Geopolitics, liberal democracy, and protracted refugee situations. *Refuge, 28*(2), 7–15.

International Detention Coalition. (2015). There Are Alternatives. Melbourne: International Detention Coalition.

IASFM. (2014). *About us*. Retrieved August 8, 2014, from International Association for the Study of Forced Migration: http://iasfm.org/about/.

Kett, M., & Trani, J. (2010). Vulnerability and disability in Darfur. *Forced Migration Review* (Issue 35), 12–13.

Koffman, E., Phizacklea, A., Raghuram, P., & Sales, R. (2000). *Gender and international migration in Europe*. Oxon: Routledge.

Milner, J. (2014). Protracted refugee situations. In E. Fiddian-Qasmiyeh, G. Loescher, K. Long, & N. Signona (Eds.), *The oxford handbook of refugee and forced migration studies* (pp. 151–163). Oxford: Oxford University Press.

Mirza, M. (2011). *Unmet needs and diminished opportunities: Disability, displacement and humanitarian healthcare*. Geneva: UNHCR.

Mostafa, A. (2015). Disability and forced migration: The experience of a Syrian Doctor. *Disability and the Global South, 2*(1), 551–555.

OCHA. (2004). Guiding Principles on Internal Displacement. New York: United Nations.

Oliver, M. (1994). *Politics and language: Understanding the disability discourse.* Paper prepared for inclusion in the MA in Disability Studies Programme: Deptartmet of Psychotherapy, University of Sheffield. Retrieved from http://disability-studies.leeds.ac.uk/files/library/Oliver-pol-and-lang-94.pdf

Pisani, M. (2011). There's an elephant in the room and she's 'rejected' and black: Observations on rejected female asylum seekers from sub-Saharan Africa in Malta. *Open Citizenship* (2).

Pisani, M. (2012). Addressing the 'citizenship assumption' in critical pedagogy: Exploring the case of rejected female sub-Saharan African asylum seekers in Malta. *Power & Education, 4*(2), 185–195.

Pisani, M. (2013). "We are going to fix your vagina, just the way we like it": Some reflections on the construction of [sub-Saharan] African female asylum seekers in Malta and their efforts to speak back. *Postcolonial Developments in Education, 2*(1), 68–99.

Pisani, M. (forthcoming). 'Illegal bodies' on the move: A critical look at forced migration towards social justice for young asylum seekers. *Perspectives on Youth* (Vol. 3). Strasbourg: Council of Europe and European Commission.

Pisani, M., & Grech, S. (2015). Disability and forced migration: Critical intersectionalities. *Disability and the Global South (DGS), 2*(1), 421–441.

Shivji, A. (2010). Disability in displacement. *Forced Migration Review, 35*, 4–7.

Soldatic, K., & Fiske, L. (2009). Bodies 'locked up': Intersections of disability and race in Australian immigration. *Disability & Society, 24*(3), 289–301.

Soldatic, K., & Grech, S. (2014). Transnationalising disability studies: Rights, justice and impairment. *Disability Studies Quarterly, 34*(2).

UNHCR. (2009). *Submissions to the 2009 Joint Standing Committee on migration inquiry into the migration treatment of people with a disability*. Canberra: UNHCR.

UNHCR. (2011). *Working with persons with disabilities in forced displacement*. Geneva: UNHCR.

UNHCR. (2015, January 7). *UNHCR report shows world's poorest countries host most refugees*. Retrieved March 11, 2015, from http://www.unhcr-centraleurope.org/en/news/2015/unhcr-report-shows-worlds-poorest-countries-host-most-refugees.html.

UNHCR and Integra Foundation. (2015). *My diversity: Age, gender and diversity perspectives in the Maltese refugee context*. Valletta: UNHCR.

WHO and World Bank. (2011). *World report on disability*. Geneva: World Health Organization.

Women's Refugee Commission. (2008). *Disabilities among refugees and conflict-affected populations*. New York: Women's Refugee Commission.

Yeo, R. (2015). 'Disabled asylum seekers?…They don't really exist': The marginalisation of disabled asylum seekers in the UK and why it matters. *Disability and the Global South, 2*(1), 523–550.

Zetter, R. (2007). More labels, fewer refugees: Remaking the refugee label in an era of globalization. *Journal of Refugee Studies, 20*(2), 172–192.

Chapter 19
The Fluid Connections and Uncertain Spaces of Women with Disabilities: Making Links Across and Beyond the Global South

Janet Price and Nidhi Goyal

Introduction: Managing Essentialisms

In this chapter we map aspects of the gendered experiences of living with and alongside disability in the global South. Our focus is on analyzing how the three intersecting ideas of the disabled southern woman, of gendered disability in the global South, and of the engendering and disabling of southern global positionality constitute terms that have been utilized, redefined, and destabilized. The tentative introductions outlined here highlight some openings in the feminist analysis of disability and gender. We make use of feminist/disability theory to develop a discursive analysis that questions the epistemic privilege and violence associated with the imposition of the category of disability, "the disabled woman"/"the woman with disabilities," as it happens within the global South, looking at some of the local forms of knowledge and ways of being that displace the notion of universalized disability (Campbell 2011; Puar 2012a; Shildrick and Price 2005).

Many myths surround disabled women. These myths are particularly powerful in relation to women with disabilities in the global South, Africa, and Asia for example, who are almost universally believed to be: living in poverty, often close to destitution; without work and without education, thus lacking skills to support

J. Price (✉)
International Public Health, Liverpool School of Tropical Medicine,
Liverpool, Merseyside L17 9PP, UK
e-mail: janeteprice41@yahoo.co.uk

N. Goyal
Independent disability and gender rights activist and writer, 702 Blossom building,
Adarsh lane, Off Marve road, Malad West, Mumbai, Maharashtra 400064, India
e-mail: nidhigoyal219@gmail.com

S. Grech, K. Soldatic (eds.), *Disability in the Global South*,
International Perspectives on Social Policy, Administration, and Practice,
DOI 10.1007/978-3-319-42488-0_19

themselves; subject to widespread magical beliefs of fate and misfortune, even of being witches; asexual and unable to establish a relationship or have children; and conversely, hypersexual and/or the victims of rape and domestic violence (Kamga 2011; Ghai 2015). Generalizations such as these do not emerge without there being an element of truth to them, but there is much in the contextual detail framed by local epistemologies that offers deeper perspectives on the lives of women living with disability in the global South, perspectives commonly ignored or dismissed.

Simultaneous discursive regimes from neoliberal, postcolonial, indigenous, and modern sources, coevally present, (of necessity) build an understanding of the fluidity of embodied lives of disabled people and of the consequent discourses that are re/constituted by and from them. Yet within these zones of discursive power, modernism exerts a constant pressure to generalize, universalize, and exclude, forcing a return to engagements with and critiques of the medical model of disability, to new emphases on the social model, and to a centrally led focus on disability's fixed nature (turning against women's strong involvement in the writing of the Convention on the Rights of Persons with Disabilities), thus serving to build an understanding of disability and the disabled body that organizes and is organized through the CRPD (Hughes 2002). Our aim is not to negate the work of those campaigning to end disability discrimination through claiming rights, nor to uncover error in this approach, but rather to address the limits of such an approach and the questions it raises.

Feminist theories have supported, informed, and been created by women with disabilities as they have worked to carve out space for themselves in their own lives and in their political organizing within a male-dominated disability movement. Although there has been a reluctance to take on the risky strategies of postconventional thought, recent developments in critical disability theory have seen a broader application of these ideas, including within postcolonial contexts (McRuer 2007; Campbell 2011; Puar 2012b). Despite significant gaps in understanding of the day-to-day experiences of women who might be termed disabled, especially in this current era of neoliberal economics, this chapter develops analyses around two foci:

1. Challenging universalized views of disability by questioning how women with disabilities are positioned, especially in the global South, and how their positionality, subjectivity, and intersectionality are understood in light of shifting global forces.
2. Addressing the feminist critique of disability, as it incorporates new gender theory and a broadened geopolitics of globalization via feminist postcolonial and postconventional thinking (Shildrick and Price 2005; Parekh 2007; Meekosha 2011). These theories have opened avenues for a provisional politics of embodied interdependency and transformative connections which lead to hopes of a geopolitically aware ethics of flourishing.

In place of addressing the whole of the highly variable global South, we take a narrower focus on two regions: southern Africa and south Asia. Even within these restricted geographic zones, the task of avoiding all essentialisms is an impossibility. And as with all theorizing, these ideas are open to further development, re/interpretation, and application.

In working together on this chapter we have attempted to acknowledge our own points of deferral to epistemic privilege, to the constraints on, and to the fixing of knowledge through the use of postcolonial and metropolitan constructs that have limited relevance to, and even misconstrue, the lived experiences of disabled women of the global South. As a woman who lives with a constantly changing body, in part due to multiple sclerosis, committed to feminist and queer ways of analyzing and working in the world, Janet writes with the limitations and privileges that accrue to a middle-aged, middle-class, cis-gendered, white lesbian who lives between Liverpool in the UK and Taranaki in New Zealand, and over the last 30 years has spent prolonged periods in India to see friends and to work. Over the last 10 years Janet has also developed close contacts with queer, feminist, and disabled activists and human rights defenders in Africa, largely southern Africa, with whom she has developed teaching, campaign, and coalition links. As a young disabled feminist who acquired a visual impairment in her teenage years and lives with the constant deterioration of sight and experience of blindness, Nidhi lives with the privileges and constraints of being a heterosexual, metropolitan, middle-class Indian. In the past 5 years, Nidhi has actively worked on disability, sexuality, and gender in India through advocacy, training, and campaigning. She brings insights stemming from the ironies of disabled and non-disabled life experiences and from belonging to a progressive positive family which is culturally a part of a conservative community. Our friendship emerged from work we are jointly involved in through an Indian-based feminist organization that works globally, CREA (n.d.). We have been brought together by the commonality and divergence of personal and work experiences, and the harmony and challenges of our ideas on the plethora of political work to be done and spaces to be reclaimed, and through shared laughter.

The short paragraphs in this chapter on the lives of particular anonymized but individual women with disabilities (Martha K., Agnes P., and Geeta) are drawn from conversations and time spent with these women during research we have been involved in. In India, Nidhi conducted several in-depth interviews with women with disabilities, one of whom was Geeta, during research for a website (Sexuality and Disability n.d.) sharing information with and supported by disabled women and men, their family, and partners, which is run and co-authored by Nidhi. Geeta hails from a conservative (middle-class, high-caste) Indian family who shared her story and responded to Nidhi's research process towards building the website. Janet discussed a range of issues with Martha K. and Agnes P. during a meeting in central-east Africa as part of a coalition-building process between disability and sexuality organizations (Coalition for Disability and Sexuality Rights in Africa), a process which sees the gathering and sharing of ideas and analyses as crucial to building women's combined strength. Their responses were recorded, the data fed back to the women, and the paragraphs written for this chapter shared for corroboration. Hopefully this chapter will serve as a source for further debate and analysis among the CDSR in African members.

Reconfiguring the Economic Potential of Disabled Embodiment

The chapter starts with a consideration of the working lives of disabled women. We use numbers and categories to solidify individuals who, as theory we subsequently address would suggest, are fluid and unfixed in time or place. But the provisional categories we utilize serve to reveal something of the challenges women with disabilities face and to reflect how economic necessity underpins transformative forces in their lives.

Countries with a low and/or highly uneven distribution of gross domestic product, those of the global South, tend to be inhabited by disproportionately high numbers of disabled people, and of disabled women in particular. The prevalence of combined moderate and severe disability in low-income countries, for example, is estimated to be higher for women than for men (at 22.1 per cent compared to 13.8 per cent) (Mathers et al. 2008; WHO and World Bank 2011: 28, 31). In both geographic North and South, data shows that many disabled women do live in the margins, surviving at or below poverty level. In all, only about 20 per cent of disabled women are recorded as in formal work (compared with 53 per cent of disabled men) although many women are active in subsistence work. But compare this to the also low figure of 30 per cent of non-disabled women in work (compared to 65 per cent of non-disabled men). Underemployment and lack of skills are situations faced by many women in poor countries, although made worse for women with disabilities by the powerful interaction of gender and disability prejudice irrespective of national economics. This leads to employment rates for disabled women that are roughly the same across low- and high-income countries. In contrast, the employment rate for disabled men in low-income countries is higher, at 59 per cent, than in high-income countries, where the rate is 36 per cent (WHO 2002–2004).

Many disabled women in the South are severely limited by these socioeconomic factors. Their lives are lived in poverty and debility, contingent and without guarantee of future security (Puar 2012b), as are the lives of women with disabilities in the global North, although the pressures upon them and the state support offered operate in different ways. Whatever statistics are available indicate that in India, South Africa, Malawi, and Nepal, among other countries, disabled women tend to live in the context of underdeveloped markets where increasing privatization of wealth, growing class inequalities, and large urban–rural divides, along with caste inequities in India, Nepal, and related south Asian communities, further marginalize many in poverty. Provisional expectations of a disabled woman would suggest that she manages the household demands of reproductive/care work, made harder by austerity's undelivered promises and the withdrawal of state services. In the face of growing market instability, she faces the necessity to develop skills to manage not only subsistence work but also paid work, seeking out scarce offers of accessible training (Akram 2011; Grech 2011).

In the global South, facing relative educational disadvantage in both gender and geopolitical terms, disabled girls who have access are driven hard to take maximum advantage of schooling. The interactions of poverty, disability, and gender lead to 45.6 per cent of boys with disabilities overall completing primary school compared with only 32.9 per cent of girls with disabilities (ignoring wide variation within low-income countries) (WHO and World Bank 2011). Lack of accessible toilets, especially post-puberty; parents' fears of their daughters being raped by assistants, teachers, or bus drivers; and the social devaluation of female education interacting with the girl's disability—these factors all act against disabled girls' education, over and above the constraints on access faced by blind and deaf girls, by those with physical and those with intellectual and psychosocial disabilities.

The general contention is that disabled women in the global South are excluded from work, both in the realm of global capitalism (with the implication, arising from the social model, that this exclusion is associated with prejudice against them) and in the sphere of the subsistence/care economy. Women, with and without disabilities, across subsistence agricultural communities in regions such as Africa and south Asia have always worked supporting household production; yet their contributions have been ignored or denied, as feminist development writers have documented (Waring 2008; Budlender and Moussié 2013). It was not until the 1970s that women were specifically included in development discourse. The women in development framework, developed in response to women's perceived passive role, was based upon the notion that women have limited access to and control over resources, despite playing a crucial role in the agricultural economy (Boserup 1970; Tinker 1990). Although often classed in census and other surveys as "non-active," ILO and other data indicate that "[i]f household duties were calculated as productive, the value of the world's GDP would increase by 25–30 per cent and women's economic participation rates would be equal to or higher than those of men" (Symington 2004: 4).

> In 2009, 20 women who had been disabled by landmine explosions and who used prosthetic arms or legs took part in a 'Miss Landmine Cambodia' competition. Of them, 10 were married, five were widows and five students. At the time, five were small-scale farmers, five were running small businesses including three selling cakes made at home, three worked for disability non-government organizations and one worked in a factory. Three were students and three (all married) looked after their children. They all had dreams of the future: 11 wanted to start or enlarge a business, four wanted to work for a disability NGO (three following up on accountancy training) and two wanted to advocate for disability rights. Two wanted to get a paid job and one wanted to care for her family. (Miss Landmine Cambodia 2009)

It is work across this broad-ranging subsistence/care economy of farm and household duties (as opposed to the established "market" economy) that appears to form the majority of work undertaken by disabled women (Mehrotra and Vaidya 2008). Working-class women with disabilities find opportunities through small-scale enterprise and home-based production, establishing local shops or market stalls, for example, while many work in rural agricultural production, ensuring both subsistence survival for their family and surplus for sale. Women with disabilities may pick up jobs in the casualized production spaces offered by the displacement of labor from North to South, taking their chances in the unsanitary, crowded workshops where health and safety are absent and wages are low.

Following the application of structural adjustment policies upon many low-income countries, women suffered as state welfare was cut, resources rationed further, and services reduced or privatized. But disabled women suffered particular difficulties, limited at every turn in their search for individual and family support, and prosthetics and access provision. And while neoliberal globalization has hit all those in poverty hard during the recent years of global austerity, the interaction of pre-existing poverty with disability and gender has made the lives of women with disabilities immeasurably harder, producing a broad picture of worsening health and disability status.

Questions of Living and Togetherness Within Precarious Situations

We aim to demonstrate that the challenges in teasing out the meaning of such socio-economic data and the successes or failures of disabled women economically depend in part upon the barriers and openings to work, whether within the family or externally mediated by factors such as local prejudice, access limitations, and glocal patterns of discrimination. But as we indicated earlier, an individual disabled woman's own embodiment is open to transformation, linked to her individual capacity, to the availability of prosthetics and the ways in which she uses them, and to her phenomenological engagement with the world. And these factors together influence the ways in which she is positioned by the state and by those around her.

> Martha K. from Cameroon is a young woman in her early thirties, noted for energy and optimism in her encounters with those around her, with one leg affected by polio. She runs a local market stall selling a variety of goods including bags and clothes made by a local disabled women's group. It serves to support not only her but also, in part, her family, her elder brothers and their wives and families, her father and his family, while bringing in a tiny amount of money for the disabled women. Although she does not give her family money on a daily basis, it is clear that in the joint family compound, M.K., as a young unmarried disabled woman, is seen as a key income generator whose contributions are expected and accepted as a family due. Alongside her own market stall, she also works with local women with disabilities to encourage them to establish economic projects and independence. And through this group she has made connections with international initiatives, of global feminist activists and of disability research, opening new channels of learning and travel. Despite the money that M.K. contributes to the family, rendering her unable to improve her own life, to buy her much-needed wheelchair or new crutches, she clearly holds her social and economic independence dear. As a woman immersed in a range of social networks, local, national and international (the latter particularly through her disability work), how she constitutes herself and the strength of her connections constantly shift as she moves from daughter to sister to income generator to activist.

Despite their clear northern origins, conceptual models of disability identity have been exported wholesale to countries around the world which occupy very different positions in relation to capitalism and social context. What distinguishes disabled women in the South from the North, as they live their consciously embodied lives

(Shildrick 2015), is that they are marked by the effects of colonialism and settler societies. Whether they come from indigenous, migrant, or colonist histories, they live with the aftermath of invasion, colonization, liberation, and, often, postliberation strife (Meekosha and Soldatic 2011). Further, the development of the CRPD has in part drawn upon distinctions made by the social model between body and society, impairment, and disability. Thus, globally disability is inflected through a northern prism with models, such as the WHO International Classification of Functioning, Disability and Health approach, "still based on the premise that disability can be objectively and universally known, mapped and treated" (Campbell 2011: 1467). And in contradiction to the promises of the CRPD, most women with anomalous embodiment, women who face discrimination and stigma of varying levels, especially in the South where access to these ideas is still limited, do not see themselves as disabled. Although individual disabled women of the South may believe in and champion rights, independence, inclusion, and the social model, as promulgated by the CRPD, whose slogan is "Nothing about us without us," they also have access to other ways of knowing and being, ways that may call into question the Convention and its commitment to liberal ideals of autonomy and rights. And there are many disabled women in the South, women unaware of their labelling, who thus function "without us," outside of any desired unity of disability identity or organization.

The origins of southern women's disability are as widely varied as in the North, from birth events to acquired disability due to accidents or physical and psychosocial illness during their lives to the impact of aging and approach of death. What differentiates women living in postcolonial contexts is that they not only live in a state of precarity engendered by neoliberal capitalism (Goodley et al. 2014) but that one consequence of the intersection of this precarity and postcolonial uncertainty is the wide range of events—"natural disasters," industrial "accidents," and state security concerns—which can be traced back to colonial origins: the 1984 Bhopal disaster where the chairman of the imploding factory, which injured and killed so many, sat across the ocean in air-conditioned security (Al Jazeera 2014); the US-initiated Iraq invasion, the start of a long-running period of fighting and population displacement leading to over one million deaths across a decade and disability linked to the invasion, insurgencies, and subsequent social breakdown (PSR 2015); and the 2013 building collapse in Rana Plaza, Bangladesh, which buried multitudes of laboring women, killing over 700 and injuring many more, while those who direct the companies, and design and wear these cheaply made clothes, are all untouched (Parveen 2014; Daly 2015). These events, whether large or small disasters, planned or accidental, reshape not only individual embodiment physically, emotionally, and socially, but also broader social and economic dynamics in both South and North. And they feed into the precarious situation in which so many exist, exacerbating the dynamics of the slow death that they face.

Work by Berlant and Puar focuses on bodily debility, the gradual loss of capacity, and "slow death," a state of prolonged exploitation of an individual's resources of survival. Berlant describes it as "the physical wearing out of the population ... very nearly a defining condition of their experience and historical existence" (2007: 754). This is a situation experienced not only by those in the global North but, as any glance at international news will demonstrate, by communities across much of sub-Saharan Africa, south Asia, and the global South where they face the ongoing depletion of resources available for subsistence living. Older disability models do not account for this reshaping of postcolonial social relations, nor for the impact of slow death whereby many live on the borders of disability, neither disabled nor untouched by disability's potential (Meekosha and Soldatic 2011; Grech 2015).

Erevelles (2011) points out that in some countries of the South, around 50 per cent of the population is closely affected by disability, living alongside and influenced by the lives of disabled others. Within the close confines of many southern households, a high degree of contact, influence, and intercorporeality is an inevitable aspect of life together. The disabled women we have encountered in southern Africa and Asia, as they strive to maintain themselves and their families, rarely work in isolation but rather in cooperation and collaboration—and even at times in internal conflict—with others, most often other women from their family and community.

For disabled women, this process of interdependent work relies not only on other individuals for support—physical, emotional, and intellectual—but also on prostheses of various sorts—the classical crutch, artificial leg, glasses, or hearing aid. And increasingly, assistance is provided through mobile phone apps, computer (designed) aids, and other electronic and mechanical tools. Thus, disabled women come together not only with other women but also with a variety of prostheses to undertake labor with a subsistence/economic aim, forming a functional entity of a heterogeneous multiplicity of elements, in Deleuzian terms an *assemblage* (Shildrick 2004). The connections between its constitutive elements are temporary, dissolving, and reconnecting ceaselessly with other elements to form different assemblages. It operates as a response not to the question of "What is a body?"; rather, Deleuze and Guattari (1987), followed by many feminist writers, have asked "What can a body do?" with a focus on capacities, potentials, and the context-dependent openings offered, as shifts occur in environment, relations, space, and time.

Such household interdependency develops as an established way of life in contrast to expectations of autonomy and individual sovereignty. And what is crucial to the operation of any group living together with close familial bonds is the role that gender plays, both in its expectations of the disabled individual and their future life path as man or woman, and in its constitution of assistance through interdependency—but an interdependency in which female household members, some disabled themselves, will play the larger part in fulfilling assistance requirements for those who are disabled. The households of Martha K. and of Agnes P. (described in the next section) both offer examples of the fluidity of assistance required and offered.

Marriage and Sexuality

One of the contexts in which individuals are most open to the possibilities of concorporeality and interdependence with another's body is when with a sexual partner. Views of the sexuality of disabled people are widely stigmatized. In many south

Asian and southern African communities, heteronormative views of sexuality constitute disabled women as unmarriageable, drawing upon concepts of impurity, danger, and barrenness (Das and Addlakha 2001; Kamga 2011). Norms that derive from the vital tasks and gender roles assigned to women in the reproductive sphere, when disrupted, as happens with "a broken body," constitute the woman as less than desired, less than the ideal of a potential successful partner and mother. Time and again, disabled women in the South refute this dominant view of themselves as single and childless of necessity, not choice.

There is much evidence that women with disabilities can bear children and that they do not inevitably, and in fact rarely pass on their disability, despite eugenic fears directed at them. Stigma against women with disabilities influences the possibility of their achieving a stable and respected marriage within a locally valued cultural context. Parents' desire to not see their sons marry a disabled woman is often a more powerful barrier than the limits against daughters marrying disabled men. Within shifting epistemological currents, across the many differing contexts of sub-Saharan Africa and south Asia, non-disabled people, in their fear of contagion, appear to believe that disabled women can bring danger and thus they will act to prevent the creation of close familial ties to them.

> Agnes P. in Malawi has three girls, the first born from a relationship when she married aged 18. While she is a Catholic, she does not believe that prayer will cure her impairment, but her mother and other women in the family felt that there was evil associated with her leg which could be both transmitted back to her natal family and onwards to a marital family. So strongly held was the fear and anxiety among some that, the night before A.P.'s first wedding, a cousin went behind her back to tell her future mother-in-law (from whom her disability had been kept secret, with the support of her father-in-law to be and of her future husband). Agnes P.'s current partner, she jokes, is perfect: 'I looked around and Matt was ideal—he had no mother and no father either! So, no interference or rumours of how badly I'll affect them, no one to see me as a danger.'

Most narratives of sexuality represent disabled women as "sexless"; yet in southern Africa women speak of "midnight husbands" who will visit and stay overnight but disappear before daybreak, a phenomenon so well known that it is represented in a health handbook for women with disabilities (Maxwell and Constantine 2007; Deepak 2013).

In India, when women with disabilities do marry, their marriage is frequently allowed to break caste and class laws, crossing what are, for many families, the essential endogamous rules by which marriages are arranged. The emphasis in a traditional marriage is on the perfection of the woman as a prospective wife, daughter-in-law, and mother. Women with disabilities, with their imperfect embodiment, have always already failed this test and so the remaining rules of a caste marriage are also loosened. So disabled women are married to disabled men; blind women marry blind men; deaf women and men become partners enabled through events run by local disability groups. Disabled women may become second or third wives, or marry men inauspicious in the Indian context such as widowers (O'Keefe 2009; Swadhikaar 2009).

> In India, Geeta hails from a conservative (middle-class, high-caste) Indian family. Already disadvantaged by her gender in the hegemonic patriarchal system, she was also discredited from being a 'true' woman owing to her disability. The prejudice and presumptions framing this attitude are that as a disabled woman she will fail to discharge her gender-assigned duties of cooking, child-bearing and caring. This in turn has resulted in her family allowing her to step out of the home and procure work, usually a non-negotiable restriction for all women of her family. She failed to fulfil the demands of womanhood, accompanied by a lack of marriage prospects which led to the limited care for her reputation shown by her family. On the other hand she experienced the freedom and growth that other women from her background were denied, illustrating with what complexity and unpredictability the confluence of various identities is reflected in different individual lives. (Goyal and Padte 2014)

For an Indian disabled woman, an advantage that may follow from always already being excluded from an ideal caste marriage, at whatever level, is that, as with Geeta, they are offered greater freedom within their families, to study and to work, to move around outside. This is especially true for middle-class disabled women, where class/caste regulation is strict.

A further aspect of this exclusion is that disabled women are concealed by their family, their existence denied for fear they may ruin the marriage chances of their sisters or simply because of the negative prejudice they may bring upon the household. Some women with disabilities are so little welcome in the family home that they are thrown out, landing on the roadside to work as beggars (Swadhikaar 2009), vulnerable to sexual assault and violence. Many disabled street dwellers have psychosocial problems, either causing their move to the street or developing consequently. Even here, however, women with disabilities may establish relationships with other street dwellers and live on the streets and in shanty towns, reliant on support from charitable and religious institutions (Price, pers. comm. with Shanti Devi, 2011). Others find a place for themselves in sex work, earning money in what is, from a middle-class Indian perspective, the lowest of female professions. Yet, as narratives from VAMP, the 5000-plus membership coalition of sex workers in Maharashtra, India, show, disabled sex workers have a regular core of clients, complicating ideas of disabled women as "sexless" in the face of contradictory ideas of sex workers as "sexmore" (Seshu and Datta 2014).

Sexuality, in any form, cannot be excluded from the embodied self nor essentialized as a given. The cultural contexts through which one strand of normative discourse appears to strip disabled women of their sexuality are deeply damaging to them. Margrit Shildrick, drawing on the disciplinary concepts of Foucault and on notions of gender performativity as developed by Judith Butler, argues that the sexuality of women with disabilities can be understood as the site "in which corporeal identity emerges—and is maintained through performance and management—and is simultaneously destabilised" (2009: 126). In southern Africa and south Asia, we see that in the face of normative notions of sexuality and of ideal relations that deny a place to disabled women, they appear to find partners and sexual expression in a number of differing, albeit devalued contexts. In opening themselves to relationships with, for example, "midnight husbands," disabled women expose themselves to vulnerability through the highly temporary interdependent and intercorporeal nature of their engagement with the other. Such phenomenological encounters are made more pointed by the ways in which the instability of disabled embodiment always already threatens ideals of autonomy, independence, and separation. These are troubled further through sexual engagement. Yet, though disturbed by a potential inability to achieve performative norms, disabled women emerge as sexual subjects through their engagement in discursive and corporeal acts of sexual desire against all external claims of their asexuality. Disabled women are, undoubtedly, active, sexy, and desiring of others and of their own pleasure, and it is these positive actions, contexts, and discourse as well as the negative—violence, war, incomprehension, and prejudice—that serve to constitute them as desiring subjects.

To unwittingly be the cause of transmitting negative energy is one issue. But the portentous notion that disabled women are complicit in superstitious rites and witchcraft is locally powerful with aspects of women's bodily difference being taken as marks of the devil. This old idea, recorded through the history of witchcraft, with early documentation from across Europe and North America in the 16th and 17th centuries, highlights how anomalous embodiment, such as skin blemishes, club foot, leprosy, and epilepsy, not only marked involvement in witching but also denoted the power of strange, fleshly matter and manner (Douglas 1991; Petherbridge et al. 2015). People with albinism, for example, especially women and children, in Tanzania and other African countries may be mutilated or murdered so that voodoo practitioners can use their body parts in ritual magic (Salinas 2013). The power of the disabled body here runs counter to the usual ideas of its lack of utility. By contrast, it is held to be saturated with force.

Disability and Fluid Embodiment

Disabled women across much of southern Africa and Asia have struggled to overcome the apparent silences that surround them, their concealment from outsiders, and the denial of their work and relationships. These silences are in fact full of debate about the management of disability, of how non-disabled people deal with their own vulnerability and reconstitute, organize, and discipline embodiment, and how disabled people represent their own strengths and learn to conceal themselves.

One aspect of this understanding of experience is language, central to how the question of disability is addressed across the globe. In the global South, many disabled women are expected to manage their experience with concepts not derived from their own understanding of embodiment. They struggle to find a place of difference for indigenous meanings and common terms addressing disability, embodiment, and impairment, which vary with place, time, and culture, against the dominant English usage. Comprehension varies of indigenous ontologies and epistemologies of the self, of perspectives of the self's gendering and embodiment, and of the origins and impact of vulnerability, guilt, shame, and prejudice around differential aspects of embodiment that have been labelled as disability, often carried and structured through religious or spiritual beliefs. Such emotional states contribute in differing intersecting ways and with variable power to the formation of identities around differing embodiments (Athanasiou et al. 2009).

But what happens when one has more than one identity: a woman, disabled, queer, and so on? A common belief all across the world, but particularly in the politics of the global South, is that these different identities converge in an additive system (Kamga 2011). Hence if a woman is considered to be oppressed, the woman with the disability is doubly oppressed, marginalized in opposition to norms of both gender and ability. Yet, the complexity of identities cannot but be multilayered and compound in its origin as well as its consequence and impact. Different identities can be seen to merge into each other, enabling a new subjectivity, a new phenomenology of embodiment, and a new political understanding to emerge. Through intersectionality, in addressing the "difference within" gender, sexuality, or disability, the different identities or the different aspects of identity neither hold a fixed position nor do they coexist in a stable relation to each other. The aspects are fluid and constantly in motion, raising shifting consciousness of, for example, disablism, sexism, and prejudice against people of the global South (Yuval-Davis 2006). Crenshaw's intersectional analysis emerged as a feminist intervention to disrupt whiteness and as a race intervention to disrupt masculinist beliefs in an identity politics growing in strength in the USA though dominated by white masculine middle-class values (Crenshaw 1991; Cho et al. 2013).[1]

Intersectional perspectives are valuable in gender analysis and political organizing as in addressing, for example, the ways southern disabled men maintain a stranglehold over most southern disability organizations, and thus southern disabled women struggle, with all the challenges they face, to find ways of continuing to meet and campaign together. Disability hierarchies intersect not only with gender but also with class, race, and nationality. In Nigeria, as in many other regions, on the one hand disabled women are faced with the patriarchal control exercised by middle-class Nigerian men, those with physical disabilities being placed high in the internal disability hierarchy of difference. On the other hand, building coalitions between Nigerian feminists and women with disabilities has taken a number of years, with both sides willing but the feminists embarrassed and uncertain, and the disabled women excluded through lack of access in feminist meeting places. Ultimately, they have found places and means whereby solidarity with Nigerian feminists can be built (Price, pers. comm. with Ekaete Umoh, 2014).

Mitchell and Snyder suggest that disability "represents an undesirable state of being that no political triage can repair … the straw that breaks the camel's back of identity politics" (2010: 36), unlike the spaces that other movements have found to claim "Black is Beautiful," for example, or to campaign for Gay Pride. Despite the importance of recognizing the differing elements constituting any individual's embodiment, disability structures inattention to issues of class, race and sexuality

[1] Crenshaw looked at intersections of structural, which addressed the intersection of racism and patriarchy; political, which addressed the intersection of antiracist and feminist organizing; and representational, which addressed the intersection of racial and gender stereotypes.

with its uneasy, uncanny presence serving to disrupt white, masculine, straight/homophobic inattention. In the uneasy focus on the non-normative body—the discomfort for a hearing person of engaging with a Deaf woman, or for a white, straight, non-disabled person to encounter a queer black man with cerebral palsy—normates have a tendency to ignore all else. Disabled feminists have drawn attention to a range of issues structured by a masculinist focus of disability theorizing and action. These include a lack of awareness of emotion; the rejection of phenomenological experience of the body, of pain, spasticity, rigidity, immobility/hypermobility, and fragility; and the inattention to and importance of psychosocial disability, now recorded as being the most common disability among women internationally.

In everyday life, disability displaces male/female difference as the founding embodied cultural norm as disability appears to ungender and desexualize individuals. The focus turns instead to the body and its foundational nature in determining "impairment." Disability theorists have worked to challenge this essentialized material basis for disability, although within the social model, impairment acts as the fixed corporeal anchor that grounds disability. Critical disability studies, conversely, work to disrupt the body's given status and establish its performative and disciplinary nature while acknowledging intersections with class, gender, sexuality, and race. Black disabled people and people of color in the global North experience a range of issues around racist disablism. Prejudice against those from the global South intersects with prejudice of the colonial period when the populations of India and Africa were regarded as essentially lower on the development hierarchy than those groups from the global North. Viewed as having malformed bodies, weaker intellect, and uncontrollable emotions, individuals such as Saartje Bartmann, the African woman exhibited as a freak in 19th-century Europe, served as examples of how gender and dis/ability could be brought into play through racist systems to pathologize and exoticize women of the South (Garland-Thomson 2002). Such prejudice may be replicated not only in the treatment of disabled people but also in the discrimination faced by tribal and indigenous groups of India and southern Africa, for example. And as recent work in Kenya has shown (for example, the Disabilities and Sexualities: Breaking the Silence project by Disability Focus Africa–Kenya, 2012–2013), LGBTQ and I disabled people are still silenced by much local disability discourse which sees gender and sexuality as secondary issues, to be dealt with once the primary issues for Kenyan people with disabilities have been confronted.

Puar argues that intersectionality is the "singular, feminist method, and the paradigmatic frame through which women's lives are understood and theorized" (2012a: 52). It sets up the "difference from," for example, normate white woman, as the primary focus of analysis rather than looking to the "difference within" which charts the continuous and unstable process of differentiation. Puar argues that reciting a list, almost a mantra of intersectional analysis, ending with the boundless "et cetera" to account for all those categories unchecked, stands in for any actual political work that seriously addresses women of color. She has a serious point.

> At a deaf and disability arts festival in the UK in 2014, there was an apparent representation of disabled people of colour. But few were from the UK. Rather they had been invited from the USA and parts of Africa, thus failing to address the issue of race discrimination affecting UK disabled artists within. A subsequent meeting of black and minority ethnic disabled artists was organised by the festival to identify ways forward. (DaDaFest 2016)

Within disability politics, an intersectional analysis opens the way to look, as Puar has indicated, despite her discomfort with intersectionality, beyond the internal comparison of "difference from" the normate individual, the never-claimed identity of non-disability, and to address "difference within" as about a continuous and unstable process of differentiation (Erel et al. 2010: 66).

On an individual level, engaging with dynamics of shifting intersectional discourses, attitudes, and representations, there may come a point where it becomes necessary to identify a point of stability, a strategic position necessarily temporary yet responsive to the context and situation. In both queer and crip movements the fluidity of identities and attention to the "difference within" rather than the "difference from" have been key points of analysis, and the idea of a fixed identity has been rejected on the grounds that it can cocoon one into the normative framework, even within individual identities.

Conclusions

Throughout the chapter, we have tried to emphasize the fluidity of disability, the multiple dissimilarities, the connections made and broken, and the ways that the varying types of anomalous embodiment across a range of cultures will be differentially influenced by events and ideas. In our writing, one of the things we have been faced with is the struggle to embrace the fluid, precarious, crip processes that emerge to persistently undermine and expose any claims to epistemic privilege, our own claims as well as those of others, especially where marked by the certainty that only a predetermined group of disabled people can *know* disability, a claim frequently made by those who follow the social model or the CRPD. We can strive to know our own disabilities—Janet with the varying impacts of a physical, sensory, and psychosocial disability, and Nidhi in living with the development of retinitis pigmentosa—but even in choosing to provide these medical diagnoses and disability definitions rather than offering you a description of our phenomenological experiences or of the origins of our disabilities, or of our ideas about how climate, geography, pollution in large cities, and the stress of modern life work upon our bodies, we are offering specifically privileged views.

While disability studies have been established as a staple unit in North American, Australo-Pacific, and European universities, demonstrating their progressive and rights-based allegiances, much of this form of disability studies have disregarded the knowledge, experience, and insight of the majority of those living with disability and debility who reside elsewhere, that is, not in the industrialized, precariously capitalized North but rather in the undercapitalized, highly precarious South, affected as it is by the ravages of climate change, war, economic maldevelopment, and growing, under-resourced populations. Globalization traces the flows, both local and global, of "hybrid identities, flexible hierarchies and plural exchanges" of anomalous embodiment, debilitated individuals, and the impact of precarity as they are mapped and engaged for their positive potential (Hardt and Negri 2001: xii).

Yet, how do disabled people in the global South relate to these fluid exchanges? There are many issues we could highlight around southern disabled women but we want to mark out three.

Knowledge

Disability studies are slowly being established in the global South, where pioneers in India, South Africa, Kenya, and Sri Lanka, among other countries, are introducing indigenous analyses. They are being followed by a wide-ranging group of activist-scholars, many of them disabled women, including some who have studied in both their home countries and in the northern metropolitan centers. Wherever their learning takes place, their lived experience is always inflected by their "difference," by their embodied knowledge of the history of colonial exploitation, and by the culturally exploitative imposition, offered and adopted, of neoliberal capitalist modernity. It is vital that disability studies develop a challenging, creative, and disruptive set of ideas that inform how disabled people—*all* people with disabilities—are enabled to live their lives (Akram 2011). And it is vital that the knowledge offers support in living, that the attempts at thinking otherwise, at "deconstruction ... offer crucial resources of thought for survival under duress" (Sedgwick 1999)—guidelines to a potentially creative future wherever disabled people may live.

Strategies

Second, disability politics needs to support women with disabilities from the South as they identify political aims and goals, as they create campaigns and advocacy strategies that speak to the hopes and ideals of the global South and indigenous disabled people. Through identifying the knowledge that speaks to the hopes of disabled women in a postcolonial future, that aims to reform neoliberal politics, and that takes along with it all those upon whom the world makes its marks of slow death, new strategies can emerge that are open to a range of critically aligned political futures. Such strategies offer crip/queer hopes and potential to build transformational ways of living against the apparent interests of a world that supports the desires of the 10 per cent, not the 90 per cent, as the Occupy movement states. And in supporting disabled women, in all their fluid and multiple ways of being, to open up to each other, to hear the voices of the poorest and the disinherited among them, women with disabilities from the global North and South have the opportunity to set radical political priorities. These come into focus as a consequence, as Saldanha writes, of letting themselves "be destabilised by the radical alterity of the other, in seeing his or her difference not as a threat but as a resource to question your own position in the world" (2007: 118).

Connections

Third, disability studies and politics across the globe need to support the formation of connections that will help disabled women weave together across temporary spaces and places, build networks and webs of connectivity, establish patterns of speech and echoes of sound, and create associations and relationships that work through touch, through hearing, smell, or sight, that move forward to welcome the creation and linkage of hybrid identities. It is not, as Shildrick (2013) argues, that disabled people living with anomalous embodiment will simply disappear, be rendered irrelevant by globalization's progress, either dying that slow death or turning into creatures of the new genetic age. Rather, new relationships may form, original concepts of ways of belonging and of becoming in a world of others may emerge, and new assemblages may come into being that build and strengthen North/South connections and disperse power differentials. Through unexpected connections, disabled women can challenge that which would destabilize or threaten their potential for human flourishing and the flourishing of all those connected to them across the global South and beyond.

References

Akram, A. (2011). *The role of women with disabilities in community based inclusive development*, March 2011. Barbara Faye Waxman Fiduccia Papers on Women and Girls with Disabilities, Center for Policy Studies. Retrieved October 21, 2013, from http://www.centerwomenpolicy.org/programs/waxmanfiduccia/2011OnlineSeriesBarbaraWaxmanFiduccia.asp.

Al Jazeera and Wire Services. (2014, October 31). *CEO blamed for Bhopal gas disaster dies*. Retrieved November 2, 2014, from http://america.aljazeera.com/articles/2014/10/31/warren-anderson-bhopal.html.

Athanasiou, A., Hantzaroula, P., & Yannakopoulos, K. (2009). Towards a new epistemology: The "affective turn". *Historein, 8*, 5–16.

Berlant, L. (2007). Slow death (sovereignty, obesity, lateral agency). *Critical Inquiry, 33*(4), 754–780.

Boserup, E. (1970). *Woman's role in economic development*. London: Earthscan.

Budlender, D., & Moussié, R. (2013). *Making care visible: Women's unpaid care work in Nepal, Nigeria, Uganda and Kenya*. Johannesburg: ActionAid.

Campbell, F. K. (2011). Geodisability knowledge production and international norms: A Sri Lankan case study. *Third World Quarterly, 32*(8), 1455–1474.

Cho, S., Crenshaw, K. W., & McCall, L. (2013). Toward a field of intersectionality studies: Theory, applications, and praxis. *Signs, 38*(4), 785–810.

CREA. (n.d.). Retrieved February 6, 2015, from www.creaworld.org.

Crenshaw, K. (1991). Mapping the margins: Intersectionality, identity politics, and violence against women of color. *Stanford Law Review, 43*(6), 1241–1299. Retrieved from http://www.jstor.org/stable/1229039.

DadaFest. (2016). *Art D'Visions?* Liverpool: DaDaFest.

Daly E. (2015, April 22). Witness: Rana Plaza factory collapse still plagues survivors. *Human Rights Watch*. Retrieved June 8, 2015, from http://www.hrw.org/news/2015/04/22/witness-rana-plaza-factory-collapse-still-plagues-survivors.

Das, V., & Addlakha, R. (2001). Disability and domestic citizenship: Voice, gender and the making of the subject. *Public Culture, 13*, 511–531.

Deepak, S. (2013). *Going beyond the taboo areas in CBR, Workshop Report, Part 1: Supporting social relationships, sexuality and reproductive rights of persons with disabilities through CBR*. Bologna, Italy: AIFO. Retrieved from http://english.aifo.it/disability/documents/cbr_sexuality/Taboo_report_part01_Social_relationships_Sexuality_ReproRights.pdf.

Deleuze, G. & Guattari, F. (1987). Becoming-intense, becoming-animal. *A thousand plateaus: Capitalism and schizophrenia*. Trans. Brian Massumi. Minneapolis: University of Minnesota Press.

Douglas, M. (1991). Witchcraft and Leprosy. *Man, 26*, 723–736.

Erel, U., Haritaworn, J., Rodríguez, E. G., & Klesse, C. (2010). On the depoliticisation of intersectionality talk: Conceptualising multiple oppressions in critical sexuality studies. In Y. Taylor, S. Hines, & M. E. Casey (Eds.), *Theorizing intersectionality and sexuality* (pp. 56–77). Basingstoke: Palgrave Macmillan.

Erevelles, N. (2011). *Disability and difference in global contexts: Enabling a transformative body politic*. New York: Palgrave Macmillan.

Garland-Thomson, R. (2002). Integrating disability, transforming feminist theory. *NWSA Journal, 14*(3), 1–32.

Ghai, A. (2015). *Rethinking disability in India*. New Delhi: Routledge.

Goodley, D., Lawthom, R., & Runswick-Cole, K. (2014). Dis/ability and austerity: Beyond work and slow death. *Disability & Society, 29*(6), 980–984.

Goyal, N. & Padte, R. K. (2014) *Women with disabilities and romance: A perspective from India*. Paper presented at the First Global Conference: Sexuality and Disability, *Inter-Disciplinary. Net*, May 6–8, Lisbon.

Grech, S. (2011). Poverty and disability. *Disability & Society, 26*(7), 888–891.

Grech, S. (2015). Decolonising Eurocentric disability studies: Why colonialism matters in the disability and global South debate. *Social Identities, 21*(1), 6–21.

Hardt, M., & Negri, A. (2001). *Empire*. Cambridge: Harvard University Press.

Hughes, B. (2002). Bauman's strangers: Impairment and the invalidation of disabled people in modern and post-modern cultures. *Disability & Society, 17*(5), 571–584.

Kamga, S. A. D. (2011). *The rights of women with disabilities in Africa: Does the protocol on the rights of women in Africa offer any hope?* Centre for Human Rights, University of Pretoria, February 2011. Barbara Faye Waxman Fiduccia Papers on Women and Girls with Disabilities, Center for Policy Studies. Retrieved October 21, 2013, from www.centerwomenpolicy.org/programs/waxmanfiduccia/2011OnlineSeriesBarbaraWaxmanFiduccia.asp.

Mathers, C., Fat, D. M., & Boerma, J. T. (2008). *The global burden of disease: 2004 update*. Geneva: World Health Organization.

Maxwell, J. & Constantine, S. (Eds). (2007). *A health handbook for women with disabilities*. Berkeley, CA: Hesperian Foundation. Retrieved October 24, 2013, from http://en.hesperian.org/hhg/A_Health_Handbook_for_Women_with_Disabilities.

McRuer, R. (2007). Taking it to the Bank: Independence and inclusion on the world market. *Journal of Literary & Cultural Disability Studies, 1*(2), 5–14.

Meekosha, H. (2011). Decolonising disability: Thinking and acting globally. *Disability & Society, 26*(6), 667–682.

Meekosha, H., & Soldatic, K. (2011). Human rights and the global South: The case of disability. *Third World Quarterly, 32*(8), 1383–1397.

Mehrotra, N., & Vaidya, S. (2008). Exploring constructs of intellectual disability and personhood in Haryana and Delhi. *Indian Journal of Gender Studies, 15*(2), 317–340.
Miss Landmine Cambodia. (2009). Retrieved February 7, 2015, from http://miss-landmine.org/cambodia/index.php/candidates.html.
Mitchell, D., & Snyder, S. (2010). Disability as multitude: Re-working non-productive labor power. *Journal of Literary & Cultural Disability Studies, 4*(2), 179–194.
O'Keefe, P. (2009). *People with disabilities in India: From commitments to outcomes*. Washington, DC: Human Development Unit, World Bank. Retrieved from http://documents.worldbank.org/curated/en/2009/07/11027298/people-disabilities-india-commitments-outcomes.
Parekh, P. N. (2007). Editorial: Intersecting gender and disability perspectives in rethinking post-colonial identities. *Wagadu*, 4. Retrieved January 15, 2016, from http://journals.cortland.edu/wordpress/wagadu/archive/v-4-2007-special-issue-intersecting-gender-and-disability-perspectives-in-rethinking-postcolonial-identities/.
Parveen, S. (2014, April 23). Rana Plaza factory collapse survivors struggle one year on. *BBC News*. Retrieved November 2, 2014, from http://www.bbc.co.uk/news/world-asia-27107860.
Petherbridge, D., Segal, L., Kokoli, A. M., & Deepwell, K. (2015). *Misogyny: Witches and Wicked Bodies*. Presented at ICA, London, 18 March.
PSR—Physicians for Social Responsibility. (2015). *Body count: Casualty figures after 10 years of the "War on Terror". Iraq, Afghanistan, Pakistan*. Trans. from German by Ali Fathollah-Nejad. Washington, DC: PSR—Physicians for Social Responsibility.
Puar, J. K. (2012a). "I would rather be a cyborg than a goddess": Becoming-Intersectional in Assemblage Theory. *PhiloSOPHIA, 2*(1), 49–66.
Puar, J. (2012b). Precarity talk: A virtual roundtable with Lauren Berlant, Judith Butler, Bojana Cvejić, Isabell Lorey, Jasbir Puar, and Ana Vujanović. *TDR: The Drama Review, 56*(4), 163–177.
Saldanha, A. (2007). *Psychedelic white: Goa trance and the viscosity of race*. Minneapolis, MN: University of Minnesota Press.
Salinas, M. A. (2013, March 12). Attacks on Albinos surge in Tanzania. *Voice of America*. Retrieved April 19, 2013, from http://www.voanews.com/content/attacks-on-albinos-surge-in--tanzania/1619907.html.
Sedgwick, E. K. (1999). Breast cancer: An adventure in applied deconstruction. In J. Price & M. Shildrick (Eds.), *Feminist theory and the body: A reader* (pp. 153–156). New York: Routledge.
Seshu, M. & Datta, B. (2014). *Through the looking glass: Sex work and disability*. Paper presented at the First Global Conference: Sexuality and Disability, *Inter-Disciplinary.Net*, May 6–8, Lisbon.
Sexuality and Disability (n.d.). Retrieved December 15, 2015, from www.sexualityanddisability.org.
Shildrick, M. (2004). Queering performativity: Disability after Deleuze. *SCAN: Journal of Media Arts Culture, 1*(3), 1–6.
Shildrick, M. (2009). *Dangerous discourses of disability, subjectivity and sexuality*. New York, NY: Palgrave Macmillan.
Shildrick, M. (2013). Sexual citizenship, governance and disability: From Foucault to Deleuze. In S. Roseneil (Ed.), *Beyond citizenship: Feminism and the transformation of belonging* (pp. 138–159). Basingstoke: Palgrave Macmillan.
Shildrick, M. (2015). "Why should our bodies end at the skin?": Embodiment, boundaries, and somatechnics. *Hypatia, 30*(1), 13–29.
Shildrick, M. & Price, J. (2005). Deleuzian connections and queer corporealities: Shrinking global disability. *Rhizomes* 11–12. http://rhizomes.net/issue11/shildrickprice/index.html.
Swadhikaar. (2009). *Monitoring the human rights of people with disabilities: Country Report: Andhra Pradesh, India*. Toronto: Disability Rights Promotion International.
Symington, A. (2004). Women's work exposed: New trends and their implications. *Women's rights and economic change* (Vol. 10). Toronto: Association for Women's Rights in

Development. Retrieved January 15, 2016, from http://www.awid.org/publications/womens-work-exposed-new-trends-and-their-implications.
Tinker, I. (1990). *Persistent inequalities: Women and world development*. Oxford: Oxford University Press.
Waring, M. (2008). Human rights and unpaid care giving. *Women's Human Rights Net Reader, 1*, 2–4. Retrieved January 15, 2016, from http://www.awid.org/sites/default/files/atoms/files/the_human_rights_of_women.pdf.
WHO and World Bank. (2011). *World report on disability*. Geneva: World Health Organization. Retrieved from http://whqlibdoc.who.int/publications/2011/9789240685215_eng.pdf.
World Health Organization. (2002–2004). *World health survey*. Geneva: World Health Organization. Retrieved March 29, 2015, from http://www.who.int/healthinfo/survey/en.
Yuval-Davis, N. (2006). Intersectionality and feminist politics. *European Journal of Women's Studies, 13*(3), 193–209.

Chapter 20
Violence Against Disabled Women in the Global South: Working Locally, Acting Globally

Leanne Dowse, Carolyn Frohmader, and Aminath Didi

Introduction

Issues of violence against women are becoming increasingly debated in countries of the global South, particularly as a human rights concern (Spratt 2013). This violence has its roots in gendered social, structural, and cultural marginalization; the feminization of poverty; and the legacies of colonialism seen in armed conflict and post-conflict displacement. These conditions differentially impact on women across multiple fronts including gender-selective abortion and infanticide, rape, domestic violence, honor killing, trafficking, forced prostitution, sexual exploitation, sexual harassment, female genital mutilation, forced marriage, and differential impact of HIV/AIDS (Vlachovd and Biason 2005).

Over 80 per cent of the world's more than one billion disabled people live in countries of the global South (Chouinard 2013), with an estimated 60 per cent of them being female (WHO and World Bank 2011). Empirical evidence confirms that men and women experience disability differently and that this difference is largely shaped by culture (Attard and Price-Kelly 2010: 43). While this influence is broadly

L. Dowse (✉) • A. Didi
School of Social Sciences, University of New South Wales, Sydney, NSW 2052, Australia
e-mail: L.Dowse@unsw.edu.au; A.Didi@unsw.edu.au

C. Frohmader
Women With Disabilities Australia, PO Box 407, Lenah Valley, TAS 7008, Australia
e-mail: carolyn@wwda.org.au

S. Grech, K. Soldatic (eds.), *Disability in the Global South*,
International Perspectives on Social Policy, Administration, and Practice,
DOI 10.1007/978-3-319-42488-0_20

recognized, Staples and Mehrotra (2016) in this volume remind us that conceptualizing disability across cultures and conceptualizing the cultures of disability remain significantly contested terrain. Different cultures maintain diverse interpretations and causal factors relating to impairments (Meekosha 2011) that result in discrimination and marginalization based on common assumptions about the status of disabled women and their capacity both as women and as people with disabilities. In some societies of the global South, women with disabilities may be likely to face multiple disadvantages as they are subject to complex discrimination related to their gender and disability, which pervades all aspects of their lives (Habib 1995). One widely recognized and significant consequence of this complex intersectional disadvantage is its contribution to and exacerbation of violence (UNHRC 2009).

Estimates of the prevalence of violence in the lives of these women are usually not more than best estimates since violence against women (and especially women with disabilities) is all too often unreported. But disabled women may be up to three times more likely to experience violence as their non-disabled sisters (Naidu et al. 2005: 16). This signals that the magnitude of the issue of violence against disabled women in the global South is significant on a global scale and the personal, social, and economic costs immense. The disproportionate lack of research on the nature, prevalence, impact, and prevention of violence against women with disabilities in these contexts signals a profound and disturbing silence and indicates that action on gendered-disability violence in the global South is crucial and urgent.

This chapter explores contemporary issues in addressing violence against women with disabilities in the global South as a pressing human rights concern. It explores some of the complex intersections across domains of ideological, ethnic, economic, social, and cultural factors that combine to produce pervasive gendered-disability violence. It also highlights the nature and foci of international activities and campaigns to address such violence. The chapter presents a case study of the work of Women With Disabilities Australia (WWDA) as an exemplar model for transnational feminist disability activism in the global human rights arena. WWDA's work, both in Australia and internationally, suggests a model to drive action on gendered-disability violence across the global North and the global South.

The Nature of Gendered-Disability Violence

Although men and women with disabilities share common experiences of isolation, marginalization, and discrimination, women with disabilities additionally experience discrimination on the grounds of their gender (Habib 1995: 50). Stubbs and Tawake (2009: 9) term this "intersectional discrimination"—a combination of disability and gender-based discrimination that adds new and separate forms of disadvantage to the lives of disabled women.

Research and field-based evidence suggest that women with disabilities experience intensified poverty, isolation, and poor health and receive less support from the family and community (Stubbs and Tawake 2009: 15). While reliable prevalence and incidence figures are unavailable, qualitative examinations of the experience of violence identify that women with disabilities experience compounding risk factors such as social and geographic isolation and physical, emotional, and financial dependency in their relationships. These experiences heighten their risk for multiple forms of abuse, which occur for longer periods of time and which also include forms of violence, abuse, and neglect specifically related to the presence of disability (Plummer and Findley 2012). Women with disabilities are also likely to have more difficulty in obtaining services and rehabilitation as their social, cultural, and economic marginalization constrains their community participation.

Although disabled women experience forms of violence similar to those experienced by other women and girls, they also experience forms of violence that are particular to their situation of social disadvantage, cultural devaluation, and increased dependency (Swift 2013: 1). This includes physical, sexual, and emotional violence and abuse (Habib 1995: 50), as well as institutional violence, chemical restraint, drug use, forced sterilization and contraception, coerced psychiatric interventions, medical exploitation, violations of privacy, humiliation, and harassment (WWDA 2010: 15). In addition to physical, mental, and sexual violence and abuse, disabled women also face unnecessary institutionalization, denial of control over their bodies, lack of financial control, and denial of social contact, employment, and community participation (INWWD 2011: 6–7). This violence is likely to occur over a longer period of time, by more perpetrators, and result in more severe injuries (Ortoleva and Lewis 2012: 16).

Disabled women face the dual processes of "silence" and "paradox" (Chenoweth 1996: 400–406), which help to explain the prevalence of violence against them. "Silence" is based on the overall societal tendency to deny the existence of violence against them. This silence is often compounded by the communicative silence of the victims themselves due to the absence of supports for recognition and reporting of violence and/or the systemic de-authorization of their voices and experiences when they do so (Dowse et al. 2013). This structural silencing is deeply embedded in social practices which ultimately result in victims' marginalization (Chenoweth 1996: 400–401). "Paradoxes" occur largely due to the protective roles assigned to disabled women. Many live sheltered lives, either within their families or in segregated settings where they have little experience of social relationships or ordinary community life (Chenoweth 1996: 403). Disabled women may also be socialized into unquestioning compliance as they age, including in schools and group residential care settings (Sobsey 1994: 164). Additionally, women with disabilities are often viewed as either asexual or sexually promiscuous, leading to the fostering of their susceptibility to abuse and violence (WWDA 2007: 51).

In recent years, the violence and discrimination experienced by women with disabilities have become more visible as a result of the advocacy work and research carried out by women with disabilities and their allies (Ortoleva and Lewis 2012: 14). Although violence against women with disabilities has been recognized as a key concern within human rights frameworks related to both gender and disability, the rates of violence against them remain high. Disabled women frequently do not report the violence they experience due to the inaccessibility (either physically or cognitively) of institutions of justice for women with different types of impairment (Ortoleva and Lewis 2012: 59). Lack of access to legal protection and representation due to inadequate training of law enforcement and legal officials, as well as lack of information in accessible formats, heightens the risk of disabled women being marginalized in the justice system. The resulting systemic and structural barriers heighten the risk of women with disabilities being seen by perpetrators as "ideal victims" (Dowse et al. 2013: 28).

Conceptualizing Gendered-Disability Violence in the Southern Context

A comprehensive picture of the extent and nature of violence experienced by women with disabilities in the global South is difficult to arrive at given the paucity of comprehensive and systematic data collection. The collection of comparable data is hampered by both the variability of approaches to the identification of disability and the extreme diversity in the recognition of acts that constitute violence in the context of gender and disability. Recent attempts by the WHO to estimate the prevalence of disability violence using a systematic review methodology of existing research suggest that adults with disabilities are at least 1.5 times more likely to be the victim of violence than their non-disabled peers (Hughes et al. 2012). This systematic review also identified that children with disabilities are almost four times more likely to experience violence than non-disabled children (Jones et al. 2012). Importantly, these studies note the lack of data from "low- and middle-income countries," indicating that specific considerations of disability violence in the global South remain conspicuously underrepresented in the agendas of governments, nongovernment organizations, and researchers in the global North.

At the international level, considerations of gendered-disability violence have been taken up by the United Nations High Commissioner for Human Rights. In examining the available evidence, the *Thematic Study on the Issue of Violence against Women and Girls and Disability* (UNHRC 2012: 5) noted that although a number of countries had undertaken research on violence against women and girls with disabilities, or had available disaggregated data on instances of violence against them, in the great majority of cases such information is not available.

Much of the work exploring the context and nature of violence at the intersection of disability and gender has emerged from interrogating the day-to-day lived experience of disability and impairment in the global North (Grech 2011: 89). As highlighted by Chouinard et al. (2016) in this volume, these discourses fail to take account of the experiences of disabled women from the global South despite the fact that the majority of the world's one billion disabled people live in countries of the global South. Meekosha and Soldatic (2011) have argued that there is a tendency for disability scholars to assume that processes of impairment and disablement are universal, thus stripping discussions of their geopolitical context. This in turn obviates the possibility to understand the implications of colonial and neocolonial power on experiences of impairment and disability in a highly unequal global capitalist order (Meekosha and Soldatic 2011: 1383).

A number of scholars have pointed to specific conditions that shape such experiences. Chouinard (2013: 342) highlights the extreme poverty in which many disabled people live in the global South as a legacy of colonial and neocolonial power and development, and which results in, for example, the human organ and global sex trades. War and conflict over resources, the arms trade, the export of toxic pollutants to poorer nations, and the exploitation of cheaper labor in sweatshops under extremely hazardous working conditions (Meekosha 2011: 675–676) are all significant considerations that need to be taken into account in southern disability studies and in particular their impact on disabled women (Chouinard 2013).

The immutable relationship between poverty, marginalization, and violence has been well documented, as has the differential experience of these along gendered lines. Throughout the world, the link between disability and poverty and social exclusion is direct and strong (Grech 2009). These historical, social, material, and cultural relations suggest that the particular position of disabled women in the global South must be understood as a complex layering of marginalization, disadvantage, and vulnerability (Quinn et al. 2002: 23). In conceptualizing violence for these women, it is also important to guard against the assumption of a totalizing or static experience. Unique assemblies of personal, civil, social, material, and cultural conditions influence the specific experiences of violence for disabled women the world over. These factors combine and mutually influence each other to give unique shape to the lived experience of violence for individual disabled women. What is understood is that in the global South, forms of violence arise at the intersection of disability and gender that encompass global, local, social, and cultural processes and are likely to be complex, pervasive, systemic, and disabling.

The Nature of Violence Against Women in the Global South

While systematic attention to gendered-disability violence as experienced by women with disabilities in the global South is scant, available evidence from relatively small-scale qualitative research suggests that the experiences of violence are likely to be multiple, pervasive, and intense (UNHRC 2009). In most countries of the global South, disabled women are often poor and/or face various other challenges unknown to most people (Stubbs and Tawake 2009: 9), giving rise to particular forms of violence. As Rees et al. (2011: 517) suggest this is evident in the significantly higher rates of gender-based violence among women with mental heath problems and intellectual disability. For example, based on research carried out in several countries in Asia, Latin America, and the Middle East, the UNHCR Thematic Study found evidence that forced sterilization was highest among women with intellectual disabilities (UNHRC 2012: 8).

Traditional gender stereotypes and cultural roles assigned to disabled women in countries in the global South shape the way violence affects such women. In some South Asian contexts, for example, Thomas and Thomas (2002: 28) argue that women are judged according to their physical appearance and their ability to look after a home, husband, and children. Traditional gender roles determined by historical, religious, ideological, ethnic, economic, and cultural factors mean that women unable to fulfil these roles are devalued by their society (Thomas and Thomas 2002: 28). In Nepal, for instance, disability has traditionally been interconnected with Hindu religious beliefs which suggest the cause as karma and the possession of bad spirits, resulting in social stigma and preventing people with disabilities and their families from accessing health services, education, and employment opportunities (Seven Women 2013). In India, social norms and the patriarchal nature of the society confine disabled women within the household where they are expected to perform only household chores, being deprived of educational opportunities and any type of vocational training for employment (Daruwalla et al. 2013). These practices make disabled women susceptible to extreme forms of violence and abuse.

A 2013 United Nations Population Development Fund study on the experiences of women with disabilities in Kiribati, Solomon Islands, and Tonga found similarly stereotypical perspectives on disabled women as asexual, unsuitable for marriage, and unable to manage their fertility or raise children. As a result, such women are unable to gain information about and access to services to support safe and healthy sexual and reproductive lives, free from violence (Spratt 2013: 10). Here too, restrictive norms surrounding sexual reproductive health intersect with beliefs about disability to create a heightened risk of violence for disabled women, where women with mental illness or intellectual disability were found to be particularly susceptible to experiencing multiple rapes, involuntary sterilization, and imposition of contraceptive use despite their inability to give informed consent (Spratt 2013: 17). Disabled women who experienced violence at the hands of an intimate partner faced extreme social pressure around reporting or responding to violence due to societal beliefs that women are "owned" by their husbands, making it almost impossible for them to break free from violence (Spratt 2013: 76). Similarly, in Cambodia, Astbury and Walji (2013: 7) found that controlling behaviors were common among partners of disabled women. Disabled women in Cambodia were four times more likely to have their activities monitored by their partners, and twice as likely to need the permission of partners before seeking health care for themselves (Astbury and Walji 2013: 20).

Societal attitudes, when condoned by the state, also have the potential to result in gross acts of violence against disabled women. In the case of North Korea, serious concerns about the human rights conditions of disabled men, women, and children, suggestive of crimes against humanity, have been raised by UN agencies, international nongovernment organizations (NGOs), journalists, South Korean human rights bodies, and individual North Korean refugees, several of whom self-identify as disabled (Lord 2013). Forced migration and internal quarantine within camps of disabled people, disability-selective forced abortion, forced sterilization of disabled men and women, infanticide, targeted killing based on disability type, and allegations of chemical and biological weapons testing on disabled people have all been documented (UNGA 2013: 12). Furthermore, gender discrimination and extreme suppression of sexual and reproductive rights of women seriously exacerbate violence against disabled women (Lord 2013).

In countries of the global South, as in other parts of the world, individual and societal violence is not only a frequent occurrence in the lives of disabled women, but also the cause of disability for many. Harmful practices such as female genital mutilation result in a wide range of physical impairments and have psychological consequences (UNHRC 2012: 10). Others acquire disability through illnesses such as polio, against which they were never vaccinated (HRW 2010: 6). In countries where there is civil unrest, war, and instability, women become disabled due to landmines or gunshot wounds, are mutilated by rebels, or sustain injuries in fires (HRW 2010: 18). In situations of conflict and natural disasters which force migration and displacement, disabled women living in camps for displaced people often have no access to provisions such as food, clothing, and shelter, and are particularly vulnerable to abuse and discrimination by strangers, neighbors, and even family members (HRW 2010: 7).

Women with disabilities in the global South also face multiple barriers in accessing support and redress for their experiences of violence. An examination of issues for disabled women in South Africa identified a range of physical, procedural, communication, attitudinal, and financial obstacles which meant that services (including the criminal justice system and gender-based violence support services), if they existed, were generally not accessible or appropriate to the needs of women with disabilities who had experienced violence (Naidu et al. 2005: 38).

Addressing Violence Against Disabled Women: Global Activism in Action

Adoption of anti-discriminatory legislation in a number of countries since the 1990s and the adoption of the Convention on the Rights of Persons with Disabilities (CRPD) and its Optional Protocol on 13 December 2006 have been seen as a landmark victory for disabled people (WHO and World Bank 2011: 261). Meekosha and Soldatic (2011: 1384) have observed that the promise of human rights in the CRPD signifies potential social, moral, and political means to redress the socio-structural processes of disability where societal attitudes and state policy regimes have been identified as the primary barriers to disabled people's full participation, representation, and inclusion. Article 6 of the CRPD, a stand-alone article on "Women with disabilities," obliges state parties to the Convention to prioritize disabled women as a group warranting specific attention, requiring governments to take positive actions and measures to ensure that they enjoy all human rights and fundamental freedoms (WWDA 2011: 13), key to which is the right to live free from violence.

The CRPD provides a framework for disability rights activists to position disability within the broader human rights family, to challenge governments on their policies and practices, and to unify disability rights-based mobilizations across the global North and global South (Meekosha and Soldatic 2011: 1385). While holding promise, there are however significant challenges in making instruments such as the CRPD "work" to address violence against disabled women. Meekosha and Soldatic are similarly guarded in relation to potential limitations when adopting Northern conceptualizations of disability rights (2011: 1384). This is particularly so in the global South where in-country contexts are often characterized by patriarchy, conflict, and limited disability and other social service provision, which often militate against effective redress, even in the presence of recognition and ratification of local, national, and international protection mechanisms. Soldatic and Grech (2014) also note how the CRPD denies debate on the production of impairment as well as impairment-based forms of resistance.

In India, for instance, it has been observed that the patriarchal nature of society which extends to all levels, including public institutions, marginalizes disabled women, resulting in their invisibility, silence, and negated identity or existence (Daruwalla et al. 2013: 8). In countries experiencing conflict and post-conflict situations, disabled women are at heightened risk of being targeted for violence due to their particular race/ethnic, religious, or linguistic identity, making access to services extremely difficult (Cornelsen 2012: 128). Even in countries where policies are in place to prohibit discrimination and codify the rights of people with disabilities, experience in Uganda suggests that attitudes of service personnel, such as health sector staff and police, act as major barriers to the realization of the rights of women with disabilities enshrined in the law (HRC 2012: 12).

With the adoption of anti-discriminatory legislation, the Convention on the Elimination of All Forms of Discrimination against Women (CEDAW) and the CRPD, many disability NGOs have shifted the focus of their activism on violence against women with disabilities to a rights-based approach in order to engage with the United Nations human rights machinery. The global disability rights movement is radically challenging citizenship status and practices in order for governments to respond to disabled people as full and equal citizens in society (WWDA 2011: 6). Although in many countries of the global South national organizations of disabled women are nonexistent or lack resources to act effectively, the recognition of the rights of people with disabilities has resonated across borders (Meekosha and Soldatic 2011: 1386). In this connection, international advocacy by NGOs led by disabled women has a significant role to play. New global alliances within the disability movement are forming to pioneer feminist disability activism locally and to drive international action on gendered-disability violence.

Women With Disabilities Australia: A Model for International Practice

Women With Disabilities Australia is the peak organization for women with disabilities in Australia, run by women with disabilities for women with disabilities. The organization utilizes a human rights-based framework linking gender and disability issues to a full range of civil, political, economic, social, and cultural rights, which recognizes that equal treatment, equal opportunity, and non-discrimination provide for inclusive opportunities for women and girls with disabilities in society (WWDA 2013). Using the international human rights normative framework, including the international human rights treaties and their optional protocols, particularly the CRPD and CEDAW as key tools, WWDA has played a leading role in bringing issues of violence and particularly forced sterilization to the international arena.

Some Hallmarks of Effective Advocacy

WWDA works nationally and internationally to increase awareness of and address human rights violations experienced by women and girls with disabilities through systemic advocacy. As a transnational advocacy network WWDA's work is motivated by shared principled ideas and values which are operationalized through its communicative structures and its members. This sees it engage in voluntary, reciprocal, and horizontal exchange of information that pursues instrumental goals and epistemic communities motivated by shared causal ideas (Keck and Sikkink 1998: 200). By building links among actors in civil society, states, and international organizations, WWDA's work blurs boundaries between states' relations with their own nationals and the recourse both citizens and the state have to the international system, which Keck and Sikkink (1998: 2) identify as the hallmarks of effective activism. This is exemplified in WWDA's campaign for advancing the sexual and reproductive rights of women and girls with disabilities globally. Based on its long-standing activism in the area, WWDA was commissioned by the UN and European governments to prepare issue papers on sexual and reproductive rights for the International Conference on Population and Development Beyond 2014 Review and for the Post-2015 Development Agenda. In this way the work of the organization has influenced the future of global population and development policy in taking account of issues for disabled women in the global South.

WWDA's strategic persistence in raising awareness and utilizing human rights mechanisms at the international level has resulted in many other tangible outcomes. WWDA's campaign on forced sterilization at the UN and at the broader international level, along with its long-standing national advocacy on the issue, resulted in the 2012–2013 Australian Senate Inquiry into Involuntary Sterilisation of People with Disabilities in Australia. Having formally stated in 2009 that the issue of forced sterilization was not on its agenda and there would be no reform in the area, this shift from the Australian Government is directly attributable to WWDA's national and international advocacy. For example, UN treaty monitoring bodies now explicitly refer to forced sterilization and violence against women with disabilities in their treaty monitoring reports and recommendations to state parties to the CRPD. The CRPD Committee has acknowledged WWDA's work as assisting in their reviews of other state parties to the Convention (HRC 2012). As a result of this success, civil society organizations the world over, including disabled people's organizations such as Disabled Women's Network Canada, utilize WWDA's work as a model in raising their profiles and issues of importance to disabled people at the UN.

WWDA has pushed to form strategic alliances and partnerships with a diversity of disabled women's organizations and networks in Africa, Nepal, Pakistan, and Palestine (WWDA 2013). Despite their differences, these organizations share a similar centrality of values, principles, and belief that they can make a difference. They share a common discourse and at the core of the relationship is information exchange (Keck and Sikkink 1998: 2). New communication technologies have been an essential part of maintaining contact with women with disabilities and their allies around the world. WWDA has spent more than 15 years methodically building extensive email distribution lists, and uses these regularly to disseminate information about its work and to seek support for its campaigns. In the global information age WWDA's framework of "information politics" (Keck and Sikkink 1998: 16) is characterized by its use of social networking through Facebook and Twitter to maximize dissemination of information, to simulate debate, and to consult with its constituency (WWDA 2013). With limited funding ruling out a physical presence at various national and international fora, the use of the Internet in disseminating information quickly and widely has played a central role in ensuring that the organization's messages are heard.

Through the effective use of online activism for persuasion, socialization, and pressure (Keck and Sikkink 1998: 12–13), as an organization in the global North, WWDA has established and nurtured key partnerships with its global southern sisters. As a deliberate priority, WWDA has also built a substantial online presence, curating extensive resources, publications, information, and research on the human rights of women and girls with disabilities. Its popular and extensive website (http://wwda.org.au) has become an important clearing house and repository for historical and contemporary information on many issues of concern to women with disabilities, particularly violence. Making these resources available and accessible to the broadest possible audience encourages other groups and organizations of women with disabilities to utilize WWDA's work.

As well as its online presence and systematic information gathering and dissemination, WWDA monitors developments in the national and international context. It actively responds to issues, initiatives, and debates relevant to the human rights of women and girls with disabilities through a sustained and relentless campaign of letter writing. In addition, taking up strategic opportunities for input into conferences, forums, inquiries, and advisory bodies ensures that the organization has a presence in key initiatives and forums where the issues of violence against disabled women are or should be addressed, including in the fields of human rights, disability, and women's issues. As a result the organization has extensive networks, alliances, and collaborative relationships that enable it to keep abreast of local, national, and international developments, and to respond to and mobilize others within a framework of "leverage politics" (Keck and Sikkink 1998: 16) in promoting accountability of governments and other duty-bearers to address issues of gender-based disability violence. This ensures that its work is placed firmly in a global context.

Conclusion

Women with disabilities in the global South face complex disadvantage shaped by patriarchy, cultural and social norms, and poverty, conflict, and displacement often grounded in postcolonial struggles. In these contexts their social exclusion leads to heightened risk and exacerbated experiences of violence. Current research in the area is largely informed by experiences and conceptualizations of disability and human rights emerging from the global North. Despite this limited focus on the specific conditions that shape the experiences of those in the global South, international recognition of the rights of women with disabilities has resonated across borders. The adoption of international human rights legislation such as the CRPD and CEDAW, as well as feminist disability activism, has led to the adoption of anti-discriminatory legislation and pressure on governments to take positive measures to protect the human rights of women with disabilities. As Chenoweth (1996: 408) suggests, disabled women must have a voice within the broader women's movement and the disability rights movement if meaningful change is to be achieved.

Disability rights activists and organizations in many countries have largely been responsible for bringing the issue of violence against disabled women to the attention of policy makers and service providers. Australia's national women's disability organization, WWDA, is one such organization internationally recognized for its approach and impact in feminist disability advocacy on violence against women with disabilities. As Meekosha and Soldatic (2011: 1386) suggest, nation states are now being compelled to respond to the demands of disability rights movements, which though locally embedded are increasingly globally connected. The innovative work carried out by WWDA provides a framework to connect activists at the global level, and to create greater awareness and impetus among governments and other institutions to address their obligations to fulfil, respect, protect, and promote human rights to support women with disabilities, both individually and collectively, to claim their right to live free from violence.

References

Astbury, J. & Walji, F. (2013) Triple Jeopardy: Gender-based violence and human rights violations experienced by women with disabilities in Cambodia. *AusAID Research Working Paper 1, January 2013*. Retrieved November 20, 2013, from http://aid.dfat.gov.au/research/Documents/triple-jeopardy-working-paper.pdf.

Attard, M., & Price-Kelly, S. (2010). *Accommodating violence: The experience of domestic violence of people with disability living in licensed boarding houses*. Redfern, NSW: People with Disability Australia. Retrieved December 12, 2014, from http://www.pwd.org.au/documents/pubs/Accommodating%20Violence%20Report.pdf.

Chenoweth, L. (1996). Violence and women with disabilities: Silence and paradox. *Violence Against Women, 2*(4), 391–411.

Chouinard, V. (2013). Precarious lives in the global South: On being disabled in Guyana. *Antipode, 46*(2), 340–358. doi:10.1111/anti.12046.

Chouinard, V., Belle, C., Khan, H., & Adrian, N. (2016). Embodying disability in the global South: Exploring emotional geographies of research and of disabled people's lives in Guyana. In S. Grech & K. Soldatic (Eds.), *Disability in the global South: The critical handbook* (pp. 583–598). New York: Springer.

Cornelsen, K. (2012). Doubly protected and doubly discriminated: The paradox of women with disabilities after conflict. *William and Mary Journal of Women and Law, 19*(1), 104–136.

Daruwalla, N., Chakravarty, S., Chatterji, S., More, N. S., Alcock, G., Hawkes, S., et al. (2013). Violence against women with disability in Mumbai, India: A qualitative study. *SAGE Open, 3*(3), 1–9. doi:10.1177/2158244013499144.

Dowse, L., Soldatic, K., Didi, A., Frohmader, C. & van Toorn, G. (2013). Stop the violence: Addressing violence against women and girls with disabilities in Australia. *Background Paper*. Hobart: Women with Disabilities Australia. http://www.stvp.org.au/documents/STVP-BackgroundPaper.pdf. Accessed 24 Nov 2013. Retrieved November 24, 2013, from http://www.stvp.org.au/documents/STVP-BackgroundPaper.pdf.

Grech, S. (2009). Disability, poverty and development: Critical reflections on the majority world debate. *Disability & Society, 24*(6), 771–784. doi:10.1080/09687590903160266.

Grech, S. (2011). Recolonising debates or perpetuated coloniality? Decentring the spaces of disability, development and community in the global South. *International Journal of Inclusive Education, 15*(1), 87–100. doi:10.1080/13603116.2010.496198.

Habib, L. A. (1995). Women and disability don't mix! Double discrimination and disabled women's rights. *Gender and Development, 3*(2), 49–53.

Hughes, K., Bellis, M. A., Jones, L., Wood, S., Bates, G., Eckley, L., et al. (2012). Prevalence and risk of violence against adults with disabilities: A systematic review and meta-analysis of observational studies. *Lancet, 379*(9826), 1621–1629. doi:10.1016/S0410-6736(11)61851-5.

Human Rights Council (HRC). (2012). *Thematic study on the issue of violence against women and girls and disability: Report of the Office of the United Nations High Commissioner for Human Rights. A/HRC/20/5*. New York: United Nations General Assembly. Retrieved October 29, 2013, from http://www.ohchr.org/Documents/Issues/Disability/ThematicStudyViolenceAgainstWomenGirls.pdf.

Human Rights Watch (HRW). (2010). *'As if we weren't human'—Discrimination and violence against women with disabilities in Northern Uganda*. New York: Human Rights Watch.

International Network of Women With Disabilities (INWWD). (2011). *Violence against women with disabilities*. Barbara Faye Waxman Fiduccia Papers on Women and Girls with Disabilities, Center for Women Policy Studies. Retrieved November 14, 2013, from http://centerwomenpolicy.org/programs/waxmanfiduccia/documents/BFWFP_ViolenceAgainstWomenwithDisabilities_TheInternationalNetworkofWomenwithDisabilities.pdf.

Jones, L., Bellis, M. A., Wood, S., Hughes, K., McCoy, E., Eckley, L., et al. (2012). Prevalence and risk of violence against children with disabilities: A systematic review and meta-analysis of observational studies. *Lancet, 380*(9845), 899–907. doi:10.1016/S0140-6736(12)60692-8.

Keck, M. E., & Sikkink, K. (1998). *Activists beyond borders: Advocacy networks in international politics*. Ithaca: Cornell University Press.

Lord, J. E. (2013, December 3). Nothing to celebrate: North Koreans with disabilities. *Foreign Policy in Focus*. Retrieved December 10, 2013, from http://fpif.org/nothing-celebrate-north-koreans-disabilities/.

Meekosha, H. (2011). Decolonizing disability: Thinking and acting globally. *Disability & Society, 26*(6), 667–681.

Meekosha, H., & Soldatic, K. (2011). Human rights and the global South: The case of disability. *Third World Quarterly, 32*(8), 1383–1397. doi:10.1080/01436597.2011.614800.

Naidu, E., Haffejee, S., Vetten, L. & Hargreaves, S. (2005) *On the margins: Violence against women with disabilities*. Centre for the Study of Violence and Reconciliation. Retrieved May 14, 2013, from http://www.csvr.org.za/docs/gender/onthemargins.pdf.

Ortoleva, S. & Lewis, H. (2012). Forgotten sisters—A report on violence against women with disabilities: An overview of its nature, scope, causes and consequences. *North-eastern Public Law and Theory Faculty Research Papers Series No. 104-2012*. North-eastern University, Boston.

Plummer, S., & Findley, P. (2012). Women with disabilities' experience with physical and sexual abuse: Review of the literature and implications for the field. *Trauma, Violence & Abuse, 13*(1), 15–29.

Quinn, G., Degener, T., Bruce, A., Burke, C., Castellino, J., Kenna, P., et al. (2002). *Human rights and disability: The current use and future potential of United Nations human rights instruments in the context of disability*. New York: United Nations. Retrieved November 14, 2013, from http://www.ohchr.org/Documents/Publications/HRDisabilityen.pdf.

Rees, S., Silove, D., Chey, T., Ivancic, L., Steel, Z., Creamer, M., et al. (2011). Lifetime prevalence of gender-based violence in women and the relationship with mental disorders and psychosocial function. *Journal of American Medical Association, 306*(5), 513–521. doi:10.1001/jama.2011.1098.

Seven Women. (2013). *Attitude towards disability in Nepal*. Retrieved December 9, 2013, from http://sevenwomenngo.wordpress.com/2013/08/12/attitude-towards-disability-in-nepal/.

Sobsey, D. (1994). *Violence and abuse in the lives of people with disabilities: The end of silent acceptance*. Baltimore: Paul H Brookes.

Soldatic, K., & Grech, S. (2014). Transnationalising disability studies: Rights, justice and impairment. *Disability Studies Quarterly, 34*(2). Retrieved September 26, 2014, from http://dsq-sds.org/article/view/4249/3588.

Spratt, J. (2013). *A deeper silence: The unheard experiences of women with disabilities—Sexual and reproductive health and violence against women in Kiribati, Solomon Islands and Tonga*. Suva: United Nations Population Fund Pacific Sub-Regional Office. Retrieved November 12, 2013, from http://countryoffice.unfpa.org/pacific/drive/ADEEPERSILENCE.pdf.

Staples, J., & Mehrotra, N. (2016). Disability studies: Developments in anthropology. In S. Grech & K. Soldatic (Eds.), *Disability in the global South: The critical handbook* (pp. 35–50). New York: Springer.

Stubbs, D., & Tawake, S. (2009). *Pacific sisters with disabilities: At the intersection of discrimination*. Suva: UNDP Pacific Centre.

Swift, K. (2013). Women with disabilities and violence: Challenges and visions in the Asia Pacific Region. *Presentation at the CSW57 Side Event, 8 March 2013*. United Nations.

Thomas, M., & Thomas, M. J. (2002). Status of women with disabilities. Selected readings in community-based rehabilitation, series 2 (2002). Disability and rehabilitation issues in South Asia. *Asia Pacific Disability Rehabilitation Journal, 9*, 27–34.

UN Human Rights Council (UNHCR). (2009). *Report of the special rapporteur on violence against women, its causes and consequences, Yakin Ertürk: Addendum: 15 years of the United Nations SR on violence against women, its causes and consequences (1994–2009): A critical review*. A/HRC/11/6/Add.5. Retrieved June 6, 2014, from http://www.refworld.org/docid/4a3f5fc62.html.

UN Human Rights Council (UNHCR). (2012). *Thematic study on the issue of violence against women and girls and disability.* Report of the Office of the United Nations High Commissioner for Human Rights. A/HRC/20/5. Retrieved May 12, 2014, from http://www.ohchr.org/Documents/Issues/Disability/ThematicStudyViolenceAgainstWomenGirls.pdf.

United Nations General Assembly (UNGA). (2013). Situation of human rights in the Democratic People's Republic of Korea. *Note by the Secretary-General, A/68/319, 14 August 2013*. Retrieved December 10, 2013, from http://www.ohchr.org/Documents/Countries/KP/A-68-319.pdf.

Vlachovd, M., & Biason, L. (2005). *Women in an insecure World. Violence against women, facts, figures and analysis: Executive summary*. Geneva, Switzerland: Geneva Centre for the Democratic Control of Armed Forces (DCAF). Retrieved June 11, 2014, from http://www.unicef.org/emerg/files/women_insecure_world.pdf.

Women With Disabilities Australia (WWDA). (2007). Forgotten sisters—A global review of violence against women with disabilities. *WWDA Resource Manual on Violence Against Women With Disabilities*. Rosny Park, TAS: WWDA. Retrieved November 28, 2013, from http://www.wwda.org.au/advpolpaper08.htm.

Women With Disabilities Australia (WWDA). (2010). *Assessing the situation of Women With Disabilities in Australia: A human rights approach*. Rosny Park, TAS: WWDA. Retrieved November 30, 2013, from http://wwda.org.au/subs2011.htm.

Women With Disabilities Australia (WWDA). (2011). Assessing the situation of women with disabilities in Australia: A human rights approach. *WWDA Policy Paper*. Rosny Park, Tasmania: WWDA.

Women With Disabilities Australia (WWDA). (2013). Information about Women With Disabilities Australia. *WWDA website*. Retrieved December 12, 2013, from http://www.wwda.org.au/about.htm.

World Health Organization (WHO) & The World Bank. (2011). *World report on disability 2011*. Geneva: World Health Organization and The World Bank. Retrieved November 12, 2013, from http://www.who.int/disabilities/world_report/2011/accessible_en.pdf.

Chapter 21
'Locked in Space': Rurality and the Politics of Location

Alexandra Gartrell and Elizabeth Hoban

Introduction

Despite rapid urbanisation, developing countries are predominantly rural, with more than 55 per cent of the world's population living in rural areas (IFAD 2011: 3). At least 70 per cent of the world's very poor people—that is, those living on less than US$1.25 a day—and those with the most insecure livelihoods are rural people (IFAD 2011: 3). While the structural disadvantages associated with rural spaces, such as disparities in access to basic health, education and other services, are widely documented (Sen 1999), insufficient attention is given to how and why these disadvantages are amplified once disability is brought into the picture. Limited research examines the intersections between rurality and disability, and the diversities and forms of disadvantage that emerge with this spatial relationship.

In this chapter, we argue that macro-level structural forces together with household micro geographies and poverty can lock disabled people in feminised, domestic home spaces, typically at the bottom of local social hierarchies. The spatial boundedness of many disabled people's lives often results in their exclusion from globalised processes of development and change that generate unequal patterns of development, increase mobility and result in livelihoods that are less local (Potter

A. Gartrell (✉)
School of Social Sciences, Centre for Geography and Environmental Sciences, Monash University, Clayton, VIC 3800, Australia
e-mail: alexandra.gartrell@monash.edu

E. Hoban
School of Health and Social Development, Deakin University, 221 Burwood Highway, Burwood, VIC 3125, Australia
e-mail: Elizabeth.hoban@deakin.edu.au

S. Grech, K. Soldatic (eds.), *Disability in the Global South*, International Perspectives on Social Policy, Administration, and Practice, DOI 10.1007/978-3-319-42488-0_21

et al. 2008). We use critical geographical theories of development and space to highlight the inherent socio-spatial unevenness of global change processes. We then apply a socio-spatial theoretical framework to examine disabled people's daily lives and draw on data from our research in rural Cambodia to support our theoretical arguments (Gartrell 2004; Gartrell and Hoban 2013). We start at where disabled people live, with their concerns and resources, and ask the question 'what is disabling for them there?' (Ingstad and Whyte 2007: 3).

Background

Rural poverty accounts for nearly 63 per cent of poverty globally, reaching 90 per cent in some countries, such as Bangladesh and in sub-Saharan African countries (Khan 2001). Poverty remains a mainly rural phenomenon (UN Habitat 2006). Echoing these global spatial patterns of poverty, the majority of disabled people (60–75 per cent) live in rural areas, and 80 per cent of these in developing countries (WHO and World Bank 2011). Yet, disabled people are essentially invisible within global discourses of rural poverty and within development theories (see Potter et al. 2008 for example), even though recent situational analyses of disability worldwide state that disabled people are the largest, most marginalised and resource-poor social group in the world (WHO and World Bank 2011).

Developing countries such as Cambodia have been dominated by rural ways of life, agriculture and land-based economic activities. The transformation of a country's economy from one that is predominantly rural and agricultural to one that is dominantly urban, industrial and service orientated in composition is central to the notion of development (Mellor 1990: 70). Development practitioners and theorists broadly agree that growth in agriculture usually generates the greatest improvements for the poorest people, particularly in poor, agriculture-based economies (World Bank 2007; IFAD 2011: 2), and they argue that improvements in agricultural productivity drive industrialisation and development (Potter et al. 2008: 444).

Historically, agriculture-led development strategies have played a critical role in economic growth, poverty reduction and structural transformation; however, in the last three decades there has been consistent neglect of agricultural development for local benefit (Bezemer and Headly 2008). Agricultural development has largely promoted mono crop production for large export markets to stimulate foreign investment. This, in turn, has often left local economies dependent on global agricultural markets, with little local control and few benefits (see Mills and Davar 2016, in this volume). The potential for agriculture and rural development to play a lead role in locally sustained growth has thus only partly been realised. Overseas development aid in the agricultural and rural development sectors has declined dramatically since the 1980s when it constituted almost 43 per cent of total aid (Chimhowu 2013: 2). By 2009, about 7 per cent of total international development aid was dedicated to activities that directly related to food security and agricultural and rural development (Chimhowu 2013: 2). Furthermore, public spending in agriculture is lowest in agricultural-based countries while their share of agriculture in GDP is highest (World Bank 2007: 7).

Rural poverty will prevail for several decades to come (World Bank 2007: 6). In light of this, geographical theories of development are useful conceptual tools to understand the spatial differentiation inherent to globalised development and change processes, and their structurally determined rural-based disadvantage.

Geographies of Development and Spatial Inequity

Historical analysis of contemporary development patterns and processes of change reveals the plurality of such processes with increasing differentiation and inequality between population groups, places, countries and regions (Potter et al. 2008). The modernist ideal that globalisation will lead to the benign development and homogenisation of the world's regions in a spatially even, positive and efficient manner has not been realised. For too long development theory has considered rural and urban areas to be discrete physical and functional entities (Potter et al. 2008: 405).

Radical and Marxist theories of development suggest that spatial and social unevenness is more than an outcome of development but is intrinsic to development itself. For example, Marxist geographer Neil Smith (1984) argues that capitalism creates unevenness within itself, and is reflected in the unevenness of the global system. Capitalism tends to centralise, create monopolies and expand into new areas and markets with profits made in tandem with social and spatial inequalities. Some theorists posit that although such inequalities are efficient for growth, they inevitably lead to deeper regional and personal income and welfare inequities because internal and external economies of scale perpetuate unevenness (Myrdal 1957). Furthermore, Friedmann's (1966) core–periphery model suggests that development becomes increasingly concentrated in space over time. Inequality will always exceed the so-called trickle down from the developed 'core' to the 'backward regions' (see Hirschman 1958) and results in urban-centric development. In the absence of state intervention to counteract these 'normal tendencies' of the capitalist system, such inequalities intensify (Hirschman 1958), as is evident in Cambodia (see Hughes and Un 2011; World Bank 2013).

Furthermore, dependency theory (Frank 1966) proposes that development and underdevelopment go hand in hand as intrinsically related manifestations of the contradictions of capitalist development. Dependency theory suggests that capitalist accumulation and divisions of labour occur at a global scale where political and economic structures serve dominant capitalist powers and urban metropolises. Underdevelopment is a direct outcome of reciprocal development elsewhere and stronger ties to core metropolises are associated with greater impediments to development in peripheral, rural agricultural areas. Underdeveloped rural areas are thus at the bottom of a hierarchy of dependency within the international division of labour (Hettne 1995).

In development planning and practice, rural areas have been regarded as true peripheries—areas that have been left behind, or as dependency theory posits held back by the accumulation of capital elsewhere (Potter and Unwin 1989: 324). Development planners have promoted urban-to-urban, or at best large urban-to-small urban, growth and insufficient attention has been given to urban–rural links and interactions. Such centre-orientated patterns of growth have further concentrated decision-making and capital both socially and spatially (Potter and Unwin 1989: 324), resulting in an 'urban bias' in development (Lipton 1977; World Bank 2007).

Lipton's theory of urban bias suggests that resource allocation has reflected urban priorities rather than equity or efficiency considerations. Urban bias theory effectively connects numbers, prices and geographies of power (Lipton 1977: 6). 'Price twists' transfer wealth from rural toward urban areas; goods originating in rural areas and sold in urban areas are underpriced, while goods flowing from urban to rural areas are overpriced against an assumed free-market price (Lipton 2005). Lipton argues that almost all reductions in poverty over the last 300 years have followed improvements in rural incomes due to increased productivity of small farms. Public policy to alleviate rural poverty must therefore focus on transforming the agricultural sector through major resource inputs and land redistribution (World Bank 2007), a policy direction currently advocated by the World Bank (2013) to address poverty in Cambodia. Such recommendations assume that agriculture is central to poverty reduction and development, an assumption that is increasingly questioned (see for example Rigg 2006; IFAD 2011).

In many developing countries, including Cambodia, rural areas are changing. Non-farm opportunities have expanded and greater mobility and migration have led to delocalised livelihoods that are more and more disconnected from farming and the land (Rigg 2006; Jones and Corbridge 2010). Unprecedented rural–urban migration has occurred in the emerging economies of Brazil, Russia, China, India, Vietnam and South Africa (International Organization for Migration 2013), and the reclassification of rural areas into urban areas is accelerating the rate of urbanisation (UN Habitat 2006). On many peri-urban fringes agricultural land has been lost to industry, particularly in areas where main roads and transport systems link industry to major cities, ports, domestic, cross-border and export markets. Rural and urban areas are increasingly connected and land ownership no longer guarantees household well-being (Rigg 2006; IFAD 2011). Given these shifting social and economic landscapes, access to non-land-based opportunities, diverse income sources and capabilities, such as education, skills and social networks, are increasingly important for households to exit poverty (see Fitzgerald and Sovannarith 2007 on Cambodia). Access to new and emerging economic opportunities associated with the occupational and industrial structure of growth and development is determined by household-level human capital, material and social resources, and this is completely disrupting the way of life in rural communities.

While these structural, political-economy perspectives broadly map how macro-level development processes produce spatial inequalities and rural disadvantage, neoliberal conceptions of development as governed by economic rationality increasingly underpin globalisation, development and international aid (Norman 2011).

While neoliberal marketisation creates new opportunities for economic advancement and even success for some, Davis (2011) argues that in rural Cambodia it is simultaneously destroying older coping strategies and reducing both the incentive and the basis for collective action. Thus in each case, the very poorest are left marginalised. Rising inequality and contested rural–urban relations are generating considerable discontent (Davis 2011). There is a growing need for geographies of development and development planners to better understand how the interactions and convergence between rural and urban areas, globalisation and neoliberal reforms are reshaping macro-structural contexts, and in turn household-level decisions regarding the use of labour, financial, social, economic and other resources that shape access to new opportunities.

Current globalised and neoliberal economic changes are characterised by insecurity and material hardship for many workers (Wilton and Schuer 2006: 188), with little knowledge on the impacts for disabled people (Eide and Ingstad 2011). Industrial capitalism and contemporary economies are geared toward an able-body/mind norm and have resulted in the systematic exclusion of disabled people (Gleeson 1999). Critical geographies must examine if disabled people's inclusion in globalised developments will provide them with a living wage, job security, dignity and meaningful social inclusion. Current approaches to disability sit at this sticky interface between market and social justice discourses with the former emphasising economic rationalism and globalisation, and the latter, citizenship, autonomy, choice and inclusion.

Disability as Socio-Spatial

Critical human geographies suggest a mutually reinforcing and reciprocal relationship between people and place, 'the social' and 'the spatial', whereby place is the outcome of dynamic social relations and power struggles between groups in society (Harvey 1996). Critical geographies articulate these socio-spatial processes where space is both an outcome and medium of social relations (Massey et al. 1999). Furthermore, spatialised processes are key to the production and maintenance of embodied identities such as disability.

Critical geographies of disability draw attention to the particular socio-spatial dynamics that entrench and distinguish disabled people's oppression from that of other social groups (see Gleeson 1999). Physical and social space(s) are politicised space(s) that are dynamic, ambiguous and contested (Kitchin 1998: 344). Space and spatial organisation reflect power relations and ideologies that underpin the (re) production of disabling social relations. Built environments are social and cultural products embedded in relations of, and spatialised contestations over, power that can be challenged and altered (Kitchin 1998). Space is thus imbued with political possibility, oppression and contestation. Viewing built environments as negotiable, dynamic and changeable can help to dislodge entrenched and disabling power relations. Changes to space alter social relations and society itself (Imrie 1996: 13).

This ‘relational’ view of space and place is an appropriate starting point for understanding disability and rurality, and the effects of globalisation on the living conditions of disabled people.

The Socio-Spatial Politics of Disability and Rurality in Cambodia

Historical, Cultural and Economic Context

The aftermath of almost three decades of war and civil unrest continues to impact on Cambodian society and development. Although soldiers and civilians were maimed in war, particularly by land mines, the greatest cause of disability in Cambodia is poverty and the general breakdown of health services (NIS 2004). Rurality holds a particular place in the historical, political and cultural landscape of Cambodia. Entire cities were evacuated during the Khmer Rouge regime and the population were forced to become rural farmers in a Maoist revolution that attempted to return Cambodia to ‘year zero’ (Chandler 1993). Instead, it resulted in the deaths of between one-and-a-half and two million people due to mass killings, disease and starvation (Ledgerwood 1992). Unresolved trauma and mental health issues are rife and intergenerational as young people today carry parental grief (McLaughlin and Wickeri 2012).

In Cambodian society, disability (*peka*) symbolizes karma and the performance of bad deeds in a previous incarnation that must be repaid in this life. Villages equate disability with suffering and while they recognise the multiple challenges and stigma associated with disability, karmic beliefs individualise and de-politicise disability (Gartrell 2004). Villagers respond to disabled people with the contradictory emotions of pity and love, and seek to protect and look after a household member with disability who is typically considered to be unproductive (Gartrell 2004).

Despite favourable economic indicators, Cambodia is one of the poorest countries in Asia, with an estimated per capita income of US$830 in 2011 (World Bank 2013). In the last decade, Cambodia has experienced ‘impressive economic growth’ which the World Bank (2013) argues has been pro-poor in its development approach and, in turn, has reduced economic inequality. Just over a fifth of the population (20.5 per cent) are said to live below the poverty line[1] with many remaining highly vulnerable to small economic shocks that could quickly return them to poverty (World Bank 2013). The introduction of a free-market economy in the 1990s has seen an increase in land ownership and landlessness, suggesting that although national economic indicators have improved some people are becoming poorer (Taksdal 2011).

[1] The World Bank (2013: 94) defines the total poverty line as equal to the food (extreme) poverty line plus an allowance for a minimum amount of non-food goods and services (housing, clothes, personal goods, entertainment and so forth). Determining the minimum amount of goods and services is done indirectly as there is no universally agreed-upon minimum.

Rural Poverty and Exclusion from Emerging Employment Opportunities

Poverty in Cambodia is mainly located in the countryside: approximately 90 per cent of Cambodia's poor live in rural areas, where the majority (80.5 per cent) of the population live (World Bank 2013). Disability rates are also higher in rural areas (NIS 2004). The poorest households tend to be headed by those employed in agriculture, a sector that remains poor and unstable (Economic Institute of Cambodia 2008: 5). The agricultural share of GDP has declined from 44 per cent in the mid-1990s to less than 29 per cent in 2004. At the same time, the industrial sector has expanded, driven by the garment industry; by 2004 industrial output had doubled to 27 per cent of GDP (World Bank 2013).

Flailing and seasonal agricultural employment leaves a large number of idle, able-bodied 18–25-year -olds with minimal skills and poor education seeking non-agricultural employment in the capital city, Phnom Penh, or in neighbouring Thailand. The feminisation of this workforce, especially among migrant workers employed in the manufacturing sector, such as in garment factories, is well documented (Chammartin 2002; Hegde et al. 2012). The receipt of remittances from migrant workers to household members enables them to remain in rural villages and to improve their diet, quality of housing and access to consumer items such as televisions, mobile phones and motorbikes (Fitzgerald and Sovannarith 2007). At the household level, income from remittances improves health and well-being, but village-level infrastructure such as roads, electricity and health services remains unchanged (Fitzgerald and Sovannarith 2007). The structural shifts in the Cambodian economy are reshaping employment opportunities, parental relationships and aspirations for their children, and the living standards of those able and unable to access these opportunities.

Able-bodied young people are keen to earn an income in the new industries, even though the employment opportunities may render them vulnerable to new forms of risk, exploitation and abuse, particularly for women (Cambodian Centre for Human Rights (CCHR) 2014). Many young people, however, experience new-found freedoms away from their family and quiet village life, and have ready access to consumer goods (Hegde et al. 2012). When able-bodied family members are in paid employment outside rural environments, disabled people remain at home with the elderly and children. In the absence of able-bodied family members to assist with household responsibilities, disabled people inevitably engage in menial unpaid, low-status domestic jobs that fulfil the social expectations of family and others.

Disabled people are frequently excluded from new economic opportunities and the social changes they bring. Typically, employment in the industrial or manufacturing sectors is not physically accessible for disabled people, and if transport and assistance are required, it is unavailable and unaffordable. Parents are concerned that companies will not accept their disabled child as an employee, and that they will not be safe in the workplace, particularly young women with a disability who are vulnerable to abuse in the workplace and shared housing facilities (pers. comm.,

Mrs Chenda,[2] interviewee and parent of a woman with disability, May 2014; see also CCHR 2014).

Spatial Disadvantage: Rurality and Disability

Few studies document the spatialities associated with rurality and disability, and yet in Cambodia the ruralisation of poverty, especially disabled people's poverty, is well recognised (Gartrell 2004; Thomas 2005). Gender differences in poverty rates have been mapped but data on disability prevalence, patterns and associated social characteristics is unreliable and prevents meaningful analysis (Thomas 2005). Recent reports on poverty in Cambodia, such as the World Bank 2013 report, fail to include disability.

Village location, that is the degree of remoteness and accessibility to basic social, education and other services, and geographical endowment are significant determinants of community well-being (Fitzgerald and Sovannarith 2007; Taksdal 2011). These structural and spatial determinants shape well-being but have been poorly examined. In the only identified study on the development challenges associated with place of residence, physical distance and poverty, the World Bank *Cambodia Poverty Assessment* found that approximately 21 per cent of people in the poorest quintile travel more than 5 km to a health clinic, while only 14 per cent of the richest quintile travel that far; and about 6 per cent of the poorest two quintiles live more than 5 km from the nearest road, compared to only 1.4 per cent in the richest quintile (World Bank 1999: 1). Furthermore, children in the poorest quintile have to walk longer distances to school—on average 7 km to the nearest lower secondary school outside the village, compared to 4 km for children in the richest quintile. Limited and poor-quality rural roads aggravate physical access to school (World Bank 1999: 4), particularly for disabled children.

Disability-specific research has found that residential location shapes access to socio-economic opportunities (World Bank 1999; Gartrell 2004; Taksdal 2011). Poverty continues to force the poorest to live with landmines in former front-line areas that are probably still infested with unexploded ordnance in north-west Cambodia (Taksdal 2011). Farmers in these so-called new areas clear bush and farm mine-suspected rice fields. They are too poor to hire others to do the dangerous work of ploughing rice fields in wet and soft soil, and too poor to avoid the dangerous land themselves (Taksdal 2011: 191). Households with a disabled child living remotely are generally poorer, and have less food security, low nutritional intake and poor access to clean water, sanitation and health services (World Bank 1999).

Disabled people's mobility beyond their immediate neighbourhood is limited; the further they are from their homes, the less mobile they become. Those with impaired mobility may be housebound for weeks at a time when roads are extremely muddy and impassable (Taksdal 2011). Furthermore, village micro-geographies

[2] Pseudonyms are used in all interview quotes.

restrict disabled people's movement to particular routes. Small paths, 'bridges'—often several pieces of bamboo, beams of wood or tree trunks tied together—and tracks running between houses and along the buns of paddy fields are unpassable, difficult or dangerous for disabled people to navigate (Gartrell 2004). The extent to which these micro-geographies shape disabled people's participation in local socio-economic opportunities and cultural activities is poorly examined.

When disabled people rely upon household members, relatives and in some cases neighbours to accompany and assist their travel to school and other places, such as health centres, travel is a negotiated socio-power relationship and makes access socially difficult (Gartrell 2004; Gartrell and Hoban 2013). Disabled people may lower themselves to their 'assistant', be very passive and adopt the 'disabled role' (Oliver 1993: 55) or alternatively draw upon feelings of pity, guilt and responsibility in their 'helper', in which case the disabled person has a semblance of control (see Gartrell and Hoban 2013 on the politics of pity). In the absence of 'assistants', disabled people must have financial resources, which they frequently do not, to pay for a motorbike taxi to take them to their destination. Social relations and physical space can lock disabled people in their 'place' of passivity and dependence upon others without access to basic socio-economic, political and cultural opportunities. Geographers refer to the 'friction of distance' as a constraint rendering women dependent on local employment (Hanson and Pratt 1995: 10); disabled people are similarly constrained by physical space and social barriers that, together with poverty, restrict them to the home.

Contribution to Household Economies and Local Employment

The commonly used Khmer expression 'solving the problem of living' encapsulates the centrality of work to physical life. Disabled people's economic marginalisation from dominant forms of employment in rural areas—largely agricultural work—leaves them feeling 'outside of society':

> If we have work to do, our life is valued … our relatives won't look down at us, no one dares … we can live in their society. They always look down at us when we are disabled … we can't live in their society. (Ta Youk, 60-year-old man with a mobility impairment)

Contribution to the household economy is a key determinant of disabled people's physical and emotional well-being, and their feelings of worthiness and entitlement to draw on household resources:

> How can I eat when I can't earn income myself? (Peap, a 35-year-old woman with a mobility impairment)

Many disabled children never attend school as their parents think that it would be a 'waste of money' because children with disability would be 'unable to learn anything' and may be the object of bullying by other children. Disabled people may not have the physical strength and mobility required to participate in the most readily available form of employment—agricultural and labouring work. Poor access to school leaves disabled people without the skills and social networks necessary to access more physically appropriate types of employment available locally, and referred to by villagers as 'big work', such as office-based work with the government or private enterprises. 'Big work' is performed by 'big people': those with power, material assets and social networks (Gartrell 2010).

Better-off households and those that have exited poverty have many adult income earners, multiple and diverse income-generation opportunities and the capacity to save and invest assets to protect the household from crisis and other unexpected events, and to fund investments in human capital such as education and health (Fitzgerald and Sovannarith 2007: 25). Social networks such as patronage relationships are increasingly important to households' upward social mobility because they provide employment opportunities, assist households in building wealth and help them secure favourable outcomes in local decision-making, conflicts and legal disputes (Fitzgerald and Sovannarith 2007: 25). In contrast, disabled people are typically socially invisible, politically silent and without a voice (see Cambodian Disabled People's Organisation 2013), particularly if they are poor.

Villagers refer to disabled people, particularly disabled women and those who do not financially contribute to their households, as 'small' and socially 'weak' people who can only perform 'small work' (Gartrell 2010). This type of work requires minimal skills and is home or village based. Women can combine small work with their domestic and childcare responsibilities. Small work keeps people poor because they only earn enough to meet their daily needs. Poorer households are more reliant on waged labour and small work (Fitzgerald and Sovannarith 2007: 25). Chronically poor households are more likely to have old, disabled or single female household heads, few income earners, more dependants, limited or no land and no capacity to invest in human capital, and are more likely to depend on common property resources (Fitzgerald and Sovannarith 2007: 25).

Waiting at Home

In the absence of accessible employment and without financial capital to establish small work such as a micro-enterprise, many disabled people 'wait at home', a Khmer phrase used to describe the unpaid home-based work typically performed by women. Waiting at home includes cooking, cleaning, collecting the firewood, childcare, guarding the home and keeping the home compound clean and, if space and resources permit, planting small crops. Two other 'work' categories are a part of waiting at home: 'minding the chickens' and 'cleaning the pots and pans'. These categories are considered to be of lower status than waiting at home and may be outsourced to a domestic worker in a 'food for work' capacity. Disabled people describe how villagers give them the job of minding the chickens—that is, keeping the chickens from eating rice husks—the very lowest status and unpaid 'work' (Gartrell 2010).

When waiting at home, disabled people describe feeling dependent and 'difficult in the heart', a Khmer phrase referring to depression, particularly when their impairments prevent them from doing the work of waiting at home (Gartrell 2004):

> I sit at home like a pig waiting to be fed. (42-year-old woman with a neurological impairment)
>
> If I stay at home … I feel complex … difficult in the heart because I have no work, no money and am not happy. (65-year-old bed ridden woman with a mobility impairment)

Restricted to waiting at home and performing poorly paid small work keep disabled people, but particularly women, in a state of poverty and reinforce their low status, at the very bottom of the Khmer social hierarchy. Like disabled women, men who are confined to the home and excluded from male gender roles as the performers of 'big work' describe feeling bored, frustrated, hopeless and in some instances suicidal. They have few choices: to depend entirely on others—typically wives, mothers or daughters—or perform low-status small work that at least gives them some money. The home space may, however, feel 'safe' as disabled people can experience negative social attitudes and feel ashamed and embarrassed when in public spaces. Disabled people tend to withdraw socially from interaction with others (Taksdal 2011).

If there is family violence within the household or a mental health problem (35 per cent of Cambodians experience a mental illness (McLaughlin and Wickeri 2012)), disabled household members are doubly vulnerable as they typically make small and non-financial contributions to their households and are unable to leave violent home spaces (Gartrell and Hoban, unpublished report). All household members are stigmatised when violence occurs and this negatively impacts informal social networks that are key to securing employment (Hegde et al. 2012).

Villagers consistently judge impairments that do not impede physical strength and mobility, such as deafness or mild learning disabilities, as less disabling (Gartrell 2010). Deaf people, for example, work in agriculture, fish and cart wood, are seamstresses and engage in many other productive tasks but they too experience social isolation (Thomas 2005). In this sense, rural life can be an enabling space, even though they are paid less than their able-bodied counterparts.

Conclusion

Rural–urban boundaries are increasingly blurred as urbanisation and development processes expand and encroach upon geographically and demographically shrinking rural areas. Rural residents have to adapt to the local impacts of the global economy and neoliberal reforms irrespective of their inclusion in, and the benefits of, such growth and change. New economic developments circumvent disabled people as they seek able-bodied youth for waged labour. Disabled people remain invisible, in poorly valued, unpaid, feminised domestic home spaces with few, if any, opportunities for social and economic advancement. Households with a disabled member are likely to fall into chronic intergenerational poverty when living in poor rural areas where the majority of the population lack ready access to education, health services, employment and viable livelihoods.

Participation in globalised economies demands mobility and freedom of movement and yet disabled people are increasingly entrapped, stuck in their place. The discrimination disabled people experience is a socio-spatial process that isolates and restricts them to the home, where household-level social relations determine disabled people's access to structurally determined life opportunities.

Greater theoretical and practical attention needs to be paid to the interaction between macro-structural changes and micro geographies of mobility at the household level to ensure that disabled people have access to basic social developments and emerging global industries. Disabled people will continue to experience multiple invisibilities associated with disability and rural-based disadvantage until they are actively included in socio-spatial analysis of economic change in increasingly globalised and urbanised societies. Analysis of household-level sociopolitical processes is critical because these shape social relations, physical movement and access to life's opportunities—education, employment and health care. Cambodia will be included in the commencement of the single market for economic development in ASEAN countries in 2015, making these issues evermore urgent. While access to the open-market economies of Asia may foster economic forms of inclusion and notions of citizenship, the social relations and structures of power and exclusion that affect the lives of the poor, including those with disabilities, continue to be neglected.

References

Bezemer, D., & Headly, D. (2008). Agriculture, development and urban Bias. *World Development, 36*(8), 1342–1364.

Cambodian Centre for Human Rights (CCHR). (2014). *Workers rights are human rights: Policy brief: The garment industry in Cambodia*. Phnom Penh: Cambodian Centre for Human Rights.

Cambodian Disabled People's Organisation. (2013). *Accessible elections for persons with disabilities in Cambodia*. Phnom Penh: Cambodian Disabled People's Organisation.

Chammartin, G. M. F. (2002). *The feminization of international migration*. International Labour Organisation, unpublished report.

Chandler, D. P. (1993). *A history of Cambodia*. Boulder, CO: Westview Press.

Chimhowu, A. (2013). *Aid for agriculture and rural development in the global South. A changing landscape with new players and challenges*. Working Paper No. 2013/14. Helsinki: United Nations University-World Institute for Development Economics Research.

Davis, E. W. (2011). Imagined parasites: Flows of monies and spirits. In C. Hughes & K. Un (Eds.), *Cambodia's economic transformation* (pp. 310–329). Copenhagen: NIAS Press.

Economic Institute of Cambodia. (2008). *Cambodia country economic memorandum: Sustaining rapid growth in a challenging environment. Cambodia's labour market and employment*. Phnom Penh: World Bank.

Eide, A. H., & Ingstad, B. (Eds.). (2011). *Disability and poverty. A global challenge*. Bristol: Polity Press.

Fitzgerald, I., & Sovannarith, S. (2007). *Moving out of poverty? Trends in community well-being and household mobility in nine Cambodian villages*. Phnom Penh: Cambodia Development Research Institute.

Frank, G. (1966, September 17–30). The development of underdevelopment. *Monthly Review*.
Friedmann, J. (1966). *Regional development policy: A case study of Venezuela*. Cambridge, MA: MIT Press.
Gartrell, A. (2004). *Flying on hope: The lived experience of disability in rural Cambodia*. Doctoral thesis, University of Melbourne.
Gartrell, A. (2010). 'A frog in a well': The exclusion of people with disability from work in Cambodia. *Disability & Society, 25*(3), 289–301.
Gartrell, A., & Hoban, E. (2013). Structural vulnerability, disability and access to non-governmental organization services in rural Cambodia. *Journal of Social Work in Disability and Rehabilitation, 12*(3), 194–212.
Gleeson, B. (1999). *Geographies of disability*. London: Routledge.
Hanson, S., & Pratt, G. (1995). *Gender, work and space*. London: Routledge.
Harvey, D. (1996). *Justice, nature and the geography of difference*. Cambridge, MA: Wiley-Blackwell.
Hegde, S., Hoban, E., & Nevill, A. (2012). Unsafe abortion as a birth control method: Maternal mortality risks among unmarried Cambodian migrant women on the Thai-Cambodia border. *Asia Pacific Journal of Public Health, 24*(6), 989–1001.
Hettne, B. (1995). *Development theory and the three worlds*. London: Longman.
Hirschman, A. O. (1958). *The strategy of economic development*. New Haven, CT: Yale University Press.
Hughes, C., & Un, K. (2011). *Cambodia's economic transformation*. Copenhagen: NIAS Press.
Imrie, R. (1996). *Disability and the city. International perspectives*. London: Paul Chapman Publishing.
Ingstad, B., & Whyte, S. R. (2007). *Disability in local and global worlds*. Berkeley, CA: University of California Press.
International Fund for Agricultural Development (IFAD). (2011). *Rural poverty report*. Italy: IFAD.
International Organization for Migration. (2013). *World migration report 2013: Migrant wellbeing and development*. Geneva: IOM.
Jones, G. A., & Corbridge, S. (2010). The continuing debate about urban bais. The thesis, its critics, its influence and its implications for poverty-reduction strategies. *Progress in Development Studies, 10*(1), 1–18.
Khan, M. H. (2001). *Rural poverty in developing countries—Implications for public policy*. Economic Issues No 26. Washington, DC: International Monetary Fund.
Kitchin, R. (1998). 'Out of place', 'knowing one's place': Space, power and the exclusion of disabled people. *Disability & Society, 13*(3), 343–356.
Ledgerwood, J. (1992). *Analysis of the situation of women in Cambodia. Research on women in Khmer society*. Phnom Penh: Consultancy for UNICEF.
Lipton, M. (1977). *Why poor people stay poor: Urban bias in world development*. Cambridge, MA: Harvard University Press.
Lipton, M. (2005). Urban bias. In T. Forsyth (Ed.), *Encyclopedia of international development*. London: Routledge.
Massey, M., Allen, J., & Sarre, P. (Eds.). (1999). *Human geography today*. Cambridge: Polity Press.
McLaughlin, D., & Wickeri, E. (2012). *Mental health and human rights in Cambodia*. New York: Leitner Centre.
Mellor, J. W. (1990). Agriculture on the road to industrialization. In C. K. Eicher & J. M. Staatz (Eds.), *Agricultural development in the third world* (pp. 70–88). Baltimore, MD: John Hopkins University Press.
Mills, C., & Davar, B. (2016). A local critique of global mental health. In S. Grech & K. Soldatic (Eds.), *Disability in the global South: The critical handbook* (pp. xx–xx). New York: Springer.
Myrdal, G. (1957). *Economic theory and underdeveloped areas*. London: Duckworth.

National Institute of Statistics (NIS). (2004). *Cambodia socio-economic survey 2004*. Phnom Penh: Ministry of Planning.

Norman, D. J. (2011). Neoliberal strategies of poverty reduction in Cambodia: The case of Microfinance. In C. Hughes & K. Un (Eds.), *Cambodia's economic transformation* (pp. 161–181). Copenhagen: NIAS Press.

Oliver, M. (1993). Disability and dependency: A creation of industrial societies? In J. Swain, V. Finkelstein, S. French, & M. Oliver (Eds.), *Disabling barriers—Enabling environments* (pp. 49–60). London: Sage.

Potter, R. B., Binns, T., Elliott, J. A., & Smith, D. (2008). *Geographies of development. An introduction to development studies*. Essex, UK: Pearson, Prentice Hall.

Potter, R. B., & Unwin, T. (Eds.). (1989). *The geography of urban-rural interaction in developing countries*. London: Routledge.

Rigg, J. (2006). Land, farming, livelihoods, and poverty: Rethinking the links in the rural South. *World Development, 34*(1), 180–202.

Sen, A. (1999). *Development as freedom*. New York: Knopf.

Smith, N. (1984). *Uneven development: Nature, capital and the production of space*. Athens, GA: University of Georgia Press.

Taksdal, M. (2011). 'My story started with food shortage and hunger': Living with landmines in Cambodia. In A. H. Eide & B. Ingstad (Eds.), *Disability and poverty. A global challenge* (pp. 189–205). Bristol: The Policy Press.

Thomas, P. (2005). *Poverty reduction and development in Cambodia: Enabling disabled people to play a role*. London: Disability KAR Knowledge and Research.

UN Habitat. (2006). *Report on the third session of the World Urban Forum, Vancouver, Canada, June 19–23*. Retrieved November 7, 2014, from http://mirror.unhabitat.org/downloads/docs/3406_98924_WUF3-Report.pdf

Wilton, R., & Schuer, S. (2006). Towards socio-spatial inclusion? Disabled people, neoliberalism and the contemporary labour market. *Area, 38*(2), 186–195.

World Bank. (1999). *Cambodia poverty assessment*. Poverty Reduction and Economic Management Sector Unit and Human Development Sector Unit. East Asia and Pacific Region: The World Bank.

World Bank. (2007). *World development report 2008. Agriculture for development*. Washington, DC: The World Bank.

World Bank. (2013). *Where have all the poor gone? Cambodia poverty assessment 2013*. Washington, DC: The World Bank.

World Health Organization (WHO). (2011). *World report on disability*. Geneva: WHO and the World Bank.

Chapter 22
Disability and HIV: Critical Intersections

Ruth Evans, Yaw Adjei-Amoako, and Agnes Atim

Introduction

The relationship between HIV and disability is complex, but critical, because disabled people are vulnerable to HIV infection, while people living with HIV are at high risk of impairment. But this relationship remains largely unexplored in disability studies, epidemiology, global health, development and associated fields, and disability issues have been largely neglected in global and national HIV policy responses. The United Nations Convention on the Rights of Persons with Disabilities (CRPD) does not explicitly refer to HIV in the definition of disability. However, UNAIDS et al. (2009: 1) note that:

> States are required to recognize that where persons living with HIV (asymptomatic or symptomatic) have impairments which, in interaction with the environment, results in stigma, discrimination or other barriers to their participation, they can fall under the protection of the Convention.

In 2009, UNAIDS in collaboration with the World Health Organization (WHO) and the Office of the UN High Commissioner for Human Rights highlighted the lack of data on the prevalence and incidence of HIV among disabled people and the need for all HIV programmes to address the concerns of disabled people. Yet disability and disabled people were mentioned in only one paragraph of the 110-page UNAIDS (2012) *Report on the Global AIDS Epidemic* and are not mentioned at all in the 2013 report, despite considerable data and attention paid to other

R. Evans (✉) • Y. Adjei-Amoako
Department of Geography and Environmental Science, University of Reading, Reading, UK
e-mail: r.evans@reading.ac.uk; adjeiyawa@yahoo.co.uk

A. Atim
Hope Development Initiative, Kampala, Uganda
e-mail: agnesapea@gmail.com

S. Grech, K. Soldatic (eds.), *Disability in the Global South*,
International Perspectives on Social Policy, Administration, and Practice,
DOI 10.1007/978-3-319-42488-0_22

vulnerable populations, such as children (aged under 15) and young people (aged 15–24) and 'key populations at higher risk', such as sex workers, people who inject drugs and men who have sex with men (UNAIDS 2013: 32). This continuing lack of data on HIV prevalence among disabled people globally obscures their specific needs and requirements in accessing HIV prevention, treatment, care and support services. It also makes invisible the links between the situation of people living with HIV and disabled people, overlooking these complex issues.

People living with HIV[1] (PLHIV) are not usually defined as disabled people, unless they have specific long-term impairments, despite some countries (including the UK and Australia) according protection to PLHIV under national disability legislation (DRC 2005; Hanass-Hancock and Nixon 2009). The disability movement has been reluctant to regard PLHIV as disabled people (Evans and Atim 2011), largely due to social model perspectives that reject the notion of disability as an 'illness' (Morris 1991; Wendell 2001). Furthermore, Groce (2005) argues that fear of the potential double-stigmatisation of disability and HIV has led many in the disability community to avoid issues of HIV. Similarly, PLHIV rarely identify as disabled, unless they have permanent physical impairments resulting from HIV that affect their quality of life. Shakespeare et al. (1996) argue that PLHIV are not prepared to identify as disabled because their understanding of disability is based on the medical model and is stigmatised. Thus, HIV activists, experts and advocates may avoid being associated with disabled people because of their own misperceptions and stigma about disability (Hanass-Hancock 2009; Groce et al. 2013).

This chapter explores this complex and critical relationship between disability and HIV, and the implications for disabled people with HIV in terms of their access to healthcare in the global South. First, we discuss conceptualisations of disability, bodies and health identities, including those of PLHIV. We then examine disabled people's vulnerability to HIV, including violence, stigma and access to sexual health and HIV prevention and treatment programmes. We focus our discussion of the relationship between disability and HIV in sub-Saharan Africa, the continent that has been most affected by the HIV epidemic to date, and examine recent policy initiatives by disabled people's organisations and networks of PLHIV to tackle discrimination and advance their claim for the right to health. We analyse the policy context of disability and HIV in Ghana and Uganda specifically in order to provide an understanding of differing local and national contexts of vulnerability, activism and policy engagement on these issues.

[1] Although the frequently used PLHA acronym includes both 'HIV' and 'AIDS', UNAIDS terminology guidelines (2011) propose use of the term that is most specific and appropriate in the context to avoid confusion between HIV (a virus) and AIDS (a clinical syndrome). People living with HIV and the HIV epidemic are the preferred terms and AIDS should be used only when referring to a person with a clinical diagnosis of AIDS or to national policy responses. We have therefore used the acronym 'PLHIV' throughout this chapter.

Disability, Health and HIV: The Medical and Social Models of Disability

Disability politics and social theories of the body, health and disability that developed since the 1970s have influenced development approaches based on multidimensional understandings of poverty that aim to enhance human capacities and well-being. Disability activists in the global North rejected medical, rehabilitative models of disability which were based on assumptions that disabled people suffer primarily from physical and/or mental abnormalities that medicine can, and should, treat, cure or at least prevent (Oliver 1990). Within the dominant 'medical model' approach, disability is perceived as an 'individual misfortune' or 'tragedy'. The disability movement in the global North (led by mainly UK-based activists and allies) instead developed a 'social model' of disability to focus attention on the sociocultural, economic, political and spatial barriers to participation that disabled people experience (Oliver 1990). An individual's 'impairment' was seen as separate from the disabling social barriers that excluded disabled people. The social model thus focuses on changing society to facilitate the participation and inclusion of disabled people, rather than on efforts to 'rehabilitate' individuals and overcome biological constraints of the body (for further discussion of the social model, see Aramayo et al. 2016 in this volume).

While these understandings of disability have been crucial to improving accessibility, achieving equality of opportunity and securing disabled people's rights in the global North, commentators have questioned the appropriateness of applying western-centric social models of disability in the global South (McEwan and Butler 2007). Furthermore, there has been growing recognition of the need to investigate the interconnections between sociocultural representations of health, illness and disability and development processes at both a local and global scale (Power 2001; McEwan and Butler 2007). Although debates about disability and chronic illness within the social sciences have been largely dominated by urban, Anglophone and western-centric concerns to date, a growing literature has highlighted that understandings of bodies, disability and illness vary according to the economic, geopolitical, sociocultural and spatial context (Power 2001; Longhurst 2005). While most cultures ascribe to notions of a 'normal' or 'ideal' body or mind, the meanings attached to different illnesses and impairments and the social responses that are deemed appropriate are not universal.

Indeed, research from the global South is increasingly challenging northern framings of the disability debate (Connell 2011). Social model approaches to disability have been criticised for failing to acknowledge the materiality of the body, such as the effects of pain and impairment on people's everyday lives, and the impacts of structural violence, such as impairments resulting from processes of imperialism and colonisation (Grech 2011; Meekosha and Soldatic 2011). Meekosha and Soldatic (2011) argue that a politics of impairment is critical for understanding 'disability' in the global South. The separation of 'impairment' from 'disability' that underpins the social model can result in impairment being constructed as 'natural' (as opposed to disability which is viewed as 'social'). However, as Meekosha and Soldatic (2011: 1393) argue, 'impairment is not in fact always natural, but the outcome of deeply politicised processes of social dynamics *in* bodies that then become medicalised and then normalised through a raft of moral discursive and real practices'. They call for a 'politics of diversity within unity' (Meekosha and Soldatic 2011: 1392) as a central strategy of global mobilisation on disability and impairment.

Recent approaches have emphasised the need to understand the changing materiality of the body and embodied experiences of health and illness in the construction of health identities (Parr and Butler 1999). Health identities are not fixed, but rather are constantly being produced, shaped and resisted through biomedical and lay discourses of health and illness, social interactions, embodied actions and resources that individuals can access within specific contexts (James and Hockey 2007). Such understandings of embodiment, health and illness have been shown to be particularly relevant in understanding the lived experiences of people with fluctuating and unpredictable chronic illnesses, such as multiple sclerosis, arthritis and HIV among others (Dyck 1995; Wendell 2001).

Drawing on Rabinow's concept of 'biosociality', Hughes (2009: 678) suggests that the interests and concerns of 'biosocial' groups and disabled people diverge in a number of ways. First, while the social model stance of the disability movement rejects biomedical discourses and has been reluctant to acknowledge lived experiences of impairment, biomedical diagnosis and impairment are central to the identification of 'biological citizens'. Second, biosocial groups are likely to 'gather and embrace the specialised medical and scientific knowledge associated with their condition' and medicine is perceived as a 'potential ally' in contrast to the disability activists. People living with HIV in Africa and others with chronic illness, for example, may identify with others on the basis of their biomedical diagnosis rather than according to a strategic notion of 'disability' and the focus of their activism may be on access to medical treatment, which may differ from the focus of disability activists (Evans and Atim 2011).

Differences in standpoint between disabled activists inspired by the social model and PLHIV are also revealed in the language each group uses to refer to themselves and in conceptualising disability and HIV. Disability activists and people living with HIV both favour terms which include the word 'people/persons' when referring to themselves. Disability activists inspired by the social model, especially those who are British and working in academia, tend to avoid the acronym 'PWDs' for 'persons with disabilities', despite the increasingly common use of this term by development agencies and in rights-based approaches. In contrast, the acronym 'PLHA' and more recently, PLHIV, is widely used by HIV activists and in the literature (Beckmann and Bujra 2010) and is not considered to dehumanise people living with HIV. Furthermore, negative attitudes, assumptions and discrimination affect the lives of both disabled people and PLHIV. The HIV literature tends to conceptualise this in terms of stigma or social processes of stigmatisation (Ogden and Nyblade 2005; Parker and Aggleton 2007), while the disability literature uses the language of 'psycho-emotional dimensions of disability' (Reeve 2002) and attitudinal barriers to equal participation in society.

Vulnerability to HIV and Access to Healthcare Among Disabled People

The 'vulnerability'[2] of disabled people to HIV has only recently been recognised and disability issues have been largely neglected in global and national HIV policy responses. Disabled people have been excluded from HIV prevention campaigns, clinical outreach efforts and social and economic support schemes (Groce et al. 2013). This is linked to underlying assumptions that disabled people are sexually inactive (Morris 1991; Shakespeare et al. 1996; Shuttleworth 2007), unlikely to use drugs and at less risk of rape and sexual violence. Recent research has refuted these assumptions and revealed that disabled people are at equal or higher risk of HIV than the wider population (Groce et al. 2013).

Some authors suggest that disabled people may be more vulnerable to HIV due to their low socio-economic status and heightened vulnerability to sexual violence, exploitation and abuse (Kvam and Braathen 2008; UNAIDS et al. 2009; Groce et al. 2013). Disabled women and girls, people with intellectual impairments and those staying in specialised institutions, schools or hospitals are identified as particularly vulnerable compared to non-disabled people. Disabled women and girls are often constructed as 'doubly marginalised' (Yeo and Moore 2003) on account of their disability and gender, which places them at greater risk of sexual violence, coercion and abuse, in turn increasing the risk of HIV transmission. Groce and Trasi (2004) suggest that in some cultures, disabled people may be raped in the belief that this will 'cure' an HIV-positive individual. Disabled people who belong to other socially marginalised groups, such as men who have sex with men, people who inject drugs or prisoners, are regarded as facing multiple layers of stigma, discrimination and social isolation which represent vulnerability factors for sexual exploitation and HIV risk behaviours (UNAIDS et al. 2009; Groce et al. 2013). Substance use (alcohol and drug) was found to be a risk factor, particularly for people with mental health problems, which increased the risk for unsafe sex and HIV infection (Groce et al. 2013).

Disabled people may also be more vulnerable to HIV due to limited knowledge of and access to sexual health and HIV prevention programmes. Article 25 of the Convention on the Rights of Persons with Disabilities (2006) commits state parties to:

> provide persons with disabilities with the same range, quality and standard of free or affordable health care and programmes as provided to other people, including in the area of sexual and reproductive health and population-based programmes.

[2] We recognise the contested, complex notion of 'vulnerability' within disability studies (Burghardt 2013). While being categorised as 'vulnerable' may have social and practical consequences in terms of being regarded as having high support needs that should be met through the provision of services, support and other resources, it may also serve to construct particular groups as passive recipients of service provision and deny their agency.

Despite this commitment from national governments to equal access to healthcare, disabled people face a number of barriers to accessing healthcare in the global South (see Swartz and Bantjes 2016, in this volume). These include stigma and negative attitudes of service providers who lack knowledge, awareness and training about the specific needs of disabled people; physical inaccessibility of clinics, hospitals and other healthcare settings and transport costs, especially in remote rural areas; and a lack of sign-language facilities or availability of information in alternative formats such as Braille, audio or plain language (UNAIDS et al. 2009; Trani et al. 2011; Van Rooy et al. 2012). In addition, the confidentiality of disabled people may be compromised in healthcare settings, including in HIV testing and counselling services, due to the need for a personal assistant or a sign-language interpreter to be present in order to access HIV-related services.

Research suggests that disabled people often have limited sexual health awareness due to low levels of literacy, poor access to education and inaccessible sexual and reproductive health education, HIV prevention resources and sexual health advice and testing centres (Hanass-Hancock and Nixon 2009; UNAIDS et al. 2009; WHO 2010). Groce and colleagues (2013) demonstrate that studies comparing disabled people to non-disabled peers show that disabled people have significantly lower levels of HIV knowledge. Attitudinal barriers on the part of service providers may restrict disabled people's access to sexual and reproductive healthcare, HIV testing and prevention information (Shakespeare et al. 1996; UNAIDS et al. 2009; Groce et al. 2013).

Many disabled children have poor access to education in the global South, which restricts their access to sexual and reproductive health education provided in mainstream school settings. Low literacy levels and a lack of HIV prevention information in accessible formats (such as Braille, sign language and audio versions or other visual formats that are accessible to those with intellectual impairments) reduce disabled people's ability to protect themselves from HIV and other sexually transmitted infections, despite evidence that peer education and specifically designed HIV prevention programmes for disabled people are successful in improving HIV knowledge and reducing risk behaviours (Groce et al. 2013).

In addition to barriers to accessing healthcare, there is evidence that disabled people living with HIV may be given lower priority in accessing antiretroviral therapy and other HIV treatment, and care and support compared to other PLHIV in resource-limited settings (UNAIDS et al. 2009; Groce et al. 2013). Even when disabled people are receiving HIV treatment, health professionals may not pay enough attention to potentially negative drug interactions between HIV treatment and the medications that disabled people are taking, and the fact that some medications may actually worsen the health status of people with mental health conditions, including depression (UNAIDS et al. 2009). There is a need for in-depth qualitative research to inform the development of appropriate interventions to tackle these crucial issues of discrimination in access to healthcare and the rights of disabled people to HIV treatment, care and support.

Disability and HIV Activism and Access to Healthcare in Sub-Saharan Africa

Organisations and networks of PLHIV in the eastern and southern African countries most affected by the epidemic have grown rapidly in recent years in order to campaign for their rights to healthcare. The principle of the 'Greater involvement of people living with or affected by HIV/AIDS' declared at the 1994 Paris AIDS Summit provided widespread international commitment (in policy rhetoric at least) to the participation of PLHIV in tackling the epidemic at all levels. The HIV Treatment Action Campaign in South Africa represents an example of an embodied health movement of citizens who successfully advocated for their rights to antiretroviral therapy and greater government involvement in efforts to tackle the epidemic (Leclerc-Madlala 2005). While PLHIV-led organisations have been able to influence policy agendas to some extent, they have tended to advocate for their rights in isolation from disabled people's organisations in the global South.

Meanwhile, disabled people's organisations (DPOs) have increasingly recognised the links between disability and HIV and advocated for national HIV and AIDS policies and programmes that are inclusive of disabled people. The Africa Campaign on Disability and HIV and AIDS, led by the Secretariat of the African Decade of Persons with Disabilities and Handicap International, was launched in 2007 at a meeting of DPOs and service providers from African countries (ACDHA 2007). Despite this growth in advocacy by HIV activists and disabled people at global, continental and national scales, the participation of both groups in policy initiatives related to HIV care and support has been limited to date. We explore recent policy developments, activism by disabled people and PLHIV and access to healthcare in two sub-Saharan African countries, Uganda and Ghana, which provide an interesting contrast in terms of the scale of HIV prevalence and impact of the epidemic.

Disability, HIV and Healthcare in Uganda

Since the condition was first recognised in the early 1980s, Uganda has been severely affected by the global HIV epidemic, although adult prevalence is now stable (at 7.2 per cent of the adult population in 2012) (UNAIDS 2013). Over three decades of the HIV epidemic have had a major impact on families and communities, as they struggle to care for large numbers of people with a highly stigmatised, chronic, life-limiting illness, with very limited public social protection or formal care services and inadequate healthcare resources (Evans and Atim 2011). The national HIV response in Uganda has been marked by a degree of commitment from politicians, civil society and development partners towards behavioural change, service delivery and policy development. Despite reliable data on the HIV prevalence of other vulnerable populations, such as children (aged under 15), young people (aged 15–24), and 'key populations at higher risk', such as men who have sex with men and sex workers, there is no data available on HIV prevalence among disabled people in Uganda. As noted earlier, however, evidence suggests that they have an equal or higher risk of HIV than the wider population.

Efforts have been made to address issues of HIV and disability globally, regionally and nationally in Uganda through the enactment of treaties, policies and initiatives such as the CRPD, the Africa Campaign on Disability and HIV and AIDS as well as research on the impact and prevalence of disability among PLHIV (ACDHA 2008; Myezwa et al. 2009; O'Brien et al. 2010). Uganda has made progress in pursuing legal reforms and developing national strategic plans, such as the Persons with Disability Act 2006 and the National HIV and AIDS Strategic Plan 2011–2012. Although the latter recognises the links between disability and HIV and acknowledges the challenges of limited access to HIV information and services among disabled people, it does not explicitly aim to target disabled people. Disabled people are instead lumped under the broad category of 'vulnerable populations', which has resulted in little attention to date being paid to their specific risks and difficulties in accessing HIV treatment, care and support.

The exclusion of disability in national HIV and AIDS responses in Uganda has led to lobbying and activism among DPOs on HIV issues at local and national levels. The DPO umbrella organisation, the National Union of Disabled People of Uganda (NUDIPU), lobbied for the inclusion of disabled people at all levels of political administration and disabled people have achieved a higher level of political representation in Uganda than in any other country in the world (McEwan and Butler 2007). Through NUDIPU and its partners, a Disability Stakeholders HIV/AIDS Committee and Uganda Disability Fraternity Five-Year HIV/AIDS Strategic Plan (2007/2008–2011/2012) were established with the purpose of mainstreaming disability issues into national HIV programmes.

Although DPOs in Uganda recognise the relationship between HIV and disability, organisations and networks of PLHIV tend to advocate for their rights without involving disabled people (Evans and Atim 2011). The CRPD definition of disabled persons[3] and the international classification of functioning, disability and health (WHO 2001) are regarded by HIV activists as bridging the disability and HIV gap and highlighting challenges related to living with HIV for disabled people. These frameworks now provide a basis for HIV and disability policy advocacy and programming for both DPOs and PLHIV organisations in Uganda.

Disability, HIV and Healthcare in Ghana

Although the first cases of HIV in Ghana were recorded in 1986, HIV prevalence has remained relatively low in West Africa in comparison to the high HIV prevalence recorded in eastern and southern Africa in the 1990s and 2000s. The

[3] The CRPD understanding of disability includes people those with long-term physical, mental, intellectual or sensory impairments which hinder their full, effective and equal participation with others in society.

government responded to the HIV epidemic by setting up the Ghana National AIDS Commission and subsequently formulated the National HIV/AIDS Policy (Agyei-Mensah 2006; Luginaah 2008; GAC 2012). The main thrust of the policy focused on reducing the impact of HIV-related vulnerability and AIDS-related morbidity and mortality. The policy identified the need to intensify behaviour-change strategies and address vulnerability due to gender, socio-economic status and marginalisation (GAC 2012). Ghana is one of the 15 sub-Saharan African countries where adult HIV incidence declined by over 50 per cent over a 10-year period, from 2.3 per cent in 2001 to 1.4 per cent in 2012 (UNAIDS 2013: 120). This reduction is due to several factors including political commitment of resources to tackling the epidemic, coordinated policy formulation and implementation, high-level advocacy and increased knowledge leading to behaviour change (GAC 2012).

As is the case in many countries in sub-Saharan Africa, however, the inclusion of disabled people in national HIV responses in Ghana is still negligible and few efforts have been made to address the specific needs of disabled people with different impairments (Tsiboe-Darko 2008; Mprah 2013). The National Strategic Plan on HIV and AIDS (2011–2015) does not specifically address the needs of disabled people, although they have an equal or higher risk of exposure to all known HIV risk factors (Groce 2005; ICAD 2008). In Ghana, most mainstream HIV education and treatment information is not provided in accessible formats such as Braille and audio versions for blind people, or in sign language for deaf people and those with hearing impairments (Tsiboe-Darko 2008; Mprah 2013). This lack of information means that disabled people often have little HIV knowledge and awareness, including about how to prevent transmission, how to live positively if one becomes infected and how to care for others living with HIV-related illness.

Under the National Health Insurance Scheme in Ghana, healthcare should be free of charge to disabled people, but physical, financial and attitudinal barriers make access to, and use of, healthcare services challenging for disabled people. Many public health facilities in Ghana, where medical services, including HIV counselling, testing and treatment, are provided, are not accessible to disabled people, as interviews with the following two women participating in the study[4] revealed:

> Just imagine going to the hospital very sick and weak and still have to climb long stairs to see the doctor. It means that you have to go with someone who is strong to carry you up the stairs, like a child … it is not nice, so I pray I do not fall sick again, even if I do I will just go to the drug store than go to that hospital. (participant with physical impairment)
>
> You go to the doctor [hospital] with a small illness and return home even more sick because no one signs, so I ask myself how they understood how I am feeling to give me drugs after checking just my temperature … God watches over people like us [the deaf]. (participant who was deaf).

[4] Interviews were conducted in 2012 as part of Yaw Adjei-Amoako's doctoral research on disability and inclusive development in Ghana, funded by The Felix Trust. The links between disability, HIV and access to healthcare were not an explicit focus of the research, although several disabled participants discussed barriers to accessing healthcare and a small proportion of the sample (3 of the 26 disabled people) identified as having 'autoimmune conditions'.

While there is a paucity of research on the links between disability and HIV, anecdotal evidence from disability advocacy groups in Ghana points to significant and unreported cases of HIV infection, HIV-related illness and death among disabled people. A considerable body of research from Ghana has focused on the disabling effects of HIV on previously healthy people; yet there is almost no mention of the impact of the HIV epidemic on people with pre-existing physical, sensory and mental or intellectual impairments.

Conclusion

This chapter has explored the critical relationship between disability and HIV in terms of the 'vulnerability' of disabled people to HIV and their often limited access to healthcare, including accessible HIV information and prevention activities, sexual health services and HIV treatment, care and support. We have also explored how the activism of PLHIV in campaigning for their rights to treatment, care and support as 'biological citizens' may differ from the activism of disabled people and DPOs, who have been more reluctant to mobilise on the basis of impairment and/or access to healthcare to date. Stigma appears to operate on multiple levels, influencing perceptions of disabled people as well as of PLHIV among healthcare professionals, members of the public and among each group. This means that networks and organisations of PLHIV have been reluctant to identify as disabled people to date and stigma further compounds the social isolation and marginalisation of disabled people living with HIV, who may face additional barriers in accessing HIV treatment, care and support in resource-limited settings.

Initiatives of disabled people and PLHIV in our two case studies of African countries with differing HIV prevalence and impacts over the last three decades—Uganda and Ghana—suggest, however, that the intersection of disability and HIV may also provide opportunities for collective mobilisation and cross-movement lobbying and campaigning on the right to health for disabled people and PLHIV. As Shakespeare and colleagues (1996) argue, the social model of disability is appropriate to those living with HIV and 'does not undermine their determination to be accepted as survivors living positively'. Building alliances between disabled people and PLHIV would bring several benefits to both groups including 'a shared voice in demanding civil rights and better services; the experiences of self-organization and social model approaches learnt in the disability movement; and the professionalism, treatment activism and resources of the HIV/AIDS lobby' (Shakespeare et al. 1996). Recent policy initiatives such as the Africa Campaign on Disability and HIV and AIDS suggest potential opportunities for PLHIV-led organisations and DPOs to form new alliances and partnerships (ACDHA 2007; GFD 2013). This would enable PLHIV and disabled people to lobby for their rights to health together, in recognition of the interconnections between HIV and disability.

African organisations of PLHIV have achieved some success in influencing the global care agenda, as demonstrated in the Agreed Conclusions of the United Nations Commission on the Status of Women 2009 meeting. The voices and needs of disabled people, however, were neglected and disabled people continue to be framed as a 'care burden' within global HIV policy debates (Bedford 2010). The rapid adoption and ratification of the CRPD in many countries have resulted in a high level of state and civil society mobilisation around disability, including in Ghana, Uganda and other African countries. This momentum could be harnessed to build alliances between DPOs and PLHIV-led organisations, in recognition of their common experiences of stigma and marginalisation and shared identifications as 'survivors' and active citizens. It is not surprising that joint advocacy by PLHIV and disabled people has already taken place in Uganda, where the lengthy duration and generalised nature of the HIV epidemic have led to a high level of sustained activism by PLHIV on the right to health since the early 2000s. In Ghana, encouraging steps are being taken to improve HIV education and promote safer sex among disabled people; in a new initiative, Ghana Federation for the Disabled is collaborating with the Ghana Health Service and Ghana AIDS Commission to promote HIV education, voluntary testing and counselling for disabled people in urban and rural areas (GFD 2013). Collective action could help to strengthen the voices of disabled people and PLHIV in lobbying for change, raising awareness of disabled people's right to health and tackling barriers to accessing HIV prevention, treatment, care and support. Finally, our analysis reveals the need for further research to provide empirical evidence about attitudinal and structural barriers to healthcare for disabled people, including health education and HIV prevention, treatment, care and support activities, in addition to documenting promising practices and policy initiatives which may help to address these barriers.

References

ACDHA. (2008). *Kampala declaration on disability and HIV & AIDS*. Declaration adopted by participants of second meeting of the Africa Campaign on Disability and HIV and AIDS, hosted by the National Union of Disabled Persons of Uganda (NUDIPU) in conjunction with the Government of Uganda, with support from Handicap International and the African Decade Secretariat, in Kampala, Uganda, 11–13 March 2008. Retrieved November 22, 2013, from http://www.africa-campaign.info/uploads/media/kampala_declaration_on_disability_and_hiv_aids.pdf.

Agyei-Mensah, S. (2006). Poverty and HIV prevalence in Ghana: A geographical perspective. *GeoJournal, 66*, 311–324.

Interagency Coalition on AIDS and Development (ICAD). (2008). *HIV, AIDS and disability*. Retrieved September 22, 2013, from http://www.icad-cisd.com/pdf/HIV_AIDS_Disability_EN.pdf.

Aramayo, M., Kagan, C., & Burton, M. (2016). Revising and using the social model in the global South: A Venezuelan exploration. In S. Grech & K. Soldatic (Eds.), *Disability in the global South: The critical handbook* (pp. xx–xx). New York: Springer.

Beckmann, N., & Bujra, J. (2010). The politics of the queue: The politicization of people living with HIV/AIDS in Tanzania. *Development and Change, 41*(6), 1041–1064.

Bedford, K. (2010). *Harmonizing global care policy? Care and the commission on the status of women*. Gender and Development Programme Paper No 7, February 2010. Geneva: United Nations Research Institute for Social Development.

Burghardt, M. (2013). Common frailty, constructed oppression: Tensions and debates on the subject of vulnerability. *Disability & Society, 28*(4), 556–568.
Connell, R. (2011). Southern bodies and disability: Rethinking concepts. *Third World Quarterly, 32*(8), 1369–1381.
Disability Rights Commission (DRC). (2005). *A guide to the Disability Discrimination Act for people with HIV, Cancer and MS, December 2005, DRC*. Retrieved October 2010, from www.drc-gb.org.
Africa Campaign on Disability and HIV and AIDS (ACDHA). (2007). *Report from the strategic planning meeting and official launch of the Africa Campaign on Disability and HIV & AIDS, Cape Town, January 2007*. Retrieved November 22, 2013, from http://africacampaign.december.fr/about-us/main-campaign-documents.html.
Dyck, I. (1995). Hidden geographies: The changing lifeworlds of women with multiple sclerosis. *Social Science and Medicine, 40*(3), 307–320.
Evans, R., & Atim, A. (2011). Care, disability and HIV in Africa: Diverging or interconnected concepts and practices? *Third World Quarterly, 32*(8), 1437–1454.
Ghana AIDS Commission (GAC). (2012). *Ghana country AIDS progress report*. Accra, Ghana: Ghana AIDS Commission.
Ghana Federation of the Disabled (GFD). (2013). *HIV and AIDS project*. Retrieved February 22, 2014, from http://www.gfdgh.org/hiv%20aids%20project.html.
Grech, S. (2011). Recolonising debates or perpetuated coloniality? Decentring the spaces of disability, development and community in the global South. *International Journal of Inclusive Education, 15*(1), 87–100.
Groce, N. E. (2005). HIV/AIDS and individuals with disability. *Health and Human Rights, 8*, 215–224.
Groce, N. E., Rohleder, P., Eide, A. H., MacLachlan, M., Mall, S., & Swartz, L. (2013). HIV issues and people with disabilities: A review and agenda for research. *Social Science & Medicine, 77*, 31–40.
Groce, N. E., & Trasi, R. (2004). Rape of individuals with disability: AIDS and the folk belief of virgin cleansing. *The Lancet, 363*, 1663–1664.
Hanass-Hancock, J. (2009). Disability and HIV/AIDS—A systematic review of literature on Africa. *Journal of the International AIDS Society, 12*, 34–45.
Hanass-Hancock, J., & Nixon, S. (2009). The fields of HIV and disability: Past, present and future. *Journal of the International AIDS Society, 12*(28). Retrieved October 2010, www.jiasociety.org/content/12/1/28.
Hughes, B. (2009). Disability activisms: Social model stalwarts and biological citizens. *Disability & Society, 24*(6), 677–688.
James, A., & Hockey, J. (2007). *Embodying health identities*. Basingstoke: Palgrave Macmillan.
Kvam, M. H., & Braathen, S. H. (2008). 'I thought…maybe this is my chance': Sexual abuse against girls and women with disabilities in Malawi. *Sexual Abuse: A Journal of Research and Treatment, 20*(1), 5–24.
Leclerc-Madlala, S. (2005). Popular responses to HIV/AIDS and policy. *Journal of Southern African Studies, 31*(4), 845–856.
Longhurst, R. (2005). The body. In D. Atkinson, P. Jackson, D. Sibley, & N. Washbourne (Eds.), *Cultural geography: A critical dictionary of key concepts* (pp. 91–96). London: I.B. Tauris.
Luginaah, I. (2008). Local gin (akpeteshie) and HIV/AIDS in the Upper West Region of Ghana: The need for preventative health policy. *Health & Place, 14*, 806–816.
McEwan, C., & Butler, R. (2007). Disability and development: Different models, different places. *Geography Compass, 1*(3), 448–466.
Meekosha, H., & Soldatic, K. (2011). Human rights and the global South: The case of disability. *Third World Quarterly, 32*(8), 1383–1397.
Morris, J. (1991). *Pride against prejudice: Transforming attitudes to disability*. Philadelphia, PA: New Society Publishers.
Mprah, W. K. (2013). Exploring knowledge and attitudes towards HIV/AIDS among deaf people in Ghana. *Disability, CBR & Inclusive Development, 24*(2), 22–39.

Myezwa, H., Stewart, A., Musenge, E., & Nesara, P. (2009). Assessment of HIV positive in-patients using the International Classification of Functioning, Disability and Health (ICF), at Chris Hani Baragwanath Hospital, Johannesburg. *African Journal of AIDS Research, 8*(1), 93–105.

O'Brien, K., Wilkins, A., Zack, E., & Solomon, P. (2010). Scoping the field: Identifying key research priorities in HIV and rehabilitation. *AIDS and Behavior, 14*(2), 448–458.

Ogden, J., & Nyblade, L. (2005). *Common at its core: HIV-related stigma across contexts.* Washington, DC: International Center for Research on Women.

Oliver, M. (1990). *The politics of disablement.* Basingstoke: Macmillan and St Martin's Press.

Parker, R., & Aggleton, P. (2007). HIV- and AIDS-related stigma and discrimination: A conceptual framework and implications for action. In R. Parker & P. Aggleton (Eds.), *Culture, society and sexuality: A reader* (2nd ed., pp. 443–458). London: Routledge.

Parr, H., & Butler, R. (1999). New geographies of illness, impairment and disability. In R. Butler & H. Parr (Eds.), *Mind and body space: Geographies of illness, impairment and disability* (pp. 1–24). London: Routledge.

Power, M. (2001). Geographies of disability and development in Southern Africa. *Disability Studies Quarterly, 21*(4), 84–97.

Reeve, D. (2002). Negotiating psycho-emotional dimensions of disability and their influence on identity construction. *Disability & Society, 17*(5), 493–508.

Shakespeare, T., Gillespie-Sells, K., & Davies, D. (1996). *The sexual politics of disability: Untold desires.* London: Cassell.

Shuttleworth, R. (2007). Introduction to special issue: Critical research and policy debates in disability and sexuality studies. *Sexuality Research & Social Policy: Journal of NSRC, 4*(1), 1–14.

Swartz, L., & Bantjes, J. (2016). Global health and disability. In S. Grech & K. Soldatic (Eds.), *Disability in the global South: The critical handbook* (pp. xx–xx). New York: Springer.

Trani, J.-F., Brown, J., Kett, M., Bah, O., Morlai, T., Bailey, N., et al. (2011). Access to health care, reproductive health and disability: A large scale survey in Sierra Leone. *Social Science and Medicine, 73*, 1477–1489.

Tsiboe-Darko, I. A. (2008). *HIV/AIDS baseline report.* Accra, Ghana: Ghana National Association of the Deaf.

UNAIDS. (2011). *UNAIDS terminology guidelines.* Revised version, October 2011. Retrieved November 22, 2013, from http://www.unaids.org/en/media/unaids/contentassets/documents/unaidspublication/2011/JC2118_terminology-guidelines_en.pdf.

UNAIDS. (2012). *Report on the global AIDS epidemic 2012.* Joint United Nations Programme on HIV/AIDS (UNAIDS). Retrieved November 22, 2013, from http://www.unaids.org/sites/default/files/media_asset/20121120_UNAIDS_Global_Report_2012_with_annexes_en_1.pdf.

UNAIDS. (2013). *Report on the global AIDS epidemic 2013.* Joint United Nations Programme on HIV/AIDS (UNAIDS). Retrieved November 22, 2013, from http://www.unaids.org/en/resources/campaigns/globalreport2013/globalreport.

UNAIDS, WHO and OHCHR. (2009). *Disability and HIV policy brief.* UNAIDS, WHO and OHCHR. Retrieved November 20, 2014, from http://www.who.int/disabilities/media/news/disabilityhivpolicy/en/.

United Nations. (2006). *United Nations convention on the rights of persons with disabilities.* Retrieved November 20, 2014, from http://www.un.org/disabilities/convention/conventionfull.shtml.

Van Rooy, G., Amadhila, E. M., Mufune, P., Swartz, L., Mannan, H., & MacLachlan, M. (2012). Perceived barriers to accessing health services among people with disabilities in rural northern Namibia. *Disability & Society, 27*(6), 761–775.

Wendell, S. (2001). Unhealthy disabled: Treating chronic illnesses as disabilities. *Hypatia, 16*(4), 17–33.

WHO. (2001). *International classification of functioning disability and health.* Resolution of the World Health Assembly, Fifty-Fourth World Health Assembly, 22 May 2011. Retrieved November 22, 2013, from http://www.who.int/classifications/icf/wha-en.pdf.

World Health Organization (WHO). (2010). *Community-based rehabilitation: CBR guidelines supplementary booklet*. Geneva: WHO. Retrieved October 2010, from www.who.int/disabilities/cbr/guidelines/en/index.html.

Yeo, R., & Moore, K. (2003). Including disabled people in poverty reduction work: 'Nothing About Us, Without Us'. *World Development, 31*(3), 571–590.

Chapter 23
Social Protection, Chronic Poverty and Disability: Applying an Intersectionality Perspective

Marguerite Schneider, Zitha Mokomane, and Lauren Graham

Introduction

When writing a chapter on social protection, poverty and disability, the notion of intersectionality comes to mind. Described as 'the interactivity of social identity structures such as race, class, and gender in fostering life experiences, especially experiences of privilege and oppression' (Gopaldas 2013: 90), intersectionality highlights the importance of considering the intersections of factors that lead to outcomes and experiences in people's lives.

This chapter uses key features of intersectionality to review the relationship between disability, poverty and social protection and how this translates into realities lived by people with disabilities. The essential thesis is that being disabled, poor or requiring social protection—in one form or another—are all ways of creating identities in their own right. When brought together in one's life, these identities

M. Schneider (✉)
Department of Psychiatry and Mental Health, University of Cape Town,
Room 30 Building B, 46 Sawkins Rd, Rondebosch, Cape Town, South Africa
e-mail: marguerite.schneider@uct.ac.za

Z. Mokomane
Department of Sociology, University of Pretoria, 19-31, HSB Building, Hatfield Campus,
Lynwood Road, Hatfield, Pretoria, Gauteng 0028, South Africa
e-mail: Zitha.Mokomane@up.ac.za

L. Graham
Centre for Social Development in Africa, University of Johannesburg,
House 9 Research Village, Auckland Park Bunting Road campus,
Auckland Park, Johannesburg, Gauteng 2006, South Africa
e-mail: lgraham@uj.ac.za

S. Grech, K. Soldatic (eds.), *Disability in the Global South*,
International Perspectives on Social Policy, Administration, and Practice,
DOI 10.1007/978-3-319-42488-0_23

intersect and create a series of outcomes that are more than the sum of the individual components. The chapter begins by setting out important features of social protection as a strategy for managing risk and promoting development, followed by an analysis of the interaction of such a strategy with poverty and disability. We present a number of examples to illustrate our arguments.

Conceptualising Social Protection

Social protection can be described as 'policies and programmes that protect people against risk and vulnerability, mitigate the impact of shocks, and support people from chronic incapacities to secure basic livelihoods' (Adato and Hoddinott 2008: 1). This chapter approaches social protection from a social development perspective (Patel 2003, 2005) which prioritises socio-economic development through a pluralist approach that acknowledges the role of all players—the state, private sector and civil society—in promoting conditions for the achievement of social and economic goals. The model highlights the importance of a commitment to pro-poor strategies and the enhancement of human agency and participation to ensure recognition of all as citizens that count. In South Africa, for example, as economic policy moved from a neo-Keynesian approach to a more neo-liberal approach, 'the notion that the role of the state and welfare expenditures should be limited because generous welfare provisions fostered dependency and consumed scarce resources, by diverting funds away from productive investments, was rejected in favour of harmonization of social and economic development' (Patel 2003: 3).

This chapter views social protection broadly as encompassing state expenditure on the provision of social grants or cash transfers, as well as, importantly, state investments in the provision of basic and social services such as water, electricity, housing, free education and limited free healthcare. All such services are provided through state mechanisms and, while available to all people, are largely intended to be targeted at and benefit poor and vulnerable groups. We understand that for approaches in other countries referred to in this chapter (e.g. Uganda and Zambia) a similar model underpins their growing social protection programmes.

Over the last decade many developing countries have adopted social protection as a key response and important policy tool to tackle poverty, vulnerability and social exclusion (Palmer 2011). The focus has been largely on social assistance and cash transfers or grants without a strong focus on a more comprehensive social protection framework that ensures a 'social contract' approach (Devereux 2013). This approach promotes beneficiaries as 'entitled claimants' rather than 'passive beneficiaries' (Devereux 2013: 13). The former are able to use such benefits as a transformative mechanism and a means to breaking intergenerational perpetuation of vulnerability and structural poverty (Devereux et al. 2011).

Indeed, when one considers social protection from the perspective of wider state investments in promoting social development outcomes, as opposed to simply cash transfers, one begins to see the impact that such investments can have on developing the capabilities of people with disabilities, and their increased sense of worthiness and recognition as full citizens. For instance, in South Africa access to basic services such as water and electricity is socio-economic rights enshrined in the Constitution. State investment to ensure a basic level of living through state expenditure bodes well for all people and ensures that potentially negative living standard outcomes related to both poverty and disability are addressed (Graham et al. 2010, 2014). Despite gaps in implementation, state investments in basic social development outcomes have far-reaching benefits that, in addition to addressing the effects of poverty, overcome the vulnerabilities of particular groups such as those with disabilities. For example, a quota of dwellings in low-cost housing developments (generally through private contractors funded by government) must be made accessible for people with mobility impairments.

There are also targeted social protection interventions such as the disability grant in South Africa. This is a means-tested grant intended to reach those people with disabilities who are living below a particular income level. It is thus intended primarily as an income protection grant, which recognises the difficulties that people with disabilities may have in accessing employment. It is not intended to address the additional healthcare, care and functioning costs that may arise as a result of a disability. These additional needs should be met by the relevant government services (e.g. health, social welfare) to both grant beneficiaries and non-beneficiaries. The income replacement orientation of the grant has meant that it has become a poverty alleviation grant and its impact is seen most notably in this outcome. For instance Loeb and colleagues (2008) found that households receiving a disability grant in the Eastern and Western Cape provinces of South Africa were better off in terms of income than those households that did not qualify to receive the grant. Similarly, in a study in Johannesburg, Graham et al. (2010) found that the disability grant was primarily used to meet household basic needs such as food and education costs.

National data in South Africa confirm that the most marked impact the disability grant has is on poverty alleviation (Graham et al. 2014). When not including any grant income, these national data demonstrate that 78 per cent of people with disabilities live below the poverty line of 502 rand (about US$50.20) per month. When income from the disability grant is included this is reduced to 69 per cent. When all grant income (e.g. from disability, old age and child support grants) is taken into account the number of people with disabilities living below the Foster–Greer–Thorbecke (Foster et al. 1984) poverty line is reduced to 41 per cent. The poverty-alleviating effects of social grants for the non-disabled population are also marked; but people with disabilities, who are more grant dependent (46 per cent of people with disabilities as opposed to 21 per cent of non-disabled people received one grant), fared better than their non-disabled counterparts with regard to income from grants (Graham et al. 2014).

What this demonstrates is that social grants have a key role to play in alleviating income poverty. However, when conceptualised primarily in terms of income protection, they do just that—alleviate poverty—with little transformative potential. A comprehensive social protection programme would ensure that the grant can retain the role of income protection with other services (e.g. health, education and basic water and sanitation services) being met by the relevant departments. The intersection of disability and poverty is further complicated by the de facto use of what is an individually targeted disability grant as a household grant. A disability grant recipient in a poor household will have less claim on the grant income for his or her individual needs than a recipient in a less poor household.

A social protection strategy includes a number of interventions and programmes ranging from cash or in-kind transfers (social assistance) through social insurance to complex labour-market interventions for development of people who are vulnerable and often marginalised (Marriott and Gooding 2007; Davies and McGregor 2009). Social assistance programmes are currently the major focus of social protection strategies and are typically non-contributory in nature, targeting the most vulnerable and poorest sectors of the population (Devereux 2013). People with disabilities are often seen as part of this vulnerable and poorest sector of the population (Marriott and Gooding 2007; Schneider et al. 2011).

Key concerns in the role of social protection as a strategy to address the disability–poverty intersection, taken up in more detail later in the chapter, include:

- Targeting through specific disability-focused social assistance versus integration of people with disabilities in general poverty-focused social assistance
- Assessing disability to determine eligibility
- Embedding social assistance within a broader social protection strategy

Unlike in high-income countries, there are few examples of disability-targeted social assistance programmes in low- and middle-income countries that make up the global South. The few exceptions include South Africa (Swartz and Schneider 2006) and Fiji (from personal experience of one author of this chapter, Marguerite Schneider), and a few other instances of some type of financial assistance with limited implementation of these programmes. Yet, there is a growing number of broader poverty-focused programmes that include disability as a consideration in determining eligibility, albeit not all in an explicit manner. Two of these are the Zambia social cash transfer programme and the Ugandan Social Assistance Grants for Empowerment (SAGE) programme (Schneider et al. 2011; Oxford Policy Management 2013).

The assessment of disability for eligibility is fraught with difficulty, even in high-income countries where there is a well-developed system of professionals specialising in this field. In low- and middle-income countries this is even more difficult with a lack of adequate skilled personnel, a high number of applicants and little time to undertake a complex assessment process (Swartz and Schneider 2006; Schneider et al. 2011). The picture is further complicated by a conflation of disability and chronic illness.

As we show in the case studies later in this chapter, the integration of social assistance programmes within a broader social protection system is not yet evident, but should be the goal to maximise the benefits of social assistance programmes.

Intersectionality as a Tool for Understanding Social Protection, Disability and Poverty

Intersectionality is rooted in feminist theory (Cho et al. 2013) but as a theoretical framework the concept has evolved beyond feminist studies to encompass other forms of identity and marginalisation such as sexual orientation, socio-economic status, nationality, health status, religion, age, attractiveness, body type and other various ways of categorising human populations (Bowleg 2012; Cho et al. 2013; Gopaldas 2013). Some examples of using the framework include understanding differential access to education by disabled children (Knoll 2009); analysing the intersectionality in the case of paralympian Oscar Pistorius killing his girlfriend (Swartz 2013) and analysing US survey data to understand the characteristics of groups of disabled people at high or low risk of experiencing harassment in the workplace (Shaw et al. 2011).

As an analytical tool, intersectionality considers the lived experiences of social (dis)advantage, identifies the historical or structural causes of the (dis)advantage and examines how different sets of identities have an impact on access to rights and opportunities (AWID 2004; Gopaldas 2013). Looking at relationships between and within categories (or groups) ensures that we can identify, for example, power relations between groups, while understanding different subgroups or experiences within one group. Inequalities are not static and part of the analysis must engage with this fluidity.

This chapter does not aim to conduct a detailed intersectionality analysis, but to use its overarching framework. We use this framework to reflect on the properties emerging from different levels of a social system as people with disabilities realise their rights as full citizens; and to grapple with how to change interrelationships when social protection systems intersect with poor and disabled sectors of the population.

The intersectionality of poverty, disability and social protection veers away from the more commonly used concept of identities (such as race and gender) being the intersecting elements. Poverty and social protection are structural factors rather than identities, and being disabled is an identity to the extent that a person sees himself or herself as disabled. There are many people who report difficulties in doing various activities (i.e. who have functional limitations) but who explicitly say that they are not disabled (Schneider 2009). While this is beyond the scope of this chapter it remains an interesting aspect to consider in future work on intersectionality in these areas.

It is also noteworthy that the difference between disability identity and functional limitation is an issue of measurement where ideally these two aspects are measured separately. Given the current status of disability measurement, it is not always clear which aspect is being measured. This is also an important discussion in its own right but not for this chapter. The findings reported in this chapter are thus not analysed in terms of the measures used as these are not made explicit in most of the studies referred to.

Interaction Between Disability and Poverty

Given the complex interaction between impairment and environment, disability is not a static phenomenon and varies as features of either the individual or his or her context changes. Applying a systems perspective, as proposed by Michailakis (2003), helps us to fully understand the implications of how society serves to marginalise those with a disability in ways that have important implications for recognition as a full citizen. Furthermore, the notion of structural deprivation (Webster 1997) highlights the ways in which society marginalises those who are living in poverty and makes poor people more vulnerable to exploitation and further marginalisation. For instance, poor people are more likely to work in exploitative conditions that may increase their risk of illness. Thus people with disabilities are marginalised by those from both 'non-disabled' and 'non-poor' contexts.

All people have an innate potential to reach a range of functionings, but achieving these is heavily dependent on the structural opportunities they have to pursue a particular course of action (Sen 1999). That is, an individual's capabilities are largely determined by his or her interaction with systems such as health services and education, and his or her socio-economic and political environments, such as a non-discriminatory/non-exploitative labour market. Such environments and services for poor people and people with disabilities as currently constructed so often serve to limit opportunities to develop people's full potential.

Poverty and disability are closely related, with poverty causing disability and disability causing poverty (Braithwaite and Mont 2009; Eide and Ingstad 2013). Typically people with disabilities are more likely to experience multidimensional poverty, increased medical care needs and other disability-related costs such as transport, assistive devices and care needs (Mont and Nguyen 2011, 2013; Mitra et al. 2013). Further intersections between poverty and disability are low educational achievement and high levels of unemployment (Braithwaite and Mont 2009; Groce et al. 2011a, b; Mitra et al. 2013). Furthermore, age of onset plays a crucial role in determining the capabilities of disabled people; the earlier the onset the more the impact of disability on education and social inclusion (Schneider et al. 1999). When poverty results in low educational achievement the combination of this with later onset of disability results in even less chance of being employed and being able to live independently than for poor, non-disabled people.

The culmination of systemic and structural determinants of poverty intersecting with disability is a loss of a sense of worthiness and ability to be seen as productive, resulting in a reduced ability to be counted as a full citizen (Ikäheimo 2009).

Current Approaches in Social Protection and Disability

There is wide recognition in high-income countries that disability is a condition that requires social assistance; hence many disability-related benefits are separate from chronic illness or unemployment benefits. In low- and middle-income countries, on the other hand, there are few examples of effective social assistance programmes for people with disabilities. Nonetheless there is growing awareness in these countries that people with disabilities are disproportionately poor and socially excluded (Palmer 2011). A number of these countries are increasingly including disability specifically as a criterion for inclusion in social assistance and poverty reduction programmes, such as cash transfer programmes.

While not disability specific, these programmes recognise the contribution of disability in generating or maintaining poverty. Poverty-focused programmes target very poor households, while disability-related grants tend to target individuals with a disability. Social assistance programmes effectively ensure survival of households, and if a household has a disabled member, access to social assistance is facilitated in countries with disability-specific social assistance programmes. To this end it could be, as suggested by Loeb and colleagues (2008), that households with a disabled member are better off than those without a disabled member at the level of basic survival (Schneider et al. 2011; Mitra et al. 2013). The disadvantage generated by the intersection of poverty, disability and a limited social protection system is that it fails to address the development of disabled individuals and their households beyond survival. If the focus is only on cash transfers, the lack of adequate healthcare, education, employment and other services combined with additional costs related to disability entrenches chronic poverty in households that have a member with disability. Disadvantage and vulnerability are maintained.

While cash transfers do make a difference (Schneider et al. 2011), they need to become transformative to restore agency and dignity for both the individual with disabilities and his or her household. Collective cultural practices that require resources to be spread out to all in a household, and the commonly occurring lack of adequate participation in decision-making by disabled people in these households, make it more difficult for them as individuals to claim their right to services and use of the grant for their specific needs. This is not necessarily an intentional lack of care or concern but often arises from lack of information (Malan 2013).

Illustrative Case Studies

Case Study 1: Intersectionality of Poverty, Disability and Presence of Basic Services

The Centre for Social Development in Africa at the University of Johannesburg undertook a rural case study in Mpumalanga Province, South Africa, as part of a broader poverty and disability project. Interviews were conducted in a circumscribed rural area, including the different services provided within that area. One interview was conducted with staff overseeing the basic community-based rehabilitation (CBR) services. CBR workers are trained to identify and refer disabled children and adults to health, education and social development/

security services. In this interview the story of family was given as an example of the effectiveness of the service provided by CBR workers.

The household comprised a mother, a largely absent father who worked about 200 kilometres away, an adolescent with severe cerebral palsy and four younger children without disability. The father contributed some money every few months but other than this, there was no regular income for the household. The adolescent with disabilities was neglected and had little interaction with others. The other children were not always going to school. The family was often hungry. They were identified by the local CBR worker as a family with a child with disabilities, and a series of visits and discussions ensued between the CBR worker and the family. The mother was referred to the agency responsible for implementing the policy on social assistance to apply for child support grants for her four non-disabled children, and an effort was made to obtain her disabled child's birth certificate to allow her to apply for a care dependency grant (disability cash transfer for children needing long-term care). Ongoing visits with the family allowed the CBR worker to engage in discussions on disability and rights of the disabled child. One of the younger daughters expressed her concern that her brother was not being looked after correctly. The disabled child was granted a care dependency grant eventually, which added to the income from the other child support grants. The trajectory of this family changed significantly with these interventions, resulting in the second child completing school and obtaining a university entrance pass in his final school exams. The level of hope increased in the family and improved relationships between all household members, including the adolescent with disabilities, who started being treated positively, with dignity, and was included as a full member of the household.

The intersections apparent in this story are that of disability, a large household and no regular income leading to a household struggling to function beyond a mere existence. The presence of what can be seen as elements of a comprehensive social protection programme (CBR workers, a functioning referral system and a social assistance programme) allowed the situation of this family to be turned around significantly.

Case Study 2: A Limited Social Protection Programme Results in Limited Improvements in Disabled People's Lives

A survey study on disability and poverty was conducted in low-resource contexts in the Eastern Cape and Western Cape provinces of South Africa (Loeb et al. 2008). In both these provinces people are struggling to get by and a large proportion of households survive thanks to the government social assistance programme. The major social assistance grants include the child support

grant, the child and adult disability grants and the old-age pension. The majority of people with disabilities do receive a disability grant. The effect of this is that households with and without a person with disabilities tend to be equal in income levels, with 'disabled' households being better off if they accessed both a disability grant and one or more other grants. The survey results showed that in other domains of functioning, however, there was a gap between those households with and without a member with disabilities. Levels of education and school attendance were much lower for people with disabilities compared to their non-disabled peers. In the Western Cape where job opportunities were higher, there was a major difference in employment rate between people with and without disabilities. In the Eastern Cape, however, where job opportunities were scarce and services limited, there were no differences noted in employment in households with and without a person with disabilities.

The intersections in this case study show that having few resources affects all households in a similar manner, but that a household member with disabilities can assist in increasing the income for that household. This ensures survival of the household. Beyond survival, the differences between disabled and non-disabled people remain stark with poor access to education and employment for people with disabilities relative to their non-disabled peers.

A comprehensive social protection programme ensures that all elements required for development are provided as a safety net to protect vulnerable people from falling into or remaining in poverty. Providing one element (social assistance grants) without the support of other elements (accessible education and health services, good transport and increased job opportunities) results in outcomes that do not go beyond mere survival.

While social assistance or cash transfer programmes are becoming more common in many African countries, few are overtly including disability as a consideration of which households are the poorest. This is associated with limited or no information being collected on disability status, making it very difficult to analyse the extent to which disability is mainstreamed into social assistance programmes (Mont 2006; Schneider et al. 2011). A small review of social cash transfer beneficiaries in Zambia showed that many of these beneficiary households included a person with disabilities and most frequently it was the head of the household who was disabled (Schneider et al. 2011). In Uganda, the government has piloted a social assistance grant that targets the poorest household (Oxford Policy Management 2013). The assessment of poverty includes an assessment of disability (or functional) status of every member of a household (Schneider et al. 2011).

Poverty-focused social assistance programmes such as the Zambian and Ugandan examples target households while disability-related grants tend to target individuals, the individual with a disability, as is the case in South Africa. High-income countries typically have a range of individually targeted, non-contributory social assistance and other contributory social insurance programmes that assist individuals in cases of illness, disability and unemployment. In low- and middle-income countries, high unemployment and high rates of poverty mean that individually targeted disability-related cash transfers tend to be used as de facto household income (Swartz and Schneider 2006; Schneider et al. 2011).

Conclusion

This chapter used intersectionality as an approach to understanding the ways in which poverty and disability further interact with social protection programmes, which currently focus on social assistance grants rather than a more comprehensive social protection strategy. Through the examples we aimed to demonstrate some advantages and pitfalls of limited social protection programmes, showing how sustainability can be achieved but with limited realisation of an effective capability set beyond survival (e.g. low educational achievement and employment rates). The South African example showed the significant advantage of providing social assistance in the context of other services.

Most social protection interventions in developing contexts focus on poverty to the exclusion of disability, and may therefore serve to reinforce the vulnerabilities and exclusions that those living with a disability may face. The examples of Zambia and Uganda and increasingly other countries too (Rohwerder 2014) show a growing recognition of the importance of including disability in broader social protection strategies, although these strategies are not yet effectively implemented.

The transformative effects of social protection, as Devereux (2013) suggests, are clearly not being met within current social protection policies related to disability in the case studies presented. This may largely have to do with the fact that social protection mechanisms such as cash transfers tend to focus either on disability or on poverty, rather than on the intersectionality of both.

When recognising the complex ways in which disability and poverty intersect to compound poverty and vulnerability, it becomes clear that dealing with disability or poverty separately cannot break this cycle. As such, it becomes important to think through social protection mechanisms that do not only address chronic poverty, but also target the specific needs of people with disabilities to ensure that they have opportunities to use and develop their capabilities (Sen 1999). The case of the disability grant in South Africa is illustrative of this. As a de facto poverty alleviation grant, it deals with chronic poverty well. However, because of inefficiencies in education and health systems, the transformative potential of social protection for people with disabilities is largely lost.

Intersectionality as an analytical approach provides a way to understand how poverty, disability and social protection can and could intersect to improve the sense of worthiness and recognition as citizens that count of poor non-disabled people and poor people with disabilities, to become 'entitled claimants rather than "passive beneficiaries"' (Devereux 2013: 13).

References

Adato, M., & Hoddinott, J. (2008). *Social protection: Opportunities for Africa*. Policy Briefs No. 5. International Food Policy Research Institute (IFPRI), Washington, DC.

AWID. (2004). *Intersectionality: A tool for gender and economic justice*. Retrieved March 13, 2014, from http://lgbtq.unc.edu/sites/lgbtq.unc.edu/files/documents/intersectionality_en.pdf.

Bowleg, L. (2012). The problem with the phrase women and minorities: Intersectionality—An important theoretical framework for public health. *American Journal of Public Health, 102*(7), 1267–1273.

Braithwaite, J., & Mont, D. (2009). Disability and poverty: A survey of World Bank Poverty Assessments and implications. *ALTER—European Journal of Disability Research/Revue Européenne de Recherche Sur Le Handicap, 3*(3), 219–232.

Cho, S., Crenshaw, K. W., & Mccall, L. (2013). Toward a field of intersectionality studies: Theory, applications and praxis. *Signs, 38*(4), 785–810.

Davies, M., & McGregor, J. A. (2009). Social protection: Responding to a global crisis. *IDS Bulletin, 40*(5), 68–77.

Devereux, S. (2013). Africa Trajectories of social protection in Africa. *Development South Africa*, (March), 37–41. Retrieved March 13, 2014, from http://dx.doi.org/10.1080/0376835X.2013.755871.

Devereux, S., McGregor, J. A., & Sabates-Wheeler, R. (2011). Introduction: Social protection for social justice. *IDS Bulletin, 42*(6), 1–9.

Eide, A. H., & Ingstad, B. (2013). Disability and poverty—Reflections on research experiences in Africa and beyond. *African Journal of Disability, 2*(1), 1–7.

Foster, J., Greer, J., & Thorbecke, E. (1984). A class of decomposable poverty measures. *Econometrica, 3*(52), 761–766.

Gopaldas, A. (2013). Intersectionality 101. *Journal of Public Policy and Marketing, 32*(special issue), 90–94.

Graham, L., Moodley, J., Ismail, Z., Munsaka, E. & Ross, E. (2014). *National study on poverty and disability in South Africa*. CSDA Monograph. Johannesburg: CSDA, University of Johannesburg.

Graham, L., Selipsky, L., Moodley, J., Rowland, W., & Maina, J. (2010). *Poverty and disability in Johannesburg*. Johannesburg: Centre for Social Development in Africa (CSDA), University of Johannesburg.

Groce, N., Kembhavi, G., Wirz, S., Lang, R., Trani, J.-F., & Kett, M. (2011a). *Poverty and disability: A critical review of the literature in low and middle-cinome countries* (No. No. 16) (pp. 1–31). London. Retrieved June 8, 2014, from http://www.ucl.ac.uk/lc-ccr/centrepublications/workingpapers.

Groce, N., Kett, M., Lang, R., & Trani, J.-F. (2011a). Disability and poverty: The need for a more nuanced understanding of implications for development policy and practice. *Third World Quarterly, 32*(8), 1493–1513.

Ikäheimo, H. (2009). A vital human need: Recognition as inclusion in personhood. *European Journal of Political Theory, 8*(1), 31–45.

Knoll, K. R. (2009). Feminist disability studies pedagogy. *Feminist Teacher, 19*(2), 122–133.

Loeb, M., Eide, A. H., Jelsma, J., Toni, M. K., & Maart, S. (2008). Poverty and disability in Eastern and Western Cape provinces, South Africa. *Disability & Society, 23*(4), 311–321.

Malan, M. (2013, 8 November). *If they are raped, then so what?* Mail and Guardian. Retrieved January 9, 2014, from http://mg.co.za/article/2013-11-08-if-they-are-raped-then-so-what.

Marriott, A., & Gooding, K. (2007). *Social assistance and disability in developing countries*. Retrieved June 8, 2014, from http://www.handicap-international.fr/bibliographie-handicap/4PolitiqueHandicap/thematique/social_protection/SOCIAL_ASSISTANCE_AND_DISABILITY_July_2007.pdf.

Michailakis, D. (2003). The systems theory concept of disability: One is not born a disabled person, one is observed to be one. *Disability & Society, 18*(2), 209–229.

Mitra, S., Posarac, A., & Vick, B. (2013). Disability and poverty in developing countries: A multidimensional study. *World Development, 41*, 1–18.

Mont, D. (2006). *Disability in conditional cash transfer programs: Drawing on experience in LAC*. Instanbul. Retrieved from http://www.gsdrc.org/docs/open/SP23.pdf

Mont, D., & Nguyen, C. (2011). Disability and poverty in Vietnam. *The World Bank Economic Review, 25*(2), 323–359.

Mont, D., & Nguyen, C. (2013). Does parental disability matter to child education? Evidence from Vietnam. *World Development, 48*, 88–107.

Oxford Policy Management. (2013). *Evaluation of the Uganda social assistance grants for empowerment (SAGE) programme Baseline report* (pp. 1–170). Retrieved June 8, 2014, from http://www.opml.co.uk/sites/opml/files/SAGE_IE_baseline_report_final_20130815_0.pdf.

Palmer, M. (2011). Disability and poverty: A conceptual review. *Journal of Disability Policy Studies, 21*(4), 210–218. doi:10.1177/1044207310389333.

Patel, L. (2003). Social development in a society in transition. *Social Development Issues, 25*(1&2), 150–161.

Patel, L. (2005). *Social welfare and social development in South Africa*. Cape Town: Oxford University Press.

Rohwerder, B. (2014). *Disability inclusion in social protection (GSDRC Helpdesk Research Report 1069)*. Birmingham, UK: GSDRC, University of Birmingham. Retrieved June 8, 2014, from http://www.gsdrc.org/docs/open/HDQ1069.pdf.

Schneider, M. (2009). The difference a word makes: Responding to questions on "disability" and "difficulty" in South Africa. *Disability and Rehabilitation, 31*(1), 42–50.

Schneider, M., Claassens, M., Kimmie, Z., Morgan, R., Naicker, S., Roberts, A., et al. (1999). *We also count! The extent of moderate and severe reported disability and the nature of the disability experience in South Africa*. Pretoria. Retrieved June 8, 2014, from http://indicators.hst.org.za/indicators/Disability/CASE_we_also_count.pdf.

Schneider, M., Waliuya, W., Munsanje, J., & Swartz, L. (2011). Reflections on including disability in social protection programmes. *IDS Bulletin, 42*(6), 38–44.

Sen, A. (1999). *Development as freedom*. Oxford: Oxford University Press.

Shaw, L. R., Chan, F., & McMahon, B. T. (2011). Intersectionality and disability harassment: The interactive effects of disability, race, age, and gender. *Rehabilitation Counseling Bulletin, 55*(2), 82–91.

Swartz, L. (2013). Oscar Pistorius and the melancholy of intersectionality. *Disability & Society, 28*(8), 1157–1161.

Swartz, L., & Schneider, M. (2006). Tough choices: The social mode of disability, social security and the challenges for implementation in South Africa. In B. Watermeyer, L. Swartz, T. Lorenzo, M. Schneider, & M. Priestley (Eds.), *Disability and social change: A South African agenda* (pp. 234–244). Pretoria: HSRC Press.

Webster, A. (1997). *Introduction to the sociology of development*. Basingstoke: MacMillan Palgrave.

Part IV
Interventions

Chapter 24
The Hauntings of Slavery: Colonialism and the Disabled Body in the Caribbean

Stefanie Kennedy and Melanie J. Newton

Introduction

'The Fact of Blackness', the fifth chapter of Martinican psychiatrist and political theorist Frantz Fanon's 1952 work *Black Skin, White Masks*, maps the journey of a black French Caribbean man coming to terms with anti-black racism as a disabling state of being. Writing in the first person, Fanon makes it clear that white French prejudices against Jews, 'cripples' and blacks each has unique historical trajectories, with consequently different lived experiences of dispossession. A moment of public humiliation, when a white child points at him and says, 'Mama, look at the Negro! I'm frightened!', leads Fanon to the realisation that his skin colour and other 'black' phenotypic characteristics have been alienated from and turned against him. He is:

> all at once responsible for my body, for my race, for my ancestors. Looking objectively at myself, I discovered my blackness, my ethnic characteristics; and my eardrums were assaulted by cannibalism, mental backwardness, fetishism, racial defects, slavery and the slave-ship, and above all else: "Dat is some good hot chocolate!"[1] (Fanon 1952: 90).

---

[1] *Y a bon banania* is a creolised reference to a chocolate-based drink popular in France, sold in a box depicting a racially derogatory image of a grinning black man in a fez. The chocolate and the man's skin are the same colour. Translations from Fanon are by Newton.

S. Kennedy (✉)
University of Toronto, Toronto, ON, Canada

Department of History, University of New Brunswick,
120 Tilley Hall, 9 Macaulay Lane, Fredericton, NB, Canada, E3B 5A3
e-mail: stefanie.kennedy@unb.ca

M.J. Newton
University of Toronto, Toronto, ON, Canada

S. Grech, K. Soldatic (eds.), *Disability in the Global South*,
International Perspectives on Social Policy, Administration, and Practice,
DOI 10.1007/978-3-319-42488-0_24

Fanon goes beyond rhetorically employing disability and impairment as a metaphor or symbol for the racist effects of colonialism. He argues that history has created an inescapable tension between blackness and disability, and explores how racist stereotypes about 'mental backwardness' and 'racial defects' rooted in the histories of black enslavement in the Caribbean still haunt and damage black bodies.[2] At the end of the chapter a 'crippled' (presumably white) World War II veteran advises a black man to: 'Resign [himself] to [his] colour as I have to my stump; we are both accident victims'. Fanon rejects the idea that he must forever accept a future determined by, in his words, 'amputation' and 'the humility of the disabled' (Fanon 1952: 113). He charts a specific history of racism that would condemn him to an existence in which he is forced to inhabit his 'blackness' as a uniquely visible and despised disability, based on a racist view of blackness as an impairment. Fanon implicitly rejects the war veteran's suggestion that there is anything 'accidental' either about soldiers being disabled in war or about black people routinely being rendered unable to fully experience their humanity because of assumptions about their racial incapacity. Fanon resolutely roots his discussion in his experience, and in Martinique's historical relationship to slavery and French colonialism, and uses Creole turns of phrase. These elements facilitate a reading of 'The Fact of Blackness' as an incipient historical analysis of how the intricate relationship between African enslavement in the Caribbean, violence and disability continues to haunt the modern world.

This chapter draws on Fanon's observations in order to demonstrate that the slave trade and plantation slavery are the historical underpinnings of systematised and violent African diasporic impairment. Slavery haunts the modern world as, in Avery Gordon's terms, a 'ghost', one of 'the unhallowed dead of the modern project [dragging] in the pathos of their loss and the violence of the force that made them, their sheets and chains …'. Tracking the ghostly history of enslavement as enforced disability helps to make 'a contact that changes you and refashions the social relations in which you are located. It is about putting life back in where only a vague memory or a bare trace was visible to those who bothered to look' (Gordon [1997] 2008: 2).

This chapter focuses on plantation slavery in the 17th- and 18th-century British Caribbean, which was one of the earliest zones of the Atlantic World to adopt a system of colonial exploitation based on African enslavement and sugar plantations (Klein and Vinson III 2007: 49–64). A focus on the racialised history of labour and Atlantic World disability leads us to rethink a key trend among disability historians, which posits mid-19th-century Europe and North America as the locations and era in which impairments took on new meanings due to the onset of industrialisation. Advocates of this approach argue that industrialisation changed the way impairment was understood and 'disability' in its modern sense emerged (Finkelstein 1980; Oliver 1990; Barnes 1990; Gleeson 1999; Borsay 2005). Although features of industrial capitalism existed in the early modern period and could cause negative social stereotyping of physical anomalies and impairments, the intensification of economic rationality that characterised the mid-19th century changed the perception of impairment, whereby

[2] For critiques of rhetorical deployments of disability and impairment as metaphors or symbols for other forms of oppression see Sherry 2007; Titchkosky (2015).

'the body *an sich* had become the body *für sich* and the impaired body had become disabled—unable to be part of the productive economy, confined to institutions, shaped to contours defined by society at large' (Davis 1995: 74).

The colonial Caribbean confounds this chronology of disability history, and undoes teleological distinctions between the early modern and modern (Paton 2004). Caribbean sugar production developed in the 17th century as an industrial enterprise, and the enslaved body was defined by its relationship to an economy driven by production and profit (James [1963] 1989; Mintz 1985). As a 'synthesis of field and factory' (Mintz 1985: 46), the sugar plantation was characterised by a division of labour according to skill, age, gender and physical condition, and a sophisticated emphasis on discipline, organisation and timekeeping. Sugar production was a precociously industrial and modern undertaking. As Trinidadian scholar C. L. R. James argued, 'from the very start [the enslaved] lived a life that was in its essence a modern life' ([1963] 1989: 392). Nevertheless, disability histories have so far reproduced a tendency, common among historians of the West, to exclude the Caribbean and the enslaved 'from the figurative time-space of "Western modernity"' (Sheller 2003: 107).

This exploration of slavery and disability emphasises that although disability may be the most universal of human conditions (Davis 1999: 502; Garland-Thomson 2005: 1568; McRuer 2006), disability must be understood within specific historical contexts. Disability is not a 'condition of being but of becoming, and this becoming is a historical event, and further, it is its material context that is critical in the theorizing of disabled bodies/subjectivities' (Erevelles 2011: 26). Shaun Grech has argued that histories of colonialism and its attendant forms of racism are a key reason why 80 per cent of the world's disabled people 'live in the poorest countries of the global South enduring some of the harshest levels of poverty' (Grech 2012: 69–70; see also Choi 2001; Szasz 2003; Sherry 2007; Grech 2011). Fanon's writings and his personal history of revolutionary itinerancy—between Martinique, France and Algeria—help us to extend such analysis further. Colonial histories are plural, and, while they certainly created distinctions between a colonising West and a global South, they created equally important distinctions *within* the global South. Read together, *Black Skin, White Masks* and *The Wretched of the Earth* (1961) illustrate Fanon's engagements with European colonialism's multiple manifestations and far-flung geographies, which placed Martinique, Algeria and France into an inexorable relationship with each other, and yet produced three radically different societies whose anti-colonial struggles both connected and diverged. In much the same way Fanon recognised the tension between disability, anti-Semitism and racism as forms of intimately interrelated and distinct dispossession.[3]

On the one hand, a disability history of the Afro-Atlantic World, focusing on the twin pillars of the sugar plantation and the slave trade in the Caribbean, offers a transnational and comparative basis for seeing the global intersections between colonial-

[3] In reading *Peau Noir, Masques Blancs* (*Black Skin, White Masks*) as a discussion of race, colonialism and disability we are mindful of Mary Sherry's critique of Fanon's 'medical model of disability' in *The Wretched of the Earth*, which was based on Fanon's interactions as a psychiatrist with patients at the Bléda Hospital in Algeria.

ism and disability. On the other hand, we advocate for histories of disability and colonialism that are attentive to different patterns of colonial exploitation and racialisation and the distinct legacies of disablement that they have produced. There are specificities to the history of disability and African enslavement that cannot simply be transferred to all other colonised contexts. The specific historical context of Caribbean slavery demonstrates that disability, colonialism and anti-black racism came into existence and relation to one another throughout the Atlantic period in complex and sometimes contradictory ways. Perhaps more than any other category of difference, Africans in the early modern Atlantic World encompass the overlapping discourses of monstrosity, disability and race. As this chapter illustrates, precolonial and colonial European discourses often equated Africans and their descendants with animality and monstrosity. These notions did not by themselves lead to African enslavement, but they served to normalise and mute opposition to African dispossession in the British Atlantic World.

The racialised historical legacies of slavery can still be seen today in the Atlantic World. 'Diaspora Africans', writes Hershini Bhana Young, 'are both inside and constitutive of modernity and outside and negated by modernity: both haunted and haunting' (2006: 47). The ghostliness of slavery permeates the Americas today—in US prisons where there is a high rate of incarceration for people with intellectual disabilities and dark skin colour, and in the Caribbean where social and political forms of disablement are linked to high rates of impairment in already marginalised (racialised, poor, indigenous, etc.) communities (Barceló et al. 2003; Young 2006; Al Snih et al. 2010; Ben-Moshe 2011). This chapter demonstrates that disability in the global South bears traces of its early modern legacy and, thus, opens a space for further thinking about bodies as texts and how history manifests itself on the bodies of the present.

Monstrosity and Emerging Notions of 'Race'

In the early colonial period, English discussions of 'exotic' peoples, in particular Africans, were shaped by a developing imperial discourse that drew heavily on existing European notions of monstrosity and deformity. Deformity in the early modern period referred to both ugliness and physical anomalies that were deemed 'unnatural' as well as functional impairments—such as a crooked spine, clubfoot or amputation (Turner 2006: 5). As late as the mid-17th century, the birth of a deformed child was interpreted as a sign that something calamitous was likely to happen. Thus, physical appearance and inner character were inextricably linked and tales of monstrous births often deployed extensive descriptions of the monster's physical appearance to sensationalise the account and prepare the reader for the moral lesson (Stagg 2006: 33).

The concept of monstrosity contained elements that anticipated more explicitly racist thinking. Monstrosity in the early modern period did not apply to one particular physical abnormality, rather, as Kevin Stagg explains, it was used to describe a variety of phenomena which were strange or striking enough to signify an offense against God (Stagg 2006: 23). Humans 'possessing features or appendages which were either of unknown origin, were rightfully the marks of another species, or were simply too large' met the criteria of the monstrous (Brammall 1996: 7). Margrit Shildrick defines monstrous bodies as 'those which in their gross failure to approximate corporeal norms are radically excluded' (2002: 2). Monstrous and disabled bodies share a history of perceived corporeal otherness to which blackness—constructed as the embodiment of corporeal insufficiency and deviance—is inextricably linked. The meaning attached to monstrosity has changed throughout history but the monster has remained the 'ubiquitous icon of physical anomaly' (Garland-Thomson 1997: 36). Although it would take centuries for Britons to explicitly justify the subordination of African descended peoples with biological arguments, 16th- and 17th-century European debates about Africans demonstrate that the so-called monstrosity of Africans raised fundamental questions for white Britons about what it meant to be human. Throughout the colonial period, the British assigned value to human life by asserting that blackness and other African phenotypes were monstrous manifestations of Africans' supposed inner depravity and aptness for servitude.

By the time British voyagers landed on African shores in the 1550s, their imaginations were already full of images of monstrous Africans taken from ancient texts and translations of European travel accounts about Africa and the New World. One of the most influential ancient texts was Pliny the Elder's *The Historie of the World* (ca. 77 CE), which was translated into English by Thomas Hacket in 1566 and remained influential well into the 17th century (Burton and Loomba 2007: 45). Pliny wrote of hybrid races and monsters—men and women with missing body parts and beast-like characteristics. Ethiopians, he wrote, had no noses or nostrils and spoke in sign with no upper lips or tongues 'but a little hole to take their breath at'. In the West were 'a people called Arimaspi, that hath but one eye in their foreheads'. The Cinamolgi were described as having heads like dogs and the people called Blemmyis as having no heads, 'but … their mouth and their eyes in their breastes' (*A Summarie of the Antiquities, and wonders of the Worlde*, 1566: images 12–13, n.p.). Pliny's depictions of Africans were repeated by several other writers, including the most widely read travel narrative of the medieval and early modern world, *The Voyages and travailes of Sir John Mandevile knight* (ca. 1366). First published in English in 1496, by 1500 it circulated in German, Italian, Dutch, Spanish, Irish, Danish, Czech and Latin. Although Mandeville's descriptions of monstrous races were repeated by a variety of writers to elaborate their own fantastic adventure tales, they were also supposedly relied on by more reputable explorers, like Christopher Columbus and Martin Frobisher, for the so-called practical geographic information they contained (Burton and Loomba 2007: 70). The perpetuation of these African mythologies demonstrates how swiftly African proto-ethnography moved across 'permeable borders' into fact-based travelogues (Curran 2013: 7).

The turn of the 17th century reflected both continuity and change with earlier European ideas about Africa and Africans. Encounters between the English and Africans increased over the second half of the 16th century due to England's emerging presence on the African coast and its developing trade in enslaved Africans. On the one hand, writers continued to draw on medieval and Renaissance texts for information about

Africa and, in doing so, perpetuated the notion that the continent was full of strange and monstrous things. On the other hand, the most extravagant, and indeed imaginary, perceptions of Africa, including the images of monstrous races, began to disappear from European writings during this period (Curran 2013: 43). A developing emphasis was being placed on ethnographic and anthropological accuracy in depictions of Africans and their descendants; yet, the English still found ways to call upon the corporeality of Africans to link them to a supposed monstrosity and animality that placed them on the borders of humanity.

The sudden and rapid expansion of the British African slave trade began in the 1660s, and, by the late 17th century, there is widespread evidence that skin colour had become a significant preoccupation in English discussions of human variety and the perceived physical, moral and intellectual differences between Africans and Europeans. Black skin perplexed the English for several reasons but many believed that 'if the cause of human blackness could be explained, then its nature and significance would follow' (Jordan 1968: 11). Roxann Wheeler (2000: 2, 7) argues that skin colour was not the primary mark of human difference until the last quarter of the 18th century; yet 17th-century debates about human variety suggest that English writers perceived black skin as the most prominent signifier of monstrosity among Africans and a sign of their inner 'difference'.

The most popular theories on the origin of blackness—climate theory, Biblical story and maternal imagination—posited an original whiteness for all humans and suggested that blackness might be a temporary aberration from the norm. In the late 17th century, the editors of the *Athenian Mercury* referred to blackness as an 'accidental imperfection'. The 'Athenian Society' was a pen name for the four Whig editors of the *Athenian Mercury*: John Dunton, a bookseller and publisher; Richard Sault, a mathematician and writer; Samuel Wesley, an Anglican clergyman, who went to school with Daniel Defoe and was the father of abolitionists John and Charles Wesley; and John Norris, a Neo-Platonist. With the exception of John Dunton, who travelled to New England in 1685, none of the contributors to the journal had any first-hand knowledge of the colonies or slavery in the Americas. Nonetheless, these writers dealt with numerous questions relating to people of African descent.

In their conceptualisation of black skin, the editors of the *Athenian Mercury* emphasised its familiarity with other so-called deformities. They claimed that maternal imagination caused both blackness and other 'monstrosities' and that individuals would be 'cur'd' of such 'defects' at the resurrection (Vol. 1 No. 12; Vol. 3 No. 28; Vol. 3 No. 29). Would Africans and blacks ascend to heaven on judgment day? If they did, would their blackness ascend as well? For the English, it was necessary for supposedly imperfect bodies—black, female or deformed—to be restored to a perfect heavenly state upon resurrection to 'maintain the homogeneity of God's plan' (Molineux 2012: 97). The editors asserted that the religious question of whether Africans would 'rise to the last day' was really a question of aesthetics—'whether *white* or *black* is *better colour*?' (Vol. 3 No. 29). They concluded that 'Black is the colour of Night, frightful, dark and horrid, but White of the Day and Light refreshing and lovely'. Therefore, 'the Negro … shall not arise with that Complexion, but leave it behind him in the darkness of the Grave, exchanging it for a brighter and a better at his return agen into the World' (Vol. 3 No. 29).

According to the *Mercury*, God's merciful correction of imperfect bodies was not reserved for people of African descent. Other supposedly 'deformed' and 'monstrous' individuals such as giants, dwarfs or those 'born with six fingers or one less than he ought' would ascend to heaven 'at the greatest *perfection* of the *natures*' (Vol. 3 No. 28). Despite these similarities, the pages of the *Mercury* reveal that blackness remained fundamentally different than other 'defects'. Slavery was key to such differences.

According to the editors, slavery generated salvation and salvation cured blackness. The *Mercury* supported slavery by arguing that it was 'the greatest *kindness* ... since otherwise they [Africans] must either be *killed* or *eaten*, or both, by their barbarous conquering Enemy—Besides, it might be a means to save their *souls* as well as *Lives* ...' (Vol. 3 No. 30). Although such argument was certainly not the only rhetoric in defense of slavery, it demonstrates that blackness, monstrosity, enslaveability and salvation were inextricably linked in the 17th-century Atlantic World. As Jennifer L. Morgan has shown, beastliness and monstrosity became 'evidence of a cultural inferiority that ultimately became encoded as racial difference' (Morgan 2004: 49). Monstrosity was, thus, one key conceptual element that enabled the enslavement of Africans and their descendants. Britain's economic interest in slavery was a significant feature of such justifications. The *Athenian Mercury* was published at the height of the metropolitan debate about the Royal African Company's monopoly on the slave trade and what emerged out of such debates was a new understanding among Britons of the slave trade and slavery's significance to Britain's economy. The *Mercury*'s discussion of blackness as a collective, inheritable and racial monstrosity, and slavery as its cure, reflected a turning point in how Britons understood their relationship to slavery and empire.

Disability and the Enslaved Body

The relationship between disability, race and slavery in the colonial period was not just one of representation; rather, disfigurement and impairment were routine results of enslavement in the British Caribbean. From the very moment of seizure in sub-Saharan Africa, enslaved bodies were methodically marked with slavery's violence. The process of capture, forced march, imprisonment and forced migration that characterised the slave trade, and the physical effects of forced labour in sugar production, malnutrition, disease and legally sanctioned punishments which characterised British Caribbean plantations, often resulted in long-term emotional and physical damage. For captives who survived the passage and years of 'seasoning', disfigurement, disease and impairment came to characterise their lives—they were 'kept alive but in a *state of injury*, in a phantom like world of horrors and intense cruelty and profanity' (Mbembé 2003: 21). In British Caribbean slave societies, the space between fitness and death constituted the majority of one's life in enslavement.

Legally sanctioned punishments were the most distinctive form of impairment and disfigurement endured by the enslaved. Throughout the colonial period, the laws that governed the enslaved were written by the white planter elite and thus reflected an 'immediate reaction of what the slave-owner conceived to be the necessities of the slave system' (Goveia 1970: 19). The 1661 Barbados slave code was the first comprehensive slave law of the Americas and greatly influenced the establishment of other English colonial laws, including Jamaica's 1664 *An Act for the better ordering and Governing of Negro Slaves*. These early laws granted slave owners almost unlimited power to punish the enslaved privately and at their own discretion. Although subsequent laws did not explicitly delegate such sovereignty, these founding laws established a mentality that it was the owner's right to govern and punish his or her property, however he or she saw fit (Paton 2001: 927). In 1717 it was made illegal for masters to dismember captives on their own property, yet, 'such provisions were by no means ubiquitous', and very little measure was taken to limit the power of owners to damage their human property (Goveia 1970: 29). The enslaved were frequently sentenced by the courts to have their ears cut off close to their heads, to have a foot removed and to have their nostrils slit for crimes such as theft and running away (Paton 2001: 937–941).

In addition to brutal punishments, the enslaved also experienced impairment caused by labour accidents, disease and malnutrition. Unsanitary water and extremely tight living quarters caused and helped spread a variety of illnesses and diseases including scabies, leprosy, yaws, parasites and worms, smallpox, diphtheria, whooping cough, measles, mumps and influenza. One 18th-century plantation management guide cautioned planters to the kinds of illness to which the enslaved were prone. The author described the yaws as:

> great ulcers that break out in various parts of the body, but chiefly on the arms, and hips; the wounds yield very little matter, nor are they very painfull [sic]; but if not cured in time will spread in hard knots all over the body, and infect the whole mass of blood; the mussels will be contracted and the features deformed; the face swell'd with large blotches, and death the consequence—unless skillfull application be had. When any negroe is soon to have this disorder, he must be taken from amongst your other slaves, or he will infect the whole. (Dovaston 1774: 253)

Other illnesses included worms, which caused an individual to appear 'as tho he was mad, and run about with desperate and ghastly looks, at other times the slaves will be taken with shakes and fitts like those of an ague, and the blood be quite chill'd to their thinking' (Dovaston 1774: 256). These diseases of unfreedom were an everyday reality for enslaved individuals and constituted a silent but powerful and highly visible debilitation of the body.

Sugar production was an extremely dangerous enterprise that caused frequent dismemberment among sugar boilers and, for field labourers, a gradual deterioration of the body. Due to their status as chattel, planters utilised enslaved bodies to their utmost benefit regardless of impairments. In the Newton plantation accounts of Christ Church Barbados, Sampson Wood, manager of the plantation, in 1796 proudly asserted that 'all who can be of any service in the plantation are put to some occupation or other' (Newton Papers MS523/288). According to Wood, the mere presence of severely ill or impaired captives on the plantation, however, was a problem. Wood commented that on the Newton plantation:

> All have something to do, except diseased people and cripples, or those who have a kind of right to be idle, as it were, by prescription & long (I must say bad) habit, for it is an ill

> example to the other people on the estate & indeed a hardship for whilst they are labouring, those are at their … leisure, & have the same daily food, cloathing, and allowed them & more than the labourers. I wish they would take themselves off to a distance, as Becky did, I am sure I should not hinder them.

Wood's complaint that the presence of impaired and diseased captives on plantation grounds caused contempt among the able-bodied can be interpreted as a projection of his own aversion to impaired bondspeople. Due to the limitations of the archival record, it is difficult to ascertain how captives themselves understood impairment among the enslaved population.

The History of Mary Prince ([1831], in Salih 2000) provides an indication, albeit limited, of how free whites and enslaved blacks responded to the impaired bodies in their midst. Prince described an enslaved man named Daniel, who was 'lame in the hip, and could not keep up with the rest of the slaves' and, thus, subjected to his master's sadistic punishments, which further incapacitated him. 'He was an object of pity and terror to the whole gang of slaves', Prince wrote, 'and in his wretched case we saw, each of us, our own lot, if we should live to be so old' (Salih 2000: 21). Prince suggested that the enslaved viewed such physical conditions as a direct result of enslavement, not as a personal tragedy but, rather, a condition to which they were all susceptible as forced labourers. She later testified that individuals whose bodies had no value for the industrial work regime of plantation labour suffered greater violence at the hands of overseers and owners than their able-bodied counterparts. Sarah, an enslaved woman 'nearly past work … who was subject to several bodily infirmities, and was not quite right in the head', endured sadistic punishments from her overseer, Master Dickey, because she 'did not wheel the barrow fast enough to please him' (Salih 2000: 22). Sarah died a few days after she received her punishment. Prince's narrative demonstrates the unremitting violence the enslaved endured and suggests that individuals whose bodies had become antithetical to the industrial work regime of plantation labour suffered greater violence at the hands of overseers and owners than able-bodied labourers.

Evidence of Things Unseen: Following Slavery's Ghost

According to Gordon, 'The presence of the ghost informs us that the over and done with "extremity" of a domestic and international slavery has not entirely gone away, even if it seems to have passed into the register of history and symbol' (2008: 168). Disability is key to how slavery and the unfinished work of emancipation continue to haunt former slave societies. The prevalence of disability caused by poor nutrition and inadequate access to health care is one key manifestation of slavery's ghost. The rate of diabetes in the Caribbean islands is consistently high and imposes a very high economic burden on Caribbean citizens. Many people with diabetes have limited access to health care, which can lead to temporary and permanent impairments (Barceló et al. 2003: 19; International Diabetes Federation 2013).

Rates of incarceration among people of African descent and people with disabilities are another sign that slavery's unquiet ghost haunts the African diaspora. Although the majority of research on incarceration, race and disability focuses on the USA, such research has relevance to and across the African diaspora, including the Caribbean. The institutionalisation of black impaired bodies in the Caribbean is inextricably bound to histories of slavery. By the late 18th century, laws were put in force in Barbados and Jamaica to ensure that owners, and not the state, had the responsibility to provide for their disabled labourers and keep them from 'wandering' the island (*The Acts of assembly of the island of Jamaica* 1788: 5). Prisons and workhouses in the Caribbean were a relatively new phenomenon in the late 18th century and reflected the modern continuum between state penal power and slave-owner sovereignty. The lodging of disabled captives in workhouses testifies to the growing problem of public displays of impaired bodies in the islands.

Today capitalism has found alternative ways to generate profit from bodies perceived as disabled by incarcerating them in total institutions such as nursing homes and prisons. Liat Ben-Moshe explains that 'disablement has become big business … [f]rom the point of view of the institution-industrial complex, disabled people are worth more to the gross domestic product when occupying institutional "beds" than they are in their own homes' (2011: 393). Race also plays a key role in rates of institutionalisation in former slave societies. Research on the USA has shown that in 2006, Latinos and African-Americans were incarcerated at a rate of 1038 per 100,000 residents and 2468 per 100,000 residents, respectively, compared to whites, who were imprisoned at a rate of 409 per 100,000 residents. What is more, nearly a quarter of prison and jail inmates who had a mental health problem had served three or more prior incarcerations (Ben-Moshe 2011: 387). 'The black body', argues Hershini Bhana Young (2005: 389), 'continues to be the site onto which the state displaces its own violent crimes, externalizing its culpability and binding the black body'. Thus, the development of modern notions of disability and race that Atlantic slavery and the slave trade set in motion can be seen today in the widespread institutionalisation of black and disabled bodies.

People of African descent and people with disabilities are still being constrained by the prejudiced and racist societal forces of capitalism today. In prisons across the Americas, a racialised and disabled workforce labours for capitalistic means yet under different structural forms of violence. Individuals labelled as 'mad', 'foolish' or 'idiots' as well as people of African descent have long been associated with notions of social danger and perceived as being prone to violent crimes (Hahn-Rafter 1997; Young 2005). Like the structures of slavery, the incarceration and institutionalisation of black and disabled peoples today demonstrates that such individuals are always seen as criminal and in need of punishment by way of constraint.

Conclusion

Like Fanon's 'The Fact of Blackness', 20th-century Afro-Atlantic fiction writers have registered the fact that there has never been anything 'accidental' about the physically destructive consequences of slavery and its legacies for people of African descent. The canonical literature of the Anglophone Black Atlantic world has produced a poignant catalogue of the ways in which enslavement routinely resulted in humiliating, painful and physically disabling conditions. The enslaved African who is the title character of British-Caribbean writer Caryl Phillips's novel *Cambridge* is horrified by the casual and disfiguring brutality revealed in newspaper advertisements that offered for sale, or sought the return of, enslaved blacks in Britain: 'To be sold, a handsome creole wench named HARMONY alias AMY. Fourteen years of age, she reads but a little. She has a scar on her breast occasioned by a burn, and a toe cut off each foot. Any person who may have a mind to the said girl, is desired to apply before the 30th' (Phillips [1991] 1993: 148). In Alex Haley's *Roots*, Kunta Kinte is still a teenager when slave catchers chop off half his foot in order to make it impossible for him to ever run away again (Haley [1976] 2007: 313).

Perhaps most powerful is Toni Morrison's celebrated novel *Beloved*, whose main characters, Sethe and Beloved, are based on the real-life story of African-American fugitive Margaret Garner and the baby daughter whom Garner killed in order to save her from reenslavement. Sethe tries to hold her family together after emancipation, but is twice scarred by slavery: first by a disfiguring scar that covers her back, the result of a vicious whipping during her enslavement, and second, by the memory of her murder of Beloved. In the same way that Sethe's beating leaves a visible record on her body, Beloved refuses to remain just a psychological wound—she spends years haunting Sethe's family as a childish, spiteful and angry ghost, only to eventually manifest corporeally as a destructive and demanding adolescent girl who moves in and slowly sucks the life out of Sethe's body. Beloved drives Sethe to physical illness and near madness until she is finally exorcised from her life (Morrison 2006).

This chapter has sought to demonstrate that, like Beloved, slavery's disabling legacy moves fluidly between the realms of representation, memory and corporeality, waging war on the bodies of the descendants of the enslaved in ways that leave them permanently scarred and impaired in disproportionate numbers. These visitations are echoes of the fact that the early modern economy of enslavement measured profit in the damaged, yet still living, bodies of enslaved labourers in the Caribbean. Modern capitalism and its attendant forms of state power continue to be characterised by systematised patterns of African diasporic disablement. Ghosts are more than memories or dreams; like Beloved, plantation slavery is 'disremembered and unaccounted' but its ghost too often takes the form of violent black disablement in the modern world. Like the traces of Beloved's existence, slavery's racialised and systematically disabling legacy is widespread and yet spectral, constantly (re)rendered invisible: 'Should a child, or an adult place his feet in them [Beloved's footprints], they will fit. Take them out and they disappear as if nobody ever walked there' (Morrison [1987] 2006: 315).

References

Al Snih, S., Graham, J. E., Yong-Fang, K., Goodwin, J. S., Markides, K. S., & Ottenbacher, K. J. (2010). Obesity and disability: Relation among older adults living in Latin America and the Caribbean. *American Journal of Epidemiology, 171*(12), 1282–1288. doi:10.1093/aje/kwq087.

Barceló, A., Aedo, C., Rajpathak, S., & Robles, S. (2003). The cost of diabetes in Latin America and the Caribbean. *Bulletin of the World Health Organization, 81*(1), 19–29. http://dx.doi.org/10.1590/S0042-96862003000100006.

Barnes, C. (1990). *Cabbage syndrome: The social construction of dependence*. Lewes: Falmer Press.

Ben-Moshe, L. (2011). Disabling incarceration: Connecting disability to divergent confinements in the US. *Critical Sociology, 39*(3), 385–403. doi:10.1177/0896920511430864.

Borsay, A. (2005). *Disability and social policy in Britain since 1750*. Basingstoke: Palgrave Macmillan.

Brammall, K. M. (1996). Monstrous metamorphosis: Nature, morality, and the rhetoric of monstrosity in tudor England. *The Sixteenth Century Journal, 27*(1), 3–21. http://www.jstor.org/stable/2544266.

Burton, J., & Loomba, A. (2007). *Race in early modern England: A documentary companion*. Basingstoke: Palgrave Macmillan.

Choi, K.-H. (2001). Impaired body as colonial trope: Kand Kyong'ae's 'underground village'. *Public Culture, 13*(3), 431–458.

Curran, A. (2013). *The anatomy of blackness: Science and slavery in an age of enlightenment*. Baltimore: John Hopkins University Press.

Davis, L. J. (1995). *Enforcing normalcy: Disability, deafness, and the body*. New York: Verso.

Davis, L. J. (1999). Crips strike back: The rise of disability studies. *American Literary History, 11*(3), 500–512. http://www.jstor.org/stable/490130.

Dovaston, J. (1774). *Agricultura Americana or improvements in West-India husbandry considered*. Vol. 1, Codex Eng 60, John Carter Brown Library.

Erevelles, N. (2011). *Disability and difference in global contexts: Enabling a transformative body politic*. New York: Palgrave Macmillan.

Fanon, F. (1952). *Peau noire, masques blancs [Black Skin, White Masks]*. Paris: Editions de Seuil.

Fanon, F. (1961). *The wretched of the Earth*. London: Penguin.

Finkelstein, V. (1980). *Attitudes and disabled people: Issues for discussion*. New York: World Rehabilitation Fund.

Garland-Thomson, R. (1997). *Extraordinary bodies: Figuring physical disability in American culture and literature*. New York: Columbia University Publishers.

Garland-Thomson, R. (2005). Feminist disability studies. *Signs, 30*(2), 1558–1587. http://www.jstor.org/stable/10.1086/423352.

Gleeson, B. J. (1999). *Geographies of disability*. London: Routledge.

Gordon, A. F. (2008). *Ghostly matters: Haunting and the sociological imagination*. Minneapolis: University of Minnesota Press. (Original work published 1997).

Goveia, E. (1970). *The West Indian slave laws of the 18th century*. Barbados: Caribbean University Press.

Grech, S. (2011). Recolonising debates or perpetuated coloniality? Decentring the spaces of disability, development and community in the global South. *International Journal of Inclusive Education, 15*, 87–100. doi:10.1080/13603116.2010.496198.

Grech, S. (2012). Disability, communities of poverty and the global south. In A. Azzopardi & S. Grech (Eds.), *Inclusive communities: A critical reader* (pp. 69–84). Rotterdam: Sense Publishers.

Hahn-Rafter, N. (1997). *Creating born criminals*. Chicago: University of Illinois Press.

Haley, A. (2007). *Roots: The saga of an American family*. 30th anniversary edition. New York: Vanguard Books. (Original work published 1976).

International Diabetes Federation. (2013). North America and Caribbean at a glance. In *IDF Diabetes Atlas* (6th ed.). Retrieved May 24, 2014, from http://ww,w.idf.org/sites/default/files/DA6_Regional_factsheets.pdf.

James, C. L. R. (1989). *The black Jacobins: Toussaint L'Ouverture and the San Domingo revolution*. New York: Random House. (Original work published 1963).

Jordan, W. (1968). *White over black: American attitudes toward the Negro, 1550–1812*. Chapel Hill: University of North Carolina.

Klein, H., & Vinson, B., III. (2007). *African slavery in Latin America and the Caribbean* (2nd ed.). New York: Oxford University Press.

Mbembé, J. A. (2003). Necropolitics. *Public Culture, 15*(1), 11–40.

McRuer, R. (2006). *Crip theory: Cultural signs of queerness and disability*. New York: New York University Press.

Mintz, S. (1985). *Sweetness and power: The place of sugar in modern history*. New York: Penguin.

Molineux, C. (2012). *Faces of perfect ebony: Encountering Atlantic slavery in imperial Britain*. Cambridge: Harvard University Press.

Morgan, J. L. (2004). *Laboring women: Reproduction and gender in new world slavery*. Philadelphia, PA: University of Pennsylvania Press.

Morrison, T. (2006). *Beloved*. New York: Alfred A. Knopf. (Original work published 1987).

Oliver, M. (1990). *The politics of disablement*. London: Macmillan.

Paton, D. (2001). Punishment, crime, and the bodies of slaves in eighteenth-century Jamaica. *Journal of Social History, 34*(4), 923–954.

Paton, D. (2004). *No bond but the law: Punishment, race, and gender in Jamaican state formation, 1780–1870*. Durham: Duke University Press.

Phillips, C. (1993). *Cambridge*. New York: Vintage International. (Original work published 1991).

Pliny the Elder. (1566). *A summarie of the antiquities, and wonders of the worlde*. Early English Books Online. Ann Arbor, MI: University of Michigan.

Salih, S. (Ed.). (2000). *The history of Mary Prince: A West Indian slave [1831]*. Toronto: Penguin.

Sheller, M. (2003). *Consuming the Caribbean: From Arawaks to zombies*. New York: Routledge.

Sherry, M. (2007). (Post)colonizing disability. *Wagadu*, special issue on intersecting gender and disability perspectives in rethinking postcolonial identities, 4, 10–22. Retrieved from http://appweb.cortland.edu/ojs/index.php/Wagadu/article/view/323/609.

Shildrick, M. (2002). *Embodying the monster: Encounters with the vulnerable self*. London: Sage.

Stagg, K. (2006). Representing physical difference: The materiality of the monstrous. In D. M. Turner & K. Stagg (Eds.), *Social histories of disability and deformity: Bodies, images and experiences*. New York: Routledge.

Szasz, T. (2003). *Liberation by oppression: A comparative study of slavery and psychiatry*. New Brunswick: Transaction Publishers.

The Acts of assembly of the island of Jamaica: To repeal several acts and clauses of acts respecting slaves and for the better order and government of slaves, and for other purposes: Commonly called, the Consolidation Act: As exhibiting at one view most of the essential regulations of the Jamaica Code noir: Which was passed by the Assembly on the 19th day of December 1787 and by the Lieutenant Governor and the Council on the 22nd of the said month. Respectfully communicated to the public by Stephen Fuller, Esq. Agent for Jamaica (1788).

Titchkosky, T. (2015). Life with dead metaphors: Impairment rhetoric in social justice praxis. *Journal of Literary & Cultural Disability Studies, 9*(1), 18. doi:10.3828/jlcds.2015.1.

Turner, D. M. (2006). Introduction: Approaching anomalous bodies. In D. M. Turner & K. Stagg (Eds.), *Social histories of disability and deformity: Bodies, images and experiences*. New York: Routledge.

Wheeler, R. (2000). *The complexion of race: Categories of difference in eighteenth-century British culture*. Philadelphia: University of Pennsylvania Press.

Wood, S. (1796). *Newton Papers (MS523/288), stored at the Main Library, University of the West Indies*. Barbados: Cave Hill Campus.

Young, H. B. (2005). Inheriting the criminalized black body: Race, gender, and slavery in *Eva's Man. African American Review, 39*(3), 377–393. http://www.jstor.org/stable/40033670.

Young, H. B. (2006). *Haunting capital: Memory, text, and the black diasporic body*. Hanover: Dartmouth College Press.

Chapter 25
From Colonialism to Postcolonialism and Contemporary Empire

Siobhan Senier and Beatriz Miranda-Galarza

Introduction

European imperialism constructed disability across the global South in profound, albeit not universal, ways. Whether by direct administration, settlement, and/or neglect, colonial rule created new ideas about and categories of (dis)ability. As shown in Kennedy and Newton's chapter (2016, in this volume), colonialism also ushered in new somatic experiences of impairment through the sheer violence of conquest, the importation of new diseases, the destruction and appropriation of indigenous land bases and resources, and the exploitation of the very bodies of the colonized for labor.

Postcolonialism describes what happened after European powers were ostensibly overthrown or otherwise resisted. The global decolonization movement is often said to have begun with the Haitian revolution (1791–1804), and to have gained momentum with the 1947 independence (and partition) of India. In such cases, historians have shown that while local populations ousted their colonizers and have worked to reclaim traditional forms of governance and social life, they have also been dogged by the persistence of colonial laws, languages, and ideologies, as well as by continued exploitation and poverty. Similar (though not identical) dynamics have appeared throughout the nationalist movements that have swept Africa, Asia, Latin America, and the Middle East from the mid-20th into the early 21st centuries. Postcolonial activists and scholars have struggled to understand and resist ostensibly colonial imports such as patriarchy, racism, heterosexism, capitalism, and ableism (for example, Thomas 1999; Campbell 2000).

S. Senier (✉)
University of New Hampshire, Durham, NH, USA
e-mail: Siobhan.Senier@unh.edu

B. Miranda-Galarza
VU University, Amsterdam, The Netherlands

S. Grech, K. Soldatic (eds.), *Disability in the Global South*,
International Perspectives on Social Policy, Administration, and Practice,
DOI 10.1007/978-3-319-42488-0_25

The historiography of disability in the global North typically begins with medicalization, moving on to segregation and stigma, and finally to the rise of group identification and activism (Braddock and Parish 2001). These teleologies are more complicated in countries struggling with ongoing legacies of colonialism, racism, and poverty. In the first place, liberation has seldom been clean or straightforward. Whether as in India, where Britain formally withdrew its administration and "granted independence," or as in Palestine, where colonizers continue to build settlements and extend their administration of daily life, colonialism is never really "over." Moreover, independence and nation-(re)building bring distinct political and economic shifts of their own, including changes in labor systems and resource distribution under the so-called modernization and development. All of these changes affect bodies, and the ways that individuals and communities experience and think about (dis)ability. Indeed, many of the scholars we cite in this chapter have shown that the emergence of transnational capital, new forms of labor, violence, and global domination continue to generate new meanings and experiences of disability.

A thorough postcolonial history of disability experience, activism, and culture in the global South is yet to be written. Indeed, scholarly and critical conversations between the two fields of postcolonialism and disability are still wholly emergent, despite the deep commitments in each to interdisciplinarity. In this chapter, we enumerate some of postcolonial theory's keywords and concerns, and ponder postcolonial studies' and disability studies' (dis)engagements. We reference just a few examples of contemporary global South disability policy, disability rights activism, and disability arts. Headed for the 21st century, many of the world's poorest and most disenfranchised populations find themselves newly beholden to the forces of neoliberalism and globalization. The latter sections of this chapter therefore suggest directions for future research on disability under these new forms of imperialism.

The Rise of Postcolonial Theory

The roots of postcolonial theory are long and deep, arguably beginning with colonialism itself, and certainly owing much to writers including Frantz Fanon and Aimé Césaire. As an academic discipline, however, postcolonial theory is usually said to have originated in the 1980s, when a cohort of British scholars known as the Subaltern Studies group began, among other projects, to interrogate South Asian historiography (Chaturvedi 2012). These scholars found narratives of Indian nationalism overly focused on the contributions of elite leaders, at the expense of those of everyday people. Their approach to "writing history from below" had strong appeal to scholars in a variety of fields, because it demanded deliberate attention to the Other by way of positions including nation, race, and gender.

For instance, in her famous essay "Can the Subaltern Speak?," Gayatri Chakravorty Spivak used the example of Indian *sati,* or the so-called widow burning, to show that it is difficult if not impossible to hear the voices of women of color in the colonial archive (Spivak 1988). Spivak refused to presume to know the widows' own desires: to be rescued from a "barbarous" ritual, or to resist colonial authority through a "Hindu" practice. In Spivak's reading, colonial archives reveal much less about their alleged subjects than about the fantasies of the British authorities who wrote and compiled them, authorities invested in a narrative of "white men saving brown women from brown men" (Spivak 1988: 297). Since the appearance of this influential essay, scholars in a wide range of fields have invoked the subaltern to represent marginalized people struggling to speak back to power while exercising caution about speaking *for* others. It is not difficult to see where disability studies could bring to the definition of subaltern an insistence on, for instance, the somatic experience of speech, while in turn postcolonial questions of nationalism and imperialism could help enrich the disability mantra, "Nothing about us without us."

Questions of otherness, alterity, and resistance to colonial power were also influentially described by the late Palestinian scholar Edward Said, author of the still widely cited *Orientalism*. Like Spivak, Said was concerned with the representation (or, more precisely, the deliberate *mis*representation) of colonial subjects in historiography and literary representations. It was his project, and that of many of his contemporaries, to show that such representations are never natural, but rather directly implicated in colonial power relations and violence. "Orientalism," he said, "was a political vision of reality whose structure promoted the difference between the familiar (Europe, West, Us) and the strange (the Orient, East, Them)" (Said 1979: 43).

One approach to such misrepresentation and domination is, as in the case of Haiti, armed revolt and overt protest. However, resistance also often takes much more subtle forms, and the relations between the colonizer and the colonized are often far more complicated, and inextricable, than a simple "Us v. Them." Bhabha (2012) is one theorist who has sought to elucidate the canny strategies that colonized people use to circumvent, accommodate, or even provisionally embrace the mechanisms of power. He uses terms like "hybridity," "sly civility," and "ambivalence" to capture the double-edged nature of postcolonial identity.

The concerns of postcolonial studies—questions of who has the right to speak for whom, of how oppressed people enact resistance, and of how forms of domination persist and change—are of great potential interest to other fields of inquiry including disability studies. But even these keywords and concerns have already been subject to questioning from below. In particular, Latin American scholars have observed that a great deal of postcolonial theory ignores the history of the 15th and 16th centuries, and the imperial experience of Spain (Méndez 2006: 358). Méndez, who has argued that postcolonial critique was in existence long before the South Asian school named it as such, has called for the articulation of a more independent Latin American postcolonial theory, one that would more clearly define what postcolonialism means in the Latin American context, and that would involve research into the colonial and postcolonial processes that occurred before or at the edge of the European presence in America (Méndez 2006: 359). Ultimately, Méndez argues that it is imperative to incorporate the work of Latin American scholars who enacted postcolonial critiques even before the term was academically implemented.

The modernity/coloniality group, including Dussel and Mendieta (1998), Quijano (1999), Mignolo (2000), Castro-Gomez (2008), and others, has articulated instead a theory of *decolonialism*. Decolonial theory uses multiple and heterogeneous conceptions that are more spatially oriented, like "border thinking" or "border epistemologies" (Mignolo 2000), insistently reminding us that knowledge and power cannot be understood outside of their specific geographical, political, and historical contexts. The year 1998 marks the fragmentation of what constituted the so-called Latin American Subaltern Studies Group (Grosfoguel 2007). Grosfoguel identifies two main discursive divisions: those who read subalternity as a postmodern critique (Eurocentric critique from a Eurocentric position) and those who read it as a decolonial critique (Eurocentric critique from a subaltern position). The process of the colonialist imposition of knowledge is what Mignolo calls the subscription of knowledge to a geopolitical space (Western Europe). Maldonado-Torres, on the other hand, insists that up to now ideas of spatiality and geopolitical relations have shaped the origin of theories of knowledge within an Enlightened Centre, Europe (2004: 29). Although each of these streams has proved immensely rich and valuable, still, neither really attends to disability.

Postcolonial and Disability Studies: Disengagements

Indeed, disability has been altogether absent from most of the postcolonial and decolonial theorizing described above; disability studies, meanwhile, have been heavily oriented toward British and American contexts. The incursion of disability studies into the field of social sciences during the 1950s and its previous anthropological approximations years before have allowed the possibility of rethinking disability beyond the functional limitations of the individual body, understanding that structure, culture, and language are responsible for shaping what is called disability. Within this framework, a constant process of changing terminology and creating theoretical models in western societies has had a major impact on their implementation in the Majority World. A local history is needed, however, in order to demonstrate that global and local sociocultural discourses construct a dominant experience of disability within a particular context, as has been suggested by some sociologists, anthropologists, and others (see for example Corker 1998; Jenkins 1999; Gleeson 2002; Yeo and Bolton 2008).

Groce (2006) has insisted that the lives of individuals with disability are limited not so much by their specific impairment as by the social interpretation of that disability. Anthropological studies have supported her argument; see, for instance, Ingstad and Whyte (1995), Gannotti et al. (2001), and Klotz (2004). The call for cross-cultural research has provoked a two-sided response. On one side are researchers who have preferred to approach disability as "difference," limiting their observation to local culture as a burden for target groups (Ingstad and Whyte 2007) isolated from the historical global context. On the other side are scholars who have looked at disability from a critical and broader concept of culture that involves not only practices but also language, interactions, discourses, and power.

More recently, scholars informed by postcolonial theory's rigorous dismantling of the idea of universality have begun to interrogate the category of disability itself from this vantage point. Introducing her fellow historians to disability as a category of analysis, Catherine Kudlick (2003) wrote a comprehensive review of a dozen groundbreaking disability histories written between 1999 and 2002, including such still-canonical texts as Stiker (2000), and Longmore and Umansky (2001). She observed that the field had been dominated by European and American analyses, concluding that, "[q]uite likely a disability studies paradigm designed in, and applied to, the modern West might not make sense in many situations. Yet the experiences of the Middle East, Africa, Asia and Latin America all have much to teach" scholars in the North (Kudlick 2003: 792). Meanwhile, in the social sciences, scholars in critical disability studies have adopted similar critiques of universality. Calling for disability studies to interrogate the knowledge produced in the global metropole (or imperial center), Connell observes that, in its eagerness to distinguish disability from impairment, mainstream disability studies may unwittingly naturalize impairment, which, she reminds us, "has to be understood in the context of the violence of colonisation and neo-colonial power" (2011: 1369). Meekosha and Soldatic also pursue this line of inquiry, arguing that while "[d]isability has now been mainstreamed within the development agenda" (2011: 1394), this has happened in a universalizing human rights framework, which can forestall claims to redistributive justice by groups disabled by colonial violence in the first place.

Eurocentric historical and theoretical accounts of disability have prevented contributions from other milieus and have generalized two tendencies: a descriptive narration of disability history as if it were a lineal and invariable history, and the reduction of the disability history of the Other to the differentiation between traditional and modern. At the same time, disability studies have avoided theorizing disability from a comparative historical perspective that should look to the global and the local. In this sense, the rich historical narratives from both the so-called metropolis and the colonies could be of great benefit. In any case, both factors must oblige us to search for traces that rebuild the map of the disability history throughout the global South.

Scarce and vague are the attempts by local researchers to create a historical framework that could offer the possibility of tracing the course of disability in Latin America. Indeed, some researchers have included a sort of general historical approach within their reports regarding disability, especially in Colombia: for instance, Pantano (1987) and her reflexion on disability as a social problem in Argentina; Portuondo Sao (2004) and a brief history of intellectual disability in Cuba; Cuadros (2005) and the perceptions of parents of disabled children in Colombia; Muñoz (2006) and the perceptions of disabled people and some practitioners regarding disability and rehabilitation in Colombia; Núñez García (1985) and a study regarding mental retardation; and Cruz and Hernández (2006) and the situation of exclusion of disabled people in Colombia. However, these studies, in hewing to a conception of western history as universal, have unwittingly suppressed the particularities of local and historical contexts that could illuminate a postcolonial disability history. Indeed Portuondo Sao (2004), in an article that discusses the evolution of the social concept of intellectual disability, presents a compilation of facts and data that starts with the work of the ancient Greeks until the introduction of the parameters of integration and normalization within the field of disability, with an emphasis on medical and pedagogical theories. Apart from a short section about Cuba, the restructuring of the *Hospital de Dementes* (psychiatric hospital), the introduction of some university programs on psychiatry and medicine, and the development of some policies, the history of disabled people in the Latin American countries is nonexistent. A similar approach is adopted by Muñoz, who gives a little more attention to events that occurred in Spain.

New Directions

Only very recently have postcolonial and disability studies begun to look to each other. Sherry (2007) made a detailed survey of each field's use of terms from the other, and came to the conclusion that each field was borrowing terms too loosely, running the danger of superficially treating the experiences of disability and colonization as somehow analogous. Postcolonial studies, he found, was invoking psychosis, pathology, infection, amputation, and other conditions as metaphors for the experience of nations, without giving due regard to the embodied experiences of material disability. Similarly, he saw disability studies appropriating terms like exile, apartheid, colonization, and even slavery to describe experiences of impairment and/or medicalization. Sherry called for scholars "to unpack the power dynamics which link the two experiences, both in practice and in rhetoric" (2007: 16).

This work is just beginning. Mark Sherry's survey appeared in Pushpa Naidu Parekh's guest edited special issue of *Wagadu* on "Intersecting Gender and Disability Perspectives in Rethinking Postcolonial Identities." In her own contribution, writing from her own experience living with polio in India and the USA, she began to sketch a "postcolonial feminist disability theory and praxis," highlighting the ways that an "intersectional approach complicates concepts of emancipation and decolonization" (Parekh 2007: 142). Her assessment of the state of the field(s) was as follows:

> Today, dominance of medical approaches to disease and disability in developing countries often find governmental sanction as well as international support through emphasis on social policy, and proliferation of institutions of health care and rehabilitation. Activists, on the other hand, are voicing the human rights issues, while academic institutions are beginning to grapple with the inclusion of disability studies as an area of intellectual as well as scholarly interest. (Parekh 2007: 157)

Additionally, Ghai (2002) has used the work of Asian postcolonial scholars to examine disability as a phenomenon involving specific meanings determined by political, cultural, religious, social, and economic realities. Other work of note includes Fedwa Malti-Douglas (1989) in compiling the history of blind people in the medieval Islamic society; Miles (1994, 1995, 2002) in reconstructing the history of disability in some Asian countries; and Lobo (1997) and Silva (2003) in recovering the institutional history of disability in Brazil. A particularly interesting thread is the research on leprosy, which places postcolonialism and disability face to face (Manton 2011; Buckingham 2006; Kim 2007; Moran 2007; Edmond 2009). Edmond, for instance, approaches leprosy in the British Asian Pacific colonies as a social, cultural, and political issue that involved colonial power. His work plays also with descriptions that connect the periphery with the heart of the Empire, London. Race and sexual stigmatization are found to be the elements that transformed leprosy from a medical subject to a vehicle for cultural, economic, and political segregation. Herman on the other hand approaches the analysis of leprosy in Hawaii from the "embodiment of racial discourses that disempowered people" (2001: 319). According to Herman leprosy was not medically conceptualized with certainty in the 19th century; however, a political and economic definition was clearly at play. Nowadays, when a cure for the disease has been found, Native Hawaiians remain "disproportionately afflicted by disease, low life expectancy, low income, and incarceration" (Herman 2001: 334).

There are distinct possibilities for pursuing this work in the Latin American context. According to Castro-Gómez (2005), for instance, the idea that there were superior and inferior races by "nature" consolidated the Spanish dominion throughout the 16th and the 17th centuries and was used as a scientific legitimization by the colonial power or what Quijano (1999) called *colonialidad del poder* (power colonization) in the following centuries. This affirmation contrasts with the position of disability scholars such as Davis (1995), who places the introduction of the linguistic use of the term "normalcy" in the European Continent in the 19th century. While the term as such could have been employed within the English lexicon by that century, the invention of the norm and the term itself in the Spanish-speaking world demands research. Colonial chronicles have registered the constant comparison between the *Indios* bodies, their intellect, and their behavior to the white ideal of personhood once the American *Indios* were taken as objects of study by the metropolis. For instance, the debate that originated between de las Casas and Sepúlveda about the human condition of the native inhabitants of America during the 16th century could offer some hints about it. Sepúlveda, who qualified the Indios as *homunculi* (nearer to the beast than the rational human being), said:

> These barbarians from the New World … in prudence, audacity, virtue and humanity are less inferior to the Spanish as the children to the adults, the women to the men; there is an immense difference among them that goes from furious people to clement people … and I could say from monkeys to human beings. (Brading 1991: 106, personal translation)

It is also important to reconsider the work of Benedict Ingstad as one of the pioneer scholars who envisioned a critical postcolonial research in the field of disability (see also Whyte 1995; Ingstad and Whyte 1995, 2007). Based on her experience as a European academic and a mother of a disabled child, Ingstad became aware of the expansion of western epistemology within the theorization of disability through her experience in Bostwana. Her work (from 1988 to 2007) regarding disabled families in developing countries and the myths of hiding and neglecting disabled members is still in force. Ingstad (1990: 188) argues that the North–South myth in the disability debate is of a more recent origin, resulting from the strategies of intervention implemented by industrialized countries in developing countries. This idea has been amplified in recent years by Connell (2011), Meekosha and Soldatic (2011), and Grech (2011: 97), who asserts that "the need to underline the primacy of the local remains a critical issue, because in the absence of this, the quest to universalise and generalise from North to South will remain a flawed, reductionist, and ethnocentric enterprise."

Contemporary Empire and Neocolonialism

Contemporary empire, arguably ruled more by transnational corporations than by geopolitical nations, in some ways seems to hark back to some of the earliest colonial productions and understandings of disability. In particular, the extractive economies that prevail in the global South are producing increasingly differential distributions of poverty, disease, and impairment. Indeed, despite affirmative actions such as inclusive education legislation, employer incentives, tax exemptions, training programs, and more apparent steps towards equality, people with disabilities in the Majority World "continue to be characterized by lower work-force participation, lower wages, lack of or limited career advancement, and discrimination in the workplace" (Kumar et al. 2012). Furthermore, issues such as violence, dehumanized policy for elderly people, and accelerated processes of technological bureaucracy that grow in the midst of an age of neocolonial rationality have posed additional challenges for survival to people labelled as intellectually disabled (Chouinard 2012).

One important critique of these new relations comes from Livingston, an anthropologist working in Botswana, who describes an exceptionally efficient mining industry that "treated African workers as disposable, drawing in the able-bodied and farming the damaged back out to the rural communities from which they had come" (2005: 111). Livingston describes a cycle that is not unfamiliar in other nations after independence, where new wealth from enterprises like mining (never evenly distributed) ushers in some changes in medicine (which she calls "partial biomedical solutions" (2005: 112)) and infrastructure that allow many people to survive their illnesses and impairments, although often in continued poverty. Livingston uses the term *debility* to encompass not only disability but also chronic illness and aging. In so doing, she challenges two major orientations of disability studies as it has been construed in the West. She emphasizes the "somatic aspects of impairment" (2005: 113) much more than Anglo scholars, and also finds that Botswanans view debility much less individualistically than do disability activists from the North.

Herein, then, lies an irony in contemporary discussions around disability: On the one hand, as Parekh observes, the medical model of disability holds inordinate power in the global South (or rather, among the entities that seek to administer and exploit the global South); on the other the social model employed by many scholars and activists in the North tends to flatten out cultural and historic difference (Grech 2009). It is for this reason, perhaps, that Barker and Murray (2010) make such a strong bid for a more precise focus on "global bodies" in their special issue of the *Journal of Literary and Cultural Disability Studies*, entitled "Disabling Postcolonialism." Following Michael Davidson's observation that disability "unsettles a global panacea for health and human welfare" and "defamiliarizes the seemingly inexorable pattern of capital movement, information exchange and market information by which globalization is known," Barker and Murray call for a disability analysis that is "*emerging from* (rather than applied to) 'cultural locatedness' in the first instance" (2010: 227). Work like Julie Livingston's fits neatly in this vein, for it shows how conceptions of "the normate" are culturally contingent and shifting—

and how local, kin-based experiences of disability may exist in tension with lingering colonial policies. Anita Ghai's critiques of heteropatriarchy in disability rights organizing also follow this call.

Another early book-length study of disability under the conditions of transnational capitalism is Nirmala Erevelles' *Disability and Difference in Global Contexts*. Building on Judith Butler's famous question, "Which bodies matter?," Erevelles asks, "Why do some bodies matter more than others?" (2011: 6). She guards rigorously against the pitfalls noted by Mark Sherry, in particular the use of either disability or colonialism metaphorically in order to examine how "the structural inequality created out of the violence of transnational capitalism" limits the capacity and agency of disabled subjects. For instance, she asks, "how can acquiring disability be celebrated as universal, if it was acquired under poverty or war?" (2011: 130). "The radical potential of disability [as the ultimate postmodern subjectivity] can only be harnessed within certain privileged material contexts that [some disability studies] scholars appear to take for granted" (2011: 129).

Despite its limitations, postcolonial theory remains salient for the lived experience of disability in the global South, especially given the force of international policy in determining that lived experience. Ingstad (2001) observed that, following the International Year of Disabled Persons (1981) and the United Nations General Assembly's institution of a World Programme of Action Concerning Disabled Persons (1983), professional interest in disability and rehabilitation increased; she cautions, however, that this interest has been largely driven by the United Nations and nongovernmental organizations based in Europe and North America. Given that, as Ingstad puts it, "the first contact that people in developing countries had with what we today call rehabilitation came through missionaries and representatives of the colonial powers" (2001: 778), it seems evermore clear that scholars and practitioners need to attend closely to ongoing effects of colonialism, to local hybrid practices, and subaltern strategies of resistance. For example, Soldatic (2013) has suggested that, despite its many successes, the UN Convention on the Rights of Persons with Disabilities perpetuates global imperialism by privileging a framework based on individual human rights and state redress. In this framework, she shows that there are no mechanisms for redistributive justice at the collective level—for claims against transnational corporations like Union Carbide, for instance, which have materially *produced* impairment in places such as Bhopal.

Soldatic and like-minded scholars and activists are duly concerned with the *representation* of disability and impairment in the political or legislative sense; but we may also consider how disability is represented in the global South in a figurative or performative sense. The experience of impairment after Bhopal, for instance, has been depicted in the acclaimed novel *Animal's People* (Sinha 2009). Again, unlike the USA and Europe, where highly visible communities of disabled activists and artists produce performance, literature, music, and art, postcolonial disability cultures are still largely under-explored. Parekh (2007) called for more collections and anthologies of writings by people with disabilities, in the interest of promoting a "culturally grounded, historically contextualized exploration of the expressive culture of peoples with disabilities" (2004: 157).

One such collection was *Across Borders* (Driedger et al. 1996), including personal narratives by women from El Salvador, Trinidad and Tobago, Barbados, Kenya, and other countries. Other notable disability autobiographies from the global South include Ved Mehta's *Face to Face* (2013), about both his loss of sight and the relations between India and England; Tito Rajarshi Mukhopadhyay's *How Can I Talk If My Lips Don't Move?* (2011), about autism; and *Gaby Brimmer*, by a Mexican woman with cerebral palsy (Brimmer et al. 2009). Other creative writers include the deaf poet and playwright Sotonwa Opeoluwa and the deaf poet Osomun Sylvester, both from Nigeria. The online journal *Wordgathering* (wordgathering.com) frequently publishes creative works by these and other global South authors.

Conclusion

Postcolonial studies and disability studies have not had a long history of mutual recognition. The new work hinted at in this chapter, however, suggests that each field can greatly enrich the other. Postcolonialism needs a more nuanced regard for bodily difference—a consideration of which bodies matter, as Nirmala Erevelles puts it. And disability studies need the insights of postcolonial theory to explain how disability and impairment have been, and continue to be, produced, both materially and discursively. Given the prevalence of community-based rehabilitation approaches to disability in so much of the global South, and given how that prevalence is still largely driven by the investments of the North, it behoves us to keep in mind how we can continue to decolonize disability itself, in theory and praxis.

References

Barker, C., & Murray, S. (2010). Disabling postcolonialism: Global disability cultures and democratic criticism. *Journal of Literary & Cultural Disability Studies, 4*(3), 219–236. doi:10.3828/jlcds.2010.20.

Bhabha, H. K. (2012). *The location of culture*. New York: Routledge.

Braddock, D., & Parish, S. (2001). An institutional history of disability. In G. L. Albrecht, K. D. Seelman, & M. Bury (Eds.), *Handbook of disability studies* (pp. 11–68). Thousand Oaks, CA: Sage.

Brading, D. (1991). *The first America: The Spanish monarchy, Creole patriots and the liberal state, 1492–1867*. Cambridge: Cambridge University Press.

Brimmer, G., Poniatowska, E., & Balch, T. (2009). *Gaby Brimmer: An autobiography in three voices*. Waltham, MA: Brandeis University Press and University Press of New England.

Buckingham, J. (2006). Patient welfare vs. the health of the nation: Governmentality and sterilisation of leprosy sufferers in early post-colonial India. *Social History of Medicine, 19*(3), 483–499.

Campbell, J. (2000). *Arguing with the phallus: Feminist, queer, and postcolonial theory: A psychoanalytic contribution*. London: Zed Books.

Castro-Gómez, S. (2005). *La hybris del punto cero: ciencia, raza e ilustración en la Nueva Granada*. Bogotá: Editorial Pontificia Universidad Javeriana.

Castro-Gomez, S. (2008). (Post)coloniality for dummies: Latin American perspectives on modernity, coloniality and the geopolitics of knowledge. In M. Moraña, E. Dussel, & C. A. Jáuregui (Eds.), *Coloniality at large: Latin America and the postcolonial debate* (pp. 259–285). Durham, NC: Duke University Press.

Chaturvedi, V. (2012). *Mapping subaltern studies and the postcolonial. (Mappings series).* London: Verso Books.

Chouinard, V. (2012). Pushing the boundaries of our understanding of disability and violence: Voices from the global South (Guyana). *Disability & Society, 27*(6), 777–792.

Connell, R. (2011). Southern bodies and disability: Re-thinking concepts. *Third World Quarterly, 32*(8), 1369–1381.

Corker, M. (1998). *Deaf and disabled, or deafness disabled? Towards a human rights perspective.* Buckingham, PA: Open University Press.

Cruz, I., & Hernández, J. (2006). *Exclusión social y discapacidad.* Bogotá: Universidad del Rosario.

Cuadros, J. H. (2005). The status of disability in Colombia and the importance of parental perceptions on the development of special education. *TEACHING Exceptional Children Plus*, 1(5). Retrieved September 19, 2014, from http://files.eric.ed.gov/fulltext/EJ966524.pdf.

Davis, L. J. (1995). *Enforcing normalcy: Disability, deafness and the body.* London: Verso.

Driedger, D., Feika, I., & Girón Batres, E. (1996). *Across borders: Women with disabilities working together.* Charlottetown: Gynergy Books.

Dussel, E., & Mendieta, E. (1998). *The underside of modernity: Apel, Ricoeur, Rorty, Taylor, & the philosophy of liberation.* Amherst, NY: Humanity Books.

Edmond, R. (2009). *Leprosy and empire: A medical and cultural history* (Vol. 8). Cambridge: Cambridge University Press.

Erevelles, N. (2011). *Disability and difference in global contexts: Enabling a transformative body politic.* New York, NY: Palgrave Macmillan.

Gannotti, M. E., Handwerker, W. P., Groce, N. E., & Cruz, C. (2001). Sociocultural influences on disability status in Puerto Rican children. *Physical Therapy, 81*(9), 1512–1523.

Ghai, A. (2002). Disabled women: An excluded agenda of Indian feminism. *Hypatia, 17*(3), 49–66.

Gleeson, B. (2002). *Geographies of disability.* London: Routledge.

Grech, S. (2009). Disability, poverty and development: Critical reflections on the majority world debate. *Disability & Society, 24*(6), 771–784.

Grech, S. (2011). Recolonising debates or perpetuated coloniality? Decentring the spaces of disability, development and community in the global South. *International Journal of Inclusive Education, 15*(1), 87–100. doi:10.1080/13603116.2010.496198.

Groce, N. (2006). Disability, public health and social injustice. In B. Levy & V. Sidel (Eds.), *Social justice and public health.* Oxford: Oxford University Press.

Grosfoguel, R. (2007). The epistemic decolonial turn: Beyond political-economy paradigms. *Cultural Studies, 21*(2–3), 211–223.

Herman, R. D. K. (2001). Out of sight, out of mind, out of power: Leprosy, race and colonization in Hawai'i. *Journal of Historical Geography, 27*(3), 319–337.

Ingstad, B. (1990). "The Cultural Construction of AIDS and Its Consequences for Prevention in Botswana." Medical Anthropology Quarterly 4(1): 28–40.

Ingstad, B. (2001). Disability in the developing world. In G. L. Albrecht, K. D. Seelman, & M. Bury (Eds.), *Handbook of disability studies (ch 35).* Thousand Oaks, CA: Sage.

Ingstad, B., & Whyte, S. R. (1995). *Disability and culture.* Berkeley: University of California Press.

Ingstad, B., & Whyte, S. R. (2007). *Disability in local and global worlds.* Berkeley: University of California Press.

Jenkins, R. (1999). *Questions of competence: Culture, classification and intellectual disability.* New York: Cambridge University Press.

Kennedy, S., & Newton, M. (2016). The hauntings of slavery: Colonialism and the disabled body in the Caribbean. In S. Grech & K. Soldatic (Eds.), *Disability in the global South: The critical handbook* (pp. xx–xx). New York: Springer.

Kim, E. (2007). Cultural rehabilitation: Hansen's disease, gender and disability in Korea. *Wagadu: A Journal of Transnational and Women's Studies, 4*, 108–124. Retrieved from http://journals.cortland.edu/wordpress/wagadu/archive/v-4-2007-special-issue-intersecting-gender-and-disability-perspectives-in-rethinking-postcolonial-identities/.

Klotz, J. (2004). Sociocultural study of intellectual disability: Moving beyond labelling and social constructionist perspectives. *British Journal of Learning Disabilities, 32*(2), 93–104.

Kudlick, C. J. (2003). Disability history: Why we need another 'other'. *American Historical Review, 108*(3), 763–793.

Kumar, A., Sonpal, D., & Hiranandani, V. (2012). Trapped between ableism and neoliberalism: Critical reflections on disability and employment in India. *Disability Studies Quarterly,* 32(3). Retrieved from http://dsq-sds.org/article/view/3235/3109.

Livingston, J. (2005). *Debility and the moral imagination in Botswana.* Bloomington: Indiana University Press.

Lobo, L. F. (1997). *Os infames da história: A instituição das deficiências no Brasil.* Rio de Janeiro: Tese de Doutorado não-publicada, Programa de Pós-graduação em Psicologia, Pontifícia Universidade Católica do Rio de Janeiro.

Longmore, P. K., & Umansky, L. (2001). *The new disability history: American perspectives.* New York: New York University Press.

Maldonado-Torres, N. (2004). The topology of being and the geopolitics of knowledge: Modernity, empire, coloniality. *City, 8*(1), 29–56.

Malti-Douglas, F. (1989). *Blindness and autobiography: Al-Ayyām of Tāhā Husayn.* Princeton, NJ: Princeton University Press.

Manton, J. (2011). Leprosy in eastern Nigeria and the social history of colonial skin. *Leprosy Review, 82*(2), 124–134.

Meekosha, H., & Soldatic, K. (2011). Human rights and the global South: The case of disability. *Third World Quarterly, 32*(8), 1383–1397.

Mehta, V. (2013). *Face to face: An autobiography.* New York: Penguin.

Méndez, C. (2006). After Spanish rule: Postcolonial predicaments in Latin America. *Hispanic American Historical Review, 86*(2), 358–361.

Mignolo, W. (2000). *Local histories/global designs: Coloniality, subaltern knowledges, and border thinking.* Princeton, NJ: Princeton University Press.

Miles, M. (1994). Disability care and education in 19th century India: Some dates, places and documentation. *Action Aid Disability News, 5*(2 Suppl), 1–22.

Miles, M. (1995). Disability in an eastern religious context: Historical perspectives. *Disability & Society, 10*(1), 49–70.

Miles, M. (2002). Some Influences of religions on attitudes towards disabilities and people with disabilities. *Journal of Religion, Disability & Health, 6*(2/3), 117–129.

Moran, M. T. (2007). *Colonizing leprosy: Imperialism and the politics of public health in the United States.* Chapel Hill: UNC Press.

Mukhopadhyay, T. R. (2011). *How can I talk if my lips don't move? Inside my autistic mind.* New York: Arcade.

Muñoz, P. (2006). *Construcción de los sentidos del mundo de la discapacidad y la persona.* Cali, Colombia: Universidad del Valle.

Núñez García, A. (1985). *Retraso mental.* Bogotá: Ediciones Morata.

Pantano, L. (1987). *La discapacidad como problema social: un enfoque sociológico, reflexiones y propuestas.* Buenos Aires: Colección Temas Eudeba.

Parekh, P. N. (2007). Gender, disability and the postcolonial nexus. *Wagadu: A Journal of Transnational and Women's Studies, 4*, 142–161. Retrieved from http://journals.cortland.edu/wordpress/wagadu/archive/v-4-2007-special-issue-intersecting-gender-and-disability-perspectives-in-rethinking-postcolonial-identities/.

Portuondo Sao, M. (2004). Evolución del concepto social de discapacidad intelectual. *Revista Cubana Salud Pública, 30*(4). Retrieved November 20, 2013, www.bvs.sld.cu/revistas/spu/vol30_4_04/spu06404.htm.

Quijano, A. (1999). Coloniality and modernity/rationality. In G. Therborn & L.-L. Wallenius (Eds.), *Globalizations and modernities: Experiences and perspectives of Europe and Latin America*. Forskningsradsnamnden: Stockholm.

Said, E. W. (1979). *Orientalism*. New York: Vintage Books.

Sherry, M. (2007). (Post)colonizing disability. *Wagadu: A Journal of Transnational and Women's Studies, 4*, 10–23. Retrieved from http://journals.cortland.edu/wordpress/wagadu/archive/v-4-2007-special-issue-intersecting-gender-and-disability-perspectives-in-rethinking-postcolonial-identities/.

Silva, A. (2003) Da fisiologia à biopolítica: discursos sobre a deficiência física na legislação brasileira. *Revista Polis e Psique 1*(1). Retrieved from http://www.seer.ufrgs.br/PolisePsique/article/view/23653/15179.

Sinha, I. (2009). *Animal's people*. New York: Simon & Schuster Paperbacks.

Soldatic, K. (2013). The transnational sphere of justice: Disability praxis and the politics of impairment. *Disability & Society, 28*(6), 744–755.

Spivak, G. C. (1988). Can the subaltern speak? In C. Nelson & L. Grossberg (Eds.), *Marxism and the interpretation of culture* (pp. 271–313). Basingstoke: Macmillan Education.

Stiker, H.-J. (2000). *A history of disability*. Ann Arbor: University of Michigan Press.

Thomas, C. (1999). Causes of inequality in the international economic order: Critical race theory and postcolonial development. *Transnational Law and Contemporary Problems, 9*, 1.

Whyte, S. R. (1995). Disability between discourse and experience. In B. Ingstad & S. R. Whyte (Eds.), *Disability and culture* (pp. 267–291). Berkeley: University of California Press.

Yeo, R., & Bolton, A. (2008). *'I don't have a problem, the problem is theirs': The priorities of Bolivian disabled people in words and pictures*. Leeds: Centre for Disability Studies. Retrieved April 24, 2014, fromhttp://disability-studies.leeds.ac.uk/publications/i-dont-have-a-problem-the-problem-is-theirs/.

Chapter 26
Global Financialisation and Disability: Can Disability Budgeting be an Effective Response in the South?

S. Janaka Biyanwila and Karen Soldatic

> *The global inequality crisis is reaching new extremes. The richest 1 % now have more wealth than the rest of the world combined. Power and privilege is being used to skew the economic system to increase the gap between the richest and the rest. A global network of tax havens further enables the richest individuals to hide $7.6 trillion. The fight against poverty will not be won until the inequality crisis is tackled.*
>
> Oxfam 2016: 1

Introduction

This chapter explores a southern disabled standpoint as a theoretical and strategic approach to examine disability with the intensification of global financialisation. The 2008 financial crisis was a significant illustration of the fragility of deregulated financial markets which directly impacted on advances in addressing issues of poverty, particularly for people with disabilities in the global South. By locating the 2008 crisis within neo-liberal strategies of financial deregulation launched in the mid-1990s, this chapter examines how the normalisation of financialisation mechanisms, processes and practices reproduces the marginalisation and exploitation of

S.J. Biyanwila
Independent Researcher, Sydney and Colombo, Australia and Sri Lanka

K. Soldatic (✉)
Institute for Culture and Society, Western Sydney University, NSW, Australia
e-mail: K.Soldatic@westernsydney.edu

S. Grech, K. Soldatic (eds.), *Disability in the Global South*,
International Perspectives on Social Policy, Administration, and Practice,
DOI 10.1007/978-3-319-42488-0_26

people with disabilities in the global South[1]. In particular, we illuminate new forms of colonialism by highlighting how global finance capital located in the global North increasingly influences the development landscape. To conclude, we explore the increasing role of identity budgeting, as first articulated in Sao Paolo through local feminist leftist movements as 'gender budgeting', as a counteracting southern tool of social justice.

Since the ratification of the United Nations Convention on the Rights of Persons with Disabilities in 2006, the enduring mainstream development discourse has increasingly engaged with the global governance of disability. Global development and governance institutions such as the World Bank and the United Nations have invested heavily in situating disability within these new practices of development as an active strategy to secure disability rights (see Soldatic 2013). Among the clearest examples is the 2011 World Report on Disability (WHO and WB 2011). These global initiatives are clearly significant for local disability movements to place downward pressure on nation-states to advance the realisation of rights (Soldatic 2015). Our concern here is to examine whether rights realisation is possible with intensified global financialisation, and the types of southern intervention that are emerging from local movements.

This chapter focuses on how people with disabilities in the global South are positioned in terms of the increasing role of finance capital in the dominant development discourse. While the World Bank discourse of good governance and microfinance has advanced the recognition of disability as a social category deserving of respect, redistribution and recognition, we argue that it also entails the production of disabled bodies and their networks into a raft of new forms of disablism and disablement. In particular, we highlight the significant ways in which these new processes of financialisation develop new forms of disability oppression. Disability scholars in the global South, such as Vandana Chaudhry (2015, 2016), have also begun to explore these new practices of disablement.

To grapple with this question and explore the contradictory positioning of disability, our analysis is situated in a southern, critical materialist standpoint. As Connell (2011: 1372–3) argues, southern knowledge on social embodiment moves beyond northern disability theories to critically situate the ontoformative processes of global politics in the periphery, where the majority of disabled people live. In this chapter, we argue for a politics of disability that combines economic redistribution with cultural elaboration of solidarity, justice and care in order for southern disabled people to transform their position of subordination and exploitation. By situating the analysis of 'disability' within a southern standpoint, the aim is to encourage deeper understanding as a necessary strategy to inform repertoires of social mobilisation and intercultural translation within the intensification of neo-liberal financialisation.

The metaphors of global North and South are more political and theoretical than geographic. The ways in which disability is constituted under neo-liberal globalisation are embedded in a historical context of colonialism and imperialism, where the global

[1]A shorthand used to refer to the countries historically conquered or controlled by the modern imperial powers. Most of these southern countries used to be colonised and are often associated with poverty, economic exploitation and dependence (Meekosha 2011: 669).

South represents the majority of the world population in poorer economies (Grech 2015). The global South highlights the oppression and injuries of colonialism and capitalism as well as anti-capitalist, anti-colonial and anti-imperial struggles (Biyanwila 2011). The South also exists in the North in the form of marginalised people, such as indigenous people, the unemployed, ethnic and religious minorities and those injured by disablism, racism, sexism and homophobia (Santos 2009). The North is also represented in the South, mostly in the urban centres of wealth and power (Connell 2007).

While the global North and South categories are differentiated and stratified realities, the dominance of the global North, in particular western modernity, is driven by the objectives of capitalism and colonialism, which marginalise and ignore an array of conceptions and theories within the South (Connell 2007; Santos 2009). Not only is this northern project of accumulation (an accumulation by dispossession) imposed upon the South by force through structural adjustment programmes via the International Monetary Fund and World Bank, injuring people and destroying their lived ecologies, but also southern states are contracting out social provisioning measures which undermine local notions of well-being, community and solidarity. In this chapter, when we refer to the South we are particularly grounded in those spaces and places marked by ongoing processes of colonial appropriation and violence, even within their 'post'-colonial positioning (see Santos 2009).

In turn, the chapter explores counterpositions to financialisation that are emerging, focusing on participatory identity budgeting, which local southern civil society movements have advanced. Rosset and Gerber (2014) have suggested that, with the advent of financialisation, identity budgeting becomes a critical feature for the full realisation of rights. In this chapter we ask this: Can collective institutional mechanisms focused on disability budgeting enable the realisation of disability rights as a localised and personalised practice?

Development in the South and Neo-liberal Global Financialisation

The dominant development discourse, grounded in a Eurocentric masculine able-bodied worldview, is intertwined with contemporary geopolitical dynamics of imperialism, based not entirely on territorial invasions, but through a forced integration with the global trading system. In this phase of 'imperialism by invitation', national projects are based on expanding markets in order to enhance 'international competitiveness'. The competition among nations to attract capital directly relates to the deregulation (reregulation) of trade and investment regimes to maintain fluid financial markets. Financialisation relates to the changing global economy that deems trading money, risk and associated products as more profitable than trading goods and services for capital accumulation. Financialisation highlights the '(I)ncreasing importance of financial markets, financial motives, financial institutions, and financial elites in the operation of the economy and its governing institutions, both at the national and international levels' (Epstein 2005: 3). The uneven processes of financialisation dominated by the

North and intersecting at various scales (transnational, national and local) directly impact on people with disabilities while reinforcing structures of impairment.

For the global South, the promotion of neo-liberal market-driven development, particularly since the late 1970s, has meant increasing integration with global financial institutions while restraining state capacities for social provisioning. The export-led industrialisation strategies promoted by the IMF and the World Bank, prioritising 'international competitiveness' and the private sector as 'the engine of growth', endure into the present, but with a new emphasis on financial markets. The privatisation of public goods and services, along with the deregulation of national financial markets, began prior to the emergence of the General Agreement on Trade in Services in 1994. The GATS highlighted the extension of markets or the scope of privatisation into health, education, social services and institutions of incarceration. The deregulation (reregulation) of trade and investment regimes under the GATS is integrated with the promotion of deregulated, or 'flexible', labour markets which restrict workers' rights.

The integration of the global South with financial markets sets up enduring structures of dependence through the mechanism of debt. The spread of market-driven development policies articulated in terms of debt repayment and 'balancing' debt locates the state in a perpetual 'fiscal crisis'. Financialisation and financial crisis are an elaboration of imperial hegemony. The role of the IMF in coordinating global monetary cooperation, financial stability and international trade directly influences the treasuries and finance ministries of the global South. IMF structural adjustment and bailout programmes illustrate how the promotion of deregulated financial markets since the 1990s has repeatedly been accompanied by financial crises across a raft of continents. Although the 2008 crisis is seen as being less disruptive than previous versions in East Asia, Russia and Latin America, it is important to locate it within enduring structures of debt dependence and instability of the financial system.

The World Bank and IMF policies of structural adjustment and monetary stabilisation directly relate to restriction of state capacities in social provisioning, such as in health, education, basic infrastructure (roads, electricity and communication) and welfare services, while extending privatisation and deregulation of these sectors. IMF 'conditionality' (known as financial programming) directly impacts on a state's capacity to raise revenue as well as plan expenditures. With its main focus on inflation (through monetary policy) rather than unemployment (fiscal policy), the IMF continues to promote monetary policies that create markets for private finance. In reinforcing the interests of global financial markets, the IMF's advice to nation-states in the global South is to retract state spending, involving wage cuts, public-sector layoffs and taxes on consumption, while restricting new public programmes (Epstein 2006; Woods 2006; Gabor 2010). The World Bank's social protection sector strategy, From Safety Net to Springboard, explicitly recommends against publicly owned and administered programmes, such as comprehensive old-age pensions, unemployment insurance and vocational training (World Bank 2001).

One example of how financialisation affects people with disabilities is in the area of food. The increasing speculation on food commodities via the future market has exacerbated food insecurity and issues of food justice. Rising food prices, mostly due to financial speculation, affect livelihoods and fuel social protests described as 'food riots'. The integration of the food system with a complex ecology is further constrained through market-driven development policies of privatisation, undermining local farmers' access to a range of public resources. Poverty and hunger enhance and/or create varying forms of impairment, and the financialised state through restrictions on state social provisioning further marginalises the needs and capacities of people with disabilities.

New Forms of Accumulation and Dispossession with Global Financialisation: Consumer Indebtedness and Labour Market Exclusion

Financialisation is significant to understanding new forms of exploitation, repression and rationalisation. With the intensification of financialisation since the 2008 global financial crisis, two primary forms of economic colonisation have become apparent: consumer indebtedness and precarious labour regimes. People with disabilities and their households are not exempt from the effects of financialisation, as we discuss.

Consumer Indebtedness

'Whereas industrial capitalism primarily exploits productive workers through the wage system, finance capitalism adds the exploitation of consumptive individuals via indebtedness' (Peetz and Murray 2012). In a context of deregulated financial markets, this indebtedness, particularly at a household level, directly impacts on the livelihoods of people with disabilities. The relationship between the micro (individual/household) context with the meso (institutions) and macro (global, planetary) levels is integral to examining the impact of financialisation on people with disabilities in the global South.

As illustrated by the aftermath of the 2008 financial crisis, financial elites remain relatively unrestrained by small reregulation reforms while the masses suffer the massive socialisation of losses with a new public austerity. Significant cuts to welfare systems and provision of public services directly impact on working-class families and communities, particularly young people, informal workers, ethnic and migrant groups, single-parent families and pensioners (disability and aged), with negative consequences for social cohesion and social justice (ILO 2014: 39). These policy choices have led to an increase in the risk of social unrest, as shown by the ILO's Social Unrest Index rising from 34 per cent in 2006/2007 to 46 per cent in 2011/2012 (ILO 2013). The Oxfam report quoted at the opening of this chapter explicitly aims to show these material inequalities.

This is most clearly illustrated in the growth of state policies that bank upon different forms of financial individualisation and entrepreneurialism, such as microfinance and international remittances. As Vandana Chaudhry (2015, 2016) has illustrated in her recent work on debtscapes with rural villages in India, microfinance and the resultant onset of household debt undermine social collective bonds that many people with disabilities rely on to maintain their well-being in rural landscapes. Rather than promoting social relations of solidarity, care and justice, microfinance loans too frequently generated forms of social tension between disabled loan recipients and their village neighbours due to many of the neo-liberal able-bodied assumptions embedded within them, such as time-limited payment conditions and the necessary forms of entrepreneurial activity required to generate revenue, for debt repayment, with interest. Moreover, as microfinance relies heavily on community surveillance for individualised debt repayment, and as household loans are recycled across village households, disabled recipients of micro-loans become extremely vulnerable to new forms of violence (Chaudhry 2016). Additional financial indebtedness heightens the vulnerability of disabled people to social stigmatisation and exclusion. Chaudhry (2015, 2016) documents clearly that women with disabilities are even more susceptible to such risks, given the intertwining cultural markers of gender and disability in poor rural settings. Thus, despite the promises of microfinance, including the intent to engineer disability entrepreneurs through microcredit schemes, the generation of increased household debt has often resulted in particularly poor outcomes for disabled households, entrenching them further into poverty and reaffirming long-standing cultural stigma.

Labour Market Restructuring

While the majority of the global labour force resides in the global South, most of this labour force works in the informal sector. According to the ILO (2014), the informal sector is characterised by employment relationships that are 'not covered in law or in practice by national labor legislation, income taxation, social protection, or entitlement to certain employment benefits'. Informal employment is particularly widespread in Africa, Asia, Latin America and the Caribbean, accounting for a cross-country average of between 40 and 50 per cent of total employment (ILO 2014: 21). In contrast to the dominant modernist narrative of linear, gradual formalisation, the informal sector is a by-product of capital accumulation and restructuring within the global economy (Castells and Portes 1989). Even within the global North, the deregulation of labour markets along with decentralisation of production structures is a reconstitution of formal work, illustrated by an increase in short-term contracts and decreased access to social protection (including rights to organise and collectively bargain).

The jobless growth trends since 2008 continued in 2014, with the bulk (45 per cent) of the increase in global unemployment located in the East Asian and South Asian regions (ILO 2014). The youth-to-adult unemployment ratio has reached a historical peak, with the youth unemployment rate three times higher than the adult rate. It is estimated that some 74.5 million young people, aged 15–24, were unemployed in 2013, an increase of almost one million in 2012 (ILO 2014). Unemployment among young women is higher than among young men, illustrating uneven geographic scales and occupational categories.

For people with disabilities to be fully engaged in the formal labour market on par with their non-disabled counterparts, formal regulatory mechanisms are required (WHO and World Bank 2011: Chap. 8). However, the promotion of labour-market deregulation within the global South as a core component of financialisation results in the winding back of key employment protections. The global competition between nations to attract transnational finance relies heavily on curtailing a range of employment protections. Issues surrounding hiring practices, workplace adjustments and hours of work are frequently compromised in order to attract foreign capital. Many people with disabilities are thus discriminated against at the point of entry or, having gained employment, are unable to maintain the hyperextended demands of these new work regimes. Global financialisation of the national economy actively discourages the very kinds of labour-market regulatory controls advocated by the 2011 World Report to advance fair, equitable and decent work for disabled people. Further, the heavy reliance on the informal sector within local southern economies means that local custom, practice and values which stigmatise disability are outside formal regulatory controls.

Countering Neo-liberal Financialisation: Budgeting for Identity Equity

One of the key interventions to transform the lived effects of neo-liberal financialisation within the global South was initially advanced by local social movements. Beginning in Sao Paolo, Brazil, with the implementation of participatory budgeting practices, 'identity participatory budgeting' has since become a key feature of global development politics, policy and practice. In Sao Paolo, identity participatory budgeting was initiated by local feminist groups who aimed to collectively make 'visible the gendered nature of assumptions, processes, and outcomes' (Walby 2005: 321) of mainline policies. In so doing, the feminist groups were able to have local and macroeconomic resources specifically targeted at areas that directly affected women, including issues around care within the household, the continued gendered division of household labour and broader cultural, economic and social politics and policies that reinforce these gendered norms.

Doing a general search on the term 'gendered budgeting' illustrates how this localised feminist intervention in macroeconomic development policies has become mainstream. There has been widespread acceptance of the need for some type of gendered budgeting within macroeconomic politics and policy. A review of international research, policy and programmes reveals that gendered budgeting has become normalised in countries such as Germany, Sri Lanka and Uganda, to name a few, and organisations such as the IMF, World Bank, UN Women and even the World Economic Forum have adopted it. As transnational governance donors, they are increasingly demanding that nation-states incorporate gendered-budgeting instruments, mechanisms and processes as a condition of grants and loans. Sharp et al. (2010) note that this has been a strong feature of transnational donor relations in Sri

Lanka since the early 2000s, for example, despite the civil conflict only coming to an end in 2009. The results are mixed. It is also difficult to demarcate the differences pre- and post-implementation due to the enduring high rates of literacy, low levels of infant mortality and other gendered indicators of human development that Sri Lanka has long experience of, compared with other countries in the global South (Chakraborty 2003).

These transnational organisations converge in some of their key principles, and yet there is also a high degree of divergence in their identity-budgeting practices. For example, the focus of many of these mainstreamed gendered-budgeting policies and programmes is often on furthering processes of neo-liberal financialisation. That is, the focus is increasingly on the microeconomic stimulus of local markets and enabling women entrepreneurs to participate in such unregulated local markets. Thus, the broader macroeconomic reforms required for widespread gender equality are often missing. Individual financial instruments that result in microeconomic stimulus, such as microfinance and gendered household indebtedness, have mixed effects. Further, when applied on their own, they often actively undermine strong state social provisioning measures, such as free childcare and gendered labour-market targets, that have been in the past universally available and freely accessible.

As noted by a range of international researchers, more inividualised and microstimulus packages are resulting in contradictory effects. Too frequently the mechanisms, processes and outcomes further reinforce other structural inequalities, particularly around class, race, age, disability, sexuality, locational disadvantage and migration. As Ong (2006) has well documented, neo-liberalism has had an uncanny ability to adopt, transform and harness some of the most progressive interventions by civil society in order to extend its reach. Gendered and participatory budgeting has not been exempt from this phenomenon. Yet feminists around the globe have not lost hope of the broader collective/macroeconomic possibilities of addressing gendered inequality. Many local and transnational feminist movements continue to advocate for gendered budgeting for its potential to intervene in the maldistribution of neo-liberal capitalism, its capacity to politically recognise the rights of women and their position of structural inequality and, most significantly, its requirement of women's representation within the budgeting process. This tripartite potential has been key to its continual support from women globally.

Coming to Disability: Is Identity Budgeting for Disability Plausible in the Global South?

The global broad-scale acceptance of gendered budgeting to address structural inequality experienced by women has led to a strong interest in identity budgeting from other groups. It is increasingly being adopted by identity movements and is now often referred to as 'diversity budgeting'. In turn, large sectors of national economies are embedding various forms of identity budgeting to meet legislative requirements in relation to anti-discrimination laws and identity-specific targets in employment and delivery, alongside identifying the costs associated with infrastructure development that is inclusive of differentiated participatory needs (see Balakrishnan et al. 2016).

This is occurring in the global North and the global South. Disability is one such identity category that is being explicitly incorporated into diversity budgeting measures, processes and instruments (Purcil 2016). Disability budgeting has long been a key demand of the global disability rights movement. Within the global North, individualised budgeting, often referred through notions of personalised support, is the financialisation of the movement's narrative of self-directed support. Since the late 1980s, individualised budgets have been argued for as critical to disabled people realising greater personalised control of services and supports. The notion of self-directed supports was a response to the historical exclusion, segregation and oppression experienced by people with disabilities. Individualised budgets were articulated as one of the primary mechanisms that could shift the relations of power between disability services and supports, via the direct purchasing of services to an individual's own defined needs, wants and desires. The aim has been for people with disabilities to achieve independence and control over their daily lives.

It was assumed that having the purchasing power of an individual consumer would improve the quality of services within the care market as disabled people would now have the market power and freedom to determine what kind of support they actually need, when it should be provided and by whom. Through monetising disability support and care, the divide between public and private radically shifts, as individualised support needs to be classified, stratified and differentiated so each component can have a financial value for market exchange. This individualised budgeting system is advocated for by many within the movement and therefore is an active process of financialisation. It is argued that disabled consumers, empowered with their individualised budgets, are able to purchase the services that they need in the open care market. However, as reknown international economist Amartya Sen (2015) has argued individualised economic empowerment does not necessarily lead to the realisation of rights for such individuals. Realising one's capabilities is grounded in a collective set of institutional, social, cultural and political structures, processes and relations, grounded and mediated by context, locales, history and power. The market alone is not enough; the consolidation of power, money and interests within open market systems results in the maldistribution of resources. The state is a contested site of money, power and interests. It is not neutral nor banal. Markets are regulated by states and regulatory forms are shaped by the power upheavals situated herein. This is why some writers have argued that individualised disability budgeting inexorably reproduces core capitalist values of exchange and exploitation (Barnes 2007). In turn, such individualised financialisation of disability is likely to reproduce many of the economic, social and political disadvantages that already exist for people with disabilities.

Financialisation via disability individualised budgets has resulted in the creation of new social care markets which are attracting a range of transnational corporations.

Disability individualised budgets, promoting cash for care, gives these market suppliers access to a new financial resource to increase their profitability. In turn, the financialisation of disability supports and services coincides with the financialisation of services provided to other marginalised groups, such as asylum seekers and refugees. In Australia, for example, the organisations that are contracted to operate off-shore refugee detention centres are the very same companies that are seeking to enter the 'disability care' market to get access to disability individualised budgets (Morton 2015). Western Australian advocates outlined these potential risks at the 2009 and 2010 public inquiries into the marketisation of consolidated public systems of care; however, such concerns were given little priority to discussions at the time.

In countries such as Sri Lanka, while there have been more concerted legislative efforts to include disability in the broader macroeconomic framework and associated social provisioning measures, as recent work by Samararatne and Soldatic (2015) suggests, these budgeting measures have differentiated outcomes as processes of financialisation are mediated by other structural locations, including class, spatial disadvantage (rural, provincial, ex-conflict areas), gender and ethnicity. For example, ex-military personnel who acquired their impairments during active service have greater access to disability pensions and cash transfer payments. Unlike rural women with disabilities, these ex-soldiers do not face the ongoing moralising gaze associated with disability stigmatisation when seeking to make claims. Rural women with disabilities, particularly those from ex-conflict zones, are often only afforded individualised cash transfers when their claim is actively supported by a disability advocate. Moreover, even when they might be awarded these forms of cash transfers to purchase disability supports and services, the women cannot necessarily realise the so-called freedoms brought on by individualised budgets, as espoused by global North disability movements, due to their rural location, the built environment of provincial towns and lack of accessible transport in such areas. Care markets are also scarce in such locations and it is therefore not possible to purchase disability supports and services.

This research with rural disabled women in Sri Lanka also demonstrates how intersectional identities lead to the perpetuation of other structural identity exclusions and inequalities within the budgeting process, even within the so-called power of consumer sovereignty that financialisation of disability supports and services affords. For many of the women interviewed, their success at obtaining cash transfers was strongly influenced by other identity markers, such as gender, rurality and ethnicity (Samararatne and Soldatic 2015). Hans et al.'s (2008) work in India, exploring the intersectional effects of gendered- and disability-budgeting practices, confirms that this occurs in other landscapes. Hans and colleagues mapped the ways that disability budgeting does not take into account the gendered dimensions of the lived experience of disability, and vice versa. That is, gendered budgeting was not sensitive to the gendered-impairment dimensions of everyday life for disabled women.

This raises the question: Can individualised disability budgeting address the structural and institutional arrangements that continue to perpetuate the exclusion of people with disabilities? Does individualised financialisation realize the full participation of people with disabilities beyond social care markets?

Southern Disability Strategies: Towards Democratic Financialisation

Across the global South, disability actors are seeking macroeconomic budgeting processes to counter the developments of neo-liberal financialisation. The conception of budgeting, that is, civil society intervention into the structural budgeting process, by such disability movement actors seeks to move beyond the claim for disability rights as practiced in individualised budgets, as outlined above, which are dominant within the North. The aim of disability budgeting at the macroeconomic scale in the South is to address enduring political, cultural, social and economic structural exclusions that occur at the institutional level through centralised budgeting and national, provincial and local governance. As Purcil (2016) documents in the case of the Philippines, disability budgeting has provided a way for local disability movement actors to first monitor central fiscal allocations towards the realisation of disability rights, and second to hold states to account under international human rights instruments when such fiscal allocations are retrogressive.

Moreover, with the onset of neo-liberal development strategies, disability movement actors are demanding macroeconomic disability strategies from central national treasuries as a process of rights realisation, particularly in relation to core areas of public life. For example, Side Events at the 9th Session on the Commission on States for the Realisation of Disability Rights (2016) explicitly engage in deliberative discussions surrounding the relationship between disability-budgeting mechanisms and processes, rights realisation and sustainable development goals. Interestingly, the aim here is to construct democratic budgeting processes at the macroeconomic scale to centrally plan and allocate resources, across all institutions, to ensure disabled citizens' right to participate in public life on par with their able-bodied counterparts (see Purcil 2016 for the case of the Philipines). Such macro-scale budgeting ensures that economic instruments, mechanisms and processes are inclusive of the collective realisation of disability rights via public provisioning, reordering and restructuring of public spending and resource allocations. In practice, such disability-budgeting processes require a range of built-in strategies and mechanisms to enable participatory decision-making at all levels of governance (national, provincial and local). This concept of rights realisation via the budgeting process is more than the right to individual choice, control and procedural fairness at the point of individual service. This notion intends to deepen disabled people's participation and self-determination in democratic governance, by enforcing disability-inclusive financial allocations across the public sphere, including but not limited to education, transport, labour-market regulation and health care. It aims to ensure representative processes of substantive equality and freedom. As economists Balakrishnan et al. (2016) have identified, this radical democratic intention of identity budgeting coalesces the tensions of collective vs. individual rights realisation, by fiscal allocations towards national, provincial and local infrastructural projects and social provisioning measures that result in freedoms for all. Thus, freedom is premised upon the embedding of substantive strategies for material equality, participation and inclusive representation.

A highly illustrative example at national budgeting level is public transport development projects. While individualised budgets enable disabled people to purchase the personal supports required within the household to 'get ready for public life', they do not have the power to ensure that public transport is readily available and accessible. Budgetary commitments are thus intended to ensure that the cost of accessibility is calculated within public infrastructure and facilities. Other areas that disability movement actors in the South are advocating for disability budgeting include sign interpreters to be available on hand, particularly in key areas of public life such as health services and schools; that educational institutions offer inclusive curriculums; and that teachers are trained in disability-accessible pedagogic practice (see Purcil 2016).

Macroeconomic disability budgeting aims to intervene in the structural and institutional landscapes of public life to enable the participation of disabled people, and ensure that the benefits of disability-centralised financing are distributed equitably across other identity markers, such as class, gender and rurality. The aim is to bring an end to the historical injustices of the past, and ensure that these are not perpetuated in the future (Sen 2015). This is significantly different to individualised budgeting, where there is growing awareness that structural inequalities can be easily reproduced (see Soldatic et al. 2014). Further, disability budgeting at the macroeconomic scale recognises the interstice between the public and the private, that is, individualised budgets are used by people with disabilities to determine their personal supports, while macroeconomic centralised fiscal allocation processes aim to realise rights and capabilities for all citizens with disabilities through transforming structures, institutions, instrumentalities, processes and practices. In other words, disability budgeting at the macroeconomic scale aims to embed disability rights into the political and institutional realm of public life for collective outcomes, and can be adjusted to take account of differences in impairment type, gender, age, ethnicity and other intersecting identity markers. This is the radical potential of macroeconomic participatory inclusive structures that are generative of representative institutions, instruments and processes at the national, provincial and local scales (Balakrishnan et al. 2016). It is transformative as it refuses to see budgeting as a purely technocratic achievement of mainstream economics. It directly establishes the TINTA principle: 'there is no technical answer' (Balakrishnan et al. 2016: 8).

Much like the women's movements of the South, civil-society disability actors in the South recognise the critical role of the nation-state's centralised budgeting processes in perpetuating the daily experience of structural violence of capitalist maldistribution under the global financial system (Purcil 2016). Through active representative politics within the budgeting process of the national, provincial and local political economy, everyday lived inequalities are forced to be recognised and responded to through distributive adjustments. Moreover, the Convention on the Rights of Persons with Disabilities enables disability movement actors of the South to directly tie macroeconomic budgetary allocations and resources to those areas of rights that they view as critical in the immediate term, and plan for future developments over the longer term, by the progressive realisations framework. Thus, the instruments, mechanisms and processes of macroeconomic disability budgeting potentially enable disability movement actors to hold states to some account (see Purcil 2016 for a full discussion of this).

Conclusion: The Potentiality of Disability Budget Regimes

The World Report on Disability documents well that people with disabilities have to spend more money on their specific needs to both maintain the same standard of living as those without disabilities and participate on par in the institutions of public life (WHO and World Bank 2011). Around the globe, people with disabilities incur large additional costs for things that remain invisible to people without disabilities. As many of the chapters in this volume illustrate (Grech and Soldatic 2016), the relationship between disability and poverty is a global phenomenon. Is promoting disability budgeting, particularly through processes of individual financialisation, really a potential intervention with global financialisation?

While individualised budgeting has been taken up by disability movements in the global North, drawing particularly on discourses of personalisation and self-directed support, collective and institutional practices of identity budgeting in the global South seek to advance collective realisation of disability rights. We are witnessing disabled actors in the South drawing on tools, mechanisms and processes not dissimilar to gendered budgeting to advance disability rights to create real material, structural, institutional and political change.

In many ways, macroeconomic budgeting for disability aims to address the inherent structural processes of maldistribution established with capitalist forms of exploitation, dispossession and expropriation. This is not to suggest that financialisation of disability is the answer to the intensification of global financialisation since the global financial crisis; clearly, disability macroeconomic budgeting falls into a model of capitalist financialisation. Yet maybe, just maybe, intervening with counter-hegemonic mechanisms, instruments and processes of financialisation can directly disrupt existing processes of maldistribution at the nation-state level, and transform structural and institutional relations of exclusion, segregation and dispossession, enabling everyday life.

References

Balakrishnan, R., Heintz, J., & Elson, D. (2016). *Rethinking economic policy for social justice*. London: Routledge.

Barnes, C. (2007). Disability activism and the struggle for change: Disability, policy and politics in the UK. *Education, Citizenship and Social Justice, 2*(3), 203–221.

Biyanwila, J. (2011). FTZ workers and politics of social protection. *Polity, 6*(1 & 2), 11–16. Retrieved from www.ssalanka.org/latest_plt.htm.

Castells, M., & Portes, A. (1989). World underneath: The origins, dynamics and effects of the informal economy. In A. Portes, M. Castells, & L. A. Benton (Eds.), *The informal economy:*

Studies in advanced and less developed countries (pp. 3–27). Baltimore, MD: John Hopkins University Press.

Chakraborty, L. S. (2003). *Budgetary allocations and gender in Sri Lanka: A categorization of financial inputs*. New Delhi: National Institute of Public Finance and Policy.

Chaudhry, V. (2015). Neoliberal disorientations: Changing landscapes of disability and governance in India. *Disability & Society, 30*(8), 1158–1173. Retrieved from http://dx.doi.org/10.1080/09687599.2015.1081093.

Chaudhry, V. (2016). Living at the edge: Disability, gender, and neoliberal debtscapes of microfinance in India. *Affilia*. doi:10.1177/0886109915622525.

Connell, R. (2007). *Southern theory: Social science and the global dynamics of knowledge*. London: Polity.

Connell, R. (2011). Southern bodies and disability: Re-thinking concepts. *Third World Quarterly, 32*(8), 1369–1381.

Epstein, G. A. (2005). *Financialisation and the world economy*. Cheltenham: Edgar Elgar.

Epstein, G. (2006). *Too much, too soon: IMF conditionality and inflation targeting*. At Issue, Bretton Woods Project, (September).

Gabor, D. (2010). The International Monetary Fund and its new economics. *Development and Change, 45*(1), 805–830.

Grech, S. (2015). *Disability and Poverty in the global South: Renegotiating development in Guatemala*. London: Palgrave Macmillan.

Grech, S., & Soldatic, K. (Eds.). (2016). *Disability in the global South: The critical handbook*. New York: Springer.

Hans, A., Patel, A. M., & Agnihotri, S. B. (2008). The need for a framework for combined disability and gender budgeting. *Indian Journal of Gender Studies, 15*(2), 233–260.

ILO. (2014). *World social protection report 2014/15*. Geneva: ILO. Retrieved from http://www.ilo.org/global/about-the-ilo/newsroom/news/WCMS_244748/lang—en/index.htm.

International Labor Organization (ILO). (2013). *Are economic stagnation and unemployment fueling social unrest? Social Unrest Index*. Geneva: ILO.

Meekosha, H. (2011). Decolonising disability: Thinking and acting globally. *Disability & Society, 26*(6), 667–682.

Morton, R. (2015, July 24). *Serco sights on NDIS Billions*. The Australian.

Ong, A. (2006). *Neoliberalism as exception: Mutations in citizenship and sovereignty*. Durham, NC: Duke University Press.

Oxfam. (2016). *An economy for the 1%*. London: Oxfam. Retrieved January 20, 2016, from https://www.oxfam.org/en/research/economy-1.

Peetz, D., & Murray, G. (2012). The financialisation of global corporate ownership. In G. Murray & J. Scott (Eds.), *Financial elites and transnational business: Who rules the world?* (pp. 26–53). Cheltenham: Edgar Elgar.

Purcil, L. (2016). The preparation of a parallel report on the CRPD: The Philippine Experience. In M. Rioux, P. Pinto, & G. Parekh (Eds.), *Disability, rights monitoring and social change* (pp. 45–54). Toronto: Canadian Scholars' Press.

Rosset, P. & Gerber, K. (2014). *Gender public policy evaluation for Brazil: Diagnosis and prospects, towards constitutional desired equality*. Retrieved from https://www.jus.uio.no/english/research/news-and-events/events/conferences/2014/wccl-cmdc/wccl/papers/ws4/w4-rosset&gerber.pdf.

Samararatne, D. W. V. A., & Soldatic, K. (2015). Inclusions and exclusions in law: Experiences of women with disability in rural and war-affected areas in Sri Lanka. *Disability & Society, 30*(5), 759–772. Retrieved from http://dx.doi.org/10.1080/09687599.2015.1021760.

Santos, B. (2009). A non-Occidentalist West?: Learned ignorance and ecology of knowledge. *Theory, Culture & Society, 26*(7–8), 103–125.

Sen, A. (2015). The economic consequences of austerity. New Statesman [online] Available at: http://www.newstatesman.com/politics/06/amartya-sen-economic-consequences-austerity [Accessed 25 Sept.2015].

Sharp, R., Elson, D., & Costa, M. (2010). *Gender responsive budgeting in the Asia Pacific region: Democratic Socialist Republic of Sri Lanka*. Adelaide, SA, Australia: University of South

Australia. Retrieved from http://www.unisa.edu.au/Documents/EASS/HRI/gender-budgets/sri_lanka.pdf.
Soldatic, K. (2013). The transnational sphere of justice: Disability praxis and the politics of impairment. *Disability & Society, 28*(6), 744–755. Retrieved from http://dx.doi.org/10.1080/09687599.2013.802218.
Soldatic, K. (2015). Postcolonial reproductions: Disability, indigeneity and the formation of the white masculine settler state of Australia. *Social Identities, 21*(1), 53–68. Retrieved from http://dx.doi.org/10.1080/13504630.2014.995352.
Soldatic, K., van Toorn, G., Dowse, L., & Muir, K. (2014). Intellectual disability and complex intersections: Marginalisation under the National Disability Insurance Scheme. *Research and Practice in Intellectual and Developmental Disabilities, 1*(1), 6–16. Retrieved from http://dx.doi.org/10.1080/23297018.2014.906050.
United Nations. (2006). *Convention on the rights of persons with disabilities*. Retrieved from http://www.un.org/disabilities/default.asp?id=264.
Walby, S. (2005). Gender mainstreaming: Productive tensions in theory and practice. *Social Politics, 12*(3), 321–343. Retrieved from http://dx.doi.org/10.1093/sp/jxi018.
Woods, N. (2006). Understanding pathways through financial crisis and the impact of the IMF: An introduction. *Global Governance, 12*, 373–393.
World Bank. (2001). *Social protection sector strategy: From safety net to springboard*. Washington, DC: World Bank.
World Health Organization (WHO) and World Bank. (2011). *World report on disability*. Geneva: WHO. Retrieved from http://www.who.int/disabilities/world_report/2011/accessible_en.pdf.

Chapter 27
Global Institutions and Their Engagement with Disability Mainstreaming in the South: Development and (Dis)Connections

Tsitsi Chataika and Judith A. McKenzie

Introduction

The historical location of disability as an individualised issue within a health and welfare framework has placed it outside the realm of development efforts that are intended to address issues of global poverty (Albert and Harrison 2006). The logic of this exclusion distinguishes development work from charity work. Poverty that is associated with disability is viewed not as structural, but as an inevitable result of personal incapacity that demands charity and not rights. This exclusion from development is evident in the Millennium Development Goals (MDGs) that were drawn up in 2000 to address global poverty (Groce 2011). Disability is not referred to in the goals, targets or indicators. This has occurred despite the mounting evidence suggesting that disabled people are more likely to be poor, hence the need for their inclusion in development efforts as a strategy of fighting global poverty (WHO and World Bank 2011).

In this chapter, we review disability-inclusion processes within development prior to the adoption of the United Nations Convention on the Rights of Persons with Disabilities (CRPD) (UN 2006). We then reflect on the impact of the CRPD and the World Report on Disability, exploring the possibilities of these being used as catalysts for inclusive development efforts by global institutions. We also make reference to the deliberations of the 2013 high-level meeting of the UN General Assembly on disability and development as this will have a major impact on local disability initiatives (UN 2013a). We offer a critique of how these global governance programmes are implemented in the global South and suggest critical areas

T. Chataika (✉)
University of Zimbabwe, Harare, Zimbabwe
e-mail: tsitsi.chataika@gmail.com

J.A. McKenzie
University of Cape Town, Cape Town, South Africa

S. Grech, K. Soldatic (eds.), *Disability in the Global South*,
International Perspectives on Social Policy, Administration, and Practice,
DOI 10.1007/978-3-319-42488-0_27

for consideration if inclusive development is to become a reality for disabled people in the global South. Finally, we look at disability-inclusive development in Africa and the quest for an African renaissance in disability mainstreaming.

Disability in Development

The connection between poverty and disability has been described as a vicious cycle, where disabled people experience stigma and exclusion, resulting in missed opportunities for education, health care and economic participation (WHO and World Bank 2011). In their study of 15 low-income countries, Mitra, Posarac and Vick established that multidimensional poverty is significantly associated with disability in most of those countries, implying that 'persons with disabilities, on average, experience multiple deprivations at higher rates and in higher breadth, depth, and severity than persons without disabilities' (Mitra et al. 2013: 11). Clearly, from a social perspective, poverty and disability are products of capitalist development, and are socially constructed and culturally produced in various communities. This suggests that it is society that is the focal point of action to deal with both poverty and disability, mainly through restructuring societal policies and provisions.

Given the growing evidence base, it would appear that people with disabilities would be a target group for development initiatives, the most notable of which are the MDGs. However, as noted above, this has not been the case. While there are no targets or indicators for disability, disabled people remain virtually invisible to most development efforts. Recently, increased attention has been paid to disability inclusion within the post-MDGs debate, based in part on the realisation that the MDGs cannot be achieved unless disabled people are included (Groce 2011). For example, education for all remains unattainable as long as one-third of the 77 million children still out of school are disabled, with less than 10 per cent of the children with disabilities in Africa attending school (World Vision 2007). Education has for a long time been perceived to be the key that unlocks economic potential, with implications for sustainable development.

The multiple crises (economic, social and environmental) facing the world today further underscore the need for an international development agenda grounded in sustainability, inclusion and equality. The international normative framework on disability, consisting of the United Nations' World Programme of Action concerning Disabled Persons (1982), the Standard Rules on the Equalization of Opportunities for Persons with Disabilities (1994) and the CPRD (2006), provides a comprehensive and holistic approach for disability inclusion, and the participation of disabled people in all aspects of economic and social development. Article 32 of the CRPD in particular was created to respond to the lack of disability inclusion and mainstreaming in the international development and cooperation agenda (UN 2006). It was expected that global instruments such as the MDGs and the Poverty Reduction Strategy Papers (PRSPs) launched by the World Bank and the International Monetary Fund would steer low-income countries to promoting opportunities, facilitating empowerment and enhancing security for their poorest citizens (Groce 2011). Yet, most governments and their development partners seem to continuously exclude people with disabilities from development processes (Chataika et al. 2011).

The PRSPs represent a lost opportunity for disability inclusion in development (Coleridge 2007). While disabled people are increasingly recognised in the PRSPs as being among the poorest of the poor, not much has been achieved in addressing this or acknowledging their exclusion. The consequence of this exclusion is that those most affected by poverty, particularly disabled people, are the least likely to participate and/or benefit from development initiatives (Grech 2009; Mwendwa et al. 2009; Wazakili et al. 2011). The estimated one billion disabled people worldwide remain excluded from equitable access to public services such as education, employment, health care and social and legal support systems (WHO and World Bank 2011).

With the increase of disability activism, some global institutions and international development organisations have initiated programmes to include disability in their development work. Drawing on the experiences of women in development, global institutions have advocated for mainstreaming specialist disability services so that mainstream services are accessible to and inclusive of all members of society (including people with disabilities). This entails the inclusion of disability issues in all areas of development in such a way that the contribution and rights of disabled people and other marginalised groups are recognised and accounted for (Chataika 2013).

Before the adoption of the CRPD, Albert and Harrison noted that the

> trickle of positive statements and disability-targeted interventions over the last few years has been transformed into an apparent flood of interest in disability and development cooperation from international and national aid agencies, as well as INGOs. (Albert and Harrison 2006: 2)

Despite this growing interest, the authors registered concern that implementation of laudable policy statements had been disappointing and attributed this to a continuing perception of disability as a medical and individualised issue, thus working against disability mainstreaming.

The Scope of Disability Mainstreaming

Disability mainstreaming entails the consideration of disability at all levels of the development cycle (planning, implementation, monitoring and evaluation) for the benefit of both disabled and non-disabled people. However, mainstreaming without specific attention to the inclusion of disabled people's needs can act as a barrier to their full participation (Wazakili et al. 2011; Chataika 2013). Where there is no deliberate effort to mainstream disability issues within development work, disabled people may continue to remain invisible and relegated to the margins of society. Funding for exclusively disability-specific projects can be significantly reduced as funds are channelled towards inclusive development. Furthermore, Fritz et al. (2009) argue that while development agencies have often developed elaborate disability mainstreaming plans, these are not accompanied by effective implementation strategies or means of enforcement. More so, those tasked with implementing these national policies barely understand disability issues.

The World Report on Disability was developed

> to provide the evidence for innovative policies and programmes that can improve the lives of people with disabilities, and facilitate implementation of the United Nations Convention on the Rights of Persons with Disabilities (WHO and World Bank 2011: xi).

Ambitiously, the report aimed to gather together and synthesise the best existing evidence on disability on a global scale (Bickenbach 2011). On the basis of this evidence, certain recommendations are made to governments and policymakers which advocate for disabled people's access to mainstream as well as disability-specific programmes. National planning and the engagement of disabled people are seen to be critical elements to the implementation of the CRPD recommendations. This also includes the provision of adequate resources, and the creation of a conducive climate for disability inclusion through public awareness. The need for credible disability data and the monitoring of disability inclusion are recommended (WHO and World Bank 2011).

In discussions of the pre- and post-2015 development agenda, disability-inclusive development has been elaborated as a twin-track approach, which promotes disability-specific as well as mainstream work (WHO and World Bank 2011). In this scenario, interventions that address disability-specific concerns are encouraged insofar as they build access to the mainstream through the equalisation of opportunity. This is reflected in the World Report on Disability recommendation that people with disabilities should have full access to all mainstream services, while at the same time being able to benefit from programmes and services specifically tailored to their needs (WHO and World Bank 2011).

Disability-specific interventions can be seen as the necessary step towards equalisation of opportunities, so people with disabilities can participate on an equal basis with others in mainstream development (UN 1994). Such interventions can in themselves become barriers, however, if they are undertaken without regard to the larger development context and become an end in themselves rather than a means to greater inclusion (Grech 2011).

The Impact of the UN Convention on the Rights of Persons with Disabilities

With the adoption of the CRPD a compelling instrument for elevating disability into a visible position in the development field was created, especially as there is an obligation on those member states that have ratified it to enshrine its articles into national legislation. There is no way to enforce it, however. Article 32 of the Convention addresses issues of international cooperation and promotes the notion of development that is inclusive of disabled people. It also encourages capacity building, cooperation in research and technical and economic assistance (UN 2006).

While community-based rehabilitation (CBR) programmes and efforts by various non-government organisations (NGOs) have demonstrated successful strategies in international development, there remains the problem of scaling up the issue of disability in developing contexts (WHO and World Bank 2011). This difficulty is attributed to the continuing dominance of the medical model, which treats disability as an individual issue. The World Report recommendations state that both mainstreaming and disability-specific efforts need to be undertaken in support of the implementation of the CRPD. Development for disabled people implies inclusion in all mainstream polices, services and programmes as well as disability-specific support, which enables people with disabilities to be part of inclusive development. The overarching principle of consultation and participation of disabled people's organisations (DPOs), therefore, should be an integral part of planning and advocating for their rights (WHO and World Bank 2011), hence the need for global institutions to interpret the development agenda from a disability-inclusion perspective, taking into account that disability is a cross-cutting, rights and development issue.

The Development Agenda and Global Institutions

The requirements of the CRPD have led global institutions to consider the issue of disability more carefully. The twin-track approach is largely accepted by many global institutions and agencies, which fall broadly into three groups. The first includes inter-governmental institutions such as the World Bank, International Labour Organization, WHO and the UN and its institutions (e.g. UNICEF, UNESCO, UNDP), which are established through multilateral treaties between sovereign states (Zacher 2001). The second group comprises INGOs which either focus exclusively on disability (such as CBM, Handicap International, Leonard Cheshire International, Sight Savers and Action on Disability and Development 2008) or embrace disability in their core business (including Save the Children, World Vision, Goal, Amnesty International and Red Cross). INGOs are created by individual citizens in different countries and expand to have a global reach that can meet a humanitarian need, with offices and staff in many countries. The third group constitutes national government aid agencies, such as the United Kingdom's Department for International Development (DfID) and GIZ (German Cooperation).

The role of the World Bank is significant in that it provides loans for investments in education, social protection, health, transport and other sectors that directly pose the greatest barriers to participation of people with disabilities. The disability and development team within the World Bank is responsible for developing the evidence base for World Bank policies and was, among other projects, a partner in the World Report on Disability. Furthermore, the World Bank established the Global Partnership for Disability and Development (n.d.), which has grown into a multisectoral alliance concerned with combating the exclusion of disabled people in developing contexts. While these are multi-government global institutions, bilateral relations between governments also have a role in disability and development. Of these, the Australian agency (AusAID) is described as the most deliberate and participatory in its processes as it explicitly adopts the approach of disability-inclusive development. DfID has developed and engaged with a series of documents advocating the twin-track approach to disability-inclusive development. In their review, Lord et al. (2010) conclude that disability has been established as part of international cooperation and development aid, frequently linked to the MDGs, mostly with regard to eradicating hunger and extreme poverty and providing access to universal primary education. Whether these agendas have been effective in responding to disabled people's needs at the local level remains unclear.

Disability-Inclusion Strategies of Global Institutions

Increased research evidence and lobbying efforts by the disability movement and its allies led the United Nations General Assembly to see the urgency of addressing the existing gap in the MDGs and other internationally agreed development goals. Accordingly, the General Assembly convened on 23 September 2013 in New York for a high-level meeting on disability and development at its 68th session, which included heads of governments (UN 2013a). Guided by the theme, 'The way forward: a disability inclusive development agenda towards 2015 and beyond', the high-level meeting adopted an action-oriented document. The document provides policy guidance that facilitates the translation of the commitment for a disability-inclusive society into concrete actions. It further seeks to strengthen global efforts to ensure inclusive development, thus acknowledging the negative impact of the exclusion of disability issues in the MDGs, and the urgency of ensuring that inclusive development becomes an integral part of the post-2015 sustainable development agenda.

According to the preparatory documents for the high-level meeting, disability must be recognised as a cross-cutting issue that links with all development areas (UN 2013b). An outcome of the meeting was the General Assembly's call for the application of the normative framework of the CRPD, coupled with the inclusion of the needs of people with disabilities within all development frameworks and policies. Recognising that the MDGs had been implemented without disability inclusion, the Assembly called for these goals to be modified so as to facilitate disability-inclusive development (UN 2013a).

Development and (Dis)Connections: Barriers to Inclusive Development

Several development actors and State Parties have identified challenges in realising Article 32 of the CRPD, making disability inclusion in development processes difficult. There are also concerns about the recommendations of the World Report on Disability. The disconnections highlighted here imply that there is bound to be unwarranted underrepresentation or absence of representation of people with disabilities in development processes. These barriers contribute to the disadvantage experienced by people with disabilities in all countries, and result in poorer health, lower education and less economic and political participation, all leading to higher rates of poverty and increased dependency and exclusion (African Union 2010).

Lack of Evidence from the Global South

The lack of reliable disability statistics is compromising the extent to which disability can be included in development processes (see Eide and Loeb 2016, in this volume); yet there is a clear and urgent need to address the links between disability and poverty (Coleridge 2007; Chataika et al. 2011). Also undermining efforts is the lack of evidence-based resources and tools to guide State Parties and development actors on the most effective and promising practices to make all development programming across all sectors fully inclusive. In addition, there is a need to raise awareness and create demand among recipient country governments for disability-inclusive programming, along with appropriate sensitisation towards disability and CRPD training for government officials and agency personnel.

Looking at the recommendations of the World Report on Disability from the perspective of the South, there are some concerns. The report presents available evidence, but there is a frank acknowledgement of the lack of research evidence from low- to middle-income countries. In addition, the report accepts the International Classification of Functioning (ICF) rather glibly as a workable model to measure disability:

> The ICF, adopted as the conceptual framework for this *World report on disability*, understands functioning and disability as a dynamic interaction between health conditions and contextual factors, both personal and environmental. Promoted as a "bio-psycho-social model", it represents a workable compromise between medical and social models (WHO and World Bank 2011: 4).

While Ptyushkin et al.'s (2011) study documented some positive aspects of the model, some participants felt that the ICF did not entertain the possibility of other models of disability. Hence, the African concept of *ubuntu*, which many Africans understand as a way of embracing diversity, is ignored. As such, western notions of disability are placed at the centre of a global understanding, and become the scientific norm around which evidence is collected and presented as scientific facts. This may well be at odds with indigenous understandings of disability.

Indigenous Understandings of Disability

Owusu-Ansah and Mji (2013) highlight the importance of indigenous knowledge in disability research as a means of understanding and addressing the needs of disabled people. While disability activists and disability development organisations might have a more contextually based understanding of disability that relates to attitudinal, institutional and environmental barriers, more often than not this understanding is not shared by other development or government agencies that should have a role to play in disability mainstreaming. A medical notion of disability as a specialised issue related to health and welfare service provision is all too often adopted by these agencies and imposed on nations of the global South with scant regard for indigenous practices (Chataika 2012).

The adoption of a development model based on a human rights perspective as embodied in the CRPD prizes individual autonomy above the collective good (Harris and Enfield 2003) and can result in contradictions and complexities in countries that adopt a more communal understanding of disability and development. Collective cosmologies that situate the individual within community can be at odds with such an individualistic point of view (Owusu-Ansah and Mji 2013). This reminds us of the *ubuntu* philosophy where the 'I' is superseded by the 'we'. Tutu (1999) noted that *ubuntu* is very difficult to render into a western language other than to say it is 'my humanity is caught up, is inextricably bound up, in what is yours'. It has to do with what it means to be truly human and to know that you are bound up with others in the bundle of life. He further said that one knows when *ubuntu* is there and it is obvious when it is absent.

In our work, the role of the extended family is critical within the African context. An example from South Africa is the provision of a social grant for disabled people. In many cases, this grant is used for the whole family, albeit in an exploitative manner at times. However, the grant also serves to meet family needs in the context of poverty and in many cases, without family support and the survival of the family unit, the person with the disability might find himself or herself far worse off. Thus, the individual rights of the person with a disability need to be considered within the context of poorly resourced families and communities (McKenzie et al. 2013).

Facilitating Self-Representation in Disability Mainstreaming

A further challenge is the establishment of mechanisms to promote and improve consultation with DPOs and other civil society organisations during all stages of development programming. Feedback from DPOs and civil society actors suggests the need for a means to connect increased donor support with government agencies and I/NGOs implementing disability-inclusive development projects (Wazakili et al. 2011). While the slogan 'nothing about us without us' communicates the idea that no policy should be decided without the full and direct participation of members of the group affected by that policy, in practice a lack of capacity among DPOs has inhibited their meaningful engagement in inclusive development processes at various levels (i.e. planning, implementing, monitoring and evaluation) (Chataika et al. 2011).

Giving voice to disabled people's experiences of social exclusion and oppression, including children and/or their parents, is a priority, particularly in Africa and other low-income regions. Different disability actors and organisations need to make the relevance of disability more visible to different stakeholders so as to broaden the debate outside the disability movement. Bridging the silos that exist within the disability movement and related services will promote the inclusion of marginalised voices on disability issues. Debates will examine assumptions that underlie policy and practice, thereby highlighting the polarisation of issues, such as language of 'us and them' that does not promote equal partnership between the global North and the global South.

Countering this, McKenzie (2011) argues that the emphasis placed on self-representation within the disability movement is problematic. Her concern is that self-representation has less relevance within non-western philosophies of care and community. The notion of the individual as autonomous and independent of their family or household is foreign in many African communities. In such settings, it may be that a disabled person cannot speak only for his or her own needs as this seems to work against the concept of *ubuntu* (McKenzie 2011).

The Neo-liberal Development Agenda and North–South Power Imbalance

The adoption of an impairment-based understanding, such as the ICF, has its own roots within a context of poverty. Grech (2009) argues that an emphasis on impairment might be entirely fitting where the absence or presence of impairment might constitute the difference between life and death. The prevention of impairment is not a priority within a human rights model and yet it seems that an injustice is done where preventable impairments are not dealt with by the health system (Grech 2009). Abberley (1987), one of the earliest social model theorists, noted the social causes of impairment as an area that needed to be addressed in pursuit of social justice. However, focusing on 'fixing' the impairment first may result in people with disabilities being excluded from development processes. Hence, policymakers and programme planners might conclude that people with disabilities are best catered for in segregated settings that are adapted for their impairment-specific needs.

The notion of 'specialness' seems to suggest that disabled people are not economically productive. Often, this level of productivity is judged by northern standards of what it is to work and generate an income (Meekosha 2008). The participation of disabled people in development projects is shaped by an understanding that the only way that they can earn an income or support themselves is through special projects and a concomitant lack of inclusion in mainstream development efforts. In addition, the implementation of disability-inclusive development work in the global South is not sufficiently sensitive to the post-colonial context of disability. The participation of southern countries in setting the development agenda is lacking and the demands of international development agencies such as the World Bank tend to favour a western, neo-liberal economic agenda that is highly individualised (Grech 2009).

Ncube (2005) brings in another interesting dimension on global North–South relations, self-representation and disability mainstreaming. He presents powerful insights into the negative impact some INGOs have had and questions their role as 'capacity builders'. He argues that the process of 'empowering' global South DPOs seems to be short-changing the global South disability movement by acting as a fine strainer, allowing only tiny particles to trickle down to those at the bottom. One then wonders if the balance of power does not tilt towards the powerful INGOs. In his study, Ncube (2005) reported that Mozambican DPOs appreciated the support offered by the international community. However, they were worried that they had not been provided, in their capacity as partners of northern NGOs, with financial reports of how funds raised for their activities were spent. They perceived that their northern NGO partners had access to considerable financial resources and they felt that their use should be discussed together more candidly and flexibly in order to explore a number of options for helping solve the wide range of problems faced by disabled people. This presents a key concern about access to and control over resources intended to support DPOs. Ncube questioned whose capacity had been strengthened more by the relationship: the INGOs or the global South DPOs?

The role of the World Bank's Global Partnership on Disability and Development becomes critical, which is to ensure that there is increased collaboration among development agencies and organisations (including global South DPOs) to reduce the extreme poverty and exclusion of the considerable number of people with disabilities living in low-income countries. A balanced relationship between the global South and global North becomes essential, hence the call for an African renaissance in disability mainstreaming.

African Solutions for African Problems

The end of the United Nations Decade for Persons with Disabilities in 1992 prompted Africa to lobby and gain United Nations support for the African Decade for Persons with Disabilities. This was because the global initiative had not brought any visible improvement to the quality of life of disabled people in Africa (African Union 2010). Only countries in the global North appeared to have benefited from the global decade. In order to apply an African lens to addressing the unacceptable situation of people with disabilities, national-, regional- and continental-level DPOs in Africa proposed the African decade, modelled after similar decades in other regions of the world (African Union 2010).

In 1999, the Organisation of African Unity (now African Union) adopted the African Decade for Persons with Disabilities (ADPD) (1999–2009). The intention was to raise awareness about disability issues in the region and identify solutions tailor-made to African experiences that would enhance full participation, equality and empowerment of Africans with disabilities. It was designed to increase the inclusion of disabled Africans in poverty reduction programmes, the number of disabled children and youth in African schools and educational programmes and the numbers of disabled Africans receiving adequate health services (African Union 2010). In 2002, the African Union adopted the Continental Plan of Action for the

ADPD, with the Secretariat mandated to facilitate its implementation (African Union 2010). The African Union sought to (1) build capacity, both in its own services and among its member organisations; (2) formulate and implement national policies, legislation and programmes that promote the full and equal participation of people with disabilities; and (3) lobby and advocate for inclusive planning and implementation of disability programmes at regional and continental levels (African Union 2010).

The first African Decade has since been extended into a second African Decade from 2010 to 2019, after a declaration to extend it was made in 2008 at the first meeting of African Union ministers in charge of social development. This mandate will hopefully draw lessons from the last decade and feed them into the second decade to ensure that disabled Africans' challenges are addressed from an African perspective. Also, a new Continental Plan of Action covering the extended decade has been endorsed by the African Union and one of the authors of this chapter was part of the roundtable think tanks. Various organisations have already made efforts to have the Continental Plan of Action implemented at a domestic level. For example, the Southern African Development Community (SADC) has come up with a draft Southern African Inclusive Education Strategy, aiming to ensure that SADC countries develop inclusive education systems that are responsive to the aspirations and needs of all learners, with emphasis on those with disabilities (Africa Disability Alliance 2014). The strategy is yet to be finalised and distributed to SADC member countries for implementation. Key to the success of this process is ensuring that self-representation of people with disabilities is evident, right from grassroots level to national level in each SADC country.

What is left now is to see how all these efforts that seem to favour disabled people are implemented in order to promote inclusive development in Africa. There have always been implementation challenges in Africa, coupled with weak technical, financial and administrative capacities and a serious lack of cooperation among relevant sectors, which have inhibited progress towards inclusive development (Wazakili et al. 2011). Consequently, despite a sizable number of African countries ratifying the CRPD, disability issues still struggle to make inroads into development policies and programmes.

Mbeki (1998) indicated that the African renaissance is a call to all people of Africa to work towards the reawakening of Africa—economically, socially, politically and spiritually. We are aware that the process of globalisation emphasises that no person is an island, sufficient to himself or herself. Rather, all humanity is an interdependent whole in which none can be truly free unless all are free, in which none can be truly well off unless none elsewhere in the world goes hungry (Mbeki 1998). No human being can be guaranteed a good quality of life unless we act together in development processes. The issue at stake is that African underdevelopment must be a matter of concern to everybody else in the world.

The stigma and prejudice linked to disability differentiate people with disabilities from non-disabled people (Abu-Habib 1997). We argue that there will be no African renaissance if disabled people continue to be marginalised and excluded from mainstream social and economic development. It is in this regard that Africa seriously needs to consider the potential contribution of disabled people in the African renaissance agenda, and thus avoid a situation where disability issues are exclusively tackled by foreign institutions.

It therefore becomes important for global institutions and other allies to consider the African renaissance agenda when implementing recommendations from the World Report on Disability, lest they continue to be accused of neocolonialism (Grech 2011). By doing so, we believe that it is a way of strengthening an awareness of global interdependence. Global institutions need to acknowledge the complexities and uniqueness of specific environments that are habitually ignored or misunderstood because of the 'imposition' syndrome in North–South patterns of administration and control (Grech 2009). Alternatively, Chataika (2012) challenges global South stakeholders to reclaim and increase their visibility within the global arena in their fight for disability mainstreaming and the eradication of global poverty.

Conclusion

We appreciate that implementing the recommendations of the World Report on Disability requires a strong commitment from a broad range of stakeholders. While national governments are expected to take a leading role, other actors such as the United Nations agencies, development partners, academics and the international disability movement have the potential to translate the report into action. Our concern, however, is the extent to which the recommendations assure that there are no power imbalances between the global North and the global South, and between disabled people and non-disabled people. Again, we are worried about the extent to which global institutions will implement the recommendations without undermining indigenous knowledge systems because of the existing power imbalances. For example, throughout the report, there is limited engagement with local practices grounded within contextual understandings of disability (see Soldatic 2013). As Soldatic suggests, at times the report universalises the disability experience between the North and the South. It rarely engages with issues of disability production caused by global imbalances of power (Soldatic 2013). Taking these concerns into account is therefore crucial in ensuring that the recommendations consider issues of power relations and diversity between the global North and global South, thus enabling the report to become a genuine catalyst for disability mainstreaming.

The efforts of global institutions are not always successful in disability mainstreaming despite policies and development strategies intended for this purpose. The CRPD offers some guidelines to ensure disability inclusion in development processes; however, we echo the words of Soldatic (2013) in using caution in the adoption of this approach. The lack of evidence, the wholesale adoption of the ICF and the lack of acknowledgement of power dynamics may hamper the promise of the CRPD to alleviate poverty in the global South. At the same time, we challenge the global South to reclaim its space and being in the fight for inclusive development. That way, we might ensure genuine engagement with disability mainstreaming between the global North and the global South, thus avoiding disconnections on the post-2015 sustainable development agenda.

References

Abberley, P. (1987). The concept of oppression and the development of social theory of disability. *Disability, Handicap and Society, 2*, 5–19.

Abu-Habib, L. (1997). *Gender and disability*. London: Oxfam.

Africa Disability Alliance. (2014). *Draft SADC inclusive education strategy*. Pretoria: Africa Disability Alliance.

Albert, B., & Harrison, M. (2006). Lessons from the disability knowledge and research programme. In B. Albert (Ed.), *In or out of the mainstream? Lessons from Research on Disability and Development Cooperation* (pp. 1–12). Retrieved November 9, 2013, from https://www.uea.ac.uk/polopoly_fs/1.3897!offprint_ch1.pdf.

Bickenbach, J. (2011). The world report on disability. *Disability & Society, 26*(5), 655–658.

CBM. (2008). *CBM and the twin-track approach to disability and development*. Retrieved March 23, 2014, from http://www.cbm.org/article/downloads/54741/TwinTrack_Paper_final_version_October2008.pdf.

Chataika, T. (2012). Postcolonialism, disability and development. In D. Goodley & B. Hughes (Eds.), *Social theories of disability: New developments and directions* (pp. 252–269). London: Routledge.

Chataika, T. (2013). *Gender and disability mainstreaming training manual*. Disabled Women in Africa: GIZ Sector Initiative Persons with Disabilities on behalf of BMZ, Germany, pp 1–75. Retrieved May 2, 2014, from http://www.diwa.ws/index.php?option=com_phocadownload.

Chataika, T., Kallon, F., Mji, G., & MacLachlan, M. (2011). *The African Policy on Disability & Development (A-PODD) project in Sierra Leone*. Dublin: A Centre for Global Health. Did What? The Global Health Press.

Coleridge, P. (2007). Economic empowerment. In T. Barron & P. Amerena (Eds.), *Disability and inclusive development*. London: Lenard Cheshire International.

Eide, A. H., & Loeb, M. (in press). Counting disabled people: Historical perspectives and the challenges of disability statistics. In S. Grech & K. Soldatic (Eds.), *Disability in the global South: The critical handbook*. New York: Springer.

Fritz, D., Miller, U., Gude, A., Pruisken, A., & Rischewski, D. (2009). Making poverty reduction inclusive: Experiences from Cambodia, Tanzania and Vietnam. *Journal of International Development, 21*(5), 673–684. doi:10.1002/jid.1595.

Global Partnership for Disability and Development [GPDD]. (n.d.). *GPDD Report for OHCHR on Article 32*. GPDD.

Grech, S. (2009). Disability, poverty and development: Critical reflections on the majority world debate. *Disability & Society, 24*(6), 771–784.

Grech, S. (2011). Comment from the field: Disability and the majority world: Challenging dominant epistemologies. *Journal of Literary and Cultural Disability Studies, 5*(2), 217–220.

Groce, N. (2011). *Disability and the millennium development goals: A review of the MDG process and strategies for inclusion of disability issues in millennium development goal effort*. New York: United Nations.

Harris, A. & Enfield, S. (2003). Disability, Equality and Human Rights: A Training Manual for Development and Humanitarian Organisations. An Oxfam Publication in association with Action Aid on Disability and Development (ADD). Oxford.

Lord, J., Posarac, A., Nicoli, M., Peffley, K., McClain-Nhlapo, C., & Keogh, M. (2010). Disability and International Cooperation and Development: A review of policies and practices. *Social Protection Discussion Paper No. 1003*. World Bank.

Mbeki, T. (1998). *Africa—The time has come*. Cape Town: Tafelberg.

McKenzie, J. A. (2011). Disability activism and participation. In T. Lorenzo (Ed.), *Disability Catalyst Africa Series 1* (pp. 13–21). Cape Town: Disability Innovations Africa.

McKenzie, J., McConkey, R., & Adnams, C. (2013). Intellectual disability in Africa: Implications for research and service development. *Disability and Rehabilitation, 35*(20), 1750–1755. doi:10.3109/09638288.2012.751461.

Meekosha, H. (2008). Contextualizing disability: Developing southern/global theory. Keynote paper presented to 4th Biennial Disability Studies Conference, Lancaster University, UK 2nd - 4th September 2008.

Mitra, S., Posarac, A., & Vick, B. (2013). Disability and poverty in developing countries: A multidimensional study. *World Development, 41*, 1–18.

Mwendwa, T. N., Murangira, A., & Lang, R. (2009). Mainstreaming the rights of persons with disabilities in national development frameworks. *Journal of International Development, 21*, 662–672. doi:10.1002/jid.1594.

Ncube, J. M. (2005). Capacity building of disabled people's organisations in Mozambique. *Disability Knowledge and Research*. Retrieved July 7, 2014, from http://hpod.org/pdf/CapacityBuilding.pdf.

Owusu-Ansah, F. E., & Mji, G. (2013). African indigenous knowledge and research. *African Journal of Disability, 2*(1), 5. doi:10.4102/ajod.

Ptyushkin, P., Vidmar, G., Burger, H., Marinček, Č., & Escorpizo, R. (2011). The International Classification of Functioning, Disability and Health (ICF) in vocational rehabilitation and disability assessment in Slovenia: State of law and users' perspective. *Disability and Rehabilitation, 33*(2), 130–136. doi:10.3109/09638288.2010.488713.

Soldatic, K. (2013). Transnational Justice: Disability praxis and the politics of impairment, *Disability & Society, 28*(6), 744–755.

Tutu, D. (1999). No Future Without Forgiveness. Pretoria: Image.

UN. (1994). *The standard rules on equalization of opportunities for persons with disabilities: UN, Unit Disabled Persons*. New York: UN.

UN. (2006). *Convention on the rights of persons with disabilities*. New York: UN.

UN. (2013a). Outcome document of the high-level meeting of the General Assembly on the realization of the Millennium Development Goals and other internationally agreed development goals for persons with disabilities: The way forward, a disability-inclusive development agenda towards 2015 and beyond. In S. General (Ed.), *Social development: Social development, including questions relating to the world social situation and to youth, ageing, disabled persons and the family*. New York: UN.

UN. (2013b). The way forward: A disability-inclusive development agenda towards 2015 and beyond. In S. General (Ed.), *New York Social development: Social development, including questions relating to the world social situation and to youth, ageing, disabled persons and the family* (Vol. Sixty eighth session). New York: UN

Union, A. (2010). *Continental plan of action for the African decade of persons with disabilities 2010–2019*. African Union: Addis Ababa.

United Nations (UN). (1982). *World programme of action concerning disabled persons*. New York: UN. Retrieved May 15, 2015, from http://www.un.org/disabilities/default.asp?id=23#10.

Wazakili, M., Chataika, T., Mji, G., Dube, A. K., & MacLachlan, M. (2011). The social inclusion of persons with disabilities in poverty reduction policies and instruments: Initial impressions from Malawi and Uganda. In A. H. Eide & B. Ingstad (Eds.), *Disability and poverty: A global challenge* (pp. 15–29). Bristol: Policy Press.

World Health Organization and World Bank. (2011). *World report on disability*. Geneva: World Health Organization.

World Vision, UK. (2007). *Education's Missing Millions: Including disabled children in education through EFA FTI processes and national sector plans*. Milton Keynes: World Vision, UK.

Zacher, M. (2001). *International Organizations. In the Oxford companion to politics of the world*. Oxford: Oxford University Press. Retrieved March 13, 2014, from http://oxfordreference.com/view/10.1093/acref/9780195117394.001.0001/acref-9780195117394-e-0366.

Chapter 28
A Local Critique of Global Mental Health

China Mills and Bhargavi Davar

Making Mental Health a Reality

The World Health Organization and the Movement for Global Mental Health are currently calling to 'scale up' mental health services, with particular emphasis on increasing access to psychiatric drugs within the global South (Lancet Global Mental Health Group 2007; Patel et al. 2011). Amid these calls, others can be heard, from local and global movements of psychiatrised peoples: people globally who have been psychiatrically diagnosed and often subjected to 'treatments', including institutionalisation and/or medical or surgical interventions, sometimes administered forcibly. The human rights abuses that occur within psychiatric institutions worldwide continue to be exposed (Mental Disability Rights International 2005, 2010; Mindfreedom et al. 2011), and forced or coerced psychiatric treatment, both within institutions and within community settings, has been recognised as a form of torture and ill treatment (Minkowitz 2011).

Groups of psychiatrised people are increasingly mobilising to counter the globalisation of psychiatry with a counter-hegemonic globalisation—a set of networks, initiatives and movements that fight against psychiatric hegemony and imagine and enact alternatives embedded in local contexts (see the work of Pan African Network of People with Psychosocial Disabilities (PANUSP) 2011; the World Network of Users and Survivors of Psychiatry (WNUSP); and Mental Health Worldwide). Much of this resistance has come about through two interrelating strands: through cross-disability advocacy that navigates the paradigmatic differences between 'disability' and 'mental

C. Mills (✉)
School of Education, University of Sheffield,
388 Glossop Road, Sheffield, S10 2JA, UK
e-mail: china.mills@sheffield.ac.uk

B. Davar
Centre for Advocacy in Mental Health, Bapu Trust, Pune 411 060, Maharashtra, India
e-mail: bvdavar@gmail.com

S. Grech, K. Soldatic (eds.), *Disability in the Global South*,
International Perspectives on Social Policy, Administration, and Practice,
DOI 10.1007/978-3-319-42488-0_28

health' in contemporary discourse on human rights and empowerment; and through mobilisations of psychiatrised peoples across geographical borders, often in the form of South–South partnerships.[1] This chapter explores how epistemologies of the South and of the psychiatrised in the South mobilise the local to challenge and resist a single psychiatric approach to mental health and well-being that claims to be global—as currently embodied in advocacy for 'global mental health'.

In the last few years, psychiatry's travels to the global South have increased with the Movement for Global Mental Health (MGMH). This is an increasingly influential international network of individuals and organisations that, alongside the World Health Organization (WHO), calls for governments 'to scale up the coverage of services for mental disorders in all countries, but especially in low-income and middle-income countries' (Lancet Global Mental Health Group 2007: 87; see MGMH 2014). While the MGMH and the WHO acknowledge that much of psychiatry's evidence base comes from research within the global North, this is not seen as problematic because it is assumed that 'mental disorders … have a physical basis in the brain … they can affect everyone, everywhere' (WHO 2001a: x), are 'chronically disabling' (Prince et al. 2007: 1) and do not differ significantly across cultures (WHO 2001a, b).

Thus, the MGMH is increasingly functioning as a global space that shapes the contours of what can be said and what can be imagined in relation to mental well-being at the local level—a discourse through which social reality (or mental health as a reality) comes into being globally. For example, in India many non-governmental organisations train community members in how to identify distress (framed as 'mental illness') and train social workers to ensure compliance with medication at a local level (see Mills 2014). The Movement's calls 'to make mental health for all a reality' (Patel et al. 2011: 90) serve to make mental health as a reality thinkable in certain ways that are dominated by ways of knowing and intervening upon distress which come from the global North.

This chapter is written out of a shared concern over the mechanisms by which certain understandings of mental health are made a 'reality'—a reality that erases the multiple realities and lived experiences, as well as overlooks the political economy, of psychosocial distress within the global South, and specifically for this chapter, within India. The chapter seeks to map the contextual landscape that psychiatry is being scaled up onto, particularly in regard to tracing psychiatry's colonial history in India. Furthermore, it traces the politico-economic terrain, and implications, of global mental health advocacy, including what possibilities this might enable for transnational advocacy for formulating resistance.

The chapter recognises the need to directly problematise Global Mental Health by questioning how a single model can claim to account for, and 'treat', psychosocial distress experienced globally, and specifically in contexts of persistent poverty and entrenched inequality. The chapter also draws upon more indirect or oblique ways of critiquing the Movement through documenting and exploring more localised ways of

[1] For example, the TransAsia group of Persons with Psychosocial Disabilities participated in a regional workshop, 'Transforming communities for Inclusion of Persons with Psychosocial Disabilities', in May 2013 in Pune, supported by the Open Society Foundation and facilitated by the Bapu Trust.

knowing and supporting people in distress in contexts of poverty through the work of survivor-led[2] and disabled people's organisations in the global South.

Specifically, this chapter draws upon the work of Bapu Trust in Pune, India. Bapu Trust is a non-governmental organisation founded by Bhargavi Davar (the co-author of this chapter) in memory of her mother, Bapu, who was subjected to violent psychiatric interventions and indignity in India because she heard voices, an experience framed by psychiatry as a 'symptom' of schizophrenia (for alternative ways of understanding this experience, see The Hearing Voices Network). Furthermore, the chapter draws upon the alliances that Bapu Trust has formed with other survivor-led groups and disabled people's organisations across geographical borders, in an attempt to map how such alliances may lay the ground for the local to speak back to the global.

A Global Norm for Mental Health

Concerns about the MGMH have been raised from a multitude of arenas, from both those who have been diagnosed and those who write the prescriptions. For example, some have pointed out the irony of 'scaling up', to countries of the global South, psychiatric interventions that are increasingly coming under criticism in the global North (Summerfield 2008; Fernando 2014; Mills 2014). Many critical psychiatrists seek to abolish psychiatric diagnostic systems, based on evidence that psychiatric diagnoses lack validity, increase stigma, do not aid treatment decisions and impose western beliefs about mental distress on other cultures (Timimi 2011); and some call for a paradigm change within psychiatry (Bracken et al. 2012) as opposed to the scaling up of psychiatry globally.

Alongside critiques of the 'evidence base' of Global Mental Health, others critique the Movement because its agenda is top-down and not home-grown within the communities it claims to serve (Fernando and Weerackody 2009). There is a further concern that because of the Movement's focus on the brain it enforces a 'global norm for mental health' that overlooks the complexity of lived experiences within diverse communities, exaggerates prevalence (Shukla et al. 2012: 292) and imposes 'western' ideas of personhood and well-being (Summerfield 2008). This means that Global Mental Health potentially serves other interests than those of people in distress, for example the financial interests of the pharmaceutical industry (Thomas et al. 2005; Fernando 2011), for whom many countries of the global South constitute an emerging market (Mills 2014).

The call to scale up access to mental health care, heavily dominated by medication, is particularly worrying because increasing evidence suggests that some psychiatric

[2] We use the terms 'user' and 'survivor' here to refer to those who currently 'use' psychiatric interventions (often not by choice), and to those who have been psychiatrised (through psychiatric categories and/or interventions). We are also referring here to the local and global self-organising of psychiatrised peoples (and sometimes those who are not (yet) psychiatrised) into heterogeneous movements made up of people who are diversely situated in relation to psychiatry and have different priorities in their struggles, but who share a commitment to challenge psychiatric hegemony in all the areas of life into which it permeates.

drug treatments are ineffective (or only slightly more effective than placebo) and in some cases are harmful (Breggin 2008; Moncrieff 2009; Whitaker 2010). This is further embedded against a background of lack of availability to many life-saving drugs in the global South, in part due to the pharmaceutical industry's refusal to distribute cheaper generic drugs. Some African countries reject loans from multilateral agencies aiming to increase access to drugs because historically the conditionality of such loans has served to increase poorer countries' dependency on the global North (Shah 2006). Furthermore, where access to medicines is pushed this seems to coincide with the conceptualisation of countries of the South as 'emerging markets', especially when (1) market saturation has been reached in the North, or (2) when a drug has never gained traction in the North, often because of adverse side effects.

The development of public–private partnerships in the global South—some of which enable companies to circumvent strict regulatory regimes—enables wide-scale promotion and distribution of medicines. This is often with the involvement of global philanthropic organisations, for example, the Bill and Melinda Gates Foundation, which purchases stockpiled drugs found to be harmful in the North and aggressively promotes them in the South (Levich 2014). There are accounts of children in the South being forcibly vaccinated (for example, with HPV or malaria vaccines) with adverse effects, including many deaths, being downplayed (Srinivasan 2010). Such aggressive promotion of drugs is often in the name of helping poor people to access medicines.

This represents a general dominance in global discourse on health by transnational corporations, and particularly the pharmaceutical industry, with their agendas of deregulation and privatisation, and tensions over prices of drugs linked to intellectual property (Soldatic and Biyanwila 2010). While Global Mental Health advocacy aims to model itself on transnational HIV/AIDS activism and argues for psychiatric drugs to be exempted from patents under intellectual property (Patel 2006), there is little critical appraisal of how the Movement is embedded in a wider political economy of global capitalism. Similarly, there is little engagement from the Movement of the ethical implications of potentially serving (even if unwittingly) to create markets for the pharmaceutical industry; and there is lack of transparency about the sources of its funding, some of which is linked to the pharmaceutical industry (Fernando 2011; Mills 2014).

In the background of the MGMH—with its increasingly international recognition, large policy launches, and publications in major medical journals—there are growing alliances between people with psychosocial disabilities (some of whom identify as users and survivors, the 'mad', or the 'mentally ill') in countries of the global South. Such alliances seek to share local knowledge and practice, and use this to speak back to the hegemonic (see the work of WNUSP for example).

The Context of Mental Health in India

In many countries of the global South users and survivors of psychiatry and people with psychosocial disabilities are often not politically organised, with the reasons for this varying across different countries and regions. In India, a multitude of incapacity laws render the psychosocially disabled as 'incompetent' 'non-persons' effectively preventing people from politically organising or establishing disabled people's organisations (Davar 2012). Whereas, for example, in Nepal, there are fewer legal barriers for participation, there may be attitudinal and societal barriers (Center for Advocacy in Mental Health 2012). Furthermore, in much of Asia, there is a dominance of parent associations that claim to speak in the 'best interests' of people with psychosocial disabilities and may be embedded within the traditional hierarchy and patriarchy that sometimes structures societal and familial organisation.

In India there is both a legislative framework calling to build more large psychiatric hospitals—one in every state (ordered by the Supreme Court)—and simultaneously to increase provision of community mental health care. While the National Mental Health Programme of India's Central Government has the goal of providing community-based care for those with 'mental illness', in actual practice there are many legal and public policy barriers to the achievement of this and much of the yearly budget allocated to community care is returned unspent (Cremin 2007). Furthermore, a large proportion of community mental health work in India is carried out by NGOs (both local and international) that tend to be strongly influenced by WHO guidelines about mental health interventions. These guidelines, in turn, operate within a national and international environment dominated by bio-psychiatry, often relying on multiple prescriptions of medication and electroconvulsive therapy (ECT) (Jain and Jadhav 2009).

Psychiatric medications are often framed as an 'essential' aspect of psychiatric treatment despite the acknowledgement by both the WHO and the MGMH of the role played by poverty, and more widely by a variety of social determinants, in contributing to distress (see Patel and Kleinman 2003; Patel 2007; WHO and the Calouste Gulbenkian Foundation 2014). The Mental Health Gap Action Programme (mhGAP) Intervention Guide (WHO 2010)—a set of guidelines specifically developed to aid treatment decisions in non-specialised health-care settings in low and middle-income countries—recommends using psychotropic medication as first-line treatment in many instances. Similarly, the World Health Report states that,

> Essential psychotropic drugs should be provided and made constantly available at all levels of health care. These medicines should be included in every country's essential drugs list ... They often provide the first-line treatment, especially in situations where psychosocial interventions and highly skilled professionals are unavailable. (WHO 2001a: xii)

Here, the 'situations' where professionals and psychosocial interventions may be unavailable are often in the global South, and thus, because these countries are constructed as resource poor, the use of psychotropic drugs as first-line treatment is seen as justified. For Jain and Jadhav, the acceptance of medication as a 'common minimum' within much mental health policy and intervention in India serves to 'reify the "pill" as central to the delivery of care at the rural clinic' in India, overlooking people's multiple and complex lived realities of the interconnections between distress and poverty, and 'silencing community voices' (Jain and Jadhav 2009: 65, 75, 60). The centrality of the pill is a key reason why community mental health policy in India often fails—'because it has been swallowed by the pills' (Jain and Jadhav 2009: 74). Similarly, attention to the socio-politico-economic context in which distress is embedded seems also to be swallowed by medication, enabling primarily biomedical organisations, such as the WHO, to frame social problems, such as chronic poverty or entrenched social inequality, as psychiatric problems (Desjarlais et al. 1995).

A painful example of this can be seen in the response from the Indian Government and some MGMH advocates to the increasing numbers of farmer suicides in India. Many small-scale farmers in India commit suicide by swallowing the very pesticides that are aggressively promoted by agribusinesses and that degrade the land on which they live and try to making a living. Some even write suicide notes to the government, telling of a life made unliveable due to agricultural reforms which open production of their crops to volatile world markets and result in enormous debt to moneylenders (Perspectives 2009). In response, some advocates of the MGMH call for increased access among farmers to antidepressants (Patel and Kleinman 2003), while the Indian Government launched a study to explore the genetic factors that influence suicide (Arya 2007). Understanding and responding to farmer suicides through a psychological and psychiatric register fails to fully acknowledge the role of the wider agrarian crisis in farmer suicides, for example, how volatile economic markets may lead to substance abuse or family conflict, which may then lead to suicide.

Thus, the MGMH promotes a technical approach to mental distress which relies 'on pharmacological solutions for psychosocial problems' (Jain and Jadhav 2009: 60)—'pills for life's ills' (Moncrieff 2009: 105). There are parallels here to the beginnings of the agrarian crisis itself in India, where the aggressive promotion of pesticides, the very chemicals now swallowed by farmers, devastated previously more sustainable agricultural practices (Sharma 2004). Despite this destruction, experts continue to push for the increased role of biotechnology and agribusiness in intervening in the agrarian crisis—interventions framed by the same neo-liberal rationales that many argue led to the crisis initially.

Yet Global Mental Health advocacy rarely explores the relationship between distress and global capitalist food production chains, thereby reducing this distress to psychiatric 'symptoms' framed as the result of brain chemistry. This was a reductionism apparent during colonisation and one that the revolutionary and psychiatrist Frantz Fanon rallied against. For Fanon, the violence and supposed laziness of colonised people in Algeria were 'the direct product of the colonial situation', and yet were constructed by psychiatry as 'biologically organised' (1963: 250, 245) and as 'mere states of mind' (Adams 1970: 811). It is such reductionism—often reliant on psychiatric technology—that a number of user/survivor groups and/or groups of the psychosocially disabled in the global South and North explicitly reject.

This colonisation of the body and mind (Thiong'o 1981) is similar to the medicalisation of the disabled body through the naturalisation of impairment and subsequent processes of normalisation through rehabilitation, or eradication through eugenics (Goodley 2011). The colonisation of the mind also has parallels to, for example, the push for the dominance of biotechnology within agriculture, or liberal individualism as the dominant epistemology of current political economy. For Shiva this push for uniformity achieved through the disappearance of diversity is more than an issue for agriculture; it is about destroying alternative ways of thinking, being and doing, and creating 'monocultures of the mind' (Shiva 1993: 5). One way in which the Indian Government and MGMH contribute to such monocultures is evident in the way that they discredit and 'weed out' alternative and indigenous forms of healing in some countries of the global South (Basu 2009; Davar and Lohokare 2009).

Psychiatrisation as a Governmental and Colonial Project

In some countries of the global South, and specifically the Commonwealth, institutions for the 'insane' arrived with colonialism. Building asylums on colonised lands has played a central role in colonial systems throughout the 19th century for managing groups considered 'unfit' for society, such as 'paupers', 'lepers', 'idiots', 'deaf mutes' and the 'insane' (Ernst 1997; Mills 2000, 2004; Mahone and Vaughan 2007; Davar 2012).

Psychiatrisation as a governmental project in India has become particularly marked since the Erwadi tragedy in 2001 in Tamil Nadu, where 25 people labelled with 'mental illness' had been chained up and died when a fire broke out in a privately run hutment that claimed to provide religious healing. As a response to this, the Indian Supreme Court began a process of intervention against local and traditional healing sites all over India, demanding that the Mental Health Act (1987) be implemented by all state governments, and that all shelters not covered by the Act be closed. Here, people's seeking of help from local healing sites is framed as due to a lack of education about 'mental illness', alongside advocating that 'mental patients' should be sent to doctors and not dargahs (traditional healing sites). This has resulted in many traditional healing sites being shut down (Davar and Lohokare 2009).

Since the tragedy at Erwadi, there has been a renewed effort in Indian Government policies to extend the reach of the 'modern' at the expense of the 'traditional' through the use of law. Thus, the last decade has seen the build-up of a complex medico-legal regime and various related laws taking over spaces provided by local indigenous healing systems, and the outlawing of grassroots spiritual treatments for affliction that have long been part of local cultural practices.

This builds on a more general thread of critique of temple and indigenous healing as being *pre*-modern and thus in need of replacement by 'modern' treatments that make claims to scientific rationality, such as psychiatry (Siddiqui et al. 2012). Such assumptions are woven throughout Global Mental Health discourse, which argues that the biomedical approach to distress should become 'the standard approach for all countries', meaning that 'irrational and inappropriate interventions should be discouraged and weeded out' (Patel et al. 2011: 1442). Questions of who gets to decide what counts as 'irrational' and who does the 'weeding out' remain unanswered here. This 'weeding out' also reproduces (neo)colonial power relationships, operating as a form of 'medical imperialism, similar to the marginalisation of indigenous knowledge systems in the colonial era' (Summerfield 2008: 992). Ernst (1997) suggests that it is through the discrediting of indigenous forms of healing as uncivilised; racially codified diagnoses that maintain and reify racial hierarchies; and the medicalisation of economic concerns about the ill health of the colonised as a threat to labour supplies (Mashingaidze 2010: 45) that psychiatry served as a tool of ideological legitimation during colonialism.

The right *not* to have psychiatric and 'western' interventions imposed within the global South is increasingly being expressed by the psychosocially disabled, whose voices are strikingly absent in the current push to scale up psychiatry. For example, the Pan African Network of People with Psychosocial Disabilities states that services and support must be delivered 'in non-paternalistic and non-patriarchal frameworks with choices available outside of the medical framework', and within the community, and must include 'the choice not to use western medical "solutions"' (PANUSP 2012: 2–3). Davar and Lohokare (2009) echo this in their claim that people experiencing distress who want to include prayer or penance as a part of their healing process should have this protected as a health-care right.

Bapu Trust: A Local Approach

Situated against a national and international background dominated by bio-psychiatry, Bapu Trust carries out a very different sort of work. Bapu Trust advocates that mental health is a local, and not a global, issue. It recognises that various local factors determine the kind of interventions needed in communities, such as local history, available social capital, commercial profile, cultural practices, local arts, spiritual and healing traditions, civic amenities and access to development.

The vision of the *Seher* (meaning 'dawn') urban mental health programme of Bapu Trust is to create psychologically sustainable communities. Seher carries out its work through creating everyday conversations about well-being within low-income communities of Pune, India, talking intimately and informally to people on the streets and in people's homes about psychosocial distress and well-being (for example at 'corner meetings', see Fig. 28.1). The programme aims to prevent development of distress and to provide necessary social and emotional support for those with psychosocial disabilities. Seher addresses a wide range of people with psychosocial disabilities, including those in extreme states—who would be framed by psychiatry as having 'severe mental disorder'—without taking recourse to involuntary incarceration.

Instead of assuming that communities lack 'scientific' knowledge about 'mental illness' and are in need of outside expert intervention (an approach that seems apparent in the work of many NGOs in India and within the literature on Global Mental Health), the Seher programme taps into the resources that already exist within the local social fabric of communities.

While at first the programme used psychiatric terminology and classificatory systems (developed in the global North), it is now more influenced by the less pathologising work of feminist disability scholarship and advocacy (Ghai 2003), as well as understandings from voice-hearing communities and peer support. Based on the fact that many communities are organised into a variety of social 'groups' and do not always have an individualistic approach to their social life, the programme has mod-

Fig. 28.1 Corner meeting, Pune, Seher Programme (with kind permission from Bapu Trust)

elled therapeutic groups as a way of creating and spreading support for people with stresses and disabilities. Eastern healing techniques that are culturally appropriate, such as mindfulness training, meditations, visualisations, drumming, body work and a variety of arts-based therapeutic support, are all widely used. This approach resonates with a widespread rejection by many user/survivor groups worldwide of the technical paradigm of psychiatry, in favour of more locally responsive understandings, with those who experience distress being understood as the 'experts'. Although psychiatric medication is a part of the support provided by Bapu Trust for some, referrals for psychiatric treatment are made only when it is felt that health care and medication can supplement the community and psychosocial strategies of recovery.

Navigating Identities of User/Survivor

Though Bapu Trust was established in response to the human rights abuses of the psychiatric system (discussed earlier), it did not at first identify itself as a 'user/survivor' organisation. Yet, over a period of time, Bapu was challenged by people carrying the label of 'mental illness' that as a third party the organisation shouldn't claim to speak on behalf of people in distress. In response to this, the Trust went through a process of restructuring and closed programmes that worked closely with institutions (such as 'beggars' homes') because they were felt to be coercive, keeping only those programmes based in the community.

As time went on, an increasing number of people who identified as users/survivors joined as staff and as users of the organisation, while simultaneously Bapu participated internationally in the negotiations of the then draft UN Convention on the Rights of Persons with Disabilities (CRPD). The issue of user/survivor identity and control became embedded within the organisational discourse, leading Bapu Trust to join the World Network of Users and Survivors of Psychiatry, with leading figures at Bapu publicly identifying themselves as survivors.

These alliances between psychiatric survivors across geographical borders continued when the Bapu Trust organised for Gabor Gombos, a leading figure of the psychiatric survivor movement in Hungary and a founder of the European Network of (Ex) Users and Survivors of Psychiatry, to come to India to facilitate workshops on self-advocacy with people who experience distress or identify as psychosocially disabled. An immediate challenge was how to get people to attend such a workshop. Few people in India self-identify as survivors of psychiatry and many people are understood, and understand themselves, within a bio-psychiatric language as 'patients'—the very term that may undermine self-advocacy. As Gombos and Dhanda recognise,

> People with psychosocial disabilities thus have good reason to be cautious before publicly speaking up as self advocates. Besides the social stigma of disability, legal incapacitation, incarceration to locked units and forced treatment with mind altering treatment methods are all realistic threats for persons with psychosocial disabilities. (Gombos and Dhanda 2009: 6)

With this in mind, Gombos and Dhanda felt that solely focusing on enabling people to become self-advocates without 'preparing the arena where the self advocates will operate' (2009: 8) could be self-limiting and lead to frustration. Yet they also acknowledged that while the stigmatisation and exclusion of people with psychosocial disability may occur across diverse contexts, the particular forms this takes may vary across cultures, thus questioning strategies of 'importing expertise to catalyze self advocacy' (Gombos and Dhanda 2009: 8).

In fact, identity categories such as 'user' and 'survivor' are to some extent embedded within the western contexts from which they emerge, and while they may be useful, they often do not reflect the lived realities of people who experience distress in countries of the global South. For example, in contexts where there is no psychiatric system, what can one be a 'user' of? Thus, the fact that many countries of the global South have no organised user or survivor networks is not necessarily because of lack of political awareness or less knowledge of human rights. It may be due to a societal context that is *not* dominated by medico-legal frameworks, or previous colonial frameworks, for responding to distress. Similarly, in areas where there is little or no institutional provision of support, violation within the system may be less of an issue.

Different organisations in the global South employ different strategies to navigate this complexity. For example, the Pan African Network of Users and Survivors of Psychiatry, based in South Africa, announced that it planned to change its name to the Pan African Network of People with Psychosocial Disabilities 'in recognition that "users and survivors of psychiatry" does not adequately reflect representation and the lived reality of this voiceless group in Africa' (PANUSP 2011: (1). In Asia, a growing network of people with psychosocial disabilities are calling themselves the Trans Asia Strategic Group of Persons with Psychosocial Disabilities as they feel that 'user survivor' frames their identities as already within the field of psychiatry. Alongside the negotiation of the user/survivor identity, the right to live independently and to be included in the community as a fundamental human right espoused in Article 19 of the CRPD has provided a key tool to enable mobilisation between users/survivors or people who identify as psychosocially disabled, and the disability movement more widely.

Resistance to psychiatry is intricately entangled within the different contexts in which psychiatry functions (or ceases to function). While the wholesale export of resistance to psychiatry from the global North to the South may arguably be just as problematic as the globalisation of psychiatry, alliances of resistance that cross geographical borders can build global networks that remain locally nuanced.

Furthermore, Bapu Trust *does* encounter some people from remote villages who articulate their experiences of psychiatry by saying that their rights have been violated. While the identity category of 'psychiatric survivor' may be relatively new in India, many have experienced abuse within the psychiatric system, and thus it can be a useful place from which to situate advocacy work with those who have been violated. This is especially true for Bapu Trust's advocacy in relation to the use of direct electroconvulsive therapy (without anaesthetic) in India, and its calls to bring those who have undergone direct ECT within human rights and medico-legal jurisprudence as victims of medical torture (see Center for Advocacy in Mental Health 2004; MindFreedom 2011).

Conclusion

This chapter has traced how the MGMH and the WHO set an increasingly global norm for understanding well-being and distress, a norm in which the local work of many NGOs in the global South is embedded within and judged by. This chapter is an attempt to reverse this logic and to use the locally contextualised work of one organisation, Bapu Trust, and its alliances with other such groups, to interrogate and rethink interventions in mental health that claim to be global.

The work of Bapu Trust stands in direct contrast to much of the current discourse on Global Mental Health. This is evident in the Bapu Trust's recognition of local complexity (of the history of a community and its myriad networks) and the effects this has on care; in its respect of indigenous and local forms of healing; its documentation and awareness raising of alternative paradigms of care than psychiatry; and in its promotion of non-medical and non-technical solutions.

Unlike the push to export psychiatric technology from the global North, the Bapu Trust promotes the expertise of those who experience distress and of local support mechanisms within communities, aiming to enhance the conditions that enrich a community's capacity to care for people in a sustainable way. Like a number of more localised organisations run by people who identify as psychosocially disabled or as users/survivors within the global South (such as PANUSP), Bapu Trust navigates an awareness of, and alliances to, global discourses of resistance to psychiatry, and yet remains always aware of the local complexities in which it is embedded.

More than global alliances that resist psychiatry, we might also begin to think about how groups acting locally to oppose the imposition of standardised approaches and monocultures (Shiva 1993) (be they monocropping in agriculture or the discrediting and closing of alternative or indigenous healing sites for distress) might connect and advocate transnationally to conserve and build diversity. This might mean the recognition that people's resistance to over-medicalisation in the Indian psychiatric field is congruent, though not always in dialogue, with other movements of resistance, such as civil society mobilisations against the increasing power of corporations in providing health care; campaigns against clinical trials on, or promotion of harmful medical interventions to, people living in poverty; the oppressive role of the army in maintaining law and order; increasing ecological degradation; and the disempowerment of a variety of vulnerable groups as socio-economic disparity and chronic poverty increase. Diverse movements could establish some threads of mutual intelligibility for joint mobilisation, for example, by recognising epistemological diversity in multiple forms as a key point of resistance to current global capitalist systems (Santos et al. 2007).

It is perhaps through such global alliances, across borders and disability identities, and between locally embedded groups, that the normative assumptions of frameworks that claim to be global (overlooking their own local conditions of possibility within the countries of the global North from which they come) will be dislodged by multiple forms of knowledge that are local, home-grown and on peoples' and communities' own terms.

References

Adams, P. L. (1970). The social psychiatry of Frantz Fanon. *American Journal of Psychiatry, 126*(6), 809–814.

Arya, S. (2007). Govt to study DNA link to suicides. *Times of India. September 27.*

Basu, H. (2009). Contested practices of control: Psychiatric and religious mental health care in India. *Journal of Medical Anthropology, 32*(1–2), 28–39.

Bracken, P., Thomas, P., Timimi, S., Asen, E., Behr, G., et al. (2012). Psychiatry beyond the current paradigm. *British Journal of Psychiatry, 201*, 430–434.

Breggin, P. R. (2008). *Brain-disabling treatments: Drugs, electroshock, and the psychopharmaceutical complex*. New York: Springer.

Center for Advocacy in Mental Health. (2012). *Mission on mainstreaming rights of persons with psychosocial disabilities—Nepal*. A report. (16th–17th May 2012). Pune: Center for Advocacy in Mental Health. Retrieved December 17, 2013, from http://camhjournal.com/2012/10/23/mission-psychosocial-nepal/?relatedposts_exclude=3.

Center for Advocacy in Mental Health (CAMH). (2004). *ECT (Electro-convulsive therapy): Need for debate*. Pune: Center for Advocacy in Mental Health Archives. Retrieved December 27, 2014, from http://camhjournal.com/2012/04/24/2004-a-campaign-against-direct-ect/.

Cremin, K. M. (2007). *General hospital psychiatric units and rehabilitation centres in India: Do law and public policy present barriers to community-based mental health services?* An Occasional Study Paper. Pune: The Centre for Advocacy in Mental Health.

Davar, B. (2012). Legal Frameworks for and against people with psychosocial disabilities. *Economic and Political Weekly, XLVII*(52), 123–131.
Davar, V. B., & Lohokare, M. (2009). Recovering from psychosocial traumas: The place of Dargahs in Maharashtra. *Economic and Political Weekly, XLIV*(16), 60–68.
Desjarlais, R., Eisenberg, L., Good, B., & Kleinman, A. (1995). *World mental health: Problems and priorities in LAMICS*. New York: Oxford University Press.
Ernst, W. (1997). Idioms of madness and colonial boundaries: The case of the European and "Native" mentally Ill in early nineteenth-century British India. *Comparative Studies in Society and History, 39*(1), 153–181.
Fanon, F. (1963). *The wretched of the earth*. (C. Farrington, Trans.). London: Penguin Books
Fernando, S. (2011). A 'Global' mental health programme or markets for big pharma? *Open Mind, 168*, 22.
Fernando, S. (2014). *Mental health worldwide: Culture, globalization and development*. Basingstoke: Palgrave Macillan.
Fernando, S., & Weerackody, C. (2009). Challenges in developing community mental health services in Sri Lanka. *Journal of Health Management, 11*(1), 195–208.
Ghai, A. (2003). *(Dis)embodied form: Issues of disabled women*. New Delhi: Haranand Publications, Shakti Books.
Gombos, G., & Dhanda, A. (2009). *Catalyzing self advocacy: An experiment in India* (Vol. 1). Pune, India: Bapu Trust, Centre for Mental Health Advocacy, Advocacy Series.
Goodley, D. (2011). *Disability studies: An interdisciplinary introduction*. London: Sage.
Jain, S., & Jadhav, S. (2009). Pills that swallow policy: Clinical ethnography of a community mental health program in Northern India. *Transcultural Psychiatry, 46*(1), 60–85.
Lancet Global Mental Health Group. (2007). Scale up services for mental disorders: A call for action. *The Lancet, 370*(9594), 1241–1252.
Levich, J. (2014). *Big pharma and the gates foundation: "Guinea Pigs for the Drugmakers"*. Global Research, May 28. Retrieved June 22, 2014, from http://www.globalresearch.ca/big-pharma-and-the-gates-foundation-guinea-pigs-for-the-drugmakers/5384374.
Mahone, S., & Vaughan, M. (2007). *Psychiatry and empire*. London: Palgrave Macmillan.
Mashingaidze, T. M. (2010). Power, disease and prejudice: Syphilis in colonial sub-Saharan Africa. *Sephis E Magazine, 6*(3), 41–53.
Mental Disability Rights International. (2005). *Behind closed doors: Human rights abuses in the psychiatric facilities, orphanages and rehabilitation centers of Turkey*. Washington, DC: Mental Disability Rights International.
Mental Disability Rights International. (2010). *Torture not Treatment: Electric Shock and Long-Term Restraint in the United States on Children and Adults with Disabilities at the Judge Rotenberg Center. Urgent Appeal to the United Nations Special Rapporteur on Torture*. Washington, DC: Mental Disability Rights International.
Mental Health Worldwide www.mentalhealthworldwide.com.
Mills, J. H. (2000). *Madness, cannabis and colonialism: The "Native-Only" Lunatic Asylums of British India, 1857–1900*. Landon, UK: Macmillan Press Ltd.
Mills, J. H. (2004). Body as target, Violence as treatment: Psychiatric regimes in colonial and post colonial India. In J. Mills & S. Sen (Eds.), *Confronting the body: The politics of physicality in colonial and post-colonial India* (pp. 80–101). London: Anthem South Asian Studies.
Mills, C. (2014). *Decolonizing global mental health: The psychiatrization of the majority world*. London: Routledge.
MindFreedom. (2011). *Global mental health empowerment handbook*. Retrieved from http://www.mindfreedom.org/globalhandbook.
MindFreedom Ghana, MindFreedom International & The Open Society Foundation. (2011). *Parallel Report to the Committee against torture on Ghana, at the 46th session*. Retrieved February 12, 2013, from http://www2.ohchr.org/english/bodies/cat/docs/ngos/Submission_Ghana46.pdf.
Minkowitz, T. (2011). *Recognizing forced and coerced psychiatric interventions against women, men and children as a harmful cultural practice*. Submission for Joint CEDAW-CRC General Recommendation/General Comment on Harmful Practices. New York: WNUSP and CHRUSP.

Moncrieff, J. (2009). *The myth of the chemical cure: A critique of psychiatric drug treatment*. London: Palgrave MacMillan.
Movement for Global Mental Health (MGMH). (2014). Retrieved November 12, 2014, from www.globalmentalhealth.org.
Pan African Network of People with Psychosocial Disabilities (PANUSP). (2011). *Cape Town declaration*. Retrieved July 12, 2012, from http://www.panusp.org/.
PANUSP. (2012). *Press package*. Retrieved July 12, 2012, from http://www.panusp.org/wp-content/uploads/2011/10/Press-Release-WHO-Launch-Toolkit-28-June-2012.pdf.
Patel, V. (2006). Beyond evidence: The moral case for international mental health. *American Journal of Psychiatry, 163*(9), 1312–1315.
Patel, V. (2007). Mental health in low- and middle-income countries. *British Medical Bulletin, 81*(1), 81–96.
Patel, V., Collins, P. Y., Copeland, J., Kakuma, R., Katontoka, S., Lamichhane, J., et al. (2011). The movement for global mental health. *British Journal of Psychiatry, 198*, 88–90.
Patel, V., & Kleinman, A. (2003). Poverty and common mental disorders in developing countries. *Bulletin of the World Health Organization, 81*(8), 609–615.
Perspectives. (2009). *Harvesting despair: Agrarian crisis in India*. Delhi: Perspectives.
Prince, M., Patel, V., Saxena, S., Maj, M., Maselko, J., Phillips, M. R., et al. (2007). No health without mental health. *The Lancet, 370*(9590), 1–19.
Santos, B., Arriscado Nunes, J., & Meneses, M. P. (2007). Introduction: Opening up the canon of knowledge and recognition of difference. In B. Santos (Ed.), *Another knowledge is possible: Beyond northern epistemologies*. London: Verso.
Shah, S. (2006). *The body hunters: Testing new drugs on the world's poorest patients*. New York: The New Press.
Sharma, D. (2004). *India's Agrarian crisis: No end to farmers suicides*. Share the World's Resources (SWTR), 27th June. Retrieved May 25, 2012, from http://www.stwr.org/food-security-agriculture/the-collapse-of-green-revolution.html.
Shiva, V. (1993). *Monocultures of the mind: Perspectives on biodiversity and biotechnology*. London: Zed Books.
Shukla, A., Philip, A., Zachariah, A., Phadke, A., Suneetha, A., Davar, B., et al. (2012). Letter—Critical perspectives on the NIMH initiative "Grand Challenges to Global Mental Health". *Indian Journal of Medical Ethics, IX*(4), 292–293.
Siddiqui, S., Lacroix, K., & Dhar, A. (2012). The temple and the asylum. *Asylum, 19*(1), 13–14.
Soldatic, K., & Biyanwila, J. (2010). Tsunami and the construction of disabled southern body. *Sephis E Magazine, 6*(3), 75–84.
Srinivasan, S.A. (2010). A vaccine for every ailment. *Infochange*, April, 2010. Retrieved February 23, 2014, from http://infochangeindia.org/public-health/healthcare-markets-and-you/a-vaccine-for-every-ailment.html.
Summerfield, D. (2008). How scientifically valid is the knowledge base of GMH? *British Medical Journal, 336*, 992–994.
The Hearing Voices Network www.hearing-voices.org
Thiong'o, N. (1981). *Decolonizing the mind: The politics of language in African literature*. Nairobi: East African Educational Publishers.
Thomas, P., Bracken, P., Cutler, P., Hayward, R., May, R., & Yasmeen, S. (2005). Challenging the globalisation of biomedical psychiatry. *Journal of Public Mental Health, 4*(3), 23–32.
Timimi, S. (2011). *No more psychiatric labels*. Retrieved January 20, 2012, from http://www.criticalpsychiatry.net/?p=527.
Whitaker, R. (2010). *Anatomy of an epidemic: Magic bullets, psychiatric drugs, and the astonishing rise of mental illness in America*. New York: Broadway Paperbacks.
WHO. (2001a). *World health report 2001: Mental health: New understanding, new hope*. Geneva: World Health Organisation.
WHO. (2001b). *Mental health: A call for action by World Health Ministers. Ministerial Round Tables, 54th World Health Assembly*. Geneva: World Health Organisation.

WHO. (2010). *mhGAP intervention guide for mental, neurological and substance use disorders in non-specialized health settings*. Geneva: WHO.
WHO and the Calouste Gulbenkian Foundation. (2014). *Social determinants of mental health.* Geneva: World Health Organization.
World Network of Users and Survivors of Psychiatry (WNUSP)

Chapter 29
Community-Based Rehabilitation and Disability-Inclusive Development: On a Winding Path to an Uncertain Destination

Pim Kuipers and Louis Paluku Sabuni

Introduction

The majority of people with disabilities who live in developing countries, predominantly in the global South, do not receive any formal disability or rehabilitation services. In those countries or regions where at least some disability services are provided, the community-based rehabilitation (CBR) approach, or some form of it, is likely to be the only approach available (Evans et al. 2001).

As a formal 'model', CBR was first promoted by the World Health Organization (WHO) in the mid-1970s to address the shortage of rehabilitation services in the global South. A key dimension of the original CBR approach was the transfer of minimum and essential rehabilitation intervention skills to families and other volunteers in the community (Thomas and Thomas 1999). The intent of the model was to provide some form of rehabilitation or disability support services through the local community, using local resources. The approach drew on the principles of primary health care, accepted international rehabilitation practices of the time and existing local practices and technologies (Hartley et al. 2009). Early CBR practices were based on a few manuals (Helander et al. 1989; Werner 1999) and emphasized basic, individually focused services, such as therapy, education, basic equipment, vocational training and referral to medical services (Thomas 2011). Historically CBR

P. Kuipers (✉)
ILEP, Geneva, Switzerland, and Menzies Health Institute Queensland,
Griffith University, Meadowbrook, QLD 4131, Australia
e-mail: p.kuipers@griffith.edu.au

L.P. Sabuni
The Leprosy Mission, Kinshasa, Democratic Republic of Congo

S. Grech, K. Soldatic (eds.), *Disability in the Global South*,
International Perspectives on Social Policy, Administration, and Practice,
DOI 10.1007/978-3-319-42488-0_29

has nearly always been promoted and implemented by international non-government organizations (NGOs) based in the global North, such as Handicap International (2014) and CBM (2014).

The most widely used definition of CBR reflects its change over time, and notes that CBR is:

> a strategy within general community development for rehabilitation, equalization of opportunities, and social inclusion of all people with disabilities … implemented through the combined efforts of people with disabilities themselves, their families and communities, and the appropriate health, education, vocational, and social services … (ILO and WHO 2004)

This statement, emphasizing not just traditional rehabilitation, but including community development, poverty reduction, equalization of opportunities and social integration, reflects something of the evolution of CBR. In recent years this evolution has been manifest in the growing shift towards the concepts and terminology of disability-inclusive development (DID) by organizations and collaborations that have traditionally emphasized CBR. The evolution towards DID approaches reflects a move beyond traditional rehabilitation to emphasizing rights and inclusion, seeking to ensure that people with disabilities are stakeholders in development processes. The goal of DID is that 'all phases of the development cycle (design, implementation, monitoring and evaluation) include a disability dimension and that persons with disabilities are meaningfully and effectively participating in development processes and policies' (IDDC 2010).

Our goal in this chapter is to examine aspects of the evolving nature of CBR, which has facilitated its emergence as a global service model. We hold that CBR and DID approaches and their evolution over past decades have both positive and negative dimensions. Likewise, we see both potentially constructive and possibly unproductive directions in the evolutionary paths ahead. We recognize that the CBR model is far from ideal, but we also advocate that with adequate vision, the CBR model can and should evolve further to more adequately respond to the needs of people with disability in the global South. Such vision must largely come from the global South, from people with disability, their families and communities.

We conclude that such a 'downstream' focus is what should characterize the evolution of CBR; however, we observe that much of the emphasis of CBR and DID is 'upstream' agendas of management, policy and international declarations. Such priorities primarily reflect the interests and priorities of some NGOs and international bureaucrats rather than people with disabilities in the global South. We also contend that the evolving nature of CBR has made it quite ill defined, resulting in a lack of identity and direction in some crucial dimensions. We suggest that adverse aspects of this unplanned evolution which characterize CBR include limited organizational leadership, inadequate global recognition, the predominance of Western values, poor educational and research infrastructure and a meagre funding stream. These issues have stunted the development of a theoretical framework or robust academic analysis. Practically, this has also hindered the clear elucidation of a leadership structure and training framework for CBR. The current reality is that the global CBR movement has not grown commensurate with the number of people in the global South who require the services, empowerment, livelihoods and social inclusion that it should facilitate.

The Evolving Identity of CBR

Given the focus on local resources, family member skills and the distinctive characteristics of local communities, it is not surprising that the implementation of CBR was never uniform and was commonly adapted, resulting in a diverse and evolving model of practice (Kuipers 1998). On the positive side, this has resulted in an approach which is readily adaptable, with great potential to be contextually responsive (Kuipers 1998). In some settings the model has evolved constructively in response to the local context (Werner 1993) and is increasingly being promoted by NGOs and by governments in the global South (CCBRT 2014). Such evolution has created the potential for greater relevance, attentiveness to local culture and responsiveness to socio-economic realities.

However, this evolution has been inconsistent across settings and across dimensions of CBR. Some examples of CBR practice have evolved very little from their Western origins in the 1970s, and maintain stereotypical treatment programmes, regardless of need or context (Giacaman 2001). Other aspects have evolved considerably, but with questionable outcomes for the majority of people with disabilities. The mercurial nature of CBR, without clear models, has permitted potentially useless or even unhelpful structures and practices to flourish in some settings. For example, in a review of 37 CBR evaluation reports, weaknesses in management and unhelpful management practices were seen as the primary cause for concern by evaluators (Kuipers et al. 2008). Such practices presumably emerged in the absence of clear management guidelines, as CBR evolved from a set of rehabilitation techniques, rather than from a considered organizational and management foundation. While key international CBR agencies have now produced formal management guidelines, and a framework for CBR is now in place (WHO et al. 2010), this wasn't undertaken until 30 years after the initial promotion of the CBR model.

The indistinct and evolving nature of CBR is not just a historical phenomenon, but is also a defining characteristic of the model. This is well illustrated in the widely used CBR Matrix (Fig. 29.1), which accompanied the CBR Guidelines (WHO et al. 2010). The matrix suggests that the scope of CBR is now so broad and all-encompassing that it is almost indefinable. The CBR Matrix consists of five key components (columns), each comprising five elements (rows). Four components (health, education, livelihood, and social) relate to development sectors; the fifth, empowerment, addresses access to development. The elements under each key component describe the range of options that could be implemented as CBR. Such breadth, coupled with the evolving nature of CBR, has made it very difficult to define, to investigate and particularly to evaluate the impact and outcomes of the

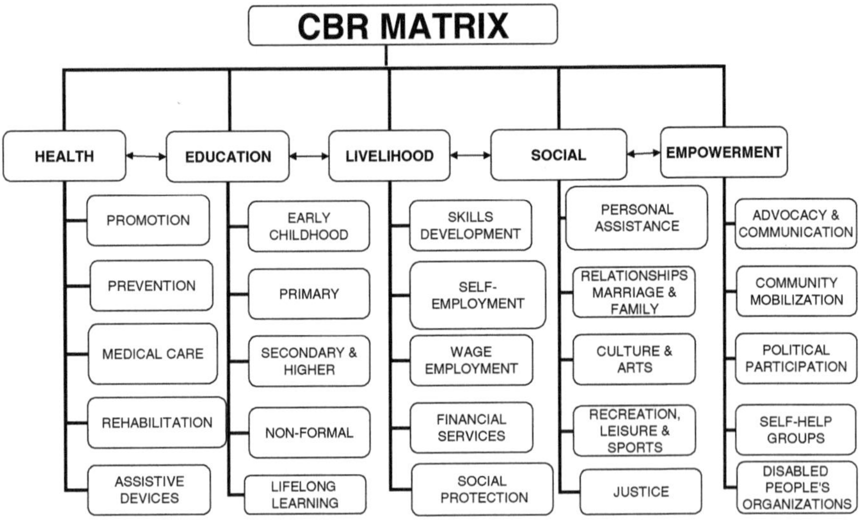

Fig. 29.1 CBR Matrix

model. As a result, questions of quality of services and cost-effectiveness of CBR have essentially not been asked, evidence of outcomes has not been demonstrated and rigorous comparative analysis at an international level has not yet occurred (Thomas and Thomas 1999; Hartley et al. 2009).

The Voice of People with Disabilities in the Identity of CBR

From relatively early, a consistent critique of CBR internationally has been that people with disabilities have had limited voice in the conceptualization of CBR services and models (Werner 1995), or in the management and running of CBR programmes (Lang 1999). In many historical and contemporary CBR projects, power resides with the professionals who manage the service, and the role of people with disabilities is as passive 'recipients' or 'beneficiaries' (Lang 2000). While these critiques remain pertinent in many CBR settings globally, and the voice and leadership of people with disabilities remain very limited, there are signs of constructive directions emerging. New training approaches have the potential to challenge traditional professional practices (Rule 2013), and new models of service delivery are evolving, which will lead to a reconceptualization of roles (Lang 2011). Such emerging models have the potential to shape CBR and DID in encouraging new ways.

The Identity of CBR Among DPOs

The decades in which CBR emerged have also witnessed the rise of disabled people's organizations (DPOs) in Western nations as well as in the global South. In many instances, relationships between CBR service providers and DPOs have been difficult. In some instances, CBR-implementing organizations have seen DPOs as peripheral and either failed to engage or actively ignored them. Conversely some DPOs in the global South, which have tended to be city based, have viewed CBR as an outdated service delivery system, suited only to rural areas (Thomas 2011).

At the implementing country level, early relationships between internationally funded and professionally supported (and usually foreign) CBR organizations and local, unfunded DPOs were quite uneasy (Miles 1996). In part this was due to the attention given to the CBR organizations by local government officials as a result of the funding that accompanied their work. More recently this situation is starting to change. With interest among international donors and aid agencies increasingly shifting towards directly funding and supporting DPOs, the identity of CBR and the relationships between CBR organizations and DPOs are being re-examined.

Some CBR leaders have advocated that the roles of CBR organizations and DPOs should increasingly be integrated at all levels (WHO 2003). Indeed, some advocate that CBR projects should instigate and strengthen DPOs, and that DPOs can also initiate and run CBR programmes (Deepak et al. 2013). This shift, in combination with the interest from donors to fund DPOs, means that they may increasingly become service providers, and that CBR organizations may see some of their area of influence diminish.

The diminution of influence of some CBR NGOs, and the potential for DPOs to become providers of rehabilitation or disability services may be a preferred model for many. Under such a structure people with disabilities may have a greater voice in management, service provision and emergence of more appropriate services. This emerging direction, however, also holds the potential for both CBR organizations and DPOs to lose their respective distinctive features and identities. For example, if DPOs become service providers, they may lose some of the 'moral authority' they hold as independent advocates and watchdogs. They may easily become conflicted, and may no longer have the necessary independence to hold service providers accountable. A potential direction for more constructive evolution may be for CBR programmes to build the capacity of people with disabilities and their families through self-help groups, which are then linked with independent DPOs, advocating to governments and service providers and providing different forms of support and capacity building (Suharto et al. 2013).

The Identity of CBR and Fundamental Values

As implied earlier, the evolving and adaptable nature of CBR has not necessarily been manifest in all dimensions of the approach. For example, a consistent critique of the early CBR model was that it naively conformed to traditional, medicalized approaches to rehabilitation (Gatjens 2009). While this is less an issue in contemporary CBR practice, there are a number of other aspects of Western conceptualization which have also been adopted without much adaptation to the diverse contexts of the global South. For example, it has been observed in the South Asian context that proponents of CBR and DID inappropriately impose a narrow Western perspective of disability development as a human rights issue, regardless of context or the strengths and weaknesses of communities (Miles 1996). This would appear to be an example of a Western colonial mindset, but in a less overt form, since such issues are seen by many in the CBR world as beyond debate or discussion.

Likewise, proponents of CBR have strongly emphasized conventional notions of empowerment of people with disabilities: from early publications (Helander 1999) to more recent frameworks (WHO et al. 2010). Western concepts of individual 'empowerment', however, are often perceived as selfish in some Asian contexts, and inconsistent with the philosophy of *ubuntu* (human interconnectedness) in some African contexts. In many developing country settings, the concerns of the family or community have precedence over individual empowerment, and indeed in some societies such notions of empowerment may be perceived as a threat to positive social order and community harmony (Thomas 2011). While such differences are not new or even necessarily contradictory, the CBR movement has not had a robust debate as to the relevance, adaptation or reinvention of concepts such as human rights, empowerment or even community-based action (Kuipers 2014). In particular, for many women with disabilities in the global South, these Western notions are peripheral at best, or at times major obstacles to achieving their aspirations for greater collective identity and growth (Lorenzo 2003).

The tendency within CBR and DID of directly transposing Western notions of empowerment, rights or other values may be seen as akin to the practice of transposing Western models of rehabilitation in the 1970s. As in the 1970s, some contemporary Western disability activists and academics appear resolute that post-enlightenment and post-modern conceptualizations should be adopted post-haste, regardless of context. Indeed, it is only in recent years that distinctly global South voices and models are being proposed for disability-related action and research (Mji et al. 2011). Without such critical analysis and debate arising from the global South, in directly importing such concepts without due regard to local contexts, cultures, beliefs and values, CBR is unlikely to advance in a contextually sustainable way.

The Identity of CBR and Religion

The roll-out of the CBR approach also appears to have strongly adhered to Western secular conceptualizations and sensitivities, deliberately ignoring issues of religion and spirituality (Crishna 1999; see also Betcher and Wangila 2016, in this volume). While religion has occasionally been acknowledged as a contextual issue in the Guidelines (WHO et al. 2010), the importance or potential of religion is not addressed in official CBR documents in any meaningful way. Recognizing that religion is a critical source of meaning and identity for the majority of people in the global South, and that disability is immersed in this meaning system (Grech 2012), this would seem a curious omission.

In part, this omission stems from the medical conceptualization that was so fundamental in the evolution of CBR. Western science-based, medical and rehabilitation models have developed away from, and have often been in conflict with, traditional religious belief systems (Miles 2010). This has aligned with Western fixations on secular and individualistic conceptualizations in development circles (Grech 2012). As a result, the CBR world has not had serious discussion about the incorporation of faith, spirituality, beliefs and religion into practice. Issues such as karma, destiny, fate or the Islamic concept of *taqdeer* have rarely, if ever, been discussed. Moreover, potential connections between religious beliefs and well-being, hope, quality of life, resilience or even the supportive and affirming potential of communities of faith and religious congregations (Grech 2012) have largely been ignored in the CBR discourse.

Recognizing the fundamental importance of religion and belief in the lives and communities of most people in the global South (Grech 2012), and that many Western CBR NGOs (such as CBM, World Vision, Caritas and numerous leprosy organizations) have come from faith-based frameworks, the silence on these issues is surprising. While they may be somewhat contentious from a Western secular perspective, without robust discussion and ongoing acknowledgement of these issues, the field of CBR is unlikely to evolve in ways that touch the lives and are coherent with the values, of the majority of people and communities in the global South.

As the emphasis in CBR evolves towards a more inclusive development approach, the prospects for addressing this shortcoming are not encouraging. The DID approach with a single-minded emphasis on rights, conventions, policy and legislation would equally appear to have little to contribute to these issues. As Grech has noted, rights, policies and legislation have replaced God in the secular conceptualization. In combination with empowerment and socio-economic advancement, they are the means by which redemption is gained (Grech 2012) in the new frameworks being imposed on people with disabilities in the global South through the DID model.

The Identity of CBR and Gender

Encouragingly, contemporary CBR literature consistently mentions the issue of gender. The need to consider gender issues and the importance of gender equality are noted throughout the new Guidelines (WHO et al. 2010) and other more recent publications (Ghosh 2011). In most instances these statements are instructions for CBR managers to support the full participation of women and girls. Given the complexity and importance of gender issues in the global South however, this level of analysis would seem somewhat superficial. We suggest that in the emerging identity of CBR, gender issues warrant much more detailed attention and nuanced analysis.

First, it is important to distinguish between sex (bio-physiological characteristics which differentiate men and women) and gender (socially constructed behaviours, expectations and roles that derive from, but may not depend on, sex) (Vlassoff and Manderson 1998). Given the socially and culturally defined nature of gender, notions of gender roles, preferred roles or even of gender equality cannot simply be transferred from one culture to another (Mohanty 1988). Unfortunately, perspectives of roles, gender and equality in global South cultures and communities are often widely discrepant from those of Western CBR professionals and NGOs (Sabuni 2004). This issue has proven somewhat problematic in CBR, which in advocating gender equality may be seen as reflecting Western views of gender. In so doing CBR may actually perpetuate Western hegemonic structures and exacerbate inequalities (Mohanty 1988) by imposing Western assumptions on families and communities of the global South.

Next, the CBR model includes numerous inherent assumptions which profoundly affect the role and place of women in settings where it is introduced. For example, most forms of the CBR model reflect an unwritten expectation of the role of women as carers (often of children with a disability). This may be seen to perpetuate the role of women in the unpaid private or domestic sphere and contribute to their marginalization and social exclusion. By relegating women to such prescribed roles they are excluded from the labour force and other important social areas (Giacaman 2001) and the role of men is reinforced in the paid public sphere (England et al. 2002). Such reinforcement of gender roles substantially diminishes the potential role women might play in economic and other forms of development (Boserup et al. 2013).

Similarly, the CBR model relies heavily on community meetings, community-level committees and dissemination of information (WHO et al. 2010). In many societies in the global South, women do not participate in such meetings or formal committee structures and decision-making (Sabuni 2004), and are more likely to be illiterate (Stromquist 1990). As such this may be seen as another way the CBR model perpetuates the marginalization of women, removing them from decision-making for an activity in which their work is actually vital.

Paradoxically, the influence of CBR on gender issues also has numerous positives. CBR engagement may create opportunities for women and girls, promoting their involvement in development activities from which they would otherwise be excluded. Indeed there is evidence that participation in CBR initiatives actually achieves substantial outcomes for women, playing a key role in their social, emotional and economic development (Lorenzo 2003).

We argue that the complexity of engaging with patriarchal social structures, the valuing and remuneration of tasks and particularly the valuing of disability and rehabilitation support activities require substantial consideration and exploration that have yet to occur in CBR. Likewise, for people with disabilities, gender issues are contentious and deserve more serious attention in the emerging models of CBR. For example, ensuring that people with disabilities attain livelihood support in gender-valued roles may not be a primary concern for CBR providers, but may be very important to all other stakeholders, particularly the person with a disability.

As a final example, in post-conflict CBR settings, the relative numbers of men and women with disabilities and the nature of their disabilities change in dramatic and complex ways. In many such societies, the esteem given to (predominantly male) war veterans, and their capacity for advocacy, may be very different from those with other disabilities. The field of CBR has yet to deal with these issues conclusively or to plan models of CBR accordingly. For CBR to evolve further on gender issues, more innovative and contextually responsive analysis is required.

The Identity of CBR Research and Education

Another challenge to the identity of CBR has been that no substantial academic and research leadership has evolved within the movement. A key characteristic of CBR is the surprising lack of dedicated research centres or academic departments focused on this area. Irrespective of the kind of research, methodology or orientation, the most commonly noted critique of CBR is that it lacks a substantial research foundation (Finkenflugel et al. 2005; Velema et al. 2008). Similarly, academic commitment to the education and training of CBR practitioners, and the development of CBR managers, has been very limited.

For a number of years the Centre for International Child Health (as it was then called) at University College London and the International Centre for the Advancement of CBR at Queens University, Kingston, Ontario, were among the only centres with a recognizable research and academic focus on CBR, but both have struggled to remain viable, to gain recognition and to achieve minimum required funding. Beyond those few centres, the dispersed academics and research-interested practitioners from elsewhere in the world have not been able to reach any substantial critical mass or momentum, nor foster a sustainable research culture to advance CBR.

The reasons for this limitation may stem from the evolution of CBR based on a manual of practical strategies to be used by family members and volunteers in the global South. This 'grab bag' of simple techniques, lacking a philosophy or coherent theory, has held little interest for conceptually oriented research institutions. Other universities and more applied research centres have similarly shown limited interest, presumably due to the absence of potential funding streams. Despite vast need and enormous potential, the world of CBR research does not have powerful patrons such as drug companies, and appears not to have fallen within the purview or key priorities of United Nations (UN) agencies.

Further, with no prospect of educating large numbers of fee-paying or Western students in degree programmes, the potential interest of training universities has been minimal. While the educational needs within CBR are equally enormous (Mannan et al. 2013), they exist in the global South, are often at a basic level and typically comprise hands-on learning, short courses or on-the-job skill development.

As noted, within development circles (and including university departments of international development), aid agencies and major funding bodies such as the World Bank have shown limited interest in CBR. It would appear that CBR is seen as having limited relevance to their organizational objectives and lacking alignment with structural adjustment priorities or their economic priorities. This in turn has limited the potential for funding of commissioned research and evaluations on which such departments depend. Likewise, the potential support for research from CBR-implementing agencies has been limited. Individual donors to such agencies are typically motivated to practically assist people with disability in the global South. In such cases, the support of academic aspirations, no matter how functional, may be seen as a luxury against the needs of individuals being emphasized by the agency.

In any field of life and endeavour, and particularly one which addresses such important issues as disability and poverty, meaningful research, critique, evidence, analysis and innovation are vital to healthy growth. For the majority of the history of CBR, this has not been the case. Serious critique and academic reflection pertaining to disability and development have mostly existed beyond the field of CBR (Priestley 2001; MacLachlan and Swartz 2009). While some academic centres and alliances have recently emerged (and encouragingly, some are emerging in the global South), they likewise continue to struggle, as reflected in the recent loss of the CBR specialty at Makerere University, Uganda. The identity of CBR depends to a considerable extent on the establishment of broad and diverse centres of research and education excellence, particularly in the global South.

The Identity of CBR in the Context of International Agencies

While the evolving and amorphous nature of CBR has been one factor constraining its advancement and improvement over the decades, another has been the neglect of disability and CBR concerns by the most important international agencies. Historically, UN agencies, the World Bank and similar bodies appear to have been indifferent to disability and CBR issues. For economically focused bodies and monetary funds, CBR as a collection of techniques for marginalized people, most of whom are not economically active, would appear to have been immaterial. For health-related agencies such as the WHO, CBR does not result in vaccines or surgical cures, and does not operate in the realm of life-saving technology or medications. Comprising relatively simple activities with people and families who are unlikely to see dramatic medical recovery, CBR has clearly not cornered the organizational priorities of these key players. For example, comparing the UN agency infrastructure for CBR with the UN service response to people with HIV/AIDS is striking. In Geneva, the Disability and Rehabilitation team tasked with this work comprises a handful of people who occupy a small section of a back corner of one floor of the WHO building. Their role is to facilitate a key dimension of the UN's response to the 190 million people who have significant disabilities globally. Within that handful of people, only a couple of individuals have some responsibility for promoting CBR as the primary global service delivery strategy. The contrast with the UN response to the HIV/AIDS crisis is stark. This condition, which affects far fewer people globally, warrants its own UN department (in addition to an array of offices in other UN agencies). It occupies a multistorey building with many hundreds of employees in Geneva alone. The UN service response is a multi-agency response with a multi-billion dollar budget. Obviously the disastrous HIV/AIDS global epidemic is devastating to millions of lives and communities, and warrants urgent and concerted attention. However, the irony of comparing the potential UN leadership of that service response with the capacity of the WHO Disability and Rehabilitation team to advocate and support CBR services indicates the challenge faced in forming the identity and underlining the relevance of CBR. The failure of CBR to engage with major systemic and structural agendas at the international level may in part be attributed to an approach which has evolved passively over the decades, without clear leadership and intention.

The 'NGO' Identity of CBR

Related to the weak identity of CBR at the international level is the slow uptake of CBR by governments in the global South. Despite nearly 40 years of activity, CBR projects are still largely implemented and sustained by international disability NGOs. The underlying NGO commitment to transitioning CBR projects to government departments of health, education, social welfare or labour has only been realized in a few cases. Instances of governments adopting and sustaining the CBR infrastructure developed by NGOs are very limited.

The causes of this enduring dependence on NGOs are numerous. They may stem from a reluctance for NGOs to fund local agencies or grassroots initiatives; they may also stem from the creation of a culture of dependence, or possibly from the imposition of a foreign model that is simply not sustainable without significant and ongoing NGO assistance. Alternatively it may stem from local governments not seeing people with disabilities as a priority. Regardless of the cause, a consequence of being predominantly implemented by NGOs, is that CBR has nearly always been implemented in the form of specific 'projects'. CBR initiatives are typically micro-level activities in discrete areas such as a rural area, a slum or a district. Further, such projects are almost always time-limited. The identity and reality of CBR in the form of micro-level, time-limited projects run contrary to the needs of people with disabilities in countries of the global South. For CBR to have an impact on the lives of people with disabilities and their families, there is a need for service initiatives to be ongoing and at a national scale, and with maximum coverage.

While CBR remains predominantly the domain of external agencies, it will be difficult for people with disabilities (and for implementing organizations) to tap into the political will, or to influence major government agendas in the global South. Even though such CBR projects may succeed at an individual level, restoring function and building participation, they will continue to only partially address many of the detrimental contextual factors that influence disadvantage (Thomas and Thomas 1999).

The Changing Identity of CBR: Evolving Towards DID

Now almost four decades since the beginning of the WHO initiative, the CBR paradigm is undergoing further change of identity in the form of a major shift of perspective and terminology. In many CBR circles, the terms 'inclusive development' or 'disability-inclusive development' are replacing CBR.

For some advocates, DID is a radically new paradigm, with a focus on making mainstream development inclusive of all people with disabilities. In this reconceptualization, the focus is not the provision of rehabilitation, or the individual person with a disability, or even their family. In such cases, DID is the application of principles of participatory community development, to maximize the inclusion of, self-determination of, participation of and social justice for people with disabilities. In other examples, the new models of DID appear more like the simple renaming of old CBR practices. Between the two poles, some CBR proponents emphasize that CBR is a strategy and that DID is the goal (Khasnabis 2011). In this more nuanced approach, inclusive development is the desired end result (making communities and society at large inclusive of all marginalized groups, including people with disability) (Thomas 2011), and CBR is a key means of attaining that end result. Such a framework may finally provide CBR with the clarity of identity and form it needs.

The shift in emphasis towards DID may be a very constructive step towards addressing some of the weaknesses of CBR, such as its 'micro' focus and failure to tackle contextual and systemic issues that affect people with disability in the global South. However, many CBR proponents and other stakeholders (Corneilje and Veldman 2011) would argue that this activity must complement the practical, physical and micro focus of people with disabilities and their families.

If CBR is to play a key part in a constructive or preferred model of disability services for people with disability in the global South, it should work more clearly with people with disabilities to address their expressed needs, build their capacity and support their families. Within the development sector, it should ensure equal opportunities and rights, and facilitate people with disability and their families to become self-advocates for inclusion in all development processes. At the social level, it should work with the community and society at large to remove barriers that exclude people with disability. Whether such a model can evolve out of the CBR context, is an issue on which the lives and aspirations of millions of people with disability in the global South depend.

Conclusion

The importance of CBR in the global South is clear. The World Report on Disability (WHO and World Bank 2011) acknowledges CBR 'as one of the significant responses to address concerns related to access to services, opportunities, participation and inclusion of persons with disabilities' globally. A key question is whether recent developments in the evolution of CBR and DID, which include the CBR Guidelines, the CBR Matrix and the adoption of disability-inclusive development as a new paradigm, will provide enough vision and direction to address the numerous limitations outlined in this chapter.

We suggest that the primary risk with these new directions and documents is that the current situation for people with disabilities in the global South will not change dramatically. First, all of the major responses and documents that have emerged in recent years have been clearly focused on 'upstream' agendas. They seek to address the limitations on CBR by looking at big picture conceptual issues, management concerns and human rights issues. Clearly these are important, but they also have limitations. For example, the breadth of the CBR Matrix may not assist in sufficiently defining and orienting CBR around the concerns of people with disabilities in the global South; the CBR Guidelines may not address the practical needs of people with disabilities; and the shift towards disability-inclusive development may result in services to people with disabilities in the global South becoming increasingly diluted across numerous international aid and development agendas. The extent to which the CBR and DID models of the future can also focus 'downstream' is a key issue. The extent to which these evolving directions can meet the practical needs of people with disabilities, foster their social participation and inclusion, address gender concerns, incorporate a human rights framework and ensure that people with disabilities are central and active partners in decisions that impact on their lives, remains to be seen.

References

Betcher, S., & Wangila, M. N. (2016). Religion after the medical miracle: Recovering 'disability' as religious analytic of social suffering. In S. Grech & K. Soldatic (Eds.), *Disability in the global South: The critical handbook* (pp. xx–xx). New York: Springer.

Boserup, E., Tan, S. F., & Toulmin, C. (2013). *Woman's role in economic development*. London: Routledge.

CBM. (2014). *Disability and development work*. Retrieved May 3, 2014, from http://www.cbm.org/Disability-and-development-work-250259.php.

CCBRT. (2014). *Comprehensive community based rehabilitation in Tanzania*. Retrieved May 3, 2014, from http://www.ccbrt.or.tz/home/.

Corneilje, H., & Veldman, E. (2011). *The dream of inclusion for all: Powerful CBR training materials*. Alphen ann den Rijn, NL: Enablement.

Crishna, B. (1999). What is community-based rehabilitation? A view from experience. *Child: Care, Health and Development, 25*(1), 27–35. doi:10.1046/j.1365-2214.1999.00087.x.

Deepak, S., dos Santos, L. R., Griffo, G., de Santana, D. B., Kumar, J., & Bapu, S. (2013). Organisations of persons with disabilities and community-based rehabilitation. *Disability, CBR & Inclusive Development, 24*(3), 5–20.

England, P., Budig, M., & Folbre, N. (2002). Wages of virtue: The relative pay of care work. *Social Problems, 49*(4), 455–473. doi:10.1525/sp.2002.49.4.455.

Evans, P. J., Zinkin, P., Harpham, T., & Chaudury, G. (2001). Evaluation of community-based rehabilitation for disabled persons in developing countries. *Social Science & Medicine, 53*(3), 333–348. doi:10.1016/S0277-9536(00)00321-X.

Finkenflugel, H., Wolffers, I., & Huijsman, R. (2005). The evidence base for community-based rehabilitation: A literature review. *International Journal of Rehabilitation Research, 28*(3), 187–201.

Gatjens, L. F. A. (2009). *A basic manual for inclusive development*. Nicaragua: Handicap International and Inter-American Institute on Disability and Inclusive Development. Retrieved August 11, 2014, from http://www.handicap-international.fr/fileadmin/documents/publications/BasicManualID.pdf.

Ghosh, N. (2011). *Challenging gender ideologies through CBR*. Retrieved August 11, 2014, from http://www.cbrglobal.org/Downloads/CS5.2.1.pdf.

Giacaman, R. (2001). A community of citizens: Disability rehabilitation in the Palestinian transition to statehood. *Disability & Rehabilitation, 23*(14), 639–644. doi:10.1080/09638280110036544.

Grech, S. (2012). Disability and the majority world: A neocolonial approach. In D. Goodley, B. Hughes, & L. Davis (Eds.), *Disability and social theory: New developments and directions* (pp. 52–69). Basingstoke: Palgrave Macmillan.

Handicap International. (2014). *Community based rehabilitation*. Retrieved May 3, 2014, from http://www.handicap-international.org.uk/what_we_do/rehabilitation/community_based_rehab

Hartley, S., Finkenflugel, H., Kuipers, P., & Thomas, M. (2009). Community-based rehabilitation: Opportunity and challenge. *Lancet, 374*(9704), 1803–1804. doi:10.1016/S0140-6736(09)62036-5.

Helander, E. (1999). *Prejudice and dignity: An introduction to community-based rehabilitation*. Geneva: World Health Organization.

Helander, E., Mendis, P., Nelson, G., & Goerdt, A. (1989). *Training in the community of people with disabilities*. Geneva: World Health Organization.

IDDC. (2010). *Contribution: OHCHR, Human Rights Council Resolution 13/11, 'Human rights of persons with disabilities'*. Brussels: International Disability and Development Consortium. Retrieved May 3, 2014, from www2.ohchr.org/english/issues/disability/docs/study/IDDC.doc.

ILO, UNESCO, & WHO. (2004). *CBR: A strategy for rehabilitation, equalization of opportunities, poverty reduction and social inclusion of people with disabilities*. Joint position paper. Geneva: ILO, UNESCO, & WHO.

Khasnabis, C. (2011). Community-based rehabilitation (CBR)—A common strategy in the developing world for rehabilitation, poverty reduction and promotion of human development. Presented at *Inclusive early childhood development—an underestimated component within poverty reduction*, Bonn, Germany, 3–4 February.

Kuipers, P. (1998). *Community based rehabilitation (CBR) as engagement: Context, parameters and potential*. PhD thesis. Brisbane: Griffith University.

Kuipers, P. (2014). Empowerment in community-based rehabilitation and disability-inclusive development. *Disability, CBR & Inclusive Development, 24*(4). Retrieved from http://dcidj.org/article/view/274.

Kuipers, P., Wirz, S., & Hartley, S. (2008). Systematic synthesis of community-based rehabilitation (CBR) project evaluation reports for evidence-based policy: A proof-of-concept study. *BMC International Health and Human Rights, 8*(3). doi:10.1186/1472-698X-8-3.

Lang, R. (1999). Empowerment and CBR? Issues raised by the South Indian experience. In E. Stone (Ed.), *Disability and development: Learning from action and research on disability in the majority world* (pp. 130–148). Leeds: The Disability Press.

Lang, R. (2000). The role of NGOs in the process of empowerment and social transformation of people with disabilities. In M. Thomas & M. J. Thomas (Eds.), *Selected readings in community based rehabilitation* (pp. 1–20). Bangalore: Occasional Publication of the Asia Pacific Disability Rehabilitation Journal.

Lang, R. (2011). Community-based rehabilitation and health professional practice: Developmental opportunities and challenges in the global North and South. *Disability & Rehabilitation, 33*(2), 165–173. doi:10.3109/09638288.2010.487923.

Lorenzo, T. (2003). No African renaissance without disabled women: A communal approach to human development in Cape Town South Africa. *Disability & Society, 18*(6), 759–778. doi:10.1080/0968759032000119505.

MacLachlan, M., & Swartz, L. (2009). *Disability and international development: Towards inclusive global health*. New York: Springer.

Mannan, H., MacLachlan, M., & McAuliffe, E. (2013). The human resources challenge to community based rehabilitation: The need for a scientific, systematic and coordinated global response. *Disability, CBR & Inclusive Development, 23*(4), 6–16. Retrieved from http://dcidj.org/article/view/157.

Miles, M. (1996). Community, individual or information development? Dilemmas of concept and culture in South Asian disability planning. *Disability & Society, 11*(4), 485–500. doi:10.1080/09687599627552.

Miles, S. (1996). Engaging with the disability rights movement: The experience of community-based rehabilitation in southern Africa. *Disability & Society, 11*(4), 501–518. doi:10.1080/09687599627561.

Miles, M. (2010). Religion and spirituality. In J. Stone & M. Blouin (Eds.), *International encyclopedia of rehabilitation*. Buffalo: CIRRIE. Retrieved August 11, 2014, from http://cirrie.buffalo.edu/encyclopedia/en/article/1/.

Mji, G., Gcaza, S., Swartz, L., MacLachlan, M., & Hutton, B. (2011). An African way of networking around disability. *Disability & Society, 26*(3), 365–368. doi:10.1080/09687599.2011.560419.

Mohanty, C. T. (1988). Under western eyes: Feminist scholarship and colonial discourses. *Feminist Review, 30*, 61–88. Retrieved from http://www.jstor.org/stable/1395054.

Priestley, M. (2001). *Disability and the life course: Global perspectives*. Cambridge: Cambridge University Press.

Rule, S. (2013). Training CBR personnel in south africa to contribute to the empowerment of persons with disabilities. *Disability, CBR and Inclusive Development, 24*(2), 6–21. Retrieved from http://dcidj.org/article/view/180.

Sabuni, L. P. (2004). *Gender differences in attitudes and practices within households in rural areas of the north east of the Democratic Republic of Congo*. Liverpool: University of Liverpool.

Stromquist, N. P. (1990). Women and illiteracy: The interplay of gender subordination and poverty. *Comparative Education Review, 34*(1), 95–111. Retrieved from http://www.jstor.org/stable/1188557.

Suharto, S., Dorsett, P., & Kuipers, P. (2013). Encouraging 'difability' thinking in community based rehabilitation: Addressing poverty and social exclusion. Presented at *Development futures: Alternative pathways to end poverty*, Sydney, 21–22 November. Retrieved August 11, 2014, from http://www.slideshare.net/DevFutures/suharto-suharto-community-exclusion-29437895#.

Thomas, M. (2011). Reflections on community-based rehabilitation. *Psychology and Developing Societies, 23*(2), 277–291. doi:10.1177/097133361102300206.

Thomas, M., & Thomas, M. J. (1999). A discussion on the shifts and changes in community based rehabilitation in the last decade. *Neurorehabilitation and Neural Repair, 13*(3), 185–189. doi:10.1177/154596839901300308.

Velema, J. P., Ebenso, B., & Fuzikawa, P. L. (2008). Evidence for the effectiveness of rehabilitation-in-the-community programmes. *Leprosy Review, 79*(1), 65–82.

Vlassoff, C., & Manderson, L. (1998). Incorporating gender in the anthropology of infectious diseases. *Tropical Medicine & International Health: TM & IH, 3*(12), 1011–1019.

Werner, D. (1993). Meeting the needs of disabled village children. *Tropical and Geographical Medicine, 45*(5), 229–232.

Werner, D. (1995). Strengthening the role of disabled people in community based rehabilitation programmes. In B. O'Toole & R. McConkey (Eds.), *Innovations in developing countries for people with disabilities*. Chorley: Lisieux Hall.

Werner, D. (1999). *Disabled village children*. Palo Alto, CA: Hesperian Foundation.

WHO. (2003). *International consultation to review community-based rehabilitation (CBR)*. Retrieved August 11, 2014, from http://whqlibdoc.who.int/hq/2003/who_dar_03.2.pdf.

WHO, UNESCO, ILO, IDDC. (2010). *CBR guidelines*. Geneva: World Health Organization.

WHO, & World Bank. (2011). *World report on disability*. Geneva: World Health Organization. Retrieved August 11, 2014, from http://www.who.int/disabilities/world_report/2011/report/en/.

Chapter 30
Disability-Inclusive Disaster Risk Reduction: Vulnerability and Resilience Discourses, Policies and Practices

Kim Spurway and Thao Griffiths

Introduction

There is very little written on the topic of disability and disaster, with the issue almost completely ignored until relatively recently in both the academic literature and the world of policy and practice (Alexander et al. 2012: loc. 11130). Very little has been written to date that could be considered critical or provide substantive alternative discourses to mainstream, traditional views regarding disasters and 'vulnerable groups', such as people with disabilities. In order to contribute to this incipient body of scholarship, this chapter takes a critical approach to disability and disasters by interrogating some of the key trends in the study and practice of disaster risk reduction and management through the lens of disability. We begin by setting out some of the conceptual parameters of current debates in disaster scholarship, and then analyse existing data on disability and disasters and the current growth in awareness and recognition by the international community of the importance of disability-inclusive disaster risk reduction and humanitarian action. The chapter compares and contrasts some key commonalities and intersections between disaster and disability theory, utilising conjoint concepts as a way to analyse emerging trends regarding vulnerability and resilience approaches in disasters and humanitarian emergencies. Vietnam is used as a case study to illustrate how these concepts are enacted in the real world with other countries introduced when appropriate.

The chapter interrogates these issues in terms of three previously distinct but now more closely integrated areas of policy and practice: human development, humani-

K. Spurway (✉)
School of Social Sciences, University of New South Wales,
Kensington, NSW 2052, Australia
e-mail: k.spurway@unsw.edu.au

T. Griffiths
Vietnam Veterans of America Foundation, Silver Spring, MD, USA

S. Grech, K. Soldatic (eds.), *Disability in the Global South*,
International Perspectives on Social Policy, Administration, and Practice,
DOI 10.1007/978-3-319-42488-0_30

tarian emergencies and disaster risk reduction. Disaster risk reduction and management, humanitarian aid and sustainable development have traditionally been framed as distinct, albeit connected, sectors with separate funding models and policy mechanisms. Yet, integration and linkages between the sectors have strengthened in line with a growing consensus that disasters are the result of unsustainable development strategies and that the best way to prevent future humanitarian crises or natural disasters is to promote sustainable, equitable and inclusive development policies and practices (Davey et al. 2013: 1; UNISDR 2011). Recent developments have also meant that climate change adaptation has increasingly been incorporated into disaster risk reduction (DRR) and management (DRM) policy and programming. In effect, DRR and DRM are currently seen as the cutting edge of adaptation to climate change, being composed of the suite of short- to medium-term strategies necessary for nations to adapt to anticipated increases in human-induced and extreme weather events worldwide (IPCC 2012; Zwi et al. 2013: 3). This gradual evolution of thinking about the causes of, and long-term solutions for, managing and reducing the risk of humanitarian crises and natural disasters has led to an international system with increasingly robust linkages at international, national and local levels in financing, funding, human resources and policies (ALNAP 2012 cited in Davey et al. 2013: 1).

The convergence of policy and practice in these formerly separate sectors makes for an extremely complex, interconnected system with different, albeit parallel, histories, shared goals and values. Within this global system, disability has slowly been emerging as a key issue that potentially highlights some of the main conceptual challenges facing the field in terms of reducing inherent societal vulnerabilities and enhancing individual, community and social resiliency. The DRR, DRM and humanitarian communities attempt to understand and model the complexities of disaster-related phenomena through the use of concepts such as vulnerability and resilience. These concepts are in many ways a genuine attempt by scholars and practitioners to describe the complex interaction of disabling social structures with the incipient, although often constrained, agency of people with disabilities. One of the problems with many of these debates, however, is that they approach the issues in a technical, neutral way (see for example Twigg 2007; Shah and Ranghieri 2012) that ignores the current context in which programmes and policies are operating: an environment in which a triumphant neo-liberal agenda has captured the field of policy and practice, shaping and controlling it in order to support the needs of global capitalism (Wisner 2001) and the associated elite capture of development processes.

As Biyanwila and Soldatic (2016) argue in this volume, the current push for economic rather than human and social development promotes a concept of resilience that has allowed some states to take a step back and renege on some of their key responsibilities in terms of mediating economic and social inequalities and the provision of public goods, such as education and health care. Within this context, the current push for a resilience approach can be criticised for sidelining the complex interplay of structural factors that results in increasing vulnerability for marginalised groups, such as people with disabilities in the global South. Discourses, policies and practices do this by sustaining and creating more potentially disabling situations that actually undermine the very outcome the international and national disaster risk reduction, humanitarian action and development communities are trying to promote: disaster-resilient individuals, communities and nations.

Disasters and Humanitarian Emergencies: Vulnerability and Resilience

In order to interrogate the trends and issues in disaster and disability, it is first necessary to introduce some of the key conceptual debates within the literature, which will later be applied to the complex intersection between social phenomena associated with disablement and disaster in the global South. The concept of what a disaster entails has been debated and contested in the literature for decades with a multitude of definitions now in play. Many of these definitions do have criteria in common: that disasters are unusual or extreme events that disrupt or destroy normal social processes and functioning as well as the built environment (Cutter 2005; Perry and Quarantelli 2005; UNISDR 2009). More traditional definitions tended to focus on the particular hazard or incident that triggered a disaster, with a clear distinction between natural and anthropogenic phenomena. Now there is a consensus in the field that there is 'nothing natural about disasters' regardless of the nature of the initiating event (Buckle et al. 2000; Alexander 2002). All disasters, both natural and anthropogenic, are thought to emerge out of failures in societal processes whether the trigger is an extreme weather event, such as a cyclone, or a complex humanitarian emergency, such as civil war (Duffield 1994: 3). The term 'disaster' used in this chapter thus includes phenomena that emerge out of both natural and anthropogenic processes and includes both slow-onset (droughts, famines) and fast-onset (floods, cyclones) disasters.

Despite this, disasters are commonly framed as extreme natural events that are outside our control and the people affected are victims of a maleficent nature. In effect, both disaster and disability are often constructed as natural events that are infrequent, extreme and outside of ordinary, everyday life whereas in reality both are commonplace, everyday social phenomena (Soldatic and Biyanwila 2006; Wisner et al. 2007: 20). In disability, more traditional and commonplace assumptions are that individual impairment leads to disablement as a natural outcome and that services for people with disabilities represent highly specialised responses for a small, minority group (Barnes 2013: 12–21; Fjord and Manderson 2009: 64).

Concepts and definitions have shifted in both areas of inquiry, however. Hilhorst (2007: 53) argues that the dominant approach in disaster studies is now that of a 'mutuality paradigm', which stresses the mutual interaction of natural and human systems. This new paradigm views disasters as the result of a complex interaction between the trigger event (natural, human or combined) and its root causes in extant social, political and economic systems and contexts (Priestley and Hemingway 2007: 64). In disaster studies there is a saying to the effect that 'there is nothing natural about disasters': like disability, disasters are believed to be caused by pre-existing structural issues within any given society or community that create 'disaster'-affected communities and increased vulnerability for certain groups, such as people with disabilities (Bankoff et al. 2007: 3–4; Pelling 2011: 6–8). It is the interplay of these kinds of factors that also determines how ‘disabled’ as well as how ‘vulnerable’ and ‘resilient’ individuals, communities and nations are.

Another trend in disaster studies is the shift in discourse, policy and practice related to defining and understanding the relative vulnerability and resilience of different social collectivities. The current tendency in disaster and humanitarian programming and policy is towards ‘building social resilience’ rather than focusing on ‘reducing social vulnerability’. This conceptual shift reflects in part an attempt to move beyond charity-based approaches that see communities (or vulnerable groups) as helpless victims in need of rescue to approaches that emphasise the agency (or resilience) of disaster-affected communities. However, this trend also reflects a shift in the field from focusing on understanding and addressing socially constructed differentiations that increase vulnerability to disasters (such as gender, class, disability) to approaches that emphasise and support developing the capacity of resilient agents ‘to resist, absorb, accommodate to and recover from the effects of a hazard’ (UNISDR 2009: 10). This shift to a resilience paradigm has not been politically neutral: a critique of the concept has been emerging within scholarship regarding the current co-option of the term by developmental elites to support the maintenance of the existing status quo, further weakening sustainable, equitable and socially just developmental processes worldwide, but most especially in the global South (Cannon and Müller-Mahn 2010; Béné et al. 2014). Ironically, the current emphasis on resilience, which could be seen as reflecting an able-bodied, western ideal (Soldatic and Biyanwila 2006), may in fact be more disabling within the international context, undermining adaptive capacities in the global South and increasing vulnerability as a result of social and economic crises emerging out of global capitalism and its local and national manifestations.

What Does the Data Tell Us?

In an ideal world, the complex interaction between disaster vulnerability and resilience would be revealed through analysis of a comprehensive set of robust qualitative and quantitative information that enables us to improve our understanding of how people with disabilities in the global South negotiate and adapt to disaster-related phenomena in their daily lives. Unfortunately, there is a relative paucity of data regarding the social and economic costs of disasters in the global South when compared with the global North, particularly information about disadvantaged groups such as people with disabilities (Spurway 2011: 174–175; Handmer and Dovers 2013: loc. 480–511). Though information about the impact and consequences of disasters on people with disabilities living in the global South is neither robust nor comprehensive, the existing data highlights very general trends in terms of disaster impact worldwide. Even after taking population numbers into account, the global South currently bears the brunt of the consequences of disasters in terms of social impact, while the global North suffers more economically in terms of total overall costs (Handmer and Dovers 2013: loc. 480–511). High-income countries make up 35 per cent of the disaster-related deaths worldwide, for example, while low- and middle-income countries together make up nearly two-thirds of all deaths (IFRC 2013: 231). High-income countries may suffer more in terms of the gross cost of disasters due to the simple fact that a higher total number of economic assets and resources are at risk in the North; however, in low- and middle-income countries a higher proportion of the gross national income is affected with longer term negative impacts on social and economic 'development' (Handmer and Dovers 2013: loc. 480–511).

Comparing Disaster Impact: Vietnam and Germany

It is difficult to make precise comparisons between countries due to the innumerable socio-economic, geographic, climatic and other factors influencing the occurrence and consequences of disasters. Using the data available, however, it is possible to roughly sketch out some of the differences between disaster impact in a country at the core of global capitalism compared with another country located on the periphery. Vietnam is a middle-income country and Germany is located in the top five very-high-income countries (World Bank 2014). Germany and Vietnam have similar sized populations (80.4 million and 88.7 million, respectively) and comparable population densities (World Bank 2014). In terms of numbers killed over the last 10 years, however, 2885 people died in 78 disasters in Vietnam compared with 191 in 32 disasters in Germany (EM-DAT 2014). The overall number of people injured in Vietnam was 4416 compared to 599 people in Germany (EM-DAT 2014). In terms of the economic impact of disasters from 2004 to 2012, Germany suffered economic damage totalling US$26.7 billion and Vietnam, a total of US$2.5 billion (EM-DAT 2014). When comparing the relative impact on each country's GDP, Vietnam lost on average 6 % of its GDP annually to disasters and Germany only 0.32 % (EM-DAT 2014; World Bank 2014).

As well as living in countries suffering higher burdens of impact and negative consequences from disasters, people with disabilities living in the global South are among the most 'vulnerable', disadvantaged and marginalised groups living in the poorest countries on the periphery of global capitalism. The literature on disasters and disabilities shows that the majority of people with disabilities live in low-income countries (80 per cent), and are often among the poorest groups in the world and encounter marginalisation, disadvantage, discrimination, stigmatisation and inaccessible built environments on a daily basis (Shakespeare 2012). In addition, people with disabilities negotiate barriers set up by cultural practices and social attitudes and are frequently viewed as burdens to their families and communities (IFRC 2007: 98–100). They encounter discrimination and disadvantage based on complex junctures of different types of social inequity based on their gender, ethnicity, religion, sect, class and race (Priestley and Hemingway 2007: 64; Mizra 2011: 1527). As a consequence, due to individual and structural factors, people with disabilities living in the global South are exposed to high levels of risk in terms of experiencing the negative consequences of disasters as well as high levels of overall social vulnerability (IFRC 2010: 90; Smith et al. 2012: 2).

In effect, these global figures reflect the ways in which social vulnerability is determined by the affected community or society's pre-existing social dynamics, power differentials and economic inequality: 'disasters expose and often magnify those inequities … predisaster inequities express themselves when disasters occur, and patterns of mortality, morbidity, loss, displacement, and recovery are inextricably linked to the social contexts in which disasters occur' (Tierney 2007: 515). Disasters lay bare existing social, governmental and organisational failings in preparing for, responding to, recovering from and mitigating against disasters (Wisner et al. 2007: 293–303). These 'failures' arise out of wide-reaching structural and contextual factors that determine the degree of risk, exposure and impact of humanitarian emergencies and natural disasters, rather than any weakness or failing by 'vulnerable groups' such as people with disabilities.

This relates directly to the ways in which resilience is constructed within the global neo-liberal project. In the current context, resilience can be used in a similar way to how the 'good governance' agenda has been used by northern elites, that is, to enforce adherence to market-led development and rebranded structural adjustment programmes in the global South (Cannon and Müller-Mahn 2010; Duit et al. 2010). Despite the superficial appeal of these terms, they can also be used as a way to condemn countries and people living in the global South for not conforming with northern norms based on market-driven development processes that undermine local knowledge, practices and resilience in favour of northern economic growth (Wisner et al. 2007: 53–54). In a similar way, the resilience concept can be used to contend that individuals and communities should rely, if not solely then at least primarily, on their own resources to survive, adapt to and recover from disasters without a strong recognition that many communities and people with disabilities have limited resources and do not have the means or ability to access inclusive, open political and social processes. It also ignores the fact that developing survival techniques or 'adaptive capacities' to negotiate and live in hostile, discriminatory and exclusionary environments is admirable but not necessarily an ideal state of affairs. As Béné and co-authors argue (2014: 40), the field runs the risk of glamorising resilience when in many cases people are forced to develop daily survival strategies in contexts in which they have few viable alternatives. In reality, many of us do not operate in some kind of idealised marketplace in which all options are on the table and are freely available and accessible to people with disabilities in the global South in terms of, for example, livelihoods, educational opportunities or political processes.

It is clear that people with disabilities living in the global South suffer from significant levels of vulnerability and it is also evident that they have extensive capacity in terms of knowing how to successfully navigate around and through social barriers, inaccessible physical environments and, at times, socially hostile contexts. Their ability to do this, however, is strongly influenced by the amount and type of resources as well as individual, cultural, natural, social and economic capitals available to them. The majority of people with disabilities are less likely to have access to large amounts of resources and to have strong social capital. In the current atmosphere of almost universally uncritical support for this new way of doing business, the critical interplay between vulnerability (structural factors and disabling contexts that constrain agency) and resilience (agency and enabling contexts) is not being analysed strongly enough. This is despite the fact that street-level policy actors and practitioners are aware of many of the inherent contradictions in this conceptual shift (Cannon and Müller-Mahn 2010; Duit et al. 2010). This lack of analysis is reflected in the ways in which international and national DRR and humanitarian policies, instruments and frameworks are not always translated into practice and often do not have enough of an impact on the daily lived experiences of people with disabilities.

Hat Mon Commune: A Model for Local Resilience?

Interrogating the term 'resilience' further poses challenges since existing data does not say much about individual, community or societal resilience in terms of either the global South generally or people with disabilities more specifically. This is partially due to the fact that it is easier to quantify deaths, economic losses and damaged infrastructure and much harder to measure the effectiveness of people's traditional knowledge, coping capacity and resilient behaviour in terms of lives saved or disasters avoided. The main way to do this currently is to interrogate key studies and publications for clues as to how resilience is expressed in real-world situations. In Hat Mon commune in Vietnam, for example, traditional forms of resilience and the adaptive capacity of community members and local authorities are demonstrated through their rich understanding of the intersection between human settlement patterns and the environment that date back 2000 years (Dao and Kaoru 2003: 124). Traditionally, people living in Hat Mon established rice fields in higher areas that were less likely to be inundated and were protected by small local dikes (Dao and Kaoru 2003: 124–125). This allowed them to avoid areas that were subject to flooding during the rainy season as well as develop strategies and solutions to adapt to and even exploit the positive consequences of flood hazards, such as exploiting the rich alluvial soil deposited during floods and accessing fish brought down by the water (Dao and Kaoru 2003: 125–126). Crucial to the overall resilience of the commune has been the government policies that critically support and enable structural and non-structural social initiatives which provide an enabling environment for the reduction of flood risk (Dao and Kaoru 2003: 128).

Current Policy and Practice

The international community has developed a suite of policy frameworks, agreements and guidelines that are comprehensive (SRSG for DRR 2013) if rather removed from the lived experiences of people with disabilities in the global South (Wisner 2006). In the humanitarian sector, Mizra (2011: 1528) traces the inclusion of disability in humanitarian policy and practice to the 1981 International Year of Disabled Persons and the creation of a Special Trust Fund for Handicapped Refugees by the United Nations High Commissioner for Refugees for use in medical treatment and rehabilitation. This was followed by several significant international events to promote the rights of people with disabilities, such as the 1991 UN Decade of Disabled Persons and UN Standard Rules on the Equalization of Opportunities for People with Disabilities (IFRC 2007: 89), as well as key operational guidelines developed for use by the humanitarian sector, such as the Code of Conduct for the International Red Cross and Red Crescent Movement and Non-Governmental Organizations (NGOs) in Disaster Relief, The Sphere Project and the Inter Agency Steering Committee's Protecting Persons Affected by Natural Disasters: IASC Operational Guidelines on Human Rights and Natural Disasters. Only the latter two frameworks have highlighted disability as an issue and recognised to some degree that international policymaking and practice have ignored the needs and rights of people with disabilities (IASC 2006; The Sphere Project 2011).

This neglect is also reflected in key international policy frameworks addressing natural disasters, such as the Hyogo Framework for Action (HFA) and its predecessors dating back to the 1980s and 1990s. These include the 1989 UN General Assembly Resolution 44/236, which declared the 1990s the International Decade for Natural Disaster Reduction (IDNDR) and established a special secretariat in Geneva for the IDNDR (UNISDR 2007), as well as important policy frameworks such as the Yokohama Strategy and Plan of Action for a Safer World: Guidelines for Natural Disaster Prevention, Preparedness and Mitigation (Alexander et al. 2012). The Hyogo Framework for Action is the most recent attempt to establish a comprehensive 10-year strategy (2005–2015) to guide nations worldwide in their attempts to reduce disaster risk (UNISDR 2005: 3). Though the needs of people with disabilities are directly highlighted only once in the entire HFA, there is an emerging consensus that disability should be prioritised; that people with disabilities have largely been ignored in DRR; and that the lack of disability in the HFA and other policy frameworks is both reprehensible and short sighted (SRSG for DRR 2013). The momentum behind the current push for disability-inclusive disaster risk reduction is in part due to the impetus that developed with the promulgation of the Convention on the Rights of Persons with Disabilities in 2006 (Soldatic 2013; WRC 2013). The CPRD includes articles that relate the rights of people with disabilities to disasters as well as international cooperation and development processes (UN 2006). These developments are significant in that, at least at the rather abstracted level of international policy, disability is at last starting to be recognised as a critical element in the degree of vulnerability of at-risk populations.

Despite these advances in global policymaking, the current impetus to recognise the needs, rights and expertise of people with disabilities is not yet comprehensively reflected in implementation and practices at street level. Evidence suggests that these kinds of global policy framework are often too far removed from the 'on-the-ground' realities and lived experiences of people with disabilities to make much of a difference (Munsaka and Charnley 2013: 756; Soldatic 2013). In real terms this means that the structural vulnerabilities and disabling contexts that make for disasters have been consistently sidelined or ignored at both national and international levels of policymaking and practice. Addressing disaster vulnerabilities in any real way means that governments have to take a lead role in meeting their obligations under international law to systematically address politically and socially contentious structural issues, such as inequality, discrimination, social attitudes and cultural norms. This kind of transformation, however, cannot be made using current resilience models that simply advocate for more economic growth, increased efficiency and neo-liberal restructuring as the universal solution to deeply ingrained societal vulnerabilities.

The gap between policy and practice reflects the relative vulnerability of individuals, communities and nations in the global South (as well as in the global North). First, the strength of cultural beliefs and attitudes at national and local levels stigmatises people with disabilities, promotes their exclusion and discriminates against them in terms of access to services, the built environment and broader developmental processes (Munsaka and Charnley 2013: 756). Second, the exclusion of people with disabilities from disaster policy processes is a result of the way in which disability has been framed within DRR and DRM as a specialised problem requiring the intervention of specialist knowledge and skills, usually of the medical or physical rehabilitation kind (IFRC 2007: 94). Third, during a disaster agencies are under intense political, temporal and resource pressure to provide protection, shelter, clean water, food, sanitation and medical care to the affected population as a whole, which may mean that the needs of minority groups are sacrificed. As a result, adapting humanitarian interventions and disaster risk reduction strategies to meet the needs of people with disabilities is frequently seen as prohibitively expensive, time consuming and a distraction from providing for essential needs (IFRC 2007: 94).

The Situation of People with Disabilities in Vietnam

The ability of individuals, groups, communities and nations to cope with both natural and anthropogenic disasters relates to their differentiated levels of poverty and access to social, economic and natural resources, in addition to the effectiveness and openness of governing institutional and social processes (Zou and Thomalla 2008: 18). On the positive side, Vietnam has a growing, albeit nascent, disability movement supported by the national government, large international donors such as AusAID and USAID and civil society actors such as Vietnam Veterans of America Foundation, Bright Future Group, Red Cross of Vietnam and Viet Nam Assistance for the Handicapped (Metts 2005: 1–3). Vietnam also has relatively robust policies, such as the National Communication Action Plan for Children with Disabilities, the National Law for Persons with Disabilities and the National Action Plan on Persons with Disabilities, which have garnered some success in certain provinces and districts (UNICEF 2011: 13).

These successes do not always translate into policies and practices on the ground, however. People with disabilities equate to about 8 per cent of the Vietnamese population, with three-quarters of people with disabilities living in rural areas (Mont and Cuong 2011: 327–335). Nearly one-third (32 per cent) of households with people with disabilities are classified as poor (two times higher than in the general population) with more than 80 per cent of households with disabled members encountering difficulties in securing employment as well as obtaining and sustaining medical care and support (Mont and Cuong 2011: 327–335). In addition, despite the success of government and civil society-sponsored awareness campaigns and events, people with disabilities in Vietnam still encounter negative attitudes and discrimination on a daily basis:

> A very significant factor hampering the advance of people with disabilities in Vietnam is attitudinal, with the general public demonstrating negative and dismissive attitudes toward disability … In large parts of the countryside, family members with disabilities are hidden in the home out of shame and are denied the same opportunities for participation and self-determination available to non-disabled family members. (USAID 2005: 17–18)

Finally, the neo-liberal push for efficiency and market-led approaches to development is not conducive to funding and implementing the kind of potentially resource-intensive and expensive programmes reliant on state intervention. This reflects broader concerns within disaster risk reduction and humanitarian action about supposedly more 'efficient', market-driven governance and public policymaking. A good example is the need to maintain teams of trained emergency service personnel and first responders, such as fire brigades and search and rescue, even when not actively operational so that these services are available and ready to respond effectively and quickly when a disaster does occur. In a complete misunderstanding of the sector's needs and operational processes, disaster and emergency management is slowly being transformed in order to make more out of 'inefficient' and underutilised resources, necessitating 'redundancies' to allow for more effective disaster risk reduction and management. This kind of market-driven 'efficiency' cannot be allowed to undermine and replace essential services usually deemed to be public goods, traditionally provided by the state, which at its best enables and supports individual and community agency and resilience.

Conclusion

Disability provides a critical lens that enhances our insights into, and critiques of, vulnerability and resilience approaches in disaster risk reduction and management. Vulnerability in the context of disasters equates to the degree and type of disabling structural and institutional barriers that translate into increased risk, impact and consequences for people with disabilities. Many of the policies and concepts in humanitarian action, DRR and DRM address the issues at a very abstract level that does not translate into action on the ground. For the most part, these frameworks and practice guidelines ignore the challenges posed by neo-liberal economic globalisation, which impact considerably on the sustainable development, DRR and DRM agendas. In the 1980s, the rise of neo-liberalism and deregulation, marketisation, privatisation and sale of public assets as well as outsourcing of services to the private sector and civil society was enforced in the global South through structural adjustment programmes set up by international financial institutions and supported by large donors like USAID and DFID in the UK (Munsaka and Charnley 2013: 758). The resulting transfer of risk from corporations to the general public through such one-sided policies (Wisner 2006: 91) led to increasing poverty and the destruction of livelihoods for the poorest and most disadvantaged, and a widening gap between the rich and poor in countries like Zimbabwe (Munsaka and Charnley 2013: 758).

There is a real need to develop better understandings of how concepts such as resilience and vulnerability interact in the global context. The vulnerability concept emphasises existing structural challenges to sustainable development and DRR strategies, whereas resilience emphasises the importance of agency and activism albeit without sufficient recognition of how this can be constrained by structural issues such as inequality, discrimination and exclusion. In order to transform current policy and practice, however, it is essential to understand, address and include both sets of factors in DRR strategies and policies. Discourses around resilience sometimes seem to assume that everyone can fit into the idealised image of an able-bodied person of considerable means who can access the political process and can adapt to adversity through the use of their own resources. What is certain is that this image does not fit that of people with disabilities in the global South who are among the poorest and most disadvantaged groups on the planet. It is also apparent that the problem is not that people with disabilities are not 'resilient', but that current approaches tend to use the term in a way that ignores the realities of marginalised populations who lack the opportunities, resources and support needed to fully actualise their capabilities and inherent capacities. Indeed, many of the existing development and resilience agendas do not advance the rights and needs of the most disadvantaged sections of the community, many of whom survive on informal livelihoods on the margins of communities and nations (Béné et al. 2014: 40). In response to this and out of harsh necessity people with disabilities have developed survival strategies to address systemic exclusionary practices. It is important to recognise that resilience can mean that people with disabilities could remain resilient victims and that 'there are limits to romanticising their "resilience", which could also be seen as a form of coping strategy, in the face of no other alternative' (Béné et al. 2014: 40). If the resilience paradigm means we simply adapt to and maintain the status quo and pre-existing social conditions that cause disaster, then resilience can be seen to be demonstrated by an acceptance of the status quo, restricting our activism and agency in order not to upset the extant social equilibrium.

References

Alexander, D. (2002). *Principles of emergency planning and management*. Hertfordshire, UK: Terra.

Alexander, D., Gaillard, J. C., & Wisner, B. (2012). Disability and disaster. In B. Wisner, J. C. Gaillard, & I. Kelman (Eds.), *The Routledge handbook of hazards and disaster risk reduction*. London: Routledge. Kindle Edition.

Bankoff, G., Frerks, G., & Hilhorst, D. (Eds.). (2007). *Mapping vulnerability: Disasters, development and people*. London: Earthscan.

Barnes, C. (2013). Understanding the social model of disability: Past, present and future. In N. Watson, A. Roulstone, & C. Thomas (Eds.), *Routledge handbook of disability studies*. Abingdon, UK: Routledge.

Béné, C., Cannon, T., Gupte, J., Mehta, L. & Tanner, T. (2014). *Exploring the potential and limits of the resilience agenda in rapidly urbanising contexts*. Evidence Report No. 63. Brighton, UK: Institute for Development Studies.

Biyanwila, S. J., & Soldatic, K. (2016). Global financialization and disability: Can disability budgeting be an effective response in the south? In S. Grech & K. Soldatic (Eds.), *Disability in the global South: The critical handbook* (pp. xx–xx). New York: Springer.

Buckle, P., Mars, G., & Smale, S. (2000). New approaches to assessing vulnerability and resilience. *Australian Journal of Emergency Management, 15*(2), 8–14.

Cannon, T., & Müller-Mahn, D. (2010). Vulnerability, resilience and development discourses in context of climate change. *Natural Hazards, 55*, 621–635.

Cutter, S. (2005). Are we asking the right question? In R. Perry & E. Quarantelli (Eds.), *What is a disaster? New answers to old questions*. Newark, DE: International Sociological Association, International Research Committee on Disasters.

Dao, P. & Kaoru, T. (2003). Flood control—Environmental and socio-economic issues: Case study of a diversion area in Vietnam. In G. Blöschl, S. Franks & M. Kumaga (Eds.), *Water resources systems—Hydrological risk, management and development* (pp. 123–129). Publication No. 281. Oxfordshire, UK: International Association of Hydrological Sciences (IAHS).

Davey, E. Borton, J. & Foley, M. (2013). *A history of the humanitarian system: Western origins and foundations*. HPG Working Paper: June 2013. London: Overseas Development Institute.

Duffield, M. (1994). Complex emergencies and the crisis of developmentalism. *IDS Bulletin, 25*(4). Retrieved February 21, 2008, from http://www.ids.ac.uk/go/publications/ids-classics.

Duit, A., Galaz, V., & Eckerberg, K. (2010). Governance, complexity & resilience. *Global Environmental Change, 20*, 363–368.

EM-DAT: The OFDA/CRED International Database. (2014). *Disasters Germany & Vietnam 2005–2014*. Brussels: Université Catholique de Louvain. Retrieved April 25, 2014, from www.em-dat.net.

Fjord, L., & Manderson, L. (2009). Anthropological perspectives on disasters and disability: An introduction. *Human Organization, 68*(1), 64–72.

Handmer, J., & Dovers, S. (2013). *Handbook of disaster policies and institutions: Improving emergency management and climate change adaptation*. Abingdon, UK: Routledge. Kindle Edition.

Hilhorst, D. (2007). Complexity and diversity: Unlocking social domains of disaster response. In G. Bankoff, G. Frerks, & D. Hilhorst (Eds.), *Mapping vulnerability: Disasters, development and people*. London: Earthscan.

IFRC. (2010). *World disasters report 2010: Focus on urban risk*. Geneva: IFRC.

IFRC. (2013). *World disasters report 2013: Focus on technology and the future of humanitarian action*. Geneva: IFRC.

Inter-Agency Steering Committee. (2006). *Protecting persons affected by natural disasters: IASC operational guidelines on human rights and natural disasters*. Washington, DC: Brookings-Bern Project on Internal Displacement.

Intergovernmental Panel on Climate Change (IPCC). (2012). *Managing the risks of extreme events and disasters to advance climate change adaptation: A special report of working groups i and ii of the Intergovernmental Panel on Climate Change*. Cambridge, UK: Cambridge University Press.

International Federation of Red Cross & Red Crescent Societies (IFRC). (2007). *World disasters report 2007: Focus on discrimination*. Geneva: IFRC.

Metts, R. (2005). *Final report and recommendations: Consultancy on the inclusion of disabled persons and disability issues in the HEPR program and on the creation of a national action plan on disability*. Hanoi: Vietnam Assistance for the Handicapped. Retrieved April 25, 2014, from http://vnah-hev.org/Robert-Metts-Report-PDF.html.

Mizra, M. (2011). Disability and humanitarianism in refugee camps: The case for a travelling supranational disability praxis. *Third World Quarterly, 32*(8), 1527–1536.

Mont, D., & Cuong, N. (2011). Disability and poverty in Vietnam. *World Bank Economic Review, 25*(2), 323–359.

Munsaka, E., & Charnley, H. (2013). 'We do not have chiefs who are disabled': Disability, development and culture in a continuing complex emergency. *Disability & Society, 28*(6), 756–769.

Pelling, M. (2011). *Adaptation to climate change: From resilience to transformation*. Abingdon, UK: Taylor & Francis. Kindle Edition.

Perry, R., & Quarantelli, E. (Eds.). (2005). *What is a disaster? New answers to old questions*. Newark, DE: International Sociological Association, International Research Committee on Disasters.

Priestley, M., & Hemingway, L. (2007). Disability and disaster recovery. *Journal of Social Work in Disability & Rehabilitation, 5*(3–4), 23–42.

Shah, F., & Ranghieri, F. (2012). *A workbook on planning for urban resilience in the face of disasters: Adapting experiences from Vietnam's cities to other cities*. Washington, DC: The World Bank.

Shakespeare, T. (2012). Disability in developing countries. In N. Watson, A. Roulstone, & C. Thomas (Eds.), *Routledge handbook of disability studies*. New York: Routledge.

Smith, F., Jolley, E., & Schmidt, E. (2012). *Disability and disasters: The importance of an inclusive approach to vulnerability and social capital*. Haywards Heath, UK: Sightsavers.

Soldatic, K. (2013). The transnational sphere of justice: Disability praxis and the politics of impairment. *Disability & Society, 28*(6), 744–755.

Soldatic, K. & Biyanwila, J. (2006). *Disability and development: A critical southern standpoint on able-bodied masculinity*. Presented at TASA Conference, University of Western Australia and Murdoch University, 4–7 December.

Spurway, K. (2011). *Decision-making in disaster management: Mapping the thematic complexities and understanding the contested rationalities of social practice*. Doctoral thesis, University of New South Wales.

The Sphere Project. (2011). *Humanitarian charter and minimum standards in humanitarian response*. Rugby, UK: Practical Action Publishing.

Tierney, K. (2007). From the margins to the mainstream: Disaster research at the crossroads. *Annual Review of Sociology, 33*, 503–525.

Twigg, J. (2007). *Characteristics of a disaster-resilient community: A guidance note*. London: Department for International Development (DFID), Disaster Risk Reduction Interagency Coordination Group.

UN Special Representative of the Secretary-General for Disaster Risk Reduction (SRSG for DRR). (2013). *Proposed elements for consideration in the* post-2015 *framework for disaster risk reduction*. Geneva: UNISDR.

UNICEF. (2011). *Rights, education and protection (REAP) AusAID-UNICEF partnership on disability: First progress report, Reporting period: April 2011—December 2011*. New York: UNICEF.

UNISDR. (2007). *A summary report of the first session of the global platform for disaster risk reduction (global platform)*. Global Platform for Disaster Risk Reduction Bulletin. Geneva: UNISDR.

UNISDR. (2009). *Terminology on disaster risk reduction*. Geneva: UNISDR.

UNISDR. (2011). *Hyogo framework for action 2005–2015: Building the resilience of nations and communities to disasters. Mid-term review: 2010–2011*. Geneva: UNISDR.

United Nations (UN). (2006). *Convention on the rights of persons with disabilities*. New York: United Nations. Retrieved January 11, 2014, from http://www.un.org/disabilities/convention/conventionfull.shtml.

United Nations International Strategy for Disaster Reduction. (UNISDR). (2005). *Hyogo framework for action 2005–2015: Building the resilience of nations and communities to disasters*. Geneva: UNISDR.

United States Agency for International Development (USAID). (2005). *Vietnam disability situation assessment and program review*. Washington, DC: USAID.

Wisner, B. (2001). Capitalism and the shifting special and social distribution of hazard and vulnerability. *Australian Journal of Emergency Management, 16*(2), 44–50. Retrieved November 7, 2014, from http://www.em.gov.au/Documents/AJEM_Vol16_Issue2.pdf.

Wisner, B. (2006). The world conference on disaster viewed through the lens of political ecology: A dozen big questions for Kobe and beyond. *Capitalism Nature Socialism, 16*(2), 89–95.

Wisner, B., Blaikie, P., Cannon, T., & Davis, I. (2007). *At risk: Natural hazards, people's vulnerabilities and disasters*. London: Routledge.

Women's Refugee Commission (WRC). (2013). *Disability inclusion in the Syrian refugee response in Lebanon*. New York: WRC.

World Bank. (2014). *World DataBank*. Washington, DC: World Bank. Retrieved January 23, 2014, from http://databank.worldbank.org/.

Zou, L., & Thomalla, F. (2008). *The causes of social vulnerability to coastal hazards in Southeast Asia*. Stockholm: Stockholm Environment Institute.

Zwi, A., Spurway, K., Marincowitz, R., Ranmuthugala, G., Thompson, L., & Hobday, K. (2013). *Do community based disaster risk management (CBDRM) initiatives reduce the social and economic cost of disasters? Research Protocol*. London: University of London, Social Science Research Unit, EPPI-Centre.

Chapter 31
Critical Silences: Disability, Networked Technologies and the Global South

Anupama Roy and Sarah Lewthwaite

Introduction

Digital networked technologies have become an increasingly integral part of human activity, shaping and being shaped by individual and collective lives. Across the world, networked economies increasingly position new technologies as key to effective governance, education, growth and the preparation of a future work force. Many countries in the global South are adopting policies and domestic strategies that seek to embed and integrate networked technologies as an essential part of everyday life (Toyama 2013). In this frame, technologies are held to 'powerfully contribute to the worldwide democratisation, civic engagement and action-orientated social responsibility' (Benson and Harkavy 2002). Policy developments such as the Convention on the Rights of Persons with Disabilities stress the role of technology in enabling people with disabilities, putting the accessibility of digital tools and services at the centre of government policies. Yet, a move beyond the habitual exoticisation of technology and its assumed benefits is important. The claims made for technology as a route to social justice have not been substantiated (Selwyn 2013).

In this chapter we examine not only the narratives that dominate mainstream understandings of technology and 'digital divides' but also the more nuanced debates in areas deemed most relevant to disabled people. We structure our account to recognise the lifecycle of mobile and networked devices, from (re) sourcing through to manufacture, usage, maintenance, disposal and governance. We do not intend to deny technology's positive impacts; we seek to highlight

A. Roy (✉)
Brighton and Sussex Medical School, University of Sussex, Brighton, UK
e-mail: onupama@gmail.com

S. Lewthwaite
University of Southampton, Southampton, UK
e-mail: s.e.lewthwaite@southampton.ac.uk

S. Grech, K. Soldatic (eds.), *Disability in the Global South*,
International Perspectives on Social Policy, Administration, and Practice,
DOI 10.1007/978-3-319-42488-0_31

silences in technology and disability discourse—disabled experiences that are missing—occluded by the arrangement of social, geopolitical, economic and cultural forces that shape our technologies and day-to-day life across the world. In the next section we situate digital technologies in a geopolitical frame, leading to a critique of these critical silences.

Situating Digital Technologies

All digital technologies are situated, originating from someone, somewhere. As Stone (1991: 111) observes, 'No matter how virtual the subject may become, there is always a body attached'. Grounding discussion in individual bodies re-establishes a connection to location and the geopolitics of the body. In disability studies, Stone (1999: 4) makes an early reference to majority experience: 'The majority world is the world that the vast majority of people live in, yet they have access to a fraction of the world's wealth and power'. As there are clear correlations between poverty and disability (see Buell et al. 2016, in this volume), any discussion of technology and disability must incorporate the geopolitics of the global South. Situating a critical perspective in this way immediately challenges the transformative claims made for technology. As Selwyn (2013: 16) observes, 'any sense of "global" transformation could be said to describe more accurately the converging nature of Western European, East Asian and North American interests, as opposed to the interests of all nations'. In this respect, networked technologies exist within, and perpetuate a power relation between, a productive, dominant North and consuming, subjected South. This power relation is obscured by claims made for technology as a context within and of itself, and tendencies for oppositional thinking; we acknowledge that the global North and South divide is neither simple nor uniform.

A Geopolitical Frame

New information and communication technologies (ICTs) have enabled a variety of nations to enter international arenas once exclusive to the economies of the global North (Sassen 2002). However, relations between the North and South predate the digital revolution, and globalisation is not simply a case of new nations grasping the opportunity to participate in wealthy economies. Digital networks are embedded within a legacy of societal structures. The features and standards of hardware and software convey underlying assumptions based on existing societal structures, and consequently re-represent those power dynamics (Latour 1991; Sassen 2002).

Dominant constructions of technology stem from the long association of technology 'with the "de-territorialisation" and "de-referentialisation" of knowledge' (Selwyn 2013). These terms identify the predominant notion of geographically detached digital networks that suggest knowledge has no boundaries and is free to travel around the world (Readings 1996; Selwyn 2013). The notion of exchanging ideas without restriction perpetuates western ideals of freedom of speech and association which contrast with non-western countries such as China or North Korea. The notion may also be at odds with communities that have different practices of storytelling. Take, for example, an Australian Aboriginal or Amazonian tribe, where the community systems permit only a certain member holding a certain status to pass the knowledge to another member of the mob or the tribe. The digitisation of such storytelling and publishing on the Web destroys the core essence of these aboriginal storytelling crafts, which can be essentially disabling for a community. Another example is that of a *hijra*, or third gender, community in India where the leader is the gatekeeper to the community/tribe. An ICT project can disable these gatekeepers or community by circumventing existing social hierarchies. Such actions highlight the geopolitical relationship between technology and disability.

Technologies are not neutral: they export particular social, physical and psychological standards and expectations from the North to the South. These standards invoke norms that divide populations into disabled and non-disabled groups according to northern conceptions of ability and necessity (see also Meekosha 2011; Meekosha and Soldatic 2011; Grech 2012; Soldatic and Meekosha 2014). In this chapter, we focus on this colonisation and the complicated relationship between technology, disability and the global South. This is not simply a story of 'forcibly imposed discontinuities' (Okoye 2014: 65) or the battle between two totalising narratives: a benevolent or oppressive North. In their way, both such histories erase the complexity and agency of indigenous cultures, their relationships with technology and alternative models of disability. For example, as Schmidt observes (1996), western views of indigenous technological cultures, in Africa, frequently claim, obscure and erase evidence of technological success. Alternatives are possible; but to begin, we establish the critical silences surrounding technology's impact on disability in a global frame.

Technology's Impact on Disability

This section looks at how new technologies construct or impact on dis/ability by examining how disability is created through resourcing and manufacturing of technology and its disposal. We also consider the maintenance of the technology and the construction of disability with the imposition of technology in the global South through global trade.

Resourcing and Manufacturing Dis/Ability

The digital divides that exist between disabled and non-disabled people are well evidenced in the global North (see Seale 2014) and there is a growing literature identifying networked technology's apparent ability to ameliorate disability by removing the physical and social barriers which otherwise exclude people with intellectual, physical or sensory impairments (as critiqued by Goggin and Newell 2005). However, the networked technologies and devices that constitute our new relationships with ourselves and others have already undertaken a journey from sourcing and manufacture to export and eventually disposal that has been neglected within disability studies. This journey is political, motivated by economic growth that surged in the 1980s with developments in the IT sector (Heeks 2008); it is also biopolitical, exporting the physical and mental risks involved in supply from the North to the South.

The manufacture of mobile and digital technologies involves processes with hazardous chemical, biological and physical agents and dangerous stamping, cutting and conveyance machines. With lax health and safety processes, inadequate personal protection equipment (safety shoes, gloves, masks, goggles and ear-plugs), disabling ergonomic conditions and poor ventilation coupled with air emissions, unnecessary and high levels of occupational injury and chronic long-term medical conditions and impairments proliferate among the workforce (Fair Labor Association 2012). The majority of this manufacturing currently takes place in China and Southeast Asia where labour is cheap and efficient.

The Taiwanese multinational Foxconn is responsible for assembling an estimated 40 per cent of all consumer electronics products sold (Duhigg and Barboza 2012). Foxconn's majority stake is located in China where it employs thousands of workers in 'factory cities' (Duhigg and Barboza 2012). Foxconn's activities have become talismanic of outsourced, global industrial practices. Levels of accidental injury at Foxconn plants have been criticised by Fair Labor Association reports (2012) and Students and Scholars Against Corporate Misbehaviour, which list Foxconn and other suppliers (such as Biel Crystal, which manufactures iPhone touch screens) among those that do not meet their obligations for compensation and assistance to injured workers, a process violating Chinese labour laws (SACOM 2013). Controversy has dogged the company as employee suicides, explosions at plants and riots in its factories make international headlines (Chan and Pun 2010; CNET 2012; Duhigg and Barboza 2012). Global organisations increasingly report on such issues, alongside underage labour, harassment and abuse of workers, involuntary/bonded labour and human trafficking. However, the outcomes for workers who are disabled by manufacturing processes or debilitated by exploitation, abuse and consequent mental health effects are unclear. There has been no coordinated attempt to engage with these issues from a disability rights perspective. The history of impairment in relation to electronics industry practices is yet to be written.

The raw materials to manufacture these devices include a number of rare and difficult to obtain materials which are often sourced from African countries. Among these coltan has become the most infamous. Coltan is an essential mineral used in the manufacture of mobile phones and other devices, including technologies used in the medical and arms industries. The Democratic Republic of Congo (DRC) is one of the world's most significant suppliers and trade in this precious mineral brings in a major source of funding for armed conflict and violence that has been perpetrated against the general population for over a decade (Poulsen 2010; Ayers 2012). It is a 'conflict mineral', also known as 'blood coltan'. Struggles to control the trade also draw in 'military forces from neighboring Rwanda, Uganda and Burundi who smuggle coltan from the DRC, and use the revenues to support their efforts in the war' (Oppong et al. 2007). The bloodshed, torture, slavery, child slavery, rape and dismemberment spurred by coltan production (Ayers 2012) has not led to boycotts or affected consumption in any meaningful way. Observers identify conflict resources within a nexus of human rights and international humanitarian law violations, and crimes under international law (Montague 2002; Renner 2002; Mantz 2008; Melcher et al. 2008).

Ayers (2012) identifies changes that are necessary to disrupt the current exploitative status quo, including shifting the burden to companies to demonstrate that they are not using minerals obtained through correlated violence. Political and activist scrutiny is slowly leading to changes and increased legislation to curb trade in conflict minerals. Major companies such as Apple and Intel are reporting conflict-free supply chains from 2014. Apple (2014a, b) released lists of the smelters and refiners whose minerals they use to establish which ones are verified as conflict-free.

Nonetheless, the ongoing creation and production of impairment in resourcing and manufacturing is yet to be recognised as a 'disability' issue. Global demand for enabling mobile technologies is underwritten by the invisible disablement of people in the global South, for example, in the DRC and neighbouring territories. This represents a global exchange in dis/ability, with the North importing new abilities in the form of technological affordances and the South receiving impairment as an output of war spurred by demand for global technologies.

Maintenance, Updates and Obsolescence

Without regular maintenance and 'updates', digital technology degrades in performance and breaks down. In addition to the cumulative effect of software defects, a computer running without the latest virus checker or updates can easily be compromised by viruses or malware, leaving it at best unusable and at worst a liability to fraud if personal and financial data is stolen (Loney and Lemos 2004). While the software assumes constant maintenance, the assumption built into the hardware is that a lifetime is short and replacement the preference rather than repair.

In resource-rich environments, bandwidth, disk space, availability of time and expert knowledge are readily available, making updates a minor chore or even a treat if the upgrade to the latest phone model is free. Experiences in the global South, where these conditions do not exist, are of a more turbulent relationship. Often we forget that developing regions often need someone to understand what a software update is and to have the connectivity and technological capacity to manage increasing and sizable updates; sometimes there is not even basic electric supply. As much as a capability is gained, a dependency is imposed on this ongoing maintenance. That might incorporate having to travel for miles to a town to access services with the associated loss of a day's income, or paying the cost of large data downloads simply to be able to start the computer. For disabled users working with assistive technologies or through a proxy family member or assistant, there are additional levels of cost, maintenance and complexity to negotiate. There has been no nuanced discussion about the implied disabling factors brought about with these dependencies. Even projects that talk about data collection (Tomlinson et al. 2009) through use of technology do not consider how these technologies are updated. Research into accessible, sustainable technologies that promote open-source approaches which do not need updates remains scarce.

Despite maintenance, devices and software are subject to 'planned obsolescence' as devices are made with an artificially limited useful life. The way in which technology is used can also become obsolete. This can be as newer technologies take over from older ones, for example, smartphones or 3G-capable models taking over from basic mobile phones. In addition, parts, servicing or repair of basic devices are slowly becoming unavailable and even new devices are creating newer waves of communication, leaving behind those who are not up to date. Perhaps in the near future a new definition of disability will arise to describe individuals that do not own the latest technology and thus do not keep pace with modern life.

The Grameen Telecom's famous Village Phone programme in Bangladesh (Lawson and Meyenn 2000; Richardson et al. 2000) is a good example of mobile phones promoting small businesses were village women could take a loan to buy the phone and subscription and then charge for use of the service within the village. But as the benefits of mobile communications were realised, competing mobile phone coverage was expanded to cover demand in these areas, and the cost of handsets and subscriptions dropped, enabling individuals rather than cooperatives to own their own connection (Boettiger et al. 2010). This then left the entrepreneurs with debt, unable to make a profit from the phone as individuals could make their own arrangements. What happened to these women? Were they encouraged to invest in the next-generation mobile system (wi-fi, 3G) to keep ahead of the game? Were they abandoned as the attention moved on to cater to the emerging mass market? Evidence is scant about how they were affected and there is little critical discussion about how legacy users or users of older versions of technology can still be supported.

Another example comes from one of the authors' involvement in an international project using mobile phones to increase the efficacy of rural health workers in promoting the health and welfare of expectant mothers. While the potential impact of the technology was carefully examined, other solutions at equal or lower cost were not considered alongside the set-up, deployment and ongoing maintenance costs of a phone-based solution. Neither was there investigation into the outreach health workers' competence and comfort with phones. There was also no understanding of the long-term lifespan of the phones as a tool: how would they be supplied, maintained, replaced and disposed of? This lack of a sustainability approach is witnessed in the majority of ICT for development (ICT4D)[1] projects (Heeks 2008).

[1] Information and communication technologies for development is a growing field that 'considers how technologies such as the personal computer, mobile phone, and the internet can contribute to global socio-economic development of economically impoverished communities' (Toyama 2010a).

There is little knowledge about whether these projects are standalone initiatives or part of a broader strategy. Are the technologies and their use sustained after the initiatives and funding end or do they fall into obsolescence as newer technologies in the North are adopted? Do they disadvantage neighbouring communities that do not have access to this technology? Finally, what happens to these obsolete technologies—where does this waste go and what are its effects?

The problem of e-waste is yet another area that bears consideration within the lifecycle of technology (Basel Action Network 2002) and its 'impairment effects' (Thomas 1999). Research shows that technological giants have often sold off or donated older versions of their technologies to the global South as a means of disposing unsellable stock in the global North. This is done in the name of corporate social responsibility and donation aid (see Operation Giving 2014) but has resulted in the global South being used as a dumping ground for unused technology. E-waste has also opened a route for exploitation through illegal exportation and fake donations of unused, obsolete and waste products in the name of aid (Basel Action Network 2005). Even legal exports of e-waste represent the export of impairment. E-waste processing involves open burning, acid baths and toxic dumping. The pollution of land, air and water exposes local populations to poisons causing ill health and long-term impairment. The costs of this are not borne by western consumers nor the waste brokers who benefit from the trade. Specific cases expose this physical toll: reports of young men in Ghana dying of cancer while trying to make a lucrative life out of processing e-wastes (Rush 2014) highlight both the risks and the silences around technology in the global South.

Technological Mis-fit and the Global South

Communications and assistive technologies have brought about vast productivity benefits throughout the world. In particular these technologies have enabled access to public life for individuals who previously faced numerous barriers to participation, echoing the hopes for the technological empowerment articulated by Finkelstein (1980). The socio-economic changes in society as a whole brought about by the widespread availability of this technology have opened up access thanks to the increasing assumption that affairs will be mediated by technology as first preference. This echoes Stone's (1991) argument regarding the separation between body and mind in a technological context. Simply put, the assumption that all affairs will be conducted online by all suggests that when one is equipped to be online, physical and social barriers are set aside.

In this context disability becomes a matter of relevance, rather than a matter of external definition. Such assumptions ignore the geopolitics of technology itself, however; little has been said about the technicist assumption that technology represents a universal good. This technicism has created new scope for disablement and a critical silence around it. In this new technologically driven paradigm, those who are left behind, marginalised, or find themselves excluded or ill equipped become as disabled as their now better-equipped peers previously were. They are socio-economically disabled as a consequence of the introduction of particular changes brought about by a technological mis-fit. There has been little debate in this regard which we open up by considering the role of technology in the global South and why this is a particularly critical issue.

The introduction of technology to the global South is often presented as intended altruistically, such as expounded by the Bill and Melinda Gates Foundation, when it is actually underpinned by profit-seeking global corporations that seek to benefit from establishing long-term technology consumers in global markets. The altruistic intention lies in using technology for development (ICT4D), but technology in the global South is promoted with specific commercial intentions which have been merged or often confused with development. The global South has been an open field for experimentation with emerging markets. These are new markets in which to make profits and new markets for existing technologies and for developing new technologies. Initial ICT4D projects were about providing quick solutions to development problems but they did not recognise the nuances of technology in this context, resulting in ill-fitting or inappropriate solutions that became apparent either immediately or as an eventual legacy. As an example, a quick solution to serving the world's poor was to set up tele-centres without regard to the capacity of communities when it came to infrastructure, social viabilities and access to other related resources. Lacking a holistic approach, these projects too often failed (Heeks 2008).

The silences in relation to promoting technology in the global South include the understanding of the longitudinal impact of these projects. Whether they were a success or a failure and whether the communities 'experimented' upon ultimately benefited from these endeavours remain serious but frequently unanswered questions. In this context, Toyama (2011) mentions that often it is thought that a computer is better than no teacher at all, especially in rural areas in developing countries where teacher absenteeism is a serious problem. Toyama argues that computers can mostly help

> good schools with good teachers … but in schools which are really struggling to teach their students … computers only suck up resources and take up space. Schools don't know how to maintain them, teachers don't know what to do with them and administrators will often even commandeer them for their own personal use. (Toyama 2010b)

The technological experiences of 'disabled' people within these communities remain mostly unknown. There is no understanding of whether these imports bring about real benefits or further disability.

In the chain of resourcing, production and disposal of technologies, capitalist and technicist structures converge to create disability, with the concept of 'development' being driven by multinationals who make and sell technology. This process can be traced within faceless global exchanges in which impairments are created as an acceptable and unreflected byproduct of consumer electronics. There is a lack of critical discussion on the mis-fit of technology solutions and their impact on both the targeted users and the wider socio-economic context in which they are applied.

Deconstructing the Digital Divide

The divide between the global North and South has been problematised within disability studies, as observed by Katsui: 'the distinction between North and South has been blurred in disability discourse, because no country has achieved equality for disabled people' (2006: 86). In terms of technology, there is additional complexity in global divides, as opposed to a simple iteration between North and South. Debates over the impact of technology suggest that the digital revolution has created divides between those with and without access to technology, often perpetuating inequality rather than challenging the status quo, particularly for disabled people. Such divides exist within the North and the South. However, there are many digital divides beyond the 'haves' and 'have-nots' (Blasiotti et al. 2001: 345). Intricate digital divides exist even between those who have access to technology, in terms of supporting infrastructure and digital literacy.

Simplistically, there is a lower level of ICT literacy and opportunity that can be observed in the global South but the variability within the global South is arguably as great as the North/South divide itself. Contrarily, attention to southern positions highlights silences in western understandings of technology and marginalisation. For example, industrialised societies require literacy for an individual to get by, and ICT is increasingly part of this. On the other hand, in more agrarian economies a person can still get by without such skills. In India, for instance, many household helps are poor women and men with little or no literacy. They clean local households and are paid in cash. There is no paperwork involved and even if they are unable to count money, a friend or family member may act as a proxy and do it for them. While questions may be raised regarding the risk of exploitation in this setting, digital literacies and print impairments are irrelevant here, highlighting their socially contingent nature. As such, some observers (Grech 2009) argue that print impairments such as dyslexia are northern impositions that do not have the same disabling impact in the global South.

We see that not only can the underlying assumption of disabling need (i.e. need for literacy) fail to traverse the deeper nuances of a North/South divide but, further, the concept of the enabling need can also fail to make this journey, with the assumed need for equivalent or specialised assistive technologies, such as mobile phone-based banking or information services.

In the global North in spheres such as education, nuanced digital divides are well evidenced (Hargittai 2002; Rice and Katz 2003). For example, digital divides between disabled and non-disabled students in anglophone higher education are well documented (see Seale 2014). This contradicts the wider perception that high levels of computer and internet access in themselves ensure inclusion (Seale 2014). The barriers within the divide include the provision of assistive technology, training in the use of assistive technologies, technical and digital literacy (Blasiotti et al. 2001) and accessible e-learning design (Burgstahler 2002).

The discussion of assistive technology in this context is aimed at this 'northern' baseline, assuming the need of a particular form of assistive technology, rather than asking what will have greatest impact. Providing a basic solution can be much more effective than a more expensive tailored or niche device for a particular problem. For example, screen readers and dictation software might be given to dyslexic students in the global North. This assumes they have a computer with microphone and speakers aiding them. This becomes problematic when transferred to the global South, as the implied additional costs may not be affordable, and the required space for the hardware and opportunity for training may not be available. An alternative such as using a dictaphone or a human assistant may be a more viable option. Hence, the known digital divides of the global North are complicated by new contexts and priorities in the South, highlighting how an imposed need for technology itself can be disabling and divisive.

Digital divides are not simply a matter of technology ownership or connectivity. Additional concerns must be raised about technical literacy and the ability to use electronic communication and information dissemination capabilities. Burgstahler (2002: 420) places accessibility at the heart of this 'second digital divide', conveyed as the 'result of the inaccessible design of many electronic resources'.

Reinforcing 'Social' Divides

The focus on disability, materials, services and systems is important, but it is not sufficient. Beyond ownership and access, a third 'digital divide' with tangible social outcomes is identified. Goggin and Newell (2003) observe how disability might be socially constructed in new media. Disability and ability continue to be 'built in' to technological networks as some disabled users are disadvantaged or locked out of mainstream interactions by technical barriers that produce them as 'disabled' (Goggin and Newell 2005; Ellis and Kent 2011). Yet, research shows that beyond this technical divide, social divides are also enabled and produced in networked public domains such as Facebook and other social media (Lewthwaite 2011). Network conditions that allow peer surveillance can enact powerful normative social pressures. In these situations, disability, as a different way of being, becomes extra visible, with perceived differences exposing disabled users to negative public scrutiny.

These factors can propel disabled people to perform or adopt 'non-disabled' modes of interaction that mask authentic, but 'extra-visible' experiences of impairment. For example, within Facebook, where upbeat and positive self-expressions are required, experiences of impairment, such as chronic pain, depression or the frustration that can be associated with degenerative health, are actively repressed to conform with network norms and resist a perceived anti-social identity (Lewthwaite 2011). In addition, the alternative modes of living that are necessitated by impairment and disability can become marked as discredited, stigmatised and deficit identities, misunderstood by a non-disabled networked public. In this way, diversity can be suppressed in social networks, while those who cannot or will not access the network on the basis of disability are seen to be doubly disadvantaged, as disability is rendered invisible and the social and digital divide of the network is reinforced (Lewthwaite 2011).

Work to bridge these digital divides is important. However, accessibility discourse has not, as yet, moved beyond the interests of the global North in examining the stratification of digital divides for disabled people in the global South. While the global divide between the haves and have-nots is problematised, disability has yet to be meaningfully represented in this debate. Inclusion, universal design and accessibility literatures have been predominantly developed in Europe, North America and Japan. To an extent, this reflects the distribution of the internet, its reach and usage. An average of only 35 per cent of the global population is connected to the internet. These rates are above average in North America (81 per cent), Western Europe (78 per cent), Oceania (63 per cent), Central and Eastern Europe (54 per cent), East Asia (48 per cent) and South America (47 per cent). Below this average fall Central America (34 per cent), Central Asia (29 per cent). South East Asia (25 per cent), Africa (18 per cent) and South Asia (12 per cent) (We Are Social 2014). As disabled people represent the poorest of the poor globally (Barnes and Sheldon 2010), access to technology is not guaranteed. Perhaps more importantly, as political debates over identity and representation increasingly occur online, disabled people in the global South can be locked out of the very systems and vehicles for digital voices that are required to challenge and reconfigure those systems. As Held et al. (1999: 28) observe, 'political and economic elites in the world's major metropolitan areas are much more tightly integrated into, and have much greater control over, global networks than do the subsistence farmers of Burundi'.

However, despite the focus of networked technologies within the metropole, social networks in the global South have led to new and unanticipated political actions, mobilising communities that have been disjointed and uncoordinated. Social networks are regarded highly for mobilising communities which are socially or politically marginalised, including disabled groups. Social technologies and global networks have mobilised 'Facebook Revolutions' and engaged global attention in new areas, across North Africa, the Middle East and parts of Central Asia.

At the time of writing, there are two billion active social network users in the world. At the beginning of the year, Facebook counted 1.184 billion users, followed by the Chinese chat app QQ with 816 million users and the Chinese social networking platform Qzone with 632 million users. WhatsApp ranks fourth with 400 million users. The Chinese chat app WeChat has 272 million users, which is a higher adoption than LinkedIn (259 million users) and Twitter (232 million). The penetration of these networks has made new research populations available. In terms of disability and technology research, this represents a potentially huge leap forward in gaining an understanding of disability in the global South that goes beyond the small-scale qualitative work that currently characterises social network research focused on disabled users. For example, Facebook has published new research on social network users with visual impairments, based on its substantial user database (Wu and Adamic 2014). This research surveyed the experiences and activities of 50,000 visually impaired social network users, numbers previously unimaginable outside government health research. While the findings of this research underline much that is already known within accessibility discourse, these developments suggest that, as networked publics are established in the global South, they may be drawn more meaningfully into the participation and development of digital and networked research.

Globalisation and International Governance of Technology

In this section we identify how international governance of technology, despite being a global phenomenon in the 21st century, represents a northern agenda. More specifically, the onus of governance is on embedding tools rather than identifying and solving a specific problem. For example, evaluation of ICT4D projects often focuses on measuring output (e.g. facilities and services) and outcome (e.g. economic benefit or not) rather than the impact on the beneficiaries (Heeks 2010). More often than not the outcome is disempowerment for those who are meant to be beneficiaries. An example is a rural health worker or farmer being given a mobile app to increase efficacy. In this scenario, the health worker not only has to learn how the mobile app works but must also learn an imposed method of using the app because research evidence indicates that a certain way of learning can enhance their efficacy, without exploring the validity of the method in the context (Ramachandran et al. 2010a, b). Thus the rural health worker who was otherwise classified disabled now faces newer 'disabilities'. Nonetheless, technology is regarded as the solution rather than one of many potential tools that can be specific to a certain disability. This technicist view of technology-as-cure perpetuates established power relations (Oosterlaken and Van Den Hoven 2011; Zheng and Stahl 2011). It represents a fundamental misunderstanding of disability as a social product when there are important political and technical elements contributing. When there is a capability to understand these assumptions there are silences around the processes that follow. Corruption and bureaucracy often play a substantial role in creating these silences because those who are complicit have no cause to disrupt a beneficial arrangement.

The lack of discussion over the processes and governance of technology entering the global South extends further from a consideration of the ethics of such practices. For example, rarely do projects based on baseline studies justify a technological intervention; that is to say, a whole ecosystem is being built around using mobile phones for development without much focus on what the population wants and how they would like to solve their issues. For example, Roy (2013) developed a mobile game-based project without discussing with the marginalised men-who-have-sex-with-men peer educators how and what they would like to enhance their efficacy or whether they would like any help at all. In these cases, participants are rather unable to opt out of the initiatives to make them technologically viable due to job obligations. Roy observed such power dynamics in her field work and research where a marginalised or poor health worker is obliged out of economic security to please the managerial staff of NGOs. Earlier we identified the critical silence not only in questioning these imposed and assumed needs, but also in having the capability to question these assumptions in the first place. Thus the notion of technology as the sole harbinger of social change is often a myth. Technology can bring positive social change when the human intent and capacity is positive, as iterated by Toyama (2011). Technology, however, is not a substitute for human intent.

We now turn to the role of international legislation which we argue embeds similar assumptions and values.

Web Accessibility and the CRPD

The UN Convention on the Rights of Persons with Disabilities (2006) continues to gain greater traction across the global North and South. The CRPD stresses the role of technology in enabling rights. Article 9—Accessibility talks about the power of technology for people with disabilities to enjoy their human rights and fundamental freedoms and to act on an equal basis with others through the use of ICTs and other facilities and services available to the public. As well as identifying and eliminating obstacles and barriers to accessibility, state parties to the CRPD shall take appropriate measures:

> 2. […] h) To promote the design, development, production and distribution of accessible information and communications technologies and systems at an early stage, so that these technologies and systems become accessible at minimum cost.

The CRPD is having an impact on global companies. For example, Microsoft has articulated its commitment to human rights through its partnership with disabled people's organisations, among other groups, in efforts to implement the Convention. Yet, the Convention positions disabled people as users and consumers of technology rather than designers, developers, fabricators or producers. It makes no reference to the rights of disabled and non-disabled people that live in communities which mine, smelt, manufacture and dispose of technologies to be free from violence and injury. The Convention is also limited in respect to the implied notion of disability as a stable, pre-existing, discrete facet of an individual. Here, the CRPD conveys a medical undertone that is at odds with social, post-structural and capability models of disability which increasingly advance the cause of disabled people's emancipation. Nonetheless, the Convention is having a significant impact on government actions, most acutely in Web accessibility. The CRPD has created a policy imperative that governments seeking to recognise the needs of disabled people must meet. This has led to many countries adopting the accessibility guidelines developed by the World Wide Web Consortium's Web Accessibility Initiative (WAI) and writing them into their legislation. This is significant, since, as Lewthwaite and Swan (2013) observe, many member parties (including China, Ethiopia, Malta and Lebanon) which have ratified the Convention do not yet have any disability legislation enforcing access to the Internet.

WAI has developed guidelines to cover all aspects of accessibility online. The foremost are Web Content Accessibility Guidelines (WCAG) used by developers to create websites that are accessible to disabled people. WCAG is a de facto standard, applied and referred to by many governments. WCAG 2.0 has been the standard for Indian government websites since 2009, for example, and the list of nations applying these guidelines as standard is growing. Web accessibility guidelines are a powerful force for creating accessible digital experiences for disabled people and anecdotal evidence suggests that WCAG is being adopted by governments keen to demonstrate an enlightened attitude towards disability (Kelly et al. 2013). The *en masse* legislative adoption is not without problems though. Technology is implied in the distribution of power and oppression and therefore possesses 'ideological qualities'. In the making of accessibility standards, critical analysis of the underlying values are rare

(Lewthwaite 2014). In this respect, standards convey implicit values that highlight the importance of meeting the requirements of disabled people, challenging regressive and ablist perspectives. However, WCAG also implicitly orders bodies in a hierarchy of impairments that is grounded strongly in the global North (Lewthwaite and Swan 2013). For example, because WCAG prioritises text over other forms of representation, Lewthwaite and Swan argue that the needs of blind and partially sighted web users who use screen-readers are given more status than more populous, southern impairment groups, such as those without assistive technologies and those with print impairments and low literacy. With respect to assistive technologies, notably, screen readers themselves are language-limited and still predominantly serve Latin alphabets, with some developments in Arabic. Provisions for many indigenous language groups are scarce. In short, WCAG implicitly exports northern views on disability to southern contexts where such views can displace indigenous knowledge with counterproductive, colonising outcomes. Since the global South is the 'majority world', there is a serious concern that western accessibility norms do not sufficiently recognise the realities of digital access for the majority of disabled people.

As governments of populous nations, such as India, adopt WCAG, there is a further concern that standardisation has crowded out opportunities for collaboration between North and South that might have ensured more robust outcomes for the majority of disabled people. As WAI guidelines are revised, it will be important for more southern voices to be meaningfully engaged in these processes and for power to devolve from western World Wide Web Consortium member organisations and individuals, to experts and rapporteurs from the global South.

Conclusion

In this chapter we have aimed to identify the silences that characterise impairment and disabled experience in relation to networked technologies in the global South. Structuring a chapter such as this is difficult, as Selwyn observes: 'the processes and outcomes of globalisation are disjointed, uneven and contradictory, and subject to various differences and imbalances in power between states, societies and communities' (2013: 17).

In this context, an overarching, totalising narrative of disability and networked technologies in the global South is inappropriate. Suggesting a pre-existing fixed-vantage point, exempt from geography and the power relations that constitute exclusion, would be erroneous. The recent history of networked technologies is still revealing itself. It is a story of unequal and fragmented relationships; of global stratification rather than global unification (Selwyn 2013). To this end, our closing point accords with Rizvi and Lingard:

> The globalised world is fundamentally heterogeneous, unequal and conflictive, rather than integrated and seamless. It is experienced differently by different communities, and even individuals, and is sustained and created by people and institutions with widely different histories and political interests. (Rizvi and Lingard 2010: 24)

This chapter has supplied a series of snapshots, each identifying gaps in scholarship, media attention and a critical gaze in global disability studies. Questions remain: How are disabled people in the global South reconfiguring global tech infrastructure to better serve their goals and recognise their circumstances? How can development and governance structures better recognise indigenous expertise and diverse contexts? To begin to answer these questions requires a sea change in how mobile and networked technologies are understood by technological elites in both the global North and global South. It requires a fundamental expansion of understandings of ability and disability, to protect human rights in view of impairment, to respect empowered choices to disconnect, and to expand existing norms to include disabled people in the global South as regular users, creators, developers and citizens of the world's global networks.

References

Apple. (2014a). Supplier responsibility standards. *Version, 4*, 2. Retrieved April 16, 2014, from http://www.apple.com/supplierresponsibility/pdf/Apple_Supplier_Responsibility_Standards.pdf.

Apple. (2014a). *Apple supplier responsibility 2014: Progress report*. Retrieved April 16, 2014, from http://images.apple.com/supplierresponsibility/pdf/Apple_SR_2014_Progress_Report.pdf.

Ayers, C. J. (2012). The international trade in conflict minerals: Coltan. *Critical Perspectives on International Business, 8*(2), 178.

Barnes, C., & Sheldon, A. (2010). Disability, politics and poverty in a majority world context. *Disability and Society, 25*(7), 771–782.

Basel Action Network. (2002). *Exporting harm: The high tech trashing of Asia*. Retrieved November 5, 2014, from http://www.ban.org/E-waste/technotrashfinalcomp.pdf.

Basel Action Network. (2005). *The digital dump: Exporting re-use and abuse to Africa*. Retrieved November 5, 2014, from http://ban.org/library/TheDigitalDump.pdf.

Benson, L., & Harkavy, I. (2002). Saving the soul of the university: What is to be done? In K. Robins & F. Webster (Eds.), *The virtual university: Knowledge* (Markets and management, pp. 169–209). Oxford: Oxford University Press.

Blasiotti, E. L., Westbrook, J. D., & Kobayashi, I. K. (2001). Disability studies and electronic networking. In G. L. Albrecht, K. D. Seelman, & M. Bury (Eds.), *Handbook of disability studies*. Thousand Oaks, CA: Sage.

Boettiger, S., Toyama, K., & Abed, R. (2010). Natural obsolescence of village phone. In *Proceedings of the Fifth International Conference on Information and Communication Technologies and Development* (pp. 221–229). New York: ACM.

Buell, S., Grech, S., & Brogna, P. (2016). Disability and poverty: Complex interactions. In S. Grech & K. Soldatic (Eds.), *Disability in the global South: The critical handbook* (pp. xx–xx). New York: Springer.

Burgstahler, S. (2002). Distance learning: The library's role in ensuring access to everyone. *Library Hi Tech, 20*, 420–432.

Chan, J., & Pun, N. (2010). Suicide as protest for the new generation of Chinese migrant workers: Foxconn, global capital, and the state. *The Asia-Pacific Journal, 37*, 1–50.

CNET. (2012). *Riots, suicides, and other issues in Foxconn's iPhone factories*. Retrieved October 17, 2013, from http://www.cnet.com/uk/news/riots-suicides-and-other-issues-in-foxconns-iphone-factories/.

Duhigg, C., & Barboza, D. (2012, January 25). In China, human costs are built into an iPad. *The New York Times*. Retrieved January 30, 2015, from http://www.nytimes.com/2012/01/26/business/ieconomy-apples-ipad-and-the-human-costs-for-workers-in-china.html.

Ellis, K., & Kent, M. (2011). *Disability and new media*. Abingdon: Routledge.

Fair Labor Association. (2012). *Foxconn investigation report*. Retrieved April 22, 2014, from http://www.fairlabor.org/report/foxconn-investigation-report.

Finkelstein, V. (1980). *Attitudes and disabled people: Issues for discussion*. Disability Archive UK. Retrieved October 17, 2013, from http://disability-studies.leeds.ac.uk/files/library/finkelstein-attitudes.pdf.

Goggin, G., & Newell, C. (2003). *Digital disability: The social construction of disability in new media*. Oxford: Rowman and Littlefield.

Goggin, G., & Newell, C. (2005). Foucault on the phone: Disability and the mobility of government. In S. Tremain (Ed.), *Foucault and the government of disability*. Michigan: University of Michigan Press.

Grech, S. (2009). Disability, poverty and development: Critical reflections on the majority world debate. *Disability & Society, 24*(6), 771–784. doi:10.1080/09687590903160266.

Grech, S. (2012). Disability and the majority world: A neocolonial approach. In D. Goodley, B. Hughes, & L. Davis (Eds.), *Disability and social theory: New developments and directions* (pp. 52–69). London: Palgrave Macmillan.

Hargittai, E. (2002). Second-level digital divide: Differences in people's online skills. *First Monday*, 7(4). Retrieved from http://dx.doi.org/10.5210/fm.v7i4.942.

Heeks, R. (2008). ICT4D 2.0: The next phase of applying ICT for international development. *Computer, 41*, 26–33.

Heeks, R. (2010). Development 2.0: The IT-enabled transformation of international development. *Communications of the ACM, 53*(4), 22–24.

Held, D., McGrew, A., Goldblatt, D., & Perraton, J. (1999). *Global transformations: Politics, economics and culture*. Cambridge: Polity Press.

Katsui, H. (2006). *Human rights of disabled people in the South*. English edition. Retrieved October 17, 2013, from http://disability-studies.leeds.ac.uk/files/library/katsui-article-for-Antti-2.pdf. (Originally published in Finnish as Vammaisten Ihmisoikeuksista Etelässä. In A. Teittinen (Ed.), *Vammaisuuden Tutkimus*, Yliopistopaino. Helsinki. 86–119.

Kelly, B., Hassell, J., Sloan, D., Lukeš, D., Draffan, E. A. & Lewthwaite, S. (2013). Bring your own policy: Why accessibility standards need to be contextually aware. *Ariadne 71*. Retrieved April 23, 2014, from http://www.ariadne.ac.uk/issue71/kelly-et-al.

Latour, B. (1991). Technology is society made durable. In J. Law (Ed.), *A sociology of monsters* (pp. 103–131). London: Routledge.

Lawson, C., & Meyenn, N. (2000). *Bringing cellular phone service to rural areas: Grameen telecom and village pay phones in Bangladesh*. Washington, DC: World Bank. Retrieved from http://hdl.handle.net/10986/11438.

Lewthwaite, S. (2011). *Disability 2.0: Student dis/connections. A study of student experiences of disability and social networks on campus in higher education*. PhD thesis, University of Nottingham. Retrieved August 14, 2014, from http://etheses.nottingham.ac.uk/2406/.

Lewthwaite, S. (2014). Web accessibility standards and disability: Developing critical perspectives on accessibility. *Journal of Disability and Rehabilitation, 36*(16), 1375–1383.

Lewthwaite, S., & Swan, H. (2013). Disability, Web Standards and the Majority World. In L. Meloncon (Ed.), *Rhetorical AccessAbility: At the intersection of technical communications and disability studies* (pp. 157–174). Amityville, NY: Baywood.

Loney, M. & Lemos, R (2004). *Study: Unpatched PCs compromised in 20 minutes*. Retrieved November 30, 2014, from http://www.drordi.com/articles/unpatched_pc_s_compromised_in_20_minutes.pdf.

Mantz, J. W. (2008). Improvisational economies: Coltan production in the eastern Congo. *Social Anthropology, 16*, 34–50.

Meekosha, H. (2011). Decolonising disability: Thinking and acting globally. *Disability & Society, 26*, 667–682.
Meekosha, H. & Soldatic, K. (Eds.). (2011). Special issue: Disability in the global South. *Third World Quarterly 32*(8).
Melcher, F., Sitnikova, M. A., Graupner, T., Martin, N., Oberthür, T., Henjes-Kunst, F., et al. (2008). Fingerprinting of conflict minerals: Columbite-tantalite ("coltan") ores. *SGA News, 23*, 7–14.
Montague, D. (2002). Stolen goods: Coltan and conflict in the Democratic Republic of Congo. *SAIS Review, 22*, 103–118.
Okoye, F. (2014). Does Africa dream of androids? *Disability and the Global South, 1*(1), 64–84. Retrieved from https://disabilityglobalsouth.files.wordpress.com/2012/06/dgs-01-01-05.pdf.
Oosterlaken, I., & Van Den Hoven, J. (2011). Editorial: ICT and the capability approach. *Ethics and Information Technology, 13*, 65–67.
Operation Giving. (2014). *Donate excess inventory*. Retrieved November 5, 2014, from http://operationgive.org/index.php/donate/donate-excess-inventory/.
Oppong, J., Woodruff, T., & Gritzner, C. (2007). *Democratic Republic of Congo—Modern World Nations*. New York, NY: Infobase.
Poulsen, F. (2010). *Blood in the Mobile*. Directed by Frank Poulson, Koncern TV- og Filmproduktion, Copenhagen, Chili Films, Hilleroed, and Gebrueder Beetz Filmproduktion, Berlin (video/DVD).
Ramachandran, D., Canny, J., Das, P. D., & Cutrell, E. (2010a). Mobile-izing health workers in rural India. In *Proceedings of the 28th International Conference on Human Factors in Computing Systems* (pp. 1889–1898). New York, NY: ACM.
Ramachandran, D., Goswami, V. & Canny, J. (2010b). Research and reality: Using mobile messages to promote maternal health in rural India. In *Proceedings of the 4th ACM/IEEE International Conference on Information and Communication Technologies and Development* (p. 35). New York, NY: ACM.
Readings, W. (1996). *The University in ruins*. Cambridge, MA: Harvard University Press.
Renner, M. (2002). *The anatomy of resource wars*. Worldwatch Paper 162. Washington, DC: Worldwatch Institute.
Rice, R. E., & Katz, J. E. (2003). Comparing internet and mobile phone usage: Digital divides of usage, adoption, and dropouts. *Telecommunications Policy, 27*, 597–623.
Richardson, D., Ramirez, R., & Haq, M. (2000). *Grameen telecom's village phone programme in rural Bangladesh: A multi-media case study. Final report*. Ontario: Canadian International Development Agency.
Rizvi, F., & Lingard, B. (2010). *Globalizing education policy*. London: Routledge.
Roy, A. (2013). *Mobile game based learning for males having sex with males peer educators in India*. PhD thesis, University of Nottingham.
Rush, J. (2014, 3 April). Think your television is recycled when you get rid of it? *Daily Mail*. Retrieved November 5, 2014, from http://www.dailymail.co.uk/news/article-2595966/Think-television-recycled-rid-This-likely-end-dumping-grounds-one-dubbed-worlds-biggest-e-waste-site.html.
SACOM. (2013, December 17). *No more iSlave on cover glass—Biel Crystal pledge to improve labour basic condition*. Retrieved January 30, 2015, from http://sacom.hk/bielcrystalpledge/.
Sassen, S. (2002). Towards a sociology of information technology. *Current Sociology, 50*, 365–388.
Schmidt, P. R. (1996). Cultural representations of African iron production. In P. R. Schmidt (Ed.), *The culture and technology of African iron production* (pp. 1–28). Florida: The University of Florida Press.
Seale, J. (2014). *E-learning and disability in higher education: Accessibility research and practice*. London: Routledge.
Selwyn, N. (2013). *Education in a digital world: Global perspectives on technology and education*. New York, NY: Routledge.

Soldatic, K., & Meekosha, H. (2014). *The global politics of impairment and disability: Processes and embodiments*. London: Routledge.
Stone, A. R. (1991). Will the real body please stand up? Boundary stories about virtual cultures. In M. Benedikt (Ed.), *Cyberspace: First steps* (pp. 81–118). Cambridge, MA: MIT Press.
Stone, E. (1999). Disability and development in the majority world. In E. Stone (Ed.), *Disability and development: Learning from action and research on disability in the majority world* (pp. 1–18). Leeds: Disability Press.
Thomas, C. (1999). *Female forms: Experiences and understanding disability*. Buckingham: Open University Press.
Tomlinson, M., Solomon, W., Singh, Y., Doherty, T., Chopra, M., Ijumba, P., et al. (2009). The use of mobile phones as a data collection tool: A report from a household survey in South Africa. *BMC Medical Informatics and Decision Making, 9*, 51.
Toyama, K. (2010a). Human–computer interaction and global development. *Foundations and Trends in Human-Computer Interaction, 4*(1), 1–79.
Toyama, K. (2010b). *The myth of scale*. TEDxTokyo—Kentaro Toyama—05/15/10—(English). Retrieved April 20, 2014, from http://tedxtalks.ted.com/video/TEDxTokyo-Kentaro-Toyama-051510.
Toyama, K. (2011). Technology as amplifier in international development. In *Proceedings of the 2011 iConference* (pp. 75–82). New York, NY: ACM.
Toyama, K. (2013). *Which comes first? Social media or social development*. Keynote presented at the IDIP International Annual Symposium. Retrieved November 30, 2014, from http://groupspaces.com/ipid/item/420051.
UN. (2006). *Convention on the rights of persons with disabilities*. Retrieved April 22, 2014, from http://www.un.org/disabilities/default.asp?navid=12&pid=150.
We Are Social. (2014). *Global digital statistics, 2014*. Retrieved April 8, 2014, from http://wearesocial.net/blog/2014/01/social-digital-mobile-worldwide-2014/.
Wu, S., & Adamic, L. A. (2014). Visually impaired users on an online social network. In *Proceedings of the SIGCHI Conference on Human Factors in Computing Systems* (pp. 3133–3142). New York, NY: ACM.
Zheng, Y., & Stahl, B. C. (2011). Technology, capabilities and critical perspectives: What can critical theory contribute to Sen's capability approach? *Ethics and Information Technology, 13*, 69–80.

Part V
Activism and Research Across Cultures

Chapter 32
Whose Knowledge, Whose Voice? Power, Agency and Resistance in Disability Studies for the Global South

JosAnn Cutajar and Casimir Adjoe

Introduction

Meekosha (2011) maintains that research and theories about disability derive mainly from the global North. Disability studies rarely include non-metropolitan thinkers. Even when it does, this research tends to be seen as context specific, and the social theories which emanate from these studies are rarely referred to in research theorizing disability in the North. This chapter sets out to investigate how this one-way transfer of knowledge affects the way disability studies is conceptualized—whose experiences are incorporated and whose are left out. Multilateral debate and dialogue between disability studies academics and activists in different locations around the world would help add to the knowledge already available in the field, while keeping others informed about what is taking place in 'similar' situations elsewhere.

Groce et al. (2011: 1493) maintain that most countries depend on North-derived concepts to differentiate between the 'normal' and those who are not. They also borrow and impose models from these locations to treat 'the disabled' (Grech 2011). The implication of this one-way transfer of knowledge, services, professionals, policies and ideas from North to South is that disability study students, academics, policy makers and activists may be 'enabled' but at the same time be constrained or 'disabled' by the global North-derived epistemology that informs perceptions, and

J. Cutajar (✉)
University of Malta, Msida, Malta
e-mail: josann.cutajar@um.edu.mt

C. Adjoe
Central University College, Tema, Ghana

S. Grech, K. Soldatic (eds.), *Disability in the Global South*,
International Perspectives on Social Policy, Administration, and Practice,
DOI 10.1007/978-3-319-42488-0_32

hence their studies, research, policies and activism. As Jamaica Kincaid (cited by Chiseri-Strater and Stone Sunstein 1997) underlines, academics writing from the periphery but immersed in western produced knowledge tend to be familiar with the lay of the land in the West. This might render them 'blind' to the fact that the theories, policies and practices they consume and promote from the global North will not always enable them to explicate and address disability in the socio-economic, cultural and political context in which they are located.

This chapter sets out to address this one-way transfer of knowledge between North and South, West and the rest and to delineate which analytical issues need to be incorporated in a disability studies for the global South. We will use Ghana and Malta as fluid case studies. We argue that theories from the global North do not always take into consideration the fact that the causes and redress of impairment lie beyond the capacity of the nation state. At the same time we need to explore the fact that the epistemologies and enunciative codes[1] 'borrowed' from the North help academics in the South re-interpret who they are. This chapter therefore explores the fine line that runs between location, positionality, dependency, neocolonialism, agency and resistance in disability studies.

The chapter relies on postcolonial Black feminist disability theory and praxis, an approach adopted also by Parekh (2007: 143). This approach helps researchers and activists to explore the nuances of social, cultural, political and economic histories and the impact these have on the representation and administration of disability in the global South (Barker 2010: 22). The implication is that national and global mobilization can take place when disability scholars and activists recognize the multiplicity of disabled and impaired identities and orient themselves towards the politics of diversity within unity (Meekosha and Soldatic 2011) while painstakingly growing their own methodologies and knowledge cultures to deal with the complexities at the local level (Tuhiwai Smith 1999).

Whose Knowledge?

Bloor (1991: 5) defines knowledge as 'those beliefs which people confidently hold to and live by'. These beliefs provide guidelines for framing, interpreting and constructing meaning. Feminists underline that what people assume to be absolute and universal truth is biased since knowledge tends to be created from the positionality and location of embodied actors situated differently in different social structures and locations around the world (Lengermann and Niebrugge 2008: 486). Knowledge is produced and varies among groups—even within groups. This means that what

[1] This concept derives from semiotics. Enunciators, those who want to relay a message, draw upon the codes of a particular language or genre to communicate. These codes tend to be influenced by the way they see the world. This means that the enunciation is structured in a way that addresses and positions its receivers, although it depends on the receivers whether or not they accept this positioning.

we regard as knowledge tends to be partial and interested, never objective. Haraway (1988) in fact sustains that there are 'knowledges' rather than knowledge.

In the academic, political and economic world, not all knowledge is given the same value, however. In these settings, western epistemologies espoused by middle-class, white, heterosexual, able-bodied males tend to be given more credibility and hence are more likely to be in circulation in the global academic circuit. Such epistemologies tend to be perceived as universal and, thus, able to be generalized and applied to other contexts.

A 2009 study conducted among Maltese Sociology students, including those attending disability study courses, found that these students tended to give more credence to knowledge produced in western countries (Cutajar 2009). This might emanate from the fact that up to 1964 Malta formed part of the British Empire. Even though the British left Malta decades ago, the Maltese still tend to believe that knowledge, products and services produced in western contexts, especially the UK and the USA, are of a higher caliber than that produced locally. Maltese students are a product of this culture. In fact they give more credibility to 'imported' knowledges because they perceive locally produced ones as inferior. They tend to consume foreign-produced knowledge while lamenting the fact that they find it too abstract and not always applicable to the local context. In the end these students become more familiar with what is taking place in English-speaking western contexts.

Disability studies in the global South need to tackle such a challenge. Students and academics in this location need to be reflexive about the type of knowledge they consume, produce and promote. Lengermann and Niebrugge (2008: 487) maintain that researchers, whether feminist, Black, postcolonial, disabled, raced and/or queer, should adopt a reflexive stance at every stage of their research. Reflexivity necessitates that students and researchers found in diverse academic seats of knowledge located in different areas around the world need to examine their own history and positionality within these educational institutions and/or structures in which they are ensconced and/or implicated, and try to understand how this might impact on which knowledge they choose to consume. Ghosh (1998) maintains that as students and researchers we need to examine the political praxis that promotes certain forms of knowledge while undermining others. These reflexive exercises will help interrupt the circuits of control and render problematic the overwhelming dependence on knowledge deriving from limited sources. At the same time this reflexivity will push us into producing more nuanced methodologies which will enable us to understand the lived and varied experiences of people with disabilities at the local level. Local research will benefit greatly if researchers are familiar with epistemologies and methodologies produced both locally and internationally. This will help them to develop a more insightful knowledge of social relations at the local, national and global levels that might give rise to inequality while exploring how disabled people and/or groups empower themselves and resist oppression on macro, meso and micro levels.

Reflexivity, therefore, helps researchers interrogate how the politics of positionality and location is implicated in every decision they make in their research practice. In the process, this will help them produce methods that help and enable political action. Researchers from the global South might feel disenfranchised when they have to depend on epistemologies and methodologies created in western contexts to explore the particular. At the same time they need to thread a fine line. The knowledge local scholars produce in the academic world can empower them while disempowering those taking part in the research. Local researchers use this particular knowledge to promote themselves in the academic world and, in so doing, help erase the agency of the actors they studied in the process of rendering their particular experiences general. To ensure that this colonization of particular knowledge does not take place, researchers need to identify and articulate the particular location from which they speak, and for whom they do so, delineating how their positionality has impacted on the conclusions they arrive at, rendering the knowledge they produce partial.

Tuhiwai Smith (1999) observes that it takes years to develop a local research infrastructure in any given field. At the same time disability studies for the South are needed so that students and activists—disabled or not—are provided with more enabling methods which promote participation, empowerment, social integration and an equitable citizenship (Hiranandani 2005). A feminist sociology of knowledge underlines how this can be done. According to Lengermann and Niebrugge (2008: 487) this can only take place when researchers take into consideration the experiences of various groups of actors as well as those of individuals within groups. At the same time, researchers need to analyze how different power relations at these different levels and locations could have led to the oppression of the said group and/or individual.

The privileging of the webbed accounts of disenfranchised groups helps to bring about their empowerment (Lengermann and Niebrugge 2008: 487). This is not the only reason why such research is important. It will also help to delineate the limitations of research deriving from more privileged academic grounds. Phoenix (2012) adds that such knowledge needs to be shared around the globe and made accessible through transnational networks of publicity and activism. Dialogue and collaboration, what Yuval-Davis (1997) refers to as transversal politics, is essential so that a political standpoint theory can be fashioned based on issues rather than identities.

Research needs to be conducted with various groups of disabled individuals to map out micro, meso and macro inequities, while at the same time underlining how different groups or individuals deal with them. Such emancipatory research does not only help give voice to disabled people, but it also provides information. Parekh (2007: 157) underlines that empowerment emerges when disabled people are allowed to make decisions based on informed choices. Knowledge is, thus, heavily implicated in enabling or dis-enabling bodies to make informed choices, to participate in society, and to seek integration and equality through empowerment.

Language and the Educational System in Ex-colonies

Educational institutions and structures in ex-colonies are almost a mirror image of those adopted by their past colonial 'masters'—Britain, in the case of Ghana and Malta, which were until some decades ago part of the British Empire. The pedagogical medium adopted in such institutions, especially at a tertiary level, tends to be English. Language, as Richardson and St. Pierre (2005) point out, is not transparent. It is a constitutive force, promoting a particular view of reality. Their competence in this appropriated medium also means that some feel outsiders within their own educational system because of the North-derived languages that constitute the realities that they perceive and work with.

In Ghana, local languages are largely ignored in almost all official domains of society, but especially in education. It is held that English is a universal language whereas the local languages 'take you nowhere' as 'job opportunities associated with the learning of indigenous languages are not lucrative' (Adjoe 2007: 175). English, thus, defines the terms of understanding and constitutes the definition of experience and its organization. This understanding is transferred to local knowledges and local authors. The Linguistic Association of Ghana, during its fourth annual conference in 2013, remarked on the preference of students for reading and citing reference works from authors outside the continent of Africa, especially from the global North. This preference is reflected in other domains of society and academic disciplines, and is not different with respect to issues concerning Disability Studies (see Ghai 2002; Adjoe, unpublished PhD dissertation, 2007). Scholars and activists located in the global South find it difficult to move beyond this dependency on western derived knowledge and enunciative modalities. This is because the texts and knowledge promoted in ex-colonies are usually imported from the global North. Locally produced texts have to compete with products deriving from the North (Karthigesu 1996) and lose out since students and academics living in ex-colonies are more likely to consume the latter.

Students' linguistic competence in English depends on their social class derivation (Cutajar 2009). Students from a working and lower middle-class background find it more difficult to grasp the concepts when these are taught in English. To render these theories even more abstract, they are taught in an 'enunciative code' with which a number of students are not that comfortable (Cutajar 2009).

Thus, according to the prevailing structure into which the southern academic and their constituencies are presently driven, only North-derived epistemologies are in operation to give a sense of what is meaningful. Kincaid's (cited by Chiseri-Strater and Stone Sunstein 1997) observation is applicable here: while our everyday experiences are situated in the local context, the landscape we read and learn about is based somewhere else. This results in a mismatch in our spatial gaze and personal landscape.

Knowledge and Neocolonialism

As outlined above, researchers, activists, government officials and professionals often borrow ideas, models and practices from the West when dealing with disability. Borrowing ideas cannot be faulted. There is, however, evidence that the tools and practices adopted are not adapted to fit the context, and they sometimes undermine more nuanced ways of dealing with disability (Grech 2011). Disability studies in the global South have not succeeded in adapting disability studies to fit the various contexts in this location since the colonial educational system, curricula and policies that govern learning and its orientation adopt neocolonial models of understanding disability and its related issues.

Neocolonialism prevails in countries where the North is perpetually positioned as the standard against which other forms of cultural experiences can be scaled. Said (1994: 223) refers to it as an 'authority based elsewhere'. This authority has managed to sustain a syndrome of dependency in these locations. Mazrui (1995) blames this dependency on the colonial form of education adopted in the global South, where the knowledge transmitted, the language of instruction used, the source and extent of library holdings, the cultural background of faculty members, the curricula structures and the pedagogic requirements rely heavily on northern ones. Academics, policy makers, activists and practitioners in the disability field use the global North as their point of reference to adjudicate what type of progress has been attained and what remains to be achieved to reach the global North standard. In the process, they lose sight of home-grown knowledge and practices that have evolved through the ages to deal with impairment, disease, social inclusion and integration (Miles 2007).

Ironically, Briskin and Coulter (1992) look to education to bring about change. In order to enable change to occur, Ghosh (1998) promotes an interventionist postcolonial pedagogy as a means of questioning and hence interrupting 'circuits of control' at the classroom level. Classrooms can be used to analyze and problematize structures, practices and content taken for granted at local, national and global levels. The classroom can also be used to demystify texts that make universalizing claims, taking them apart, analyzing them and constructively building them up collaboratively. This space is not always provided in educational institutions where academics are positioned or position themselves as the seat of knowledge in a bid to retain power.

Students may not be aware that experiences and knowledge are embodied, partial and hence subjective, rendering all knowledge situated (Rich 2003). It is this partiality which can be used to reach out and learn about the 'Other'. The knowledge produced in the process might lead to consciousness-raising and empowerment of subordinate groups (Grewal 1996), and can lead to change at the individual, group, national and global levels. This is one way to begin to break down the academic dependency syndrome which Alatas (2003: 601) refers to as 'academic neocolonialism'.

Re-contextualizing Knowledges

When introduced in countries in the global South, Disability Studies served as a tool to counter local myths that explained disabilities as mystical inflictions and afflictions. It provided a means of explicating the mundane conditions under which disabilities occur through North-derived epistemologies and enunciative codes. These borrowed, essentialized knowledges need to be re-contextualized locally, however, to ensure that the borrowed tools explicate what is happening at the local level. To be able to do this, countries in the global South need to conduct evidence-based research before a policy deriving from the North is applied. Where financial resources are limited, this process cannot always be undertaken.

Even when undertaken, the need to emulate or live up to northern paradigms makes us lose sight of the cultural context in which we are embedded. This is not only because academics prefer northern paradigms, but because the sources of funding and the authorities behind such research tend to emphasize, understand or accept only northern-derived paradigms. A case in point is the implementation of 'independent support living' in the Maltese Islands. Independent research was undertaken before this policy was adopted (see Spiteri Gingell 2011). This report starts by scrutinizing international policies (of the United Nations and European Union) to underline what still needs to be done at the local level. In another section of the report, statistical information is given on the number of disabled people in Malta, their disabilities, their level of education, their rate of employment, and so on. Agencies funding such research often demand this type of data. Yet such data, and the significance attributed to it, works to objectify its subjects, denying the validity of their lived experiences. Statistical data makes it easier for policy makers to take certain decisions and not others. Spiteri Gingell (2011) wrote this study to promote independent living, but policy makers, too engrossed by this western model, did not consider that almost "half of Maltese young people aged 25–34 live with their parents" (Chetcuti 2014: n.p.). The majority of young Maltese people tend to live with their family of origin until they get married. Those who do not get married do not always set up their own living arrangements.

In Ghana, a similar pattern of borrowing and implementing concepts and policies can be observed. Statistical information is increasingly preferred over real-life situation studies, such as ethnographic and heuristic studies, in determining valid knowledges and their use in society. The implication is that real-life situations are relegated to the background as figures assume lordship in decision-making. This orientation gives rise to the equalization of diverse experiences, situations and conditions under figures, and conceals the multi-dimensional and ethical nature of the problems faced by people with disabilities. Figures help to sanitize and obliterate a person's actual situation. Such approaches also make it easier for disability issues to be converted into political issues, with the statistics cited to back baffling and dodgy claims.

Hiranandani (2005) asserts that the prevalence of certain ideas, models and inferences of disability over others means that alternative ways of defining embodied differences and dealing with them are automatically rejected in contexts where North-derived knowledge percolates. This knowledge tends to obfuscate more nuanced ways of dealing with issues on a contextual and situational level. As Grech (2011) also points out, where northern-derived knowledge and practices are adopted and used without taking the socio-economic, cultural and political context into consideration, the policies, research and services which ensue tend to be similar in outlook to those found in northern contexts, and might not be responsive to what is needed on a local basis, resulting in new forms of colonization.

Knowledge and Identity Formation

A lack of responsiveness to what is needed on a local basis arises from the disregard for local identities and the diversities that lie therein. Parekh (2007: 143) maintains that "identity formations are informed by geopolitical, socio-economic, cultural or ideological discourses", where these formations are "conflicting, competing, co-opting and intersecting, depending on locatedness and positionality". It should be underlined at this stage that Parekh draws upon the work of key postcolonial scholars such as Spivak (Landry and Maclean 1996), Mohanty (1984) and Grewal (1996), among others to come up with this synthesis.

Connell on the other hand speaks about social ontoformativity (Soldatic 2013). She also believes that southern impaired bodies are socially embedded in geopolitical relations of power, which means that disability is caused by structural, social and attitudinal factors both internal to and external to the nation state (Connell 2011). Meekosha and Soldatic (2011) argue that this theory helps to reconcile the politics of impairment with that of disability—two aspects to the equation which North-derived epistemologies tend to keep apart.

Although the above-mentioned exponents underline that there have been alliances between different disability movements within and without particular nation states, there is also competitiveness among various disabled groups and individuals on the basis of gender, age-differentiated constituencies, ethnicity, type of impairment, caste and/or marital status, among others, even within one given nation state. It is for this reason that postcolonial Black feminist disability theory and praxis also adopts an intersectional approach. Hill Collins (1991), one of the first exponents of this approach, underlines that change can only occur when those standing at the intersection of hegemonic systems of oppression use this position to understand where systems of inequality come together.

Those who study social inequality in countries situated in the global North tend to blame this on structural and attitudinal factors embedded in one particular geopolitical space. They look to the nation state to remove barriers to participation, inclusion and representation (Meekosha and Soldatic 2011). Countries situated in the global South, however, are not always in a position to protect their citizens from the atrocities committed in the name of neo-liberalism and globalization.

We adopt postcolonial Black feminist disability theory (Parekh 2007) because it seeks to destabilize the normalizing and homogenizing impulses found in imperialist and nationalist practices and discourses in the field of disability studies. The validity of this theory and praxis stems from the fact that it seeks to study lived experiences, and by so doing helps give value to collective knowledge, political engagement and the ethics of responsibility adopted by those involved in these stories. The postcolonial Black feminist disability framework is therefore concerned with how neocolonial or imperialist systems and operations of power conflate at the intersection of gender, race and disability in particular spaces and moments. The way disabled people are perceived impacts on the way they position and locate themselves, which in turn affects how they are treated by others (Grech 2011). Thus,

Parekh (2007: 144) maintains that the advantage of this framework is that it projects the idea that the self is constantly in the making, and reconstituted by multiple and intersecting identities which have an effect on the person's agency in the community, nation and the world.

While this theoretical framework analyzes the politics of the body, it also sustains that the body is political (Butler 1990). The body, whether female, disabled, racialized, queer and/or postcolonial, is the object of scrutiny by policy makers and resource providers. For this reason, Parekh (2007: 149) maintains that bodies tend to be contested sites of denied or suppressed citizenship. The manner in which the bodies of disabled people are treated through policy must therefore be a critical object of concern and scrutiny to ensure they do not become sites of denied or suppressed citizenship in the global South. At the same time postcolonial Black feminist disability theory conflates positionality and situatedness with resistance and change.

In effect, this theoretical framework underlines the relevance of situatedness and locatedness even when appropriating knowledge and tools envisaged for other contexts. Since disability intersects with class, gender, nation, sexual orientation and religion, among other identities, resistance and solidarity are generated based on transversal politics (Grewal 1996). Individuals or groups undergoing oppression on one or multiple levels can understand the oppression faced by others on another level.

The Social Construction of 'Normality'

Parekh (2007: 157) notes that a number of governments—ex-colonies or neocolonized—tend to favour certain types of approach to disease and disability when they want to attract international support and/or investment. It is these paradigms which need to be critiqued, and hence the relevance of disability studies within certain contexts. In the case of Malta, a country at the fringes of Europe, our policies in the economic, cultural, educational and social fields have to abide by the directives issued by the various entities that make up the European Union. In the social field, policy makers and service providers are constantly mulling over who is 'normal', 'normalcy', 'normality', 'norm' and 'average' when it comes to designing policies and implementing them (see Wendell 1997).

In Ghana, the economic, cultural, educational and social fields depend on the directives of international financial and lending institutions and other supporting agencies, and on the conditionalities of loans and grants in financing budgets. Concepts such as normalcy and the normal are thus usually defined, essentialized and imposed by such institutions, especially insurance agencies and state bureaucracies (Hiranandani 2005), rather than by the local experiences and lived contexts of the recipients.

Stone (1999: 4) suggests that the concept of disability in the global North arose from a particular emphasis on "urbanisation, industrialisation, the rise of the medical and rehabilitative professions, and the creation of the welfare state which differentiated between the disabled and the non-disabled." This is not always the case in some contexts in the global South. The differentiation between the abled and the disabled in the global North sets down a basis for inequality deriving from the ability or fitness to work or not to work (Wendell 1997). States, corporations and employers in the global South dependent on financial packages deriving from the global North tend to adopt such distinctions between those who have the capacity to work and those who do not. At the same time, this is not the paradigm that is used in different contexts to decide who is disabled or not.

Social Justice in Disability Issues

Governments and disability activists in the global South promote human rights-based policies and programs for people with disabilities (Groce et al. 2011: 1495). Soldatic (2013) feels that this approach will not help activists, policy makers and/or scholars redress the situation beyond the means offered by the Convention on the Rights of Persons with Disabilities, an issue which needs to be taken into consideration in a disability studies for the global South. Meekosha and Soldatic (2011) observe that impairment is often caused by policies and decisions enacted beyond the borders of a given nation state in the global South. Transnational companies as well as supranational organizations with their headquarters in the global North promote the deregulation and liberalization of the market. Governments in the global South, in a bid to attract foreign investors or in response to structural adjustment directives foisted on them, retract social protection and state social provision (Soldatic and Biyanwila 2010). This means that people are often forced to work in abysmal working conditions which can lead to death or impairment. The nation state, the locus of redress according to the CRPD, is powerless to do anything about this since it is dependent on foreign handouts from powerful countries or agencies.

When studying the experiences of disabled people living in the global South, we cannot limit the analysis to personal, group or systemic levels. Instead, we need to go beyond the nation state to find the causes of impairment and for redress (Soldatic 2013).

Conclusion

We have tried to delineate what a disability studies for the global South should incorporate. We have dwelt mainly on underlining why dependence on western knowledge does not always explicate what is happening in the South. Empowerment, argues Hill Collins (1991: 230), "involves rejecting the dimensions of knowledge, whether personal, cultural, or institutional", and acquiring "a way of knowing that enables individuals to grasp the relations between history and biography".

Epistemologies deriving from the North tend to forget that a country's geopolitical position, histories, experiences and knowledges need to be taken into consideration in policies and decisions intended to empower disabled people. These also need to be taken into consideration when promoting inclusion into diverse social milieus. An interventionist postcolonial pedagogy is therefore needed to recuperate "alternative" experiences and knowledges. Ghosh (1998) argues that in spite of these limitations, we need to continue doing research which will help us translate grass roots knowledge into meaningful concepts and actions.

As Said (1994: 245) postulates, the revisionist task of explaining ourselves to ourselves is facilitated by the fact that we are placed at an intersection of a system of differences (Abu-Lughod 1991: 140). Abu-Lughod (1991) defines scholars whose identity is shaped by their exposure to knowledge produced, published and/or disseminated abroad as caught in this intersection of difference. The inherent contradictions within enunciative positions derives from our liminal location as the global order interacts and intersects with our local social milieu. This split in the self can help generate awareness of one's positionality within the structures within which we are implicated.

Kaplan (1994: 143) observes that scholars can use the dialectical space emanating from these inherent contradictions within enunciative positionalities to explore the interplay between repression and resistance. New research methods and theories can develop when researchers explore situated experiences (Hill Collins 1991: 7; Tuhiwai Smith 1999). The revisionist or recuperative projects undertaken by subaltern subjects need to historicize and theorize the position of the present and the past in order to map action for the future.

Greenman (1996: 50) subscribes to the idea that when subalterns make use of western epistemologies, methodologies and enunciative codes to explore a given context, they should be deconstructing static perceptions of the 'Otherized' group, individual or nation. Pratt (1992: 7) adds that in the process of depiction, idioms and tools appropriated from the colonizer are transformed, challenging western and ableist notions of resistance and agency. These revisionist projects also help disrupt the prevailing image that disabled people in developing countries are victims of circumstance, which renders them passive or lacking in creativity. As Wolf (1996) underlines, when western epistemologies and enunciative codes are adapted or disrupted in this way, researchers learn more about their communities of derivation while teaching the minority world about themselves.

Postcolonial feminists recommend an ethic of reciprocity when carrying out research with, for, by and from silenced individuals and groups (Lal 1996). This ethic of reciprocity can be attained when the research is undertaken with and for the benefit of the participants, since its main objective is to bring change through consciousness raising among the participants themselves as well as the authorities concerned (Hastrup 1992). The knowledge created and the process through which it was created should serve as a site of resistance (Hondagneu-Sotelo 1996: 109).

Some academics situated in the global South are afraid that by appropriating western epistemologies and enunciative codes they are assisting in the replication and consolidation of the language of power and privilege (John 1989: 72). Ghosh

(1998) is also concerned that by using English as our means of communication with diverse communities, we are at the same time restricting access to knowledge produced collaboratively in the field, as we have already noted.

We believe that the English language cannot be ignored in discussing and communicating knowledge. Instead, the language can be used to "talk back" (Pennycook 1994) through the deconstruction of assumptions and by interrogating situations. Nonetheless, the study of life experiences should take into consideration the collaborative production of knowledge on disability and new conceptual models that can be developed through the interaction with the vernaculars since they are the main communicative vehicles of the majority of people in the global South.

References

Abu-Lughod, L. (1991). Writing against culture. In R. Fox (Ed.), *Recapturing anthropology* (pp. 137–162). Santa Fe, NM: School of American Research Press.

Adjoe, C. (2007). *Language policy and planning in Ghana: A monolingual ideology, ethos and discourses in a multilingual society?* Unpublished PhD dissertation, London University.

Alatas, S. F. (2003). Academic dependency and the global division of labour in the Social Sciences. *Sociology, 51*(6), 599–613.

Barker, C. (2010). Interdisciplinary dialogues: Disability and postcolonial studies. *Review of Disability Studies: An International Journal, 6*(3), 15–24.

Bloor, D. (1991). *Knowledge and social imagery*. Chicago: The Chicago University Press.

Briskin, L., & Coulter, R. (1992). Feminist pedagogy: Challenging the normative. *Canadian Journal of Education, 17*(3), 247–263.

Butler, J. (1990). *Gender trouble. Feminism and the subversion of identity*. New York: Routledge.

Chetcuti, K. (2014, February 2). *Half of 25-34 year-olds still living with parents*. Timesofmalta.com. Retrieved April 6, 2014, from http://www.timesofmalta.com/articles/view/20140202/local/half-of-25-34-year-olds-still-living-with-parents.505083.

Chiseri-Strater, E., & Stone Sunstein, B. S. (1997). *Fieldworking: Reading and writing research*. Upper Saddle River, NJ: Prentice Hall.

Connell, R. (2011). Southern bodies and disability: Re-thinking concepts. *Third World Quarterly, 32*(8), 1369–1381.

Cutajar, J. (2009). "Let me learn". The use of Western derived epistemologies and in/dependence in Maltese classrooms. Paper presented during *The First Malta International Forum on Learning*, Dolmen Hotel, 25–29 June 2009.

Ghai, A. (2002). Disabled women: An excluded agenda of Indian feminism. *Hypatia, 17*(3), 49–66.

Ghosh, B. (1998). *The postcolonial bazaar: Thoughts on teaching the market in postcolonial objects*. Retrieved April 30, 2008, from http://jefferson.village.virginia.edu/pmc/text-only/issue.998/9.1ghosh.txt.

Grech, S. (2011). Recolonising debates or perpetuated coloniality? Decentring the spaces of disability, development and community in the global South. *International Journal of Inclusive Education, 15*(1), 87–100.

Greenman, N. (1996). More than a mother. Some Tewa women reflect on Gia. In G. Etter-Lewis & M. Foster (Eds.), *Unrelated kin. Race and gender in women's personal narratives* (pp. 49–67). New York: Routledge.

Grewal, I. (1996). *Home and harem: Nation, gender, empire and the cultures of travel*. Leicester: Leicester University Press.

Groce, N., Kett, M., Lang, R., & Trani, J. F. (2011). Disability and poverty: The need for a more nuanced understanding of implications for development policy and practice. *Third World Quarterly, 32*(8), 1493–1513.

Haraway, D. (1988). Situated Knowledge: The science question in feminism and the privilege of partial perspective. *Feminist Studies, 14*(3), 575–599.

Hastrup, K. (1992). Writing the ethnography. State of the art. In J. Okely & H. Callaway (Eds.), *Anthropology and autobiography* (pp. 116–133). London: Routledge.

Hill Collins, P. (1991). *Black feminist thought. Knowledge, consciousness, and the politics of empowerment*. New York: Routledge.

Hiranandani, V. (2005). Towards a critical theory of disability in social work. *Critical Social Work*, 6(1). Retrieved September 9, 2013, from http://www1.uwindsor.ca/criticalsocialwork/towards-a-critical-theory-of-disability-in-social-work.

Hondagneu-Sotelo, P. (1996). Immigrant women and paid domestic work. Research, theory and activism. In H. Gottfried (Ed.), *Feminism and social change. Bridging theory and practice* (pp. 105–122). Urbana: University of Illinois.

John, M. E. (1989). Postcolonial feminists in the western intellectual field: Anthropologists and native informants. *Inscriptions, 5*, 49–73.

Kaplan, C. (1994). The politics of location as transnational feminist practice. In I. Grewal & C. Kaplan (Eds.), *Scattered hegemonies. Postmodern and transitional feminist practices* (pp. 137–152). London: University of Minnesota Press.

Karthigesu, R. (1996). *Mass media and cross cultural communication: Malaysian study*. Interim Report. Singapore: AMIC.

Lal, J. (1996). Situating locations: The politics of self, identity and 'Other' in living and writing the text. In D. L. Wolf (Ed.), *Feminist dilemmas in fieldwork* (pp. 185–214). Boulder: Westview Press.

Landry, D., & Maclean, G. (1996). *The Spivak reader: Selected works of Gayati Chakravorty Spivak*. New York: Routledge.

Lengermann, P. M., & Niebrugge, G. (2008). Contemporary feminist theory. In G. Ritzer (Ed.), *Sociological theory* (pp. 450–498). Boston: McGraw-Hill Higher Education.

Mazrui, A. (1995). The 'Other' as the 'Self' under cultural dependency: The impact of the postcolonial university. In G. Brinker-Gabler (Ed.), *Encountering the other(s)* (pp. 333–362). Albany: Suny P.

Meekosha, H. (2011). Decolonising disability: Thinking and acting globally. *Disability & Society, 26*(6), 667–682.

Meekosha, H., & Soldatic, K. (2011). Human rights and the global South: The case of disability. *Third World Quarterly, 32*(8), 1383–1397.

Miles, M. (2007). *International strategies for disability—related work in developing countries: Historical, modern and critical reflections*. Retrieved July 28, 2014, from http://www.independentliving.org/docs7/miles200701.pdf.

Mohanty, C. T. (1984). Under western eyes: Feminist scholarship and colonial discourses. *Boundary 2, 12*(3), 333–358.

Parekh, P. N. (2007). Gender, disability and the postcolonial nexus. *Wagadu: Journal of Transnational Women's and Gender Studies, 4*, 142–161.

Pennycook, A. (1994). *The cultural politics of English as an international language*. Harlow: Pearson Education.

Phoenix, A. (2012). De-colonising practices: Negotiating narratives from racialised and gendered experiences of education. In H. S. Mirza & C. Joseph (Eds.), *Black and postcolonial feminisms in new times. Researching educational inequalities* (pp. 101–114). London: Routledge.

Pratt, M. L. (1992). *Imperial eyes. Travel writing and transculturation*. London: Routledge.

Rich, A. (2003). Notes towards a politics of location. In R. Lewis & S. Mills (Eds.), *Feminist postcolonial theory: A reader* (pp. 29–42). Edinburgh: Edinburgh University Press.

Richardson, L., & St. Pierre, E. A. (2005). Writing: A method of inquiry. In N. K. Denzin & Y. S. Lincoln (Eds.), *Handbook of qualitative research* (3rd ed., pp. 959–978). Thousand Oaks, CA: Sage.

Said, E. W. (1994). *Culture and imperialism*. New York: Knopf.
Soldatic, K. (2013). The transnational sphere of justice: Disability praxis and the politics of impairment. *Disability & Society, 28*(6), 744–755. Retrieved from http://dx.doi.org/10.1080/09687599.2013.802218.
Soldatic, K., & Biyanwila, S. J. (2010). Tsunami and the southern disabled body. *Global South: SEPHIS, 6*(3), 75–84.
Spiteri Gingell, D. (2011). *Policy on independent supported living for disabled persons in Malta*. St. Venera: Kummissjoni Nazzjonali Persuni b'Dizabilita'.
Stone, E. (1999). Disability and development in the majority world. In E. Stone (Ed.), *Disability and development: Learning from action and research on disability in the majority world* (pp. 1–18). Leeds: The Disability Press.
Tuhiwai Smith, L. (1999). *Decolonizing methodologies: Research and indigenous people*. London: Zed Books Ltd.
Wendell, S. (1997). Towards a feminist theory of disability. In L. J. Davis (Ed.), *The disability studies reader* (pp. 260–278). New York: Routledge.
Wolf, D. L. (1996). Situating feminist dilemmas in fieldwork. In D. L. Wolf (Ed.), *Feminist dilemmas in fieldwork* (pp. 1–55). Boulder: Westview Press.
Yuval-Davis, N. (1997). *Gender and Nation*. London: Sage.

Chapter 33
Revising and Using the Social Model in the Global South: A Venezuelan Exploration

Manuel Aramayo, Mark H. Burton, and Carolyn Kagan

Introduction

In this chapter we consider the 'social model of disability', developed largely by disabled activists in the UK, in relation to the different context and social realities of the global South, via a case study of disability theory and policy in Venezuela. We all value this approach to understanding the nature of disability, the realities of life as experienced by disabled people, and 'what is to be done' to improve the situation. However, we also take the view that ideological, theoretical and institutional reforms can be hard to understand, and that enthusiasm for the positive elements can obscure other elements that are less helpful (Burton and Kagan 2006).

The so-called British social model of disability arose from the disabled activists' movement in the UK (Union of the Physically Impaired Against Segregation (UPIAS) 1974) in the context of their struggle against segregation and exclusion. This small group of physically disabled activists questioned received beliefs about the cause of their dependency, re-framing it in terms of the disabling barriers created by a world designed for able-bodied living.

M. Aramayo
Monteávila University, Caracas, Venezuela

M.H. Burton (✉)
Independent scholar-activist/Manchester Metropolitan University, Manchester, UK
e-mail: mark.burton@poptel.org

C. Kagan
Manchester Metropolitan University, Manchester, UK

S. Grech, K. Soldatic (eds.), *Disability in the Global South*,
International Perspectives on Social Policy, Administration, and Practice,
DOI 10.1007/978-3-319-42488-0_33

> This interpretation involved a clear distinction between 'impairment' and 'disability'. The meaning of disability was radically redefined … promoting the argument that disability can be interpreted … as being socially created. (Finkelstein and French 1998: 170)

This redefinition both resulted from and implied a conscious prioritisation of political effort towards the changing of society—emancipation—rather than towards ameliorative or compensatory strategies. Oliver (1990) took this thinking further with a materialist theoretical account. While it had some similarities with other approaches that emerged in the context of critiques of the 'medical model' (e.g. deviancy theory, normalisation and social role valorisation theory), this social model was not so much a theory as an explicitly political orientation that problematised the oppression of disabled people, as segregated and excluded by physical and social barriers.

The social model did not deny the reality of physical impairment. As Finkelstein makes clear,

> The agreed UPIAS interpretation was that, although it may be a *tragedy* to have an impairment, it is *oppression* that characterises the way our society is organised so that we are prevented from functioning [author's emphasis]. (Finkelstein 2001: 2)

Within the social model, disability is a social construction whereby the physical problem is used ideologically to construct the relations of oppression and discrimination. For example, the inability of a person to perform the actions of conventional writing becomes a barrier to educational participation and achievement. In this example disability is the product of the failure of educational provision to make it possible for the person to take part, for example through appropriate technology and personal support.

So, as the product of a social movement, the social model was, at least initially, more a counter-hegemonic ideology than a theory of disability and social relations: its protagonists varied in their emphasis, from a more environmental focus to a more explicitly political one. Nevertheless, the social model became a powerful tool in the fight against exclusion, helping to prioritise social and environmental adjustments, a key feature of present British anti-discrimination legislation.

There is something of a problem in referring to *the* social model. Our point of departure is the materialist social model stemming from UPIAS, Finkelstein, French, Oliver and Barnes. Oliver (1990) himself explores cultural and ideological dimensions within the framework of critical political economy (Priestley 1998), but later writers have added other emphases, to the extent that these have tended to stretch and maybe rupture the boundaries of the social model (Thomas 2004). There have been culturalist and feminist versions, and postmodern thinking has also been imported. More recent work on the body itself, and hence impairment, has challenged the original prioritisation of socially imposed disability. We have not the space to explore these paths, but acknowledge the intersectionality of oppressive domains: disabled people are disabled-in-society, at the same time as being women or men, gay or straight, black or white and so on, and these dimensions are not reducible to one another. This is not to replace the materialist social model but to enrich it.

The social model was the product of subaltern action within the global North. But that subalternity was within the context of a welfare system in a core country of the world system, so much of the critique of social model protagonists was orientated to a developed but paternalist system of health, education and welfare. The social model incorporated elements of the modernist world view, not least the idea of the rational administration of a cadre of welfare workers (health, education, social service, etc.) and the use of the concept of 'independence'. As such the approach had something in common with the radical critiques of writers such as Illich (see for example Illich et al. 1977), which identified problems arising from the rationalised social arrangements of late modernity. The British social model, then, is ambiguously located within, and also in opposition to, aspects of the modern paradigm of social administration, and within that it is contextualised in the specific social reality of the western European post-war welfare settlement. It may therefore be interesting to see what happens when the approach is transported to a different context, in the global South (some decades later), in critical dialogue with disabled people and their allies: there has been little discussion of this question (Grech 2009; Díaz 2012) and so far as we know, no empirically based study.

The first author of this chapter (Aramayo) became interested in and studied the social model during a post-doctoral fellowship in Manchester in 1999. On his return to Caracas, he worked with a group of disabled students at the Universidad Central de Venezuela (UCV) to critically explore the social model from a Venezuelan, and Latin American perspective (Aramayo 2005a). We describe this process and perspective on the social model that emerged from it. We then look at the parallel development of disability policy in Venezuela from the 'Punto Fijo' period into the 'Bolivarian' period that followed the election of the reforming government of Hugo Chávez in 1999, drawing upon this new local interpretation of the UK social model. Finally, we reflect on the difficulties of interpretation and implementation of the social model in Venezuela, in order to address the question: how relevant is the social model to the lives of disabled people in low- to middle-income countries?

Reviewing and Revising the Social Model in Venezuela

The project of reviewing the UK social model in Venezuela began in 2000, coinciding with the first years of the government of Hugo Chávez, who had come to power in 1999 on a wave of popular support with a reforming agenda under the banner of 'Bolivarismo' and (later) '21st Century Socialism', two broad and associated but poorly defined ideological tendencies with a populist, egalitarian, nationalist (anti-imperialist) and democratic orientation. The impact of the disaster of floods and landslides in late 1999 that affected Vargas State and parts of Caracas coincided with the work described here. The country, meanwhile, was beginning to become politically polarised between supporters of the government and its policies and its opponents, culminating in the attempted coup of April 2002; the 2-month struggle over the lock-out and re-establishment of control over the management of the state oil company (December 2002); and the 2004 campaign for the recall of President Chávez and its defeat, with massive demonstrations by the two sides. This all made for a difficult context, politically and economically, and the tensions extended to the university where engagement with the social model was beginning. The context in which a locally appropriate model of disability would be making its proposals was a combination of possibility for radical change and frustrating factors that also impacted on civil society.

The situation for disabled students was not easy. In the year 2000, as Aramayo describes it:

> Some professionals suffering from blindness or motor problems have graduated from the UCV since the 70's; they are survivors of the battle against inequality. There are no people or procedures responsible for their admission, support or monitoring. Their admission was the only benefit received from the University. Many spend years fighting and suffering from frustration without receiving the smallest sign of support or assistance! (Aramayo 2008: 67)

The differing socio-historical development of the two countries ruled out the possibility of simply applying the English vision to this Latin American context. Aramayo decided to undertake a small qualitative research study with disabled students, to reformulate, rebuild and rethink the model with those most affected—Venezuelans with disabilities—to understand the meaning and nature of the experience of being disabled in Venezuela and how to define actions to improve the situation.

> The main proposed objective led us to select a method of working that would allow us to apprehend a personal subject, specific to the socio-familial context, influenced both by the moment and circumstances of each disability and determined by the circumstances that differentiate a deaf from a blind person or from someone who has spent their life in a wheelchair. (Aramayo 2005a: 88)

An unstructured, depth interview method was chosen with data to be analysed using the method of grounded theory (Strauss and Corbin 1990). Eleven students, aged between 20 and 60, from the university's faculty of political science in the year 2001 participated. Four were female and seven male, and they came from different socio-economic classes. They all had severe motor, visual or auditory impairments, variously of congenital, developmental or traumatic origin.

The students described objects, people, settings, events, actions, emotions and aspirations in their everyday conversations. A vision for a new social system was revealed, one in which disabled people, their concerns and their participation were at the core, and in which all the contributory elements were in constant and reciprocal interaction, as shown in Fig. 33.1: the legal setting; the state as a promoter of policies and executor of plans and programmes; institutions working towards inclusion; professionals as active agents of social change; support groups, the community and family, as partners; and most importantly, the organised movement of Venezuelans with disabilities. This is what became known as the Venezuelan social model of disability. Like the British model it is less a theory of disability than an action-oriented depiction of the situation facing disabled people and what needs to be done.

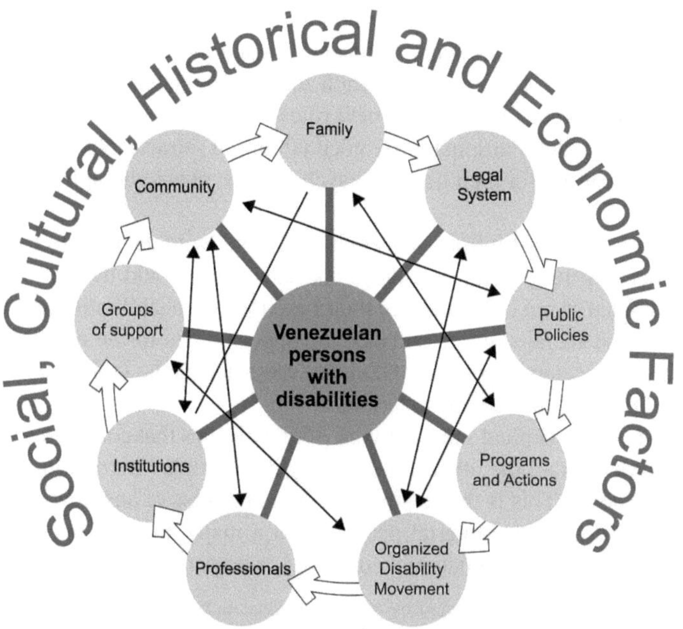

Fig. 33.1 Elements of the Venezuelan social model that emerged from the qualitative study

Issues that emerged from the data, which help us see both the similarities with and differences from the British social model, are summarised below.

1. Participants' responses to and perceptions of their own and others' impairments and disabilities were a highly emotionally charged area, with the expression of strong feelings of shame, hopelessness and difficulty, sitting alongside determination and a yearning to be seen as people and be included in everyday life. Their feelings were rooted in the responses of others and the contradictory social dimensions of admiration, support, respect and acceptance as well as rejection and maltreatment.
2. Elements of both medical and social thinking were present. The salience of a medical perspective and references to impairments and medical terminology arose spontaneously. However, participants also saw the restrictions on their activity and participation as a social phenomenon.

   The social burden of disability is not how we see ourselves, but how others see us. Being in a wheelchair is synonymous with begging, it's synonymous with being unable to work, because society itself, in one way or another, sees it that way.
3. The role of positive self-esteem was recognised, and participants considered that collective identity was built from social interaction, friendships, groups, and participation in rights-based organisations.

   Disability is a great social problem. The problem is not personal; it is collective.

4. Individual problems (such as mobility, transportation, Braille) were embedded in and inseparable from social problems (including information, sensitisation, awareness (conscientisation), education and the sluggishness of the institutions).
5. Professionals were visualised in new roles, appropriate to the as-yet unarticulated social model. Participants avoided talking of miracles, but did design new role specifications for their doctors, psychologists, physiotherapists and the other experts.
6. Reform of social institutions was envisaged along with the need to form support networks. Institutions for assistance and education would need to be renewed and redefined to not only embrace their functions of rehabilitation, but also offer personal and social skills to enhance the opportunities for an equal, active participation in society. However, the family remained as the indispensable starting and end point of this interactive system.
7. The primary conceptual mini-network of experiences that conditions everything else and defines all the other dimensions with multiple interrelations was at the economic level. This is the leit-motif or basic premise of any new model of disability in Venezuela. Material poverty was a major theme—not just personal poverty but poverty in a national context. As one participant pointed out.

> We are disproportionately affected by poverty in Venezuela. There are three million disabled "poor" and we know what the situation of the poor person is in Venezuela. They do not have access to healthcare [this was in 2000], they do not have access to education, they do not have access to work, they do not have access to many things, including all the social limitations they face because of the environment or architecture. They are culturally deprived.

Disability worsened the grave financial situation in which participants found themselves.

> Venezuela is not designed for disabled Venezuelans. In fact, it's not even designed so one can eat because what it says in the [old] constitution about 2 per cent of employees having to be disabled has never been enforced. That upsets me, I have to eat also, I have basic needs that I need to take care of and I can't because I'm disabled and it really angers me.

A dramatic panorama of helplessness and hopelessness was presented, but at the same time a refusal to be cast in the position of objects of charity was evident.

> Unfortunately, what happens in this country is that most people who end up in a wheelchair are poor. It's not about giving them things. I have never asked anyone for anything. I have been through difficult situations. My family did not have enough to eat after my accident, never enough to eat.

The daily hassles of being disabled in Venezuela put further financial strain on participants.

> I can't get around by bus because I can't get on them. That means I have a lot more expenses than you because you can get around just fine.

In sum, the complex reality of disability in Venezuela is both a social and collective problem, well beyond the personal level, because the impact of limitations and impairments is felt more deeply due to the way society is constituted and organised.

Participants described not just the social realities of being disabled but also provided a vision of what is needed to improve the situation of disabled people. It is this that gives the model its prescriptive form. Fundamental to the implementation of change is a solid foundation of a movement of disabled people.

> There is no way to navigate from the individual to the social and explain disability within a new paradigm without the involvement of the *movement of people with disabilities* that in our country is still incipient and, rather like the wider Venezuelan problem, is marked by disunity, rivalry, disorganization, politicking and lack of communication. (Aramayo 2005a: 189)

The integration of these basic ideas and concepts gradually created (as in the UK in the 1970s) a new, paradigmatic *theory of disability from a social perspective.* It is summed up as:

> The establishment of a legislative framework, that articulates new requirements and rights, is followed by the preparation of well defined policies, complemented by plans and programs that are translated into concrete action. The responsibility is both individual and collective. Leadership comes from the organized movements that keep vigil that their rights be upheld. The State, professionals, family and communities are only active companions in this process, in most cases co-participants, but never the leading protagonist. (Aramayo 2005b: 9)

Policy Development, Advances and Disappointments

Since the social model can be interpreted, both in the UK and in Venezuela, as a call for social change, it can be used as a kind of standpoint from which to review and evaluate policies and their implementation. This also subjects the model to an evaluation in terms of its relevance to the social reality to which it claims to speak. When confronted with the reality of policy formulation and implementation in complex and contradictory circumstances, does the social model (in general, or in its Venezuelan manifestation) help to navigate these contexts, conceptually and practically? We will therefore briefly sketch the characteristics of Venezuelan social policy for disabled people, with particular focus on educational settings, in the 1990s (before the Chávez Government) and afterwards, the periods immediately before and after the adoption of Venezuela's new constitution in 1999. It should be noted that the earlier period predates the work to describe a Venezuelan social model.

Before 1996, there had been gradual but very uneven change in the understanding of disability, with medical and educational models dominant. In concert with these developments there was a slow professionalisation of the field and the establishment of some services, particularly for school-age children (Torres 2007). In this, the picture is not unlike that in most middle-income countries, where specialist provision developed in the context of considerable unmet need.

In December 1996 the Ministry of Education, with its Resolution 2005, established a framework for school integration of the population defined as having special needs. Admission, continuation and completion was to be guaranteed in ordinary schools. There were to be support services, coordination of diagnoses, objectives, learning strategies, and assessments according to the characteristics of the students to adapt the curriculum. The Ministry of Education would develop courses, workshops and events for professional improvement.

However, the resolution paid insufficient attention to the resources and processes of pedagogy and support for the students and teachers needed for true inclusion (Aramayo 1999). As a result the resolution was poorly implemented. This is not unusual: in the enthusiasm of a new model (in this case integration) an over-optimistic estimation is made of what will be required and as a result there is poor planning and poor implementation. What became more evident, though, was the de-activation of special education; it continued to be the 'Cinderella' of the system. Government staff, including the Ministry of Education, effectively ignored it. The continued ignorance and prejudice towards disability and special education confined it to being a minority concern, forgotten, unproductive, and irrelevant to the country, absorbed as it was by other tasks arising from the crisis of neo-liberalism of the 1990s, which also brought the gradual decline in services to all Venezuelans.

A New Century

The Venezuelan constitution of 1999, produced by a constituent assembly and ratified by popular referendum, among other things provided a legal framework for the complete inclusion of disabled people in society. The *Constitution of the Bolivarian Republic of Venezuela* (Government of Venezuela 1999) and the *Law for People with Disability* (Government of Venezuela 2007) can be considered as 'advanced' in the Latin American context, emphasising the rights of disabled people as citizens and the State's responsibilities to them (see articles 81 and 86 of the constitution).

The question is whether this has led to lasting change. The state can establish the best policies, programmes and actions, and ensure that they should be upheld and invest the necessary resources, and the professionals and institutions can know and internalise the postulates of a social model, reinterpreted within the socio-historical context of the country. All of these factors will become agents of a new order, with the interactive factors comprising the new system underpinning the Venezuelan social model (see Fig. 33.1). However, the *sine qua non* condition is that they are led by a solid movement of disabled Venezuelans. This is another point of difference between the two countries. While in the UK, a social movement of people in situations of disability led the formulation of the social model and agitated for policy change, in Venezuela that movement is still incipient and changes in formulation and in policy have been adopted and promoted by internationally connected professionals. The emergence of some new groups, movements and associations claiming rights has been encouraging, although the organised movement of Venezuelans with disabilities has not manifested itself to the magnitude of those in England, Spain and other countries. It had seemed that everything was going to be different. The new constitution and disability law created high expectations. From 1999 a few social changes could be observed although the overall sadness of the situation became more acute as it became clear these expectations would not be realised. Disabled people remain marginalised in many ways. They may have the vote, but assuming public office is rarely a possibility. Unlike other sectors of Venezuelan society, they do not protest about their situation. Like other poor Venezuelans they tend to live in settings characterised by high levels of violence. Their economic, social and cultural rights are vulnerable. Many live in situations of poverty similar to or worse than the student participants in the research group and this perpetuates their discrimination, dominating their lives. People with physical and visual impairments are still begging on the streets and the 5 per cent mandatory employment targets (an advance on 2 per cent) are not being met, despite official announcements and inspections from the government-sponsored National Council for Disabled People (CONAPDIS).

So, for the Bolivarian period of the Fifth Republic led by the Chávez/Maduro Governments, the aims of policy have been set appropriately high, with an emphasis on citizenship and participation. There have been improvements in this period with positive redistributive policies but, as in many other areas of Venezuelan social policy, this has been uneven, marred by problems of implementation, including a vagueness as to how those social goals are to be realised. Although there has been some progress in reducing poverty, it has been difficult to provide decent jobs for poor Venezuelans. Economic problems still dominate the lived reality of disabled Venezuelans.

Perhaps this is not so surprising: it is important that we do not de-contextualise the field of disability policy here, any more than elsewhere. The following considerations are relevant.

1. At the outset of the Bolivarian period, the new government was faced with a distorted economy, and severe social and economic division, with some 80 per cent living in poverty at the start of the century.
2. The government's policies have been impaired by political polarisation and conflict (including the kind of sabotage that had by late 2013 led to a serious problem of price increases, and the violent opposition protests of early 2014), as well as by corruption and poor administrative capacity/competence.

It is in this turbulent political and economic context that we should consider failures to deliver on the vision of social inclusion for disabled Venezuelans as another demonstration of how disabled people are everywhere disadvantaged economically and politically, if to differing degrees in different contexts. Politically, the prospects for a strong and effective political movement of disabled people will be limited in a polarised political context where people are playing for high stakes—put simply, it is difficult for disabled people and their allies to be heard in such a storm! This is not a counsel of despair but a reminder that social change does not happen without a strong and 'politically canny' coalition, a social movement, that works inside and outside the official system, creating concrete examples of principled change and pressing for their wider adoption (Burton 1989). What this tells us about the social model in the Venezuelan context is that any change in the position of disabled people will be brought about by not only dealing with the multiple oppressions that society imposes, but also by navigating a turbulent social and political environment.

Reflecting on the Social Model on the Basis of the Venezuelan Experience

What, then, can we conclude about the nature of the social model in the two national contexts? What are the similarities and the differences?

It may help to view the model, borrowing metaphorically from Lakatos's (1970) theory of scientific research programmes, in terms of a hard core of essential propositions and an auxiliary set of propositions and adjustments that are not integral to the model. For Lakatos the test of the theory underpinning the research programme is whether it continues to lead to new discoveries without being disrupted by them. Applying the idea to the social model, we might ask whether the materialist core of the model enables its protagonists to develop praxis in other social contexts, in terms of both space-geography and time-history, where praxis means both understanding the social reality and prioritising action on it.

It should be clear by now that the core propositions of the social model have a robust generality across the two contexts. Disabled people are not disadvantaged because of their impairments, but because of the way they are treated by the society in which they live. Their impairments are real and the social nature of disability does not mean they can be ignored: there is a biomedical component in the social model in that access to adequate treatment and care is a right. But the pressing problem is social, which in turn calls for a politically effective movement to secure, and keep, real citizenship. Nevertheless, Venezuela has achieved the establishment of an emancipatory agenda at a political level which has contributed to a small degree to cultural change for disabled people (thus there seems to have been some progress towards the criteria established by Goodley (1996) of citizenship: struggle against a disabling culture and the establishment of an emancipatory agenda). The need for an effective social movement of disabled people is acknowledged by the model's protagonists but so far it is only at the beginning stages, a situation that in turn reflects the extreme disadvantage experienced by disabled people, for example in being able to get around, or to have time away from the day-to-day economic struggle of survival for the political struggle.

The setting may be different but the central theme of the agenda is the same in both places: this is the social model—the social account of how disability is constituted and what needs to be done about it. But that difference in national setting brings about a number of further differences.

Firstly, a greater emphasis is given to economic questions in the Venezuelan articulation of the model. The most obvious difference is the lack of the northern European welfare state with its safety net of economic support. This means disabled Venezuelans are inserted more fully into the daily economic struggle, with poverty a reality for most: in many cases they are economic actors rather than recipients of welfare payments. That makes the economic dimension in Venezuela more salient in individual lived experience. It is also there in the UK, but to a relatively lesser degree, being 'covered' by the state and its agencies, at least up to the present vicious onslaught of neo-liberal austerity policies (which have targeted welfare payments and housing subsidies for many disabled people). The two countries may be moving in opposite and convergent directions in this sense and it will be interesting to see what the eventual impact on their social models is.

Secondly, the British model emphasises 'independence' in a way that the Venezuelan model does not. While the British activists of UPIAS used the term a great deal, their meaning was not necessarily identical to the ideological usage that became dominant in British social policy, especially as the neo-liberal influence became hegemonic. For these activists, independence meant the right to live as they wanted and not in the kind of institutional settings that were the main option until the 1980s. It was perhaps an unfortunate term to have used since it is also a key building block of the individualism that characterises the neo-liberal assault on collective responsibility for welfare, which simultaneously valorises choice and turns clients and patients not into citizens but into consumers (Burton and Kagan 2006), recuperating the language of the original social model.

The Venezuelan model does not mention this notion of independence. In Venezuela, collectivism does seem to be stronger, culturally and politically, especially in the poorer sections of the population. This has been eroded in the UK, while the shortcomings of welfare bureaucracy have legitimated consumerist models. For British disability activists the struggle was *against* services, or rather against uniform, restrictive, segregative and de-humanising services. For disabled (and poor) Venezuelans the struggle is more a struggle *for* services, or rather for the provision of the assistance that is required. In both cases the ideal would be to have intelligent and effective supports when and where needed, but the difference in starting point means a different background against which emerges the social model, both as description of reality and agenda for change.

Thirdly, in the UK, the social model is the expression of the social movement of disabled people and their allies (families, policy activists, academics and reform-orientated workers in human services). There is an emerging movement in Venezuela, and the adoption of the social model has been more the result of scholar-activists and professionals, aware of experiences elsewhere.

And finally, the models emerged in different decades. In the UK the social model came into being in the 1970s while in Venezuela it only became formally known from 2001 as a result of Aramayo's work of reformulation described in this chapter.

Today it is used within the framework of the social inclusion policy orientation of the government's 21st-century socialism, if without a solid conceptualisation, being used more as a political slogan.

Conclusion

In the introduction to this chapter we noted that the British social model was not a theory of disability. Likewise, the Venezuelan social model that emerged from the research described here was also not a theory of disability. In both cases the aim was pragmatic and activist. Yet it is difficult to isolate such a model, as guide to action, from its meta-theoretical assumptions. Perhaps it makes more sense to see these social models as pragmatic theories of action that include some explicit and implicit propositions about the nature of disability in the national social context of the time. It seems to us that in this the Venezuelan social model is similar to the original materialist British social model in terms of its (Lakatosian) core.

If we consider this core, there is perhaps not really such a thing as a social model that belongs to a particular country. The particularities of each national context are those elements of the disabling system that will be emphasised differently in those national contexts (so, economics/poverty in Venezuela but independence in the UK). As we have seen, the social model has an invariant, materialist core that is ontological, epistemological and ethical. In that sense it is that unfashionable but necessary thing, a universal (Doyal and Gough 1984; Gómez and Dussel 2001: 63). This common core can be shared across cultures as a social and political vision of disability that demands an agenda of actions according to the distinctive contexts of each country and location.

So what does the experience of developing a Venezuelan social model tell us about the relevance of the social model for other low- and middle-income regional and national contexts? Our overall conclusions are suggestive but plausible. If the (material, theoretical) core of the model is the same in both the UK and Venezuela and this reflects a basic reality about disability in social contexts—but that the priorities for struggle and the balance of forces among actors are distinctive, reflecting the national political, social, cultural and economic context—then it seems possible that the same formula could apply elsewhere. Thus we suggest that disability is everywhere best understood as the imposition and limitation by social arrangements on people who are impaired, while the particular way of improving the situation will depend on the particularities of the context, not least the capacities of disabled people and their close allies (typically, but not exclusively, families) to organise in ways that define the problem and begin to act on it, while expanding their consciousness of themselves as social actors and of the social reality in which they are embedded. Just as in the Venezuelan case, we anticipate that social models will emerge with a similar invariant core but distinctly different pragmatic and programmatic elements that speak to and from the local cultural, political and economic reality.

References

Aramayo, M. (1999). *La Integración Escolar del Discapacitado: Una Revisión Crítica de la Resolución 2005* [Educational Integration of the Disabled: A Critical Review of Resolution 2005] (No. 07-18-4181). Caracas: CDCH: Universidad Central de Venezuela.

Aramayo, M. (2005a). *La discapacidad: Construcción de un modelo teórico venezolano [Disability: Construction of a Venezuelan theoretical model]*. Caracas: Fondo Editorial de la Facultad de Medicina: Universidad Central de Venezuela.

Aramayo, M. (2005b). *Universidad y Discapacidad [University and Disability]*. Caracas: Cátedra Libre de la Discapacidad, Universidad Central de Venezuela.

Aramayo, M. (2008). La UCV La casa que vence las sombras de la discapacidad? [The UCV: The house that defeats the shadows of disability?]. *Visión Ucevista, 9*, 66–72.

Burton, M. (1989). *Australian intellectual disability services: Experiments in social change: Working Paper in Building Community Strategies, No 1*. London: Kings Fund College. Retrieved from https://www.academia.edu/1193439/Australian_Intellectual_Disability_Services_Experiments_in_Social_Change.

Burton, M., & Kagan, C. (2006). Decoding valuing people. *Disability & Society, 21*(4), 299–313.

Díaz, R. (2012). Discapacidad y mirada colonial. Reflexiones desde perspectivas feministas y descoloniales [Disability and the colonial gaze. Reflections from feminist and de-colonial perspectives]. In M. E. Almeida & M. A. Angelino (Eds.), *Debates y perspectivas en torno a la discapacidad en América Latina* [Debates and perspectives on disability in Latin America] (pp. 27–61). Paraná, Argentina: Universidad Nacional de Entre Ríos. Retrieved from http://www.bibliotecavirtual.info/2013/05/debates-y-perspectivas-en-torno-a-la-discapacidad-en-america-latina/.

Doyal, L., & Gough, I. (1984). A theory of human needs. *Critical Social Policy, 4*(10), 6–38. doi:10.1177/026101838400401002.

Finkelstein, V. (2001). *The social model of disability repossessed. Disability studies archive UK*. University of Leeds. Retrieved from http://disability-studies.leeds.ac.uk/files/library/finkelstein-soc-mod-repossessed.pdf.

Finkelstein, V., & French, S. (1998). Towards a psychology of disability. In J. Swain, V. Finkelstein, & M. Oliver (Eds.), *Disabling barriers: Enabling environments* (pp. 26–332). London: Sage.

Gómez, F., & Dussel, E. (2001). Ethics is the original philosophy or, the barbarian words coming from the third world: An interview with Enrique Dussel. *Boundary, 28*(2), 19–73. Retrieved May 8, 2010, from http://bibliotecavirtual.clacso.org.ar/ar/libros/dussel/artics/gomez.pdf.

Goodley, D. (1996). Tales of hidden lives: A critical examination of life history research with people who have learning difficulties. *Disability & Society, 11*(3), 333–348. doi:10.1080/09687599627642.

Government of Venezuela. (1999). *Constitución de la República Bolivariana de Venezuela (1999)* [Constitution of the Bolivarian Republic of Venezuela (1999)]. Retrieved from http://www.tsj.gov.ve/legislacion/constitucion1999.htm.

Government of Venezuela. (2007). *Ley para las Personas con Discapacidad (2007)* [Law for People with Disability (2007)]. Retrieved from http://www.conapdis.gob.ve/index.php/ley-para-las-personas-con-discapacidad.

Grech, S. (2009). Disability, poverty and development: Critical reflections on the majority world debate. *Disability & Society, 24*(6), 771–784. doi:10.1080/09687590903160266.

Illich, I., Zola, I. K., McKnight, J., Caplan, J., & Shaiken, H. (1977). *Disabling professions*. London: Marion Boyars.

Lakatos, I. (1970). Falsification and the methodology of scientific research programmes. In I. Lakatos & A. Musgrave (Eds.), *Criticism and the growth of knowledge* (pp. 91–195). Cambridge: Cambridge University Press. Retrieved from http://www.csun.edu/~vcsoc00i/classes/s680f11/Lakatos.pdf.

Oliver, M. (1990). *The politics of disablement*. Basingstoke: Macmillan Education.

Priestley, M. (1998). Constructions and creations: Idealism, materialism and disability theory. *Disability & Society, 13*(1), 75–94.

Strauss, A., & Corbin, J. (1990). *Basics of qualitative research: Grounded theory procedures and techniques*. Newbury Park, CA: Sage.

Thomas, C. (2004). How is disability understood? An examination of sociological approaches. *Disability & Society, 19*(6), 569–583. doi:10.1080/0968759042000252506.

Torres, M. (2007). *La Educación Especial en Venezuela* [Special Education in Venezuela]. Caracas: Universidad Pedagógica Experimental Libertador, Instituto Pedagógico de Caracas.

Union of the Physically Impaired Against Segregation (UPIAS). (1974). *Aims and policy statement*. Retrieved from http://disability-studies.leeds.ac.uk/archiveuk/UPIAS/UPIAS.pdf.

Chapter 34
Disability Research in the Global South: Working from a Local Approach

Marcia Rioux, Paula Campos Pinto, Jose Viera, and Rados Keravica

Walking into the unregulated slum for the first time and as the only non-Indian participatory action researcher, I thought I had some ideas for getting children with disabilities into pre-schools and schools. I stepped cautiously through the sewage running on the pathways (in my sandals). And tried not to look horrified by the live wires hanging down nearly to the pathway and the children romping around those wires. I held the grant along with my Indian partner who ran a disability organization. But I was not in charge of the project—I had lots of ideas but I had been approached only after there was a pretty concrete plan for the work. I was technical support. That project (lasting five-plus years and still ongoing) taught me a lot. It was not my first experience in international North–South work but one in which I was able to reflect on the meaning of emancipatory research and the role that northern researchers can play constructively and proactively. (Marcia Rioux, unpublished field notes)

M. Rioux (✉)
York University, Toronto, ON, Canada

Disability Rights Promotion International, Toronto, ON, Canada
e-mail: mrioux@yorku.ca

P.C. Pinto
University of Lisbon, Lisbon, Portugal

Disability Rights Promotion International, Lisbon, Portugal

J. Viera
Disability Rights Promotion International, Buenos Aires, Argentina

R. Keravica
Disability Rights Promotion International, Belgrade, Serbia

S. Grech, K. Soldatic (eds.), *Disability in the Global South*, International Perspectives on Social Policy, Administration, and Practice, DOI 10.1007/978-3-319-42488-0_34

Reflection on research models and agendas comes to the surface when northern and southern colleagues work together on research in the global South.[1] Here we do not distinguish between quantitative and qualitative methodologies, nor do we differentiate which development agency or funder supports the research. The research methodology does not drive the research, but is a tool used to meet the needs of the research question(s). In this chapter we talk about the way in which northern researchers see their role in research and the role they play during the process of the work. Projects start and are carried out with very different impacts and have very different potential for sustainability and transformation.

Thomas Kuhn in his famous book *The Structure of Scientific Revolutions* (Khun 1962) suggested that there are paradigm shifts in science. They occur when fundamental theories, hypotheses, data, and underlying assumptions are questioned and demonstrated to be wrong and new fundamental concepts replace them. Sometimes one will occur during a century. Occasionally, they will be more frequent and sometimes less (Zubrow 2014). There have been several important paradigm shifts in the field of disability over the past 40 years. The first one was the move from the medical/charity or rehabilitation model to the social model (Oliver 1992) and then to the human rights model (Rioux 2003; Rioux et al. 2013). This paradigm shift has had a significant influence on the way in which disability has been conceptualized and the way in which governments have moved forward in working on inclusive models that respect human rights. This paper does not address the criticisms that have been leveled at the disability rights model as a model imposed from the North, rather it takes at face value the work and effort that were expended by disabled people in both the global North and the global South in structuring and politicizing this model during the construction of the Convention on the Rights of Persons with Disabilities (see Meekosha and Soldatic 2011).

A second, emerging paradigm shift underlies the importance of the changing North–South paradigm dynamic in terms of how services, programs, policy and rights are incorporated and put in place in the South, based on the research and development agendas. A few of the non-mutually exclusive, identifiable models of North–South research projects that can be distinguished in this second paradigm shift include:

1. Researchers from the North design research with or without collaboration of southern partners (usually with southern partners as that is now a common requirement of most international development agencies which fund these projects), and pay lip-service to engagement or consultation of those with disabilities in the South and with universities in the South.
2. Researchers from the North engage in research in the South in which they are invited to participate and to provide expertise to southern researchers.

[1] This chapter does not refer to those who work in the South using a model of engagement that does not include southern actors in the work or in the execution of projects. Though that model is certainly still common in some rehabilitation and medical work, we do not include it in this analysis.

3. Researchers from the North design the research (often rationalized as participatory action research) and carry out the research (in collaboration with local people either with or without disabilities). When it is "successfully" completed, there are some "knowledge mobilization" tools (manuals or work books) developed and distributed. The outcome of the work is that it answers the research questions, driven by the northern researchers (often themselves disabled people's organizations) or by the northern development agencies with some evidence-based knowledge. Generally with this model there are assumptions that qualitative research, in itself, makes the research legitimately inclusive.
4. Researchers from the North build collaborative research projects that include people with disabilities in the core of the planning and as key players in the collection of evidence-based research. Where the methodology is unfamiliar to the southern partners, the role of the northern researchers is to work with those in the South so that they can continue carrying out the research, independent of their northern colleagues.
5. Transformational research, which is driven by the interests and concerns of those in the South, is based upon their leadership of the research process, contributes to their ownership of the research outcomes, and includes an independent long-term strategy, built from the ground up.

This chapter will explore one piece of transformational research in which we consider the importance of recognizing that rights, justice and power cannot be separated in the fundamental design and implementation of research and in the transfer of knowledge. Knowledge is not uni-directional but bi-directional. There are no established rules for doing this kind of research successfully, yet one of the key elements is the philosophy of organizations in how they see their role in development work and in human rights work.

The fundamental principle of human rights work is to entrench the rights of people who are marginalized, wherever and for whatever reason. So human rights goals include social justice actions aiming at fighting oppression experienced by people with disabilities, the LGBTQ community, women, indigenous people, and others. These actions include the southern partners who identify the bases of systemic discrimination and address those as central to the research in which they are involved. The nature of the research itself has to be grounded in more than conventional notions of disability and service and policy guidelines, to address the denial of rights that occurs in the everyday lives of people with disabilities. The process of the research and development is as important as the outcome if there is to be bi-directional learning on how to implement and entrench disability rights.

The implementation of the Convention on the Rights of Persons with Disabilities (CRPD) is exemplar of the wide gap between theory and practice; that is, between the promises of governments and what is happening at the grassroots level. The goals of full participation and equality, which are recognized and adopted as fundamental principles in the CRPD, are currently more an illusion than a concrete reality for most people with disabilities throughout the world.[2] Not surprisingly then, a disability rights approach is still considered by many people with disabilities as an abstract framework, empty of any practical impact that improves their lives (Boucher et al. 2011; Pinto 2011). And it does not extend to the design, implementation, and outcome of research itself, which often appears as the imposition of northern disability rights or disability theory or disability research methodology on those in the South.

This chapter will look at ways of building into the research itself notions of rights and the power to sustain the work outside the context of the northern researchers who are likely to be the grant holders. We note the obstacles and barriers currently preventing the full enjoyment of rights by people with disabilities in the global South, by exploring how increasing participation and decision-making power in monitoring rights can lead to more sustained social change.

In evaluating a cross-disability, collaborative, participatory research project carried out by Disability Rights Promotion International (DRPI),[3] we bring a critical perspective to the process of monitoring rights. There are a number of approaches and methodologies in place to monitor disability rights and to carry out that work in southern environments. The DRPI in its monitoring has tried to move beyond traditional North–South research paradigms by making the process of the research and methodology itself central to the work. It is an iterative process that engages both the northern and the southern collaborators and always places people with disabilities in central decision-making roles.

The DRPI monitoring model facilitates data collection and the collation of evidence that shows discrimination on the basis of individuals' own experiences and perceptions. This is done through research tools that have been field tested and adapted in numerous countries of the global North and South. People with disabilities themselves, in their local environments, adapt the tools, carry out the field research and write the reports that come from the analyses they have conducted. Using this model provides a snapshot of the erosion of dignity and the discrimination and limited scope for self-determination that people with disabilities experience in their daily lives. It delivers evidence-based findings which highlight the ways in which communities are slow to change when it comes to including people with disabilities. The methodology is designed to show the gaps, tensions and contradictions in existing legislation and policy in any particular jurisdiction, when assessed from a rights-based perspective. Drawing from information about both systemic discrimination and individual experiences collected and collated by people with disabilities themselves, the methodology also bridges the gap between the North and South, providing an evidence-based picture of the lives of people with disabilities (Rioux et al. 2015). It is a progressive, emancipatory and critical model of monitoring that grounds itself in the experiences of those who are most affected

[2] This is clearly evident in the several shadow reports submitted so far to the CRPD committee by disability organizations in the context of national monitoring processes (for a complete list visit http://www.ohchr.org/EN/HRBodies/CRPD/Pages/CRPDIndex.aspx).

[3] A project hosted by York University, Canada and funded by the Swedish International Development and Cooperation Agency and others. http://drpi.research.yorku.ca

by the denial of rights. While solid and well structured, the methodology is flexible enough to take into account the needs at the grassroots and of the monitoring agenda of each specific country or region.

To provide a clearer perspective of the impact of both the model of research and the new North–South relationship paradigm, this chapter articulates the ways in which DRPI's monitoring research has fostered the engagement of people with disabilities in critical research in the South in which northern partners are involved. This chapter outlines some ideas for a transformative model of North–South research with an agenda based on disability rights, where people with disabilities play a proactive and activist role, rather than being passive beneficiaries, of fact-finding, monitoring, and reporting.

A New Methodology for Old Problems

There are multiple perspectives from which to assess human rights. DRPI offers one approach that is made up of a number of techniques and tools used in other areas of rights monitoring including interviews, focus groups, policy and legal research and surveys of public attitudes. It triangulates the findings, and in that way, arguably, it is innovative. The monitoring tools have been designed and developed so that the work can be repeated at periodic intervals, based on decisions by country organizations of the need to re-evaluate the reality of the on-going policies, laws and individual experiences. The information is updated through this process and enables a means to assess a country's progressive realization of rights. Launched in 2000, with a think tank of people with disabilities and international organizations designing the basic tenets of a comprehensive methodology (Rioux 2000), DRPI has developed into a collaborative global network working to build the capacity of people with disabilities to monitor the human rights of people with disabilities. This monitoring is, by design, an empowering process through which marginalized groups can document violations and abuses and provide their own description of reality.

The DRPI structure currently includes five regional offices (in Africa, Eastern Europe, Asia Pacific, Latin America, North America), each staffed with a regional officer who works in their own country. To conduct the monitoring work, the project partners with disabled people and human rights organizations, universities, statutory human rights bodies, government agencies and the United Nations. Funders include international development agencies, NGOs who work in the field of disability, donor organizations, research institutes, and universities.

As a way to engender full engagement of the South, bi-directional research and a transformational model, four central ideas are at the core of the DRPI initiative: (1) disability rights monitoring is led by people with disabilities; (2) the rights of people with disabilities are recognized as the same as the rights of all other citizens; (3) there is an agreed and negotiated commitment to create sustainable networks of disability rights monitoring; and (4) the work has to be transformational and provide people with disabilities an opportunity to define how they see the issues identified and addressed. Recognizing the vast cultural and regional differences, DRPI has grounded its monitoring in five key human rights principles, which can be found in the CRPD but also in other international human rights instruments: dignity; autonomy (or self-determination); equality and non-discrimination; inclusion, participation and accessibility; and respect for difference. These are the standards against which we measure and they are built into the research tools for individual monitoring, systemic monitoring and media monitoring. This has important practical implications as it mandates that any program or policy that falls within the scope of the Convention—whether it is, for example, education, employment, legal capacity or rehabilitation—has to uphold those principles. For example, transportation has to be designed that respects those principles, precluding forms of segregation or discrimination in service and mandating the fundamental notion of dignity in using that transportation. Employment has to meet a basic test of how it is secure, non-exploitative, meets the minimum wage, is not precarious or dangerous, and is not classified as training when it is a job. The research and findings do not proscribe particular programs or policies but look at outcomes rather than at inputs, in terms of whether rights are being respected (Rioux and Riddel 2011). It is not an accounting of how many children go to school but rather if those children are receiving an education of equivalent quality to those without disabilities, without discrimination and with dignity and autonomy.

The DRPI methodology for monitoring disability rights incorporates three types of information collection and blends the three elements to provide a grounded holistic picture. The three types of monitoring are: systemic, individual and media. Systemic monitoring (the most common type of rights monitoring) involves an accounting of constitutions, laws, policies and programs. For that purpose, DRPI has developed a template that is web-based and can be easily updated. Individual monitoring involves semi-structured interviews to get the first-hand stories of how people live and feel about their lives. In DRPI projects, monitors conduct approximately 100 interviews in each country, covering rural, metropolitan, and small urban areas. Finally, DRPI undertakes media monitoring to explore public attitudes towards disability and people with disabilities.

Monitoring country projects begin with the establishment of a partnership and collaborative work among the DRPI regional officer (himself or herself a person with disability), DRPI international staff and a local cross-disability organization that will take leadership in monitoring activities, from recruitment of monitors and interviewees to the processes of data collection, analysis and reporting. A core dimension of the DRPI monitoring process is the empowerment of individuals with disabilities and collective actors within the disability community. This goal is achieved through the direct involvement of people with disabilities as monitors and that of local disability organizations in all stages of monitoring.

Once the partnership is formally agreed to with the signing of a memorandum of understanding among all parties, the local partner initiates the preparation of the monitoring project. This first phase involves choosing a place to organize the training seminar and recruiting participants, on the basis of cross-disability and gender criteria, as well as personal interest and motivation. All participants are people with disabilities themselves. These monitors will take part in an intensive training seminar that addresses the human rights approach to disability and the holistic methodology, including internationally adapted tools related to monitoring activities. A significant part of the training is dedicated to learning and practicing skills on how to conduct monitoring interviews in the field (including specific interview techniques; how to use the interview guide; how to obtain free and informed consent of the interviewees; how to protect data confidentiality). The fact that people with disabilities will be the monitors in charge of interviewing other people with disabilities is a clear advantage of the DRPI approach, in creating a context of mutual trust and respect between the interviewer and the interviewee that facilitates information sharing within a rigorous methodological framework.

Following the training, monitors go into the field to collect data including gathering and analyzing individual experiences; collecting and analyzing laws, policies and programs in the country; and collecting and carrying out the analysis of media sources. Compiling a holistic report involves bringing together the field researchers and others to reflect on the findings obtained. A further step based on disability rights issues identified in the research is a process of determining priorities at the local level for political action.

The DRPI model incorporates what has been termed the emancipatory research paradigm (Oliver 1992, 2002; Barnes 2001), setting in motion dynamic processes that ensure control of the research process by people with disabilities and their organizations; accountability to people with disabilities and their organizations; practical results; the use of the human rights model of disability; and a plurality of research methods *granting scientific* rigor. The research process recognizes the central role of the lived experiences of people with disabilities to highlight the rights issues that are critical in each social and cultural context. By working within the framework of human rights, the DRPI approach can make a contribution to the process of emancipation and the collective struggle of disabled people, as knowledge about rights violations remains in the hands of those who can best do something with it.

Critical Reflexive Engagement

More recently, a number of authors including Meekosha and Soldatic (2011), Soldatic et al. (2014) have questioned the usefulness of human rights discourses to support struggles for disability justice in the global South. They have been calling for research that includes the voices of southern people with disabilities to avoid making them "'victims' of human rights rather than agents in their own social change" (Meekosha and Soldatic 2011: 1394). The DRPI work has been carried out in both the North and the South, recognizing that the process of engagement has to be interactive and bi-directional as disability rights are as precarious in the North as in the South (see for example UN OHCHR Concluding Observations country reports). This also recognizes that the transposing of ideas uni-directionally from

North to South has led to many services, programs and laws which inhibit rather than enhance rights. As one of our colleagues in Africa said, there would not be any total care institutions in Africa if the North had not built them. Similarly segregated schools, care and treatment based on models of rehabilitation (e.g., behaviour modification) that are not liberating, do not respect dignity, and are culturally inappropriate, have been imported from North to South.

Through the joint development of a methodology that places people with disabilities at the center of disability rights monitoring processes and that has been used both in the global North and the global South, DRPI embraces the challenge of providing space to give adequate consideration of cultural and regional differences, while working to create new opportunities to find a common ground and foster solidarity on disability rights that cuts across the North–South divide. Since 2002, the DRPI approach has been applied in over 45 countries around the world. About 550 people with disabilities have participated in DRPI trainings and have engaged in participatory monitoring. How have their voices been heard? Has engagement with disability rights monitoring made a difference in their lives? How has it contributed to their struggles? These questions are critical as they speak to the fundamental criteria that define transformational research. We address them here.

Hearing People, Building Disability Solidarity

Transformational research and participatory monitoring need, above all, to respond to local interests and needs. While DRPI advances a holistic approach to monitoring, not all projects follow the same script. On the contrary, projects are tailored to suit local priorities. It is up to local organizations to decide where they will place their focus, and therefore in some countries only individual monitoring is conducted while in others systemic or media monitoring is prioritized. For instance, a DRPI project recently concluded in Algeria focused only on individual monitoring, while another project developed in five countries of the Middle East and North African region a few years ago focused exclusively on the assessment of law and policy (Rioux and Pinto 2013). Tailoring the DRPI approach has also involved adapting our materials to best address issues defined as critical at local level. In Colombia, for example, our local partner was particularly interested in rights violations affecting people with psychosocial disabilities, a largely neglected issue in that country. As such, without overlooking a cross-disability perspective, our training materials, data collection tools and the monitoring study were adapted in order to be accessible to this group. In South Asia, a major project under way in India, Bangladesh and Nepal is focused on employment, thus responding to what appears to be one of the major arenas of disability discrimination in the region. Similarly, the Middle East project provided an opportunity to strengthen the gender lens in DRPI's work—addressing the concerns of our local partner, the DRPI systemic assessment tool was adapted to reflect both a disability and women's rights perspective. In Canada, a project is ongoing that engages First Nations/Aboriginal people with disabilities in a number of communities, providing an opportunity to adapt the tools to be culturally sensitive to this population.

Once the focus of the study is defined in dialogue with local partners, a training seminar is organized. The knowledge gained throughout more than a decade of DRPI work suggests that this initial training is a fundamental stage in the process of transformational research. It is during these intensive seminars that participants start to place their own individual experiences into the broader framework of the social, economic, and political forces and structures that create disability oppression in our societies. As disability services in most countries (both North and South) have traditionally been organized around types of impairment, itself a reflection of the prevailing medical approach to disability, for many people with disabilities participation in a DRPI training constitutes the first opportunity to encounter and interact with people with a variety of impairments. Throughout discussion and the hands-on practice of monitoring, participants are encouraged to work in small groups that often also involve sign language interpreters and other assistants. One participant remarked:

> What I've noticed as the greatest problem in general for people with disabilities is that one category of people with disabilities do not know about the problems of people with a different type of disability, so I think that in some way they have to learn about each other's problem, to not close ourselves off in a circle according to diagnosis, but for it to be a bit wider.

In a training seminar in Manila, Philippines in 2008, a long-time disability activist with a mobility impairment noted it was for her the first time she had communicated and worked with a deaf person. She was not alone in that comment. In practicing interview techniques, in particular, we encourage participants to pair up with someone with a different ability. We often meet with some initial resistance but throughout the days attitudes typically change in a more positive way, as participants gain a better understanding of each other's skills and possibilities. This contributes to breaking down the isolation and marginalization in which so many people with disabilities live and lays the ground for new forms of solidarity, not just among the members of the group, but indeed more broadly across the disability movement.

Raising Awareness of Disability Rights

This process continues throughout fieldwork, when the pairs of monitors conduct their monitoring work. As they collect individual stories from the people they interview, monitors gain new insights about disability discrimination and the meaning of rights in the lives of disabled people. Once again, for many of them, this new awareness starts during the training. The practice component involves several instances of interviewing each other and reporting back to the group and these moments of sharing are crucial in creating a new understanding of their own story and the root causes of disability-based discrimination. In Moldova, a participant noted:

> The training served as an arena, where the gaps in the field of persons with disabilities' rights were shown in their real light. The training was totally adapted for the persons of different types of disability and the personal needs of each participant were taken into consideration which allowed us a safe space for equal participation and full inclusion.

Historically, the consequence of the individualization and medicalization of disability—brought about by capitalism and increasingly spread around the world, even to more traditional societies, due to globalization (Barnes 2009)—is that people with disabilities have been made to believe "they" are the problem and that it is their "fault" if they are not included. Many have never been exposed to the social and human rights models and lack the language to name their experiences in terms of rights violations. The DRPI training begins by creating a space where that knowledge is provided and reflected upon on the basis of participants' personal experiences. A site coordinator from Serbia acknowledged:

> My conclusion is that people with disabilities are not familiar with the term "discrimination". Many are discriminated but most of us are not aware of it at all. People don't have information about what it is, and what rights they, as persons with disabilities, can exercise.

Gaining that understanding becomes the foreground on which a new, stronger and liberating sense of self is built. And while human rights discourses have been criticized as being imposed by the West, we are always humbled and struck by the immediate response and identification that participants in the seminars, whether taking place in the global North or the global South, express towards notions such as disability oppression, disability discrimination and a basic sense of dignity. At the closing of the Middle East project one female monitor confided to us:

> Before the training I could not leave the house after 4 pm. My mother wouldn't allow me. But after the training I felt a free woman. Now I go everywhere. I've even been abroad and I go alone. This power, this big mouth is given to us by talking about ourselves, talking about our problems, that we are here, and others need to give us space; it's our space!

The impact of a monitoring study in raising awareness about disability discrimination is not restricted to the training seminar or even the data collection stage. In fact, it is felt when data analyses are being conducted and the larger patterns of disability discrimination in a particular country start emerging and can be compared with those obtained in different socio-cultural contexts. People with disabilities also participate in data analyses and in many projects results are discussed with the larger group who took part in data collection and analysis, before final reports are issued. In other words, knowledge about disability rights and rights violations is produced with and by people with disabilities. This knowledge is fundamental for the advocacy work of local disability organizations, as it legitimizes community claims to funds to improve the rights situation of people with disabilities, thus helping to build a stronger disability movement at the local level.

Building Capacity and Taking Ownership of the Monitoring Process

During the pilot phase of DRPI in 2003, training seminars were mostly facilitated by the DRPI international team. Yet from the inception of the initiative, training seminars were organized following a train-the-trainer format. The focus was on training local leaders, who would then be able to replicate the methodology in their own communities. A great emphasis has been placed, since the beginning, in creating accessible training materials and making them available with no copyright on the project's website.

The DRPI initiative has gained a global dimension with training seminars being held all over the world, mostly led by regional officers and co-facilitated by local leaders from neighboring countries who have previously conducted DRPI projects themselves. This again is done with the explicit purpose of fostering linkages, sharing power and building solidarity and justice around disability rights beyond national borders. People with disabilities and their organizations are central in all these processes: they are trainers, participants, monitors and coordinators. They take responsibility and control over the study, defining its focus, direction, resources, actions, and timing. They take an active role in data analysis and decide how and when to use the knowledge gathered for their ongoing disability activism. As researchers, our role is to be available as technical resources, sharing our knowledge and expertise as requested. This is not to say we are mere spectators. We continue to participate in trainings and often use the data collected and analyzed in these projects to add to our own academic purposes of publishing and presenting at conferences. As much as possible, though, presentations and articles are co-authored, and the invisible work of all those behind the scenes who have contributed to the outcomes is regularly acknowledged in our publications.

Moreover, beyond just providing training for participation in a singular monitoring study, our focus has been on building capacity within a long-term strategy by sharing knowledge about research methodology that can be used in other arenas. One participant in a recent training in Macedonia commented:

> [The training] provided me with the skills that I could use in the work of my organization and enabled me to understand deeper disability rights. I learned the methods of interviewing and qualitative research as the solid ground for revealing the hidden life stories of people with disabilities.

Monitoring has long been the exclusive field of human rights experts. Providing solid and hands-on training, free and accessible materials and monitoring tools, and adequate support throughout the monitoring process, the DRPI approach shifts the balance of power and justice from academia and NGOs onto the disability community. This approach encourages disability organizations to take ownership of research and monitoring work, thus taking the mystique out of monitoring. This knowledge can be, and has been, successfully transferred to other areas of rights work (e.g. women's rights, HIV/AIDS, indigenous rights), strengthening and broadening DPOs' ability to advocate and take their place, as equal players, in disability and human rights politics, at national and international levels.

Concluding Remarks and Challenges Ahead

Looking at development policies and the research projects that are funded within their parameters suggests that the paradigm shift from the charity model to the rights model in disability is addressed only peripherally. This shift is reflected even less in the processes of the projects themselves, which have a strong focus on consulting with people with disabilities and little focus on transformational change. The reliance on northern development agencies has been the model for services for people with disabilities for many years and there is little evidence of this changing, even within the context of a paradigm change to rights that the CRPD has fostered. There is also little evidence to date of a paradigm shift that includes justice and power—to transformational change residing in the disability community. This might have been expected with the impressive number of countries so quickly ratifying the CRPD.

Transformational research is the new disability research paradigm that, rather than imposing northern research agendas and models onto the global South, is considerate of South-North politics, addresses local priorities and concerns, provides a voice to local communities, and thus contributes to building from the ground up a sustainable, long-term, independent strategy in which disability organizations take ownership of research processes and outcomes. DRPI participatory monitoring is an illustration of transformational research practices.

Yet despite its many strengths and advantages, the DRPI model still faces a number of challenges. The first comes from within academia. From a positivist point of view, such an approach is not without criticism. Concerns about the reliability of participatory research methods have been raised (Friderers 2008) and the quality of data that is collected, analyzed and reported by people with disabilities, with no full academic training and record, is often questioned. To address such criticisms in the context of DRPI we have strived to improve the quality of our training, ensuring sufficient practice and discussion time. As trainings are intensive and follow an in-house format, in addition to regular daytime workshops we reinforce important skills through more leisurely activities in the evenings. We have also worked hard to develop accessible training materials and make them freely available, on-line, in a variety of formats.

DRPI participatory monitoring studies work in solidarity with people with disabilities to document personal experiences and the social, legal and policy contexts in which people live, in order to provide a comprehensive evidence-based picture of their ability to exercise their rights in their own environments, and to build that knowledge into an advocacy agenda. The participation of people with disabilities in collecting, analyzing and reporting data leads to the framing of the issues from the perspective of people with disabilities in their own countries and their own regions. Concerns about the cost of implementing such a model are often raised. We argue that, although it can be more expensive in the beginning, mostly due to the requirements of the initial training and the resources involved in conducting individual monitoring, the model is cost effective and provides for better reporting over time. If we do not challenge ourselves to hear what people with disabilities have to say about their own lives we will hardly know what has to be changed.

People with disabilities debated, argued and struggled for consensus during the development of the CRPD and became a political voice in that process. They/we and their/our organizations now have an active role to play in promoting a more inclusive global South, in which equality is part of the collective project. Their/our participation does not only help bring to the forefront issues of autonomy, diversity, disability-based discrimination and difference, but it also constitutes an expression of empowerment and the basis for transformation in developing a political agenda, which can be shared with the global North. In this sense, it will increase the pressure on governments and other actors to achieve societies in which all citizens are able to exercise their rights. More than a material presence, this contribution is essential to reshape a new political and social reality, not just in the global South, but indeed around the world.

References

Barnes, C. (2001). *'Emancipatory' disability research: Project or process?* Public lecture, City Chambers, Glasgow, 24 October. Retrieved February 11, 2015, from http://disability-studies.leeds.ac.uk/files/library/Barnes-glasgow-lecture.pdf.

Barnes, C. (2009). *Disability in the majority world context: A materialist account*. Presented at Disability and Economy Conference, Manchester Metropolitan University, Manchester, 29–30 April. Retrieved February 11, 2015, from http://disability-studies.leeds.ac.uk/files/library/Barnes-majority-world-2.pdf.

Boucher, N., Fiset, D., Pinto, P., Dinca-Panaitescu, M., Carpenter, S., Killoran, I., et al. (2011). Droits humains et personnes ayant des incapacités: Analyse comparative de l'utilisation des services de soutien en contexte ontarien et québécois. *Journal of Human Development, Disability and Social Change, 19*(2), 23–41. Retrieved from http://www.ripph.qc.ca/revue/journal-19-02-2011-03.

Friderers, J. (2008). Participatory research: An illusionary perspective. In J. Friderers (Ed.), *A world of communities: Participatory research perspectives* (pp. 1–13). Toronto: Captus University Publications.

Khun, T. S. (1962). *The structure of scientific revolutions*. Chicago: The University of Chicago Press.

Meekosha, H., & Soldatic, K. (2011). Human rights and the global South: The case of disability. *Third World Quarterly, 32*(8), 1383–1398.

Oliver, M. (1992). Changing the social relations of research production. *Disability, Handicap and Society, 7*(2), 101–114.

Oliver, M (2002). *Emancipatory research: A vehicle for social transformation or policy development?* Presented at 1st Annual Disability Research Seminar, Dublin, 3 December. Retrieved February 11, 2015, from http://disability-studies.leeds.ac.uk/files/library/Oliver-Mikes-paper.pdf.

Pinto, P. C. (2011). At the crossroads: Human rights and the politics of disability and gender in Portugal. *European Journal of Disability Research, 5*(2), 116–128.

Rioux, M. (Ed.) (2000). *Let the world know: Report on a seminar on human rights and disability*. Office of the Special Rapporteur on Disability of the United Nations Commission for Social Development. Retrieved February 11, 2015, from http://www.un.org/esa/socdev/enable/stockholmnov2000.htm.

Rioux, M. H. (2003). On second thought: Constructing knowledge, law, disability and inequality. In S. Herr, L. Gostin, & H. Koh (Eds.), *The human rights of persons with intellectual disabilities: Different but equal* (pp. 287–317). Oxford: Oxford University Press.

Rioux, M. H., Gilmour, J., & Angel-Cabo, N. (2013). Negotiating capacity: Legally constructed entitlement and protection. In B. McSherry & I. Freckelton (Eds.), *Coercive care: Rights law and policy* (pp. 51–75). Abingdon, Oxon: Routledge.

Rioux, M., & Pinto, P. (2013). *Are we moving forward? Regional study on rights of women with disabilities in the Middle East*. Palestine: Stars of Hope. Retrieved February 11, 2015, from http://oddh.iscsp.utl.pt/index.php/pt/2013-04-24-18-50-23/publicacoes-dos-investigadores-oddh/item/143-mulheres-direitos-humanos-e-defici%C3%AAncia-no-medio-oriente.

Rioux, M., Pinto, P. C., & Parekh, G. (Eds.). (2015). Disability, Rights Monitoring and Social Change: *Building power out of evidence*. Toronto: Canadian Scholars' Press.

Rioux, M. H., & Riddel, C. (2011). Values in disability policy and law: Equality. In M. H. Rioux, L. A. Basser, & M. Jones (Eds.), *Critical perspectives on human rights and disability law* (pp. 36–56). The Hague: Martinus Nijhoff.

Soldatic, K., Morgan, H., & Roulstone, A. (Eds.). (2014). *Disability, spaces and places of policy exclusion*. London: Routledge.

UN Office of the High Commissioner for Human Rights. *Concluding observations reports by the committee on the rights of persons with disabilities*. Retrieved from http://tbinternet.ohchr.org/_layouts/treatybodyexternal/TBSearch.aspx?Lang=en&TreatyID=4&DocTypeID=.

Zubrow, E. (2014) Silences of sound: A prologue. In L. Eneix (Ed.), *Archaeoacoustics: The archaeology of sound*. Publication of proceedings from the 2014 conference in Malta. Sarasota: OTS Press.

Chapter 35
Australian Indigenous People with Disability: Ethics and Standpoint Theory

John Gilroy and Michelle Donelly

> *In order to understand our position better and to ultimately act to improve it, we must first immerse ourselves in and understand the very system of thought, ideas and knowledge that have been instrumental in producing our position. (Nakata 1998: 4)*

Introduction

The 370 million Indigenous[1] people around the world take great pride in their cultural and language diversity (United Nations 2006, 2008). The United Nations (2008) defines Indigenous peoples as:

> communities, peoples and nations … which, having a historical continuity with pre-invasion and pre-colonial societies that developed on their territories, consider themselves distinct from other sectors of the societies now prevailing on those territories, or parts of them.

It is almost impossible to calculate the number of 'nations', 'tribes' or 'clans'. The World Health Organization reported in 2010 that Indigenous peoples lived in 70 countries around the world (Pulver et al. 2010).

Colonisation is widely understood as a process whereby one ethnic or cultural group invades and occupies the lands of another. Europe's self-perceived 'need' to conquer and colonise other lands over centuries was underpinned by a range of desires, such as economic and resource prosperity, militarism, imperialism, spread of Christianity and global domination (Reynolds 1981; Harris 1990; Pétré-

[1] We use the term Indigenous in this paper to include both Aboriginal and Torres Strait Islander peoples. This term makes it easier to read when discussing Indigenous Standpoint Theory to an international audience.

J. Gilroy (✉)
Centre for Disability, Research and Policy, University of Sydney, Sydney, NSW, Australia
e-mail: john.gilroy@sydney.edu.au

M. Donelly
Health and Human Sciences, Southern Cross University,
Locked Mailbag 4, Coolangatta, QLD 4225, Australia
e-mail: michelle.donelly@scu.edu.au

S. Grech, K. Soldatic (eds.), *Disability in the Global South*,
International Perspectives on Social Policy, Administration, and Practice,
DOI 10.1007/978-3-319-42488-0_35

Grenouilleau 2004). The European colonisers occupied the land and deprived Indigenous communities of their sources of food, spirituality and community. Frontier warfare extended over decades as occupation spread into new areas. This included the systematic extermination, forced labour, segregation, detention, abduction, sexual assault and starvation of Indigenous people. Indigenous peoples of colonised lands were not recognised as citizens when their lands were conquered and occupied. High rates of incarceration, impoverishment, youth suicide and intergenerational trauma are currently experienced among Indigenous peoples. The largest socially determined life expectancy gap within any nation in the world currently exists between Indigenous and non-Indigenous people in Australia (Cohen 1999; Pulver et al. 2010).

The WHO has described the high rates of disability and poor health among various Indigenous populations as a historical legacy of colonisation (Alderete 1999; WHO 2008; Pulver et al. 2010). 'Science' has typically reflected the social relations of colonisation and global difference. For example, science has been employed to justify the colonisation of Indigenous peoples' lands by providing 'proof' of the 'evolutionary superiority' of particular races or cultures (Connell 2007: 17). One of the main features of European colonialism was the West's desire to study and document the 'Indigenous' or 'native' inhabitants of the lands. Scholars in post-colonial studies and Indigenous studies have long argued that the West, through its Eurocentric scientific enquiries, labelled, defined and categorised how the 'Other' (Indigenous, Aboriginal, native) was *different* and *inferior* to white European races (Said 1978; Attwood 1989; Tuhiwai Smith 1999). Connell's (2007) critical historical review of social scientific literature concluded that much of the social science literature represented the West (Metropole) as superior in comparison to Indigenous peoples (Periphery) of other nations and continents.

International research in the area of disability and impairment has been engaged in what has been called "academic neo-colonialism" or "academic neo-imperialism" (Alatas 2003; Grech 2012). These terms define the exportation of theories and epistemologies from the West (primarily Europe and, in the 20th century, North America) across cultures. Research in the area of disability and impairment has been an important mechanism in the legitimisation and spread of global European/north Atlantic imperialism. Since colonisation began, notions of 'defectiveness', 'impairment' and 'normality' have been imposed upon Indigenous communities. Colonial administrators, officers, physicians and scientists set about naming, framing and claiming the colonised continents and its peoples, including renaming and framing impairment and disability among Indigenous peoples. Grech states that 'backing this exportation of epistemologies is the inherent assumption that theories and writing from the West are transferable to the rest, sustained by the continuation of western imperialism in knowledge production and its dissemination' (2012: 59).

This chapter examines research about the Indigenous peoples of Australia to explore the historical foundations of colonisation, colonialism and research on impairment and disability. The first section presents a critical historical analysis of ethnographic and anthropological literature from the 1800s. This is followed by a critique of the current approaches used to address the ethics of research involving

Indigenous people with disability. In a bid to address concerns regarding practices employed in human and social research, the Australian government and the academic community, in consultation with Indigenous stakeholders, have developed national ethical guidelines on research involving Indigenous people. These guidelines, however, as we argue in this chapter, have not been effective in addressing the manner in which Australian Indigenous people with a disability are framed and disempowered in disability research methodology and epistemology.

In response to the continued gap between the prevalence of disability in Australian Indigenous communities and their low participation rates in support services (AIHW 2011), this chapter proposes that Indigenous Standpoint Theory (IST) can be used to critique how research represents, frames and defines Indigenous people with disability. IST is a way of merging local Indigenous communities' philosophies and cultures into the research process. It is argued that IST can also be used to augment current ethics guidelines in order to promote the decolonisation of research in the area of disability and to empower Australian Indigenous people with disability. This idiographic examination will focus on the application of IST in an Australian context so that theory might be grounded in the land on which we stand and in order to 'illuminate a situation in its concreteness' (Connell 2007: 207).

Australian Indigenous People with Disabilities

The half-million Indigenous people of Australia represented around 3 per cent of the Australian population in 2011. Interestingly, Indigenous people had higher rates of disability than the non-Indigenous population and represented around 5 per cent of all people with a disability (AIHW 2011). Research has demonstrated a link between the 200 years of British settlement and the high prevalence of disability in the Indigenous population (Hollinsworth 2013).

Australian researchers have attempted to identify specifically 'Indigenous' conceptualisations of disability and impairment within a racialised Eurocentric conceptual framework ever since the 19th century (Gilroy et al. 2013). Australian colonial researchers Curr (1886), Lindsay (1893) and Brodsky (1943) conducted and reported on ethnographic, linguistic and anthropological research all around Australia. Their studies found no concept equivalent to the English words 'disability' or 'impairment' (or in the language of the researchers in the late 19th century, 'handicapped') in any Indigenous language. On the other hand, analysis of Curr's reports found 12 different phrases describing hearing impairment, 10 for blindness, four relating to 'madness/insanity' and three relating to speech impairment. Even Australian Indigenous communities in proximity to each other within the same language groups used different terms and words to describe these characteristics of people. As such, the generic concepts of 'disability' or 'impairment' were not recognised by any Australian Indigenous community before European colonisation. Therefore, the identification and demarcation of a group of 'disabled Indigenous people' did not exist in the language or culture of Indigenous Australians.

Although the concept of disability did not exist in Australian Indigenous communities, non-Indigenous administrators, officers, researchers and scientists continued to impose the concepts of 'handicap' and 'impairment', as generic concepts, on Indigenous people according to Eurocentric, colonising methodological frameworks. According to Cawte, in the first half of the 20th century, health and behavioural sciences were interested "on the one hand with the crop of mental illness that characterises a native culture, and on the other with the mental illness that occurs as [Indigenous] people emerge from native culture into western" (1964: 170). Researchers categorised Indigeneity and Indigenous practices and cultures on the basis of the level of skin melanin, physiological features and lifestyle in comparison to western norms. Researchers have quantified, documented and reported on intellectual disability (identified variously in early research using terms such as 'intellectual handicap', 'mental retardation' or 'mental delay') and mental health conditions (also identified as insanity or mental illness) of so-called 'traditional' and 'non-traditional' people in Australian Indigenous communities. Indigenous people who attributed 'psychosis' or 'paranoia' to spiritual or magical cursory or witchery were identified as 'traditional people' and those who described their 'conditions' as a result of being excluded from their traditional communities and western colonial communities as "non-traditional people" (Bostock 1924; Kidson 1965, 1967; Cawte 1966). This approach dichotomised and pathologised Australian Indigenous community members and distanced the researchers from the impact of colonisation on health and well-being. Consistent with a biomedical model, this research sought to explain the trauma experienced by Australian Indigenous people by identifying impairments inside the person rather than examining the impact of colonisation. This also precluded research being undertaken in Australia during this period from the perspective of the person with a disability themselves using constructivist or emancipatory paradigms.

Western sciences' thirst for knowledge about disability, impairment or any embodiment of similarity or difference among Indigenous people resulted in the desecration of Indigenous sacred sites in the name of scientific 'progress'. For example, research on Boomerang Leg resulted in the bodies of some Indigenous communities' deceased ancestors being exhumed for study. During the 1900s, disability researchers quantified the prevalence of Boomerang Leg to ascertain the level of impact this condition had on the quality of life of Indigenous people (Chewings 1936; Stirling 1950). Hackett (1936) reported that the 'condition' was prominent in most Australian states and territories. Interestingly, most studies on Boomerang Leg found that the 'physical deformity' did not restrict the physical abilities of the individual. Shown in Fig. 35.1 are some pictures taken by Hackett (1936) and Chewings (1936).

Indigenous people were culturally *othered* in the development of government disability policy and programs in Australia. The critical historical reviews by Gilroy (2012) and Gilroy et al. (2013) of the evolution of Australian Government Indigenous disability research and policy found that Indigenous people were represented and treated as a specialised field together with migrants and disadvantaged people categorised by three factors: remoteness, cultural difference and disadvantage. The dominance of the biomedical model, or impairment-based view, of disability has persisted in research among Indigenous people in Australia despite decades of cri-

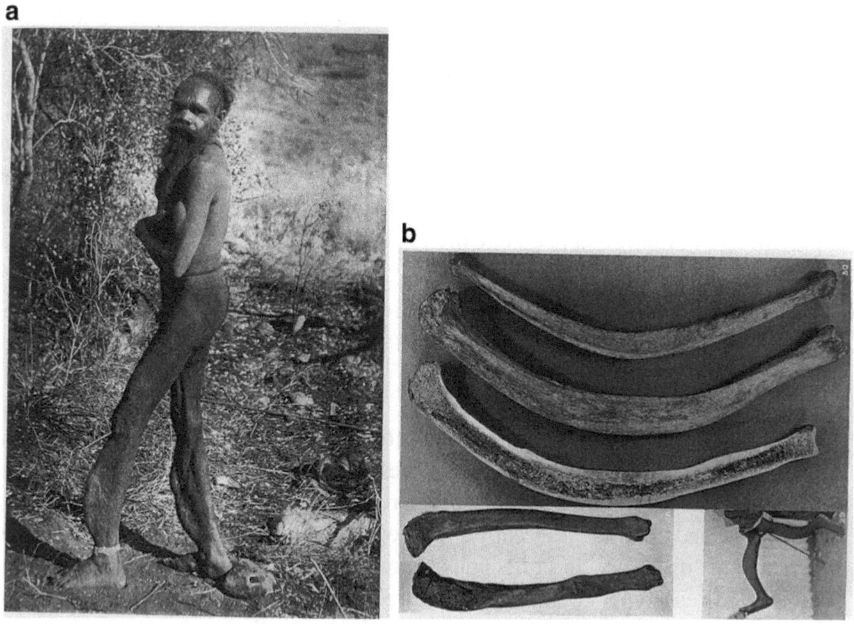

Fig. 35.1 Photos of boomerang leg (Chewings 1936: 35; Hackett 1936: 76–77)

tiques of this model and the parallel rise of structural models of disability in the northern Atlantic nations (Oliver 1990; Shakespeare and Watson 1997). Of course when disability is identified as residing within an individual, the condition becomes the focus of research and intervention either to ameliorate functional incapacity or decrease prevalence, neatly dovetailing with the dominance of scientific positivism in research and the rise of the neo-conservative economic agenda (Oliver 1990). Interestingly, some of the first critics of the structural models among northern Atlantic nations argued that the models themselves privileged the views of particular gender and social strata and ignored complex and embodied experiences (Morris 1991; Crow 1996). This in turn has led to calls for the development of emancipatory political agendas that acknowledge and address the structural factors which create and promote disability as well as the lived experience of a person (Hughes and Paterson 1997).

Consistent with Connell's (2007) analysis of the global division of power, the study of disability in Australia has been caught up in an *Us* (Metropole/abled/white/normal) versus *Them* (Periphery/Indigenous/disabled/non-normative) method of enquiry. Researchers have defined, framed and classified what is 'abled' and 'disabled' with limited input from Indigenous people. Researchers have dichotomised indigeneity based on how the West defined 'traditional' and 'non-traditional' Indigenous cultures (Gilroy 2010, 2012; Meekosha 2011). Colonial, racialised constructions of Indigeneity and disability have emerged from the earliest periods of colonisation with limited input from Indigenous people. This is consistent with the experience of Maori, where the non-Indigenous researchers had a 'storehouse' (Tuhiwai Smith 1999: 44) of research on Maori even before colonisation, which continued to serve the 'interests of the researcher's own making, defined and accountable in terms of the researcher's own cultural world-view' (Bishop 1998: 200). Research has failed to identify, investigate or address the structural factors that contributed to the prevalence of disability. The research enterprise focused on impairment and sought out biomedical justifications for the social marginalisation experienced by Aboriginal people. Gilroy et al. state that:

> There are volumes of knowledge, a whole epistemological library in fact, on Indigenous people with a disability. This knowledge is not owned by Indigenous people, rather this library operates as a resource for non-Indigenous researchers and government decision makers to legitimate themselves as the controllers and bearers of the 'truth' on disability. (Gilroy 2012: 116)

Disability research which assumes and substantiates this power hierarchy cannot address the social marginalisation and oppression of Australian Indigenous people with disability. Non-Indigenous disability researchers define their knowledge as authoritative and continue to occupy a privileged position in defining the nature and experience of 'disability' in Indigenous communities in a similar process to that of non-disabled researchers defining the nature of disability research. The legacy of colonisation is that Australian Indigenous people are the 'known' or the 'objects' of science rather than the 'knowers' or 'actors'. Indigenous people with disability are characterised as a research issue.

Research Ethics in Australia

The evolution of the research ethics review process in the northern Atlantic nations has been described as a form of punctuated equilibrium. Periodic crises arise from controversial cases leading to moral panic (Jones 1990; Fitzgerald 2004) and changes in ethical requirements. Some commonly cited cases that have influenced the development of various statements governing research ethics have included the Nazi experimentation among concentration camp prisoners (Proctor 1992), allegations of misconduct by anthropologist Chagnon and medical scientist Neel regarding research conducted in South America (Tierney 2000), and Indigenous cultural destruction (Kowal et al. 2005; Fredericks 2006).

Not surprisingly, the populations represented among these crisis cases typically include people who have been 'othered', disadvantaged and/or marginalised (Fitzgerald 2004). This suggests that there may be underlying structural factors which are not necessarily understood, acknowledged or addressed in current ethical and methodological guidelines governing research practice nor by the commonly recognised philosophical principles underpinning theorising in this area, such as utilitarianism[2] and deontology.[3] Moral panic about such research practices typically spark a formal inquiry (for example the recommendations of the United States National Commission for the Protection of Human Subjects of Biomedical and Behavioural Research (1979)). This has led to the development and adoption of various codes of ethical practice such as the 'Georgetown Four' (Beauchamp 2007) in the USA, referring to the research principles of autonomy, beneficence, non-maleficence and justice. These principles stipulate that research must be significant; participation must be informed, voluntary, confidential and anonymous; the research does no harm to participants; and the risks and benefits of research are evenly distributed.

As important as these principles are for Australian researchers, they predominantly address ethics and ethical considerations as an interaction between individuals and affecting the rights of individuals rather than addressing systematic or structural inequities that may already exist. Research ethics are typically understood to protect the interests, safety and rights of both the researcher and the research participants. Conventionally, disability researchers rely on state-sanctioned ethical guidelines when proposing research involving people with a disability (National Health and Medical Research Council [NHMRC] 2007, 2013). For research involving Indigenous people in Australia, disability researchers were required to meet the Guidelines on Ethical Matters in Aboriginal and Torres Strait Islander Research (NHMRC 1991). These guidelines were non-enforceable, however. In 2003, the NHMRC developed new enforceable ethical guidelines, Values and Ethics (2003, 2006), later accompanied by the Road Map (NHMRC 2010) and other supporting principles to help guide all researchers (not just non-Aboriginal researchers) in the planning, design and implementation of research with Aboriginal people. Many Australian university ethics guidelines and review processes are modelled on the NHMRC Values and Ethics Guidelines.

The NHMRC guidelines identify six key values that lie at the heart of ethical research with Indigenous communities, displayed in Fig. 35.2. Reciprocity acknowledges that a culture of mutual obligation exists within Indigenous communities. This 'mutual obligation extends to the land, animals and other natural elements and features … in various forms, and may vary between locations' (NHMRC 2003: 10).

Complementing the value of reciprocity, respect is characterised as appreciating the diversity of Aboriginal cultures, traditions and languages. A research project is to be based on respect between all parties as this 'induces trust and co-operation' (NHMRC 2003: 11). Respectful relationships minimise the risk of 'difference blindness' impacting on the Aboriginal people participating in the research (NHMRC 2003: 11).

[2] Theories of ethical decision-making guided by the view that the morally right action is the action that produces the greatest amount of good for the greatest number of people (Driver 2009).

[3] Theories of ethical decision-making guided by duty and moral rules such as maintaining respect for people and that no matter how morally good their consequences, some choices are morally forbidden (Alexander & Moore 2012).

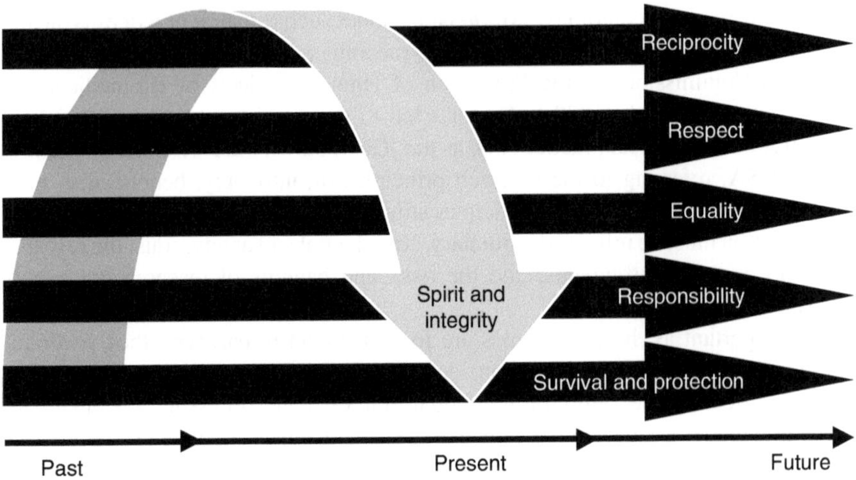

Fig. 35.2 The NHMRC values and ethics guidelines. *Note*: Adapted from NHMRC 2003: 9, *Diagram 1*: Aboriginal and Torres Strait Islander Peoples values relevant to health research ethics

A relationship based on reciprocity and respect will also involve equality between Aboriginal people participating in research and Aboriginal or non-Aboriginal researchers as they share power and control throughout the research process. Equality must not be confused with 'sameness'. Equality in research practice affirms that Aboriginal people are equal drivers of the research process and benefits (NHMRC 2003) and recognises their responsibilities to family, kin and country[4]. The NHMRC states that responsibility also includes 'to do no harm, including avoiding having an adverse impact on others' abilities to comply with their responsibilities' (NHMRC 2003: 16).

Survival and protection acknowledges that research must protect traditional cultures, languages and identities from 'erosion by colonisation and marginalisation' (NHMRC 2003: 18). The repeated devaluation of Aboriginal cultures, languages and knowledge in research has produced an intergenerational perception of research as 'an exploitative exercise' (NHMRC 2003: 18). The final value that binds the previous five values is spirit and integrity. This value has two components. First, researchers must acknowledge the continuity of cultures, languages and knowledge and the continuum between past, present and future. The second component is that the behaviour and values of researchers are consistent with those of the Aboriginal communities participating in research (NHMRC 2003).

In the 10 years since the introduction of the Values and Ethics Guidelines, Australian Indigenous people have raised concerns about the impact of these guidelines. The guidelines do not address the need to decolonise the research process

[4]Country, in Indigenous language, is the traditional homelands of a person's Aboriginal and/or Torres Strait Islander ancestry. It is the geographic region where their spiritual ancestors were born.

regarding the experiences of people with a disability in Indigenous communities. Concerns have also been raised about the difficulty that people have experienced in using these guidelines effectively. Many researchers have reported to the NHMRC that they do not understand how to implement the values and principles of the guidelines in practice (Henry et al. 2002; NHMRC 2013). Aboriginal communities have criticised the values and principles as being too broad and complex. Many Aboriginal communities still do not feel that they are adequately involved in the research process. The preliminary findings of the NHMRC's evaluation of the guidelines concluded that 'there needs to be better ways for communities to have a greater role in the monitoring of research and the research process from the community perspective' (2013: 1). The NHMRC reported that researchers are addressing the guidelines as a token gesture in the research 'process':

> Ethics is often an afterthought and the methods are already developed, so there is limited scope to change this. Researchers are approaching community with methods in place and are usually not willing to change this. (NHMRC 2013: 2)

Henry et al. (2002) and Anderson (1996) suggest that many researchers and research institutions are heavily focused on conforming to funding grant requirements at the expense of research performance and social impact. Researchers and research institutions are under pressure to obtain research funds, often limiting their availability and capacity to properly engage with Indigenous communities. Although an ethics committee may include or consist of Aboriginal and Torres Strait Islander people, there exists no accountability measures to monitor, or to change, the behaviour of researchers once they have obtained ethical approval.

In addition to the difficulties in operationalising these principles in practice, they do not go far enough to challenge the hegemony of western science in naming, framing and claiming the experience of Indigenous people. The problems that arise from an imposed epistemology are particularly concerning in research about the experience of Indigenous people with disability. Researchers are not encouraged to question and challenge how past Eurocentric, and now northern Atlantic, methodological frameworks continue to define indigeneity and disability in the Australian context. Indigenous people are given limited opportunity to scrutinise how they and their communities are represented, framed and defined in epistemological frameworks that underpin current research practice. Rather, non-Indigenous researchers want Indigenous people to engage in and with a pre-existing set of conceptualisations and research processes without critique or question (Anderson 1996; Henry et al. 2002).

Consequently, the Values and Ethics Guidelines contribute to the bureaucratisation of Australian Indigenous research in the human sciences as researchers are encouraged to circumnavigate abstract rules and procedures rather than fully conceptualise research practice (Humphery 2001). Meanwhile gaps in understandings about phenomena compromise efforts to address areas of significant disadvantage, such as the prevalence of disability among Indigenous communities and the lack of support. To be able to address these concerns about the current ethical guidelines in a manner that will move beyond the punctuated equilibrium of crisis cases, it is necessary to look more closely at academic colonialism and the creation of knowledge.

Indigenous Standpoint Theory and Decolonisation

A possible mechanism for informing and deepening our understanding of ethical research practice with Indigenous communities is to adopt a research framework or frame of reference that is articulated with Indigenous knowledge, cultures and understanding. Indigenous Standpoint Theory offers a solution to the problem of northern Atlantic disability sciences undermining Indigenous people as the cultural Other. Nakata (2004) describes IST as a distinct form of analysis where the Indigenous researcher's personal experiences elevate attention to aspects of the research enquiry that might not have been uncovered in a traditional research approach. IST breaks away from the Us versus Them approach and its definitions of 'traditional' versus 'non-traditional' knowledge. Foley defines IST as:

> a process and ontology, an epistemological approach to learning within research applications that enables the Indigenous person to maintain/regain or learn their own epistemological standpoint that has been lost due to colonisation and the adoption of ethnocentric Western forms or approaches to knowledge. (Foley 2006: 29)

Foley, drawing from feminist standpoint theory, claims that "non-Indigenous Australia cannot and possibly will not understand the complexities of Indigenous Australia at the same level of empathy as an Indigenous Australian researcher" (2003: 46). IST has evolved into a global community of Indigenous scholars.[5] These Indigenous scholars contest the privileged position of western science in defining and re-representing Indigenous people. This has entailed an exchange of skills and knowledge between Indigenous and non-Indigenous researchers and the conceptualisation of research epistemologies that are culturally appropriate for Indigenous people. In Australia, the application of IST has informed decolonising research in education (Nakata 1997), women's studies (Moreton-Robinson 2004) and the proliferation of Indigenous knowledge. Yet, there has been limited investigation of how IST can be developed and applied to decolonise research in the area of disability (Gilroy et al. 2013).

IST is not an Indigenous way of doing research, either at a local or macro level. IST is framed in the Indigenous person's ancestry, 'which informs the methodology in a science that is possibly tens of thousands of years old' (Foley 2006: 29–30). IST includes emancipatory philosophies developed by Indigenous people, for Indigenous people and with Indigenous people. These have developed out of their skills, experience and advocacy of Indigenous people's rights to self-determination and autonomy. For example, Moreton-Robinson (2000: xvi) suggested an IST for feminist studies as influenced by how an Indigenous woman experiences the following:

- Sharing an inalienable land
- Sharing a legacy of dispossession, racism and sexism

[5] These include Jackie Huggins (1993), Marcia Langton (1993), Martin Nakata (1997), William Oates (2003), Errol West (2000), Manulani Aluii Meyer (2008), Aileen Moreton-Robinson (2004), Wendy Brady (1992), Lester Irabinna Rigney (2007), John Gilroy (2012) and Linda Tuhiwai Smith (1999).

- Resisting and replacing disparaging images of women with self-defined images
- Continuing Indigenous people's activism as mothers, sisters, aunts, daughters, grandmothers and community leaders
- Negotiating sexual politics across and within cultures

In this case, an Indigenous woman's standpoint is shaped by how and where she was socialised as an Indigenous woman. This standpoint was developed in response to the western feminist standpoint, what Moreton-Robinson (2000) calls 'white feminism', which does not properly consider the position of Australian Indigenous women. In doing so, Moreton-Robinson prioritises Indigenous women's power and subjectivity in knowledge production. Moreton-Robinson claims that the researcher's subjectivity and biases are connected to 'relations of ruling whereby white racial difference shapes those on whom it confers privilege as well as those it oppresses' (2000: xxi). She suggests that contrary to western science's focus on race and ethnicity, Indigenous standpoint 'does not deny the diversity of Indigenous women's experience, as Indigenous women will have different concrete experiences that shape our relations to core themes' (2000: xvi).

Martin Nakata's (1997, 2004) IST takes a different approach to research, based on his experiences as a Torres Strait Islander scholar in Indigenous education. He suggests that Indigenous and non-Indigenous people operate in a contested knowledge space at the cultural interface (Nakata 2004). The cultural interface is the domain where the trajectories of Indigenous and non-Indigenous knowledge and experiences intersect. 'For in this space there are so many interwoven, competing and conflicting discourses that distinguishing traditional from non-traditional in the day-to-day is difficult to sustain even if one were in a state of permanent reflection' (Nakata 2004: 27–29). As such, the researcher must acknowledge that Indigenous agency is conditioned and framed within the cultural interface. The Indigenous researcher must identify how the experiences of Indigenous and non-Indigenous people are established and intersect at the cultural interface (Nakata 2004).

Linda Tuhiwai Smith (1999: 185) and Graham Smith (1997, 2008) found that western science was not inclusive of the diversity of Maori cultures and principles. Furthermore, western methodologies did not accommodate Maori cultural protocols. One approach developed by Maori scholars was *Kaupapa Maori* research, which attempts to guide the development of respectful cultural protocols in research that take into account experiences of colonisation and dispossession among Maori peoples (Smith 1997; Tuhiwai Smith 1999). Such research:

- Is related to 'being Maori'
- Is connected to Maori philosophy and principles
- Takes for granted the validity and legitimacy of Maori, and the importance of Maori language and culture
- Is concerned with the struggle for autonomy over our own cultural well-being

A challenging aspect of the development of cultural protocols is the wide diversity of experiences of indigeneity among specific cultural and language communities and the wide diversity of experiences of colonisation and dispossession. Gilroy

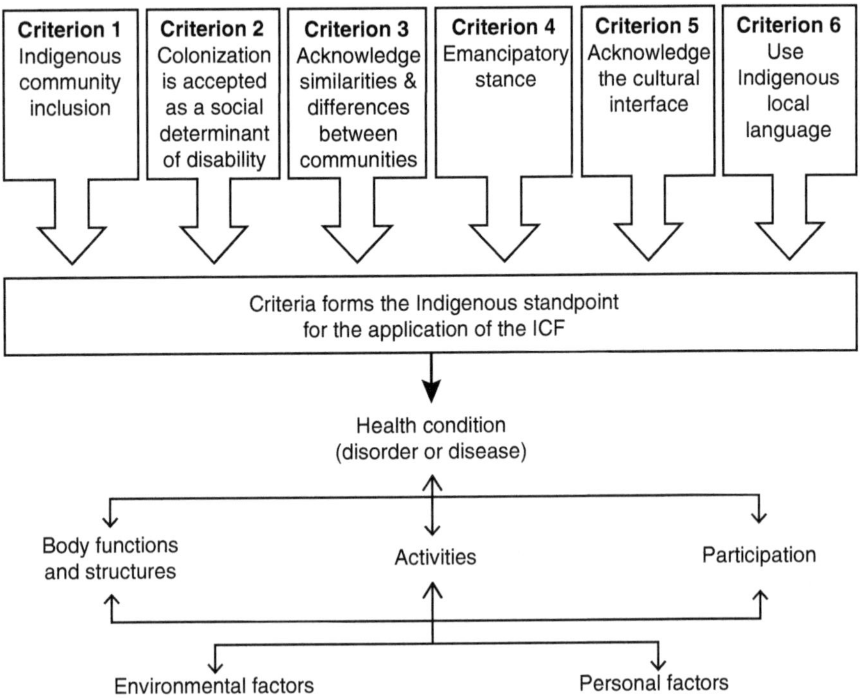

Fig. 35.3 Conceptual framework for research on disability with Indigenous communities (Gilroy et al. 2013: 54)

and colleagues established an IST as a foundation to examine the factors currently considered to influence human functioning identified in the International Classification of Functioning (WHO 2002; Gilroy et al. 2013). The six criteria listed in Fig. 35.3 are suggested as a starting point to help researchers and policy advisers develop a localised IST for working with Indigenous communities that acknowledges the cultural diversity within the population.

Gilroy et al. (2013) suggested that 'utilizing IST with the ICF could help ameliorate the current weaknesses of the global contextual framework in disability research and policy development'. The listed criteria could help increase the likelihood that the researchers and policy advisers (or team) identify and address structural factors, functional limitations within Indigenous communities, the lived experience of Indigenous people with disability, and the contradictions and complexities in this field. It acknowledges that both individual and social approaches to disability need to be adopted in research and policy development that impact on people with disability and Indigenous people.

In developing his standpoint theory, Foley (2006) built upon the work of Indigenous scholars in Australia (Rigney 1999; Moreton-Robinson 2004), New Zealand (Tuhiwai Smith 1999) and Hawaii (Meyer 2001). Foley took a philosophical approach that consists of three parts, displayed in Fig. 35.4. First, the spirit

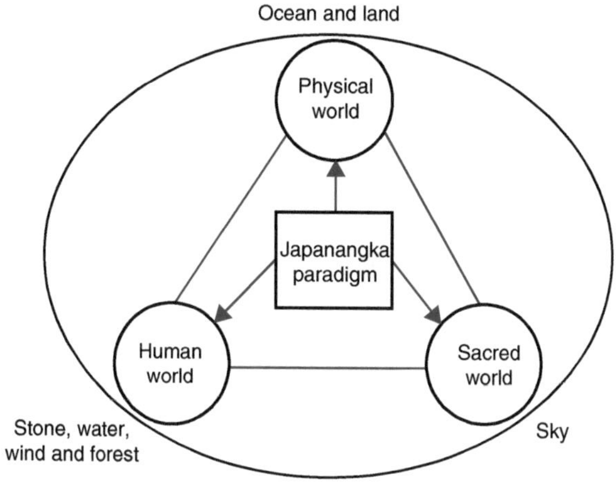

Fig. 35.4 Foley's Indigenous Standpoint Theory. *Note*: Adapted from Foley 2003: 49, Fig. 35.2

world equates to the land, creation, natural resources and spirituality of the Indigenous person's traditional homelands. Second, the human world acknowledges the importance of including all people, family, cultural protocols and ceremony. Third, the sacred world is not based on the metaphysical but is foundational to healing, spiritual and physical well-being of all creatures, lore, oral history, care of country, the laws and their maintenance (Foley 2003, 2006).

Similar to the development of IST, many Australian Indigenous scholars have incorporated cultural protocols into their methodologies due to the absence of a culturally appropriate conceptual framework within western sciences (Rigney 2007). For example, Miriam Rose Ungunmerr's (2002) cultural standpoint called *Dadirri*, which provides principles to foster communication between the researchers and research participants, was incorporated into many Australian Indigenous scholars' decolonising research methodologies, such as 'Indigenist Research' (Rigney 2007: 225). Ungunmerr was concerned about researchers not properly engaging with the Aboriginal community and failing to provide feedback on research findings (Ungunmerr 1995). Building on these developments, Foley (2003, 2006) and Rigney (2007) suggest the following three principles for research regarding Indigenous people:

1. The research must be counter-hegemonic to western ideologies and promote Indigenous people's recognition and self-determination in the production of knowledge.
2. The research must privilege Indigenous voices, which is fundamental to exposing the diverse experiences of Indigenous people as unique.
3. The research must be done by Indigenous researchers. IST has an emancipatory imperative in research regarding Indigenous people.

Oates disagreed with Foley's and Rigney's suggestion that only Aboriginal people can do research that involves Indigenous people, saying that 'the problem with this position is that insight and understanding are not dependent on the amount of melanin in the skin or whether the person can do a "kangaroo dance" or "Irish jig"' (Oates 2003: 5). Therefore the development of a single protocol or entitlement approach remains controversial.

The disability movement can learn from the lessons of Indigenous community development and Indigenous education in applying IST. For example, non-Indigenous researcher Walker adopted Nakata's IST in a community development research project. Walker stated that researchers needed to acknowledge they 'are all located within the cultural interface and this allows for the idea of leaving cultures intact in all their diversity while recognising that we are all becoming something different than we were because of our interactivity in this space' (2004: 173). Similarly, Nakata's IST has been adapted to assist Indigenous and non-Indigenous educators in developing curriculum and pedagogy that educates Indigenous children and youth to navigate the two worlds of Indigenous cultures and western cultures. This approach to education is now used by educational researchers in the planning and implementation of research and research practice (Choy and Woodlock 2007). The Ngaanyatjarra Pitjantjara Yankunytjatjara (NPY) peoples of central Australia approach is similar to Foley's model for aged-care research, exploring the challenges NPY people face in receiving culturally appropriate services for older people (NPY Women's Council 1995).

Academic Decolonisation: Indigenous Standpoint Theory and Disability Research

After two centuries of colonisation in Australia, western science in the area of disability research has not proven effective in understanding and addressing the health and well-being of Indigenous people with disability. Research on disability in Indigenous communities can also be argued to be *disabling* Australia's Indigenous peoples in a variety of ways, not the least of which is imposing northern Atlantic views of 'disability'. Meekosha (2004, 2011), Gilroy (2012) and Hollinsworth (2013) call for ethically sound and culturally appropriate research methods to help decolonise research involving Indigenous people with disability.

Mirroring the example of Indigenous education, women's studies and health studies, disability research needs to establish an IST for research with Indigenous people. Meekosha rightly states that researchers "cannot meaningfully separate the racialised subaltern from the disabled subaltern in the process of colonisation" (2011: 673). It is important that disability studies acknowledges the interplay between the parallels of 'race', 'culture' and 'disability'. Foley (2003) suggests four criteria to inform the development of an IST:

1. The research team must consist of Indigenous people. Research students must be supervised by Indigenous scholars.

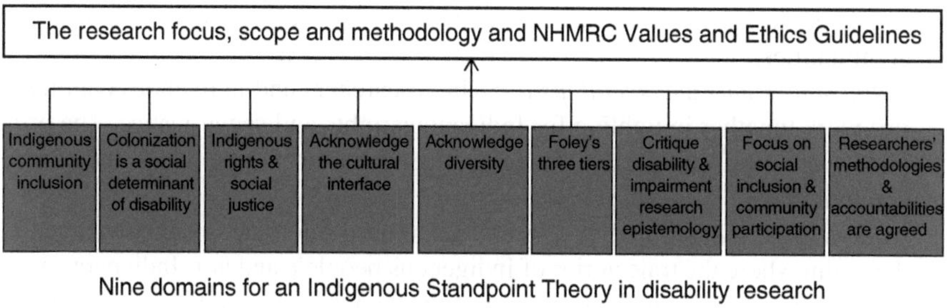

Fig. 35.5 Merging IST and Australian Indigenous research ethics in disability studies

2. The research team must be well versed in western social science discourses, such as social theory, critical sociology, post structuralism and post-modernism to name a few. The research team must be 'acutely aware of the limitations of these discourses to ensure that Indigenous research is not tormented or classified in the physical and metaphysical distortions of these western approaches' (Foley 2003: 50).
3. The research is designed to and does benefit the Indigenous communities or the wider Indigenous population.
4. Wherever possible, use Indigenous languages.

Figure 35.5 proposes an IST framework for Indigenous communities and research teams that would strengthen research methodology and address some of the shortcomings of the current NHMRC guidelines in decolonising disability research. While this has been developed in an Australian Indigenous research context, it may be a relevant point of reference for researchers among many Indigenous nations. The framework includes nine domains for Indigenous disability research planning and development and acknowledges the cultural diversity within the populations of Indigenous people. These domains acknowledge the strengths of the NHMRC Centre for Clinical Research Excellence (CCRE) (Fredericks 2006; Gilroy 2012; Gilroy et al 2013). The IST framework must be developed before the research scope, methodology and ethical guidelines are developed. There is no assumption in the following as to whether the research team or researcher is Indigenous or non-Indigenous.

1. *Indigenous community inclusion*: The research team includes Indigenous people, "bringing with them their own experiences as an Indigenous person" (Gilroy et al. 2013). This ensures that the researchers are meeting Indigenous local cultural protocols in undertaking research. Exchange in skills and knowledge should occur between Indigenous and non-Indigenous people. Indigenous communities could also have a research committee, project committee, yarn-up or reference group specifically to drive local disability research. This may involve complex and highly sensitive negotiations over time, for example, where family factions exist in local Aboriginal communities (Peters-Little 2000).
2. *Colonisation is accepted as a social determinant of disability*: The researchers and Indigenous communities have a shared understanding on how colonisation

and dispossession has influenced the experience of disabilities in local Indigenous communities.

3. *Indigenous rights and social justice*: The researchers and Indigenous communities work together in fighting for Indigenous rights and social justice. The principles and philosophies of social justice come from the local Indigenous communities.
4. *Acknowledge the cultural interface*: The cultural interface is acknowledged as the realm where the trajectories of Indigenous people's and non-Indigenous people's experiences of disability, colonisation, dispossession and indigeneity intersect. Research can then break away from the Us versus Them mentality.
5. *Acknowledge diversity*: The experience of functional limitation will be different and similar for each Indigenous community and between non-Indigenous and Indigenous communities in the same geographical region.
6. *Foley's three tiers*: Foley's (2003) three tiers—physical world, human world and sacred world—acknowledges the diversity and complexity of Indigenous knowledge systems from a macro level to a micro level. Wherever possible, these three tiers can be included in the research methodology to keep the research philosophies grounded and localised in Indigenous knowledge systems.
7. *Critique disability and impairment research epistemology*: Disability researchers and Indigenous people critique the way disability and impairment research represents and frames Indigenous people. Indigenous people must challenge the current western knowledge system in how it oppresses Indigenous people with disability as the Other without Indigenous people's input. A good example is the CCRE approach in Indigenous health research.
8. *Research methodologies and accountabilities are agreed on Indigenous communities' terms*: Planning and embedding research methodologies and accountabilities into the IST ensure that the researchers are accountable to the Indigenous communities. Furthermore, the research methodologies are culturally appropriate for Indigenous people and reflect Indigenous cultures, protocols and customs.
9. *Focus on social inclusion and community participation*: The concept of disability is either a new or a foreign term in many Indigenous communities. The concepts of disability and research are unacceptable in many Indigenous communities due to the practices of past researchers. Research in the area of disability and Indigenous communities can establish a shared understanding on 'social inclusion', 'community participation', 'health and well-being' to break away from the stigma associated with 'disability'.

An IST should be developed and embedded into the research focus, scope, methodology and ethics. The proposed IST framework will help Indigenous communities and research teams respond to the NHMRC Values and Ethics Guidelines. The NHMRC guidelines do not necessarily need to be changed because IST, at its core, is an ontological and epistemological approach for the application of research that enables an Indigenous person to establish their own standpoint to address the research objectives. IST allows the researchers to consider the cultural nature and meaning of knowledge and knowledge acquisition (Guba and Lincoln 2005) and therefore deepens and extends the understanding and application of the current NHMRC guidelines.

By grounding research in Indigenous communities the IST complements the NHMRC guidelines by establishing a bridge between western and Indigenous knowledge. This framework enables research in the area of disability to be scrutinised in relation to the representation and engagement of Indigenous people. Research can then be critiqued and held accountable for research outcomes including the emancipation and/or oppression of Indigenous people in Australia and perhaps also among other Indigenous nations. Once the IST is developed, it can inform the use of the NHMRC guidelines.

A good example of how IST is merged with research ethics is the CCRE, which focuses on circulatory and associated diseases in Indigenous communities. The CCRE merged IST with the NHMRC Values and Ethics Guidelines (NHMRC 2003, 2006; Fredericks 2006). Fredericks states that:

> If we are to bring about change to the way people think about us, know us as Aboriginal and Torres Strait Islander peoples in theoretical, learnt settings, we must be part of these environments … [and] challenge the current knowledge bases and ways of acquiring knowledge about us. (Fredericks 2006: 9).

As such, we must deconstruct and challenge how Europeans have defined and described Aboriginal identity to presently situate Aboriginal people as the most disadvantaged subgroup of the Australian population.

Concluding Points

Consistent with the international works of Alatas (2003), Connell (2007), Moreton-Robinson (2004) and Tuhiwai Smith (1999), this chapter has deconstructed the history of research in Australian Indigenous communities, showing that historically research in the area of 'disability and impairment' as a form of knowledge construction has involved academic imperialism or academic neo-colonialism. Australian Indigenous peoples' experience of research as a form of academic neo-colonialism has been detrimental to the health and identity of Indigenous people with disability. Reflecting the international literature, the scientific study of 'disability' and 'impairment' among Australian Indigenous communities has developed and maintained the hegemony of able-bodied non-Indigenous people (Metropole/abled/white/normal), in effect further marginalising Indigenous people with disability (Indigenous/disabled/non-normative) as the 'Other'. Research which assumes and substantiates this power hierarchy cannot address the social marginalisation and oppression of Indigenous people with disability.

There is a global movement towards decolonising Indigenous research and epistemologies. This chapter has highlighted some of the weaknesses of Australia's approach to research ethics in this area. Developing and merging an IST with the

NHMRC ethical guidelines shows promise in assisting researchers and research participants to decolonise disability research. In particular, this approach can assist in addressing the potential for research to contribute to marginalisation and oppression. The proposed framework engages Indigenous communities with the research from conceptualisation as opposed to the current process where engagement occurs only after the research has been conceptualised and planned. This approach to the examination of research practice extends our understanding of research ethics beyond the punctuated equilibrium of crisis cases, individual freedoms and bureaucratised ethical procedures which characterise current research practice.

A community-grounded, structural enquiry framework, such as IST, is proposed to include the following key elements:

- Focus on social inclusion and participation of the Indigenous community and Indigenous people with a disability
- Accepting and addressing colonisation as a social determinant of disability
- Adopting an emancipatory approach to social rights and justice, and critique of disability and impairment research
- Acknowledging the cultural interface
- Acknowledging the diversity and complexity of Indigenous perspectives and world view and adopting a critical disability research epistemology and methodology accountable to Indigenous communities

Such a comprehensive framework could assist international research communities and Indigenous communities to understand and address fundamental patterns of social and community marginalisation in the history of research practice. In addition, disability researchers and Indigenous communities can work together to create new perspectives, insights and theories of the impact of colonisation, inclusion and participation for people with disability, their families and communities.

References

Alatas, S. F. (2003). Academic dependency and the global division of labour in the social sciences. *Current Sociology, 51*(6), 599–613.

Alderete, E. (1999). *The health of indigenous peoples*. Geneva: World Health Organization.

Alexander, L. & Moore, M. (2012). Deontological ethics. In E. N. Zalta (Ed.), *The Stanford encyclopedia of philosophy* (Winter 2012 edn.). Retrieved February 2014, from http://plato.stanford.edu/archives/win2012/entries/ethics-deontological/.

Anderson, I. (1996). Ethics and health research in Aboriginal communities. In J. Daly (Ed.), *Ethical intersections* (pp. 153–165). Sydney: Allen & Unwin.

Attwood, B. (1989). *The making of the aborigines*. Sydney: Allen & Unwin.

Australian Institute of Health and Welfare (AIHW). (2011). *Aboriginal and Torres Strait Islander people with disability: Wellbeing, participation and support*. Canberra: AIHW.

Beauchamp, T. (2007). The 'four principles' approach to health care ethics. In R. Ashcroft, A. Dawson, H. Draper, & J. McMillan (Eds.), *Principles of healthcare ethics* (pp. 3–10). Chichester: Wiley.

Bishop, R. (1998). Freeing ourselves from neo-colonial domination in research: A Maori approach to creating knowledge. *International Journal of Qualitative Studies in Education, 11*, 199–219.

Bostock, J. (1924). Insanity in the Australian Aboriginal and its bearing on the evolution of mental disease. *The Medical Journal of Australia, 5*(July), 459–464.

Brady, W. (1992). Indigenous control of Aboriginal and Torres Strait Islander research. *2nd Aboriginal Studies Association Conference*, University of New South Wales, pp. 311–315.

Brodsky, I. (1943). Congenital abnormalities, teratology and embryology: Some evidence of primitive man's knowledge as expressed in art and lore in Oceania. *The Medical Journal of Australia, 8*(May), 417–420.

Cawte, J. (1964). Tjimi and tjagolo: Ethnopsychiatry in the Kalumburu people of north-western Australia. *Oceania, 34*, 170–190.

Cawte, J. (1966). Australian aborigines in mental hospitals. *Oceania, 36*(4), 264–282.

Chewings, C. (1936). *Back in the stone age: The natives of central Australia*. Sydney: Angus and Robertson.

Choy, S., & Woodlock, J. (2007). Implementing indigenous standpoint theory: Challenges for a TAFE trainer. *International Journal of Training Research, 5*(1), 39–44.

Cohen, A. (1999). *The mental health of indigenous peoples: An international overview*. Geneva: World Health Organization.

Connell, R. (2007). *Southern theory: The global dynamics of knowledge in the social sciences*. Sydney: Allen & Unwin.

Crow, L. (1996). Including all of our lives: Renewing the social model of disability. In C. Barnes & G. Mercer (Eds.), *Exploring the divide: Illness and disability*. Leeds: Disability Press.

Curr, E. M. (1886). *The Australian race: Its origin, languages, customs, place of landing in Australia, and the routes by which it spread itself over that continent*. Melbourne: John Ferres, Government Printer.

Driver, J. (2009). The history of utilitarianism. In E. N. Zalta (Ed.), *The stanford encyclopedia of philosophy*, (Summer 2009 edn.). Retrieved February 2014, from http://plato.stanford.edu/archives/sum2009/entries/utilitarianism-history/.

Fitzgerald, M. (2004). Punctuated equilibrium, moral panics and the ethics review process. *Journal of Academic Ethics, 2*, 315–338. doi:10.1007/s10805-005-9004-y.

Foley, D. (2003). Indigenous epistemology and indigenous standpoint theory. *Social Alternatives, 22*(1), 44–52.

Foley, D. (2006). Indigenous standpoint theory: An acceptable academic research process for Indigenous academics. *International Journal of the Humanities, 3*(4), 25–36.

Fredericks, B. (2006). Aboriginal and Torres Strait Islander lead and governed research: A sign of social change. In *Proceedings of the Social Change in the 21st Century Conference 2006*, Queensland University of Technology, Brisbane.

Gilroy, J. (2010). History of Aboriginal people with disability in NSW: How are Aboriginal people with disability positioned and represented in the NSW disability services sector? *Interaction: Special Edition on Aboriginal People with Disability, 24*(1), 6–29. Retrieved from http://aiidd.org.au/interaction/24/24.1.pdf.

Gilroy, J. (2012). *The participation of Aboriginal persons with disability in disability services in New South Wales, Australia*. Doctoral dissertation, University of Sydney, Australia.

Gilroy, J., Colmar, S., Donelly, M., & Parmenter, T. (2013). Conceptual framework for policy and research development with Indigenous persons with disability. *Journal of Australian Aboriginal Studies, 2*, 42–58.

Grech, S. (2012). Disability and the majority world: A neo-colonial approach. In D. Goodley, B. Hughes, & L. Davis (Eds.), *Disability and social theory*. Basingstoke: Palgrave Macmillan (Chapter 4).

Guba, E., & Lincoln, Y. (2005). Paradigmatic controversies, contradictions and emerging confluences. In N. Denzin & Y. Lincoln (Eds.), *The sage handbook of qualitative research* (3rd ed., pp. 191–215). Thousand Oaks, CA: Sage.

Hackett, C. (1936). *Boomerang leg and yaws in Australian aborigines*. London: Royal Society of Tropical Medicine and Hygiene.

Harris, J. (1990). *One blood: 200 years of Aboriginal encounter with Christianity—A story of hope*. Sutherland, NSW: Albatross Books.

Henry, J., Dunbar, T., Arnott, A., Scrimgeour, M., Matthews, A., Murakami, L., et al. (2002). *Indigenous research reform agenda: Changing institutions* (Links monograph series). Darwin: Cooperative Research Centre for Aboriginal and Tropical Health.

Hollinsworth, D. (2013). Decolonizing Indigenous disability in Australia. *Disability & Society, 28*(5), 601–615.

Huggins, J. (Ed.). (1993). *Pretty deadly tidda business*. Sydney: Allen and Unwin.

Hughes, B., & Paterson, K. (1997). The social model of disability and the disappearing body: Towards a sociology of impairment. *Disability & Society, 12*(3), 325–340.

Humphery, K. (2001). Dirty questions: Indigenous health and western research. *Australian and New Zealand Journal of Public Health, 25*, 197–202.

Jones, D. (1990). Contemporary medical scandals: A challenge to ethical codes and ethical principles. *Perspectives on Sciences and Christian Faith, 42*, 2–14.

Kidson, M. (1965). *Ethnopsychiatry in central Australia: A survey of mental illness in the Walbiri.* Unpublished manuscript. Sydney: Prince Henry Hospital.

Kidson, M. (1967). Psychiatric disorders in the Walbiri Central Australia. *Australian and New Zealand Journal of Psychiatry, 1*, 14–22.

Kowal, E., Anderson, I., & Bailie, R. (2005). Moving beyond good intentions: Indigenous participation in Aboriginal and Torres Strait Islander health research. *Australian and New Zealand Journal of Public Health, 29*, 468–470.

Langton, M. (1993). *Well I heard it on the radio and I saw it on the television*. Sydney: Australian Film Commission.

Lindsay, D. (1893). *Journal of the elder scientific exploring exhibition 1891–2*. Adelaide: Corkwood Press.

Meekosha, H. (2004). Drifting down the gulf stream: Navigating the cultures of disability studies. *Disability & Society, 19*(7), 721–733.

Meekosha, H. (2011). Decolonising disability: Thinking and acting globally. *Disability & Society, 26*(6), 667–682.

Meyer, M. (2001). Our own liberation: Reflections on Hawaiian epistemology. *The Contemporary Pacific, 13*(Spring), 124–309.

Meyer, M. (2008). Indigenous and authentic: Hawaiian epistemology and the triangulation of meaning. In N. Denzin, Y. Lincoln, & L. T. Smith (Eds.), *Handbook of critical and Indigenous methodologies* (pp. 217–232). London: Sage.

Moreton-Robinson, A. (2000). *Talkin' up to the white woman: Aboriginal women and feminism*. Brisbane: University of Queensland Press.

Moreton-Robinson, A. (2004). Whiteness, epistemology and Indigenous representation. In A. Moreton-Robinson (Ed.), *Whitening race: Essays in social and cultural criticism* (pp. 75–88). Canberra: Aboriginal Studies Press.

Morris, J. (1991). *Pride against prejudice: A personal politics of disability*. London: Women's Press.

Nakata, M. (1997). *The cultural interface: An exploration of the intersection of western knowledge systems and Torres Strait Islander positions and experiences*. Doctoral dissertation, James Cook University, Townsville, QLD.

Nakata, M. (1998). Anthropological texts and indigenous standpoints. *Australian Indigenous Studies, 3*, 3–15.

Nakata, M. (Ed.). (2004). *Indigenous knowledge and the cultural interface: Underlying issues at the intersection of knowledge and information systems*. Sydney: Post Press.

National Commission for the Protection of Human Subjects of Biomedical and Behavioural Research. (1979). *Ethical principles and guidelines for the protection of human subjects of research (Belmont Report)*. Washington, DC: US Department of Health, Education, and

Welfare. Retrieved November 7, 2014, from http://www.hhs.gov/ohrp/humansubjects/guidance/belmont.html.

National Health Medical Research Council (NHMRC). (1991). *Guidelines on ethical matters in Aboriginal and Torres Strait Islander health research*. Canberra: NHMRC. Retrieved November 2013, from http://www.nhmrc.gov.au/_files_nhmrc/publications/attachments/e11.pdf.

NHMRC. (2003). *Values and ethics: Guidelines for ethical conduct in Aboriginal and Torres Strait Islander health research*. Canberra: Commonwealth of Australia. Retrieved November 2014, from http://www.nhmrc.gov.au/_files_nhmrc/publications/attachments/e52.pdf.

NHMRC. (2006). *Keeping research on track: A guide for Aboriginal and Torres Strait Islander peoples about health research ethics*. Canberra: NHMRC. Retrieved November 2014, from https://www.nhmrc.gov.au/guidelines/publications/e65.

NHMRC. (2007). *National statement on ethical conduct in human research*. Canberra: NHMRC. Retrieved October 2013, from http://www.nhmrc.gov.au/health-ethics/human-research-ethics-committees-hrecs/human-research-ethics-committees-hrecs/national/.

NHMRC. (2010). *NHMRC road map II: A strategic framework for improving the health of Aboriginal and Torres Strait Islander people through research*. Canberra: NHMRC. Retrieved June 2013, from https://www.nhmrc.gov.au/guidelines/publications/r47.

NHMRC. (2013). *Researching right way Sydney consultation notes: Stakeholder experiences of using the NHMRC values and ethics guidelines and keeping research on track*. Unpublished.

Ngaanyatjarra Pitjantjatjara Yankunytjatjara Women's Council. (1995). They might have to drag me like a bullock. In *The Tjilpi Pampa Tjutaku Project*. Alice Springs: NPYWC.

Oates, W. (2003). Bastards of the bush: Towards an Indigenous Australian research. In P. Jeffrey (Ed.), *AARE Conference Proceedings, Auckland, New Zealand*. Retrieved November 7, 2014, from http://www.aare.edu.au/publications-database.php/3929/bastards-of-the-bush-towards-an-indigenous-australian-research-methodology.

Oliver, M. (1990). *The politics of disablement*. London: Macmillan.

Peters-Little, F. (2000). *The community game: Aboriginal self definition at the local level*. AIATSIS discussion paper, 10. Retrieved November 7, 2014, from http://epress.anu.edu.au/caepr_series/no_20/mobile_devices/ch19.html.

Pétré-Grenouilleau, O. (2004). *From slave trade to empire: European colonisation of black Africa, 1780s–1880s*. New York: Routledge.

Proctor, R. (1992). Nazi doctors, racial medicine, and human experimentation. In G. Annas & M. Grodin (Eds.), *The Nazi doctors and the Nuremberg code*. New York: Oxford University Press.

Pulver, L. J., Haswell, M. R., Ring, I., Waldon, J., Clark, W., Whetung, V. et al. (2010). *Indigenous health—Australia, Canada, Aotearoa New Zealand and the United States—laying claim to a future that embraces health for us all*. Background paper 33. Geneva: World Health Organization.

Reynolds, H. (1981). *The other side of the frontier: An interpretation of the Aboriginal response to the invasion and settlement of Australia*. Townsville, QLD: James Cook University.

Rigney, L. (1999). Internationalisation of an Indigenous anticolonial cultural critique of research methodologies: A guide to indiginist research methodology and its principles. *Wicazo SA Review, 14*(2), 109–121.

Rigney, L. (2007). *Indiginist research epistemologies: A historical journey of conviction, contradiction and transformation*. Doctoral thesis. Flinders University, Adelaide.

Said, E. (1978). *Orientalism*. London: Routledge & Kegan Paul.

Shakespeare, T., & Watson, N. (1997). Defending the social model. *Disability & Society, 12*(2), 293–300.

Smith, G. (1997). *Kaupapa Maori: Theory and praxis*. Auckland: The International Research Institute for Maori and Indigenous Education.

Smith, G. (2008). *Theorizing, transforming and reclaiming ourselves*. Presented at the International Health—Wellbeing Course, University of British Columbia, Canada.

Stirling, E. (1950). Sir Edward Stirling, F.R.S.: Boomerang legs, the marsupial mole and diprotodon remains. *The Medical Journal of Australia, 29*(April), 556–557.

Tierney, P. (2000, November 6). The fierce anthropologist. *The New Yorker*, 1–15. Retrieved from http://www.old.li.suu.edu/library/circulation/Dean/anth1010edTiernyFierceAnthropologistFall08.pdf.

Tuhiwai Smith, L. (1999). *Decolonising methodologies: Research and Indigenous peoples*. Dunedin: University of Otago Press.

Ungunmerr, M. R. (1995). Dadirri. In E. Stockton (Ed.), *The Aboriginal gift: Spirituality for a nation* (pp. 179–184). Alexandria: Millennium Books.

Ungunmerr, M. R. (2002). *Dadirri: Inner deep listening and quiet still awareness*. Melbourne: Secretariat of National Aboriginal and Islander Child Care.

UN. (2006). *Convention on the rights of persons with disabilities*. New York: United Nations. Retrieved from http://www.un.org/disabilities/convention/signature.shtml.

United Nations (UN). (2008). *Declaration on the rights of indigenous peoples*. New York: United Nations. Retrieved from http://www.un.org/esa/socdev/unpfii/documents/DRIPS_en.pdf.

Walker, R. (2004). *Transformative strategies in indigenous education: A study of decolonisation and positive social change, the indigenous community management program*. Doctoral dissertation, University of Western Sydney, Bansktown, NSW.

West, E. (2000). *An alternative to existing Australian research and teaching models: the Japanangka teaching and research paradigm, an Australian Aboriginal model*. Doctoral thesis, Southern Cross University.

World Health Organization (WHO). (2002). *Towards a common language for functioning, disability and health ICF*. Geneva: WHO.

WHO. (2008). *Commission on social determinants of health—Final report*. Geneva: WHO.

Chapter 36
Global South–North Partnerships: Intercultural Methodologies in Disability Research

Karen R. Fisher, Xiaoyuan Shang, and Jiawen Xie

Introduction

Adopting critical research methodologies in the global South requires straddling national and international expectations about what, how and why the research is done. One approach to deal with the competing tensions in these questions is through a global South–North research partnership that continuously reflects on and adjusts the methodology as part of the research process itself. In this chapter, we use a South–North research partnership between Chinese and Australian researchers as an example to explore how practical tensions might be managed in the choices made about the disability research subject, design, methods, analysis and knowledge translation.

K.R. Fisher (✉)
Social Policy Research Centre, UNSW Australia,
Gate 9 High Street, Kensington, Sydney, NSW 2052, Australia
e-mail: Karen.fisher@unsw.edu.au

X. Shang
Social Policy Research Centre, UNSW Australia,
Gate 9 High Street, Kensington, Sydney, NSW 2052, Australia

Beijing Normal University, Beijing, China
e-mail: x.shang@unsw.edu.au

J. Xie
Beijing Normal University, Beijing, China

Institute of Sociology, Shanghai Academy of Social Sciences,
17043 NW Reuben Ln, Portland, OR 97229, USA
e-mail: xjw@sass.org.cn

S. Grech, K. Soldatic (eds.), *Disability in the Global South*,
International Perspectives on Social Policy, Administration, and Practice,
DOI 10.1007/978-3-319-42488-0_36

Approaches to disability research are contested in any context, perhaps even more so in the global South. Even the very concept of disability, what it is, who experiences it, why and how, will always remain a political question, therefore shaped by the context in which these questions are asked (Meekosha and Soldatic 2011). Similarly, disability research is subject to unresolvable epistemological and methodological differences in disciplinary approaches. Claiming global norms to these questions is a foolhardy activity. Yet global South disability researchers are often expected to do just that, in order to resource, conduct and communicate their research nationally and internationally.

Critical studies researchers have sought to explain these pressures on research in the global South, including on indigenous and disability research, as an expression of neo-liberal and neocolonial oppression (e.g. Grech and Goodley 2012; Connell 2014). In response, global South researchers sometimes adopt conservative approaches to research to placate the multiple demands of and on global South research actors—people with disabilities, researchers, the audience and funders. This is despite a well-established alternative body of practice that seeks to recognise the authority and legitimacy of global South methods (e.g. Bishop 1998; Denzin et al. 2008). How can global South and North researchers and people with disabilities work together to overcome the risk of reductionist approaches to disability research?

This chapter uses the empirical experience of a mixed team of researchers to explore these questions. First, it introduces concepts about collaborative research in the global South. It then illustrates the dilemmas by analysing the actions of the research team from the conception of a disability research project through to communication and application, using the case example published in Shang et al. (2011). It draws conclusions for confronting those who claim universal application of global North disability research methods is desirable, good enough or even possible.

Collaborative Research

International collaboration is not new, but partnerships that prioritise the value and utility of local knowledges are more recent. Collaboration between global South–North researchers has the potential to exchange assumed research authority in a global South research context. International collaboration also raises questions about the conditions required to organise the research such that the global South partners control the project. Otherwise, the collaboration itself retains the risk that the global North methodologies continue in their propensity to dominate. This chapter explores an approach that might inform some of these conditions.

Researchers draw from a range of knowledge frameworks, including their personal position and community, national and international expectations. They make choices about how to balance these knowledges, depending on their political positioning of the purpose and audience for the research. These decisions can be difficult especially when the frameworks conflict about which knowledge is valued by whom. Global South disability researchers can face many such epistemological conflicts which then affect their methodological choices. Their choices about which audiences to prioritise will privilege particular knowledges and methodologies. For example, the choice of methodologies could be informed by local and other understandings of disability; lived experiences; indigenous, customary and traditional knowledges; policy, practice and professional knowledge; or disciplinary, national and international norms of research (Grech and Goodley 2012). Contrasting methods that might arise from these knowledges include a wide range of qualitative or quantitative processes.

In a simplified example of this tension, global South researchers might simultaneously be expected by local people with disabilities to conduct research with them as participants in order to understand and improve their living conditions; be expected by national policymakers to conduct large-scale quantitative instrumental research using internationally validated instruments for consistency with a policy evidence base (Urwick 2013); and be expected by international journal editors to use other global North methods in order to demonstrate the rigour of the research and the relevance of the findings to other settings. Research about disability and poverty could take the form of action research with local people with disabilities so as to also contribute to alleviating poverty; alternatively, it may involve conducting economic analysis based on national census data about the number and characteristics of people with disabilities and their incomes.

Global North disability researchers negotiate these conflicts, too, of course, but the conflicts they face are usually fewer because their geopolitical location dominates in the positioning of international knowledge. Sometimes they can be freer than many global South researchers to adopt less conventional methodologies because they are less likely to need to demonstrate their global North legitimacy (Grech 2011). For example, disability-inclusive research practices, action research, narrative life history research, and indigenous methodologies are gaining acceptance by some decision-makers in parts of global North countries. In some cases, these approaches are expected or even mandated in policy frameworks, if the research is to be government funded and the results are to have utility for the community (e.g. NHMRC 2002; NDRDA 2011).

Published reflections on the reasons for collaborative research that prioritises global South knowledges are generally from the perspective of the global North partner (for a recent summary, see Lombe et al. 2013). Other global North partners lament the futility of international collaborations that perpetuate the status quo and generate research for display, where the research fails to contribute to socially progressive change (such as development grants that tick boxes rather than engage with the political context—see Urwick 2013). While collaborations driven by global South researchers do not necessarily achieve immediate national or international policy influence, Urwick emphasises the capacity of collaborations to influence wider understandings about the issues in the research question by the people involved in it. This newer partnership approach coincides with other global North epistemological positions that value inclusion, participation and control by people with disabilities of disability research (e.g. Nind 2014).

Of interest in this chapter is the utility of international collaboration from the perspective of global South researchers. What can international partnering add to local disability research, while still prioritising local knowledge and retaining local control over the research process and product? As suggested by Meekosha (2011), can social solidarity between global South and North researchers bridge power gaps in the conceptualisation and contribution of global South disability research to the local demands of people with disabilities, national utility and international theorisation?

As a starting point, we apply the interesting analytical reflections from Samuel and Mariaye's (2013) South–South collaboration in a joint PhD program between South Africa and Mauritius. They analysed the steps they took in setting up a partnership, including creating bridges between the different approaches of the partners; their mutual reciprocity in contributing to the partnership and learning from it; and generating a local knowledge resource for theorising on an international platform. They emphasised that as global South researchers, they did not uncritically romanticise local knowledge because all knowledge has a potential for exploitation. Their aim was to disrupt power hierarchies and speak back to coloniality by decolonising their contributions to international theorisation. A strength of their reflections was the acknowledgement of their specific political histories and the hierarchies even within and between these two colonised countries.

We apply several relevant conclusions from the Samuel and Mariaye analysis. First, the quality of the collaboration depended on the reflective relationships between the parties, including acknowledging their past, current and future political and cultural context, both with respect to their own countries and the relationships between them. They used this reflection to disrupt hierarchies that would continually recur. Second, they looked inward to privilege the generation of local knowledge and outward to contribute to international theorisation. This way they were able to critically generate and analyse local knowledge that was relevant to their context and challenge international theoretical assumptions. We take this frame to analyse our intercultural collaborative approach.

Methodological Choices in a South–North Context

Choices about research methodology reflect power dynamics in any research program (Hunter 2002). We analyse our experience in a collaborative disability policy research project to describe the points at which methodological choices were affected by power in the global South–North partnership. First, we describe how we adopted a reflective relationship approach to negotiate the diverse expectations of the research in the national and international context. Then we discuss the operation of the partnership in the research context in each country, Australia and China; the roles of the research team members; the methods adopted; and the process of analysis and impact.

In this chapter we look critically at a single case study of qualitative, participatory research (Shang et al. 2011), which was part of a larger national research project in China. In this case study we analysed the experiences of children with hearing and speech impairments in a poor Chinese county and conducted the research by focusing on the social networks around a young man in a rural village. The research was conducted and applied in China, with joint funding from Australia and China, detailed later. The team operates in China and Australia, working with local, national and international researchers. It seeks to respect local research priorities and methods, but with the intention of publishing the results nationally and internationally.[1]

The main finding of the case study, and an important finding of the whole project, is that children with disabilities socially participate through communication, social relationships and interest representation with their family, school friends and schools during childhood, and also in informal community disability groups during teenage years. In contrast, the formal local government disability organisation had less direct impact on participation. The implications for policy to fulfil children's rights were to increase direct government engagement with people with disabilities and to fund information, support, resources and formal structures to assist children, their families, communities, schools and local non-government organisations.

The Chinese disability policy researchers in the team work in a Chinese research context, where conservative approaches from the global North tend to dominate. These researchers are generally expected to use standard approaches so that their findings hold some authority with national and international audiences. And yet the research is conducted in a country of diverse and changing lived experiences of people with disabilities across the vast geography and population of China. In the highly structured policy research context of communist China, the government funds official channels for disability policy research. The agency responsible for disability policy, the Chinese Disabled Persons Federation (CDPF), funds five university disability research institutes,[2] and these and other researchers have formed a China Disability Research Society. Their work is largely traditional social science analysis using standard quantitative or mixed-methods research (e.g. Zheng et al. 2012). CDPF is also informed by the affiliated China Rehabilitation Research Centre (n.d.), which conducts medically oriented research about rehabilitation and technology. Other research organisations, like the China Research Centre on Ageing, organise policy research about older people with disabilities.

In addition to these formal disability research organisations, other academic researchers contribute knowledge from various disciplinary approaches, most of which do not prioritise lived experience (e.g. Yang 2009, 2013; Liu 2011; Qin and Zeng 2014; Yan and Li 2014; Yang and Wang 2014). A small number of researchers contribute alternative voices through more grounded approaches. For example, Hua

[1] The case study was published in Chinese first (Xie and Shang 2009). It was later published in English as a chapter in an edited collection aimed at an international social science audience (Fisher et al. 2011b). The larger research project followed a similar pattern of Chinese followed by English publication (Fisher and Li 2008; Shang 2008, 2012, 2013; Shang et al. 2011; Shang and Wang 2011; Fisher and Shang 2013, 2014).

[2] Nanjing University, Renmin University of China, Peking University, Shandong University and Jilin University.

Lan (2008) studied social participation barriers that people with disabilities faced by interviewing 30 people with disabilities about their daily life in a community of Tianjin. Our collaborative example also used this approach.

Within the partnership, the Australian disability policy researchers are also affected by tensions between global South and North disability research in several ways, despite their privileged global North position. Most directly challenging to dominant global North disability research methods in Australia are Indigenous Australian disability experiences; global South migrant experiences in Australia (the largest migrant groups are now from India and China); and the global South geographical position of Australia in Asia (or Pacific or Oceania, depending on perspective) in tension with its global North colonial history (Meekosha 2011). As a result, even in the Australian context, the diversity of experience of disability is sometimes recognised in disability research methods and occasionally in policy responses. These methods are consistent with principles of critical disability studies (Goodley 2013) and critical policy studies (Bartels and Wittmayer 2014), which encourage reflective, inclusive methods to shift power within research and policy towards positions and methods relevant to people's lived experiences.

This is an interesting example of where a cultural positioning of global South–North (China–Australia) is the opposite of the geographical position (Australia–China). China and Australia have a short history of research collaboration, with Australia generally taking the researcher expert role. Until 2013, China was a priority country for Australian international aid, including research. More recently, collaboration has included greater reciprocity, largely driven by the obvious changes to trade and migration relationships and China's growing international economic and political status. As a consequence of the changes in these national relationships, expectations in bilateral research partnerships have also changed. For example, Chinese studies in Australia now has a generation of Chinese researchers rather than just Australian experts on China (see CSAA 2015). Included in this newer approach to collaboration is our example of partnership between Chinese researchers and an international disability policy researcher.

Research Team

Collaborative research teams need to consider how they manage power in the dynamics and roles of the team members given their cultural and knowledge hierarchies. Samuel and Mariaye's (2013) framework relies on reflective relationships to disrupt recurring hierarchies. Our research team is led by Xiaoyuan Shang and Karen Fisher at UNSW Australia (see Shang and Fisher 2013, 2015). Shang is also affiliated with Beijing Normal University, where she supervises higher degree candidates who participate in the research. She is the pre-eminent expert on social policy about Chinese orphans, most of whom are children with disabilities. Shang maintains relationships nationally and internationally with Chinese researchers, academics, policy officials, NGOs and other social networks of people who initiate, participate and use the disability policy research. For example, the research team maintains close relationships with many child welfare institutions in China, where over 90 per cent of children in care are children with disabilities. Shang's research team in China also works with organisations established by parents of children with autism, to assist them to voice the interests of their children. She also develops relationships with international organisations in China that focus on program and policy development for children with disabilities, such as UNICEF, Save the Children UK and Right To Play. Some of these organisations also fund disability research.

Jiawen Xie managed the fieldwork for this research during her PhD in a project led by Shang and Fisher. The other fieldwork researchers relevant to the analysis in this case study were 28 higher degree and undergraduate students at Beijing Normal University who conducted the research in their dispersed hometowns. The research could build on their strong community relationships (Denzin et al. 2008). To select this team, Xie interviewed students and asked them to talk about their understanding of disability. Before the fieldwork, only two students had direct experience of disability in their family and neighbourhood. The others had only indirect contact with people with disabilities in their hometowns.

The global North researcher is Karen Fisher, who specialises in disability policy. She has regularly visited or lived in China since 1985, which gives her an understanding of the cultural and political context of the research and language. In Australia, she prioritises inclusive methodologies by investing in relationships with disability advocacy organisations, facilitating disability research capacity building and working with colleagues with disabilities.

None of the team has a personal experience of disability. Our methods attempted to privilege direct disability voices to overcome this limitation. The mixed-methods team structure enabled research capacity building for each of the members and the research partners. Bringing a reflexive approach to relying on internal and external relationships in the research team created opportunities to share and challenge each other's experiences and expectations, discussed in the next section.

Methods and Fieldwork in a Collaboration

The first way of managing the risk of global North dominance within the collaboration is the team designing the projects based on local needs and knowledge. In Samuel and Mariaye's (2013) framework, this local contextual focus is the first of a two-part step towards challenging international theoretical assumptions. The team uses two strategies to maintain this global South control: the research questions are generated from local discussions; and the data are collected by researchers with local relationships. The global North contribution to the collaboration in this stage is reactive only.

Local Research Focus

Shang takes primary responsibility for initiating the research questions, managing and conducting the data collection and analysing the results. She discusses each of these steps with the many Chinese collaborators mentioned earlier so that the research has community, policy and research relevance. She then discusses with Fisher the questions that emerge from the priorities of local collaborators and the choice of international policy, theory or methods to fit the research. Their reflective discussions take the form of asking questions of each other, rather than assuming a static knowledge base from which to build. Examples of how this is done are described in the following sections.

The research topics prioritised in this way are usually not yet dominant policy priorities in China because the topics are generated from listening to a wider range of people. Yet, the outputs from topics researched this way often attract popular focus. For example, when we began this child disability policy research in 2005, other Chinese researchers or policymakers were not concentrating on the area nationally. The team publishes a report in Chinese each year on emerging issues and leading research to try to influence academic policy research trends in China (Shang et al. 2010; Shang and Wang 2011, 2012, 2013).

For the overall research project (Shang and Fisher 2015), Shang discussed the possible research priorities and design with her Chinese policy contacts over a prolonged period to develop questions that had theoretical and policy relevance. The partnership funding in China eventuated from an international NGO based in Beijing, Right To Play China, whose personnel had asked Shang for earlier policy advice. The NGO needed empirical evidence about children's experiences to support the design and implementation of local programs. Their most urgent policy need was basic empirical research about the experience of children with disabilities within their families. The researchers chose to adopt a human rights framework for the project because it resonated with the partners in China and internationally and held policy currency with the Chinese Government (Fisher et al. 2011a).

The funding for the project was an Australian academic grant (Australian Research Council Linkage grant), which requires partnership funding from China and demonstrated collaboration in the project design. The academic partnership and the nature and source of funding had an impact on the research questions and methods. The NGO partnership funding allowed the researchers to pursue research questions relevant to short-term policy interventions, while the academic funding enabled investigation into conceptual research questions in a relatively longer period of 3 years. This longer timeframe suited the research questions, facilitating local research relationships and drawing out international implications, consistent with the Samuel and Mariaye framework.

Local Data Collection Methods

The choices about methods for the project were driven by practical questions of funding resources, available datasets, Chinese policy expectations, the program needs of the NGO partner, and national and international research expectations, within the constraints of the budget and available researchers. The mixed-methods research design included quantitative analysis of a national dataset (Second Chinese National Disability Survey 2006) and qualitative fieldwork. Access to the dataset was negotiated through Shang's earlier government and academic research connections in China. Ethics approval was from the international university, UNSW Australia, and endorsed by the Chinese university. This chapter focuses on the qualitative data collection and analysis.

The fieldwork was designed around the capacity of the fieldwork researchers to conduct research in their hometowns—regional and remote villages around China. The advantage of this method was that diverse experiences of disability could be included. Researchers could draw on their local knowledge and social relationships to arrange the research; respectfully engage with the community members with disabilities; adapt the methods to locally specific expectations; and understand the context of the data to interpret it for analysis. The risks were that they might feel pressure to extend a research relationship or exert pressure on people with whom they had a social relationship. Shang recruited Xie to conduct fieldwork and to manage the fieldworker team. Fisher's role was to comment on the fieldwork design, including ethical practice (such as disability-inclusive methods, observation with children, arms-length recruitment and confidentiality), training, questions, process and framework.

Xie met the young deaf man and his family at the centre of this case study through convenience sampling and voluntary participation. Xie had visited the organisation responsible for disability in her local community (the DPF (Disabled Persons Federation), the local level of the CDPF), and randomly selected families with children with different impairments from the list of people in the county. An informal community group of people with hearing and speech impairments in the county gathered at a hair salon. The salon is not an incorporated NGO or a government community organisation, although they would like to have this formal status. Xie decided to pursue this particular case study after spending extra time observing and participating in the activities of the young man's household and community and the salon, which revealed interesting social networks.

Xie collected the data over 9 months of visits whenever she returned to her hometown. Methods were semi-structured observation, conversations and in-depth interviews with the young man, his family and people in his community from his social networks. Xie also conducted repeat interviews with the DPF staff and local people, such as neighbours, doctors and other people who knew the young man and his family. She learned basic sign language during the research to improve her participatory methods. With their consent, most of the interviews with people who only used sign language were assisted by a hearing member of the salon, sometimes supplemented with pen and paper for independent conversation. Because social media, texting and online communication were preferred means of communication for the young man and some of the other deaf community members, Xie also used these media for follow-up interviews and conversations.

During the participatory fieldwork Xie was frequently asked to assist the people she was interviewing. The most common request was to help them get more financial support from local government. The parents of the young man also asked her to help them speak with their son because they had difficulties with sign language. These requests were culturally and methodologically appropriate as forms of reciprocity in exchange for the time they spent contributing to the research.

Analysis and Application Through a Collaboration

The last step in Samuel and Mariaye's (2013) framework for contributing to international theorisation is analysing local knowledge to critically challenge international theoretical assumptions. The way the research team approaches this step is to generate local research outputs for immediate impact, followed by international outputs for academic impact.

Local Impact

The publications are generally discussed and published first in Chinese language for government and academic audiences, in the form of confidential and public reports to government and non-government partners; journal articles; and academic books. These publications are authored by Shang and her local research colleagues, including other academics, officials and the fieldwork researchers. The impact of the research was that it immediately informed disability policy and could be adopted by local policy and disability community actors as evidence to support claims for change, such as the local DPF paying people with disabilities to implement the DPF responsibilities. The researchers then contributed to academic debates around Chinese research about disability policy. At the time, this research was the only example of Chinese disability research that used in-depth analysis of experiences in a rural community using participatory methods and a rights-based conceptual framework. The novel approach stimulated national and local action.

This case study had local impact on the disability social organisations through the participatory data collection process itself. It generated opportunities for the local DPF and informal disability organisation to reflect on the utility of their interaction and how that might change to their mutual benefit. It indicated to them potential ways to remedy the common problem of under-representation of people with disabilities within the DPF and how to address the informal organisation's desire for greater political participation. For the young man and his family it was a chance to reaffirm how his life had improved through the intervention of the informal group. The research interactions also helped the family to trust the informal organisation. They had initially been wary about the organisation because they were unable to directly communicate with their son and they were afraid of the risk of exploitation, which he had experienced earlier in his youth.

International Impact

The local knowledge research outputs are then prepared for international publication and presentation in English. It is another point of difference between global South and North expectations that the research team resolves through successive stages. Shang or the fieldworkers translate the data or Chinese research outputs. Shang then prepares a draft of the analysis for the international output. Fisher does not re-analyse the raw data in Chinese or English, rather she works directly from Shang's draft. This way she can discuss the analysis with Shang, who returns to the raw data as necessary. The benefit of this approach is that they each concentrate on their area of comparative expertise. The disadvantage is that Fisher is one step removed from the actual data. The iterative publications through this partnership approach provide an opportunity to consider and debate different styles of analysis and writing for different audiences. Unsurprisingly, the English-language versions most directly refer to international conceptual frameworks and include comparison to international literature.

In this case study, Xie took the lead in making a first draft analysis from the data so that the research team could discuss the findings and analyse them in a way that would contribute to international literature. Their discussions took the form of questioning each other about the meanings of the data from contrasting local, national and international perspectives to decide what interpretation might be consistent between the observed lived experiences, local and national policy implications, and international conceptualisation of critical understandings of disability. Through these discussions, the influence of the global North framework became most obvious: the data were reframed to be from the perspective of the young man (rather than the family), and ordered using an ecological model of social relationships so as to analyse how the parts of the framework fitted together (Bronfenbrenner 1979). This meant that tentative implications for other people in other contexts could be generalised from the experiences. And analysis in this context could challenge the culturally specific assumptions in the framework, such as social networks that young people with disabilities might be expected to access (Shang et al. 2011).

The data were originally collected to address a general question about the young man and his family's social participation and support. Through the prolonged and in-depth analysis, this focus was expanded to explain the broader social context and social institutions. This was only possible because Xie's curiosity about the young man's experience led to her following up with repeat interviews and investing time in developing reciprocal relationships for participatory observation opportunities. It is unusual for qualitative data to stand alone in policy research in China (large quantitative datasets are the preferred method and so they usually dominate even in studies with qualitative components), and it is almost unheard of to concentrate on a single case study. Xie's persistence in the data collection and analysis, combined with the discussions with Shang and Fisher, meant that these conservative assumptions about what qualifies as quality research in China could be challenged. The success of justifying the approach to governments and academics was also helped by positioning this piece of work within the larger project that included some of these other methods, including quantitative secondary data analysis (e.g. Fisher and Shang 2013; Shang 2013).

Implications for Approaches to Global South Disability Research

This chapter used an example of a South–North collaboration to examine how practices in a partnership can reflectively resist reductionist approaches to disability research in a global South context. The question is important because of the tendency of global South researchers to feel pressure to adopt conservative global North methodologies for their contribution to be heard outside their local context. While international partnerships can add to local disability research, is it possible to avoid the same pressure within the relationship so that local knowledge can be prioritised and local control over the research process and product can be retained?

The goals of international collaborations can include intentionally privileging local knowledge and contributing to international theorisation (Samuel and Mariaye 2013) in ways that may not have been open to local researchers without the collaboration. In the example in this chapter, the partnership enabled the researchers to address questions about the lives of people with disabilities of local and national priority that would contribute to policy, including the social institutional arrangements in this particular community, while also questioning the international concepts about child disability rights and social institutions in mixed welfare systems.

The capacity of the research team to achieve these goals relates to an additional aim of international partnerships; that is, to bridge power gaps between local demands, national utility and international theorisation (Meekosha 2011). The researchers each had unique strengths that contributed to the effectiveness of the collaboration. For example, Xie was a local community member, which enabled her to build from social relations of trust with the research participants and return frequently for further formal and informal research activities as the relationships developed. Shang had deeply embedded academic and policy relationships, which enabled the generation of research questions relevant to policy, feasible research methods and high national policy impact. Fisher was an established disability researcher available to question the positioning of the research in the international context in the methodological choices.

This combination of partners meant that methods that could otherwise have been challenged by external audiences or questioned by team members could be discussed throughout the project to bridge the interpretations between contexts and lend international legitimacy to the locally appropriate methodological choices. Examples included the participatory methodology in the community, the opportunistic data collection and publication of the single case study, which would otherwise not have been usual in Chinese social research.

Certain conditions of the partnership might achieve these goals. Samuel and Mariaye (2013) summarise these as reflective relationships that acknowledge the histories and hierarchies between the collaborating contexts to overcome the propensity of global North methodologies to dominate. In the example in this chapter, we found that this needed to be applied at both the personal and geopolitical contextual level. That is, the research team members had to personally reflect on their position and reciprocity in relation to the young man and the local community. Within the research team they also had to reflect on their differences in disability experience, research role and cultural competence. As described earlier, recognising the strengths of the community, the researchers and their practice of discussion through raising questions with each other assisted in that reflection. Each was more familiar with some aspect of the research process, which probably disrupted the tendency for the international experience to override other choices. For example, after she was trained and supervised within the team, Xie made discretionary decisions in the community, which only she could know were locally appropriate, about what contributions to make and methods to pursue in response to the participatory opportunities as they arose.

Acknowledging the histories and hierarchies at the contextual level was less demanding because it was more obvious. The contrast between rural China and urban Australia is stark. Attempting to directly apply international literature or Australian experience about methodological choices was almost absurd. The researchers each brought a critical research position to the team, which meant that they did not struggle with rebutting assumptions that international research practices were better or historically determined and appropriate to rural China. What this condition of acknowledgement did enable, however, was the space to reflect on why the methods might be different. This led the researchers to decide, for example, that it was methodologically appropriate for the fieldworkers to follow the local cultural expectation that they would build on their personal contacts to arrange meetings with officials, to meet participants or to intervene locally on behalf of the people with disabilities in order to assist them.

Limitations in this analysis are the political specificity of the research example. China and Australia are large, relatively wealthy countries, each with their particular history and politics. The three authors do not have a personal experience of disability and they all have global North research experience.

In conclusion, the analysis in this chapter demonstrates that the partnership approach to South–North disability research methodologies can purposefully share research privilege between research team members, research contexts and local community members. As Samuel and Mariaye (2013) argue, this is not to say that it is possible to eliminate power hierarchies within a partnership, but rather that the cultural specificity of the power can be highlighted and intentionally challenged. We found that the key to the collaborative practice was to prioritise the relationships in the research team, in the research setting and in the research application. Reflective relationships have the capacity to address the apparently conflicting expectations about research in a way that incrementally adjusts the intercultural methodology. The goal of speaking to local, national and international audiences complicates research methodology, but a partnership can be one way to achieve the goals of prioritising local methodologies and facilitating the possibilities of global South researchers speaking back to the North.

References

Bartels, K., & Wittmayer, J. (2014). Symposium introduction: Usable knowledge in practice. What action research has to offer to critical policy studies. *Critical Policy Studies, 8*, 397. doi:10.1080/19460171.2014.957335.

Bishop, R. (1998). Freeing ourselves from neo-colonial domination in research: A Maori approach to creating knowledge. *International Journal of Qualitative Studies in Education, 11*(2), 199–219.

Bronfenbrenner, U. (1979). *The ecology of human development*. Cambridge: Harvard University Press.

China Rehabilitation Research Centre. (n.d.). Retrieved April 26, 2015, from http://www.crrc.com.cn/html7/index.cbs.

Connell, R. (2014). Using southern theory: Decolonizing social thought in theory, research and application. *Planning Theory, 13*(2), 210–223.

CSAA. (2015). *Chinese studies association of Australia*. Retrieved April 26, 2015, from www.csaa.org.au.

Denzin, N., Lincoln, Y., & Smith, L. (2008). *Handbook of critical and indigenous methodologies*. Los Angeles: Sage.

Fisher, K. R., & Li, J. (2008). Chinese disability independent living policy. *Disability & Society, 23*(2), 171–185.

Fisher, K. R., & Shang, X. (2013). Access to health and therapy services for families of children with disabilities in China. *Disability and Rehabilitation, 35*(25), 2157–2163.

Fisher, K. R. & Shang, X. (2014). Protecting the right to life of children with disabilities in China. *Journal of Social Service Research*. doi:10.1080/01488376.2014.922521.

Fisher, K. R., Shang, X., & Blaxland, M. (2011a). Review Article: Human rights based social policies—Challenges for China. *Social Policy and Society, 10*(1), 71–78.

Fisher, K. R., Shang, X., & Xie, J. (2011b). Support for social participation of children and young people with disability in China. In B. Carrillo & J. Duckett (Eds.), *China's changing welfare mix: Local perspectives*. London: Routledge.

Goodley, D. (2013). Dis/entangling critical disability studies. *Disability & Society, 28*(5), 631–644.

Grech, S. (2011). Recolonising debates or perpetuated coloniality? Decentring the spaces of disability, development and community in the global South. *International Journal of Inclusive Education, 15*(1), 87–100.

Grech, S., & Goodley, D. (2012). Doing disability research in the majority world: An alternative framework and the quest for decolonising methods. *Journal of Human Development, Disability, and Social Change, 19*(2), 43–55.

Hunter, M. (2002). Rethinking epistemology, methodology, and racism: Or, is White sociology really dead? *Race and Society, 5*(2), 119–138.

Lan, H. (2008). [*The reconstruction of social welfare system for disabled people in China: From the succor pattern to the 'remove obstacle' pattern*] (trans. from Chinese). Doctoral thesis, Nankai University, Tianjin.

Liu, J. (2011). The strategic transformation of disability welfare policy model in China and a "positive" disability welfare policy framework. *Renwen Zazhi* [Journal of Humanities], 3, 136–146. (Chinese).

Lombe, M., Newransky, C., Crea, T., & Stout, A. (2013). From rhetoric to reality: Planning and conducting collaborations for international research in the global South. *Social Work, 58*, 31–40.

Meekosha, H. (2011). Decolonising disability: Thinking and acting globally. *Disability & Society, 26*, 667–682.

Meekosha, H., & Soldatic, K. (2011). Human rights and the global South: The case of disability. *Third World Quarterly, 32*, 1383–1397.

National Disability Research and Development Agenda (NDRDA). (2011). Retrieved October 15, 2014, from www.dss.gov.au/our-responsibilities/disability-and-carers/program-services/government-international/national-disability-agreement/national-disability-research-and-development-agenda.

National Health and Medical Research Council (NHMRC). (2002). *Statement on consumer and community participation in health and medical research*. Retrieved October 14, 2014, from www.nhmrc.gov.au/guidelines/publications/r22-r23-r33-r34.

Nind, M. (2014). *What is inclusive research?* London: Bloomsbury Academic.

Qin, Q. & Zeng, D. (2014) Relationship among the Chinese government, the CDPF and the civil organizations for the disabled. *Shehui Kexue* [Journal of Social Sciences], 4, 90–98. (Chinese).

Samuel, M. A., & Mariaye, H. (2013). De-colonising international collaboration: The University of KwaZulu-Natal-Mauritius Institute of Education Cohort PhD programme. *Compare: A Journal of Comparative and International Education, 44*, 501–521.

Shang, X. (2008). *The system of social protection for vulnerable children in China*. Beijing: Social Sciences Academic Press (Chinese).

Shang, X. (2012). Looking for best practice in caring for disabled children: A case of socialized foster care in China. *Asia Pacific Journal of Social Work and Development, 22*(1–2), 127–538.

Shang, X. (2013). *Experiences of families with children with disabilities*. Beijing: Social Sciences Academic Press (Chinese).

Shang, X., & Fisher, K. R. (2013). *Caring for orphaned children in China*. Lanham: Lexington Books.

Shang, X., & Fisher, K. R. (2015). *Disability policy in China: Child and family experiences*. London: Routledge.

Shang, X., Fisher, K. R., & Xie, J. (2011). Discrimination against children with disability in China: A case study in Jiangxi Province. *International Journal of Social Welfare, 20*(3), 298–308.

Shang, X., & Wang, X. (Eds.). (2011). *Discovery report: Emerging issues and findings for child welfare and protection in China (2011)*. Beijing: Social Sciences Academic Press (Chinese).

Shang, X., & Wang, X. (Eds.). (2012). *Discovery report: Emerging issues and findings for child welfare and protection in China (2012)*. Beijing: Social Sciences Academic Press (Chinese).

Shang, X., & Wang, X. (Eds.). (2013). *Leading research on child welfare and protection in China (2013)*. Beijing: Social Sciences Academic Press (Chinese).

Shang, X., Wang, X., & Tao, C. (Eds.). (2010). *Discovery report: Emerging issues and findings for child welfare and protection in China (2009–2010)*. Beijing: Social Sciences Academic Press (Chinese).

Urwick, J. (2013). Who will listen to educational researchers? Reflections on the research–policy relationship in the global South, with illustrations from Africa. *Compare: A Journal of Comparative and International Education, 44*, 545–565.

Xie, J. & Shang, X. (2009). Functions of social organizations in the realization of rights of children with disabilities. *Qingnian Yanjiu* [Youth Studies] 1, 36–44. (Chinese).

Yan, N. & Li, J. (2014). Analysis about the construction of medical aid system for the rural disabled. *Shehui Baozhang Yanjiu* [Social Security Studies], 1, 14–19. (Chinese).

Yang, L. (2009). From residential care to social participation: Evolution of social protection policies of disabled in China. *Shehui Baozhang Yanjiu* [Social Security Studies], 4, 67–77. (Chinese).
Yang, L. (2013). Construction model of China's disability welfare: From charity to social rights. *Renmin Daxue Xuebao* [Journal of Renmin Univiersity of China], 2, 11–19. (Chinese).
Yang, Y. & Wang, L. (2014). Study on social security needs among people with metal disabilities in different ages. *Heilongjiang Shehui Kexue* [Heilongjiang Social Sciences], 1, 90–97. (Chinese).
Zheng, X., Chen, R., Li, N., Du, W., Pei, L., Zhang, J., et al. (2012). Socioeconomic status and children with intellectual disability in China. *Journal of Intellectual Disability Research, 56*, 212–220.

Chapter 37
Embodying Disability in the Global South: Exploring Emotional Geographies of Research and of Disabled People's Lives in Guyana

Vera Chouinard, Cora Belle, Halima Khan, and Norma Adrian

Although an estimated 80 per cent of the world's disabled people live in countries of the global South (Grech 2011), most of what we know about impairment and disability is based on experiences of the minority in developed western nations. And despite critiques of this western-centric focus of disability studies emerging in recent years (e.g. Grech 2011; Meekosha 2011; Meekosha and Soldatic 2011; Chouinard 2012, 2014), there remains a pressing need for analyses that situate processes giving rise to impairment and disability in the context of colonial and neo-colonial relations of power and a highly unequal global capitalist order. Further, as Soldatic (2013) points out, there is a need to unsettle western conceptions of impairment as 'natural' that render the production of impairment in the global South invisible and uncontestable in terms of transnational justice claims.

In this chapter, we explore two aspects of our research on disabled people's lives and disability activism in the developing nation of Guyana. First, we draw on feminist conceptions of reflexivity to explore the emotion-laden nature of the research process itself. In doing this we place particular emphases on the contradictory positionality of the first author as both 'outsider' and 'insider' and on the challenges of negotiating emotional reactions of researchers and participants in the interview process. We also illustrate some of the ways in which research encounters altered our research practices. Second, we use a feminist, embodied, emotional geographic conceptualization of forces shaping disabled people's lives and activism in a global capitalist order to explore impairment, disability and responses to disability issues by activists in Guyana.

V. Chouinard (✉)
McMaster University, Hamilton, Canada
e-mail: chouinar@univmail.cis.mcmaster.ca

C. Belle • H. Khan • N. Adrian
Red Thread, Georgetown, Guyana

S. Grech, K. Soldatic (eds.), *Disability in the Global South*,
International Perspectives on Social Policy, Administration, and Practice,
DOI 10.1007/978-3-319-42488-0_37

In what follows, we first outline the feminist concept of reflexivity including some of the challenges of doing research reflexively. Next, we draw on this concept to help understand emotional geographies of research encounters and the implications these had for our research practices. Following this, we outline an embodied, feminist and emotional geographic conceptualization of forces giving rise to impairment and disability in the context of an unequal global capitalist order. Next, we draw on this conceptual approach to consider how an embodied emotional geography of impairment and disability that takes global power inequities seriously can help us better understand the lives of disabled women and men in a country such as Guyana. The chapter concludes with reflections on the implications of our work for future research on impairment and disability in the global South and for efforts to create more enabling and inclusive spaces of everyday life.

Reflexivity and Understanding Emotional Geographies of the Research Encounter

The feminist concept of reflexivity is of crucial importance in efforts to better understand emotional geographies of the research encounter. Simply put, reflexivity is critical self-reflection on how the positionality of the researcher (i.e. the way she or he is situated in relations of power such as class, gender, race and ability) influences research practices, including ways of relating to the persons who are 'researched'. Reflexivity, then, seeks to situate knowledge as partial and constructed from particular vantage points. As Rose (1997) reminds us, however, doing research reflexively is not a straightforward or easy task. She is critical, in particular, of approaches that posit what she terms a 'transparent reflexivity'—that is to say a researcher self and a research context that is transparently and fully knowable. She likens this to a 'goddess trick' that assumes an all-seeing researcher. But, she argues, other types of reflexivity are possible:

> the landscape of power produced by transparent reflexivity is not the only space through which the power of the academic to produce knowledge can be situated. There is also a much more fragmented space, webbed across gaps in understandings, saturated with power, but also, paradoxically, with uncertainty: a fragile and fluid net of connections and gulfs. Seen from this perspective, the research process is dangerous. It demands vigilance, a careful consideration of the research process: another kind of reflexivity, in fact, but one which can acknowledge that it may not be adequate since the risks of research are impossible to know. (Rose 1997: 317)

Ward and Wylie, drawing on Pillow's concept of a 'reflexivity of discomfort', are also critical of approaches to reflexivity that presume a transparently knowable researcher self and research context. They write:

> On Pillow's (2003) account reflexivity may in fact rescue rather than interrupt modernism's assumptions about the knowable subject. To counter this tendency reflexivity must become a critical practice of 'vigilance from within' in order to expose the 'difficult and often uncomfortable task' (Pillow, 2003: 177) of acknowledging that the world cannot be entirely

> known and that the researcher's knowledge of self may become uncontainable and uncomfortable (2003: 188). This Pillow calls a 'reflexivity of discomfort'—a reflexivity that seeks to know, while at the same time, situates this knowing as tenuous (2003: 188). Pillow's call is for researchers to inhabit 'unease, tentativeness and uncertainty' and to push always, towards the uncomfortable (Burdick and Sandlin, 2010: 353–354). Drawing on Pillow's idea in response to their engagement with critical public pedagogies, Burdick and Sandlin (2010) propose a 'methodology of discomfort': nudging the researcher into a mode of consciousness that, following Said, can be termed that of 'exile', characterized by transgression of inherited dominant narratives. (Ward and Wylie 2014: 253–254)

It is also important to recognize that engaging in critical reflexivity is necessarily a provisional and ongoing, life-long process. Maxey expresses this well when he writes:

> the empowering potential of engaging critically and reflexively with our research, and all aspects of our lives, remains there for us all, whether we choose to embrace this potential or not. I make sense of this, as I outlined above, by attempting to do as much as I can from 'where I am at'. For me, this approach emphasizes the provisional, ongoing nature of engaged critical reflexivity. Once we are able to celebrate the value of our contingent, flawed efforts, we will be far freer to add our next contribution to the conversation. (Maxey 1999: 206)

However provisional and tentative the knowledge outcomes of reflexivity are, engaging in reflexivity does provide important opportunities to explore, even if only in a partial way, some of the dynamics of the research encounter. So, for example, it creates openings to consider the emotion-laden nature of the research process and the implications of this for research practices and for experiences of being a research subject.

In doing so, it can help us to better understand emotional geographies of research encounters—that is the complex, and often contradictory, ways that emotions shape researchers' and research subjects' senses of what their engagement in places of research means (e.g. with respect to the former a sense of guilt or entitlement at the privileges they enjoy in the production of knowledge; with respect to the latter feeling empowered or disempowered in the production of knowledge about their lives).

In the following section, we illustrate how engaging in critical reflexivity contributed to at least partial insights into the emotional dynamics of our encounters in the research field and how these, in turn, helped to shape research practices. Insights into these facets of the research process are perhaps especially important with regard to research that crosses borders between the global North and global South. This is because such research encounters challenge us to better understand how the research we do is embedded in tensions arising from neo-colonial relations and global imbalances of power, and how this, in turn, creates challenges for researchers from both the North and South. Exploring emotional geographies of the research process itself in a critically reflexive way encourages us to reflect on how researchers and research subjects feel about their encounters in the places where the research unfolds. It also requires efforts to illuminate how positionality matters in shaping research encounters—that is striving to better understand how differences such as gender, class, ability and geographic location shape research relationships and practices.

The reflexive account of the research journey that follows is undertaken from a feminist disability standpoint. This approach recognizes that disability is a feminist issue (e.g. with women being especially likely to experience impairment and disability as a result of domestic violence, and also being more likely than men to care for disabled family members) and that gender is a disability issue (e.g. with disabled women being poorer than men). For further discussion of these points see Ferri and Gregg (1998). Following Valentine (2007), this approach also recognizes the need to think intersectionally about the differences researchers and research subjects embody and how this affects the research encounter. By this we mean being attuned to how particular differences become more and less salient to how researchers and research subjects engage with each other as the research process unfolds.

Critical Reflexivity and Exploring Emotional Geographies of Research

The study on which this paper draws originated in the global North, specifically Canada. The principal investigator, Vera (first author), is a disabled woman and a professor of geography at a university in southern Ontario. Cora (second author) was an Afro-Guyanese woman who belonged to the women's advocacy and development organization known as Red Thread (based in the country's capital Georgetown). She and Vera worked closely together to conduct many of the life history interviews with disabled women and men and interviews with disability activists about the challenges they faced in promoting change. Halima Khan and Norma Adrian (third and fourth authors, respectively), also members of Red Thread, conducted additional life history interviews with disabled women and men using the same interview guide used in Vera and Cora's interviews.

Here we share some key insights about our engagement in this research, the emotions involved and how these informed our research practices. Before sharing our stories of journeying through the research process, however, it is important to note how this section was written. Sadly, Cora died about 1 year ago and so can no longer give voice to her research experiences. This has meant that I, Vera, have had to do my best to weave Cora's story into my written account. This is far from ideal but because Cora played such a central role in the research project it would be problematic not to make her presence felt in this account. (Note: throughout the next section 'I' refers to Vera).

Vera's and Cora's Stories

When I first began to contemplate doing research on disability in Guyana I knew it was out of my 'comfort' zone intellectually and emotionally. While I had studied developing countries and visited one as a tourist, I had not conducted research in the global South. Although I was enthusiastic about the project, especially in light of the pressing need for research on disability in the global South, I was also nervous and apprehensive about the possibility that I might not do justice to the stories people shared. I was also very conscious that this possibility reflected my privilege in being a researcher from Canada albeit one who was also female and disabled. Being nervous and apprehensive about my own involvement in the research made it very important indeed that the research journey was made in collaboration with Guyanese women from Red Thread. A complete autoethnography of my research journey is beyond the scope of this chapter. Instead, I share select key moments in my own and Cora's encounters with people and places to begin to flesh out emotional geographies of the research process. These draw on my recollections and field notes.

It is 8:30 a.m. and I'm about to land at the Georgetown airport for the very first time. I feel very nervous and unsure as to what to expect. I also feel very naïve and sheltered as a northern white woman. I noticed upon boarding the Caribbean Airlines aircraft that it was older and its cabin in need of more repair than the planes that I usually fly on. I wondered, with some trepidation, if this was a sign as to the kinds of living conditions I'd encounter while in Guyana. The taxi ride to my hotel seemed to confirm this as indicated in the following excerpt from my field notes:

> The ride up the coast from the airport [to Georgetown] is interesting. We pass many small villages. Some of the houses appear to have been improved a lot but others are weathered grey wood and almost look as if they will fall down any moment [this impression is heightened by the fact that the houses are elevated on stilts because of risks of flooding when the coastal seawall is breached]. A lot of animals (e.g. cows, horses, donkeys, lambs and goats) meander at the edges of the road—occasionally wandering onto it. Trucks, cars and minibuses use the road but also many horse-drawn wagons which are more affordable than motor vehicles for transporting things such as lumber. It is certainly a different world than what I am used to and yet, strangely, not quite as different or 'foreign' as I was worried I might find it…

My emotional reactions to being in Guyana for the first time are perhaps best described as 'mixed'—part apprehension, part fascination, part vulnerability and part insecurity as an 'outsider' researcher:

> Still I feel very much a stranger and outsider here and realize I have a huge amount to learn—which is probably a very good thing although it makes me feel much more insecure than I am used to feeling as a privileged white academic woman from the North (maybe a good thing too although it definitely feels uncomfortable).

These sights and feelings, combined with warnings from women in Red Thread that I would be in danger as a clearly foreign, white, disabled woman in a country where violence against women is common, heightened both my sense of not belonging and being vulnerable here and my concern for the well-being of women in Guyana. While my feelings of fear and vulnerability subsided somewhat as time passed and we took safety precautions in the research process, such as ensuring that Cora was with me for interviewing and that I had a reliable Guyanese driver, they still lingered on as the research progressed.

While all of our research encounters were important and complex, certain encounters stand out as especially revealing of emotional geographies of conducting research in the global South. One of those encounters took place in a dilapidated house in Georgetown.

Here Cora and I were interviewing two physically disabled female relatives sharing the home. Before the interviews began the two women started to apologize for the poor state their home was in—this reminded me of how intrusive it must feel to them to have researchers in a home they are ashamed of and how especially intrusive it must feel to have one of those researchers embody a white northern female identity, even with my use of a cane signalling that I too was visibly disabled. While I wondered what to say Cora replied in a 'no nonsense' tone, 'We have come to talk to you, not to see your home'. Cora's intervention was a pivotal moment in this research encounter as it was only after this clarification as to why we were here in their home that the women appeared to relax and we were able to begin the interviews.

Another research encounter that comes to mind is when Cora and I travelled to West Berbice to interview a woman who had lost her right forearm in a chopping attack by her then husband (chopping involves maiming or killing with a cutlass, the tool still used to chop sugar cane in a sugar export industry dating from colonial times). Guyanese women are the vast majority of victims of this type of violence. This was the first woman I had met who had been 'chopped' although a number of other interviewees had also been subjected to this, even though this was not a selection criterion for participating in the study. I felt shocked and deeply angered at her loss, especially as Cora and I learned as we talked to her that this loss had meant she couldn't continue with the electrical training she was doing at the time of the attack. This, and the general lack of access to prostheses in Guyana as well as discrimination against disabled people in the labour market, meant her job prospects were dim. I also felt a sense of helplessness—wondering how an 'outsider' from the North could make a positive difference in the lives of women like her. Having tried, and unfortunately failed, to find ways of getting prosthetic arms from Canada to Guyana (partly due to the lack of trained technicians to fit such devices in Guyana), I still wonder about this. This wondering and the sense of frustration that it entailed did encourage me to incorporate other ways of making a difference into the research process, for example by sending books and other materials to a school for disabled children and learning more about the challenges facing disability activists in Guyana.

Not too long after that, Cora and I encountered another woman who had been 'chopped'. In her case both forearms were lost and at the time of the interview the prostheses provided on a one-time basis by a foreign aid agency were broken and not repaired. There were many memorable moments in this research encounter, including shared moments of profound sadness as the woman recounted how she was often blamed for the attack and that, as a result, people would avoid and shun her, even members of her own family. Another emotion-laden moment was when this interviewee began to recount all the things she was no longer able to do, such as fetch water from the trench (there was no piped water or electricity in her home), turn on the lights or do the sewing she loved to do before the attack. We sat quietly saddened by her losses. Then Cora spoke in a firm voice, 'You can still talk. You can give talks'. This was her way of trying to evoke feelings of hope in a research encounter dominated by expressions of loss. In this case, however, Cora's intervention in the interview did not seem to elicit hope and this interviewee summed up her losses by saying that they made her feel no longer a part of Guyanese society. Part of being critically reflexive about the research encounter is acknowledging that interventions in the research process in response to emotions such as profound sadness do not always have the intended effect. Following Rose (1997) we need to see such moments of 'failure' as indicative of how dangerous, fluid and unpredictable our research encounters are.

Many of the disabled women and men that Cora and I interviewed related mundane acts of violence (e.g. name-calling, taunting and avoidance) that they experienced on a daily basis. They also, as I discuss elsewhere (Chouinard 2012), experienced the violence of poverty. Almost all of the 80 men and women Cora and I interviewed were struggling to survive on less than one US dollar per day. It was difficult and disturbing to hear their accounts of this. For example, some spoke of how difficult it was to save the money needed for transportation to places of health care. Others talked about having to choose between medication and food as well as having to beg from family members and strangers. Others spoke about how they had to rely on remittances from family living outside Guyana and how unreliable this was as a source of income. These accounts were disturbing to me in part because of the depth of poverty among disabled men and women in Guyana and in part because it underscored just how privileged I was as a disabled white academic woman from the global North. While I tried to be mindful of this privilege throughout the research process, for example by reflecting on how it informed my engagement in the research in my field notes, I also have to admit that I did not at the time the research was conducted nor do I now have anything approaching a full understanding of the differences my privilege made in the research encounter and process. This is something I continue to wonder about and it reflects both the tenuousness and partiality of the knowledge we obtain through critical reflexivity.

There were important, if often fleeting, moments when Cora and I were able to forge some common ground and mutual understanding with those we interviewed, particularly in the case of disabled women, despite the differences we embodied. For Cora this was particularly so in the case of disabled women experiencing domestic violence; her experience dealing with domestic violence issues through Red Thread and her concerns to assist women experiencing domestic violence offered at least a tenuous basis for mutual solidarity and understanding. Forging such a sense of connection was arguably more difficult for me, who, unlike Cora, was not a woman of colour interviewing other women and men of colour and whose class privilege created an experiential gulf between myself and the disabled women and men interviewed (e.g. with respect to fully appreciating how desperate their economic circumstances were). When a sense of connection was at least temporarily forged it was usually on the basis of experiences of having an impairment and being disabled. Even then, however, how research subjects read my embodiment of disability made a difference in the extent to which a sense of solidarity developed. I recall, for example, an interview with a woman of colour and a wheelchair user in which she assumed that I could not understand what it was like to be in a wheelchair since at the time of the interview I 'only' used a cane. It was only when I revealed that in the past I had used both a scooter and a wheelchair that there was some sense of common ground between us.

A final research encounter stands out as much as for what it concealed as for what it revealed about disabled men's and women's lives. Early in the research process Cora, our driver and I visited a facility located outside of Georgetown (the capital). Staff gave us a 'tour' of the facility, which was home to severely physically disabled men and women, some of whom had been abandoned at birth. Conditions at the home spoke of how difficult it is to maintain a facility with very limited funding in the context of a developing nation. Old ceiling fans that whirred above the mattresses on which these men and women lay provided the only partial relief from the sweltering heat. Most women and men lay on mattresses without sheets as flies buzzed about them; however, staff seemed to care about those in their charge. I only learned later that while Cora and I were out of earshot one of the staff members confided to our driver that these disabled women and men were being abused. This was a humbling reminder that not only researchers from the North but also their collaborators from the South are rarely, if ever, in positions that allow them to grasp the reality of the research field in any transparent way. Acknowledging this is an important facet of being critically reflexive and grappling with the dangers of the research process.

An Embodied, Feminist and Emotional Geographic Conceptualization of Impairment and Disability in the Global Capitalist Order

Recent critiques of the western-centric focus of disability studies have helped to highlight the dualistic nature of social models of disability that treat impairment as 'natural' and disability as social (e.g. Meekosha and Soldatic 2011). In doing so, they have helped to problematize disability scholars' tendencies to neglect the socio-spatial production of impairment and to universalize social models of disability based on experiences in the minority world. Connell (2011) echoes these concerns and suggests that impairment and disability need to be rethought as processes of social embodiment.

Such a perspective considers how social dynamics have bodily effects, notably impairment, and how bodies become embroiled in social dynamics in ways that are disabling. At the same time, Connell stresses the importance of understanding these processes as unfolding in the context of a global order shaped by colonial and neocolonial relations of power and oppression. This is an important theme in the small but growing literature on disability in the global South (Grech 2011; Meekosha 2011; Meekosha and Soldatic 2011; Chouinard 2014). Although Thailand was never a formally colonized nation, King and King (2011) contend that the forces of globalization have had 'colonizing effects' on the lives of men with spinal cord injury in northeast Thailand. These effects include the adoption of western biomedical approaches to treatment as opposed to traditional healing practices, and increasing reliance on money and monetary exchange rather than mutual aid. These effects did not go uncontested, for example some of the men interviewed for their study reported continuing to use traditional healing as well as biomedicine.

A feminist conceptualization of impairment and disability as arising from processes of social embodiment recognizes that these processes are shaped by the differences people embody, such as gender, class, race, ability and geographic location. Such an approach also directs our attention to the emotion-laden nature of encounters among and between non-disabled and disabled people and the implications this has for the particular ways in which people experience impairment and disability. Related to this is a concern with complex processes of identity formation and re-formation. Finally, an embodied feminist approach that is committed to understanding impairment and disability within a geopolitical context must consider how political identities and actions are shaped by local and transnational ways of knowing about disability. Berghs (2011), for example, considers how those impaired through conflict in Sierra Leone lived their embodiment and identities as amputees and/or war victims in terms of an inability to forgive and 'reconcile' with a post-conflict society. She also shows how the identity of being 'disabled' was embraced only insofar as it permitted access to NGO resources.

King and King's (2011) research in northeast Thailand also highlights the importance of attending to how impairment and disability are lived emotionally. They point out Buddhist beliefs in reincarnation and in the idea that if something unfortunate happens to someone when they've done nothing wrong, the cause of this must lie in transgressions in a past life. This encouraged the men with spinal cord injury as a result of a motor accident to blame themselves for the event and to feel shame. Such beliefs encouraged others in their community to also blame them for their fate, thus fuelling negative social stigma.

It is important to recognize that our emotional lives have geographies. That is to say, that our emotions help to situate us in particular ways in different places, influencing for example the extent to which we feel included or excluded, valued or devalued. There is also a recursive relation between place and emotion whereby being in a place that has affective meanings (such as not belonging) elicits emotions such as feeling 'out of place' and alone. An emotional geography lens can, then, help to advance our understanding of living with impairment and disability as an embodied, emotion-laden process of negotiating different places of everyday life such as the workplace and home. These negotiations include dealing with particular types of encounters and non-encounters with others in these places. The forces shaping emotional geographies of impairment and disability unfold across multiple scales ranging from the local, micro-scale (e.g. the home) to the global scale. An example of the latter with respect to Guyana is the outmigration of trained health professionals and volunteers to developed countries. This not only serves to limit access to health care and severely restrict access to assistive devices such as prostheses, but also elicits emotions such as frustration, despair and resignation.

Embodied, Emotional Geographies of Impairment and Disability in Guyana

We now want to explore selected aspects of the embodied, emotional geographies of impairment and disability experienced by the disabled women and men interviewed (the names of all interviewees are pseudonyms). Our account draws on interviews conducted by Cora and Vera as well as those by Halima and Norma. It also draws on some of the results of interviews with representatives of disability organizations. Our discussion is organized around five key themes: experiences of abandonment and loss; poverty, impairment and disability; discrimination in employment; barriers to accessing health care and spaces of disability activism; and identity formation, human rights and the prospects for social change.

Abandonment and Loss

Feelings of abandonment and loss were common among the disabled women and men interviewed. For some people, such as Sean, abandonment took the form of finding that friends drifted away following, in his case, mobility impairment. He spoke with great sadness about no longer having friends: 'I feel sad because I done tell myself that I don't have friends'. When asked by Cora if his friends had 'given up on him', he agreed: 'they just give up'. In other instances, abandonment was linked to disabling constructions of women impaired by chopping violence as being insufficiently subordinated by men and thus deserving of impairment and disabling conditions of life. This was very much the case for Sarah, the woman noted earlier as having lost both forearms to chopping violence. She experienced shunning and avoidance by both family members and friends who accepted accounts of her behaviour prior to the attack as promiscuous and non-obedient. Such masculinist discursive accounts of chopping violence and what kind of woman it was directed against served to construct women like Sarah as deviant and in need of male discipline. Clearly such gendered discourses about impairment and disability were aimed at reasserting male domination in a violent post-colonial context. For Sarah her resulting socio-spatial isolation evoked powerful feelings of abandonment and loss, leading her to feel like she no longer belonged or counted in Guyanese society.

It is important to recognize that abandonment and loss also diminished the assistance available to the men and women interviewed. Michael recounted how, 6 months after he became physically impaired as the result of a stroke and was no longer able to work, his wife withdrew her initial assistance with cooking and instructed his children to no longer interact with him. He summed up his feelings of being abandoned by family by saying that he was being treated 'worse than a dog'. In his case being abandoned even while present in the family home reflected warnings by relatives to his wife that if she interacted with a 'strokes man' she might also get the stroke.

Overt hostility and acts of hatred also evoked feelings of abandonment and loss. Allen, who also became mobility impaired as the result of a stroke, explained how members of his community would taunt him pejoratively, calling him 'stink nasty' and other derogatory terms. He interpreted such acts as meaning that he was hated and excluded in his local community.

Poverty, Impairment and Disability

Almost all of the women and men interviewed lived in poverty, struggling to get by on less than one US dollar per day. The poverty associated with their disadvantaged class locations both caused and exacerbated impairment and disability, for example forcing interviewees to choose between medication or food and disabling them in various ways. The latter included experiencing difficulty saving the money needed for the transportation to get to places of health care or meetings concerned with disability activism. Representatives of various disability organizations commented on how poverty caused membership to dwindle because disabled people lacked the money needed to get to meetings. Poverty was also disabling in terms of heightening dependence on others for income and necessities such as food. Sam related how an income insufficient to maintain his family had forced him to beg on the streets, something that he found very demeaning and distressing. Some interviewees, such as April, relied on remittances sent home from relatives abroad, a survival strategy that provoked uncertainty and anxiety about when and how much additional income would be coming her way.

Most interviewees struggled to survive on very low levels of government income assistance and consistently noted how this assistance was inadequate to meet basic needs.

Interestingly, despite inadequate assistance levels, several female interviewees expressed deep gratitude for this assistance. This was not an emotional response seen among male interviewees, suggesting that emotional geographies of class oppression, impairment and disability were gendered in significant ways.

Discrimination in Employment

Although most interviewees did not engage in paid work, at least two of those who struggled to secure additional income from sporadic employment commented with frustration and anger on how their work was devalued compared to that of able-bodied people. Sheila, a wheelchair user, talked about how people would try to pay her less for the chair backs she knitted because she was visibly impaired. Tom, also a wheelchair user, commented on how, when employed to do odd jobs such as painting or tiling, employers paid him less than if he was able-bodied even though he insisted that his work was ‘as good or better’ than that of many non-disabled workers. These discriminatory acts helped to construct their disabled bodies as defective and less valuable. In addition, experiences of being subject to such constructions of their embodiment fuelled feelings that they were being unjustly treated in the labour market and wider society.

Even for interviewees who did not report discrimination in employment, income generated by paid work was relatively low. Michael, who was mobility impaired and used a wheelchair, repaired shoes to support himself. Prices for the repairs varied but some were as low as 300 Guyanese dollars (or US$1.50). Sarah, a visually impaired woman, tried to augment her income by selling small packets of drink crystals for 10 Guyanese dollars. Trying to scrape together enough income for basic necessities such as food prompted feelings that their economic situation was precarious and this was a basis of anxiety about managing in the future. Although feelings of apprehension about being in a precarious class location and facing a very uncertain economic future were shared, to some extent, by interviewees who were seeking but had not yet secured employment (e.g. due to discrimination in hiring) and those who were not in paid employment, it was encounters with non-disabled people involving overt discrimination in hiring or pay that elicited especially intense feelings of anger and a sense of being subject to injustice.

Barriers to Accessing Health Care and Spaces of Disability Activism

As already noted, the poverty associated with disadvantaged class locations was a major factor exacerbating impairment and acting as a disabling barrier to accessing places of health care and spaces of disability activism. The disabled women and men interviewed frequently stressed that their incomes were insufficient to cover the costs of transportation to places of health care, medication and doctors' fees. Representatives of disability organizations commented on how difficult it was to sustain the involvement of disabled members because their incomes were insufficient to cover the costs of transportation to meetings or public protest actions. Small numbers of participants at such protest actions in turn made it difficult to impress upon politicians how many people were impaired and disabled in the country and to create a sense of urgency for action on disability issues.

Poverty and other barriers to accessing health care reflected the disadvantaged places of disabled people and of Guyana in a neo-colonial global capitalist order. The emigration of trained health professionals to more affluent countries in search of higher wages has, for example, severely constrained the government's ability to train replacement workers (resulting in a shift from more intensive specialist training to shorter and less involved or specialized training programmes). This in turn has translated into a lack of trained health-care professionals in areas such as prosthetics, leaving women such as Sarah (who lost her forearms in a chopping attack) without access to the prostheses that would allow her to be more independent in the home and wider community. The heightened dependency arising from lack of prostheses has left Sarah feeling intensely frustrated and sad about the abilities she has lost. The high costs of imported mobility aids such as wheelchairs has also been a barrier to mitigating impairment and ensuring access to spaces of health care, activism and community life more generally. The government lacks the resources to ensure that all people who need a wheelchair have one and this has meant that people with mobility impairments have to hope that a charitable or foreign aid agency will provide them with one.

Other barriers to accessing health care and spaces of activism and to being included in community life are cultural and attitudinal. Representatives of disability organizations noted how many families were deeply ashamed of having a disabled family member and therefore 'shut them in the home', denying them opportunities such as receiving job training or participating in disability activism. The head of the Guyana Mission for the Deaf, for example, estimated that for every deaf person who took advantage of their training services, two more were locked away in the home. Emotions such as shame and embarrassment are thus a crucial part of processes devaluing disabled women's and men's lives, and isolating and excluding disabled people in Guyana. To socially embody impairment and disability is, then, often to be rendered invisible and silenced.

Identity Formation, Human Rights and the Prospects for Social Change

Although this study did not explicitly examine identity formation, at least two aspects of this process emerged which are relevant to considering the prospects for enabling social changes in Guyana. First, it was clear that the vast majority of disabled women and men interviewed associated being disabled with having an embodied self that was lacking and defective. This can arguably be seen as an outcome of replicating western ableist regimes of power in the global South. These are replicated through the internalization of ableist discourses that construct disabled people as 'lesser' than their non-disabled counterparts. Second, the disability activists interviewed tried to counter such devaluing discourses by framing disability issues primarily as matters of individual human rights. This, too, reflects the dominance of western conceptions of disability activism in the global South.

Understanding disability activist identities as 'champions' of human rights worked, at least partially, to limit the kinds of social change advocated by activists. Overwhelmingly, activists stressed the need to have human rights legislation for disabled people passed in the national parliament (something which happened in 2010 after a lengthy delay). It was rare, in this context, that issues of distributive injustice in disabled people's lives were considered. An exception to this was the recognition by some activists that participation in disability organizations and political events was limited by lack of income to pay for transportation costs. However, and crucially, transnational distributive injustices, such as the 'drain' of health-care specialists from Guyana to the global North, were never flagged during interviews with disability activists. Activists also did not problematize the production of impairment through phenomena such as male engagement in chopping violence against women, something that, as noted earlier, is among the legacies of a violent, male-dominated colonial order.

It appears, then, that framing disability issues in Guyana in terms of human rights has been associated with the neglect of processes giving rise to impairment and of issues of distributive injustice that, as Meekosha and Soldatic (2011) contend, are central to understanding disabled people's disadvantaged locations in countries of the global South.

Conclusions: Toward Enabling Emotional Geographies of Impairment and Disability in the Global South

We want to conclude by sharing some reflections on the implications of our work for future research on impairment and disability in the global South. We also reflect on its implications for efforts to create more enabling and inclusive spaces of everyday life in a southern context.

What are the implications of the work shared in this chapter for future research?

One is that it is critical that researchers concerned with impairment and disability in the global South consider the tensions, contradictions and emotions involved in the research encounter itself. As we have argued in this chapter, the feminist concept of reflexivity provides a useful basis for such work as long, that is, as it does not assume a transparently knowable researcher and research context. Being reflexive is perhaps especially critical when researchers from the North are involved in research in the global South. Relatedly, it is important to further explore how intersectional differences help to position researchers and participants in particular relations of power in the research process. For example, one aspect of my own (Vera's) and other northern researchers' neo-colonial privilege deserving of further analysis is our class locations. While conducting research in Guyana I was acutely aware that, at least initially, my class location as a well-paid white female disabled professor made it difficult for me to fully appreciate the depth of poverty in which the interviewees lived, how desperate their struggles for survival were and how hard those struggles were to maintain. A related important avenue for inquiry is closer consideration of the emotions of disabled participants and how these influence their views of their 'place' in the research process. Another challenge is to ensure that the voices of our research collaborators in the global South are part of the stories of the research encounter that we tell. In this chapter, we have started to do this by weaving Cora's voice into the account of the research encounters.

Future research is needed on the lives of disabled women, men and children in countries of the global South. How common is it, for example, for feelings of shame and embarrassment to fuel practices such as shutting disabled family members in the home? How do family members try to justify such actions? And what does this tell us about why they feel shame? There is also a need for more detailed research into the many ways in which poverty causes or exacerbates impairment and creates barriers to the socio-spatial inclusion of disabled people. How common is it, for instance, for poverty to prevent engagement in the disability movement? Do disabled people give other reasons for not becoming involved or ceasing involvement and, if so, what are these? Future research into disabled people's lives in the global South needs to explore in greater detail how neo-colonial relations of power in the global capitalist order shape experiences of impairment and disability. We have illustrated some facets of this in Guyana with respect to the perpetuation of a violent masculine colonial and neo-colonial order in which a tool used in a colonial export industry is used to maim or kill women. How common is it for women to become impaired in this way in other countries of the global South? What other forms of violence contribute to impairment and ultimately disabling conditions of life? To what extent are women who experience male violence blamed for it and ostracized from their communities? We also illustrated neo-colonial processes of development at work in the exodus of trained health-care professionals from Guyana to nations in the global North. More research is needed to determine how common this phenomenon is and the reasons professionals give for leaving their countries. We also need to better understand how professionals make their decisions to leave. Is it, for example, only due to comparatively low wages or are there other factors involved?

The work we have shared in this chapter has implications for efforts to create more enabling and inclusive spaces of life for disabled people in Guyana and other countries of the global South. One of these is how important it is to consider the production and exacerbation of impairment as the embodied outcome of the transnational injustices of a neo-colonial global capitalist order. Disabling conditions of life such as deep poverty also need to be framed in this way. When this is done it becomes clearer that justice for disabled people requires a fundamental redistribution of resources between countries of the global North and South—in terms of, for example, trained health and rehabilitation professionals and debt forgiveness to enable governments in such countries as Guyana to spend more on income and other forms of assistance, such as the provision of mobility aids and prostheses. As disability scholars such as Barnes and Sheldon (2010) have argued, in this era of globalization ableist attitudes and practices are being replicated worldwide. Among the manifestations of this in Guyana are the practices of shutting family members with disabilities in the home due to shame and embarrassment and paying disabled people less for the work they do. Thus a key facet of struggling for more enabling and inclusive spaces of life in countries of the global South is challenging the devaluation of disabled lives and of the contributions of disabled women, men and children that is endemic in the global North. Among the strategies that might be used to do this are public education campaigns that showcase the accomplishments and hopes and dreams of disabled people. Tackling the extreme poverty in which so many disabled people live and other barriers to accessing spaces of community life, such as places of health care and activism, is also crucial. In addition to raising income assistance levels, expanding government and NGO job training programs for disabled people is important. Transportation itself also acts as a barrier to inclusion. In the case of Guyana there is no public transportation, only private minibuses. Those buses often do not stop for disabled people because aids such as wheelchairs take up the room that could otherwise be occupied by a paying customer. An accessible paratransit system could help to address this problem; however, to make this feasible in Guyana a redistribution of resources from the North to South would be essential. Finally, creating more inclusionary and enabling spaces of everyday life for people with impairments and illnesses in countries such as Guyana requires public education efforts that could help highlight the emotional costs and suffering associated with ableist attitudes and practices. This includes, as illustrated in this chapter, feelings of abandonment and loss that rob disabled people of a sense of belonging and of mattering as members of society.

As we hope to have helped illustrate, tackling impairment and disability in the global South requires nothing less than a sea-change in how we view and address disability issues. Until we understand the production of impairment and disability as embodied, emotional processes that unfold in the context of an unequal neo-colonial capitalist order and as matters of transnational injustice, disabled people's oppression will be perpetuated in countries of the global South.

References

Barnes, C., & Sheldon, A. (2010). Disability politics and poverty in a majority world context. *Disability & Society, 25*(7), 771–782.

Berghs, M. (2011). Embodiment and emotion in Sierra Leone. *Third World Quarterly, 32*(8), 1399–1417.

Chouinard, V. (2012). Pushing the boundaries of our understanding of disability and violence: Voices from the global South (Guyana). *Disability & Society, 27*(6), 777–792.

Chouinard, V. (2014). Precarious lives in the global South: On being disabled in Guyana. *Antipode, 46*(2), 340–358.

Connell, R. (2011). Southern bodies and disability: Rethinking concepts. *Third World Quarterly, 32*(8), 1369–1381.

Ferri, B. A., & Gregg, N. (1998). Women with disabilities: Missing voices. *Women's Studies International Forum, 21*(4), 429–439.

Grech, S. (2011). Recolonising debates or perpetuated coloniality? Decentring the spaces of disability, development and community in the global South. *International Journal of Inclusive Education, 15*(1), 87–100.

King, J. A., & King, M. J. (2011). The lived experience of families living with spinal cord disability in Northeast Thailand. *Third World Quarterly, 32*(8), 1475–1491.

Maxey, I. (1999). Beyond boundaries? Activism, academia, reflexivity and research. *Area, 31*(3), 199–208.

Meekosha, H. (2011). Decolonising disability: Thinking and acting globally. *Disability & Society, 26*(6), 667–682.

Meekosha, H., & Soldatic, K. (2011). Human rights and the global South: The case of disability. *Third World Quarterly, 32*(8), 1383–1398.

Rose, G. (1997). Situating knowledges: Positionality, reflexivities and other tactics. *Progress in Human Geography, 21*(3), 305–320.

Soldatic, K. (2013). The transnational sphere of justice: Disability praxis and the politics of impairment. *Disability & Society, 28*(6), 744–755.

Valentine, G. (2007). Theorizing and researching intersectionality: A challenge for feminist geography. *The Professional Geographer, 59*(1), 10–21.

Ward, E., & Wylie, G. (2014). 'Reflexivities of Discomfort': Researching the sex trade and sexual trafficking in Ireland. *European Journal of Women's Studies, 21*(3), 251–263.

Index

A
Ableism, 100, 256, 393
Ablenationalism, 118
Academic colonialism, 553
  academic dependency syndrome, 508
Academic decolonisation, 558–561
Academic neo-colonialism, 546
Academic neo-imperialism, 546
Addis Ababa, 188, 196
Africa, 188, 191, 194–197
  African Decade for Persons with Disabilities (ADPD), 432, 433
  African Disability Forum (ADF), 196
  African Union, 188, 196
  African Union Disability Architecture (AUDA), 196
  Ubuntu, 77–78
Afrocentricity, 77
Agricultural economy, 307
Agriculture-led development strategies, 338
Albinism, 313
Anglo-Saxon social model, 153, 155, 156, 163
Anthropology
  alterity, 42
  Benedict's essay, 36
  cross-cultural comparison, 42
  cultural change, 37
  and culture, 36–39, 42, 43
  of disability studies, 37, 38
  ethnographic approach, 36
  ethnographic documentation, disability, 42
  historical interest in disability, 37
  positioning disability scholarship, 38–40
  radical alterity, 43
  social movements and state policy, 43
  theoretical and methodological contributions, 36
  theoretical orientations, 43
Anti-black racism, 379, 382
Anti-capitalism, 409
Applied theatre programs, 108
Arabs, 258, 262
Armed conflict, 323
Art literacy programmes, 107
Assistive devices, 25, 144, 145, 175, 179, 227, 244–246, 263, 276, 370, 591
  mobility devices, 25
Assistive technology, 491
Association of Disabled Ex-Service Personnel (ADEP), 104
Asylum seekers, 290, 291, 293, 295, 296
Australian disability policy, 572

B
Bapu trust
  Eastern healing techniques, 445
  electroconvulsive therapy, 447
  Seher vision, 444
  'user/survivor' organisation, 445, 446
Begging
  amor fati, 154
  case study, 159, 160
  charitable response, 162
  charity, 153, 154
  contradictory and cynical attitude, 161
  marginal economy, 157
  mercantilization, 153

S. Grech, K. Soldatic (eds.), *Disability in the Global South*,
International Perspectives on Social Policy, Administration, and Practice,
DOI 10.1007/978-3-319-42488-0

Begging (*cont.*)
motor disability, 154
social perception, 157
vulnerability, 153
Biopsychosocial model of disability, 55 (*see also* Conceptualising disability)
Biosociality, 354 (*see also* Conceptualising disability)
British social model of disability, 517 (*see also* Conceptualising disability)
Building Disability Solidarity, 538–539 (*see also* Disability politics)

C
Canada, 256, 260, 261, 264
Capitalism
anti-capitalism, 409
and disability, 156
Caribbean
anti-black racism, 379 (*see also* Anti-black racism)
mental backwardness and racial defects, 380
Caribbean Airlines aircraft, 587
CBR. *See* Community-based rehabilitation (CBR)
Charity, 8, 52, 92, 97, 112, 153, 154, 157, 160–163, 187, 224, 279, 423, 472, 522, 532, 542
Charitable organizations, 160
Childhood, 9, 167–169, 182, 571
Childhood development
check-ups and surveillance, 170
erroneous judgements, 171
impairment recognition, 170
parents and caregivers, 168–170
policies and strategies, 171
social protection scheme, 170
structurally violent processes, 170
Children, 188–196
Chinese disability policy, 571
Chinese social networking platform Qzone, 493
Christianity, 258, 263
Christian history of salvation, 120
Christianising mission, 120–122, 127
Christian literature, 124
and colonialism, 70, 117, 121, 122, 125, 127
and disability, 117, 119, 122
missionaries, 120, 121
Citizenship, 291, 298, 299
non-citizen, 287, 289, 296–299
Civil society organisations (CSOs), 188, 192
Collaborative research partnerships, 572, 573 (*see also* Disability Research)
Colonial mission
salvation, 120
Colonialism, 11–12, 380–382, 443, 560
colonial destruction, 393
colonising discourses, 12, 14
and impairment, 12, 14, 224, 548
modern colonialism, 121
Coloniality, 3, 14, 224, 395, 570
Colonizing consciousness, 122
Communications and assistive technologies, 489
Community, 242–244
Community participation, 73
Community-based rehabilitation (CBR), 61, 143, 144, 273, 371, 372, 427
CBR Matrix, 455, 465
characteristics, 461
definition, 454
DID, 454, 463, 464
DPOs, 456–457
empowerment programme, 179
and fundamental values, 457–458
and gender, 459, 460
International agencies, 462–463
local community, 453
local resources, 455
management guidelines, 455
NGO identity, 463
and religion, 458–459
research and education, 461
western conceptualization, 457, 458
Conceptualising disability
adoption of anti-discriminatory legislation, 329
anti-discriminatory legislation, 73
complexities, 70, 133–146, 255–266, 554
geopolitical boundaries, 74
global North conceptualisations, 70–73
hegemonic status of models, 75
heterogeneity, 15, 16, 171
ICF, 53, 72, 73
medical model of disability, 304, 381, 400
models of disability, 53, 54, 308, 353–354, 429, 485
place, 69–80
social model of disability, 4, 24, 55, 71, 86, 151–153, 155, 163, 221, 227, 298, 353–354, 360, 517, 520
space, 70, 73, 74
theoretical framework, 73
Conflict, 257–259, 263–266, 276–278
biomedical/epidemiological measurement, 270
CRPD (*see* United Nations Convention on the Rights of Persons with Disabilities (UNCRPD))

DPOs, 275
impairment, 13, 270–280
indigenous communities, 271
intersectional consideration, 275
long-term effects
environmental, 278
infrastructural, 278
mental, 276–277
physical, 276
reproductive/demographic, 277
social structural, 277
medical and rehabilitative, 272
medical humanitarianism, 271–272
non-physical impairments, 273
post-conflict interventions, 273
post-traumatic stress, 258
pre-conflict populations, 272
psychological dimensions, 272
terrorism, 271
UNHCR (*see* United Nations)
vulnerability, 274
wars, 107, 244, 258, 259, 269–281, 286, 287, 327
Constitution of the Bolivarian Republic of Venezuela, 524
Consumer indebtedness, 411–412
Contemporary empire
transnational corporations, 400
Context, 16, 24–29, 39, 42, 55, 70, 71, 76, 78, 79, 87–89, 99–101, 105–110, 112, 113, 120, 134–137, 139, 142, 143, 153, 155, 159, 161, 163, 168, 174, 178, 188, 193–196, 202, 208, 222–225, 227, 232, 249, 256, 259, 260, 266, 270, 275, 285, 289, 290, 294, 304, 306, 308, 309, 316, 326, 328, 332, 341, 352, 353, 370, 374, 381, 382, 395–397, 399, 408, 411, 415, 426, 430, 431, 440–443, 446, 455, 457, 458, 462–463, 470, 472, 474, 478, 479, 484, 489–492, 496, 503–505, 507, 509, 513, 517–520, 522–526, 528, 534, 537, 542, 547, 553, 559, 568–573, 575, 577, 578, 583, 584, 590–592, 595, 596, 598
Contextualising disability, 7, 11, 16, 163, 225, 231, 299, 401
Contextual locations, 42
Coping strategies, 341
Corporeality and interdependence, 310
Counting disability
complexities, 52, 64, 65
conceptual models, 53, 54
limitations, 55, 60
personal factors, 62
qualitative research, 62
restrictions in social participation, 55
screening procedure, survey, 59
Crenshaw's intersectional analysis, 314
Criminal justice system, 329
Critical disability studies, 230
Critical Transnational Disability Studies, 298
Critique disability and impairment research epistemology, 560
Cross-cultural research, 396
CRPD. *See* Convention on the Rights of Persons with Disabilities (CRPD)
Culture
cultural knowledge, 42 (*see also* Anthropology)
cultural locations, 89, 91 (*see also* Anthropology)
cultural practices, 87, 90, 161, 162 (*see also* Anthropology)
cultural production, 73 (*see also* Anthropology)
cultural religious practices, 125 (*see also* Anthropology)
cultural theory, 37, 38, 40, 45 (*see also* Anthropology)

D

Dalit theology, 125 (*see also* Religions understandings of Disability 1009)
Daoism, 118
Decolonization, 547, 554–561
Decolonizing discourse, 559
Decolonizing methodologies, 557
Deformities, 384 (*see also* Conceptualisation of disability)
Demobilisation and reintegration (DDR), 104, 105 (*see also* Conflict)
Democratic budgeting, 417
Democratic Republic of Congo (DRC), The, 486 (*see also* Africa)
Dependency theory, 339
Deprivation
guilt-ridden accommodation, 241
low-income countries, 240
unemployment, 240
Development, 260, 264, 266
colonial roots, 12
neocolonising development, 15
neoliberal globalised development, 308

Development and disability, 429, 430
connections, 3–17, 218, 316, 423–434
disability mainstreaming, 430–432
disability targeting, 368, 425
disability inclusive development, 3–6, 14, 217, 221, 230, 424, 426, 428, 430, 431, 453–465
disability inclusion, 15, 141, 146, 242, 423–426, 428, 434
disability exclusions, 221
ICF, 429 (*see* World Health Organisation International Classification of Functioning, Disability and Health (ICF))
nexus, 4
rights based approach to development, 8, 188
disability and poverty, 6–8, 14, 23, 139, 218–233, 237–239, 247, 249, 286, 327, 369–372, 374, 419, 429, 462, 569
poverty reduction, 4, 5, 10, 13, 14, 221, 229, 230, 338, 340, 371, 424, 432, 454
Devised/applied theatre process, 111 (*see also* Sri Lanka)
Digital divide, 279, 483, 485, 491–493
Digital Divide deconstruction, 491, 492
Digital networked technologies
action-orientated social responsibility, 483
adopting policies, 483
civic engagement, 483
"de-referentialisation", 484
disability discourse, 484
domestic strategies, 483
geopolitical relationship, 485
"global" transformation, 484
habitual exoticisation, 483
human activity, 483
in global South, 490
manufacture of mobile phones, 486
models of disability, 485
policy developments, 483
production and disposal, 490
regular maintenance and 'updates', 487–489
societal structures, 484
socio-economic context, 490
territorialisation, 484
Disabled students, 191–193
Disability, 187–190, 192–196, 255–266 (*see also* Conceptualising disability)
contextualising disability, 7, 8, 11, 73, 200, 213, 239, 288, 304, 430, 455, 460, 464, 509, 556, 573
cultural framings, 272
disability measurement, 59, 63, 369
job quota, 158
medical tragedy, 156
models of disability, 53, 54, 308, 353–354, 485, 495, 549, 590
and poverty, 6–7
social and economic vulnerability, 159
symbolic violence, 157
world's population, 3
Disability and development. *See* development and disability
complexity and heterogeneity, 15, 16
connections, 3–17
empirical work on disability, 10
environmental disasters and forced migration, 9
field of thought and practice, 107
mainstream development programmes, 10
theoretical questioning and reflexive practice, 4
theorising, 9, 11, 36, 70, 286
Disability and fluid embodiment, women, 313, 314
Disability and poverty
critique of cycle, 7, 231–232
disability and poverty cycle, 218–224
discourse on, 73–75, 167
relationship, 6–7, 23, 217–233, 288
research and empirical work, 10, 221
research gaps, 570, 578
vulnerability, 26, 217, 228, 229, 274–275, 374
Disability and poverty cycle
atheoretical, ahistorical and uncritical analyses, 223–224
cyclical representation, 220, 230
disabled families, 231
disabled households, 231
intergenerational poverty, 219
quantitative and qualitative studies, 223
vulnerability, 229
Disability and the Global South, 286
Disability and rehabilitation team, 462
Disability budgeting, 409, 415–417, 419
Disability children, 172–181
adaptations, 178
assistance and impairment-related aids, 178
exploratory projects, 177
impairment-focused problems and solutions
in rural Sri Lanka, 175
impairment-related and access needs, 178
in South Asia and Uganda, 167

parents and caregivers
in Orange Farm, South Africa, 178–181
participatory research
education and work, 174
physical impairments, 172
problematic relationships, 173
school/community-based rehabilitation programmes, 172
social relationships, 172–173
12–18-year-olds, urban India, 177
8–11-year-olds
rural India, 176–177
Urban India, 176
and young people, 171–172
Disability definitions, 51 (*see also* Conceptualising disability)
Disability history, 37, 125, 381 (*see also* Colonialism and colonisation)
Disability-inclusive development (DID), 6
Disability intervention, 167 (*see also* Community-Based Rehabilitation (CBR))
Disability knowledge systems. *See also* Conceptualising disability; Disability Research
colonial and neo-liberal interests, 79 (*see also* Capitalism; Colonialism)
social model, 79 (*see also* Conceptualising disability)
Disability mainstreaming, 5 (*see also* Community Based Rehabilitation (CBR))
Disability measurement systems, 59
Disability performance. *See also* Sri Lanka
applied theatre practitioners, 111
post-dramatic, 113
Samanalayaya performances, 112
Samanalayaya workshops, 110
workshops, 110
Disability policy
feminist disability activism, 333
international human rights legislation, 333
rights activists and organizations, 333
social exclusion, 333
Disability politics, 316, 317 (*see also* Conceptualising disability)
Disability rehabilitation, 104 (*see also* Community Based Rehabilitation (CBR))
Disability research
analytical issues, 504
decolonizing disability research, 547, 554–561
epistemologies, 513
gaps, 3–17, 570
in global South, 505
knowledge cultures, 504
multilateral debate and dialogue, 503
neocolonising research, 400–402, 507–508
North-derived concepts, 503
postcolonial pedagogy, 513
repression and resistance, 513
revisionist/recuperative projects, 513
theories, policies and practices, 504
Disability rights awareness, 539–540 (*see also* United Nations Convention on the Rights of Persons with Disabilities (UNCRPD))
Disability rights movement, 151
Disability Rights Promotion International (DRPI), 534
Disability statistics. *See also* Conceptualising disability; Counting disability
activity and participation, 62
cross-national comparability, 65
disability measurement, 63
economic development activities, 63
equalisation, 52
functional limitation, 63
human rights approach, 63, 64
impairment-based, 52
in census, 57
measurement scales, 64
participation restrictions, 65
participatory approaches in research, 53
population data, 63
prevalence rates, 52
statistical and research data, 63
survey enumerators, 52
survey sample prevalence measures, 59
theoretical model, 52
Washington City Group, 58
Disability street culture, 158–160
Disability studies (DS)
Eurocentric, 286
global North origins, 70–73, 219, 286
and the global South, 503–514
Disability-adjusted life year (DALY), 54, 55
Disability-inclusion processes, 428–432 (*see also* Disability and Community-Based Rehabilitation (CBR); Disability and development; Disability mainstreaming)
AusAID, 428
barriers (*see* Development and disability)
CRPD / UNCRPD / United Nations Rights on the Persons with Disabilities, 424
DfID, 428

Disability-inclusion processes (*cont.*)
  disability mainstreaming, 425, 426
  global institutions strategies, 428
  INGOs, 427
  MDGs, 424
  and poverty, 424
  PRSPs, 425
  twin-track approach, 427
Disability-inclusive development (DID), 454
Disability-inclusive disaster risk reduction
  disaster scholarship, 469
  DRR and DRM, 470
  issues, 469
  vulnerability and resilience, 470
Disability-inclusive education
  in India, 204, 205
  in South Africa, 205
Disability-inclusive livelihood assessments, 142
Disability-specific interventions, 426
Disability-specific research, 344
Disabled bodies, 381, 383, 388
Disabled children's agency, 182
Disabled embodiment, 306–308
Disabled families, 231
Disabled households, 231
Disabled people, 264–265
  economic potential, 306–308
Disabled people's mobility, 344
Disabled people's organizations (DPOs), 51–52, 86, 357, 427, 456, 457
  Disabled Persons Federation (DPF), 575
Disabled soldiers, 101, 102, 112
Disablement, 99, 100
Disablism
  definition, 27
  and exclusion, 219
  psychology, 238
Disaster and humanitarian programming and policy, 472
Disaster risk management (DRM), 470
Disaster risk reduction (DRR), 470
Disasters, 471, 474
DISTAT, 57
District Information System for Education (DISE), 204
District Primary Education Programme (DPEP), 204
Diversity budgeting, 414
Donor-funded interventions, 212
Down's syndrome, 112
DPOs. *See* Disabled people's organizations (DPOs)
Drama therapy, 111
DRPI monitoring model
  advantage, 537
  bi-directional research and transformational model, 535
  denial of rights, 535
  disability community empowerment, 536
  DRPI trainings, 538
  emancipatory research paradigm, 537
  evidence-based findings, 534
  human rights principles, 536
  monitoring tools, 535
  monitoring types, 536
  North–South relationship paradigm, 535
  pilot phase, 541
  responsibility and control, 541
  training seminar and recruiting participants, 536
  transformational research, 539
Dystopian literature, 126, 127

E

Eastern healing techniques, 445
Economic marginalisation, 345
Education, 188–197
  inclusive education, 180, 181, 195, 199–213, 400, 433
  special education, 201, 211, 524
  special schools, 174, 180, 190, 192, 193, 205, 207, 211
Education and training, 138–141
Education for All, 195
Electroconvulsive therapy, 447
Emotional dynamics, 585
Emotional geographies of research, 592–595
  colonial and neo-colonial relations of power, 583
  emotional reactions, 583
  in Guyana
    abandonment and loss, 592
    discrimination, employment, 593
    health care and spaces of disability activism, 594
    human rights and social change, 595
    identity formation, 595
    poverty, impairment and disability, 593
  of impairment and disability, global capitalist order, 590–591
  and reflexivity, 586–590
Environmental disasters and forced migration, 9
Epistemic privilege, 305
Essentialisms
  discursive regimes, 304

Ethiopia, 188–195 (*see also* Africa)
Ethnicity, 255–266
Ethnographic fieldwork, 44
European capitalist system, 122
European colonialism, 546
E-waste, 489

types, 316
VAMP, 312
Forced migrants, 286, 287, 290–293, 295, 298
Forced migration, 286–289, 291, 292, 295, 298, 299
Full Service School (FSS), 207

F
Feminism, 40, 555
Feminisation, 108
Feminist concept of reflexivity, 584, 585
Feminist conceptualization of impairment and disability, 591 (*see also* Conceptualising disability)
Feminist method, 315 (*see also* Disability Research)
Feminist standpoint theory, 554 (*see also* Disability Research)
Feminist theories, 304 (*see also* Conceptualising disability)
Feminization of poverty, 323
Financial capital, 136 (*see also* Capitalism; Democratic budgeting)
Financialisation, 414–416 (*see also* Capitalism; Democratic budgeting)
budgeting process, 417
capitalist maldistribution, 418
colonialism and capitalism, 409
consumer indebtedness, 411–412
crisis, 407
democratic budgeting, 417
gender budgeting, 408
governance, 417
identity budget (*see* Identity budgeting)
IMF, 410
labour market restructuring, 412–413
macroeconomic disability, 417, 418
microfinance, 408
participatory budgeting, 413
south and neo-liberal, 409–411
Fluid connections, women
colonial exploitation, 317
corporeality and interdependence, 310
disability studies, 317
disability studies and politics, 318
household interdependency, 310
impairment, 315
internal conflict, 310
intersectionality, 315
performance and management, 312
sexual engagement, 313
strategies, 317–318

G
GATS, 410
Gender. *See also* Feminism
Gender analysis and political organization, 314
Gender budgeting, 408
Gender Equitable Men (GEM) Scale, 101
Gender-based violence, 248
Gender-based violence support services, 329
Gendered biopolitics, 106
Gendered-disability violence
colonial and neocolonial power, 327
communicative silence, 325
cultural devaluation, 325
discrimination, 324
global capitalist order, 327
in Southern context, 326–327
justice system, 326
legal protection and representation, 326
physical, sexual and emotional violence, 325
poverty and social exclusion, 327
research and field-based evidence, 324
social disadvantage, 325
social relationships, 325
structural silencing, 325
violence and discrimination, 325
Gender-selective abortion, 323
Geographies of disability
human geographies, 341
power relations, 341
socio-spatial dynamics, 341
Ghana Health Service and Ghana AIDS Commission, 361
Global activism against violence
cultural roles, 328
forced sterilization, 327
gender discrimination, 329
gender stereotypes, 328
harmful practices, 329
impairment-based forms of resistance, 330
intellectual disability, 328
mental illness, 328
patriarchal nature, 328
restrictive norms, 328
small-scale qualitative research, 327
social norms, 328

Global activism against violence (*cont.*)
  societal attitudes, 328
  vocational training for employment, 328
Global burden of disease (GBD) study, 54
Global European/north Atlantic imperialism, 546
Global health
  care resources, 22
  conceptual and ideological issues, 23
  disability activism, 27–28
  disability movements, 24
  economic system, 25
  ethics of distribution and exclusion, 26
  health policies, 22
  medical discourse and practice, 25
  "medical model", 24
  neoliberal policies, 25
  and power, 23–24
  sexual and reproductive health service, 22
  social networks, 29
  sociopolitical and human rights issue, 25
  transformation, 29
Global health and disability-specific international organisations, 3–4
Global Institutions, 427–428
Global mental health
  global norm, 439
  global South, 440
  in India, 440–443
  MGMH, 438–440
  pharmaceutical industry, 440
Global Mental Health advocacy, 442
Global migration policy, 285, 288
Global neo-liberal project, 474
Global South
  vulnerability, 474
Global Southern response, 76–78
Global South–North partnerships
  authority and legitimacy, 568
  communication and application, 568
  cultural positioning, 572
  data collection and analysis, 574
  disability research, 568
  disability social organisations, 576
  epistemological and methodological differences, 568
  histories and hierarchies, 579
  international publication and presentation, 577
  international theoretical assumptions, 573, 576
  national and international expectations, 567
  neo-liberal and neocolonial oppression, 568
  opportunistic data collection, 579
  political specificity, 579
  power dynamics, 570
  reductionist approaches, 568, 578
  social institutional arrangements, 578
Globalisation, 433, 447
  neo-liberal, 408
Globalisation and International Governance, networked technologies, 494–496
Government-sponsored National Council for Disabled People (CONAPDIS), 525
Grameen Telecom's famous Village Phone programme, 488
Greece–Turkey border, 291

H

Hat Mon Commune, 475
Health, 21–30, 137–138, 247–248, 351–354, 437–448
Health issues, 137, 138
Health systems, 25, 55, 261, 276, 374, 431
Health-care systems, 25
Hearing and speech impairments, 571
Hegemonic patriarchal system, 312
Hegemony, 298
Heteronormative views of sexuality, 311
Historiography of disability, 394
HIV and disability, 351
  activism, Sub-Saharan Africa, 357–360
  antiretroviral therapy, 356
  collective action, 361
  healthcare, 355–356
  healthcare in Ghana, 358–360
  healthcare in Uganda, 357, 358
  prevention programmes, 356
  sexual and reproductive health education, 356
  UNAIDS, 351 (*see also* AIDS)
HIV testing
  and counselling services, 356
  and prevention information, 356
Homogenisation, 289
Honduras, 264
Household economies and local employment, 345, 346 (*see also* Capitalism; Disability and development)
Human capital, 137
Human rights, 187, 188, 190, 192–197, 265–266, 285–288, 290, 291, 293, 294, 296 (*see also* CRPD / UNCRPD / United Nations Convention on the Rights of Persons with Disabilities)
Human rights abuses, 437

Human rights model, 532
Human rights principle, 533, 536
Human rights-based approach to disability (HRBAD), 187, 188, 190, 194–196
Humane imperialism, 117, 120, 121
Hurricane Mitch, 264
Hyogo Framework for Action (HFA), 476

I

ICF model, 56, 61 (*see* International Classification of Functioning, Disability and Health)
Identity budgeting. *See also* Democratic budgeting; Financialisation
  consumer sovereignty, 416
  diversity budgeting, 414
  macroeconomic framework, 416
  market systems, 415
Illegal bodies, 289, 290
Illegal immigrants, 289
Immigration Restriction Act, 261
Impairment, 518
Inclusion, 188, 190, 278–280
Inclusive development, 5, 6, 15, 17, 359, 423–432, 459, 463, 464, 470
Inclusive education
  cost effectiveness, 200
  country-based stakeholders, 202
  discriminatory attitudes, 200
  economic issues, 199
  educational systems, 201
  enthusiasm, 200
  evidence-based policy developments, 213
  global enactments, local spheres, 209–211
  growth, 202
  in southern contexts, 200
  international declarations, 212
  national and international policies, 200
  passionate debates, 199
  policy imperatives in India and South Africa, 202
  policy implementation programmes, 213
  realisation, 201
  school improvement and pedagogy, 200
  service provision for children with disabilities', 199
  social justice, 200
  teacher development programmes, 212
  toolkits, 200
  training and development packages, 200
India, mental health care
  agrarian crisis—interventions, 442
  community-based care, 441
  farmer suicides, 442
  mhGAP Intervention Guide, 441
  psychiatrisation, 443
  psychotropic drugs, 441
  research projects, 206–207
  tragedy at Erwadi, 443
  WHO guidelines, 441
Indian disability activists, 40
Indian-based feminist organization, 305
Indigeneity, 393
Indigenous community inclusion, 559
Indigenous disability understandings, Australia
  biomedical model, 548
  colonisation, 545
  conceptual framework for research, 556
  disability and impairment, 547
  disability research, 550
  ethnographic and anthropological literature, 546
  Eurocentric, 548
  frontier warfare, 546
  health and behavioural sciences, 548
  physical deformity, 548
  pre-invasion and pre-colonial societies, 545
  social relations, 546
  Western sciences', 548
  WHO, 546
Indigenous rights and social justice, 560
Indigenous standpoint theory (IST), 547, 554–556, 558–560
Information and communication technologies (ICTs), 484
Institutional *vs.* community-based rehabilitation, 246 (*see also* Community-based rehabilitation)
Inter Agency Steering Committee's Protecting Persons Affected by Natural Disasters, 476
Interactional model of disability, 55, 75
Intercategorical, 256
Intergenerational poverty, 219
Internally displaced person (IDPs), 289
International Classification of Functioning, Disability and Health (ICF), 429
International Classification of Impairments, Disability and Health (ICIDH), 54
International Committee of the Red Cross, 105
International community policy and practice
  DRR and DRM, 477
  HFA, 476
  humanitarian sector, 476
  vulnerabilities, 477

International Decade for Natural Disaster Reduction (IDNDR), 476
International monetary fund (IMF), 410
International non-governmental organisations, 279
International Organization for Migration, 105
Intersectional discrimination, 324
Intersectionality, 255, 256, 265
Intersectionality analysis, 369
Irregular migrants, 289, 291

K

Knowledge contestations
- disenfranchised groups, 506
- and identity formation, 510–511
- integration and equality, 506
- publicity and activism, 506
- reflexivity, 505
- social relations, 505
- transversal politics, 506

Knowledge production, 546, 555
North-derived epistemologies, 507
Knowledge transfer. *See also* Conceptualising disability; Colonialism; Disability and the Global South
- definition, 504
- north-derived epistemologies, 507
- Northern epistemologies, 70–73
- power, 533, 541
- social structures and locations, 504

L

Labour market restructuring, 412–413 (*see also* Capitalism; Disability and Development; Disability and poverty)
Language and educational system, Ex-colonies, 506, 507
Latin America, 151
Law for People with Disability, 524
Lebanon, 279, 280
Levitical laws, 119
LGBTQI disabled people, 315 (*see also* sexuality)
Libya, 290
Lipton's theory of urban bias, 340
Livelihoods
- CBR interventions, 144
- data collection and analysis, 145
- definition, 134
- economic disadvantage, 133
- education and training, 138
- employment, 135
- financial capital, 136
- health issues, 137, 138
- human capital, 137
- microfinance movement, 143
- natural capital, 140, 141
- physical capital, 140
- poverty, 137
- social capital, 138, 139
- social protection interventions, 143

Living and togetherness, 308–310
Local data collection methods, 575
Local knowledge systems, 44, 93, 94 (*see also* Knowledge contestations)

M

Macroeconomic
- broader collective, 414
- democratic budgeting, 417
- inherent structural processes, 419
- politics and policy, 413 (*see also* Capitalism; Financialisation)

Mainstreaming disability, 425, 426 (*see also* Disability and Development)
Malta, 295
Manus Island, 296
Masculinities study, 100, 101, 113
MDGs. *See* Millennium Development Goals (MDGs)
Medical Humanitarianism
- physical and indirect consequence, 272
- post-conflict security, 272

Medical model of disability, 518 (*see also* Conceptualising disability)
Medicalisation, 442 (*see also* Conceptualising disability)
Mental Health Gap Action Programme (mhGAP) Intervention Guide, 441
Microfinance, 408, 411, 412, 414
Microfinance and entrepreneurship programmes, 143
Migration, 261, 262, 266, 286, 287, 289, 290, 292, 294, 296, 298, 299
- asylum seekers, 290–293, 295–296
- forced migration, 9, 13, 285–299, 328, 385
- refugees, 9, 108, 223, 244, 256–257, 259, 270, 272, 274–275, 280, 286–287, 289–290, 293–299, 328, 416

Millennium Development Goals (MDGs), 5, 7–8, 65, 221, 424
Mobile technologies, global demand, 487 (*see also* Digital Divide)
Mobility, 245

Modernity/coloniality group, 395
Morphological disabilities, 127
Movement for Global Mental Health (MGMH)., 438
Muslim, 258, 262, 263 (*see also* Religious Understandings of disability)

N

Nagi models, 53, 54
Nagi models of disability, 54
National Health Insurance Scheme in Ghana, 359
National Security, 296–298
Natural capital, 140–141
Neocolonialism, 257, 259, 400–402, 434
 academic dependency syndrome, 508
 and knowledge, 507–508
 neo-colonial power, 397
 neo-liberal assault, 527
 neo-liberal autonomy and humanistic, 246
 neo-liberal financialisation, 413–414
 neo-liberal globalisation, 12–14, 288, 298, 308
 neo-liberalism, 14–15
Neo-liberalism, 14–15, 276, 289, 414, 479, 510, 524 (*see also* Capitalism; Financialisation; Disability and development)
Normative masculinity, 99
Northern feminisms, 317 (*see also* Feminism; Gender)

O

Online activism, 332
Ontological and epistemological approach, 560 (*see also* Knowledge transfer)
Oppression, 249
Organisations of people with disabilities (DPOs), 188, 189 (*see also* Disabled People's Organistions (DPOs))

P

Pan African Network of Users and Survivors of Psychiatry, 446
Partial biomedical solutions, 400
Participatory budgeting, 413, 414
People living with HIV and AIDS (PLHA)
 Anglophone and western-centric concerns, 353
 definition, 352
 disability community, 352
 illnesses and impairments, 353
 medical and social models, 353–354
 UNAIDS terminology guidelines, 352
Personhood, 36
Place of disability. *See also* Geographies of disability
 ontological and theoretical complexity, 69
 political, cultural, social and material issues, 69
Plantation slavery
 anti-black racism, 379
 colonialism, 380
 disability, 385–387
 disability history, 381
 disabled bodies, 381
 enslaved body, 385–387
 ghostly history, 387–388
 industrialisation, 380
 modern capitalism, 389
 modernity, 382
 race, 382–385
Policy and Programme Imperatives, 144–145 (*see also* Disability Policy)
Political-economy perspectives, 340 (*see also* Capitalism; Financialisation)
Politicised processes of social dynamics, 354
Pollution, 489
Post-Cold War, 297
Postcolonial condition, 14, 41, 78, 112, 119, 224, 304–305, 309, 317, 394–398, 402, 505
Postcolonial and dystopian literatures, 127
Postcolonial Black feminist disability theory, 504, 510
Postcolonialism
 colonial power, 399
 contemporary empire, 400–402
 disengagements, 396–398
 emancipation and decolonization, 398
 historiography of disability, 394 (*see also* History of disability)
 medicalization, 398
 misrepresentation and domination, 395
 modernity/coloniality group, 395
 Subaltern studies, 394
 western epistemology, 399
Post-conflict conciliation, 270, 271
Post-conflict displacement, 323
Post-Fordist capitalist societies, 155
Post-global financial crises, 409

Poverty, 139, 157
and disability, 7, 11, 138–139, 155, 230–233, 249, 365–374, 424, 484 (*see also* Disability and poverty)
intersectionality, 369
non-disabled population, 367
social assistance programmes, 373
unemployment, 370
Poverty and disability, 155, 424 (*see also* Disability and Poverty)
Poverty Reduction Strategy Papers (PRSPs), 9, 424
Psychiatrisation, 443
Psychoemotional disablism, 16, 231, 354
Psychological and relational networks, 73
Psychology
'bottom-up' epistemology, 239
disablism, 238
neo-liberal autonomy and humanistic, 246
social positioning, 239
Psychological dimensions of disability, 54, 71, 238–239, 249
Public spending in agriculture, 338–339

Q
Quality-Adjusted Life Year (QUALY), 55

R
Rabinow's concept of 'biosociality', 354
Race, 255–266, 365, 369
accidental imperfection, 384
and sexual stigmatization, 398
deformities, 384
humanity, 384
monstrosity, 382
practical geographic information, 383
Race and racism, 554
Racial and gender stereotypes, 314
Racialised, 255–264, 266
Racist disablism, 315
Radical and Marxist theories of development, 339
Rana Viru Seva Authority, 104
Rana Viru Sevana rehabilitation centre, 103
Re-contextualizing knowledges, 508–509
Reductionism, 442
Reflective practice and reflexivity, 207–209
Refugees, 286, 287, 289–291, 293–299
Rehabilitation model, 532, 538
Religion, 258, 262–264
Religious understandings of disability
biblical archaeology, 126
Buddha or Christ, 127
Christian bible, 119
miraculous remediation of disability, 122
Western Christianity, 120
Western religions, 118
Reproductive health and dignity, 247–248
Research advocacy, 540, 542
disability and poverty, 569
geopolitical location, 569
international collaborations, 568, 569
political histories and hierarchies, 570
political positioning, 568
social solidarity, 570
Research ethics review process, Australia, 550–553
Research Imperatives, 145
Research process
CRPD, 533
DRPI, 534
North–South research projects, 532, 533
Resilience, 95, 229, 232, 270, 273, 459, 469–479
Resourcing and manufacturing disability, 485, 486
Rights of Persons with Disabilities, 255
Rights-based approach to development (RBA), 8
Rural areas, 3, 6, 8, 10, 142, 190–191, 207, 217, 221, 226, 227, 288, 337–340, 343, 345, 347–348, 356, 361, 371, 457, 463, 478, 490
Rurality
and agriculture, 338
economic developments, 347
'food for work' capacity, 346
food security, 338
geographical theories of development, 339
geographical theories of development and space, 338
global spatial patterns of poverty, 338
globalised economies, 348
informal social networks, 347
Khmer social hierarchy, 347
learning disabilities, 347
livelihoods, 133–146, 227–228, 288, 337, 366, 411, 455, 460, 474, 479
macro-level structural forces, 337
marginalised and resource-poor social group, 338
theoretical and practical attention, 348
transformation of a country's economy, 338

S
SAFOD Research Program, 53
Salamanca Statement and Framework for Action on Special Needs Education, 199
Sanitation, 247

Scenario policy implementation, 208
Schizophrenia, 439
Schools
  barriers, 242
  exclusion factors, 241
  family/community factors, 241
SDGs, 7, 9, 16
Seher programme, 444
Selfhood, 247
Senses, movement, 93–96
Sensing disability
  Accra, Disability Vantage Point, 90–93
  critique of binary thought, 86
  and ethnographic context, Accra, 87–89
  extero-receptive sensory modalities, 87
  Ghana, 86, 87
  labeling discourse, 85
  sensory-rich stories, 86
  underrating of abilities, 85
Serbian–Hungarian border, 292
Sexual health care, 248
Sexuality, 312 (*see also* Feminism; Gender)
Sexually transmitted infections (STIs), 277
Slavery, 380 (*see also* Colonialism; Race and racism)
  plantation (*see* Plantation slavery)
Social capital, 138, 139
Social and community marginalisation, 562
Social inclusion and community participation, 560
Social justice, disability issues, 512
Social marginalisation, 561
Social model approaches, 353
Social model of disability, 151, 152, 163, 519–523
  issues, 518
  social movement, 518
  Venezuela (*see* Venezuela social model)
Social networks, 346
Social positioning, 239
Social protection
  cash/in-kind transfers, 368
  disability, 370, 371
  government services, 367
  high-income countries, 368
  intersectionality, 369
  poverty, 370
  'social contract' approach, 366
  social grants/cash transfers, 366
  socio-economic development, 366
Social protection interventions, 143
Social suffering, 124
Social vulnerability, 474
Social' Divides reinforcement, 492, 493
Social-relational forms of disablism, 181
Socio-spatial politics, disability. *See also* Capitalism; Disability and development; Financialisation
  economic indicators, 342
  free-market economy, 342
  historical, cultural and economic context, 342
  national economic indicators, 342
  rural poverty and exclusion, 343–344
  seasonal agricultural employment, 343
  unresolved trauma and mental health issues, 342
Somalia, 191 (*see also* Africa)
South Africa. *See also* Africa
  research projects, 207
Southern African Development Community (SADC), 433 (*see also* Africa)
Southern epistemologies, 89
Southern feminisms, 303, 309, 310, 314, 317 (*see also* Feminism; Gender)
Southern global positionality, 303
Space, 3, 8, 12, 16–17, 30, 39, 43, 70, 79, 90, 94, 101, 107–109, 111–112, 201, 219–220, 224–232, 257, 259, 274–275, 286–287, 293–295, 303–318, 337–348, 385, 396, 409, 438, 508, 510, 540, 555, 584, 592, 594–597
Spatial inequalities
  agricultural sector, 340
  coping strategies, 341
  dependency theory, 339
  development planning and practice, 340
  economic rationality, 340
  globalisation and neoliberal reforms, 341
  historical analysis, 339
  household-level human capital, 340
  macro-level development processes, 340
  material and social resources, 340
  urban-centric development, 339
Spatialities associated with rurality and disability, 344, 345
Special educational needs (SEN), 201 (*see also* Inclusive Education)
Special School as Resource Centre (SSRC), 205, 207 (*see also* Inclusive Education)
Sphere Project, 476
Sri Lankan civil war, 105
  disability visible, 103–105
  disabled female LTTE ex-combatants, 107
  disabled soldiers, 101, 102
  disablement, 99, 100
  gender inequitable decision-making, 102
  masculinities study, 100, 101, 113

Sri Lankan civil war (*cont.*)
'normative' masculinity, 99
programme of disability rehabilitation, 104
SF (*see* Sunera Foundation and butterflies theatre)
songs, disabled soldiers, 103
Stigmatisation, 354
STIs. *See* Sexually transmitted infections (STIs)
Subaltern studies, 394
Sub-Saharan African countries, 188, 189, 191
Sudan, 256–259, 262, 263, 265, 266
Sudanese, 256, 258, 262–265
Sudanese Arabs, 258
Sunera Foundation, 100
Sunera Foundation and butterflies theatre
An Inspired Swan Lake, 107, 108
applied theatre definition, 108
disabled dance and performance, 110
disabled performance art, 105
disabled soldier, 109, 112
feminisation, 108
performance, 106
sexual and romantic expressions, 109
Support teacher system, 201
Sustainable Development Goals (SDGs), 4
Sustainable livelihood frameworks, 134, 135
Syria, 285, 286, 291
System of Comprehensive Protection of the Disabled, 158
Systematic information gathering and dissemination, 332

T
The Structure of Scientific Revolutions, 532
Theological archaeology, 124
Theory of disability from a social perspective, 523
Theory of domination, 155
Third World, 257
Trans Asia Strategic Group of Persons with Psychosocial Disabilities, 447
Transformational research, 533
Transformational research and participatory monitoring, 538
Transnational justice claims, 583
Tunisia, 290
Twin-track approach, 427

U
ubuntu, 429, 430, 458
UN Convention on the Rights of Persons with Disabilities (UNCRPD), 187, 188, 190, 195, 196, 230, 265, 266, 296, 426, 427, 446
Article 1a, 287
Article 11, 294, 295
United Nations, 287
Convention on the Elimination of All Forms of Discrimination against Women (CEDAW), 330
Convention on the Rights of Persons with Disabilities (CRPD), The, 152, 203, 270, 294–296, 329, 330, 424, 476, 495, 496, 533
United Nations ESCAP 2012 report, 134
United Nations High Commissioner for Refugees (UNHCR), 274
2013 United Nations Population Development Fund study, 328
United Nations Security Council Resolution 1325, 265
United Nations Statistical Division (UNSD), 56, 58

V
Values and Ethics Guidelines, 552, 553
Venezuela social model. *See also* Conceptualising disability
Bolivarismo' and '21st Century Socialism', 519
British model, 527
disability policy, 525
disabled students, 520
economic problem, 527
economic problems, 525, 526
elements, 521
emancipatory agenda, 526
policy development, 523–526
poverty, 522, 525
social movements, 523, 524
space-geography and time-history, 526
Vietnam
disabilities discrimination, 478
disability movement, 477
market-driven governance and public policymaking, 478
Vietnam and Germany, disaster impact
cultural practices and social attitudes, 473
economic impact, 473
resilience concept, 474
Violence
against women, 323
armed conflict and post-conflict displacement, 323
discrimination and marginalization, 324
empirical evidence, 323
gendered-disability violence, 324
human rights concern, 323, 324

personal, social and economic costs, 324
prevalence, 324
Vulnerability, 26, 29, 92, 94, 108, 139–140, 153, 157–159, 163, 217, 228–229, 244–246, 271, 274–275, 280, 312–313, 327, 355–356, 359–360, 366, 371, 469–479, 587
and resilience, 470
disability, 471
disaster, 471
DRR strategies and policies, 479
global South, 472
social impact, 472–473

W
WAI guidelines, 496
Wars, 257–259
civil, 269, 270, 279
Iraq, 271
Sri Lanka, 99–114
Sudan, 257–259, 262–266
Washington City Group on Disability Statistics, 61
Web accessibility, 495–496
Web Content Accessibility Guidelines (WCAG), 495
WG's approach, 58
White Australia Policy, 261
White settlement, 395
WHO International Classification of Functioning, Disability and Health, 309
Widow burning, 394
Women With Disabilities Australia (WWDA), 324, 331, 332
forced sterilization, 331
forced sterilization and violence, 331
strategic alliances and partnerships, 332
World Health Organization (WHO), 286, 438
World Health Organization Disability and Rehabilitation team, 462
World Health Organization Disability Assessment Schedule (WHODAS), 56
World Health Survey (WHS), 55
World Programme of Action, 56
World Report on Disability, 21, 73, 155

Y
Youth
with disabilities, 205

MIX
Papier aus verantwortungsvollen Quellen
Paper from responsible sources
FSC® C105338

FSC
www.fsc.org

If you have any concerns about our products,
you can contact us on
ProductSafety@springernature.com

In case Publisher is established outside the EU,
the EU authorized representative is:
Springer Nature Customer Service Center GmbH
Europaplatz 3, 69115 Heidelberg, Germany

Printed by Libri Plureos GmbH
in Hamburg, Germany